CONGRESS v. THE SUPREME COURT

CONGRESS v. THE SUPREME COURT

RAOUL BERGER

HARVARD UNIVERSITY PRESS

CAMBRIDGE, MASSACHUSETTS

PREFACE

It is a commonplace of contemporary historiography that complete objectivity is a delusion and that one should hope for no more than the historian's awareness and avowal of his prejudices. Such avowal is especially important when the subject matter is wrapped in emotion-laden controversy. Currently, detractors of the Supreme Court charge that it has embarked upon a course for which it holds no charter, nothing less than a revolution in Constitutional theory and social relations. Its admirers are rejoiced by the Court's creative leadership in areas where the Legislative and Executive branches have faltered.

As a lawyer accustomed to invoking judicial protection against Congressional or Executive invasions of Constitutional rights, I have shared in the general assumption of bench and bar that this judicial role is both constitutionally established and proper. Probably that assumption is shared by the citizen who looks for protection against arbitrary governmental action. Nevertheless I am not an uncurbed partisan of the Supreme Court. At various times and for different reasons I have had considerable misgivings about the manner in which the Justices have performed their role,[1] though I shall have nothing to say here about current challenges to Supreme Court decisions.

During a sojourn at the University of California, Berkeley, I undertook to ascertain for myself whether judicial review—that is, power to set aside legislative acts—was conferred or usurped, and if conferred, what the Founders envisaged as its scope; and whether

[1] Berger, "Constructive Contempt: A Post-Mortem," 9 *U. Chi. L. Rev.* 602 (1942).

the Congress was empowered to deprive the Supreme Court of appellate jurisdiction to hear Constitutional cases. Historical methodology was a source of some uneasiness until I learned that two eminent practitioners of the historical art, Professors Hugh Trevor-Roper and C. R. Elton, though not in accord on some important aspects of the art, were agreed that the essence of "historical method" is to ground "detail upon evidence and generalization upon detail."[2] Like Moliere's bourgeois who discovered that he had been talking prose all his life, I was much edified to find that throughout my law practice I had unwittingly employed "historical method." Law practice, I may add, conditions a lawyer to discount his predilections, for he who selects only the favorable and ignores the adverse facts risks having the "evidence" blow up in his face. That is not a risk which can comfortably be postponed for the verdict of posterity—a judge is apt to render judgment with somewhat more promptitude. Experience, as well as the fact that I have no axe to grind, still less, passionate convictions rooted in social or economic prejudices, led me to make as dispassionate a search for the "facts" as I could, and to consider and weigh every objection to easy conventional assumptions. If the "truth" has eluded me, let my failure serve as still another illustration of human fallibility.

In examining the legitimacy of judicial review, I have skirted Charles Beard's "economic interpretation" wherewith he bolstered his analysis of the Framers' utterances,[3] not only because it lies outside my competence but because the subject has become enmeshed in controversy.[4]

A word about the massive annotations. Long before I entered the domain of legal research, Frank Sullivan's parody on a page of footnotes to a line of text had turned me against the pedantry that often

[2] Trevor-Roper, Book Review of Elton, *The Practice of History*, in London *Times*, October 15, 1967, p. 33.

[3] Beard, *The Supreme Court and the Constitution* 84–107 (Prentice-Hall, 1962).

[4] McDonald, *We the People* (1958); Westin, Introduction to Beard, supra, note 3 at 31–32; Boorstin, Book Review: "Paperbacks and History, Benson, Turner and Beard: American Historical Writing Reconsidered," *New York Times Book Review*, November 28, 1965. Professor Samuel Eliot Morison states that "This Federalist-Antifederalist contest was largely personal; it was not a class, a sectional or economic cleavage. Some of the wealthiest men in the country were Antis." Morison, *Oxford History of the American People* 313 (1965). See also De Pauw, *The Eleventh Pillar* xii, xiii (1966).

lurks behind excessive footnoting. Notwithstanding, the writer who would persuade rather than pontificate must furnish to the reader the materials whereby he can conveniently test controversial statements for himself. To expect the reader to scurry to the library to ascertain whether innumerable statements are supported by the citations is in the result merely to add still another flock of *ipse dixits* to the field.

Finally, I am indebted to Professors Louis Henkin, Paul J. Mishkin, and Dean Robert B. McKay for reading the manuscript. They must, of course, be absolved of all responsibility for the views herein expressed.

CONTENTS

CONTENTS

CONTENTS

CONGRESS v. THE SUPREME COURT

AUTHOR'S NOTE: To facilitate citation, frequently cited authorities are cited by the author's name only unless more than one work by the same author is used. For further identification see bibliography, p. 391. Where notes refer to other notes to this text, citation is to the chapter in which the citing note appears unless otherwise identified by chapter. Italics throughout are in the quoted original unless otherwise indicated.

INTRODUCTION

"Is there anybody so simple minded as to feel that we can deprive the U.S. Supreme Court of the right to protect your constitutional rights?"[1] Congressman Rogers' rhetorical question, in the course of the August 1964 debate on the Tuck bill to deprive the Supreme Court and inferior federal courts of all jurisdiction over "reapportionment" controversies, was answered in the affirmative by a considerable majority of the House.[2] The majority was thereby far from proving that it was "simple-minded." It could and did summon to its support a series of incautious, all-too-sweeping Supreme Court pronouncements,[3] stretching from Chief Justice Marshall to the present, in which the Court repeatedly stated that Congress, by virtue of Article III of the Constitution, possesses power that "may be uncontrollable" to give or withhold from the Supreme Court all appellate jurisdiction, and that the Court has only such appellate jurisdiction as is conferred by statute.[4]

[1] 110 *Cong. Rec.* 20227 (August 19, 1964).

[2] Id. at 20300. For citations to Congressional attempts to limit the Supreme Court's appellate jurisdiction, see Elliot, "Court-Curbing Proposals in Congress," 33 *Notre Dame Lawyer* 596 (1958); Ratner 159; Wechsler, *Courts & Constitution* 1005. On May 2, 1968, the *New York Times* (p. 39) reported a Senate Judiciary Committee recommendation of a bill that would "abolish the Supreme Court's jurisdiction to review state courts' decisions to admit confessions . . . and to abolish the right of a person convicted in state courts to seek habeas corpus release in Federal courts." Compare infra, Chapter 8, text accompanying note 257.

[3] Hart, *Dialectic* 1362; 110 *Cong. Rec.* 20224, 20228, 20247, 20249 (1964).

[4] Hart, Book Review 1473 n. 54. The cases are analyzed in Ratner 173–183. See also Glidden v. Zdanok, 370 U.S. 530 (1962); Hughes 25; cf. Frankfurter & Landis, *The Business of the Supreme Court* vii, 86 (1928).

Small comfort is to be derived from "distinguishing" cases in which sweeping dicta carry the weight of 150 years of reiteration. A row of district courts seized upon such utterances to hold that the provision of the Fair Labor Standards Act ("Portal to Portal") 61 Stat. 84, 29 U.S.C. §251, that "No court . . . shall have

Article III, section 2 provides that "the Supreme Court shall have appellate jurisdiction, both as to law and fact, with such exceptions and under such regulations as the Congress shall make." The high-water mark of judicial abnegation in construction of this provision is represented by *Ex Parte McCardle*,[5] where the Congress had withdrawn jurisdiction to consider a Reconstruction measure upon a petition for habeas corpus that was then "in the bosom of the Court."[6] Although Andrew Johnson, then under shadow of impeachment because of his resistance to Radical Reconstruction measures, had vetoed the proposed measure (which was then passed over his veto) because it "establishes a precedent which, if followed, may eventually sweep away every check on arbitrary and unconstitutional legislation,"[7] the Court meekly declared that its appellate jurisdiction was subject to regulation by Congress. In view of the Radical lightning that played about the head of President Johnson— the impeachment proceedings were "one of the most disgraceful episodes in our history"[8]—*McCardle* may be regarded as a cautious

---

jurisdiction . . . to enforce liability" arising out of an employer's failure to pay "portal to portal" claims had deprived the courts of jurisdiction to hear them. For citations see Moeller v. Eastern Gas & Fuel Associates, 74 F. Supp. 937, 938 (Mass. 1947). In the courts of appeal, decision turned on the view that employees had no "contractual" claims. The Second Circuit alone declared, before reaching that issue, that Congress "must not so exercise its undoubted power to give, withhold or restrict the jurisdiction" of the federal courts "as to deprive any person of life, liberty or property without due process of law or to take private property without just compensation." Battaglia v. General Motors Corp., 169 F. 2d 254, 257 (2d Cir. 1948).

The Supreme Court has had no occasion squarely to decide that the "exceptions" power may be employed with the effect of foreclosing *all* judicial review of a Constitutional claim. Compare New York Times Co. v. Sullivan, 376 U.S. 254, 268 (1964): "Respondent relies heavily . . . on statements of this Court to the effect that the Constitution does not protect libelous publications. Those statements do not foreclose our inquiry here. None of the cases sustained the use of libel laws to impose sanctions upon expression critical of the official conduct of public officials."

[5] 7 Wall. (74 U.S.) 506 (1869). McCardle was approved in passing in Glidden v. Zdanok, 370 U.S. 530, 367 (1962), although Justice Douglas, dissenting, questioned whether that decision would be reached today. Id. at note 11. Professor Hart remarks that in McCardle, "The circuit courts of the United States were still open in *habeas corpus* and the Supreme Court itself could still entertain petitions for the writ which were filed with it in the first instance," citing Ex Parte Yerger, 8 Wall. (75 U.S.) 85 (1869); Hart, *Dialectic* 312.

[6] Roberts, "Fortifying the Supreme Court's Independence," 35 *A.B.A.J.* 1, 3 (1949).

[7] 6 Richardson, *Messages & Papers of the Presidents* 646, 647 (1897).

[8] Morison 721.

attempt to ride out the Reconstruction storm. Had the Radicals prevailed in those proceedings, then "in all probability the Supreme Court would have been battered into submission."[9]

Nevertheless *McCardle,* wrote Justice Burton in 1955, *"disclosed"* the "Achilles heel of the Supreme Court's right of judicial review," a "weakness" deriving from the fact that the Constitution "does not give the Court absolute appellate jurisdiction."[10] Justice Roberts, advocating an Amendment which would insulate that jurisdiction, asked, "what is there to prevent Congress taking away, bit by bit, all the appellate jurisdiction of the Supreme Court."[11] Since then, Professor Wechsler, citing *McCardle,* declared that "Congress has the power by enactment of a statute to strike at what it deems judicial excess by delimitations of the jurisdiction of the lower courts and of the Supreme Court's appellate jurisdiction." And he dismissed the notion that "cases that have constitutional dimension" must be exempted from the Congressional power, on the ground that it is "antithetical to the plan of the Constitution for the courts— which was quite simply that the Congress would decide from time to time how far the federal judicial institution should be used within the limits of the federal power."[12] This view carries not only the weight of Professor Wechsler's great learning but can draw on the unqualified terms of Article III and the literal effect[13] given to those terms in many Supreme Court pronouncements.

Conventional acceptance of judicial power to declare Acts of Congress unconstitutional—herein termed "judicial review"[14]—rests

[9] Ibid. The story is recounted in Marke, *Vignettes of Legal History* 141–168 (1965).

[10] Burton, "Two Significant Decisions: Ex Parte Milligan and Ex Parte McCardle," 41 *A.B.A.J.* 124, 176 (1955).

[11] Roberts, supra, note 6 at 4.

[12] Wechsler, "Courts & Constitution" 1005. In announcing hearings on the manner in which the Supreme Court is carrying out its constitutional responsibilities, Senator Sam J. Ervin, Jr., Chairman of the Senate Subcommittee on Separation of Powers, stated that "the power of Congress to change the appellate jurisdiction of the Supreme Court" was designed to enable Congress "to discipline and correct a Supreme Court which had overstepped its constitutional bounds," to "discipline it when in their judgment the Court is behaving improperly." Subcommittee Press Release, May 17, 1968.

[13] "Literalism," said Judge Friendly, is "peculiarly inappropriate in Constitutional adjudication." Friendly, "In Praise of Erie—and of the New Federal Common Law," 39 *N.Y.U. L. Rev.* 383, 396 (1964).

[14] "Judicial Review" will also include review of State statutes in terms of constitutionality. It is not a "general right" to set aside State or federal statutes, but

on the assumption that the Court was empowered to prevent Congress in a proper "case" from acting in excess of Constitutional authority. If such a power was indeed conferred, as most lawyers unquestioningly assume, why should the Founders simultaneously authorize the Congress to prevent the Court from taking such action? This is but one of a number of perplexing questions that arise when the "exceptions" power is given literal effect. Yet the disturbing fact is that Congress' power to make "exceptions" to the Supreme Court's appellate jurisdiction is expressly conferred whereas judicial review, some stoutly maintain, is derived from questionable implications and debatable history.[15] For me it therefore became necessary to reexamine whether the power of judicial review was a questionable arrogation or a function contemplated by the Founders, to examine once more the presuppositions from which they proceeded, if only better to understand the role of the "exceptions" clause in the entire scheme. The more deeply I delved into the historical materials the more the wisdom of the tenet that a Constitutional grant is not to be read in isolation but in the context of the whole document[16] was brought home to me. As the larger purposes of the Founders emerged, they helped to illumine the scope of the "exceptions" clause, which also has its own special history. What began, therefore, as a study of the Congressional "exceptions" power irresistibly grew into a reexamination of the sources of judicial review.

Such a reexamination may well be thought stale and unprofitable because for upwards of 150 years the Court has never questioned

---

a power asserted in the course of litigation between parties, Hart, Book Review 1457–1458; or, in the words of Madison, "limited to cases of a Judiciary Nature." 2 Farrand 430. See also Iredell, quoted infra, Chapter 3, text accompanying note 168; cf. Wechsler, "Courts & Constitution" 1006, quoted infra, Chapter 9, note 5.

[15] Beard's remark that the "usurpation" argument gives the "color of legality" to "a movement designed to strip the courts of their greatest political function," Beard 37, is even more relevant to a literal reading of the "exceptions" clause for the same purpose.

[16] James Wilson made the point in urging adoption of the Constitution before the Pennsylvania Ratification convention: "Take the detached parts of any system whatsoever, in the manner these gentlemen have hitherto taken this Constitution, and you will make it absurd and inconsistent with itself." After recounting an illustrative anecdote, he concluded, "This story may convey an idea of the treatment of the plan before you; for although it contains sound sense when connected, yet, by the detached manner of considering it, it appears highly absurd." 2 Elliot 451. See also Hart, Book Review 1465, quoted infra, Chapter 8, note 90.

nor reexamined the doctrine enunciated by Chief Justice Marshall in *Marbury v. Madison*.[17] Over the same period, however, the Court has also uttered sweeping dicta about the all but "uncontrollable" power of Congress over the several segments of federal jurisdiction. It would be incongruous to regard judicial review from the vantage point of 150 years of acceptance while turning back to 1787 for the meaning of the "exceptions" clause.

Writing in 1924 against the background of Charles Beard's classic study of the Framers' views on judicial review, Professor Frankfurter impatiently attributed the "persistence" of talk of "usurpation" to "lack of historical scholarship, combined with fierce prepossessions," and stamped it as an "empty controversy" which should have come to an end with "the publication of Beard."[18] No sooner had Beard's findings been published, however, than they became the subject of vigorous controversy;[19] and criticism—notably Professor Crosskey's assault in 1953[20]—has become more astringent over the years. If Crosskey's views are themselves open to large doubts,[21] there is Professor Bickel's subsequent impeachment of the conventional textual argument and his guarded treatment of the historical materials,[22] bridging over Judge Learned Hand's "left-handed welcome" to judicial review "as the twilight child of a doctrine of

[17] 1 Cranch 137 (1803); see Westin 9–10.
[18] Frankfurter, "A Note on Advisory Opinions," 37 *Harv. L. Rev.* 1002, 1003 n. 4 (1924). Beard, *The Supreme Court and the Constitution* (1912), gathered the statements of the Framers respecting judicial review, and his tally of opinions pro and con will be discussed infra, Chapter 3.
[19] Davis, "Annulment of Legislation by the Supreme Court," 7 *Am. Pol. Sci. Rev.* 541 (1913); Corwin, Book Review, 7 *Am. Pol. Sci. Rev.* 330 (1913), quoted by Westin 28–29. Davis was disputed by Melvin, "The Judicial Bulwark of the Constitution," 8 *Am. Pol. Sci. Rev.* 167 (1914). Corwin had published studies indicating that the matter was more complicated and subtle than the Beard count would suggest. Corwin, "The Establishment of Judicial Review," 9 *Mich. L. Rev.* 102 (1910); and see, Corwin, *The Doctrine of Judicial Review* (1914); Corwin, *Court Over Constitution* 33 (1938).
[20] Crosskey 938–1064.
[21] The Crosskey position was subjected to a vigorous critique by Professor Hart, Book Review 1456, which my own study confirms. Notwithstanding the Hart critique, Crosskey's work continues to be cited: Westin 27, 33; Rossiter, 58, 282, 296, 297. Rossiter calls it "as useful as it is exasperating." Id. at 296. Compare Friendly, "In Praise of Erie," 393 n. 52.
[22] Bickel 5–16. There is more than a little resemblance between the Crosskey and Bickel analyses, though Professor Bickel would "make plain [his] disavowal of an analysis by Professor William Winslow Crosskey, which is in some respects similar but which is also quite different, having regard to its context and supports and the purposes it is made to serve." Bickel 7.

necessity."[23] The "ghost of usurpation," as Professor Westin remarks in his valuable 1962 summary of the long debate, continues to "clank its chains"; he considers that the issue remains a "murky question."[24] So, although I shrank from yet another wearisome canvass of the historical materials, I felt driven to review the sources for myself, not in the "hope to carry off a coup from the library stacks,"[25] but because continuing criticism of conventional reliance on the sources demands such reappraisal.

One who would meet such criticism runs the danger of inditing a debater's screed and of inviting charges that "scholarship" has been forsaken for disputation. That is an unavoidable risk; clarification of the "murky question" requires patient point-by-point analysis of attacks upon the conventional view based upon a comparison with the sources. Inescapably counter-criticism is polemical in tone,[26] but it is not here meant to be dogmatic. The fact that the meaning of the text and its historical background continue to be involved in controversy counsels against dogmatism. Nevertheless, one who pores over the sources afresh may not shrink from avowing his conclusions forthrightly.

[23] Pollak, "Racial Discrimination and Judicial Integrity: A Reply to Professor Wechsler," 108 *U. Pa. L. Rev.* 1, 3 (1959). In his Holmes Lectures (1958), Judge Learned Hand concluded that the power of judicial review is "not a logical deduction from the structure of the Constitution but only a practical condition upon its successful operation," Hand 15, "being unwilling to rest on the historical evidence." Bickel 46.

The limited nature of Professor Bickel's reliance on the historical evidence is indicated by his invocation of Holmes's aphorism that continuity with the past is not a duty but merely a necessity, and that it is revolting to rely upon a rule, the grounds of which have "vanished long since," so that ultimately, states Bickel, we must justify judicial review "as a choice in our own time." Bickel 16.

[24] Westin 2, 33. Farrand, *Framing* 22, steeped in the Records and literature of the Convention, said of judicial review, "This power has been the subject of much dispute, and many have looked in vain in the proceedings of the convention for authority to exercise any such power." Professor Westin more recently stated that "Several dozen books and perhaps a hundred articles have persisted in treating this as still a debatable proposition, and not all of the commentators are to be dismissed as incompetents or outraged partisans deprived of reason." Westin 2. Cf. Hyneman, *The Supreme Court on Trial* 114 (1963). On the other hand, Professors Hart and Wechsler say that "Despite the curiously persisting myth of usurpation, the Convention's understanding on this point emerges from its records with singular clarity." Hart & Wechsler 14.

[25] Westin 33.

[26] In addition, "refutation of an argument," as Chief Justice McKean told the Pennsylvania convention, "begets a proof," 2 Elliot 541, a view also expressed by Fisher Ames in the First Congress, citing the maxim *destructio unius est generatio alterius.* 1 *Ann. Cong.* 560.

INTRODUCTION

The focus of this study is the "appellate" jurisdiction of the Supreme Court both because its "original" jurisdiction is of relatively slight significance to the private litigant who would assert constitutional rights[27] and because the original jurisdiction is beyond the reach of Congress.[28] But the appellate jurisdiction is threatened not alone by the Congressional power to make "exceptions" thereto, but by the power of Congress to control appeals by drying up the source. Under the doctrine of *Sheldon v. Sill*, the creation of inferior courts, the extent of their jurisdiction, and their disestablishment is said to rest in the complete discretion of Congress.[29] Presumably it was this that led Henry Hart to say that State courts "are the primary guarantors of constitutional rights, and in many cases they may be the ultimate ones."[30] State courts too, however, may be excluded from jurisdiction;[31] they may fail to effectuate constitutional guarantees.[32] So the question remains whether Congress' powers to "exclude" State jurisdiction and to "ordain and establish" inferior federal courts stretch so far as to enable it to bar *both* State and federal jurisdiction for vindication of constitutional rights, as it did in the Fair Labor Standards Act ("Portal to Portal").[33] These and related problems must be noted if only because an appellate jurisdiction of the Supreme Court without State or inferior federal court jurisdiction from which appeals may be taken is a phantom husk.

[27] Hamilton, *Federalist* No. 81 at 533; Davis, *Veto* 116; cf. Hughes 26.
[28] Cf. Hart & Wechsler 218.
[29] 8 How. 441 (1850); cf. Wright, *Federal Courts* 24.
[30] Hart, *Dialectic* 1401.
[31] Hart & Wechsler 373–374.
[32] Some State courts have proved sorry "guarantors" of civil liberties, and a bar to the appellate jurisdiction of the Supreme Court would calamitously affect, for example, Negroes in Alabama and Mississippi. See infra, Chapter 8, note 90. "Only the Supreme Court can enforce" federal rights "if the state courts balk." Hart & Wechsler 312. See infra, Chapter 8, text accompanying note 265.
[33] 61 Stat. 84, 29 U.S.C. §251 (1938), quoted Hart & Wechsler 301.

HISTORICAL BACKGROUND

FEAR OF "LEGISLATIVE DESPOTISM"

One who would understand the significance of judicial review for the Founders does well to start from the fact that in 1787 there was widespread fear of oppression by a remote federal government, centered largely in dread of "legislative despotism." By 1787 it was clearly perceived that the alternative to Union was disunion, foreign oppression of the disunited states, internecine strife, and a string of lesser calamities. Few in the Constitutional Convention and in the Ratifying conventions were not alive to these evils;[1] but to many they seemed not nearly so perilous as a potentially tyrannical central government.[2] Only a despotism, some believed, could effectively

[1] Melancton Smith said in the New York Ratification convention that "the defects of the old confederation needed as little proof as the necessity of a union." [2] Elliot 223–224. See 2 Madison, *Writings* 361–369 (April 1787); 1 Farrand 24, 25, 317, 464, 466; 2 Farrand 220, 388, 584; 3 Elliot 36, 38, 75, 88, 105, 119, 238, 399, 470, 603, 606; 4 Elliot 14, 17, 18, 19, 20, 25, 89, 98, 183, 222, 230, 253. The sober Washington wrote after the close of the Convention that the choice was between "the Constitution or disunion," "anarchy." 2 Bancroft 279–280.

[2] In a recent study of the New York Ratification proceedings, it was said that *The Federalist* "mistakenly assumed that it was necessary to convince the anti-federalists of the need for a stronger federal union, when what was needed was to convince them that the stronger union proposed by the Philadelphia Convention would not endanger personal liberty." De Pauw, *The Eleventh Pillar* 116 (1966). "[T]here was more concern," said Haines 209, "as to the restrictions under which the government should operate than as to the functions to be performed." Summarizing the Virginia debate, van Doren 179 said, "The central government . . . was magnified into a monstrous overriding force . . . which would be free to dominate, tax and enslave a helpless people." In Pennsylvania, the dissenters condemned the Constitution as an "iron-handed despotism." Id. at 186. There Robert Whitehill prophesied that "in its probable operation," the proposed government would be "oppressive and despotic." McMaster & Stone 258; and see id. at 255, 267, 284. Samuel Chase said in the Maryland convention that the "powers to be vested in the new government are deadly to the cause of liberty." Quoted 2

govern the vast land mass.[3] To our generation, resting confidently on 175 years of democratic practices, the specter of despotic government in these United States, even against the backdrop of contemporary totalitarianism, may seem to be a figment of the imagination.[4] It was real enough to the generation which framed and adopted the Constitution. A "great majority of the American people," said Henry Adams, "shared the same fears of despotic government."[5] Such fears had Congress as their focal point, for to it was to be confided the bulk of the new governmental powers.

The popular mood is reflected in Hamilton's remark to the New York Assembly just before the Convention:

> Upon every occasion, however foreign such observations may be, we hear a loud cry about the danger of intrusting power to the Congress.[6]

Bancroft 282. In New York, Thomas Tredwell feared "the total extinction of our civil liberties." 2 Elliot 405. William Goudy said in North Carolina, "Let us beware of the iron glove of tyranny." 4 Elliot 10. See also 2 Elliot 28, 68, 391; 3 Elliot 30, 208, 396, 456; 4 Elliot 55, 56, 124, 132, 337; 1 Bryce 26.

[3] The widely prevalent view was voiced by George Mason in the Virginia convention: "Is it to be supposed that one national government will suit so extensive a country, embracing so many climates, and containing inhabitants so very different in manners, habits and customs. It is ascertained, by history, that there never was a government over a very extensive country without destroying the liberties of the people." 3 Elliot 30. In his *Spirit of the Laws*, 150–151 (trans. 1802), Montesqieu had said that only a despotism can govern a large area. And there were proposals that there be several lesser confederations rather than one large confederation. See also Charles Pinckney, 4 Elliot 262, and note 116.

[4] In our own time, Professor Jaffe stated: "We may grant that power is benign and without it we can do nothing. But it is also malign, fearsome, hateful and dangerous . . . [W]e cannot forget that our age has produced elsewhere, and even in our own country, the most monstrous expressions of administrative power." Jaffe, "The Right to Judicial Review," 71 *Harv. L. Rev.* 401, 404–405 (1958).

[5] H. Adams, *John Randolph* 38, 18 (1882).

[6] Quoted Rossiter, *Hamilton* 168. Hamilton's note of reproach hardly does justice to acute 18th century Colonial concern with the problem of "power." Bailyn tells us that the Colonists dwelt on it endlessly, centering on "its essential characteristic of aggressiveness: its endlessly propulsive tendency to expand itself beyond legitimate boundaries . . . What gave transcendent importance to the aggressiveness of power was the fact that its natural prey, its necessary victim, was liberty, or law, or right." Bailyn 56–57. Distrust of power continued to haunt those who were asked to ratify the Constitution. Said Patrick Dollard in the South Carolina convention, "Lust of dominion is natural in any soil, and the love of power and superiority is as prevailing in the United States, at present, as in any part of the earth." 4 Elliot 337.

By 1787 a contributing factor was jealous insistence upon "independent" State sovereignty which, Washington observed, was "so ardently contended for." 3

Suspicion of legislative power arose in good part from the post-1776 experience, a result of the grant of virtually unchecked powers to the State legislatures.[7] By 1781 Jefferson could write that the Virginia constitution, the first of the State constitutions, "was formed when we were new and unexperienced in the science of government . . . No wonder then that time and trial have discovered very capital defects in it." One such defect was that under the paper separation of powers

All the powers of government, legislative, executive, and judiciary result to the legislative body. The concentrating these in the same hands is precisely the definition of despotic government. It will be no alleviation that these powers will be exercised by a plurality of hands. 173 despots would surely be as oppressive as one . . . An *elective despotism* was not the government we fought for.[8]

In the Convention John F. Mercer asked, "What led to the appointment of this Convention? The corruption and mutability of the Legislative Councils of the States."[9] Madison noted that there had been a tendency "to throw all power into the legislative vortex . . . If no effective checks be devised for restraining the instability and encroachments of the latter . . . a revolution . . . would

---

Farrand 51. Essential power was originally withheld from the central government because of a "bias in favor of local autonomy." Corwin, *Progress* 535. See also infra, Chapter 8, text accompanying notes 155–182.

[7] Haines 68–72. The 1780–1787 "constitutional reaction" "embraced two phases, that of nationalism against State sovereignty, that of private rights against uncontrolled legislative power, but the point of attack in both instances was the State legislature." Corwin, *Doctrine* 37.

[8] 3 Jefferson, *Writings* 222–224. Madison later quoted these remarks *in extenso. Federalist* No. 48 at 324. Jefferson's complaints were echoed in the 1784 Report of the Pennsylvania Council of Censors, to which Madison also refers in No. 48, listing the Council's condemnation of various legislative violations of the State constitution and bill of rights. No. 48 at 325. See also 3 Elliot 66; cf. Rossiter, *Hamilton* 186; Hamilton, infra, Chapter 3, text accompanying note 226; Corwin, *Doctrine* v; Corwin, *Progress* 514.

[9] 2 Farrand 288. "The state legislatures, whose malignant course affecting rights of creditors and similar interests had been a principal cause of the Convention." Corwin, *Twilight of the Supreme Court* 52 (1934). Madison said that interference with "the security of private rights and the steady dispensation of Justice" "were evils which had more perhaps than anything else, produced this convention." 1 Farrand 134. See also remarks of Mercer, 2 Farrand 285, and of Mason, id. at 362.

be inevitable."[10] Gouverneur Morris concurred with Madison "in thinking that the public liberty is in greater danger from Legislative usurpations than from any other source"; he considered "Legislative tyranny the greatest danger to be apprehended."[11] James Wilson said that "we have seen the Legislatures in our own country deprive the citizen of Life, of Liberty, & Property, we have seen Attainders, Banishment, & Confiscations."[12]

These strictures, to be sure, were aimed at State excesses, but the Framers were not slow to draw the moral, to discern that a national legislature might ape the State assemblies. Mason, discussing proposed judicial participation in revision of federal enactments prior to effectiveness, said that the national Legislature "would so much resemble that of the individual States, that it must be expected frequently to pass unjust and pernicious laws. This restraining power was therefore essentially necessary."[13] Madison, after referring to the "strong propensity" of State legislatures "to a variety of pernicious measures," said that "one object" of an executive veto "was to controul the Natl. Legislature, so far as it might be infected with a similar propensity."[14] "Is there no danger of a Legislative despotism," asked Wilson? "Theory & practice both proclaim it. If the Legislative authority be not restrained, there can be neither liberty nor

[10] 2 Farrand 35. He sounded the same note in *Federalist* No. 48 at 322. In a letter to Jefferson of October 24, 1787, Madison stated the "injustice" of State laws had "been so frequent and flagrant as to alarm the most stedfast friends of Republicanism . . . and the evils issuing from these sources contributed more to that uneasiness which produced the Convention . . . than those which occurred . . . from the inadequacy of the Confederation to its immediate objects." 5 Madison, *Writings* 27. See also Wilson, 2 Farrand 300.

[11] 2 Farrand 76, 551.

[12] 1 Farrand 172; see also *Federalist* No. 44 at 322–323. Gorham said that "Rh. Island is a full illustration . . . of the length to which a public body may carry wickedness and cabal." 2 Farrand 42. For similar criticism by Charles Pinckney in the South Carolina convention, see 4 Elliot 327.

Such remarks were not confined to proponents of the Constitution. After submission of the Constitution by the Convention, R. H. Lee, a critic of the Constitution, said that "Our governments have been new and unsettled; and several legislatures, by making tender, suspension, and paper money laws, have given just cause of uneasiness to creditors. By these and other causes, several orders of men in the community have been prepared by degrees, for a change of government; and this very abuse of power in the legislatures, which in some cases has been charged upon the democratic part of the community, has furnished aristocratical men with these very weapons." *Letters of a Federal Farmer* (October 1787), reprinted in Ford, *Pamphlets* 279, 283.

[13] 2 Farrand 78.

[14] Id. at 110. See also Madison, infra, Chapter 9, text accompanying note 47.

stability.[15] "All agree," said Nathaniel Gorham, "that a check on the Legislature is necessary."[16]

In the Ratification conventions, one opponent of the Constitution after another descanted on the dangers of Congressional oppression, tyranny, despotism. Leading the opposition in Virginia, Patrick Henry said: "I trust that I shall see Congressional oppression crushed in embryo."[17] In North Carolina Timothy Bloodworth warned that "Without the most express restrictions [going beyond those contained in the Constitution], Congress may trample on your rights."[18] So often was the tocsin rung that Lee, a friend of the Constitution, was impelled to say in Virginia that the friends "will oppose the efforts of despotism as firmly as its opposers."[19] In Pennsylvania, Wilson, arguing for adoption, said that "the legislature should be restrained; . . . for of all kinds of despotism, this is the most dreadful and the most difficult to be corrected. With how much contempt have we seen the authority of the people treated by the legislature of this state."[20] Whatever the New Direction was to be, it seems plain that the point of departure was disenchantment with an all-powerful, uncurbed legislature.[21]

[15] 1 Farrand 254.
[16] 2 Farrand 79; see remarks of G. Morris, id. at 75.
[17] 3 Elliot 546, 396.
[18] 4 Elliot 167. And he stated, "no one can say what construction Congress will put upon it . . . I distrust them." 4 Elliot 50. William Lenoir said, "When we consider the great powers of Congress, there is great cause for alarm." 4 Elliot 203. "Let us," said William Lancaster in North Carolina, "exclude the possibility of tyranny." Id. at 213. And William Goudy warned, "beware of the iron glove of tyranny." Id. at 10.
[19] 3 Elliot 177. Marshall felt constrained to say thereafter, "The friends of the Constitution are as tenacious of liberty as its enemies." 3 Elliot 226.
[20] McMaster & Stone 304. Wilson had said in the federal Convention, "May there not be legislative despotism if in the exercise of their power they are unchecked or unrestrained by another branch." 1 Farrand 261.
[21] "The experiment of entrusting the welfare of the American community to the practically unlimited discretion of thirteen state legislatures proved a dismal failure, thus producing a constitutional reaction which led eventually not only to judicial review and the gubernatorial veto within the states, but also to the summoning of the Philadelphia Convention." Corwin, Court Over 24. He had earlier made the point in Corwin, Doctrine v, 62. See also his 1913 statement quoted infra, Chapter 3, text after note 311. Charles Merriam had noted in 1906 the common belief in 1787 that "the greatest danger to liberty arises from the expanding power of the legislative body." Quoted, Haines 208.
Haines 205 states that "the attempt to account for judicial review of legislation as a result of the abuse of powers by early state legislatures fails to give weight to other factors . . . which undoubtedly aided in strengthening the position of the

"LIMITS" AND "CHECKS" ON CONGRESS

Bloodworth's insistence on "the most express restrictions" was but one of many outcries against "unlimited powers." As Jefferson was later to say,

> It is jealousy and not confidence which prescribes limited constitutions to bind down those whom we are obliged to trust with power. Our Constitution has accordingly fixed the limits to which, and no further, our confidence will go. In questions of power, then, let no more be heard of confidence in man, but bind him down from mischief by the chains of the Constitution.[22]

There was oft-voiced anxiety whether the Congressional powers were "distinctly bounded,"[23] whether there was an adequate "fence" "against future encroachments," such as would be provided by a bill of rights.[24] To quiet such fears there were repeated assurances that Congress "has no power but what is expressly given it,"[25] that it has "no authority" to make a law "beyond the powers" enumerated,[26]

---

courts." Among these were the principle that there were certain rights which no government dared violate, that there were limits especially appliable to legislatures, that there was a general duty to resist interference with such rights. Id. at 206. Even so, it was the violation of those rights by the legislatures which lent motive power to those principles.

[22] Quoted by Warren, *Congress* 153. In the Massachusetts convention W. Bodman complained that the taxing power "was certainly unlimited, and therefore dangerous." 2 Elliot 60. In the New York convention, Tredwell declaimed that to force a people "to give unlimited power to their rulers" was to "give their rulers power to destroy them." Id. at 397. In the Pennsylvania convention Whitehill affirmed that Article I conferred powers "so unlimited in their extent" as to afford a foundation for the most "arbitrary sway." McMaster & Stone 284; and see id. at 277 ("power supreme and unlimited"). In the Virginia convention Monroe protested that "There are no limits pointed out. They are not restrained or controlled from making any law, however oppressive in its operation." He desired security from destruction of "inalienable rights" by a bill of rights. 3 Elliot 218. Patrick Henry there inveighed against the grant of "unlimited, unbounded authority." 3 Elliot 437.

Compare with such statements Boudin's remark at 121 that "In so far as the legislature was concerned, *their* [the Framers'] *great anxiety was that it should have sufficient and ample powers,* not that it should have limited powers." And see infra, text accompanying notes 23-32.

[23] 2 Elliot 77; 4 Elliot 137; McMaster & Stone 256.
[24] 4 Elliot 171, 168.
[25] 3 Elliot 464.
[26] 4 Elliot 161. In Massachusetts, Samuel Stillman acknowledged that the Congressional powers were "great and extensive," but maintained that they are "defined and limited, and . . . sufficiently checked." 2 Elliot 166.

that "If Congress, under pretence of executing one power, should, in fact usurp another, they will violate the Constitution."[27] "The legislature," said Archibald Maclaine in the North Carolina convention, "cannot travel beyond its [the Constitution's] bounds";[28] it cannot, Governor Johnston there said, "assume any other powers than those expressly given them, without a palpable violation of the Constitution."[29] A law "not warranted by the Constitution," said James Iredell in that convention, "is barefaced usurpation."[30] Lee assured the Virginia convention that "the liberties of the people are secure . . . When a question arises with respect to the legality of any power, exercised or assumed by Congress [the question will be] . . . *Is it enumerated in the Constitution?* . . . It is otherwise arbitrary and unconstitutional."[31] As Iredell said of the related Supremacy Clause in the North Carolina convention, "the question . . . under this clause, will always be, whether Congress had exceeded its authority."[32]

Underlying such assurances was the familiar common law principle that the act of an agent beyond the scope of his authority was simply void. Lee explained to the Virginia convention the consequences of the "limited powers" delegated by the people to the government, saying that "it would be an insult upon common sense to suppose that the agent could legally transact any business for his principal which was not contained in the commission whereby the

[27] 4 Elliot 179.
[28] Id. at 63; see also id. at 14–141.
[29] Id. at 142. Governor Johnston said that Congress' powers "are all circumscribed, defined . . . So far they may go, but no further." Id. at 64. In Pennsylvania, Chief Justice McKean told the Ratification convention that "the powers of Congress . . . being . . . enumerated and *positively* granted, can be no other than what this positive grant conveys." 2 Elliot 540.
[30] 4 Elliot 194.
[31] 3 Elliot 186. Even in 1938, after the New Deal repulses at the hands of the Supreme Court had led Corwin to reevaluate the problem, he could still say that "the new government was constantly presented by its advocates as one of delegated powers only, thus suggesting, as in Hamilton's argument in Federalist 78, the legal analogy of a limited agency subject to a judicial reading of its powers." Corwin, *Court Over* 81. Such representations emerge most sharply in the Ratification debates in order to allay the opposition's fears of unbounded legislative oppression. See infra, Chapter 4, text accompanying notes 26–147.
[32] 4 Elliot 179. Earlier, Iredell expressed the "utmost satisfaction" with the "jealousy and extreme caution with which gentlemen consider every power to be given this government." 4 Elliot 95.

powers were delegated."[33] Hamilton alluded in *The Federalist* to the "clear" principle that "every act of delegated authority, contrary to the tenor of the commission, under which it is exercised, is void. No legislative act, therefore, contrary to the Constitution, can be valid."[34] The question that troubles some scholars—who was to declare it out of bounds and void—was unhesitatingly answered by George Nicholas in the Virginia convention. Replying to the query "who is to determine the extent of such [Congressional] powers," he said, "the same power which, in all well-regulated communities, determines the extent of legislative powers. If they exceed these powers, the judiciary will declare it void."[35] In the Massachusetts convention, Samuel Adams said that "any law . . . beyond the power granted by the proposed constitution . . . [will be] adjudged

[33] 3 Elliot 186. Iredell said of the enumeration of powers given to Congress, "It may be considered as a great power of attorney, under which no power can be exercised but what is expressly given." 4 Elliot 148. In *The Law of Nations* 18 (1760 ed.), which was the manual of students and statemen, infra, note 95, Vattel stated that since the State "was first established by the nation, which afterwards trusted certain persons with the legislative power, the fundamental laws are excepted from their commission." In his "Memorial and Remonstrance Against Religious Assessment" (1785), Madison stated that Rulers "who overleap the great barrier which defends the rights of the people . . . exceed the Commission from which they derive their authority, and are tyrants." 2 Madison, *Writings* 185. In the Convention, Roger Sherman said of the proposed Congressional veto of State statutes that "Such a power involves a wrong principle, to wit, that a law of a State contrary to the Articles of Union would, if not negatived, be valid and operative." 2 Farrand 28.

[34] *The Federalist* No. 78 at 505. Sir George Bowyer traced application of the principle to public law from Roman private law through Vattel and Grotius. See B. Coxe 114–119. Coxe cites an opinion of the English Attorney General in 1730, respecting action under the Connecticut charter, that any Connecticut laws "repugnant to the laws of England . . . are absolutely null and void." Id. at 198–199. The colonists were familiar with the principle that Acts which "conflicted with the colonial charters" were void. Haines 49.

Corwin states that "the colonial charter came to embody a conception of governmental power which, as applied to principal governments, was absolutely revolutionary. This was the idea, invoked for example by Hamilton in *Federalist* No. 78, that governmental authority is a limited *commission* or *agency* postdating government, rather than an attribute of government as such, and hence coeval with it . . . Congress . . . was presented by the advocates of the Constitution themselves as a legislature of *delegated* powers—indeed, of powers delegated piecemeal. It was, therefore, entirely legitimate for Hamilton to argue in *The Federalist,* and for Marshall to argue in the Virginia Ratifying convention and later on in his famous decisions, to the effect that the grants of power to Congress implied limitations which were judicially construable no less than the prohibitions on those grants—in short, for judicial review of unlimited *scope.*" Corwin, *Court Over* 20–21.

[35] 3 Elliot 443.

by the courts of law to be void."[36] Oliver Ellsworth told the Connecticut convention that "If the general legislature should at any time overleap their limits, the judicial department is a constitutional check"; "a law which the Constitution does not authorize" is "void," and the judges "will declare it to be void."[37] Similar statements were made by Wilson in Pennsylvania,[38] and by John Marshall in Virginia.[39] And in his 1790–91 "Lectures on Law," Wilson, then a Justice of the Supreme Court, declared that under the Constitution the courts would render "vain and fruitless" every legislative "transgression" of Constitutional bounds—"a noble guard against legislative despotism!"[40]

PROTECTION OF PRIVATE RIGHTS

Congressional withdrawal of federal jurisdiction needs also to be considered in the light of its impact upon private rights and the Founders' concern lest those rights be impaired. To begin with, there was a deeply-felt need for protection of private rights from State and Congressional encroachments. "Interference" with "the security of private rights and the steady dispensation of justice," said Madison in the Convention, "were evils which had, more perhaps than anything else, produced this convention."[41] Washington wrote to Lafayette in June 1787 that he had responded to the Convention call to determine "whether we are to have a Government . . . under which life, liberty, and property will be secured to us."[42] In the Convention, Gouverneur Morris said that "Every man of observation had seen . . . excesses against personal liberty,

36 2 Elliot 131.
37 Id. at 196.
38 He said that if the legislature "transgress the bounds assigned to it," and the judges "find it to be incompatible with the superior power of the Constitution,—it is their duty to pronounce it void." 2 Elliot 446. See also McKean, infra, Chapter 4, text accompanying note 37.
39 If the Congress "were to make a law not warranted by any of the powers enumerated, it would be considered by the judges as an infringement of the Constitution which they are to guard . . . They would declare it void." 3 Elliot 553. James Otis, Pamphlet 109, made the point in 1764, as did Iredell in 1786. 2 McRee 148.
40 1 Wilson, *Works* 462. In these Lectures, Wilson drew "on his experience as one of the most active members of the Constitutional Convention," Wesberry v. Sanders, 376 U.S. 1, 17 (1964), as well as leader in the Pennsylvania convention.
41 1 Farrand 134.
42 3 Farrand 34.

private property and personal safety."[43] Madison urged a presidential veto in the Convention "for the safety of a minority in danger of oppression from an unjust and interested majority."[44] The propertied minority had found that its rights were "too often decided, not according to the rules of justice . . . but by superior force of an interested and over-bearing majority."[45] Today this vibrates with anti-democratic overtones,[46] but it is one of the ironies of history that the protection then engineered for a propertied minority is now available for the benefit of propertyless minorities. In the Virginia Convention, Randolph urged adoption of the Constitution "because it secures the liberty of the citizen, his person and property."[47] There were many, like Bloodworth in the North Carolina Convention, who feared that the Congress "may trample on the rights of the people of North Carolina if there be not sufficient guards and checks."[48] The prevalence of such fears served to block ratification in North Carolina notwithstanding the prior adoption by ten states;[49] and it is worth recalling that in Virginia, despite knowledge that eight States had already adopted the Constitution, ratification just

[43] 1 Farrand 512. In *Federalist* No. 10 at 54, Madison adverted to the "alarm for private rights which [is] echoed from one end of the continent to the other." He wrote in October 1787 to Jefferson that "A reform therefore which does not make some provision for private right must be materially defective." 5 Madison, *Writings* 27. In the First Congress, James Jackson valued "the liberties of [his] fellow citizens beyond every other consideration"; and said Alexander White, the "limits described in the Constitution" were "to secure the liberties of our fellow citizens." 1 *Ann. Cong.* 505, 534–535.

[44] 1 Farrand 108; cf. id. at 51, 27, 486; 2 Farrand 362. Beard stated that "Every page" of Madison's Notes of the Convention shows that the members were striving "to set up a system of government that would be stable and efficient, safe-guarded on one hand against the possibilities of despotism and on the other against the onslaught of majorities." Beard 93.

[45] Madison, *Federalist* No. 10 at 54; and see id. No. 51 at 339. To Jefferson, Madison wrote in 1788 that he "has seen the [Virginia] bill of rights violated in every instance where it had been opposed to a popular current." 5 Madison, *Writings* 269, 272. In the Convention he said, "Experience had evinced a constant tendency in the States . . . to oppress the weaker party." 1 Farrand 164.

[46] Bowen 70, remarks that "if the word property today carries sinister philosophical overtones, to the Convention of 1787 it had an altogether different connotation: property was not a privilege of the higher orders but a right which a man could defend." See also id. at 71–72.

[47] 3 Elliot 67. Madison said that "The primary objects of civil society are the security of property and public safety." 1 Farrand 147.

[48] 4 Elliot 187. And see id. at 68, 93, 203, 212. Samuel Spencer stressed that the "rights of individuals ought to be properly secured." Id. at 163, 153.

[49] See infra, Chapter 4, note 78.

squeaked by, as was the case in Massachusetts, New Hampshire, and New York.[50]

The struggle for more assured protection against feared federal encroachments continued and eventuated in the Bill of Rights. That story has been happily summarized by Chief Justice Marshall, who, it must not be forgotten, had been a member of the Virginia Ratification convention:

> the great revolution which established the constitution of the United States, was not effected without immense opposition. Serious fears were extensively entertained, that those powers which the patriot statesmen . . . deemed essential to union, and to the attainment of those invaluable objects for which union was sought, might be exercised in a manner dangerous to liberty. In almost every convention by which the constitution was adopted, amendments to guard against the abuse of power were recommended. These amendments demanded security against apprehended encroachments of the general government . . . In compliance with a sentiment thus generally expressed, to quiet fears thus extensively entertained, amendments were proposed by the required majority in congress, and adopted by the states.[51]

In sum, the purpose of this "magnificent" "structure of government," to paraphrase Justice Wilson's Lecture in 1791, was for the accommodation "of the sovereign, Man," and the "primary and principal object" was "to acquire a new security" for *his* rights.[52] Any shuffling of power as between Congress and the Supreme Court which im-

---

[50] Van Doren 230, 202, 206, 235. In both Virginia and North Carolina opponents of the Constitution insisted that it would impair rights and liberties. 3 Elliot 236, 268, 325, 588; 4 Elliot 68, 203, 213.

[51] Barron v. Mayor & City of Baltimore, 7 Peters 243, 250 (1833). For remarks in the Convention, see 2 Farrand 587–588; in the Ratification conventions, 2 Elliot 131, 154, 435; 3 Elliot 150, 217, 271, 314, 315, 446, 454; 4 Elliot 152, 315; in First Congress, 1 *Ann. Cong.* 443, 445, 448, 449, 450, 454, 463, 464, 687, 689, 730, 733, 734, 759, 775, 778, 787. And see infra, Chapter 10, note 79; Chapter 5, note 23.

[52] 2 Wilson, *Works* 453–454. In the Pennsylvania Ratification convention, Wilson, justifying the provisions for judicial independence, said, "The servile dependence of the judges, in some of the states that have neglected to make proper provision on this subject, endangers the liberty and property of the citizen . . . I hope that no further objections will be taken against this part of the Constitution, the consequence of which will be, that private property, so far as it comes before their courts, and personal liberty, so far as it is not forfeited by crimes, will be guarded with firmness and watchfulness." 2 Elliot 480. It may be ventured that Wilson was not unaware of legislative assaults on judges who *had* stood firm. See infra, text accompanying notes 162–165.

pairs that "security" contravenes the "primary and principal object" of the Constitution.

For Crosskey, however, the view that "the Court was to be the special protector of the people against their legislatures . . . is easily shown to be imaginary."[53] Certainly it was not "imaginary" to

[53] Crosskey 938. Contrast this with the statement in 1803 by Judge St. George Tucker of the Virginia court and Professor of Law at William and Mary, where he succeeded George Wythe:

and herein consists one of the great excellencies of our constitution: that no individual can be oppressed whilst this branch of the government remains independent and uncorrupted; it being a necessary check against the encroachments, or usurpations of power by either of the other [branches] . . . The judiciary, therefore, is that department of the government to whom the protection of the rights of the individual is by the Constitution especially confided, interposing its shield between him and the sword of usurped authority. Tucker's Blackstone, App. to vol. 1, pp. 356-357.

This was written in 1802, though published in 1803, and probably antedates the Marshall analysis in Marbury v. Madison.

Crosskey had been anticipated by Boudin 115, who flatly declared that the judicial power *"was not intended as a means for the protection of individual rights, that is to say as a protection of the minority against the 'tyranny of the majority' in the domain of general or social legislation."* For proof Boudin pointed to "the conclusive circumstance that, as the Constitution came from the hands of the Framers, there were no fundamental rights in it and the Judicial Power would have been utterly useless for that purpose . . . *when the Constitution came from the hands of the Framers, it had no Bill of Rights."* (Boudin's italics) Id. at 115-116. But the proponents in the Ratification conventions maintained, among other things, that in a government of limited and enumerated powers a bill of rights was superfluous, even dangerous, because rights which would not be enumerated would be threatened. 2 Elliot 87, 121, 436; 3 Elliot 246, 251; 4 Elliot 148-149; infra, Chapter 5, note 23. See also Barrett, *Constitutional Law* 577. Boudin 107, himself quotes Hamilton's No. 78, *The Federalist:* "If the courts are to be considered as the bulwarks of a limited constitution against legislative encroachments, this consideration will afford a strong argument for the permanent tenure of judicial offices . . . This independence of the judges is equally requisite to guard the Constitution and the rights of individuals."

Boudin, who acidulously adverts to Beard's "fancy 'canons of historical criticism,'" Boudin 581, who not too delicately intimates that Beard had not "really been making an impartial historical inquiry," id. at 582, who wishes that Beard "were less the advocate and more the historian," id. at 579, is himself guilty of serious inaccuracy when he asserts that in the Convention Hamilton advocated a "scheme of government for the United States *which did not include the Judicial Power in any of its phases,"* id. at 580. Hamilton did not profess to submit a complete "scheme" of government but merely "to suggest the amendments which he should probably propose to the plan of Mr. R[andolph] in the proper stages of its future discussion," 1 Farrand 291 (a plan which provided for a judiciary as a "check" on the legislature, id. at 28). In fact, Hamilton suggested changes in the "Supreme Judicial authority" in his "scheme," id. at 292, and at the close of the Convention he urged that "every member should sign" the finished document, 2 Farrand 645, so that he swallowed his differences and then became a mighty protagonist of judicial review in *The Federalist.*

Edmund Randolph, Marshall, and Iredell. Randolph stated in the Virginia convention that "If Congress wish to aggrandize themselves by oppressing the people, the judiciary must first be corrupted."[54] "To what quarter," Marshall there said, "will you look to protection from an infringement on the Constitution, if you will not give the power to the judiciary."[55] Said Wilson in the Pennsylvania Ratification convention, "personal liberty, and private property, depend essentially upon the able and upright determination of upright judges."[56] The "real reason" for judicial review "in the mind of its advocates," said Corwin, was stated by Iredell: "In a republican form of government (as I conceive) individual liberty is a matter of utmost moment, as, if there had been no check upon the public passions, it is in the greatest danger."[57]

Various other checks, of course, had been suggested: a presidential veto,[58] a Council of Revision which would include the judiciary and which would "negative" a law *prior* to its effectiveness,[59] a Congress divided into a "popular" branch and the Senate, considered by Madison to be a "check on the democracy,"[60] periodic elections,[61] and still other expedients.[62] But these were cumula-

---

[54] 3 Elliot 205.

[55] Id. at 554; compare 4 Elliot 157. This was also the view of Patrick Henry, speaking for the opposition. See infra, Chapter 4, text accompanying note 111.

[56] 2 Elliot 480–481; see also supra, note 52.

[57] Corwin, 9 *Mich. L. Rev.* 120. See also Madison, infra, text accompanying note 77. In his 1791 Lectures, Justice Wilson quoted a statement in the Congress by Elias Boudinot, wherein, adverting to an objection that a bill might be adjudged "contrary to the constitution, and therefore void," he said that this judicial power "is my boast and my confidence," and rejoiced that "there is a power in the government, which can constitutionally prevent the operation of a wrong measure from affecting my constituents." 1 Wilson, *Works* 463. Cf. 3 Farrand 135. Hart & Wechsler 11 n. 19 say that "Courts were thought of in part, of course, as instruments for the protection of individuals."

[58] To check a legislative "propensity" to "pernicious measures." 2 Farrand 110.

[59] 1 Farrand 21, 97–104, 108–110, 138-140; 2 Farrand 73–80, 298.

[60] 1 Farrand 222; and see id. at 51, 254, 511–512, 517.

[61] So, Gerry pressed for "annual elections as the only defense against tyranny." 1 Farrand 214–215; cf. id. at 368; 2 Elliot 348, 446.

[62] The peril of building an exclusive preference for a particular check upon isolated remarks advocating one or another of these alternatives may be illustrated by a few examples. Wilson said, "If the legislative authority be not restrained, there can be neither liberty nor stability; and it can *only* be restrained by dividing it within itself, into distinct and independent branches." 1 Farrand 254 (emphasis added). Plainly this does not mean that Wilson placed his trust "only" in a division of the legislative branch, for he was one of the most vigorous proponents of judicial review. See infra, text accompanying note 64; Chapter 4, id at notes 39–41;

tive;[63] fear of an all-consuming Congressional power led not to one proposed check but to many. Charles Pinckney told South Carolina the judiciary "might be the keystone of the arch."[63a] Wilson, after alluding in the Pennsylvania convention to the several sources of "efficient restraints upon the legislative body," stated that such restraints "may proceed from the great and last resort—from the people themselves. I say, under this Constitution, the legislature may be restrained, and kept within its prescribed bounds, by the interposition of the judicial department."[64] The people themselves, this may be understood to mean, had delegated to the courts the function of keeping the legislature within bounds, and this not out of an abstract passion for neatly drawn lines but to make private rights secure against Congressional invasion.

Before assaying the evidence commonly adduced for judicial review—the Beard tally of remarks made by the Framers—let us examine what Professor Crosskey apparently regards as a presumption of "legislative supremacy" which allegedly barred the way to judicial review. Armed with this presumption, Crosskey asks at

---

Chapter 5, at notes 26–30. Similarly, though Elbridge Gerry pressed for "annual elections as the *only* defense of the people agst. tyranny," 1 Farrand 214–215 (emphasis added), he was a proponent of judicial review. Infra, Chapter 3, text accompanying notes 13–17; Chapter 5 id. at note 25. John Dickinson, a member of the Convention, said in his *Letter of Fabius* (published after the close of the Convention, and reprinted in Ford, *Pamphlets* 165, 184), "Our government will be guarded by a repetition of the strongest cautions against excesses," naming a divided Congress, and "the president, and the federal independent judges, so much concerned in the execution of the laws, and in the determination of their constitutionality."

In the Massachusetts convention, James Bowdoin, meeting arguments that "this great power may be abused, and instead of protecting, may be employed by Congress in oppressing, their constituents," urged that the possibility of abuse is "no sufficient reason for withholding the delegation" for "no power could be delegated" on that reasoning. But the "possibility" "should make us careful, that, in all delegations of importance, like the one contained in the proposed Constitution, there should be such checks provided as would not frustrate the end and intention of delegating the power, but would, as far as it could be safely done, prevent the abuse of it; and such *checks* are provided in the Constitution." Among the checks, he recited the fact that all officers of the government, including "the judicial officers, both of the United States and the several states, shall be bound, by oath or affirmation, to support this Constitution." 2 Elliott 85–86.

[63] See Corwin, quoted infra, Chapter 8, notes 190, 191.

[63a] The judicial he conceived to be at once the most important and intricate part of the system . . . this department might be the keystone of the arch." 4 Elliot 257–258. Pinckney had been a delegate to the federal Convention. Id. at 253.

[64] 2 Elliott 445.

every step: where is the *clear* provision which alone can override it? It is therefore important to clear the way at the outset in order that the Founders' utterances may be weighed on their merits, unencumbered by a presumption that finds little or no support in the facts.

CROSSKEY'S PRESUMPTION AGAINST JUDICIAL REVIEW

Starting from the proposition that "there was, when the American Revolution occurred, no judicial right, under English law, to review the validity of acts of Parliament," Crosskey affirms that the Framers "must have concluded" that the Supreme Court would not possess the right of judicial review "as to Acts of Congress, unless that right was in some clear way provided," unless they had "a perception of something in the character of the new national government they were about to create" which would make "English rules and ideas" inapplicable.[65] Written "limits" and "checks" on the legislature were so revolutionary as alone to suggest a new "character" to which English rules could not be "applicable."[66] Crosskey also posits "the complete normalcy of the duty of absolute obedience which every system of courts was then deemed to owe to the acts of its particular legislature."[67]

With Crosskey I believe that in the task of interpretation "our interest is in the state of American opinion at the time the Federal Convention met."[68] Although he makes a brave show of hunting for that opinion,[69] it undergoes a strange metamorphosis at his hands. That opinion, it develops, is not what men actually believed in those days but what, he concludes on the basis of 19th century research

[65] Crosskey 941–942.
[66] See comments of Maclaine and Johnston, infra, text accompanying notes 129, 130.
[67] Id. at 986. For comments on this statement see infra, Chapter 3, text accompanying notes 137–144. To mention only one stumbling block to this theory of "absolute obedience," Sherman, *before* the Supremacy Clause was adopted, stated that "the Courts of the States would not consider as valid any law contravening the Authority of the Union." 2 Farrand 27.
[68] Crosskey 943. And he states that "only in the light of the facts about [judicial review] which were then true and *known* to the men who drew the document, can the words of the Constitution, as they relate to judicial review, be justly interpreted." Id. at 941 (emphasis added).
[69] Crosskey vii, 1–5.

and his own 20th century analysis of certain cases,[70] they "must" have believed. For the 1787 opinion we must look to what men *then* believed, whether that belief was mistaken or not, and this will become plainer as we examine the particulars under three heads: the influence of Coke; the influence of Blackstone; and the influence of pre-1787 State court "precedents."

Coke's Influence

The Framers did not pluck the concept of judicial review from the void. It harked back to Coke's 1610 statement in Bonham's case: "when an Act of Parliament is against common right and reason . . . the common law will control it and adjudge such act to be void."[71] The footing of Coke's statement has been impeached by modern scholars;[72] and some have read it as a canon of construction rather than a constitutional theory.[73] Crosskey calls it an "ill-founded idea," the effects of which "were almost immediately wiped out by the 'glorious Revolution' of 1688."[74] That Revolution, to be sure, established the power of Parliament vis-à-vis the King; but Chief Justice Holt apparently concluded that it left the relation of courts to Parliament untouched, for shortly thereafter—in 1702—he stated that Coke's statement is a "very reasonable and true saying."[75] The fact that "Tenure during good behavior . . . had been secured in

---

[70] E.g. "Bearing in mind . . . that there was, when the Federal Convention met, not a single *supporting* precedent for judicial review of a *general* character . . . and remembering, further, that the men of the Convention probably regarded the English law as the standing *national* law upon this subject anyway, it seems a completely certain inference that they did not rely upon the bare grant of a 'supreme' 'judicial power' to the United States Supreme Court, as sufficient to invest that body with a general right of judicial review against Congress." Crosskey 982.

[71] 8 Coke 114a, 118a, 77 Eng. Rept. 647, 652 (1610). Corwin, 9 *Mich. L. Rev.* 104, 107, remarks that one "idea" borrowed by the Framers was "Coke's dictum in Bonham's case."

[72] For citations to the literature, see Gough 32; Boudin 76–77. For a caustic discussion of Coke's citations see Boudin 498–503. The Coke statement is discussed in detail, infra, Appendix A.

[73] For summary of such views, see editorial note, 2 John Adams, *Legal Papers* 118–119.

[74] Crosskey 941.

[75] City of London v. Wood, 12 Mod. 669, 687, 88 Eng. Rept. 1592, 1602 (1702). See infra, note 78. "The issue which developed in the seventeenth century was between parliament and the king, and in this the courts and parliament were allies." Gough 49. See also Appendix A, note 52.

23

England by the Glorious Revolution"[76] might have persuaded the Colonists that the Revolution sought to strengthen rather than weaken the judiciary. Certainly Madison did not conceive in 1785 that Parliament had become paramount for he stated: "The *Judiciary Department* merits every care. Its efficacy is demonstrated in G. Brittain where it maintains Private Right against all corruption of the two other departments."[77]

There was little or no incentive in the pre-1787 years to go behind Coke's statement, the more so because it was congenial to the Colonial forces that were mounting an attack on parliamentary supremacy. Blackstone, who had first articulated the case for an uncontrollable Parliament in 1765, stated that Coke was an object of "great veneration and respect," a "man of infinite learning in his profession," whose "writings are so highly prized, that they are generally cited without the author's name."[78] Jefferson recorded that there never was "one of profounder learning in the orthodox doctrines of the British Constitution or what is called British rights" than Coke.[79] Coke's statement had been repeated in 1615 by Chief Justice Hobart;[80] it was taken up in the Abridgments;[81] and it had been approved by Chief Justice Holt in 1702;[82] so that a Colonial lawyer may be pardoned for not going behind Coke to the Year Books cited by Coke, if they were indeed accessible.[83] In the eyes of

---

[76] Morison 168. True, the Act of Settlement of 1700 made judges removable on an address of both Houses of Parliament, but that procedure had not been employed prior to 1787, and in fact has since been employed only once, in 1830, when an Irish judge was removed. Wade, *Administrative Law* 281 (1967).

[77] 2 Madison, *Writings* 166, 170.

[78] 1 Bl. 72. Sir Frederick Pollock said, "The omnipotence of Parliament was not the orthodox theory of English law, if orthodox at all, even in Holt's time. It was first formally adopted . . . in Blackstone's Commentaries . . . Down to the Revolution, the common legal opinion was that statutes might be void as 'contrary to common right.' " Pollock, "A Plea for Historical Interpretation," 39 L.Q.R. 163, 165 (1923).

[79] Quoted Corwin, *Doctrine* 31.

[80] Day v. Savadge, Hob. 85, 87, 80 Eng. Rept. 235, 237 (1615).

[81] 19 Viner's *Abridgment* 512–513, "Statutes" (E.6) (1744); 4 Bacon's *Abridgment* 639, "Statutes" (E) (1759); 4 Comyns' *Digest* 340, "Parliament" (R.10) (1766). "A lot of American law came out of Bacon's and Viner's Abridgments." Goebel, "Ex Parte Clio," 54 *Colum. L. Rev.* 450, 455 (1954). James Otis cited Bonham's case "from the extract of it in 19 Viner, Abridgment." 2 John Adams, *Legal Papers* 128 n. 13. In his argument in Trevett v. Weeden (R.I. 1786), discussed infra, text accompanying notes 145–150, Varnum quoted Bacon's *Abridgment*. Haines 105, 108.

[82] City of London v. Wood, 12 Mod. 669, 687–688. Holt was cited in 1764 by Otis, Pamphlet 110.

[83] See Plucknett, 40 *Harv. L. Rev.* 45. Only one Year Book appears in several

the Colonists, "reiteration of the dictum by Coke's successors on the bench and by commentators had given to it, by the middle of the eighteenth century, all the character of established law."[84]

Sound or not, Coke's statement became a rallying cry for Americans in 1761 when it was resoundingly invoked by James Otis. If an Act of Parliament had the effect claimed for it, he argued in the Writs of Assistance case, it would be "against the Constitution" and therefore void,[85] an argument that John Adams, with Otis concurring, repeated in 1765 in opposition to the Stamp Act.[86] Otis' argument stirred mens' souls; it put a legal footing under Colonial resistance; and it became "a permanent memory with men of the time."[87] The currency that Otis gave Coke is illustrated by a number

catalogues of well-known private libraries in New York, in the library of Judge William Smith. Hamlin, *Legal Education in Colonial New York*, App. VII, pp. 171–176 (1939). Then too, Chief Baron Comyns of the Court of Exchequer lists in his *Digest*, as late as 1766, the medieval precedents cited by Coke, under Comyns' citation of Bonham, giving them credit in reliance on Coke. 4 Comyns' *Digest* 340 ("Parliament").

[84] Corwin, 9 *Mich. L. Rev.* 104. Horace Gray made a similar observation 100 years ago. Quincy's Repts. (Mass. 1761–1772), App. I, p. 525 (1865).

[85] John Adams, *Legal Papers* 127; Corwin, *Doctrine* 30. In his pamphlet, Otis left no doubt that it was for the courts to declare such Acts "void," e.g. "the judges of the executive courts have declared the act 'of a whole parliament void.'" Id. at 71. Again, "it will not be considered as a new doctrine that even the authority of the parliament of *Great Britain* is circumscribed by certain bounds, which if exceeded, their acts become those of *meer power* without *right*, and consequently void. The judges of England have declared in favor of these sentiments . . . that *acts against the fundamental principles of the British Constitution are void*," citing Coke, Hobart, and Holt. Id. at 109; cf. id. at 61–62.

It is true that in the same pamphlet Otis said that the Parliament was "uncontrollable but by themselves . . . They only can repeal their own acts." Quoted Bailyn 179. Here Otis exhibits some of the confusion that earlier beset Chief Justice Holt, infra, Appendix A, text accompanying notes 81–83; but as Professor Bailyn notes, Otis' contemporaries were "unencumbered by Otis' complexities," Bailyn 180, and they fastened on the idea that an Act contrary to the Constitution is void. This was the argument made by John Adams, with Otis concurring, in 1765 in opposition to the Stamp Act. Quincy's Mass. Reports (1761–1772) 200, 203 (1865). See also infra, note 88.

[86] Quincy's Mass. Reports (1761–1772) 201, 203.

[87] Corwin, *Doctrine* 31. Sixty years after the event, the aged John Adams, who had been a spectator, recorded the Otis impact in "impassioned language" that "shows what feelings were aroused at the time." Morse, *John Adams* 24 (1890). See also Page Smith, *John Adams* 55–56 (1962). For a balanced evaluation of Otis' impact, see editorial note, 2 John Adams, *Legal Papers* 120–122.

In 18th century America, Bailyn tells us, "It was taken as a maxim by all . . . that it was the function of the judges 'to settle the contests between prerogative and liberty . . . to ascertain the bounds of sovereign power, and to determine the rights of the subject.'" Bailyn 74. When the Colonists were threatened by Parliamentary oppression they not unnaturally looked again to judges to "settle the bounds of sovereign power and to determine" their rights.

of citations in the years that immediately followed;[88] and the point received extended exposition in the 1786 argument made by James Varnum in the Rhode Island "paper-money" case, *Trevett v. Weeden,* a *cause célèbre,* which Varnum broadcast in pamphlet form.[89] Though these citations are scattered, they are countered by only one citation of Blackstone. And Lieutenant-Governor Hutchinson's statement in Massachusetts that "the people in general" relied on Coke[90] indicates that such reliance went beyond published citations. The argument that Coke had been "discredited" does not rest upon more numerous citations of Blackstone but on inferences drawn from his principle of "legislative omnipotence" which, as will appear, the Founders categorically rejected.

Is pre-Convention reliance on Coke vitiated by the fact that modern critics consider his statement vulnerable? The animating force of an idea is not necessarily measured by its verity. For example, "we may deny the validity of belief in the supernatural, but we cannot deny its tremendous power."[91] Mohammedanism swept

[88] In 1766, a Court of Hastings in Virginia said that a "law of Parliament imposing stamp duties in America binding on Virginia" was "unconstitutional." 5 McMaster, *History of the People of the United States* 394–395 (1913). In 1766, Judge William Cushing, "later one of the original bench of the Supreme Court . . . charged a Massachusetts jury to ignore certain acts of Parliament as 'void' and 'inoperative.'" Corwin, *Doctrine* 32. And John Adams wrote Cushing, "You have my hearty concurrence in telling the jury of the nullity of Acts of Parliament." 9 Adams, *Works* 390–391 (1854). In 1772, Mason argued, citing Bonham's case, that a Virginia Act making certain Indians slaves was "contrary to natural right and justice," and therefore void. Robin v. Hathaway, Jeff. (Va.) 109, 114 (1772).

[89] Trevett v. Weeden (R.I. 1786), 1 Thayer, *Cases on Constitutional Law* 73 (1894); Haines 105–112. The Varnum pamphlet is generously quoted in B. Coxe 235–246.

[90] Blackstone was invoked in Rutgers v. Waddington (N.W. 1784), Thayer, supra, note 89 at 63; Haines 98–104. The Blackstonian argument is quoted by Haines at 99–100.

Lieutenant-Governor Hutchinson of Massachusetts wrote in September 1765, "the prevailing reason [among "the people in general"] at this time, is that the Act of Parliament is against the Magna Charta and the natural rights of Englishmen and therefore according to Lord Coke null and void." Quoted by Plucknett, 40 *Harv. L. Rev.* 63, Iredell's 1787 statement likewise indicates acceptance of the Coke doctrine. While noticing the alleged "absolute power" of Parliament, he stated that "any act passed, *not inconsistent with natural justice* (for that curb is avowed by the judges even in England)" would be binding. 2 McRee 172. In his App. I to Quincy's Repts. (1761–1772), p. 527, Horace Gray states that the Bonham doctrine "was a favorite in the Colonies before the Revolution" and appends numerous citations.

[91] Muller, *Uses of the Past* 36 (1954). For years France was wracked by dis-

the world though one may doubt a divine revelation to Mohammed. The importance of Coke for judicial review does not therefore turn on whether he was "right" but rather on the fact that "at the time of the Convention" Americans believed he was, and proceeded to act on that belief.

Other ideas merged into the Cokean stream, of which only a few can here be noticed. Otis drew in his 1764 pamphlet upon Vattel's proposition that "legislators derive their power" from the Constitution and cannot "change it without destroying their authority."[92] Translated by the Massachusetts Circular Letter of 1768 as "the supreme legislative . . . cannot overleap the bounds of [the Constitution] without destroying its own foundation,"[93] it was reiterated by Varnum, who borrowed the very "overleap the bounds" phrase,[94] and echoed by Ellsworth in the Convention.[95] Thus the concept emerged that a constitution was a "fundamental law" to which other laws must conform.[96] Among other conceptual influences was the idea that a constitution is itself a "law" and that it is the function of the courts, not the legislature, to interpret the law,[97] that a law

---

sension about the Dreyfus case largely because of popular belief in a false version of his "guilt" propagated by the Army. "What acted on public opinion in the affair was never what happened but what the Nationalist press and whispered rumor said happened." Tuchman, *Proud Tower* 181–182, 171–226 (1965). Haines 9 n. 7, noted the influence "on legal thinking of incorrect facts and incorrect assumptions, when such facts and assumptions are believed to be true." See also Corwin, *Progress* 522.

[92] Otis 109; cf. B. Coxe 240; Vattel, *The Law of Nations* 18 (1760).

[93] Quoted Haines 60–61; Corwin, *Doctrine* 20, states that the Vattel apothegm "was a commonplace in Massachusetts before the Revolution." A 1768 reference in South Carolina is quoted by Meigs, *Relation* 45. See also Madison's paraphrase in 1785, 2 Madison, *Writings* 185.

[94] Quoted B. Coxe 243.

[95] Quoted supra, text accompanying note 37. Cf. 2 Farrand 92. Vattel's treatise was then "the manual of the student, the reference work for the statesman, and the text from which the political philosopher drew inspiration." Fenwick, "The Authority of Vattel," 7 *Amer. Pol. Sci. Rev.* 395 (1913); cf. McMaster & Stone 772. The Vattel apothegm was paraphrased by Iredell, 2 McRee 148, and seeped into the 1787 opinions in Bayard v. Singleton, 1 Martin 5, 7 (N.C. 1787) (1901 Reprint); see B. Coxe 120, and was quoted shortly after adoption of the Constitution in Kamper v. Hawkins, 1 Va. Cas. 20, 38, 75–76 (1793). See also infra, Chapter 6, note 91.

[96] Haines 59, 64; see infra, Chapter 6, text accompanying notes 85–125.

[97] Corwin regards acceptance of the idea that the interpretive function is exclusively judicial as the great breach with English and American tradition. *Doctrine* 26, 27. It may be doubted that it constituted a breach with the tradition of Coke: "According to Coke's view the common law was the supreme law in the state, and

which overleapt constitutional bounds was "void,"[98] and still others.[99] Conceptual tools were thus at hand and had been invoked by prominent figures in the struggle to secure private rights from Parliamentary infringement.

Blackstone's Influence

The "true view," says Crosskey, "unquestionably was that of Blackstone," and his ideas of "legislative supremacy" "affected American ideas quite as much as they did those which were current in England," where "Coke's ideas" were "entirely discredited."[100] In

---

the judges, unfettered and uncontrolled save by the law, were the sole exponents of the supreme law." Holdsworth, *Some Makers of English Law* 115 (1938).

The idea was sharply expressed in 1786 by Varnum, quoted B. Coxe 242, and by Iredell, 2 McRee 148–149. In the Convention Caleb Strong said that "the power of making ought to be kept distinct from that of expounding the laws. No maxim was better established." 2 Farrand 75. The distinction was recognized by others. 2 Farrand 73–80. See also infra, Chapter 3, text accompanying notes 31–38, for discussion of "expounding" as employed in the Convention.

Corwin concludes that "in one form or another, the notion of legislative power as *inherently limited power*, distinct from and exclusive of the power of interpreting the standing law, was reiterated again and again and was never contradicted." Corwin, *Doctrine* 42. The matter was summed up by Hamilton in *Federalist* No. 78 at 506:

> The interpretation of the laws is the proper and peculiar province of the courts. A constitution is in fact, and must be regarded by the judges, as a fundamental law. It therefore belongs to them to ascertain its meaning as well as the meaning of any particular act proceeding from the legislative body.

For extended discussion of the Founders' view on the issue where the function of "interpretation" was to be lodged, see infra, Chapter 6, text accompanying notes 126–194.

[98] Supra, text accompanying notes 34–39.

[99] For example, protection of minorities against oppression by the majority, supra, text accompanying notes 43–45. Then there was the familiarity with disallowance of Colonial Acts by the Privy Council because violative of Colonial Charters or Acts of Parliament. Corwin, *Court Over* 17–21. Much has been made of the fact that these were largely "legislative" vetoes, but Meigs, *Relation* 27, properly stresses that thereby it became widely known that a "law" *could* be overturned because in excess of powers conferred. Cf. Corwin, *Court Over* 20–21, quoted supra, note 34. The Founders considered and rejected legislative vetoes, infra, Chapter 8, text accompanying notes 1–25, but they clung to the concept that laws violative of the Constitution were "void," supra, text accompanying notes 33–40, and by the Supremacy Clause replaced a legislative veto by a judicial negative. Infra, Chapter 8, text accompanying notes 18–25.

Those who would pursue the several facets may consult Corwin, *Doctrine* 26, 34–44; Corwin, "Progress" 511 et. seq., Haines 204–231. See also Corwin quoted infra, Chapter 6, text accompanying note 232.

[100] Crosskey 941, 943. Here too Crosskey was anticipated by Corwin: "Throughout the Revolution the Blackstone doctrine of 'legislative omnipotence' was in the ascendant," Corwin, "Progress" 517, and his "influence" "retarded the growth of

the main, Crosskey relies on Blackstone's reasoning, in the teeth of acknowledged judicial statements, from debatable political principles:

> I know that it is generally laid down more largely, that acts of parliament contrary to reason are void. But if the parliament will positively enact a thing to be done which is unreasonable, I know of no power that can control it; and the examples usually alleged in support of this sense of the rule do none of them prove, that where the main object of a statute is unreasonable the judges are at liberty to reject it; for that were to set the judicial power above that of the legislature, which would be subversive of all government.[101]

The developing Whig notion of an absolutist Parliament had never harmonized with the facts of Colonial life, because the vast Atlantic gulf conduced to local autonomy limited by English suzerainty only on the "outer fringes of Colonial life."[102] Far from winning adherence, "legislative omnipotence" fed the flames of revolt, for as Edmund Burke, pleading the cause of the Colonists said of deductions drawn from "illimitable sovereignty," "if that sovereignty and their freedom cannot be reconciled, which will they take? They will cast your sovereignty in your face. Nobody will be argued into slavery."[103]

---

judicial review." Corwin, *Doctrine* 52, 32, 34. In 1938 Corwin reiterated that the "powerful authority of Blackstone was directly opposed to judicial review." Corwin, *Court Over* 23.

[101] 1 Bl. 91. In fact Blackstone had not shaken down his own analysis. Although he stated that parliament enjoyed uncontrollable power, even to enact unreasonable laws, ibid., he uneasily noted that "the omnipotence of parliament" is "a figure rather too bold," id. at 161. He repeated the traditional learning that "no human law has any validity, if contrary to" natural law, id. at 41, 42; he emphasized that the "absolute rights" of Englishmen included "personal security," "personal liberty," and "private property," id. at 127–129; and stated that the law "will not authorize the least violation of" private property, id. at 139.

F. W. Sherwood states in his contribution to the *Encyc. Brit.* (14th ed.) on Blackstone that "Whether through the natural conservatism of a lawyer, or through his own timidity and subservience as a man and politican, he is always found a specious defender of the existing order of things."

[102] Bailyn 201; cf. id. at 19–20, 51, 202–204.

[103] Quoted Bailyn at 208 n. 50. On the touchy issue of representation, Arthur Lee rejected an unpalatable Blackstonian assertion and said, "The British Constitution is not to be new modelled by any *court lawyer*." Quoted id. at 171. Professor Bailyn has convincingly shown that the mind of the American Revolu-

Crosskey would have us accept as an article of faith that publication in 1765 of Blackstone's "legislative omnipotence," which would enthrone the very supremacy that the Colonists bitterly opposed, "affected" the "ideas" of those who went on to throw off the parliamentary yoke. Without doubt Blackstone enjoyed Colonial prestige as a commentator on the common law; 2,500 copies of his *Commentaries* had been sold in America by 1787.[104] But this furnishes no index of his influence on an explosive political issue. That "legislative omnipotence" ran counter to deeply-rooted Colonial convictions was spelled out in the Declaration of Independence: "We have warned ["our British brethren"] from time to time of attempts by their legislators to extend an unwarrantable jurisdiction over us." And though Marshall and Iredell read Blackstone,[105] as did Hamilton,[106] all three nonetheless flatly plumped for judicial review.[107]

Yet how are we to account for the fact that notwithstanding Colonial rejection of "unwarranted" interference by the British Parliament, the Colonists then entrusted comprehensive powers to their own State legislatures?[108] This, I suggest, was not an illogical return to the doctrine of "legislative omnipotence" but rather a pragmatic response to Colonial experience. As James Wilson explained, local assemblies were trusted because they had been chosen by the Colonists themselves, not thrust upon them by the King as were the governors and judges.[109] "[A]ll through colonial times,"

tionary generation was shaped by an early 18th-century group of English radical publicists and opposition politicians who carried forward the "peculiar strain of anti-authoritarianism bred in the upheaval of the English Civil War." Id. at viii, xi, 34–45, 53. As Corwin, *Twilight of the Supreme Court* 102, said, "The 'founding fathers' owed their mental sustenance much more to seventeenth century England than to the England with which they were themselves contemporary." A dispassionate English scholar has since written that "American political leaders had been nurtured in the same natural-law tradition as Blackstone himself, but they drew exactly opposite conclusions as to the capacity of the British Parliament." Gough, *Fundamental Law in English Constitutional History* 192 (2d ed. 1961).

[104] Corwin, "Progress" 517.

[105] Ibid.

[106] *Federalist* No. 84 at 557.

[107] Infra, Chapter 3, text accompanying notes 227–229, 168; id. Chapter 4 at note 123.

[108] Haines 68–72.

[109] Wilson explained that before the Revolution "the executive and judicial powers were" not derived from the people but from a "foreign source . . . directed to foreign purposes." "On the other hand, our assemblies were chosen by ourselves

says Corwin, "the legislature had stood for the colonial interest against the imperial interest."[110] But, because "legislative supremacy" was enjoyed by some of the early State legislatures[111]—and before long harshly criticized—it does not follow that the Framers meant to confer similar powers upon the national legislature. First, by 1787 public sentiment had been alienated by the excesses of the legislatures, and what remnant of respect for Blackstonian theory may have survived had been dissipated by disenchanting experience. Jefferson, it will be recalled, said in 1781 that "173 despots would surely be as oppressive as one . . . And elective despotism was not the government we fought for."[112]

Second, to the partisan of local interests in the far-off hinterland, the proposed Congress seemed little less distant or remote from his interests than the Parliament in London.[113] Men were oppressed by the immensity of the country; the great American land-mass, many thought, was simply too huge for one effective, democratic government. There was the unsettling historical fact that republics had "been extremely limited in territory,"[114] and Montesquieu had laid

---

. . . Every power, which could be placed in them, was thought to be safely placed." At the Revolution, "the same fond predilection, and the same jealous dislike, existed and prevailed . . . The legislature was still discriminated by excessive partiality." 1 Wilson, *Works* 398. The "executive and judicial power are now drawn from the same source, are now animated by the same principles, and are now directed to the same ends, with the legislative authority." Id. at 399.

Morison, 273, remarks that the Virginia constitution, which gave the legislature most of the power, "was a bad example of seeking political guarantees against past dangers, in this instance the arrogant royal governors." And he states that "John Adams' Massachusetts constitution [1780] was based, not on Locke's principle of legislative supremacy, but on Polybius theory of 'mixed government' . . . which by this time had been renamed 'checks and balances' . . . Adams own contribution—you needed an independent judiciary as a balance wheel." Id. at 275. Commenting on John Adams' subsequent "Defense of American Constitutions," Boudin 95–96, asks, "What did *he* have to say on the subject [judicial review]? Nothing. Literally and emphatically: Nothing." But Adams had also written Judge Cushing in 1766, "You have my hearty concurrence in telling the jury of the nullity of Acts of Parliament." Supra, note 88.

[110] Corwin, *Doctrine* 35.

[111] Haines 68–72.

[112] 3 Jefferson, *Writings* 222–223; supra, note 21.

[113] "It took as long to travel by land from Charleston to Boston as to cross the ocean to Europe, nor was the journey less dangerous." 1 Bryce 26. "Newspapers from London reached Savannah faster than mail sent overland from Massachusetts or Connecticut." Bowen 83.

[114] C. Pinckney, 4 Elliot 325–326.

down that only a despotism could govern a large area.[115] As Mason asked in the Virginia convention: "Is it to be supposed that one national government will suit so extensive a country, embracing so many climates, and containing inhabitants so very different in manners, habits and customs? It is ascertained by history that there never was a government over a very extensive country without destroying the liberties of the people."[116] Pierce Butler asked in the federal Convention: "Will a man throw afloat his property and confide it to a government a thousand miles *distant?*"[117] In South Carolina James Lincoln declaimed that adoption of the Constitution meant the surrender of self-government "into the hands of a set of men who live one thousand miles distant from you."[118] Melancton Smith, a leader of the opposition in New York, said that "In a country where a portion of the people live more than twelve hundred miles from the centre, I think that one body cannot possibly legislate for the whole."[119] Sent in 1785 to Congress from Georgia, William

[115] 1 Montesquieu, *Spirit of the Laws* 150–151 (1802 translation). His view was noted by Hamilton, *Federalist* No. 9 at 49–51. "It was a *communis opinio* that 'democracy' was suited to small territories only . . . 'The natural limit of a democracy,' Madison wrote, 'is that distance from the central point which will just permit the most remote citizens to assemble as often as the public functions demand.'" Salvemini, "The Concepts of Democracy and Liberty in the Eighteenth Century," in Read, *The Constitution Reconsidered* 105, 106 (1938).

[116] 3 Elliot 30, 84. In the federal Convention Hamilton had expressed "great doubt whether a more energetic government can pervade this wide and extensive country." 1 Farrand 295; and see id. at 303. He thought the "immense extent" of the country "unfavorable to representation," felt that there was a "Difficulty of judging local circumstances," and noted that "Distance has a physical effect upon mens' minds." Id. at 305. Delegates John Lansing and Robert Yates wrote to Governor Clinton of New York, "however wise and energetic the principle of the general government might be, the extremities of the United States could not be kept in due submission and obedience to its laws, at the distance of many hundred miles from the seat of government." 3 Farrand 245, 246. Later *The Federalist* devoted considerable space to meeting such fears, and to rebutting the view that several small confederacies were to be preferred to one grand Union. No. 1 at 7; No. 5 at 24; No. 13 at 77; No. 14 at 82.

[117] 1 Farrand 173.

[118] 4 Elliot 313. What distance meant is suggested by Hamilton: "several of the states, particularly New Hampshire, Connecticut and New Jersey, thought it would be difficult to send a great number of delegates from the extremes of the continent to the national government." 2 Elliot 273–274. Rebutting the argument for annual elections, Thomas Hartley stated in the Pennsylvania convention, "If, for instance, a delegate to the Congress were obliged to travel 700 or 800 miles from Georgia and Carolina, he could scarcely have entered upon the duties of his appointment, before the year would be past, and his authority annulled." McMaster & Stone 291.

[119] 2 Elliot 334. Van Doren 236-237, explains that the isolated farmers or fron-

Houstoun "thought of himself as leaving his 'country' to go to 'a strange land amongst Strangers.' "[120] Madison, "perhaps better informed than any other," had said that "Of the affairs of Georgia I know as little as of those of Kamskatska."[121]

The sense of distance was accentuated by sectional suspicions. Joseph Taylor of North Carolina declared that the men of New England "cannot with safety legislate for us."[122] "When I was in Congress," said Bloodworth in North Carolina, "the southern and northern interests divided at Susquehannah. I believe it is so now."[123] Joseph M'Dowall feared that the northern States, being in the majority, might make laws which "will be oppressive to the last degree upon the Southern States."[124] There were fears that "large states will crush the small ones,"[125] the divergent interests of importing and nonimporting States.[126] Although compromises to rec-

---

tiersmen of North Carolina "suspected the proposed federal government, which seemed vast, remote, and not likely to be attentive to the people's interests."

[120] Van Doren 45.

[121] Id. at 15. The corollary, expressed by Spencer in North Carolina, was a fear of taxation by representatives "who cannot sufficiently know our situation and circumstances." 4 Elliot 80. In New York, Melancton Smith said, "It is not possible to collect a set of representatives who are acquainted with all parts of the continent. Can you find men in Georgia who are acquainted with the situation of New Hampshire, who know what taxes will best suit the inhabitants, and how much they are able to bear?" 2 Elliot 335. "America's magnitude, the distance between states, remained the pivot [in the federal Convention] on which great questions hung." Bowen 99.

[122] 4 Elliot 24. Rawlin Lowndes asked, "was it consonant with reason . . . to suppose, in a legislature where a majority of persons sat whose interests were greatly different from ours, that we had the remotest chance of receiving adequate advantages? Certainly not." 4 Elliot 272. Charles Pinckney said that North Carolina, South Carolina, and Georgia "in their Rice and Indigo had a peculiar interest which might be sacrificed." 1 Farrand 510.

[123] 4 Elliot 186. In the Convention Madison said, "The great danger to our general government *is the great southern and northern interests of the continent being opposed to each other. Look to the votes in congress, and most of them stand divided by the geography of the country.*" 1 Farrand 476. And see Randolph, id. at 510.

[124] 4 Elliot 211, 124. "Pierce Butler of South Carolina wrote home that the interests of the Southern and Eastern States were 'as different as the interests of Russia and Turkey.' " Bowen 92; see also id. at 272. Reporting to the French government about the federal Convention, a "shrewd charge d'affaires, Monsieur Otto," stated "there is not a resolution of Congress which can be equally useful and popular in the South and the North of the Continent. Their jealousy seems an insurmountable obstacle." Bowen 142.

[125] 1 Farrand 167.

[126] 4 Elliot 157; 2 Farrand 363; cf. 4 Elliot 20. For survey of some of the conflicts, see Hamilton, 2 Elliot 236. Van Doren 225, summarizing Patrick Henry's

oncile such differences had been fashioned, it remained to implement them, and the men of 1787 were no more ready to concede "legislative omnipotence" to the Congress that was to do so than to Parliament.[127]

But we are not left to generalities, for the Fathers clearly recorded their rejection of "legislative omnipotence." In 1785, Gouverneur Morris stated before the Pennsylvania Assembly that the "boasted omnipotence of legislative authority is but a jingle of words . . . freemen must feel it to be absurd and unconstitutional."[128] In the North Carolina convention, Maclaine noticed Blackstone's view that "the power of Parliament is transcendent and absolute" and then asked, "Has any man said that the legislature can deviate from this Constitution. The legislature . . . cannot travel beyond its bounds."[129] Governor Johnston immediately added that the Parliament "can, at any time, alter the whole or any part" of the Magna Charta, but that Congress had "no such power. They are bound to act by the Constitution. They dare not recede from it."[130] The inappropriateness of the Blackstonian doctrine to the American scene was pointed up by Wilson before the Pennsylvania convention,[131]

---

tirade in Virginia, stated, "Virginia, the mother of states and of American liberties, must not be lost in the general government with its head elsewhere. The agricultural South must not be put at a disadvantage with the commercial North. The West must not be sacrificed to the interests of the East," etc.

[127] In New York, John Williams asked, "What reason have we to suppose that our rulers will be more sympathetic, and heap lighter burdens upon their constituents than the rulers of other countries? If crossing the Atlantic can make men virtuous and just, I acknowledge that they will be forever good and excellent rulers; but otherwise, I must consider them as I do magistrates of other countries." 2 Elliot 340.

"There were many who regarded federal authority in the light of a foreign government, and transferred to it the hostility they had felt to the mother country under the colonial regime." Jameson, *Essays on Constitutional History* 58 (1889). The opposition sentiment was "Why fight a war to achieve independence only to be taxed by a powerful Congress instead of by a powerful Parliament." Bowen 11. Cf. Chapter 8, note 163. Professsor McCloskey remarks on the then current "illusion that localism is inevitably linked to democracy that a potent central government is the instrument of minority control and the enemy of liberty." McCloskey, Introduction 4.

[128] 3 Sparks, *Life of Gouverneur Morris* 438 (1832). Unconstitutional, he explained, "because the Constitution is no more if it can be changed by the Legislature," echoing Vattel. Ibid.

[129] 4 Elliot 63.

[130] Id. at 64.

[131] Said Wilson, "Sir William Blackstone will tell you that in Britain . . . the Parliament may alter the form of the government and that its power is absolute,

and it had been contemptuously dismissed, in favor of the lessons drawn from experience, by Iredell, "mastermind" of the North Carolina convention[132] and later a Justice of the Supreme Court. In an address published in 1786 respecting the formation of the North Carolina constitution, he said:

> It was, of course, to be considered how to impose restrictions on the legislature . . . [to] guard against the abuse of unlimited power, which was not to be trusted, without the most imminent danger, to any man or body of men on earth. We had not only been sickened and disgusted for years with the high and almost impious language from Great Britain, of the omnipotent power of the British parliament, but had severely smarted under its effects. We . . . should have been guilty of . . . the grossest folly, if in the same moment when we spurned at the *insolent despotism* of Great Britain, we had established a *despotic* power among ourselves. Theories were nothing to us, opposed to our own severe experience.

In the process of forming a State government, he said, "we decisively gave our sentiments against" the "theory of the necessity of the legislature being absolute in all cases."[133] Compared to such statements by leaders of public opinion, the materials relied upon to exhibit the hold of "legislative supremacy" in the pre-Convention

---

without control . . . To control the power and conduct of the legislature, by an overruling constitution, was an improvement in the science and practice of government reserved to the American states." 2 Elliot 432. The chief instrument of this "control," he made plain, was to be "interposition of the judicial department." Quoted, supra, text accompanying note 64. And in his 1791 Lectures, he returned to the "lately introduced" Blackstone doctrine and rejected the notion that judicial power to control unreasonable legislative action "would be subversive of all government," pointing to the "miserable consequence" of that view, and affirming that under the Constitution the courts were to render "vain and fruitless" every legislative "transgression" of Constitutional bounds—"a noble guard against legislative despotism." 1 Wilson, *Works* 457–458, 462.

[132] 2 Bancroft 348. See alsos Yates, quoted infra, Chapter 3, text accompanying note 187.

[133] McRee 145–146. Commenting on parliamentary supremacy, *Federalist* No. 53 at 348, said that "the dangerous practices [thereunder have] produced a very natural alarm in the votaries of free government." And in No. 81 at 523, 524–525, Hamilton met the argument that the "Parliament of Great Britain, and the legislatures of the several States, can at any time rectify by law, the exceptionable decisions of their respective courts," whereas the errors of the Supreme Court "will be uncontrollable and remediless," not by abjuring the connotations of the latter phrase but by demonstrating the necessity of judicial finality.

period are feeble indeed.[134] The unmistakable rejection of Blackstone's doctrine refutes Crosskey's assumption that it represented the reigning American view.

No crystal-clear grant of judicial review power was required to displace a repudiated premise. The evidence, I suggest, calls for a quite different approach. Having plainly repudiated "legislative omnipotence," having recorded their aversion to legislative "excesses," the Founders may be credited with enough horse sense to erect every possible "bulwark" against both. Instead therefore of beginning with an untenable presumption against judicial review, we are better justified in presuming that the Founders would embrace every alternative that promised to make "legislative despotism" a thing of the past.

The Influence of the State "Precedents"

Professor Crosskey makes yet a third attempt to "approximate" the "background of ideas on the subject of judicial review, which was

[134] Corwin's citations "for illustrations of the Blackstonian influence" to "arguments of attorneys in 4 Halstead (N. J.) 427 and 1 Binney (Pa.) 416," Corwin, *Doctrine* 52 n. 82, carry less weight than the statements of the leadership for adoption of the Constitution, let alone that the cited arguments of counsel were made in 1827 and 1808.

Crosskey's citations, p. 1325 n. 25 are even less convincing. For the statement that "The idea of legislative supremacy occurs over and over again in American writers of the period," he cites "Tucker's reference to Congress as 'the *supreme national council*' in his edition of Blackstone of 1803." St. George Tucker said, however, in the same edition, that Blackstone's doctrine of legislative supremacy "does not apply to governments of the American states, by whose respective Constitutions, as also by the Constitution of the Federal Government, the legislative power is restrained within certain limits," and that "in case the federal government should exercise powers not warranted by the constitution . . . the remedy is to be sought by recourse to that judiciary, to which the cognizance of the case properly belongs." 1 Tucker's *Blackstone* 48–49, and App. 153. As a judge, Tucker had participated in Kamper v. Hawkins, 1 Va. Cas. 22, 46, 60 (1793), wherein Judge Tyler, asserting the duty to declare a State law unconstitutional, declared that the "supposed 'omnipotence of parliament' . . . is an abominable insult upon the honor and good sense of our country."

Crosskey's citation of Otis' 1764 statement that "There can be *but one supreme power, which is the legislative, to which all the rest are and must be subordinate,*" Crosskey, 1325 n. 25, overlooks Otis' reliance on Coke's dictum for a judicial power to declare an Act of Parliament void. In the same 1764 statement, Otis said that

even the authority of the parliament of *Great Britain* is circumscribed by certain bounds, which if exceeded . . . [are] void. The judges of England have declared in favor of these sentiments, when they expressly declare that *acts of parliament . . . against the fundamental principle of the British Constitution are void.* Otis 109.

possessed by the Federal Convention when it drew and proposed the Constitution, and by the American people when they read and adopted it"—he turns to the pre-1787 State precedents.[135] His approach to these precedents exhibits the same defect as his treatment of Coke, for he spends his ammunition—and is not alone in this[136]— in a minute attempt to establish what the cases actually held, and makes little or no allowance for the fact that official reports of the cases were virtually inaccessible and that the men of the period gathered their "ideas" of the cases from quite disparate accounts. By his own testimony, "there was virtually no reporting of judicial decisions during [this] period."[137] "Cases of the kind," he remarks, "got into the newspapers; they were apt to be reported in pamphlets; men wrote letters about them and petitioned legislatures about them; and action was taken by the legislatures, or attempted to be taken by factions in them, against the judges who participated in such decisions.[138] Now such accounts of cases may and often do differ markedly from what courts actually have "held." But if such versions were generally accepted and men acted upon them, the possible incorrectness of the accounts does not vitiate the action.[139] Professor Crosskey's considerable labors to demonstrate what the early cases

---

[135] Crosskey 944.

[136] E.g., Boudin 51–65, 531–563.

[137] Crosskey at 943; and see Haines 94.

[138] Crosskey 943. Boudin 532 remarks that because Rutgers v. Waddington (N.Y.) "was thought by some people at the time to be an attempt by the Judiciary to disregard legislation, it was reported at great length in special pamphlet form and created great excitement and commotion. The same is true of Trevett v. Weeden [R.I.]."

[139] One must "give due weight to the influence on legal thinking of incorrect facts and incorrect assumptions when such facts and assumptions are believed to be true." Haines 91 n. 7. As Haines states, such "impressions were in certain instances important factors in determining men's views regarding judicial control over legislation." Id. at 89. And see supra, text accompanying note 91.

Crosskey himself furnishes a remarkable example of how little influence "true facts" had on the views of the 1789 Virginia convention. In his account of the Josiah Philips case, he relates that Philips had been executed under circumstances of unimpeachable validity. Ten years later, Edmund Randolph, the Attorney General in the prosecution, instanced the case in the Virginia convention as a "horrid" example of legislative abuse via a bill of attainder. Crosskey 945–946. In the convention were Patrick Henry, "who had been governor . . . at the time of the Philips execution" and "Benjamin Harrison, who had been chairman of the House of Delegates when the act attainting Philips had been passed . . . But remarkable as it may seem, none of these men, apparently, did know the true facts of what had happened." For both Henry and Harrison defended "the legislative attainder of Philips [a notorious outlaw] and his execution in consequence." Id. at

"held" are therefore beside the point; for we cannot filter into the 1787 "background of ideas" the Crosskey analysis of cases that were then inaccessible, but rather must be guided by what the men of the Convention had read and said about them. That must be our touchstone if our search is truly for the ideas "possessed" by the Convention and the Ratifiers. And several cases at least, by Crosskey's own admission, furnished a solid basis for a belief in the existence of judicial review.

In the New Hampshire "Ten Pound Act" case (1786) the courts, states Crosskey, treated as " 'unconstitutional and therefore not binding' upon them" an Act providing for the expeditious recovery of small debts without trial by jury.[140] This case, said by Crosskey to be a "strong precedent for judicial review," received notice "in several of the Philadelphia papers while the Federal Convention was in session" as repealing an "unconstitutional" Act. "It is not likely," observes Crosskey, that "the members of the Convention failed to observe this interesting item," and two delegates from New Hampshire "arrived with full information of all that had occurred," including the judicial defiance of the legislature's attempt to impeach the judges, "So it is not to be doubted," he states, that members of the Convention "knew the facts of these New Hampshire cases."[141]

Then there was *Bayard v. Singleton* (1787), which Crosskey considers with the New Hampshire case the "only real supportive precedents,"[142] where the North Carolina court held a state act "unconstitutional and void," and of which a brief notice "appeared in the Philadelphia papers towards the end of June" 1787.[143] In addition, Richard Spaight, a North Carolina member in attendance at the Convention, wrote a letter of criticism of the decision to

---

946. So the case, to borrow from Crosskey, was "mistakenly" known as one "wherein a man's rights, under the state's vaunted Bill of Rights, had been unceremoniously denied to him by the legislature, without his having any remedy whatever for this wrong." Id. at 947.

Parenthetically, if one accepts Crosskey's conclusion that this was not "a great landmark of judicial review," ibid., it nevertheless had a powerful impact upon the Virginia convention, being cited to demonstrate the need for judicial protection against legislative excesses.

[140] Crosskey 969.
[141] Id. at 970–971.
[142] 1 Martin 5 (N.C. 1787) (1901 Reprint); Crosskey 974.
[143] Crosskey 972–973.

Iredell, one of counsel who procured it. William Davie, Iredell's co-counsel, who was also a Convention member, was, "there can be little doubt," says Crosskey, "fully and promply informed of the case," so that, he concludes, the decision "must have been familiar to the men of the Federal Convention."[144]

Consider a case more open to doubt, the Rhode Island "paper money" case of *Trevett v. Weeden* (1786) which, Corwin concluded, "produced the most evident impression on the membership of the Convention."[145] James Varnum, counsel in the case, a general who had served by Washington's appointment in the Revolution, and later in the Continental Congress,[146] had reported the case in a pamphlet that was broadcast and indeed was "offered for sale in Philadelphia, at about the time the Federal Convention assembled. In addition to this, the case had been reported very widely in the newspapers at the time of its occurrence and in the fall before; its facts were familiarly mentioned during the debates in the Convention; and no doubt seems possible" says Crosskey, "that the existence of the case, the general nature of the decision in it, and what hap-

---

[144] Ibid. And see Corwin, *Doctrine* 39 n. 59. Crosskey dismisses both the New Hampshire and Bayard cases because they pertained to "legislative attempts to invade the judiciary's own peculiar prerogatives," i.e., to "self-defense," of which more will be said anon. Trevett v. Weeden allegedly "had also been a case of this character." Crosskey 974. The challenged New Hampshire Act curtailed the right to trial by jury, id. at 969, as did the Rhode Island Act involved in Trevett v. Weeden, id. at 965–966. It is no mean feat to convert denial of the individual's right to trial by jury into an invasion of "judicial prerogatives." Apparently Bayard v. Singleton regarded this as a personal right: "by the Constitution every citizen had undoubtedly a right to a decision of his property by a trial by jury." 1 Martin (N.C. 1787) 5, 7 (1901 Reprint). And in 1793 Judge Spencer Roane stated in Virginia, "In cases where the controversy before the court *does not* involve the private interest, or relate to the powers *of, the judiciary* . . . e.g. if the legislature should deprive a man of the trial by jury." Kamper v. Hawkins, 1 Va. Cas. 20, 39 (emphasis added). So much for the 20th-century conversion of the right to jury trial into a "judicial prerogative." See also Hart, Book Review 1463 n. 16.

Additionally, Bayard is thrust aside by Crosskey because "a large and influential *minority* in the state disapproved of any court's possessing such a power; and . . . were, furthermore, firmly convinced the North Carolina court did not justly possess it." Id. at 973 (emphasis added). But an even larger majority—58 to 24— beat back the minority proposals which sought to give effect to that view. Id. at 971–972. See infra, text accompanying note 162.

[145] Corwin, "Progress" 523. "Paper money" was a flaming issue. In *Federalist* No. 44 at 290, Madison commented on "The loss which America has sustained since the peace, from the pestilent effects of paper money." Feelings continued to run high about the issue. See the harsh condemnation in the South Carolina convention by General C. C. Pinckney and by Charles Pickney, 4 Elliot 306, 334.

[146] 19 *Dic. Amer. Biog.* 227.

pened to the judges who had participated in the decision, were facts more or less familiar to every member of the Federal Convention."[147] Weeden, in violation of a Rhode Island statute, had refused to accept payment for meat in paper money. The Act provided that such violations were to be tried without a jury, and Varnum maintained that the Act was therefore unconstitutional and void. Crosskey states that the judgment "simply was 'that the information was not cognizable before [the court].'" But he himself quotes from the account of the case in the *Newport Mercury* that Judge Howell went on to declare "himself independent as a judge—the penal law to be repugnant and unconstitutional—and therefore gave it as his opinion that the court could not take cognizance of the information!" As Crosskey states in a footnote, "three judges, at least, thought the legislative exclusion of jury trial unconstitutional."[148] In short, by newspaper account the court refused to take jurisdiction of a criminal prosecution under an unconstitutional statute. Certainly the legislature thought the decision had constitutional implications for it required the judges to "'assign their reasons'" for declaring "an 'act of the supreme legislature . . . to be unconstitutional, and so absolutely void.'" When the judges appeared before the legislature, it was "totally unimpressed" by their "highly technical" explanation and moved to deprive them of their offices.[149] Brinton Coxe concluded that "The bar, the legislature and the public all understood the reason why the court rendered such a judgment, *viz.* because the statute was, as the defendant's plea asserted, 'unconstitutional and so void.'"[150] And so a member of the Convention who read the published accounts might well have concluded.

Of another "precedent," *Holmes v. Walton* (N.J. 1780),[151] Crosskey says that "In *1929*, it was convincingly shown" that "no decision having anything to do with the institution of judicial review can possibly have occurred" in this case.[152] Be it so. But sixty petitioners complained to the Assembly that the justices had "set aside some of the laws as unconstitutional." These petitioners, explains Crosskey,

[147] Crosskey 965. For the widespread publication see 1 McMaster 339.
[148] Crosskey 766.
[149] Id. at 967–968.
[150] B. Coxe 245; Haines 112.
[151] Crosskey 948–952; Haines 92–95.
[152] Crosskey 948.

probably had an axe to grind; they were "probably men interested in the forfeitures that had been upset; they were, therefore, naturally desirous of presenting the New Jersey Supreme Court's action in the light most likely to discredit it."[153] Nonetheless, he prudently notes that the petition "may indicate a common view of *Holmes v. Walton,* at the time, and may in addition, be the fact principally responsible for the opinion, that the case had been a true instance of judicial review, which seems, a little later, to have been current." As evidence of such currency, Crosskey quotes the 1785 remark of Gouverneur Morris, later a member of the Convention, that "a law was once passed in New Jersey, which the judges pronounced to be unconstitutional, and therefore void."[154] But Crosskey regards it as improbable that the case was so viewed in the Convention because the chief justice, Brearley, who sat in the case, was a member of the Convention, and had the case "come into discussion in any way, Brearley *surely* would have set the Convention right as to what had been decided in it."[155] To accept the "improbability" it is essential to assume first that Brearley viewed the case as does Crosskey in a situation where, according to Crosskey, the action of the court "was easy to misinterpret as a setting aside of the legislature's act";[156] and second, that Brearley communicated such views to the Convention members. One may with equal plausibility speculate that if Brearley felt strongly enough about misconceptions of *Holmes v. Walton* to communicate his views to fellow members, that he was "probably" opposed to judicial review. Why then did he preserve complete silence in the face of repeated declarations that it would be available?[157]

A last "precedent," the 1784 New York case of *Rutgers v. Waddington,*[158] where the issue was whether a New York statute was repugnant to a treaty of peace of the Continental Congress. The

---

[153] Id. at 950.

[154] Id. at 951–952. Morris' remark "has commonly been assumed—and, no doubt correctly—to refer to Holmes v. Walton." Id. at 951.

[155] Id. at 952, 961 (emphasis added).

[156] Id. at 951.

[157] As a member of the Committee of Eleven, to which was referred unfinished portions of the Constitution, 2 Farrand 483, 496, 508, who recorded the obstinate and earnest reargument over each Article, 3 Farrand 73, and over certain suggested changes in Article III, 2 Farrand 621, Justice Brearley must have been well aware of such declarations.

[158] Citations in Crosskey 1370 n. 51; Haines 98–104.

Mayor's court, for once following the Blackstone doctrine, said that there was no judicial power to control the legislature, but it was "accused, and with good reason, it would seem—of having in fact, 'assumed and exercised power to set aside an Act of the State.' "[159] The case was "reported, at the time, in a pamphlet"; it was "widely noted in the newspapers"; and, concludes Crosskey, "it seems completely certain that *Rutgers v. Waddington* was well-known to the men in the Federal Convention."[160] Once again popular reports and impressions were that a court had attempted to overrule a statute, and on a ground that presented a grave national problem—State noncompliance with national treaties.[161] Whether or not *Rutgers v. Waddington* be regarded as a "precedent" for judicial review, its lesson was not lost on the Convention: by the Supremacy Clause State judges were directed to set aside State laws that collided with national treaties.

In a number of instances there had been subsequent legislative attempts to punish judges who, so it was thought, had the temerity to declare statutes unconstitutional. An attempt in North Carolina to put through an instruction to the court to treat statute and constitution "on a footing of complete equality . . . was defeated by a vote of 58 to 24." Then a legislative committee reported that the judges were guilty of "disregarding or suspending one of the legislature's acts" "but no recommendation was made. They were eventually discharged on the suggestion of another committee that they had not actually been guilty of malpractice in office."[162] In New Hampshire the judges, despite a 44 to 14 legislative vote that the act was constitutional, "remained obdurate" and refused "to execute the law." Upon motion for impeachment, the representatives voted 56 to 21 for approval of a committee report that the judges were "not Impeachable for Maladministration as their conduct [was] justified by the constitution" of the State. The legislature then passed an act "to repeal the act the judges had disapproved."[163] In New York, the legislature condemned the mayor's court but defeated a motion "to oust the mayor . . . from office." In Rhode Island judges who

---

[159] Crosskey 963–965; Haines 101.
[160] Crosskey 963–965.
[161] Corwin, "Progress" 529–530.
[162] Crosskey 971–972.
[163] Id. at 970.

set a statute aside failed of reappointment.[164] This mixed bag is regarded by Crosskey as "evidence of the widespread hostility of the time, to the judicial setting aside of legislative acts"![165] The leaders of the Convention wasted no sympathy on such legislative reprisals. Madison castigated Rhode Island, where "the judges who refused to execute an unconstitutional law were displaced, and others substituted, by the Legislature who would be the willing instruments of the wicked and arbitrary plans."[166] Wilson indignantly rejected a suggestion in the Pennsylvania Ratification convention that judges might be impeached if they were to "decide against the law":

> The judges are to be impeached, because they decide an act null and void, that was made in defiance of the Constitution! What House of Representatives would dare to impeach, or Senate to commit, judges for performance of their duty?[167]

In no other convention was it intimated that legislative punishment could pursue judges who declared an Act unconstitutional; instead delegates were repeatedly assured that unconstitutional laws would be annulled by the courts. Nevertheless Crosskey surmises that the several legislative "reprisals" "must surely have enforced the necessity of clearly stipulating the right of judicial review if the Supreme Court was to have that right, and of so constituting the court as to make exercise of the right secure and safe against Congress if judicial review of that body's acts were desired."[168] Again Crosskey would substitute his censorious 20th century view for that of the Founders, for the evidence hereafter collated shows that the Founders considered they were "clearly stipulating the right of judicial review."[169] How, moreover, would Crosskey reconcile his implication that judicial review was not made "safe and secure against Congress"[170] with

---

[164] For New York, id. at 964; for Rhode Island, id. at 968.

[165] Id. at 964. Speaking of North Carolina, Crosskey said, "a large and influential *minority* in the state disapproved of any court's possessing such a power." Id. at 973 (emphasis added).

[166] 2 Farrand 27–28.

[167] 2 Elliot 478; and see infra, Chapter 9, note 34.

[168] Crosskey 964, 968, 970, 971.

[169] Chapter 7, text accompanying notes 15–22.

[170] Compare his "natural conclusion" that "the Federal Convention expected the Supreme Court to exercise" certain rights "without regard to any acts of Con-

the provisions for judicial tenure and fixed compensation, which avowedly were designed to make courts "independent" of Congress.[171] Legislative attempts to discipline judges in fact fueled the resolve of those who dreaded "legislative despotism" to protect judges against such sanctions.[172]

Certainly the Fathers did not regard the "lately introduced position" of Blackstone[173] as a stumbling block; and they did not start from a doctrinaire assumption that a court owed a duty of "absolute obedience" to the legislature.[174] Their initial, empirical reliance on local legislatures had been badly shaken by legislative excesses, and they were determined that the national legislature should not be left free to follow the "propensity" of State legislatures for "pernicious measures."[175] If judicial review be regarded as an innovation—as Wilson was prepared to do in order to meet Blackstone's "lately introduced" departure from Coke's doctrine[176]—the Founders did not shrink from "change."[177] From the past the Founders learned both what to do and what to avoid. Plainly they had no stomach for "legislative omnipotence"; and such "precedents" as had come within

---

gress interfering unconstitutionally with them" through the "excepting power." Crosskey 1003; see id. at 616; Hart, Book Review 1473 n. 54.

[171] Chapter 3, text accompanying notes 323–334.

[172] Ibid. Sporadic legislative revision of judicial decisions had been harshly criticized by Jefferson and by the Pennsylvania Council of Censors. Reference to both was made by Madison in *Federalist* No. 48 at 324–325.

[173] 1 Wilson, *Works* 457. Wilson disputed Blackstone as to the English law. Id. at 182–183.

[174] Quoted supra, text accompanying note 67. Meigs, *Relation* 76–79, notes that a debating club in far-off Danville, Kentucky, concluded on May 5, 1787, that "when an Act of Assembly is contrary to the Constitution, the judge ought to govern his decision by the Constitution."

[175] Quoted supra, text accompanying note 14.

[176] See supra, note 131.

[177] Madison bluntly declared in *Federalist* No. 14 at 85 that

Had no important step been taken by the leaders of the Revolution for which a precedent could not be discovered, no government established of which an exact model did not present itself, the people of the United States might, at this moment, have been numbered among the melancholy victims of misguided councils . . . Happily for America . . . they pursued a new and more noble course. They accomplished a revolution which has no parallel in the annals of human society. They reared the fabrics of government which have no model on the face of the globe.

In so far as judicial review is concerned, these remarks are to be read against the currency of the Vattel and Coke influence. My search of the various convention records did not persuade me that the Fathers regarded judicial review as a remarkable innovation but rather that for them it had the ring of the familiar.

their ken seemed to them an important, not necessarily exclusive, means for dealing with legislative excesses, as will more clearly emerge when we examine the utterances of the Founders in the Federal Convention and then in the Ratification conventions.

If State "precedents" were few—a not surprising fact in view of the narrow gap between 1776 and 1787[178]—the salient fact is that they *were* thought to exemplify judicial review.[179] The case for

[178] Cf. Hart, Book Review 1463.
[179] Compare Madison's reference to the Rhode Island "judges who refused to execute an unconstitutional law," 2 Farrand 28; Gerry's statement that "In some States the judges had set laws aside as being agst. the Constitution," 1 Farrand 97. After earlier discussion of "independence of judges" as an "essential safeguard against infractions of the Constitution," Hamilton said, "The benefits of the integrity and moderation of the judiciary have already been felt in more States than one." *Federalist* No. 78 at 509. And in *Federalist* No. 81 at 524, he stated, "the law ought to give place to the Constitution . . . There can be no objection therefore, on this account, to the federal judiciary which will not lie against the local judiciaries in general."

In the Virginia convention, Judge Pendleton stated, "My brethren" in the judicial department "have prevented the operation of some unconstitutional acts." 3 Elliot 299. Patrick Henry, who conducted an all-out fight against adoption, commented that "The honorable gentlemen did our judiciary honor in saying that they had the firmness to counteract the legislature in some cases. Yes sir, our judges had the fortitude to declare that they . . . would oppose unconstitutional acts . . . I take it as the highest encomium on this country, that the acts of the legislature if unconstitutional, are liable to be opposed by the judiciary." 3 Elliot 324–325. What better index of the contemporary understanding than agreement by opposing leaders, in the midst of the hard-fought campaign, that judicial review had precedent?

As Professor Hart stated, "What the materials do show incontestably, as other records of the time confirm, is that the idea of judicial review was in people's minds. The power had been repeatedly asserted, seldom if ever negatived, and on at least three occasions actually exercised before the Constitution was signed." Hart, Book Review 1463.

Professor Crosskey has made overmuch of Judge Pendleton's statement in 1782 that the question whether the Virginia court could declare null an act passed by the legislature was "indeed a deep, important, and . . . tremendous question, which he found no occasion to decide because there had been no violation of the Constitution." Crosskey 954–955. Some of his brethren, at least, did not share his reserve. Id. at 958–959. When the issue arose in 1788, Pendleton joined with his brethren in the Remonstrance which the Court of Appeals sent to the Virginia legislature, wherein it was stated that "the constitution and the act are in opposition and cannot exist together, and that the former must conrol the operation of the latter." Appended to Kamper v. Hawkins, 1 Va. Case. 22, 98, 100–102 (1793). To obviate the argument that the court was encroaching on the legislature "when they decide between an act of the people and an act of the legislature," the judges said in the Remonstrance that they were acting "within the line of their duty," and that to maintain harmony with the legislature the "court most sincerely wish that the present infraction of the constitution may be remedied by

judicial review does not therefore hinge upon whether there existed an established *practice* of judicial review, but rather on the Founders' *belief* that existing precedents, apparently fortified by Coke and Holt, furnished a means to curb Congressional excesses and enforce Constitutional limits.[180] As Corwin stressed, the "indebtedness" of the Fathers

> to the past was for ideas rather than for institutions. Whenever therefore they borrow from the past any of the really distinctive features of our constitutional system, for example, Federalism, checks and balances, judicial review, they will be found to have taken them, not in the form of institutions tested and hammered into shape by practice, but as raw ideas.
>
> The case of judicial review furnishes a particularly good example of the issue between those who, like myself, would insist upon the rationalistic background of American constitutional history and those who would insist upon its institutional background.[181]

---

the legislature themselves . . . But should their wishes be disappointed by the event, they see no other alternative for a declaration by the legislature and the judiciary than an appeal to the people." Id. at 107–108. Crosskey 957, says that in the Remonstrance "the Virginia judges did not say to their legislature: 'Hither shall you go, but no further.' They displayed, instead, the greatest diffidence that the legislature would heed their views." Nevertheless, the court did not shrink from declaring that a legislative act was opposed to the constitution, and since problems of enforcement were yet to be resolved the court felt constrained to appeal to the people if the legislature did not join in the court's "declaration." In 1793, Judge Tucker read the Remonstrance as authority for a square holding that an Act was unconstitutional. Kamper v. Hawkins, 1 Va. Case. 22, 93, 98. Then there is Pendleton's own remark in the Virginia convention in 1789, quoted above, which was immediately confirmed by Patrick Henry, both of which follow the Remonstrance in time. In that convention Pendleton also said that "oppressive laws will not be warranted by the Constitution" and "independent judges will never admit an oppressive construction." 3 Elliot 548.

[180] See e.g., supra, G. Morris, text accompanying note 154; Madison, text accompanying note 166; Gerry, infra, Chapter 3, text accompanying note 13.

[181] Corwin, 9 *Mich. L. Rev.* 103.

THE FEDERAL CONVENTION

AND BEARD'S TALLY

Possibly encouraged by Professor Frankfurter's remark in 1924 that Charles Beard's study of the Framers' views on judicial review should have put an end to "empty controversy,"[1] Beard affirmed in 1938 that his book had "settled the controversy . . . The ghost of usurpation was fairly laid."[2] Despite this certificate of burial the ghost has continued to frequent scholarly haunts, and in the persisting controversy the opposition has in fact preempted the center of the stage.[3] It is time to reappraise the conclusions in Beard's 1912 study in the light of subsequent criticism and to test both conclusions and criticism against the original records so that each reader may consider the evidence and determine for himself which way the scales tilt.

Beard based his study on the utterances of the Framers before, during, and after the Convention. Of the fifty-five members of the

[1] Supra, Chapter 1, text accompanying note 18.

[2] Beard 35–36.

[3] Supra, Chapter 1, text accompanying notes 19–24. Because much criticism of the conventional view will be drawn from Boudin and Crosskey, it may be noted that in 1962 Professor Westin referred to their books as being "in the grand manner," Westin 27, and to Crosskey's "massive two-volume study," id. at 33. See also Rossiter, *Hamilton* 296; Friendly 393 n. 52. In his "Practicing Lawyers' Guide to the Current Law Magazines," Professor Keeffe says that Crosskey "argues with great force that, except for alteration of *its* Article III powers [self-defense], the Court should be powerless to declare Congressional legislation unconstitutional." 53 A.B.A.J. 91, 93 (1967) (emphasis added).

Crosskey who, like Boudin, attacks the Beard view, and who is not himself given to understatement, says that Boudin "is inclined to argue much beyond his evidence." Crosskey 1368 n. 22.

Convention who were present at its meetings, says Beard, at least one-third "took little or no part in the proceedings or were of little weight or were extensively absent." There were twenty-five "whose character, ability, diligence and regularity of attendance . . . made them the dominant element in the convention . . . Among these men were leaders of whose words and activities we have the fullest records." Seventeen of these men, he states, "declared directly or indirectly for judicial control." Adding eight of the less prominent members, he arrives at a total of twenty-five who "favored or at least accepted some form of judicial control."[4]

The primary evidence, of course, is what was said on the Convention floor. Next come utterances of the Members outside the Convention not too far removed in time, which afford a clue to their views, on the premise that they voted in accordance with their opinions. On this premise, subsequent utterances which are at war with what the speaker said in the Convention are discounted because it is reasonable to assume that he acted in the Convention in accordance with what he said on the floor. That assumption is not undercut by a subsequent change of opinion. Men's opinions shift over the years, but such shifts do not prove that the earlier belief was spurious. No reliance is placed on utterances in the midst of the sharpening power struggle between Federalists and Jeffersonians in the late 1790's. This is not to say that the Convention was unmoved by political considerations, but the Framers were seeking to reconcile political differences—for example, when the States Righters accepted federal supremacy over State laws and constitutions, rather than to blow them up for purposes of political conflict. They were acting like statesmen rather than politicians.[5] Even in

[4] Beard 47, 69.
[5] When Washington, who presided over the Convention, transmitted the Constitution to the Congress, he wrote,

> in all our deliberations on this subject we kept steadily in our view, that which appears to us the greatest interest of every true American, the consolidation of our Union . . . [T]hus the Constitution, which we now present, is the result of a spirit of amity, and of that mutual deference and concession which the peculiarity of our political situation rendered indispensable.

2 Farrand 667. In the 1780's, de Pauw says of New York, "Party was an evil," and refers to 1787 as "a time when party and faction were not respectable." De Pauw, *The Eleventh Pillar* 102, 52 (1966).
"The Convention," says Donald G. Morgan, "was an exercise in detachment,

the First Congress, in which sat a considerable group of Framers, recognition of the availability of judicial review cut across incipient party lines.[6]

REMARKS IN THE CONVENTION

Remarks about judicial review in the Convention are not clustered around a systematic analysis of Article III, which came late in the Convention, but bob up as one facet or another of the Legislative power was under discussion.[7] Perhaps this may account in part for the casualness of these remarks, a quality which itself suggests that the availability of judicial review as a necessary instrument of the new system was taken for granted.[8] For the most part, these remarks were made during the debate on the Virginia proposal to include the judiciary[9] in a Council of Revision which could negative a Congressional Act *before* it was effective. It needs to be emphasized at once, Crosskey to the contrary notwithstanding, that judicial review did not emerge as a substitute for the rejected Council,[10] but that the two were regarded from the beginning as complementary and cumulative. In explaining the Virginia Plan, Randolph set out

---

in the creation of conditions which enabled representative leaders . . . to put political pressure aside and conduct a search for principles of constitutional government appropriate for the purpose." Morgan, *Congress and the Constitution* 42 (1966). But the "calm communication between minds that had marked the 1789 episode was gone in 1798." Id. at 65. Debate on the Sedition Act engendered "party rancor." Ibid. When Speaker Dayton, a Framer, charged Abraham Baldwin of Georgia, another Framer, with "grossly misrepresenting the intent of the framers," Baldwin "decried the tone of the proceedings. Never, he said, had the 'councils of the United States' exhibited such harshness of manner and indecorum as in this Fifth Congress." Id. at 66. The "record of the House debate clearly reflects the ascendancy of party conflict." Id. at 59. Compare infra, note 76.

[6] Infra, Chapter 5, text accompanying notes 11–18.

[7] Cf. van Doren 47.

[8] It is when a position is assumed to have general acceptance that it is casually stated. Cf. McGowan, "The Problem of Historical Perspective," 33 *Notre Dame Lawyer* 527, 538 (1958). See also infra, Chapter 3, note 315.

[9] Reference to the "judiciary" or to "judges" generally meant the Supreme Court. Ratner 162 n. 23.

[10] The "men in the Convention who were most interested in using the Supreme Court justices as guards against Congressional excesses *at first* attempted to provide for the Justices' functioning in this way, by making them . . . the dominant members of a 'Council of Revision'" (emphasis added). Crosskey 1013; see also infra, Chapter 6, note 16. Compare Crosskey's own statements, infra, text accompanying note 79, and note 84.

Checks upon the Legv. and Ex. Powers
1) A Council of Revision to be selected out of the ex. and Judcy Departments, etc.
2) A natl. judiciary to be elected by the natl. Legr.[11]

These "checks," as earlier appeared, in large part responded to fear of legislative excesses.[12]

Elbridge Gerry

When the Council of Revision came up for consideration, Gerry doubted

> whether the Judiciary ought to form a part of it, as they will have a sufficient check agst. encroachments on their own department by their exposition of the laws, which involved a power of deciding on their Constitutionality. In some States the Judges had actually set aside laws as being agst. the Constitution. This was done too with general approbation.[13]

From remarks such as "encroachments on their own department," first Corwin and then Crosskey deduced that only judicial "self-defense" was in contemplation, that is defense against invasion of their own judicial prerogatives.[14] A number of such "self-defense"

---

[11] 1 Farrand 28. These are Paterson's notes and therefore free from the "falsification" imputed to Madison by Crosskey, 1009. For the Virginia Plan Resolutions themselves see 1 Farrand 21.

By "checks" the Framers embraced a power to "negative" a law. Madison, speaking on behalf of the Congressional "power to negative legislative acts of the States," labeled it a "check" on State encroachments and oppressions. 1 Farrand 164. Compare Luther Martin's rejection of judicial participation in an Executive veto on the ground that the judiciary would "have a double negative." Infra, text accompanying note 43. Randolph's explanation also casts doubt upon Corwin's statement that "in the so-called Virginia Plan . . . the idea of judicial review was entirely overlooked." Corwin, *Court Over* 25.

[12] See supra, Chapter 2, text accompanying notes 6–21.

[13] 1 Farrand 97. Boudin 565, states, "*It may also be assumed safely that Mr. Gerry's opinion on the point would not have carried any weight with the Convention* since he was not even a lawyer." No more was Madison, and yet no one was more influential. It is not pretended that Gerry could "decide" for the Convention; his remarks do however register his own opinion, and it is most significant that a veteran legislator should be aware of what judicial review entailed and consider that it was available, and that no "lawyer" rose to correct him.

[14] Corwin, *Court Over* 29, asserts that Gerry "evidently regarded" judicial review "as mainly a self-defensive weapon of the judiciary." Crosskey maintains that "it was the theory of Gerry and, apparently, of others in the Convention" that

remarks will be examined. Here let us consider Crosskey's remark that what Gerry said "probably" was "imperfectly recorded" because of "difficulties" which arise from his alleged distinction between "actually set aside laws as being agst. the Constitution" and merely "deciding on their Constitutionality." The latter, says Crosskey, resembles the "advisory opinions, for which specific provision was made" in the Massachusetts Constitution.[15] "Deciding" is not so easily transformed into "advice," particularly since Gerry illustrated the "power of deciding on Constitutionality" by instances where judges "had set aside laws as being against the Constitution." This it was, not "advisory opinions," that Gerry meant by "deciding."

Gerry is cited by Boudin to show that "the Framers were not particular admirers of the Judiciary" and that "*he did not want* the judges in the particular role which Professor Beard says the Framers *must* have intended to assign to them," relying on one of Gerry's subsequent objections to judicial participation in a Council of Revision: "It was making statesmen of the judges, and *setting them up as guardians of the people. He relied, for his part, on the representatives of the people as the guardians of their rights and interests.*"[16] This was but one of a number of objections, among them, "It was combining & mixing together the Legislative & the other departments." Gerry meant to leave the *enactment* of legislation to the legislators without judicial intermeddling in the *enacting* process, as is pointed up by his closing remark: "A better expedient for correcting the laws, would be to appoint as had been done in Pena. a person or persons of proper skill to draw bills for the Legislature." There is no good reason to read these remarks as a repudiation of his earlier recognition of the judicial function of setting "aside laws as being agst. the Constitution." In any event, the speculations of both Crosskey and Boudin are set at rest by Gerry's unequivocal expressions in the First Congress during the debate on the Presidential "removal" power, when he said that "judges are the constitutional umpires on such questions," and

---

judicial review "was a right existing for the judiciary's protection of its own Constitutional prerogatives only" Crosskey 1013–1015.

[15] Id. at 1372 n. 10, 1013–1014.

[16] Boudin 579; 2 Farrand 75. Both Boudin and Crosskey are given to generous use of italics.

asked whether the judges "would not be bound to declare the law a nullity, if this clause is continued in it, and is inconsistent with the Constitution."[17]

Rufus King

King also wished to exclude judges from the Council of Revision, "observing that the Judges ought to be able to expound the law as it should come before them, free from the bias of having participated in its formation."[18] What "expound" was understood to mean is

[17] 1 *Ann. Cong.* 492, 524. Gerry emphatically rejected Congress as the expounder of the Constitution:

> The people of America can never be safe, if Congress have a right to exercise the power of giving constructions to the constitution different from the original instrument . . . But if the power of making declaratory acts really rests in Congress, and the judges are bound by our decisions, we may alter that part of the constitution which is secured from being amended by the fifth article. Id. at 523, 557.

Horace Davis, *Veto* 48, accepts Gerry as one who *"favored* judicial control" but wavers in his evaluation of Gerry, citing his refusal to sign the Constitution, one reason being that "the judicial department will be oppressive." Id. at 52; 1 Elliot 493. Gerry's letter of explanation exhibits concern over the impact of the Constitution on the States, over loss of individual liberties and the "indefinite and dangerous powers" of Congress. It is therefore unlikely that his "oppressive" judiciary remark expressed concern that Acts of Congress might be set aside. Then too, on the Convention floor Gerry assigned as one reason for not signing the Constitution that it would "establish a tribunal without juries, which will be a Starchamber as to Civil cases." 2 Farrand 633. This reflected widespread concern that the appellate jurisdiction of questions of "fact" would invade trial by jury. See infra, Chapter 9, text accompanying notes 8–19, and it may be that his later "oppressive" remark referred to this. Compare 2 Farrand 635. Remains Davis' citation of Gerry's pre-ratification statement that "There are no well defined limits of the Judiciary Powers; they seem to be left as a boundless ocean." Davis, *Veto* 52. Consequently Davis cannot believe that Gerry *"approved* of giving to the Supreme Court the highest power imaginable—that of annulling an Act of Congress." Id. at 53. Throughout, such fears as were expressed of the Judiciary were in a context of States Rights, the swallowing up of the State courts and the like. See e.g., 2 Farrand 638; 3 Elliot 542, 565, 527; Address by Melancton Smith, reprinted Ford, *Pamphlets* 103; 1 *Ann. Cong.* 846, 865. Though he would not sign the Constitution, Gerry assumed the availability of judicial review in the Convention, and later in the First Congress, as Davis recognizes. Davis, *Veto* 53. And see infra, Chapter 5, text accompanying note 18; id. Chapter 8 at note 244.

[18] 1 Farrand 98. These notes of Madison are confirmed by Yates, id. at 105, by Rufus King himself, id. at 108, and by William Pierce, id. at 109, a striking disproof on a telling point of Crosskey's charge that Madison falsified his notes. See Hart, Book Review 1477 n. 64. Compare Madison's faithful rendition of Pinckney's remarks, 4 Farrand 28 n. 1. Boudin 565, on the other hand, says that "as to Mr. King, there is very serious doubt whether he even conceded it [judicial review] in the Constitutional Convention. At least, Madison's minutes

made clear by William Pierce, who records King as saying that "the Judicial ought not to join in the negative of a Law, because the Judges will have the expounding of those Laws when they come before them, and they will no doubt stop the operation of such as shall appear repugnant to the Constitution."[19] Mark too that King postulates an available judicial power, not a substitute conceived after the Council was voted down. Gerry's motion to exclude the judiciary from participation in the veto prevailed.[20]

According to Crosskey, King's statement "was apparently . . . in connection with the judiciary's right to protect its own peculiar constitutional prerogatives."[21] That inference finds little support in the facts. The topic under discussion was the Virginia proposal for a Council "to examine *every* act of the National Legislature before it shall operate,"[22] not merely those which affected judicial "prerogatives." Gerry, it is true, had objected to judicial participation on the ground that "they will have a sufficient check agst. encroachment on their own department by their exposition of the laws."[23] But King did not pick up this phraseology; instead he spoke in broadest terms: "Judges ought to be able to expound the law as it should come before them,"[24] which responded to the proposed judicial participation in a veto of "every" law.

James Wilson

When Wilson reopened the matter on July 21st,[25] he said,

The Judiciary ought to have an opportunity of remonstrating agst. projected encroachments on the people as well as themselves. It has been said that the Judges, as expositors of the Laws would have an opportunity of defending their constitutional rights. There was weight in this observation; but this power of the

---

do not make any mention of it." Thus King's own notes, confirmed by Yates and Pierce, are deemed insufficient, let alone that it stretches the facts to maintain that Madison did not "make any mention of it."

[19] 1 Farrand 109.
[20] Ibid.
[21] Crosskey 1014.
[22] 1 Farrand 97, 21.
[23] Id at 97.
[24] Id. at 98.
[25] 2 Farrand 73. For intervening ineffective attempts, see Crosskey 1014.

judges did not go far enough. Laws may be unjust, may be unwise, may be dangerous, may be destructive; and yet not be so unconstitutional as to justify the Judges in refusing to give them effect. Let them have a share in the Revisionary power, and they will have an opportunity of taking notice of these characters of a law, and of counteracting, by the weight of their opinion the improper views of the Legislature.[26]

In short, let the courts share in *preventing the passage* of unwise laws which fall short of unconstitutionality and therefore cannot be set aside judicially. On August 23d he added, "The firmness of judges is not of itself sufficient. Something further is requisite—It will be better to prevent the passage of an improper law, than to declare it void when passed."[27] The Council was for him merely cumulative, adding another safety factor. In the Pennsylvania Ratification convention, and later in his 1790–91 Philadelphia "Lectures on Law" while serving both as professor and as Justice of the Supreme Court, Wilson made these views clear beyond cavil.[28]

Wilson's name has cropped up frequently in these pages and it will appear more often in the pages to come, so that it is appropriate to notice the attributes which lend special force to his views. In his Introduction to the 1967 edition of Wilson's *Works*, Professor McCloskey lists some preliminary and more obvious claims of Wilson to our esteem:

He was one of six men who signed both the Declaration of Independence and the Constitution; and his contribution to the deliberations of the Federal Convention was second only to Madison's. He was the principal figure in the struggle to secure ratification of the Constitution in Pennsylvania, the approval of that state being indispensable to the success of the whole constitutional movement . . . He was . . . commonly accepted in a nation already much dominated by lawyers as the most learned and profound legal scholar of his generation.[29]

[26] 2 Farrand 73.
[27] Id. at 391.
[28] Infra, Chapter 4, text accompanying notes 39–41; id. Chapter 5 at note 28.
[29] McCloskey, Introduction 2. For similar statements by other scholars see id. at 6.

From 1768 onward he had been an incisive student of the perplexities that beset Colonial relations with an authoritarian Parliament,[30] and he was to become a Justice of the Supreme Court.

"Expounding"

Now Gerry renewed his objections to "mixing the Legislative and other departments," and said, "It was making the Expositors of the Laws, the Legislators which ought never to be done,"[31] a clear expression of the idea that the legislature was excluded from "the power of interpreting standing law."[32] "Expounding," "exposition," and "expositors" will recur and the meaning these words had for the Fathers bears emphasis. It appeared in Gerry's statement that the judiciary's "exposition of the laws . . . involved a power of deciding on their constitutionality."[33] The judges, said King, "will have the expounding" of the laws "and will no doubt stop the operation of such as shall appear repugnant to the Constitution."[34]

In opposing judicial participation in a Council of Revision, George Mason said that "in their expository capacity of judges they would have one negative" and "in this capacity . . . they could declare an unconstitutional law void."[35] The dissenting John Mercer "disapproved of the Doctrine that judges as expositors of the Constitution should have authority to declare a law void."[36] Madison pressed for judicial independence lest Congress be the "expositor as well as the maker of the laws," that is to say, interpretation was not for Congress but the courts, who must be free to call laws into question without "complaisance" to Congress.[37] With good reason did Corwin

---

[30] Id. at 9–10. Wilson "was recognized as one of the most learned men in the young nation; he did know more about history and government than almost any one else." Id. at 24.

[31] 2 Farrand 75.

[32] Corwin, *Doctrine* 42, notes that "in one form or another" this "notion . . . was reiterated again and again and was never contradicted."

[33] 1 Farrand 97. Almost 100 years earlier Chief Justice Holt stated in The King v. Earl of Banbury, Skinner 517, 526, 90 Eng. Rep. 231, 236 (1693), that the judges "construe and expound Acts of Parliament, and adjudge them to be void."

[34] 1 Farrand 109.

[35] 2 Farrand 78.

[36] Id. at 298.

[37] Id. at 34. The idea that courts would frustrate legislative "usurpation" when "expounding . . . legislative acts" was again expressed by Madison in *Federalist* No. 44, quoted infra, text accompanying note 146. Compare Madison's letter to Washington, April 16, 1787, 2 Madison, *Writings* 347. When Madison later

state that "the function of judicial review is almost invariably related by Members of the Convention to the power of the judges as 'expositors of the law.' "[38]

Caleb Strong and Nathaniel Gorham

Strong and Gorham maintained that the "expository" function should be uninfluenced by prior judicial participation in law-making through membership in a Council of Revision. Strong "thought with Mr. Gerry that the power of making ought to be kept distinct from that of expounding, the laws. No maxim was better established. The Judges in exercising the function of expositors might be influenced by the part they had taken, in framing the laws."[39] Similarly, Gorham said that "the Judges ought to carry into the exposition of the laws no prepossession with regard to them."[40] When these remarks are viewed in the framework of the earlier remarks of King and Gerry, it seems not unreasonable to assume that Gorham and Strong attached their meaning to "expositors" and "exposition." That this was the accepted connotation is again suggested by Mason's subsequent remark.[41] Beard included Strong on the basis of his vote for the Judiciary Act,[42] a vote which strengthens the inference I would draw from his use of "expounding"; and I would add Gorham, recognizing, however, that his case is weaker.

---

stated in the Virginia convention, "with respect to treaties, there is a peculiar propriety in the judiciary's expounding them," 3 Elliot 532, there can be little doubt that he contemplated that courts would set aside State laws in contravention of a treaty. See infra, Chapter 4, text accompanying note 92; Appendix B, text accompanying notes 70–72. Cf. Kamper v. Hawkins, 1 Va. Cas. 20, 78–79 (1793), where Judge Tucker tied the power to "expound" the laws to the power to declare them unconstitutional, precisely as had Holt, C. J. 100 years earlier. Supra, note 33. To the same effect, Judge Spencer Roane, Kamper v. Hawkins, supra, at 38–39.

[38] Corwin, *Doctrine* 43–44. In the First Congress, Gerry again stated that "the judges are the expositors of the Constitution and the acts of Congress. Our exposition therefore would be subject to their revisal. But a further reason why we are not the expositors, is, that the Judiciary may disagree with us, and undo what all our efforts have labored to accomplish." 1 *Ann. Cong.* 596.

[39] 2 Farrand 75.

[40] Id. at 79.

[41] Infra, text accompanying note 49.

[42] Beard 68–69. From this vote, Davis, *Veto* 63, draws exactly the opposite conclusion. My reasons for concurring with Beard are hereinafter set forth. Strong is not included by Hart, Book Review 1477; Ratner 162–163 n. 25.

Luther Martin

Luther Martin objected to judicial participation in the veto, saying, "as to the Constitutionality of laws, that point will come before the Judges in their proper official character. In this character they have a negative on the laws. Join them with the Executive in the Revision and they will have a double negative,"[43] parenthetically, confirming Randolph's proposal to have *two* checks on the Legislative, namely the Council of Revision *and* the Judiciary. Despite this unmistakable statement, which Mason took to mean that "judges could declare an unconstitutional law void,"[44] Horace Davis lists Martin in opposition to judicial review because he later argued to the Maryland Legislature *as a reason for rejecting the Constitution* that "Whether . . . any laws or regulations of the Congress . . . are contrary to or not warranted by the constitution, rests only with the judges."[45] Minimally this constitutes recognition that the Constitution *provided* for judicial review. The reason for Martin's opposition, indicated in a subsequent communication to Ellsworth, was not that judicial review was undesirable, but that he was opposed to trial of such questions in "the inferior federal courts . . . it was my wish and hope that any question of that kind would have been determined *in the first instance* in the courts of the respective states" and, it may be added, he admitted, having been charged by Ellsworth with so doing, that he "voted an appeal should lay to the supreme judiciary of the United States."[46]

Crosskey would disparage Martin's utterance on a different ground. He regards that utterance as "vaguely general" (as contrasted with review limited to "self-defense"), "*if* taken in strict literality." But Crosskey does not take him literally because Martin allegedly "was against the proposal to use the judges to protect the people,"[47] a manifest warping of Martin's objection to giving the judiciary a second, "double" negative by participating in a veto at

---

[43] 2 Farrand 76.

[44] Infra, text accompanying note 49.

[45] Davis, *Veto* 54; 3 Farrand 172, 220.

[46] 3 Farrand 287, 273. Davis, *Veto* 55–56, notices the point without mention of its implications. See also Martin's statement, infra, note 192.

[47] Crosskey 1017.

the legislative stage.[48] Certainly Mason took Martin with "strict literality."

George Mason

Mason anticipated that the Legislature

> would so much resemble that of the individual States, that it must be expected frequently to pass unjust and pernicious laws. This [Revisionary] restraining power was therefore essentially necessary . . . It has been said (by Mr. L. Martin) that if the judges were joined in this check on the laws, they would have a double negative, since in their expository capacity of judges they would have one negative. He would reply that in this capacity they could impede in one case only, the operation of the laws. They could declare an unconstitutional law void. But with regard to every law however unjust oppressive or pernicious, which did not plainly come under this description, they would be under the necessity as Judges to give it a free course. He wished further use to be made of the Judges, of giving aid in preventing every improper law.[49]

Because Mason said that in "their expository capacity . . . they could impede in one case only . . . They could declare an unconstitutional law void," Crosskey concludes that "Mason plainly did not think that the power of judicial review amounted to much."[50] Unmistakably, however, Mason did recognize an existing judicial power to declare laws unconstitutional, and it is precisely that power that is in issue.

Without mention of Mason's above-quoted statement, Horace Davis concludes that Mason's "approval of the theory of judicial control seems on the whole to rest on a slender foundation."[51] He

[48] Parting company with Crosskey, Boudin 565, stated, "The only ones who asserted it [that judicial review was available] were the same Gerry and Martin." He goes on to say, "The others named conceded it in debate–some with reservations. And everybody knows the difference between an assertion and a concession in debate." Presumably Wilson was one of those who so "conceded," and yet his conduct in the Pennsylvania convention, and his 1791 Lectures prove him to be a staunch advocate of judicial review. "Concessions" are generally made when points cannot be controverted. Of "concessions" made *arguendo* I found no trace.

[49] 2 Farrand 78.

[50] Crosskey 1017. Crosskey concedes that Mason, like Martin, had reference to judicial review in "general," i.e., not confined to "self-defense." Ibid.

[51] Davis, *Veto* 57.

notices Mason's remarks respecting judicial enforcement of the prohibition of ex post facto laws,[52] and says that "With the exception of these remarks," Mason's "whole attitude seems adverse to vesting such power in the judiciary."[53] First he points out that Mason "favored Madison's plan for a Council of Revision";[54] but, as the above quotation shows, this was in order to reach *beyond* the judicial power respecting unconstitutional laws to embrace laws (by judicial participation in a veto) that though constitutional were yet "improper." Again, Davis invokes Mason's letter of October 1787 to Washington, in which he objected to the prohibition against ex post facto laws because inevitably legislatures must make them, and because such a "breach" will "afford precedents for other innovations." "Evidently," Mason was "not then relying on the courts to check such legislation."[55] The bearing of this statement on judicial review, at best ambiguous, may be contrasted with Mason's subsequent express recognition in the Virginia convention of judicial enforcement of the prohibitions of both State and federal ex post facto laws,[56] and in the federal Convention of the "restraining power" of the courts over unconstitutional laws of Congress.[57] Finally, Davis refers to the fact that Mason "is credited with the authorship of the Virginia convention amendments intended to limit the power of the federal judiciary"[58] by omitting from the "arising under" clause the words "Constitution, laws," leaving solely "treaties."[59] In recommending that federal courts be deprived of jurisdiction to enforce federal laws, Virginia cannot be understood to mean that those laws would be altogether unenforceable, but rather that

[52] Id. at 56; Article I, §10 (1); 3 Elliot 479–480. In the Virginia convention Mason was fearful that the *ex post facto* clause embraced civil as well as criminal laws, and said, "When this matter comes before the federal judiciary, they must determine according to this Constitution. It says, expressly, that they [Congress] shall not make *ex post facto* laws. Will it not be the duty of the federal court to say that such laws are prohibited? . . . an express power is given to the federal court to take cognizance of such controversies, and to declare null all *ex post facto* laws." 3 Elliott 479–480. Though this remark was made in opposition to adoption of the Constitution, it recognizes judicial power to set aside federal laws.

[53] Davis, *Veto* 57.
[54] Ibid.
[55] Ibid.
[56] See supra, note 52.
[57] Supra, text accompanying note 49.
[58] Davis, *Veto* 57.
[59] 3 Elliot 660.

the State courts, to which Patrick Henry and others looked for protection,[60] would be the judges whether federal laws complied with State constitutions and their bills of rights. State court primacy, subject to appeal to the Supreme Court, was soon the path taken in the Judiciary Act of 1789.[61] Davis' strained inferences do not overcome Mason's express recognition of judicial review.[62]

John Rutledge

Rutledge "thought the Judges of all men the most unfit to be concerned in the revisionary Council. The Judges ought never to give their opinion on a law till it comes before them."[63] Having in mind that both Council and judiciary had been explained by Randolph as "checks" on the Legislature, that the purpose of the negative by the Council on laws prior to effectiveness was minimally to reach laws that were unconstitutional if not merely "improper," one may fairly deduce that Rutledge had in mind a judicial "opinion" that would be parallel in effect with the Council negative. Later, during the debate on a proposed removal of judges by the Executive, Rutledge said, "If the supreme Court is to judge between the U.S. & particular States, this alone is an insuperable barrier,"[64] thereby implying that the Court would decide conflicting claims to constitutional boundaries between Congress and the States, for to men of that time the United States largely spelled Congress.[65] On the strength of these two utterances, Corwin lists Rutledge among those who accepted "the idea of judicial review as applying at least in some sense to Acts of Congress";[66] and I would concur, though Beard does not include Rutledge in his list of proponents.

[60] Infra, Chapter 4, text accompanying notes 110–111; Chapter 8, note 202.

[61] Infra, Chapter 8, text accompanying notes 182–187, 216, 234.

[62] Supra, note 49. Seemingly Mason was one of the first to argue (Corwin, *Doctrine* 32) in Robin v. Hathaway, 1 Jeff. (Va.) 109, 114 (1772), that "all acts of legislature apparently contrary to natural right and justice, are . . . considered as void . . . Such have been the adjudications of our courts of justice," citing Coke. See Haines 63.

[63] 2 Farrand 80.

[64] Id. at 428.

[65] Compare supra, Chapter 2, text accompanying notes 17–18, 23–32, and Wilson's awareness that "it was delusory . . . to regard the legislature alone as the people's branch." McCloskey, Introduction 25. Cf. supra, Chapter 2, text accompanying notes 109–110.

[66] Corwin, *Court Over* 30. Davis, *Veto* 62, regards Rutledge as "doubtful or noncommittal."

Charles Pinckney

When Madison reopened the matter on August 15th, Charles Pinckney "opposed the interference of the Judges in the Legislative business: it will involve them in parties, and give a previous tincture to their opinions."[67] Unlike the earlier statements of Strong and Gorham, Pinckney did not employ the words "expound" or "expositors," but the fact that Mercer, who spoke after Pinckney, "disapproved of the Doctrine that the Judges as expositors of the Constitution should have authority to declare a law void," suggests that Mercer may so have understood him.[68] In a continuing debate one may assume that after a point has been made repeatedly it no longer needs spelling out in detail. Corwin also relies on Pinckney's earlier statement that the judges "will even be Umpires between the U. States and individual States,"[69] and lists him among those who recognized judicial review.[70]

To these remarks by Pinckney may be added his statement in the South Carolina legislature which was to call the Ratifying convention that the judicial "department might be made the keystone of the arch . . . whose duty it would be not only to decide all national questions which would arise within the Union . . ."[71] If this be deemed equivocal, his statement to the ratifying convention seems quite clear: "With this powerful influence of the purse, they [Congress] will always be able to restrain the usurpations of the other departments, while *their own licentiousness* will, in its turn, be *checked and corrected by them*."[72] In their totality Pinckney's remarks seem to indicate an assumption of judicial review, and one may, with Corwin, regard Pinckney as a proponent.

Davis states that "Pinckney did not express himself in the federal convention, but in 1799 he wrote '. . . that it is an unsafe and dangerous doctrine . . . to suppose that a judge ought to possess

---

[67] 2 Farrand 298.

[68] Melvin 179: "The very obvious inference that Pinckney expected the court to have to decide later, in the ordinary course of judicial business, upon the validity of acts of Congress seems unavoidable when we find that Mercer at once arose and protested against this general theory that the courts could negative an unconstitutional act."

[69] 2 Farrand 248.

[70] Corwin, *Court Over* 30.

[71] 4 Elliot 257–258.

[72] Id. at 330 (emphasis supplied).

CHAPTER 3

the right of questioning or deciding upon the Constitutionality of treaties, laws, or any act of the legislature . . . a doctrine which is not warranted by the constitution.'"[73] Statements made in this period, ten years after adoption of the Constitution, by Framers who were now immersed in party strife, are suspect. Pinckney was a Republican;[74] in 1799 occurred the first "determined political attack" by Republicans on the Justices of the Supreme Court, arising out of their decisions while serving as judges of circuit courts under the Alien and Sedition laws,[75] which they declined to declare unconstitutional. The Virginia and Kentucky Resolutions declared these laws unconstitutional and claimed the right of each State to decide for itself whether Congress had exceeded its powers. As Samuel Eliot Morison remarks, "Both state legislatures had their eyes on the coming presidential elections and were really engaged in lighting a fiery cross to rally the Republican clans."[76] Inevitably the controversy colored the entire problem of judicial review, so that statements on the subject by political participants may well be viewed with reservation. What Pinckney said in the federal and State conventions, rather than his subsequent politically-motivated shifts, must be the guide to the meaning he attached to the Constitution prior to its adoption.[77]

[73] Davis, Veto 59.
[74] Warren, Congress 122.
[75] Id. at 194; see also supra, note 5. Warren remarks that this attack "was not because the Court [i.e., the individual Justices] held these Acts of Congress unconstitutional, but because it failed to do so." Warren, Congress 194; cf. Boudin 160.
[76] Morison 354. Salvoes in opposition were fired by the legislatures of Delaware, Rhode Island, Massachusetts, New York, Connecticut, New Hampshire, and Vermont. 4 Elliot 532–539. Davis himself states that "the Virginia and Kentucky Resolutions and their reception indicate the politics of the moment, rather than any fixed philosophical views about the method of determining the constitutionality of laws," pointing to a reversal of State attitudes "at the time of the Hartford Convention in 1814." Davis, Veto 45–46, 127 n. 4. Boudin 161 remarks upon the "great change which had occurred in a little less than a decade" and the fact that the Federalist-Republican struggle had "assumed a somewhat geographical character." "The history of the federal bench in those early days is thus part and parcel of a fierce party strife." Frankfurter & Landis, The Business of the Supreme Court 21 (1928). See also infra, Chapter 5, text accompanying notes 35–36.
The impact of political considerations was illustrated afresh when Corwin, testifying in 1937 on the "Court-packing" plan, said, "I don't think I gave the weight that should have been given to the objections made by Dickinson and by Madison and afterwards [1799] by Charles Pinckney and by Baldwin." Westin 26.
[77] See supra, note 5.

John Mercer
Mercer

heartily approved of the motion [for a Council of Revision]. It is an axiom that the Judiciary ought to be separate from the Legislative; but equally so that it ought to be independent of that Department. The true policy of the axiom is that legislative usurpation and oppression may be obviated. He disapproved of the Doctrine that the Judges as expositors of the Constitution should have authority to declare a law void. He thought laws ought to be well and cautiously made, and then be uncontroulable.[78]

Note first that Mercer's reference to a "Doctrine that the Judges . . . should have authority to declare a law void" recognizes that the Doctrine had been mooted in terms that he understood. Even that jealous reader, Crosskey, says that it "is not to be denied" that "there is a certain implication" in Mercer's remarks that "he understood the discretionary Supreme Court veto which Madison and Wilson had just proposed, as intended by them to be a substitute for an already-provided general power of judicial review."[79] Mercer's disapproval of judicial review may also have been provisional. He wanted laws "well and cautiously made," and "*then* to be uncontroulable"; for this reason he espoused the Council of Revision, being desirous that "legislative usurpation and oppression may be obviated." But if the Council was voted down, does it follow that he wanted legislative "oppression" altogether insulated? Crosskey concludes that "it can hardly be said, with any degree of certainty just what he intended."[80] Though Mercer's statement does not therefore express ineluctable opposition to judicial review, his was the clearest dissenting voice, and I shall list him as opposed to judicial review.[81]

[78] 2 Farrand 298.
[79] Crosskey 1018. Crosskey persistently misreads Wilson as offering a "substitute" for, rather than a supplement to, judicial review. See Hart, Book Review 1476–1477.
[80] Crosskey 1019.
[81] Beard state that Mercer "stands on record as distinctly disapproving the doctrine" of judicial control. Beard 70. And see Davis, *Veto* 66–67. Mercer was decisively repudiated by his own State, Maryland. Infra, Chapter 4, note 50.

John Dickinson

Shortly after Mercer spoke, Dickinson said that he

> was strongly impressed with the remark of Mr. Mercer as to the power of the Judges to set aside the law. He thought no such power ought to exist. He was at the same time at a loss what expedient to substitute. The Justiciary of Aragon he observed became by degrees the lawgiver.[82]

Horace Davis classes Dickinson as "doubtful," and in 1937 Corwin classified him as an opponent of judicial review.[83] Both do less than justice to Dickinson's remarks. Dickinson does not say that the power is nonexistent but rather that "no such power ought to exist," suggesting, as even Crosskey concedes, that there is an existing power of judicial review.[84] One who dislikes a "power" but is "at the same time at a loss what expedient to *substitute*" indicates that in the absence of a "substitute" he sees no alternative to the "power." It is reasonable to deduce that Dickinson voted for judicial review, albeit reluctantly, in the absence of a "substitute." This deduction is bolstered by the fact that after the Convention Dickinson said in his *Letters of Fabius* (1788) that "Our government . . . will be guarded by a repetition of the strongest cautions against excesses [for example, a Congress divided into two Houses] . . . and in the president, and the federal *independent judges,* so much concerned in the execution of the laws, and in the *determination of their constitutionality* . . . the people of the whole union, may be considered as conjointly represented."[85] The bulk of his *Letter* was addressed to objections leveled against the Constitution, and his easy, passing reference to judicial review confirms that in the Convention he assumed that it existed, and as Beard stated, he presented

---

[82] 2 Farrand 299.

[83] Davis, *Veto* 62; Westin 26. In 1914 Corwin counted Dickinson among the Framers who were "definitely asserting" that the Constitution secured to the courts "the right to pass on the validity of acts of Congress." Infra, text accompanying note 267.

[84] Crosskey 1019, states that Dickinson "certainly" sounds as if he had reference to a "guard . . . *which was already provided,*" an "existing guard," and he says that "This interpretation of Dickinson's remarks . . . certainly is a natural one *as they are recorded.*"

[85] Ford, *Pamphlets* 165, 184 (emphasis added).

"this implication to the public as a commendable feature of the Constitution,"[86] again suggesting that he had voted for it.

Gouverneur Morris

Morris followed Dickinson and said that he

could not agree that the Judiciary which was part of the Executive, should be bound to say that a direct violation of the Constitution was law. A controul over the legislature might have its inconveniences. But view the danger on the other side . . . Encroachments of the popular branch of the Government ought to be guarded agst.[87]

Crosskey alone rejects Morris as a proponent, and suspects that the "Dickinson-Morris colloquy may be spurious." The "slightest consideration of the actual situation in which these men were speaking," he says, "makes perfectly clear that this one thing [a "general right of judicial review"] that *seems* to be clear, from the record of their remarks, could not have been intended by them at all. For the legislative follies that Morris feared [which he had mentioned after Mercer and before Dickinson spoke] were national emission of paper money and national legislative acts repudiating, or altering, prior national commitments involving the 'public Credit' . . . Judicial review could of course have been no guard against these ills, unless national paper emissions and national 'ex post facto laws' were forbidden to Congress. Yet, on August 15th, neither of these things were forbidden to the proposed new national legislature." Moreover, he finds it *"difficult to see why, in that context, judicial review was mentioned at all."*[88] Professor Crosskey's "perfectly clear" and "could not have been intended by them" shatter on the facts.

---

[86] Beard 49. Davis, *Veto* 49–50, finds this doubtful evidence because in the same paper Dickinson said that "when the several parts abuse their respective power . . . *the people* must restore things to that order from which their functionaries have departed." As appears from the quotation in the text, supra, Dickinson considered that the "people" were represented by the courts who would determine "constitutionality." Only if that proved unavailing need the people interfere, an idea he shared with Wilson. Infra, Chapter 6, text accompanying notes 128–141. And see Madison's remarks, infra, text accompanying note 146; cf. Hamilton's remarks, infra, text accompanying note 216.

[87] 2 Farrand 299.

[88] Crosskey 1020.

Morris had spoken for judicial review in 1785, as Crosskey himself notices,[89] and had said that "Such power in judges is dangerous; but unless it somewhere exists, the time employed in framing a bill of rights and form of government was merely thrown away."[90] And prior to the allegedly "spurious" colloquy Morris had said in the Convention that "Legislative alterations not conformable to the federal compact, would clearly not be valid. The judges would consider them null and void."[91] Why in the "colloquy" context was "judicial review mentioned at all"? Morris had first suggested for the ills he feared "the idea of requiring three-fourths of each House to repeal laws where the President should not concur," that is, to override a Presidential veto.[92] And immediately after Dickinson's short interjection, Morris went beyond that to "the expedient of an absolute negative in the Executive." The context, as Crosskey resolutely would not see, was a negative *prior* to effectiveness, and in this context those who opposed judicial participation in a veto had repeatedly referred to the fact that the judiciary would later have the opportunity to declare invalid laws unconstitutional. When Mercer at last spoke up, he quite reasonably addressed himself to such earlier remarks.[93] Then spoke Morris, and Dickinson did not reply to Morris but picked up Mercer's prior disapproval of judicial review. Morris, after first recurring to the remedy for the fears he had expressed—an absolute executive veto—turned to the Mercer-Dickinson remarks. Having earlier espoused judicial review, it is

[89] Id. at 951; and see supra, Chapter 2, text accompanying note 154.

[90] 3 Sparks, G. Morris, 438 (1832). Corwin, *Doctrine* 72, was therefore mistaken in saying that Morris "did not . . . want the judges in Pa. to exercise any such power."

Crosskey 1026, rejects the inference that remarks by Members, "before the Convention," show that they were advocates *in* the Convention of judicial review, because they "had a confidence in government organized on a national scale, which they lacked in the smaller-scale governments of the states," citing *Federalist* No. 10. Madison, it is true, thought that factionalism was likely to be diluted because of the "greater number of citizens and extent of territory" which the Union would have, id. at 60. But the fact is that widespread attachment to the State, accompanied by distrust of a remote central government, persisted. See supra, Chapter 2, text accompanying notes 13–32, 114–127; infra, Chapter 8, text accompanying notes 156–191. Moreover Gouverneur Morris weighs against the Crosskey view, for he reiterated on the floor of the Convention the view he had expressed in 1785.

[91] 2 Farrand 92.

[92] 2 Farrand 299.

[93] Id. at 298.

not strange that Morris should now pause to defend it against criticism. Extemporaneous remarks in a running debate cannot be tested by the demands of rigorously coherent organization.

It would be inexcusable to pass by in silence Crosskey's parting shot at Morris: "There remains the question of what happened to Morris' motion. And the answer is that, though it was favored by Maryland and Delaware, it was overwhelmingly voted down by all the other states. This indicates the indisposition of the Convention on August 15th, to provide any check on the two houses of Congress, beyond the overridable executive veto for which the Constitution eventually provided," and "forbid[s] the usual view that the Supreme Court was looked upon, by the framers of our government, as an agency of protection against Congress."[94] The only reference to a "motion" by Morris is his statement that "he wished the section to be postponed, in order to consider of some more effectual check than requiring ⅔ only to overrule the negative of the Executive."[95] Shortly before, he had stated that "requiring ¾ to repeal would, though not a compleat remedy, *prevent the hasty passage* of laws."[96] The vote to which Crosskey refers was on "The question for postponement [which] passed in the negative,"[97] and immediately thereafter a motion to change ⅔ of each House to ¾ was adopted.[98] The inclusion of the Judiciary in the "negative" to "prevent passage" of laws had been voted down *before* Morris spoke, and it bears reemphasis that much of the opposition to such inclusion arose from the fear that it would bias the judges in the performance of their later "expounding" function.[99] In summary, Morris, seeking to "prevent the hasty *passage* of laws," first proposed a ¾ overriding veto, then an absolute Executive veto, and then moved to postpone for consideration of a "more effectual check than requiring ⅔ only to

[94] Crosskey 1021–1022.
[95] 2 Farrand 300.
[96] Id. at 299 (emphasis added).
[97] Id. at 301.
[98] Ibid.
[99] Hamilton explained in *Federalist* No. 73 at 481 that one reason judges were excluded from the Executive veto was that "the judges, who are to be the interpreters of the law, might receive an improper bias, from having given a previous opinion in their revisionary capacities . . . . It is impossible to keep the judges too distinct from every other avocation than that of expounding the laws." See supra, Strong, text accompanying note 39; Gorham, id. at note 40; Pinckney, id. at note 67; cf. Rutledge, id. at note 63.

overrule" the Executive veto. Judicial review *after* enactment was not in issue, and the immediately following vote to substitute ¾ for ⅔ confirms that the Convention, at this point, was solely concerned with reinforcing the Executive veto, nothing else. To wring from these unpromising facts an "indisposition" of the Convention to contemplate judicial review is to indulge in wishful thinking.

Hugh Williamson

Williamson said, in the course of discussion of the prohibition against federal ex post facto laws, that "Such a prohibitory clause is in the Constitution of N. Carolina, and tho it has been violated, it has done good there and may do good here, because the judges can take hold of it,"[100] that is, to enforce the prohibition. Corwin and Davis concur with Beard in viewing Williamson as a proponent of judicial review.[101] But Crosskey states that "Whether Williamson meant, by this remark, that 'the judges could take hold of' the clause as a basis for setting aside acts of Congress deemed by them to conflict with the Constitution in this respect, or as a basis for a presumptive rule of construction, it is impossible, with certainty to say." In part Crosskey bases this on the apparent fact that North Carolina courts had not yet used the ex post facto clause to set a State law aside.[102] Even so, Williamson might have believed, if mistakenly, that North Carolina judges *had* done so, for a State law had been set aside in *Bayard v. Singleton,* and various attempts by a legislative minority to undo the decision had fallen flat.[103] It would not be straining unduly to assume that these facts were known to a North Carolina delegate to the Convention. Crosskey's reading of Williamson's remarks as suggesting a "rule of construction" borders on the droll. State legislatures had passed ex post facto laws, Charles Carroll reminded the Convention, and Gerry urged that the need for the prohibition "was greater in the National than in the State Legislature."[104] To meet the need by giving the courts the power merely to construe ex post facto laws, a "construction" which

100 Art. I, §9 (3); 2 Farrand 376.
101 Corwin, *Court Over* 30; Davis, *Veto* 62; Beard 63–64.
102 Crosskey 1025.
103 Supra, Chapter 2, text accompanying notes 142–144, and note 144. Crosskey 971–972.
104 2 Farrand 376, 375.

the Congress could wipe out merely by passing an amended law, would be like restraining a bull with a pink ribbon. It is not too much to credit Williamson with a desire for a more effective restraint,[105] as events in the North Carolina Ratification convention were to prove.

Gunning Bedford

Bedford is commonly listed against judicial review.[106] In the course of the initial debate on the Council of Revision he said that he "was opposed to every check on the Legislative, even the Council of Revision first proposed."[107] This remark was directed to the Council, not judicial review.[108] In his opposition to *all* checks on the Legislature Bedford was swimming against the current.[109] The history of the Convention and the Ratification conventions is a tale of insistence on more and more checks on Congress. It may therefore be doubted whether Bedford influenced the votes of other Framers. But the sweeping nature of his expression requires that he be regarded as opposed to judicial review.

Benjamin Franklin

Franklin was classed by Charles Haines among those "who opposed judicial review" on the ground that "it would be improper to put it in the power of any man to negative a law passed by the legislature because it would give him control over the legislature."[110] Franklin opposed an *Executive* veto because in Pennsylvania "The negative of the Governor was constantly made use of to extort money. No good law whatever could be passed without a private bargain with him."[111] Notwithstanding, Franklin was not absolutely

[105] Compare Mason's remark in the Virginia convention that the federal courts would be under a duty to enforce the prohibition against federal ex post facto laws. Supra, note 52.

[106] Beard 69; Davis, *Veto* 66; Corwin, *Court Over* 30.

[107] 1 Farrand 100.

[108] Corwin, *Doctrine* 12.

[109] He was repudiated by his own State; Delaware unanimously ratified the Constitution, van Doren 193, with all its "checks"; and Bedford joined in the vote. 1 Elliot 319.

[110] Haines 131.

[111] 1 Farrand 99. Madison's version is confirmed by Yates and King, id. at 106, 107. Pierce recorded that "Dr. Franklin thinks it would be improper to put it in the power of any Man to negative a Law passed by the Legislature—because it would give him control of the Legislature; and mentioned the influence of the

opposed: "If the Executive was to have a Council such a power would be less objectionable."[112] At no point did Franklin go beyond his fear of the corrupting influence of executive demands for money upon the legislature. At most Franklin is classed as doubtful.[113]

James Madison

Critics of the conventional view draw heavily on Madison, and Beard himself said "That Madison believed in judicial control over legislation is unquestionable, but as to the exact nature and extent of that control he was in no little confusion."[114] Corwin said in 1938 that "his attitude at Philadelphia respecting judicial review of acts of Congress was unsympathetic, and it was presently to become pronouncedly antipathetic towards sweeping views on the subject."[115] Boudin goes so far as to maintain that *"Madison had no doubt that the Framers did not intend to put the Judicial Power into the Constitution."*[116]

Undeniably Madison was inconsistent over the years, as his biographer, Irving Brant, acknowledged.[117] So, he fathered the Virginia Resolutions in 1798,[118] which asserted a State's right to determine issues of constitutionality for itself. But before long he tempered those views,[119] and subsequently recognized judicial review repeatedly.[120] Crosskey concludes that "Obviously Madison could

British King, and the influence which a Governor of Pennsylvania once had in arresting (for the consideration of an increase of salary [for a Crown-appointed Governor, cf. Wilson, 1 Farrand 100]) the power out of the hands of the legislature." 1 Farrand 109.

[112] Id. at 99.

[113] Davis, *Veto* 62.

[114] Beard 55.

[115] Corwin, *Court Over* 33. Compare his 1914 statement, "On the floor of the Convention, as we have just seen, [Madison] had espoused the doctrine of judicial review in unmistakable terms." Corwin *Doctrine* 47, 43. For Corwin's shifts see also infra, note 162, 230, and Chapter 6, note 63.

[116] Boudin 90.

[117] Brant, "Mr. Crosskey and Mr. Madison," 54 *Colum. L. Rev.* 433, 445 (1954).

[118] Hockett, *Political & Social History of the United States, 1492–1828*, 264 (1929).

[119] He "admitted the finality of judicial construction of the Constitution as against the *other* branches of the National Government [as distinguished from "against the States"], and in the end he abandoned his case completely." Corwin, *Doctrine* 56.

[120] 3 Farrand 537-538, 424; Crosskey 1011.

not have 'believed' *all* the various inconsistent things he had said about judicial review,"[121] imparting a fixity to men's convictions that everyday experience contradicts. Experience, the impact of events, the stresses of political battle, have often led men to espouse views radically opposd to those they earlier held,[122] and such change does not impeach the genuinness of the "belief" at either period. To embark upon an inquiry into what Madison really "believed" at any given time is a task for psychoanalysts, not for those who would assay the votes in a Convention. The undisclosed convictions of a speaker do not influence voters; voters are swayed by what he advocates in the assembly.[123] Crosskey himself would attach weight to Madison's remarks during the 1789 debate on the President's "removal" power because it was those views "upon which the majority in the House [allegedly] acted."[124] With Jefferson, I would hold that the meaning of the Constitution is "to be found in the explanation of those who advocated it" to the delegates who in voting presumably acted on that explanation.[125]

When we look to what Madison said in the course of the federal and State Conventions—and it is these utterances that are germane to the convictions he held while framing and fighting for adoption of the Constitution—there is actually little or no inconsistency. By way of introduction let us begin with his remarks on July 17, 1787, when he explained that judicial tenure was designed to forestall "undue complaisance" to the Legislature, which would "render the Legislature the virtual expositor, as well as the maker of the laws."[126] Judicial independence was designed to insulate judges from legisla-

[121] Crosskey 1012.

[122] Compare Corwin's changing appraisal of Madison, supra, note 115, and infra, Chapter 6, note 63.

[123] Hart, Book Review 1481, comments on the "ineffability of [Crosskey's] assumption that in the interpretation of a doctrine embodying a grant of fundamental powers from the people to their government the representations made to the people to obtain the grants are irrelevant, and what alone counts are the secret thoughts of men who drew the document the people approved."

[124] Crosskey 1034.

[125] Warren, *Congress* 68.

[126] 2 Farrand 34. A few minutes later he said that "If no effective check be devised for restraining the instability and encroachments of the [Legislature], a revolution of some kind or other would be inevitable." Id. at 35. At this point, to be sure, he was discussing strengthening the Executive, but no one was more alive to the danger of "legislative omnipotence." Beard 55: "His fear of the legislature is expressed repeatedly in his writings." And see 2 Farrand 74.

tive pressure on constitutional decisions,[127] and the fact that Madison employed "exposition" after hearing Gerry and King use "exposition" and "expounding" to embrace constitutional decisions,[128] that he separated the law *makers* from exposition, indicates that Madison envisaged judicial review of Congressional Acts.

On July 21st Madison spoke for Wilson's motion to include the judiciary in the "Revisionary power":

> It would be useful to the Judiciary department by giving it an *additional* opportunity of defending itself agst. Legislative encroachments . . . It would moreover be useful to the community at large as an *additional* check agst. a pursuit of those unwise & unjust measures which constituted so great a portion of our calamities . . . Experience in all the States had evinced a powerful tendency in the Legislature to absorb all power into its vortex. This was the real source of danger to the American Constitutions; and suggested the necessity of giving *every* defensive authority to the other departments that was consistent with republican principles.[129]

"Additional" indicates Madison's belief that the judiciary already enjoyed the "opportunity of defending itself agst. Legislative encroachments,"[130] and his reemphasis on the "dangers" of unbridled legislative authority, counsels a hospitable approach to "every" means of "checking" it. But let us move on to clearer testimony.

On July 23d Madison was advocating ratification of the Constitution by the people rather than by the State legislatures, largely because the Constitution "would make essential inroads on the State Constitutions, and it would be a novel and dangerous doctrine that a Legislature could change the constitution under which it held its existence." And he

> considered the difference between a system founded on the Legislatures only, and one founded on the people, to be the true difference between a *league* or *treaty* and a *Constitution* . . . A

[127] Infra, text accompanying notes 323–334.
[128] Supra, text accompanying notes 13 and 19.
[129] 2 Farrand 74 (emphasis added); and see 1 Farrand 139.
[130] For discussion of "self-defense" see infra, Chapter 6, text accompanying notes 1–62.

law violating a treaty ratified by a preexisting law, might be respected by the Judges as a law, though an unwise or perfidious one. A law violating a constitution established by the people themselves, would be considered by the Judges as null and void.[131]

Those who rely on the last sentence for judicial review of Congressional Acts, says Crosskey, wrench it "out of context"; read with what precedes it, "it is perfectly plain that Madison was not talking about *national* 'laws' at all."[132] It is by no means "perfectly plain" that Madison addressed himself solely to State "law." He insisted upon ratification by the "people" rather than by State legislatures because the Constitution would alter existing State constitutions and because no "Legislature could change the Constitution under which it held its existence," an enunciation of broad general principles. Assuming the validity of Crosskey's exclusion of "national" laws, State laws remain, and he neglected to explain why Madison denied State legislatures power to make "changes" in State constitutions— the broad Vattel doctrine—but left the national legislature free to "change" the national constitution.[133] Was it for this that Congress was being "fenced" about with prohibitions and with "limits" derived from a specific "enumeration" of powers? The logic of Madison's "A law violating a constitution established by the people themselves, would be considered by the judges as null and void" extends equally to violations by State or federal law. Nothing in the context compels a contrary conclusion, and as will appear, the Framers were far more concerned about the impact of judicial review on the States than upon Congress.[134]

To continue with Madison's statements in the Convention. On August 27th, he urged that the "jurisdiction of . . . cases arising under the Constitution" ought "to be limited to cases of a Judiciary

---

[131] 2 Farrand 92–93.
[132] Crosskey 1023.
[133] See infra, text accompanying notes 138–144.
[134] See infra, Chapter 8, text accompanying notes 155–191. Boudin reads Madison's statement as "actually an assertion that in sovereign governments the Judiciary is bound to obey *any* law passed by the Legislatures, no matter how *immoral, unwise or perfidious*." But the italicized words were uttered by Madison about laws which violated "a *treaty* ratified by a pre-existing law." Madison postulated that nothing inhibited a legislature from passing "a law violating a treaty," but he expressly distinguished a "law violating a constitution," which "would be considered by the Judges as null and void."

Nature. The right of expounding the Constitution in cases not of this nature ought not to be given to that Department."[135] If the case *was* of a "Judiciary Nature" the implication is plain that Madison thought "the right of expounding" was *given;* and "expounding," as he himself recorded, had been employed by the Members to include decisions on constitutionality. Then too, there is his answer, as the Convention drew to a close, to the question what redress would there be if there was State violation of the duties proviso: "There will be the same security *as in other cases*—the jurisdiction of the Supreme Court must be the source of redress."[136] Violations of the Constitution by the Congress had been mooted again and again, and it is not stretching unduly to conclude against the earlier background that such violations were included by him "in other cases."

In arguing on June 8th for a Congressional negative of *"all* laws to be passed by the state legislatures which *they* [Congress] may judge improper," Madison said, "The judges of the state must give state laws their operation, although the law abridges the rights of the national government."[137] From this Crosskey concludes that Madison "could have rested upon only one thing: the complete normalcy of the duty of absolute obedience which every system of courts was then deemed to owe *to the acts of its own particular legislature;* and this, even though the acts of the legislature might, in the particular courts opinion, contravene a constitution *established by the legislature's superiors, the people of the state concerned.* In other words . . . [Madison] had no notion at all, in the Federal Convention, of any right of judicial review as a normal and usual incident of judicial power under a popularly enacted constitution

---

[135] 2 Farrand 430. Beard 56, deduces from this clause that "complete judicial paramountcy over the other branches of the federal government [Madison] certainly deprecated." "Complete paramountcy" was, of course, cut down to cases of a "Judicial Nature" and outside of such cases the courts had no visitorial function. But if "expounding" within that jurisdiction did not confer "paramountcy," there was little occasion to limit the jurisdiction, because without "paramountcy" unlimited judicial jurisdiction would leave each Department free to "interpret" the Constitution for itself.

[136] 2 Farrand 589 (emphasis added).

[137] 1 Farrand 169. More than five weeks were to pass before Sherman made the point that the Congressional negative on State laws "involves a wrong principle, to wit that a law of a State contrary to the articles of the Union, would if not negatived, be valid and operative." 2 Farrand 28. And the paramount allegiance of State judges to the States which created them remained to be solved.

which imposed limitations on the legislative authority."[138] Because a State judge was bound by a State law that "abridged" *national* rights it does not follow that he was bound by a State law that violated a *State* constitution. Not judicial "obedience" to a State legislature, right or wrong, was then in issue but the overriding allegiance at that juncture of State judges to the States. Their duties to the as yet unborn Nation were still to be determined; June 8th was early in the Convention; all was in flux. Whether federal was to supersede State law lay in the future. The problem was solved in part on July 17th when, in place of the Congressional negative which had become a sticking point, Martin proposed the Supremacy Clause. Although it made federal law paramount over State *laws,* it pointedly excluded State *constitutions* from the "notwithstanding" phrase.[139] As Martin explained to his native Maryland, if national laws "were inconsistent with our [Maryland] constitution and bill of rights, the judiciaries of this state would be bound to reject the first and abide by the last"; national laws "were not proposed nor meant to be superior to our constitution and bill of rights."[140] Thus State judges, whose first duty ran to the State whose creatures they were, were thought by Martin, and presumably by the Convention which unanimously voted for his proposed Supremacy Clause, to be bound to prefer State constitutions to conflicting *federal* laws in the absence of a Supremacy provision. This is the frame, I suggest, in which Madison's June 8th remark is to be read. Neither Martin nor Madison implied that State judges were bound to enforce State laws that conflicted with *State* constitutions; and such an implication must surmount the fact that legislative excesses had placed State legislatures in disrepute. Indeed, Madison expressly stated on July 23d that "A law violating a constitution . . . would be considered by the Judges as null and void";[141] if Madison "was not talking about national laws," as Crosskey insists,[142] he must have been talking about State laws; and there is nothing in the context to suggest that Madison thought such laws could not "violat[e] a constitution" or that State judges could not consider *them* "null and void." This

138 Crosskey 986-987.
139 2 Farrand 28–29.
140 3 Farrand 287.
141 Supra, text accompanying note 131.
142 Supra, text accompanying note 132.

analysis is confirmed by Madison's remark on August 28th—after adoption of Luther Martin's primitive version of the Supremacy Clause on July 17th, which resolved the problem of State court allegiance to valid State law—that the prohibition of State "*ex post facto* laws . . . will oblige the judges to declare such interferences null and void."[142a] Mark the tacit assumption that judicial machinery exists for such a purpose and that judges are *obliged* to nullify infractions of Constitutional prohibitions.

Weightier evidence against Crosskey's "duty of absolute obedience" to the legislature is furnished by Madison's statement, immediately before Luther Martin's proposal, that "In R. Island the Judges who refused to execute an unconstitutional law were displaced, and others substituted by the Legislature who would be willing instruments of the wicked and arbitrary plans of their masters."[143] In condemning legislative displacement of judges who held a law unconstitutional, Madison repelled the notion of a judicial "duty of absolute obedience" to the legislature. So too, his argument on the very same day for secure judicial tenure to forestall "undue complaisance" to the Congress[144] is irreconcilable with such a "duty."

Perhaps the totality of Madison's remarks in the Convention does not quite add up to Corwin's 1914 statement that Madison "had espoused the doctrine of judicial review in unmistakable terms,"[145] but they are sufficiently clear to justify his inclusion among its proponents. That inclusion is confirmed by his statement in *The Federalist,* and it is not shaken by his statements in the Virginia Ratification convention.

In No. 44 of *The Federalist,* Madison addressed himself to the question: What if Congress "shall exercise powers not warranted by" the "true meaning" of the "necessary and proper" clause?

> I answer . . . the same, in short, as if the State legislatures should violate their respective constitutional authorities. *In the first instance, the success of the usurpation* will depend on the

---

[142a] For adoption of the Martin version, see 2 Farrand 32; for Madison's August 28th remark, see id. at 440.

[143] 2 Farrand 28.

[144] Supra, text accompanying note 126; cf. infra, Chapter 9, text accompanying note 47.

[145] Corwin, *Doctrine* 47.

executive and *judiciary* departments, which are to *expound* and give effect to the legislative acts; *in the last resort* a remedy must be obtained from the people, who can, by the election of more faithful representatives, *annul the acts* of the usurpers.[146]

Madison looked to the courts "in the first instance" to check Congressional "usurpations" when they "expounded . . . legislative acts," and that check necessarily included the power to declare such usurpations unconstitutional, as is confirmed by the fact that "in the last resort," for example where, as in Rhode Island, the legislature had defied judicial decrees (so Madison thought), the "people" themselves could "annul the acts of the usurper." That last resort would become necessary only if the judicial "annulment" "in the first instance" was not respected.

In the Virginia Ratification convention Madison spoke often and at length and replied to almost every objection that was made. Here he heard Pendleton, Nicholas, Marshall, and others speak forthrightly for judicial review of Acts of Congress,[147] and this was the place to express misgivings, to counter, for example, Tyler's fear that the "federal judicial power" was unlimited.[148] Toward the end of

[146] *Federalist* No. 44 at 295. In subsequent numbers of *The Federalist* Madison discussed Jefferson's early suggestion of appeals to the people from differences among the departments, only to dismiss them as impractical and to rely on reciprocal departmental checks and counterbalances of conflicting social interests, without mention of judicial review. Nos. 49, 50, 51. Again in No. 57, he stated that the restraints on discrimination by the House are to be found in "the genius of the whole system; the nature of just and constitutional laws; and above all, the vigilant and manly spirit which activates the people of America," and that these are all "that government will admit, and that human prudence can devise." No. 57 at 373. Though there is no mention here of judicial review, Madison can hardly be charged with repudiation of what was said by himself and others on that score in the Convention, particularly since his reference to the "genius of the whole system" and to "constitutional laws" can account for those remarks.

In his Introduction to his 1961 edition of *The Federalist,* Benjamin F. Wright attaches great weight to the alleged fact that prior to No. 78 there is 'little aid or comfort" in *The Federalist* for a judicial interpretation that will be "superior" to that of the other branches, id. at 71–73. This is not at all remarkable, to my way of thinking, because *The Federalist* attempted a systematic treatment of large general problems, arriving in due course at "The Judiciary Department" in No. 78 et seq., where a coherent rather than disjointed exposition could be presented. As an experienced advocate, Hamilton doubtless knew the impossibility of stating a whole case in one breath and the danger inherent in sketchy allusions to issues which require full statement to be understood. His few anticipatory allusions have been a subject of unceasing debate. Infra, text accompanying notes 212–221.

[147] Infra, Chapter 4, text accompanying notes 116–118, 123.

[148] 3 Elliot 638–639.

the debate, George Mason read "The judicial power shall extend" clause and asked, "What objects will not this expression extend to?" And he reiterated that the judicial jurisdiction "may be said to be unlimited."[149] Mason, to be sure, was concerned with the impact of the federal courts on State sovereignty,[150] but the fact that he expressed no concern about the effect on Congress is itself revealing. When Madison replied, he said of the "judicial power" clause,

> It may be a misfortune that, in organizing any government, the explication of its authority should be left to any of its coordinate branches. There is no example in any country where it is otherwise. There is a *new policy of submitting it to the judiciary* of the United States . . . With respect to the laws of the Union, it is so necessary and expedient that the judicial power should correspond with the legislative, that it has not been objected to. With respect to treaties, there is a peculiar propriety in the judiciary's expounding them.[151]

That courts were expected to set aside State laws which conflicted with "treaties" seems scarcely open to question,[152] and this was the implication of "expounding them." The *"peculiar* propriety" of "expounding" treaties implies the normal propriety of expounding "laws of the Union," with its concomitant connotation of setting unconstitutional laws aside. The most feared part of the "authority" that was to be "explicated" was, as has appeared, that of Congress. Madison's "the judicial power should correspond with the legislative" is further illuminated by R. H. Lee's *Letters of a Federal Farmer* (October 1787, that is, prior to the Virginia convention): "It is proper that the federal judiciary should have power co-extensive with the federal legislature—that is the power of deciding finally on the laws of the union."[153]

Other remarks of Madison, made in the First Congress, are best considered in the framework of the several debates. Let it be noted

---

[149] Id. at 521, 523.

[150] Id. at 521–522.

[151] Id. at 532.

[152] See infra, Appendix B, text accompanying notes 71–73, 97, 99, and note 73.

[153] Ford, *Pamphlets* 279, 306–307. The "coextensive" jurisdiction point was frequently made. 2 Elliot 469; McMaster & Stone 301, 330, 402, 771; 3 Elliot 517; 4 Elliot 156–158; *Federalist* No. 80 at 516. Federal laws required enforcement but, as Iredell stated, judges would not enforce unconstitutional laws. Infra, note 168.

only that when speaking for the proposed Bill of Rights, he stated that courts will "be an impenetrable bulwark against every assumption of power in the legislative or executive."[154]

All this is thrown into the discard by Boudin on the strength of a statement made by Madison in October 1788,[155] that is, after the Convention and the Virginia Ratifying convention, in a letter written to a Mr. Brown, who sought advice "relative to a projected Constitution for Kentucky." Others also have been troubled by that statement;[156] but when the letter is studied in its entirety, it falls short of demonstrating Boudin's claim that *"Madison had no doubt that the Framers did not intend to put the power into the Constitution."*[157] The letter was addressed to Jefferson's draft of a constitution for Virginia. Madison steadfastly preferred a Council of Revision as the means of dealing with legislative excesses, and although it had been rejected by the Convention, he recurred to it in this letter. He now suggested with respect to such a Council that in the enacting process laws should be sent to both the executive and the judiciary and

> If either of these object, let ⅔, if both, ¾ of each House be necessary to overrule the objection; and if either or both protest against a bill as violating the Constitution, let it moreover be suspended notwithstanding the overruling proportion of the assembly, until there shall have been a subsequent election of the H of D's & a repassage of the bill by ⅔ or ¾ of both Houses, as the case may be. It is *not to be allowed* the Judges or ye Executive to pronounce a law *thus enacted* unconstitutional and invalid.[158]

Lacking the extraordinary measures he was suggesting, it seems unlikely that Madison intended that the legislature should be left

---

[154] 1 *Ann. Cong.* 457.

[155] Boudin 90; 5 Madison, *Writings* 284.

[156] Davis, *Veto* 53; Corwin, *Doctrine* 47; Beard 56; Haines 234. Crosskey 1010–1011, employs it to suggest Madison's "want of candor" and to demonstrate "his true and candid views."

[157] Boudin 90.

[158] 5 Madison 284, 294 (emphasis added). This is a variant of several unsuccessful proposals for which he strove in the Convention, 2 Farrand 27, 390, 440, 589, to which he now added suspension of the proposed law until a newly elected Assembly repassed the bill.

altogether without curbs.[159] And the statement that if enacted in accord with his proposed safeguards the judges are "not to be allowed . . . to pronounce a law thus enacted unconstitutional" implies that judges presently enjoyed such power.

Immediately following the words "unconstitutional and invalid," however, comes the oft-quoted statement:

> In the State Constitutions & indeed in the Fed'l one also, no provision is made for the case of a disagreement in expounding them; & as the courts are generally the last in making ye decision, it *results* to them by refusing or not refusing to execute a law, to stamp it with its *final character*. This makes the Judiciary Dept. paramount in fact to the Legislature, which was never intended and can never be proper.[160]

Apparently Madison considered that the failure to make express provision for who was to have the last word "resulted" "in fact" in judicial "finality," though that was "never intended." Yet at the outset of the letter, he alluded to the necessity of preventing "sudden modifications of the [judiciary] establishment, or addition of obsequious judges [Court-packing], for ye purpose of evading the checks of the Constitution and giving effect to some sinister policy of the Legislature."[161] An attack on judicial independence for the purpose of evading constitutional checks is thus to be "prevented," and it seems reasonable to conclude that judges were to administer the checks.

The sharp internal contradictions in this letter strongly indicate that Madison had in fact not succeeded in sorting out his own ideas, and consequently there is no need to view his "never intended" statement as a clear repudiation of all that he had earlier said on the subject of judicial review.[162] Nor is there a compulsion to posit a

159 In 1818 he said of the Council, "Such a control restricted to constitutional points . . . would have precluded the question of judiciary annulment of Legislative Acts." 8 Madison, *Writings* 406–407.

160 5 Madison, *Writings* 294 (emphasis added).

161 Id. at 291.

162 Corwin, *Court Over* 49, juxtaposing this 1788 letter with Madison's statement in the 1789 Congress that courts "will be an impenetrable bulwark against every assumption of power in the Legislature," asks "is it reasonable to suppose that it was Madison's intention, in speaking thus [in 1789] to discard views to which he had given such positive expression eight months prior." Cf. Corwin, *Doctrine* 47 n. 72. It is not unreasonable to suppose that in proposing a Bill of

necessary correlation between the public utterances of a political leader and his private views. As Sir Robert Menzies, former Prime Minister of Australia, said, "When a man is politically engaged, and particularly when he is a political leader, he must, in a substantial sense, speak for others. He cannot indulge in the luxury of 'going on a frolic of his own.' "[163] The Madison 1788 letter may well have represented his private—and confused—as distinguished from his public view of judicial review.

Whatever the effect attributable to Madison's views in the 1788 letter, those views cannot be attributed to the Framers, for they were not put before them. And on the very subject of the Council of Revision he was voted down time and again because, among other reasons, it was stated, the matter would come before the courts. In arguing for it anew in his undisclosed letter, his conflicting expressions at best reflect his own views, not those of the Convention or the Virginia convention. Boudin could ill afford to argue that the undisclosed letter rose above Madison's remarks in those conventions, for it was he who insisted that "The individual opinions of the members not expressed on the floor itself, as reasons for their actions therein, are practically valueless as a guide to the intention of the Convention."[164] In sum, Madison's remarks in the Convention, *The Federalist*, and the Virginia convention show that, although he preferred a Council of Revision, he was ready to accept judicial review; and his letter of October 1788, so charged with internal contradictions, does little to shake that appraisal.

REMARKS OF FRAMERS OUTSIDE THE CONVENTION

Richard Spaight

While attending the Convention, Spaight wrote a letter on August 12th to Iredell concerning *Bayard v. Singleton*, wherein a

---

Rights Madison wanted more than parchment guarantees, and that when faced with the need for taking a position as leader of Congress who had to muster votes, rather than parsing the analytic components in private correspondence, he took a more mature view of the problem, a view which reflected his several earlier Convention utterances. Account will hereafter be taken of his seemingly conflicting utterances in the First Congress during the debate on the President's "removal" power.

[163] Quoted London *Times*, October 18, 1967, p. 11.
[164] Boudin 93.

North Carolina court had somewhat earlier declared a State law unconstitutional. Iredell was co-counsel in the case, and his associate,
Davie, who argued the case, was also a delegate to the Convention.[165]
Spaight condemned the court's "usurpation" of authority to declare
a law void, and said that "no judiciary ought ever to possess" an
"absolute negative on the proceedings of the Legislature." He added
that "It must be acknowledged that our [State] Constitution, un-
fortunately, has not provided a sufficient check, to prevent the
intemperate and unjust proceedings of our Legislature, though such
a check would be very beneficial, and, I think, absolutely necessary
to our well-being," and he closed by asking, "what is the general
opinion on that transaction?"[166] By August 12th, Spaight had heard
frequent espousals of judicial review in the Convention but never
registered a dissent. Notwithstanding his disapproval of judicial
review one may speculate that his condemnation of legislative "in-
temperance," his emphasis on the "absolute necessity of a check,"
coupled with his inquiry as to the state of "general opinion," betrayed
some irresolution.

Iredell met Spaight head-on in a reply that anticipates the Hamil-
ton-Marshall reasoning:[167]

> it has ever been my opinion, that an act inconsistent with the
> Constitution was void; and that the judges, consistently with their
> duties could not carry it into effect . . . Without an express
> [State] Constitution the powers of the Legislature would un-
> doubtedly have been absolute . . . The experience of the evils
> which the American war fully disclosed, attending an absolute
> power in a legislative body, suggested the propriety of a real,
> original contract between the people and their future Govern-
> ment . . . The Constitution, therefore, *being a fundamental law*
> . . . the judicial power, in the exercise of their authority, must
> take notice of it . . . either . . . the *fundamental unrepealable*
> law must be obeyed, by the rejection of an act unwarranted by
> and inconsistent with it, or you must obey an act founded on
> authority not given by the people . . . It is not that the judges

[165] Crosskey 972–973; Corwin, *Court Over* 25 n. 22; id. at 31.
[166] 2 McRee 170.
[167] Corwin, *Court Over* 25 n. 22.

are appointed arbiters, and to determine as it were upon any application, whether the Assembly have or have not violated the Constitution; but when an act is necessarily brought in judgment before them, they must, unavoidably, determine one way or another.[168]

Came the North Carolina convention in which Spaight, Iredell, and Davie were participants. According to Crosskey, only a "large and influential *minority* ["58 to 24"] in the state [had] disapproved of any court's possessing such a power" as had been asserted in *Bayard v. Singleton*.[169] Here Spaight heard repeated assaults on legislative excesses, on unbounded Congressional powers, plus assurances that the courts would set legislative usurpations aside.[170] Now Spaight could freely speak his mind; he did speak to other matters but said not a word against judicial review. Perhaps he had found in Iredell's searching analysis[171] and in the popular anti-

---

[168] McRee 172–173. A year earlier Iredell had set forth his views in an Address printed in the Newbern papers, August 17, 1786, respecting formation of the North Carolina constitution. His rejection there of Blackstonian legislative supremacy was quoted supra, Chapter 2, text accompanying note 133. Because this Address has been little noticed, I venture upon a further quotation:

> The duty of that [judicial power], I conceive, in all cases, is to decide according to the *laws of the State*. It will not be denied, I suppose, that the Constitution is a *law of the State*, as well as an act of Assembly, with this difference only, that it is the *fundamental law*, and unalterable by the legislature, which derives all its power from it . . . An act of Assembly cannot repeal the Constitution, or any part of it. For that reason, an act of Assembly, inconsistent with the constitution, is *void*, and cannot be obeyed, without disobeying the superior law to which we were previously and irrevocably bound. The judges, therefore, must take care at their peril, that every act of Assembly they presume to enforce is warranted by the Constitution, since if it is not, they act without lawful authority.
> . . . *if the power of judging rests with the courts,* their decision is final as to the subject matter.

2 McRee 148–149.

[169] Crosskey 973, 972. So too, Crosskey regards a motion in the New York legislature to remove judges, which was "defeated," as "part of the evidence of the wide-spread hostility of the times, to the judicial setting aside of legislative acts." Id. at 964.

[170] Infra, Chapter 4, text accompanying notes 71–98.

[171] Not a word of Iredell's reply to Spaight is mentioned by Crosskey as he dwells on Spaight's letter to Iredell. Crosskey 972–973. Iredell later was to play a leading role in the North Carolina convention. Like his parallel failure to notice a central paragraph in Hamilton which vitiates the Crosskey gloss, Hart, Book Review 1483, this omission constrains one to conclude that Crosskey has a blind spot for materials which are adverse to his thesis. Compare his use of quotations from St. George Tucker and James Otis, supra, Chapter 2, note 134.

congressional mood a resolution of his conflicting emotions.[172] At least his failure publicly to record his earlier private dissent suggests a consciousness that his earlier view was not generally shared.[173]

William Davie

Davie is not included by Beard among the proponents, but in 1938 Corwin so classified him on the ground that as Iredell's co-counsel "he had urged the constitutional argument upon the court" in *Bayard v. Singleton.*[174] He argued to the court that "the Assembly had clearly exceeded the limits of the power which the people . . . had delegated to their representatives met in general assembly, . . . and that an act so illegally passed, was not to be looked on as a law";[175] and the court thereafter held the Act unconstitutional. Later, meeting objections to the "arising under" clause in the North Carolina convention, Davie said that "Without a judiciary, the injunctions of the Constitution may be disobeyed, and the positive regulations neglected or contravened."[176] True, he employed illustrations of restrictions upon States, but North Carolina dreaded *Congressional* incursions on State and private rights, and proponents were hardpressed on the one hand to assure the convention that Congress would be kept within bounds and on the other to plead

---

[172] Cf. infra, note 294.

[173] Compare the above with Boudin's statement that

It is absurd to assume that the many [?] avowed opponents of judicial control of legislation who sat in the convention would have agreed to the [judiciary] article without a murmur had they suspected that it contained even a part of the enormous power which our judiciary now exercises. Richard Spaight for one, whose fiery denunciation of this power I have quoted above, would have made the halls in which the Convention met ring to the echo with his emphatic protest, had he suspected any such implications.

Boudin, "Government by Judiciary," 26 *Pol. Sci. Quart.* 248–249 (1911), quoted by Beard 71–72. But, as Beard remarks, "The view was more than once clearly voiced in the Convention, and any delegate who was not aware of such implications must have been very remiss in the discharge of his duties;" id. at 72; all the more because Iredell had spelled out plainly to him the foundation of judicial review, and his co-counsel, Davie, who had established judicial review in North Carolina, sat with Spaight in the Convention. See also, Corwin, *Doctrine* 12. In the North Carolina convention, Spaight spoke for adoption of the Constitution; he heard an unequivocal assurance by his co-proponent, John Steele, that judicial review would curb legislative excesses and uttered not one word to the contrary. Infra, Chapter 4, text accompanying note 79.

[174] Corwin, *Court Over* 31, 24 n. 22.

[175] Meigs, *Relation* 114.

[176] 4 Elliot 156.

that a national government could not function without some enforceable restrictions on the States.[177] He also stated that "the judiciary ought to be competent to the decision of *any* question arising
out of the Constitution itself . . . the judicial power should be coextensive with the legislative," explaining that "The federal government ought to possess the means of carrying the laws into execution."[178] Davie did not contemplate that the courts would carry into
"execution" laws that were unconstitutional, for he had prevailed
on the court in *Bayard v. Singleton* to hold that a State law inconsistent with the State constitution was unconstitutional. And the
frequently encountered coextensive phrase, it will be recalled, had
been explained by R. H. Lee to mean "the power of deciding finally
on the laws of the union."[179]

Robert Yates

Yates, a justice of the New York Supreme Court and a delegate
from New York who opposed ratification, published a trenchant
critique of the Constitution after the Convention in his "Letters of
Brutus."[180] Though he opposed judicial review, the Letters powerfully demonstrate the actual understanding—to borrow Crosskey's
"standard of discrimination"—"of an intelligent and informed man
of the time, based on a reasoned analysis of the Constitution"[181] that
it provided for judicial review. He opposed judicial review in part
because it would "operate to a total subversion of the state judiciaries,
if not to the legislative authority of the states,"[182] and because judges
were irremovable and uncontrollable whereas "the people . . . could
remove" legislators if they rejected a legislative construction of the
Constitution.[183] The importance of the judiciary, he repeatedly

[177] Infra, Chapter 4, text accompaning notes 71–98.
[178] 4 Elliot 156, 158 (emphasis added). See infra, Chapter 8, note 55.
[179] Ford, *Pamphlets* 279, 306–307; see also supra, note 153.
[180] Extensive extracts from "Brutus" are reprinted in Corwin, *Court Over* 231–
262. Yates was made a justice of the New York court in 1777, "where he earned
a reputation for his legal abilities," and became chief justice in 1790. De Pauw,
The Eleventh Pillar 56, 83 (1966).
[181] Crosskey 1028, 712.
[182] Quoted Corwin, *Court Over* 234. Yate feared that the judicial power "will
lean strongly in favour of the general government . . . [and] will favour an
extension of its jurisdiction." Id. at 238, 243.
[183] Id. at 261.

emphasized, derives from the fact that "No errors they may commit can be corrected by any power above them."[184] The "arising under" clause, he stated, "vests the judicial with a power to resolve *all* questions that may arise on *any* case on the construction of the constitution.[185] Moreover, "there is no power provided in the constitution that can correct their errors, or controul their adjudication . . . And I conceive that the legislature themselves, cannot set aside a judgment of this court, because they are authorized by the constitution to decide in the last resort. The legislature must be controuled by the constitution, and not the constitution by them."[186] Yates noted that the

> judges in England . . . in no instance assume the authority to set aside an act of parliament under the idea that it is inconsistent with their constitution . . . The judges in England are under the controul of the legislature . . . But the judges under this constitution will controul the legislature, for the *supreme court are authorized in the last resort to determine what is the extent of the powers of Congress;* they are to give the constitution an explanation and there is no power above them to set aside their judgment.[187]
>
> The power of this court is in many cases superior to that of the legislature . . . If, therefore, the legislature pass any laws, inconsistent with the sense the judges put upon the constitution, they will declare it void; and therefore in this respect their power is superior to that of the legislature.[188]

Yates, states Crosskey, was "the ablest of the opposition writers in New York."[189] Undeniably Yates opposed judicial review, but it is equally clear that he considered that such review had been provided by the Convention.

Corwin dismissed Yates's statement on the ground that it is "argumentative," and that Yates "was no longer in Philadelphia

[184] Id. at 232.
[185] Id. at 235 (emphasis supplied).
[186] Id. at 237.
[187] Id. at 251–252 (emphasis supplied).
[188] Id. at 257–258.
[189] Crosskey 712. The essays of "Brutus" "were clipped and published all over the country." De Pauw, *The Eleventh Pillar* 130 (1966).

when Article III was elaborated."[190] Nonetheless, Yates's reading constitutes the contemporary interpretation of an intelligent man—a delegate to both the federal and New York conventions—who construed the document for himself and opposed it because, for one thing, it provided for judicial review. Two other critics of the Constitution, the "Centinel" in Pennsylvania,[191] and Luther Martin in Maryland,[192] who also opposed ratification, read the judicial power much as did Yates. No apologist for the Constitution hastened to rebut such inferences. To the contrary, Hamilton replied by "going [Yates] one better" in New York,[193] and Alexander Hanson, who advocated ratification and was a member of the Maryland convention, like Martin, considered that the Constitution provided for judicial review.[194] These were not obscure voices but people who commanded attention. For a year the "Centinel" kept up a drumfire of criticism in Philadelphia;[195] the "Letters of Brutus" were published over a period of several months in the New York *Journal;*[196] and there is good reason to believe that such views were widely cir-

[190] Corwin, *Court Over* 36. In the preface to this same work, id. at viii, Corwin states that Yate's "Letters of Brutus" comprise the "most thorough examination that was made prior to the Constitution's adoption of the power of the Supreme Court in interpreting it."

[191] The "Centinel" said "should Congress be disposed to violate the fundamental articles of the constitution for the sake of public justice [the settlement and payment of accounts due under the Confederation] . . . still it would be of no avail, as there is a further barrier opposed, namely, the supreme court of the union, whose province it would be to determine the constitutionality of any law that may be controverted . . . it would be their sworn duty to refuse their sanction to laws made in the face of and contrary to the letter and spirit of the constitution." McMaster & Stone 659. Davis, *Veto* 79, considers "Centinel" "one of the ablest Anti-Federal publicists." And Crosskey relied on what the "Centinel" perceived. Crosskey 690.

[192] Martin reported adversely to the people of Maryland and said "Whether therefore, any *laws* or *regulations* of the *Congress* . . . are *contrary* to or not *warranted* by the constitution . . . rests *only* with the judges." 3 Farrand 172, 220. The reasons for his opposition are discussed supra, text accompanying notes 43–44.

[193] Corwin, *Court Over,* 47.

[194] Hanson said, "But say the objectors, 'The congress being itself to judge of the necessity and propriety, may pass any act which it may deem *expedient,* for any other purpose . . .' They may reflect however, that every judge in the union, whether of federal or state appointment . . . will have a right to reject any act, handed to him as a law, which he may conceive repugnant to the constitution." "Remarks, etc. to the People of Maryland," reprinted, Ford's *Pamphlets,* 221, 234.

[195] McMaster & Stone, 565–672.

[196] Corwin, *Court Over* 231–262 (reprints excerpts pertaining to judicial review).

culated.[197] "Existence of the power," says Meigs, "was nowhere denied by any writer of repute."[198]

Alexander Hamilton

Hamilton's views were expressed mainly in *The Federalist*. Both are subjected to harsh criticism by Crosskey, and Hamilton was not more gently treated by Boudin. Crosskey dismisses such pre-Ratification remarks because it is "utterly impossible" to "accept statements made in that [ratification] campaign as proof of the true opinion of the makers thereof."[199] Crosskey himself does not take his wholesale dismissal of Hamilton and *The Federalist* seriously; he is ready enough to cite Hamilton to bolster his own pet theory that the Supreme Court has erroneously declined to exercise a "common law" jurisdiction allegedly conferred by the Constitution. For this purpose Hamilton becomes a Daniel come to judgment: "Brutus [Yates] and

[197] In Pennsylvania, Pelatiah Webster published "The Weakness of Brutus Exposed," reprinted in Ford's *Pamphlets*, 116, but exposed no weakness in Yate's statements on judicial review. The "Centinel" in Pennsylvania praised the "masterly" analysis of "Brutus," McMaster & Stone, 600, criticized the *Federalist,* id. at 635, and cited Martin's "Information" to the Maryland Legislature, id. at 633, 646, while Ellsworth of Connecticut criticized Martin's publication. 3 Farrand 271.

To further illustrate the circulation of debating materials: Wilson's speech in Philadelphia was promptly reprinted in New York and Richmond, 2 Bancroft, 241–242. Davie of North Carolina thanked Iredell for *The Federalist* and for the Pennsylvania debates. 2 McRee 230. In the Massachusetts convention, Stillman referred to Randolph's letter to the Virginia legislature explaining his refusal to sign the Constitution, 2 Elliot 163, 124. Madison referred in the Virginia convention to the debates in other States, 3 Elliot 619, and said that Georgia now knew of New Hampshire affairs, id. at 254. In the North Carolina convention, Jones cited a letter from Jefferson to Madison that had been quoted in the Virginia convention. 4 Elliot 226. Hamilton referred to Lee's "Letters From the Federal Farmer" in the New York convention. 2 Elliot 256. Lee's "Letters" "were circulated by thousands in the central states. They were designed to counteract the powerful impression the papers of Publius [*The Federalist*] were producing." Jameson, *Essays in Constitutional History* 59 (1889).

As to *The Federalist*, Rossiter, *Hamilton* 56, states that "Fifty-two copies of the collected edition were rushed to Richmond at Hamilton's direction and used by advocates of the Constitution in the climactic debates over ratification." And he states, id. at 282 n. 98, that "A letter of Charles Thomason to James McHenry, April 19, 1788 . . . makes clear that at least a few men of influence were rushing copies of *The Federalist* to friends of the Constitution in other States." See id. at 55 for list of newspapers which republished portions of *The Federalist*. In North Carolina, Spencer stated that he had "paid attention . . . to the writings on both sides." 4 Elliot 51.

[198] Meigs, *Relation* 160.

[199] Crosskey 1026.

Hamilton . . . seem sufficient to show that the ideas of the national judiciary here presented [by Crosskey] were current when the Constitution was adopted."[200] Now Hamilton also concurred in unmistakable terms with Yates—although they were on opposite sides—that the Constitution provided for judicial review, and therefore we might pardonably conclude that their remarks on this score were no less representative of "current" views, especially as they are buttressed by unequivocal remarks in the several conventions and in the dissenting views of Luther Martin and the "Centinel."

To recur to Crosskey's assault on the "fable" that has grown round *The Federalist*, before publication of his charge that *The Federalist* teems with "sophistry, innuendo and near-falsehood"[201] one could cite it without more ado. With Crosskey's critique before him, Clinton Rossiter recently said,[202]

These papers are, by common consent of both scholarly and popular opinion, the most important work in political science that has ever been written . . . in the United States . . . It would not be stretching the truth more than a few inches to say that *The Federalist* stands third only to the Declaration of Independence and the Constitution itself among the sacred writings of American political history.[203]

Little time need be wasted in multiplying citations; recall only the remarks of Washington and Jefferson. Washington, who presided over the Convention and doubtless learned something in the process, wrote Hamilton in 1788 that "the work will merit the notice of posterity; because in it are candidly and ably discussed the principles of freedom and the topics of government which will always be interesting to mankind."[204] Presumably Crosskey would discount this because Hamilton was "a great favorite of Washington's."[205] But Jefferson, "the fiercest of [Hamilton's] opponents in the formative years," wrote in his old age, when the smoke of battle had long

[200] Id. at 711–712.

[201] Id. at 10, 8–9. For critical comment, see Brown, Book Review of Crosskey, 67 *Harv. L. Rev.* 1439, 1444–1445 (1954).

[202] Rossiter, *Hamilton* 282 n. 100. And see Marshall's estimate in 1805, quoted Brown, supra, note 201 at 1446.

[203] Rossiter, *Hamilton* 51–52.

[204] Quoted id. at 52.

[205] Crosskey 10.

since cleared, that *The Federalist* is a document to which "appeal is habitually made by all, and rarely declined or denied by any as evidence of the general opinion of those who framed, and of those who accepted the Constitution of the United States, on questions as to its genuine meaning."[206]

As "proof" that it is "utterly impossible" to accept such pre-Ratification "campaign" statements as indicative of the maker's "true opinion," Crosskey instances Hamilton's "about face." First he is said, by his advice as defense counsel to prosecute no appeal from a "partial success" in *Rutgers v. Waddington* in 1784, to have indicated his own belief that there was no "right of judicial review, in the courts of New York."[207] Hamilton had argued in *Rutgers* that the state statute was contrary to the treaty of peace and the Articles of Confederation and therefore void on the ground that a "Legislature of one State cannot repeal a law of United States."[208] True it is that he apprehended an "unfavorable issue in the supreme court" of New York,[209] but it does not necessarily follow that he therefore jettisoned his own belief in the position which he had argued to the court. Still less does it indicate his belief as to what the *national law* ought to be. Indeed, his argument in *Rutgers* was given expression in the Supremacy Clause, which made treaties binding on State judges notwithstanding State provisions to the contrary.[210] And the fact that in his "Letters from Phocion" Hamilton clung to the view he had urged in *Rutgers*[211] repels an inference that he had

---

[206] Rossiter, *Hamilton* 52, 227. Writing on November 18, 1788, to Madison, Jefferson said *The Federalist* was "the best commentary on the principles of government which was ever written." 7 Jefferson, *Writings* 183 (Lib. ed. 1903). In his edition of Blackstone (1803), St. George Tucker praises Nos. 78 and 79 of *The Federalist* and quotes them extensively because "too valuable to be abridged." Id. App. 127. In 1793, the Virginia court, in Kamper v. Hawkins, 1 Va. Cas. 22, 81–84, quoted Hamilton's definition of judicial supremacy as "conclusive." In his "Answer to George Mason's Objections" in 1788, Iredell referred to *The Federalist* as "That great writer." Ford, *Pamphlets* 335, 365. See Cohens v. Virginia, 6 Wheat. 264, 418 (1821) (per Marshall, C.J.).

[207] Crosskey 1026-1027, 964.

[208] Quoted Corwin, "Progress" 530.

[209] Haines 104 n. 39.

[210] Corwin, "Progress" 529–531.

[211] Hamilton continued to maintain that "the states are bound by it [treaty] and ought religiously to observe it," and denied that "we then can do by act of legislature, what the treaty disables us from doing," because the delegation to the Confederation of the "right of making treaties" abridges "the sovereignty of each particular state." "Letters from Phocion," 4 Hamilton, *Works* 239, 238. It strains

abandoned his own belief in judicial review, be the New York law what it may. Hamilton's exposition in *Federalist* No. 78 thereafter was therefore no *volte-face*.

Having converted Hamilton's advice to settle rather than appeal into evidence of Hamilton's "belief" as to the *New York* law of judicial review, having then transmogrified this "belief" into his view that "*Congress* was the constitutional judge of its own constitutional powers," Crosskey next invokes *Federalist* No. 33 to show that Hamilton's "initial position was in essential accord with his earlier view."[212] The "simple and candid views" of No. 33 upon which Crosskey builds are Hamilton's answer to the question "Who is to judge of the *necessity and propriety* of the laws to be passed for executing the powers of the Union?":

> the national government, like every other, must judge in the first instance, of the proper exercise of its powers, and its constitutents in the last.[213]

Crosskey argues that "As the Supreme Court has no 'constituents,' it is evident that Hamilton must have been speaking of Congress and the President . . . And that Hamilton regarded the people, through their rights of election, direct and indirect, as the true constitutional check on Congress and the President, is shown by his next ensuing sentence. 'If the federal government should overpass the just bounds of its authority, and make a tyrannical use of its powers, the people, whose creature it is, must,' he says, 'appeal to the standard they have formed, and take such measures to redress the injury done to the Constitution as the exigency may suggest and prudence justify.'"[214]

Although the Supreme Court has no "constituents," that is, it is not elected, Crosskey too hastily read it out of the "national government" which "must judge in the first instance." When conflicts between State and national claims arise—and it is to these that the

---

belief that he abjured his conviction that judicial review must lend teeth to these propositions. Says Miller, *Alexander Hamilton: Portrait in Paradox*, 201 (1959), Hamilton "had long advocated that the interpretation of the fundamental law be committed to the judiciary."

[212] Crosskey 1026–1027 (emphasis supplied).
[213] Ibid.; *Federalist* No. 33 at 200.
[214] Crosskey 1026–1027.

Crosskey quotation was directed—it is neither Congress nor President who determines the scope of national power but the courts. "The majesty of the national authority," said Hamilton in *Federalist* No. 16, "must be manifested through the medium of the courts of justice."[215] For him the "people" were a last resort if judicial relief proved unavailing. Considering a "usurpation of authority" by a State in No. 16, Hamilton said that "The success of it would require not merely a factious majority in the legislature, but the concurrence of courts of justice *and* of the body of the people. If the judges were not embarked in a conspiracy with the legislature, they would pronounce the resolutions of such a majority to be contrary to the supreme law of the land, unconstitutional and void."[216] In terms of Crosskey's quotation from No. 33, the "national government" would "judge" of its powers "in the first instance" through the medium of the courts, and only if the courts concurred in the "usurpation" need the "people" themselves take hold. Mark also that No. 16 enunciates the principle, later amplified in No. 78, that a law "contrary to the supreme law of the land [is] unconstitutional and void," and though Hamilton was concerned in No. 16 with State action—recognizing that State judges could set aside State legislative action—jealous opponents of sweeping Congressional powers were more tender of State's rights than of federal laws.

Evidence of such jealousy is furnished by No. 33 itself. Its purpose was to allay the fears of those who dreaded the breadth of Congressional authority "to make all laws which shall be necessary and proper for carrying" federal powers into execution. Such fears led Hamilton to say that acts which are *"not pursuant* to its [Congress'] constitutional powers, but which are invasions of the residuary authorities of the smaller societies . . . will be merely acts of usurpation, and will deserve to be treated as such."[217] How they were to be treated had already been outlined in No. 16: "usurpations" were to be pronounced "unconstitutional and void" by the courts.[218]

215 *Federalist* No. 16 at 98–99.
216 Id. at 100 (emphasis supplied).
217 *Federalist* No. 33 at 201–202. Professor Hart, Book Review, 1482–1483, notes that Crosskey ignored this statement.
218 When Corwin, *Court Over* 45, says of the "acts of usurpation" that Hamilton "does not say" "who is to determine such matters," he overlooks the above statement in No. 16.

Those who were being asked to surrender cherished State powers, who anxiously inquired "Who is to judge of the *necessity* and *propriety* of the laws to be passed for executing the powers of the Union,"[219] would scarcely want Congress, in Crosskey's phrase, to be "the constitutional judge of its own constitutional powers"[220] to invade the "residuary authorities" of the States. Hamilton's purpose and assurances in No. 33 are therefore at war with the meaning Crosskey pins onto the word "constituents";[221] indeed the implications of No. 33 not only do not oppose, but they foreshadow, the views No. 78 more carefully delineated.

Boudin maintains that No. 78 and Hamilton's No. 81 "are entirely contradictory" and concludes that "this supposed great pillar of strength of the Judicial Power among the Framers was but a broken reed."[222] He singles out Hamilton's statement in No. 81 that "It is not true that the Parliament of Great Britain, or the legislatures of the particular States, can rectify the exceptionable decisions of their respective courts, *in any other sense than might be done by a future legislature of the United States.*" Inquiring whether this means that after the Supreme Court's decision in "*Pollock v. Farmers Loan & Trust Co.,* the Congress . . . could proceed to enact and enforce another income tax law, although it could not reverse the judgment in [that] particular case." Boudin concludes "*that is exactly what Hamilton seems to have meant.*"[223] True it is that in meeting one argument, that "the Parliament . . . and the legislatures of the several States, can at any time rectify, by law, the exceptionable

---

[219] Federalist No. 33 at 200.

[220] Crosskey 1026.

[221] When Crosskey finds that some expressions in *The Federalist* are "artfully contrived to leave an impression contrary" to alleged Hamiltonian views that he prefers, he states, "But the opponents of the Constitution were not deceived by these inconsistent things *The Federalist* said. This is sufficiently shown, so far as the judiciary powers are concerned, by what one 'Brutus' . . . had to say upon the subject." Crosskey 712. We too may invoke "Brutus," i.e., Yates. *Federalist* No. 16, which foreshadows judicial review, was published December 1787; No. 33, which on Crosskey's reading obscurely plays against judicial review, was published on January 3, 1788. On January 31, "Brutus" published his first piece on judicial review, Corwin, *Court Over* 231, and not at all deceived by the "inconsistencies" of No. 33, read Article III to provide unmistakably for judicial review. Needless to say, I recount the incident merely to show again how Crosskey plays both sides of the street.

[222] Boudin 113 n. 3.

[223] Id. at 112–113.

decisions of their respective courts,[224] Hamilton said that "The theory, neither of the British, nor the State constitutions, authorizes the revisal of a judicial sentence by a legislative act . . . A legislature, without exceeding its province, cannot *reverse* a determination once made *in a particular case;* though it may *prescribe a new rule for future cases.*"[225]

But this statement of the ordinary rule had no play where constitutional decisions were concerned. There, as No. 81 itself plainly shows, the Supreme Court was to have the final word:

> the Constitution ought to be the standard of construction for the laws, the law ought to give place to the Constitution . . . There can be no objection, therefore, on this account, to the federal judiciary which will not lie against the local judiciaries in general, and which will not serve to condemn any constitution that attempts to set bounds to legislative discretion.

In a word, it was for the courts to decide when laws "must give place to the Constitution" which "set bounds to legislative discretion." That the courts must have the last word appears from what follows:

> From a body which had even a partial agency in passing bad laws, we could rarely expect a disposition to temper and moderate them in the application. The same spirit which had operated in making them, would be too apt in interpreting them; still less could it be expected that men who had infringed the Constitution in the character of legislators, would be disposed to repair the breach in the character of judges . . . There is an absurdity in referring the determination of causes, in the first instance, to judges of permanent standing; in the last, to those of a temporary and mutable constitution. And there is a still greater absurdity in subjecting the decisions of men, selected for their knowledge of the laws, acquired by long and laborious study, to the revision and control of men who, for want of the same advantage, cannot but be deficient in that knowledge.[226]

[224] *Federalist* No. 81 at 523, 526.
[225] Ibid. (emphasis added).
[226] Id. at 524–525.

Quite plainly, Hamilton rejected revision of constitutional decisions by the legislature. How Boudin could distill from No. 81 the proposition that Hamilton asserted the power of Congress to change a constitutional interpretation passes understanding.

So well knit is Hamilton's argument in No. 78 of *The Federalist* that it is hazardous to excerpt it, and I shall follow the general example in making copious quotations. Judicial tenure based on good behavior, he said, is an

> excellent barrier to the encroachments and oppressions of the representative body . . . The complete independence of the courts of justice is peculiarly essential in a limited Constitution . . . Limitations [such as on bills of attainder, ex post facto laws] can be preserved in practice in no other way than through the medium of courts of justice, whose duty it must be to declare all acts contrary to the manifest tenor of the Constitution void. Without this, all the reservations of particular rights or privileges would amount to nothing.[227]

Addressing himself to the objection that the judicial right "to pronounce legislative acts void, because contrary to the constitution . . . would imply a superiority of the judiciary to the legislative power," he stated,

> There is no position which depends on clearer principles, than that every act of a delegated authority, contrary to the tenor of the commission under which it is exercised, is void. No legislative act, therefore, contrary to the Constitution, can be valid. To deny this, would be to affirm that the deputy is greater than his principal . . . that men acting by virtue of powers, may do not only what their powers do not authorize, but what they forbid. If it be said that the legislative body are themselves the constitutional judges of their own powers, and that the construction they put upon them is conclusive upon the other departments, it may be answered, that this cannot be the natural presumption, where it is not to be collected from any particular provisions in the Constitution. It is not otherwise to be supposed, that the Constitution could intend to enable the representatives of the people to sub-

[227] Id. No. 78 at 503, 505.

stitute their *will* to that of their constituents. It is far more rational to suppose, that the courts were designed to be an intermediate body between the people and the legislature, in order, among other things, to keep the latter within the limits assigned to their authority. The interpretation of the laws is the proper and peculiar province of the courts. A constitution is, in fact, and must be regarded by the judges, as a fundamental law. It therefore belongs to them to ascertain its meaning, as well as the meaning of any particular act proceeding from the legislative body. If there should happen to be an irreconcilable variance between the two, that which has the superior obligation and validity ought, of course, to be preferred; or, in other words, the Constitution ought to be preferred to the statute, the intention of the people to the intention of their agents.

Nor does this conclusion by any means suppose a superiority of the judicial to the legislative power. It only supposes that the power of the people is superior to both; and that where the will of the legislature, declared in its statutes, stands in opposition to that of the people, declared in the Constitution, the judges ought to be governed by the latter rather than by the former.[228]

If, then, the courts of justice are to be considered as the bulwarks of a limited Constitution against legislative encroachments, this consideration will afford a strong argument for the permanent tenure of judicial offices, since nothing will contribute so much as this to that independent spirit in the judges which must be essential to the faithful performance of so arduous a duty.[229]

In sum, Hamilton explained that (1) the Constitution is the fundamental law and as such must be interpreted by the courts; (2) Acts contrary to the Constitution are void; (3) Congress cannot be left to be the judge of its own constitutional powers; this function is for the courts if Congress is to be kept within Constitutional bounds; and (4) independence of judges secures their function as bulwarks of a limited Constitution; only thus can judges safely declare statutes unconstitutional. The several analytical components of his statement will be hereinafter examined.

[228] Id. at 505, 506.
[229] Id. at 508.

It has often been thought that the doctrine of judicial review sprang full-grown from the brow of Hamilton, but as Corwin justly stated in 1925, after reviewing the statements of Varnum and Iredell, "Here are all the premises of the doctrine of judicial review . . . the superiority of the Constitution to statute law . . . its qualities as law knowable by Judges . . . the exclusion of 'legislative power' . . . from law interpretation. The classical version of the doctrine of judicial review in the Federalist, No. 78, improves upon the statement of these premises but adds nothing essential to them."[230] As he said in 1914, "It cannot be reasonably doubted that Hamilton was here, as at other points, endeavoring to reproduce the matured conclusions of the Convention itself. And not less certain is it that he was thus notifying those to whom the Constitution had been referred for ratification of the grounds upon which its framers and supporters based the case for judicial review."[231] The fact that such opponents as Yates, Martin, and the "Centinel" read the Constitution in the same way furnishes powerful confirmation for the Corwin conclusion.

Oliver Ellsworth

In the Connecticut Ratification convention, Ellsworth said, "If the general legislature should at any time overleap their limits, the judicial department is a constitutional check. If the United States go beyond their powers, if they make a law which the Constitution does

---

[230] Corwin, "Progress" 526–527. In this, as in other aspects of judicial review, Corwin blew hot and cold over the years. See supra, note 115; infra, Chapter 6, note 63. In 1938, influenced by the Court's invalidation of New Deal legislation, ibid., and cf. Corwin, *Court Over* vii, he found no answers in No. 33, and concluded that "Hamilton's later argument in Federalist 78 and 81 seems to have been inspired by the effort of Yates." Corwin now stamped No. 78 as "a tour de force" and concluded that it came too late to influence ratification outside New York. Corwin, *Court Over* 45, 47. As to the last point, see supra, note 197. My submission is that the earlier Corwin was closer to the mark. Hamilton himself made the argument in Rutgers v. Waddington in 1784, Corwin, "Progress" 529; he cannot have been unfamiliar with the widely disseminated Varnum argument in Trevett v. Weeden in 1785; and since he was a well-publicized advocate of judicial review because of his advocacy in Rutgers v. Waddington, it is not too far-fetched to surmise that Iredell's 1786 address was called to his attention. Above all, some of the ideas which he pulled together in No. 78 had been in the air because of the wide currency of Vattel, and James Otis' invocation of Coke in 1764. See quotations from Corwin, supra, text accompanying notes 230–231.

[231] Corwin, *Doctrine* 44. See Jefferson, quoted supra, text accompanying note 206.

not authorize, it is void; and the judicial power, the national judges, . . . will declare it to be void."[232] This statement "clearly" expressed the "doctrine of judicial control as an argument in favor of the Constitution."[233]

Abraham Baldwin

In the Congressional debate of 1789 on the President's "removal" power, Baldwin said, "Gentlemen say it properly belongs to the Judiciary to decide this question. Be it so. It is their province to decide upon our laws and if they find this clause to be unconstitutional, they will not hesitate to declare it so."[234] But in 1800 Baldwin made a statement in the Senate that appears to run counter to his earlier view.[235] Such utterances of Southern statesmen in the wake of the Virginia-Kentucky Resolutions may be discounted,[236] and allowance must be made for the fact that men change their minds over the years without impeaching the actuality of the earlier belief, which was in this case much closer to the Convention.

Edmund Randolph

Governor Randolph, in explaining the Virginia Plan to the Convention, stated that a "Council of Revision" and a "national judiciary" were to be "Checks upon the Legv. and Ex. Powers."[237] That such "checks" embraced judicial review is illustrated by the compromise he submitted—apparently directed to the proposed congressional negative of State laws—in which it was provided that "any State may appeal to the national Judiciary against a Negative; and that such negative if adjudged to be contrary to the power granted

[232] 2 Elliot 196.
[233] Davis, *Veto* 51. But Davis classifies him as "disapproving" of judicial review because he was for the Act of 1789, a matter hereinafter discussed. Compare also, infra, text accompanying notes 244–247.
[234] 1 *Ann. Cong.* 582.
[235] "Suppose either of the other branches of the Government, the Executive or Judiciary, or even Congress, should be guilty of taking steps which are unconstitutional, to whom is it submitted, or who has control of it, except by impeachment." 3 Farrand 383. Warren, *Congress* 123 n. 1, doubts whether this expression indicates a change in Baldwin's earlier view; but I would give it broader scope. Even so, it does not deprive the clear, earlier expression of its effect.
[236] Supra, note 5, and text accompanying notes 74–76, and note 76.
[237] 1 Farrand 28.

by the articles of the Union, shall be void."[238] Thus the test whether
Congress had unconstitutionally invaded State powers was to be
left to the Supreme Court. Randolph also opposed "weakening . . .
the independence of the judges,"[239] but he refused ultimately to sign
the Constitution, assigning among other reasons that it was deficient, among other things, "in limiting and defining the judicial
power."[240] The suggested limitation carries no implication of opposition to judicial review because in the very same document he found
the Constitution deficient "In drawing a line between the powers
of congress and individual states; and in defining the former . . .
to prevent the one from being swallowed up in the other."[241] Anxiety
lest Congress swallow up the States is incompatible with opposition
to judicial review which would limit such invasions, and as was
earlier noted, Randolph had suggested recourse to the courts for
just such protection.

In the Virginia convention he abandoned his opposition, argued
on behalf of adoption,[242] and said that "If Congress wish to aggrandize themselves by oppressing the people, the judiciary must first be
corrupted,"[243] plainly implying that judicial review was to thwart

[238] 3 Farrand 56; 2 Farrand 17; Melvin 177.

[239] 2 Farrand 429.

[240] 3 Farrand 127. In the Convention Randolph had objected to the "want of
a more definite boundary . . . between the General and State Judiciaries." 2 Farrand 564.

[241] 3 Farrand 127. In the Virginia convention Randolph stated that were he
to propose an amendment, "it would be to limit the word *arising* [in Article III].
The jurisdiction of the judiciary in cases arising under the system, I should wish
to be defined, so as to prevent it being extended unnecessarily; I would restrain the
appellate cognizance as to fact, and prevent oppressive and vexatious appeals."
3 Elliot 602. Opponents had dilated on the "stupendous magnitude" of the
"arising under" jurisdiction, id. at 565, 523; they feared that the judiciary would
destroy state courts and the states themselves, id. at 521, 522, 527, 542; and it
was to this that Randolph responded. Significantly there is no hint of depriving
the courts of jurisdiction to declare Acts of Congress unconstitutional—a question
of law—though it had been stated more than once in the Virginia convention that
courts would have such power. Infra, Chapter 4, text accompanying notes 109–128.

[242] 3 Elliot 24–29.

[243] Id. at 205. Referring to oppression by the federal government, Randolph
said that if the federal judiciary "will not do justice to the persons injured, may
they not go into our own state judiciaries to obtain it?" 3 Elliot 468. Contrast this
with the reliance by Davis, *Veto* 59–60, on Randolph's statement, "Can Congress
go beyond the bounds prescribed in the Constitution? Has Congress a power to
say that she [Virginia] shall pay fifteen parts out of sixty-five parts [of a direct
tax]? Were they to assume such a power it would be a usurpation so glaring, that
rebellion would be the immediate consequence." 3 Elliott 121. The fact that a

"aggrandizement." After enactment of the Judiciary Act of 1789, Randolph, then Attorney General, was asked to report on it to the House.[244] He had preferred federal to State courts in the Convention,[245] and he now urged that the federal courts had exclusive jurisdiction in certain categories and that State courts be excluded therefrom.[246] He recognized, however, the right of State courts under the Act to declare federal Acts unconstitutional,[247] and presumably were the jurisdiction taken from the State courts and restricted to the federal courts, the latter would exercise a similar power. Randolph, it need scarcely be added, had no criticism of the power of the Supreme Court to "affirm or reverse" in the premises, and, after noting the provisions for appeal from the State courts to the Supreme Court, stated "That the avenue to the federal courts ought, in these instances to be unobstructed is manifest."[248] His desire was that the federal courts should take over the initial jurisdiction as well. Davis classifies Randolph as "doubtful,"[249] but he overlooked the bulk of the foregoing materials.

Other Members

Those who participated in drafting the Judiciary Act of 1789, worked for it on Committees, and voted for it are listed by Beard as proponents of judicial review.[250] Davis deduces from precisely the

---

"glaring" malapportionment of taxes among the States might incite to rebellion does not compel the inference that judicial relief is unavailable. It is also significant that in citing an example of the argument against the judiciary, Randolph concentrated on the appellate jurisdiction of questions of fact, 3 Elliot 205, which was widely considered to imperil trial by jury. Infra, Chapter 9, text accompanying notes 7–14.

[244] Amer. State Papers, Misc. I (1789–1809) 21.
[245] 2 Farrand 46.
[246] Supra, note 244 at 22, 26.
[247] Id. at 23; Davis, Veto 60.
[248] Supra, note 244 at 23.
[249] Davis, Veto 61. Hear Boudin 582: "while Randolph did say in his speech introducing the Virginia or Randolph plan 'that some check was therefore to be sought against this tendency of our governments' to 'the turbulence and follies of democracy,' he also said, in the same breath, *that a good Senate seemed most likely to answer this purpose.* He then proceeded through the weary months that the Convention continued its sessions, *but never once mentioned the Judicial Power.* What warrant have we then to saddle him with responsibility for the Judicial Power?" I would not saddle him with "responsibility," but the materials above set forth show that he was a proponent of judicial review. Supra, text accompanying notes 237–248.
[250] Beard 48, 65, 67, 68–69.

same fact that they were opponents.[251] The Members involved are Richard Bassett, John Blair, William Few, Oliver Ellsworth, William Johnson, Robert Morris, William Paterson,[252] George Read, Caleb Strong, and George Washington. Analysis of the Act is postponed for discussion in chronological sequence; my submission is that the Act empowered State courts to set aside unconstitutional federal laws and on appeal the Supreme Court could reverse or affirm.[253] Consequently I would concur with Beard that votes for the Act may be taken to indicate approval of judicial review, all the more since the debate on the President's "removal" power, which took place some six weeks earlier, displayed substantial unanimity with respect to the availability of judicial review.[254] Here it may be noted that the gloss placed by Beard upon the votes is confirmed in at least three and possibly four instances by action taken prior to or not long after the Act. Ellsworth had unmistakably declared in the Connecticut Ratification convention that the judiciary could declare Acts of Congress void.[255] Strong joined Gerry in separating the

[251] Davis, *Veto* 58, 61–62, 63, 114–120.

[252] Beard does not mention William Paterson, who voted for the Act in the Senate. 1 *Ann. Cong.* 18, 51.

[253] Davis, *Veto* 119–120, himself states that "The Supreme Court is given the power to reverse or affirm the decision of a state court adjudging a federal statute unconstitutional. In other words, the Supreme Court may acquiesce in [affirm] the action of a State annulling a federal statute; or it may reverse the State's decision and pronounce the law constitutional and valid. But it has no jurisdiction to decide of its own accord that the law is unconstitutional." For purposes of my discussion of the appellate jurisdiction, it suffices that in the exercise of that jurisdiction the Supreme Court may affirm a State court decision that a federal law is unconstitutional. It may be added, however, that the statute which governs the appellate jurisdiction only, can not cut down the Supreme Court's power under the *original* jurisdiction. Power to declare a statute unconstitutional derives from the Constitution, and the Judiciary Act on which Davis relies and which relates to the appellate jurisdiction draws thereon.

Davis, *Veto* 113–114, also reads the Tenth Amendment reservation to the States of powers not delegated to the Nation as evincing an intention "to reserve to the States the authority to decide upon the constitutionality of acts of Congress." If I understand this rightly, it is a variant of the discredited Virginia-Kentucky Resolutions which later ripened into the rejected Nullification doctrine. Morison, *History* 432. And it overlooks Madison's statement in the First Congress, when proposing the Bill of Rights, that the courts would act as a bulwark of the rights thus enshrined. 1 *Ann. Cong.* 457.

[254] Infra, Chapter 5, text accompanying notes 11–18. Corwin, *Doctrine* 49, n. 74, says that "If Mr. Davis had turned to the debate, just reviewed on the establishment of the Department of Foreign Affairs [re the "removal" power], he would have found at least half a dozen men championing the notion of judicial review who [a few weeks] later voted for the Act of 1789."

[255] Supra, text accompanying note 232.

"making" from "expounding of laws,"[256] and expounding, it will be recalled, contemplated declarations of unconstitutionality. Blair had advised Washington in *Hayburn's Case* in 1792 that the court could not act under a statute which unconstitutionally delegated non-judicial powers to it.[257] Paterson, as a Supreme Court Justice sitting on Circuit in 1795 in *Vanhorne v. Dorrance,* held that "if a [State] legislative act oppugns a Constitutional principle [of the Pennsylvania constitution], the former must give way and be rejected on the score of repugnance."[258]

Pierce Butler and John Langdon voted against the Judiciary Act, and Beard questions "whether a vote cast against the Act as a whole is evidence of opposition to the principles of judicial control over federal legislation recognized in the twenty-fifth section of the

[256] Supra, text accompanying notes 39, 31–38.

[257] 2 Dallas (2 U.S.) 409, 411. Boudin 182 ridicules this as a "suppliant 'remonstrance'" that "proclaims loudly" the difference from views that "now prevail on the subject," i.e., that courts may "declare legislative acts unconstitutional." He mistakes politeness for subservience. To say that a court cannot act under an unconstitutional statute is merely a polite way of declaring the act unconstitutional. Cf. supra, Chapter 2, text preceding note 148.

[258] 2 Dallas 304, 309. Although I do not rely on Vanhorne as a "precedent" but merely as an expression of Paterson's view, it may not be amiss to note that Boudin 185 dismisses Vanhorne because Paterson was merely giving the jury the "benefit of his expert opinion" in a charge telling them that *"they were the judges of the law as well as of the fact."* I failed to find such a statement. To the contrary, Paterson stated in his charge to the jury that "The great points on which the case turns, are of a legal nature; they are questions of law; and therefore . . . they ought to be put in train for ultimate adjudication by the Supreme Court." 2 Dallas at 304. After a lengthy exposition of the law, Paterson said, "plaintiff is, by law, entitled to recover the premises in question, and, of course, to your verdict." Id. at 320. In the face of this, Boudin concludes that Paterson merely held that "the constitutionality of a legislative act is a matter which every one called upon to act must decide for himself!" Boudin 185.

Davis, *Veto* 58, argues that since Vanhorne involved the validity of a Pennsylvania statute under the Pennsylvania constitution, "there can be no positive inference that Paterson believed that the federal Supreme Court should have the power conclusively to determine the constitutionality of acts of Congress." Paterson's broad statement of basic principles cannot be so narrowed. Why should the relationship between a federal court and a national legislature under the Constitution be different from that of a State court—Paterson was deciding a diversity case as he conceived a State court would—to a State legislature under a State constitution?

It may be asked why should we lend credence to Paterson's 1795 judicial statement while excluding the Pinckney-Baldwin statements in 1798–1800. The latter are suspect as politically motivated because they follow on the heels of strife over the Alien and Sedition Acts. But Paterson's statement preceded these events by some years; it was made in a judicial capacity about a State law under a State constitution; and it is not easy to perceive political motivation.

act."[259] Although a vote for the Act necessarily involved acceptance of Section 25 with all of its implications, while a vote against it may perhaps be deemed ambiguous, vote-counting should not only be but seem even-handed, and I would therefore class Butler and Langdon as opponents.

From Beard's list of proponents I would also delete David Brearley, William Livingston, and George Wythe. Wythe was included by Beard on the strength of his opinion in *Commonwealth v. Caton* (1782). Livingston and Brearley were included by Beard because through their connection with *Holmes v. Walton* they "went on record as understanding and approving the doctrine of judicial review."[260] Both *Caton* and *Holmes* were subjected to full-scale attack by Boudin and Crosskey,[261] and though I am little disposed to rely on either,[262] some confirmatory evidence which I descried respecting *Caton*[263] raised doubts that suggest suspension of reliance

[259] Beard 71. So too, Davis, *Veto* 65, states that Pierce Butler and John Langdon "may have had a score of reasons for voting against the judiciary act; I do not feel that such action is indicative of a view either in favor or against judicial control?"

[260] Beard 68, 69 n. 2.

[261] Crosskey 948–961; Boudin 531–555.

[262] Crosskey 1368 n. 22, who does not shrink from extreme interpretation of evidence, is driven to say that Boudin "is inclined to argue much beyond his evidence," though he concludes that the factors mentioned by Boudin "make it very improbable" that Holmes v. Walton was a case of judicial review.

Consider too Boudin's invidious remarks about Austin Scott's article on Holmes v. Walton, 4 *Am. Hist. Rev.* 456 (1899) (Boudin 536), wherein Scott at worst mistakenly attributed an unlocated opinion to Chief Justice Brearley: "The fastening of an opinion in this case on Chief Justice Brearley is just one of those little details which are sometimes added by this class of historians in order 'to give versimilitude to a bald and unconvincing narrative.'" Boudin 544–545. Instances of similar intolerant criticism can be multiplied. Id. at 519, 557–558, 578, 581–582. One who so intemperately attacks follow scholars that hold opposing views betrays his own partiality.

[263] Both Boudin 534, and Crosskey 952, 960, virtually charge Daniel Call, the reporter of Commonwealth v. Caton, 4 Call 5 (1782) with fabricating, or to use an uglier word, with falsifying, the constitutional aspects of the opinion for political purposes. Unpalatable as such charges are, I was disturbed to find for myself that when the judges decided Kamper v. Hawkins, 1 Va. Cas. 22, 107 (1793) (among whom was John Tyler, whose opinion in *Caton* is reported by Call) and cast about for authority, no one thought to cite *Caton*; instead the Remonstrance of 1788 was cited. And Tucker, a judge of the Virginia court, stated in his 1803 edition of Blackstone that "more than one instance might be adduced where the judiciary department have doubted, or denied the obligation of an act of the legislative, because contrary to the constitution," App. 81, but he too omitted to cite *Caton* though he referred to a 1783 "case of the district court clerks in the court of appeals," and to Kamper v. Hawkins "in the general court."

on Wythe, and for good measure on Brearley and Livingston, until the unclouded authenticity of *Caton* and *Holmes* as judicial review precedents is established.

Now to tally the Members. Beard listed seventeen of the twenty-five most influential Members as having declared, directly or indirectly, for judicial control: Blair, Dickinson, Ellsworth, Gerry, Hamilton, Johnson, King, Madison, Martin, Mason, Gouverneur Morris, Robert Morris, Paterson, Randolph, Washington, Williamson, and Wilson. To these he added eight men of lesser eminence: Baldwin, Bassett, Brearley, Few, Livingston, Read, Strong, and Wythe.[264] From the latter list I would strike Brearley, Livingston, and Wythe, and with Corwin I would add Davie, Charles Pinckney, Rutledge, and Gorham as well. The total comes to twenty-six out of fifty-five who recognized or favored judicial review. The dissenters noted by Beard were Bedford, Mercer, and Spaight;[265] I would add Butler, Langdon, and Yates, with emphasis that Yates unmistakably indicates that the Convention went the other way. Out of a membership of 55, 26 were for and only 6 against judicial review. The remainder of the 55 left no record of their views.

Let Corwin draw the inferences in his 1914 *Doctrine of Judicial Review*:[266]

That the members of the Convention of 1787 thought the Constitution secured to courts in the United States the right to pass on the validity of acts of Congress under it cannot reasonably be doubted. Confining ourselves simply to the available evidence that is strictly contemporaneous with the framing and ratifying of the

---

[264] Beard 47, 65–69. Professor Westin suggests that "Beard uses support of review over state laws as though such a position automatically placed its adherent in favor of the other review power" of federal statutes. Westin 29. Beard cited some references to State courts which set aside State laws, and one case where Paterson, sitting in a diversity case and deciding as would a State judge, laid down the principle that a law which offended a constitution was void. Beard 48, 50, 60, 63. From these it is reasonable to deduce that federal judges may set aside federal laws under the federal Constitution. As far as my search goes, Beard at no point cited to a statement that a *federal* court could set aside a *State* law. The analogy rather is that if a State court may set aside a State law, a federal court may annul a federal Act. Nor would I discard the federal-State examples, had Beard in fact employed them, for reasons developed infra, Chapter 8, text accompanying notes 151–193.

[265] Beard 69–71.

[266] Corwin, *Doctrine* 10–13.

Constitution, as I think it only proper to do, we find the following members of the Convention that framed the Constitution definitely asserting that this would be the case: Gerry and King of Massachusetts, Wilson and Gouverneur Morris of Pennsylvania, Martin of Maryland, Randolph, Madison and Mason of Virginia, Dickinson of Delaware, Yates and Hamilton of New York, Rutledge and Charles Pinckney of South Carolina, Davie and Williamson of North Carolina, Sherman and Ellsworth of Connecticut.[267] True these were only seventeen names out of a possible fifty-five, but let it be considered whose names they are. They designate fully three-fourths of the leaders of the Convention . . . men who expressed themselves on the subject of judicial review because they also expressed themselves on all other subjects before the Convention. They were the leaders of that body and its articulate members . . . Altogether it seems a warrantable assertion that on no other feature of the Constitution with reference to which there has been any considerable debate is the view of the Convention itself better attested.[268]

When Corwin is cited for the opposition, this 1914 statement is strangely overlooked, and reliance is placed instead on his 1913 book

[267] Corwin added Davie, C. Pinckney, Rutledge, Sherman, and Yates to the list of those who thought the Constitution provided for judicial review, but does not mention the voters for the Judiciary Act of 1789. See supra, text accompanying note 252.

[268] Of Hamilton's exposition of judicial review in *Federalist* No. 78, Corwin said in 1914, "It cannot be reasonably doubted that Hamilton was here, as at other points, endeavoring to reproduce the matured conclusions of the Convention itself." Corwin, *Doctrine* 44.

Apparently this was the view of Washington, who presided over the Convention. Upon receipt of the bound *Federalist* from Hamilton, Washington wrote him in August 1788, "I have read every performance which has been printed on one side and the other of the great question lately agitated . . . and, without an unmeaning compliment, I will say, that I have seen no other so well calculated (in my judgment) to produce conviction on an unbiased mind, as the *Production* of your *triumvirate*." Quoted, Brown, Book Review 1455.

Corwin again endorsed the Beard view in his 1925 article, "Progress" 536. But in 1938 he said, "it is obvious that Hamilton is not professing in *Federalist* 78 to speak as a witness, but is making an argument." Corwin, *Court Over* 48–49. In 1910, Corwin, 9 *Mich. L. Rev.* 118, 119, alluded to Gerry's reference to the judiciary's "power of deciding upon the constitutionality of laws," which "was reiterated or applauded at times by King, Martin, Strong, Charles Pinckney and Rutledge . . . Madison, Wilson, and Mason accepted explicitly the idea of judicial review." He found only Bedford and Mercer in clear dissent, and noted Spaight's opposition in his letter to Iredell.

review of Beard.[269] But Corwin returned to his 1913 views after the judicial ordeal of the New Deal,[270] so that the still-cited 1913 review merits close analysis. Comment is facilitated by breaking up the lengthy passage.

In 1913 Corwin concluded that the Convention regarded the question of judicial review "as still an open one when it adjourned," for

> of the twenty-five members set down by Mr. Beard as favoring judicial review of acts of Congress seven are so classified simply on the score of their voting two years after the Convention for the Judiciary Act of 1789, the terms of which do not necessarily assume any such power, though they do not preclude it.[271]

The First Congress, in which sat a goodly number of Framers and Ratifiers, has been regarded almost as an adjourned session of the Convention.[272] To it fell the task of filling out the governmental structure provided by the Constitution. That the Act of 1789 assumed a power in the State courts to set aside Congressional acts,

---

[269] Corwin, Book Review 330–331. Boudin 570–571; Haines 134–135; Westin 28.

[270] See infra, note 312. In his 1938 "Court Over Constitution," 33, Corwin said, "First and last, only a small portion of the members expressed themselves regarding the matter; and while among them were some [¾] of the leaders of the Convention, and a majority appeared to favor the idea, yet their language was sometimes tentative, the grounds upon which they rested their belief was not uniform, and when this belief was challenged, the only effort they made—if indeed it is interpretable as such—toward putting the matter beyond doubt was the insertion of the words 'this' Constitution in the 'arising under' clause." His remarks on "finality," "self-defense," and other problems that allegedly obscure the intention of the leadership will hereafter be examined in detail. It suffices for the moment that Yates and Martin, vigorous critics of the Constitution, found no difficulty in discerning that the "arising under" clause provided for judicial review, as the Founders contemplated. See infra, Chapter 7, text accompanying notes 16–17.

[271] For the entire quotation see Westin 28. Three of the "seven" did not "simply" vote for the Act of 1789; Ellsworth, Blair, and Paterson made confirmatory statements elsewhere. Supra, text accompanying notes 255–258.

[272] Madison wrote in 1832, "It deserves particular attention, that the Congress which first met contained sixteen members, eight of them in the House of Representatives, fresh from the Convention which framed the Constitution, and a considerable number who had been members of the State Conventions which had adopted it." 3 Farrand 518. See Warren, *Congress* 98–99. Those who would substitute present day speculation against the views of the First Congress might well ponder the remarks of Congressman William Vans Murray in 1796, quoted infra, Chapter 5, note 1.

subject to an appeal to the Supreme Court, which was authorized to reverse or affirm, will hereafter appear.[273] Subject to that proof, a vote for the Act is not unjustifiably regarded as an index of the Framer's view in the Convention, particularly because three of the voters confirmed Beard's inference by other action.[274]

Next, says Corwin,

Of another six, only utterances are quoted which postdate the Convention, sometimes by several years. Furthermore, by far the two most important members of this group are Hamilton and Madison, the former of whom apparently became a convert to the idea under discussion between the time of writing Federalist 33 and Federalist 78, and the latter of whom is proved by the very language which Mr. Beard quotes to have been unfavorable in 1788 and 1789.

Hamilton's espousal of judicial review in *Rutgers v. Waddington*, and his subsequent "Letters from Phocion," wherein, as Corwin stated in 1925, "Hamilton was reiterating his views,"[275] remove him from the ranks of a recent "convert." Justifiably we may discern in *Federalist* No. 33 as well as No. 16 merely a reflection of his earlier views.[276] Corwin's statement that Madison was "unfavorable both in 1788 and 1789" relies first on the undisclosed letter of October 1788, which "postdated" both the federal and Virginia conventions.[277] In this self-same critique Corwin is the first to prefer statements made "on the floor of the Convention" to those made outside.

---

[273] Corwin does not find the implications of §25 of the Act of 1789 "clear-cut": "It was there provided that a decision final under the state law of a state court which was adverse to a claim set up under the Constitution or a treaty or statute of the United States, and which purported to rest on the invalidity of the national law or treaty in question, might 'be re-examined, and reversed or affirmed in the Supreme Court on writ of error.' The section thus *inferred* the possibility of a state court holding 'invalid' for a case before it a national treaty or statute, and authorized the Supreme Court to *affirm* such a holding; that is to say, the language was that of *authorization* rather than of *recognition*." Corwin, *Court Over* 52–53. Congress may only "authorize" action which the Constitution permits, and such "authorization" constitutes "recognition" that the power to "authorize" is conferred by the Constitution.

[274] See supra, text accompanying notes 255–258.

[275] Corwin, "Progress" 529–530.

[276] Supra, text accompanying notes 208–221.

[277] Supra, text accompanying notes 155–163.

"On the floor of the Convention," said Corwin in 1914, Madison "had espoused the doctrine of judicial review in unmistakable terms."[278] Against the 1789 statement in the course of the "removal" debate, hereinafter noticed, must be balanced Madison's unequivocal statement in the very same First Congress when proposing the Bill of Rights, that the courts will be "an impenetrable bulwark against every assumption of power in the Legislature or Executive."[279] What Madison said *in the Convention* rather than his subsequent statements seems to me to be controlling.

Since it is not possible to identify the other four of the "six" with certainty, I shall comment on six post-Convention utterances by Ellsworth, Randolph, Dickinson, Baldwin, Blair, and Paterson. Ellsworth spoke plainly for judicial review in the Connecticut Ratification convention,[280] and then voted for the Judiciary Act of 1789;[281] and both Jefferson and Madison attached controlling weight to explanations given to the Ratifiers who were being asked to adopt the Constitution.[282] Randolph's 1790 *Report to the House*[283] confirmed views he had expressed in both the Convention and the Virginia Ratification convention,[284] though to do Corwin justice, these expressions were not cited by Beard. Dickinson's 1788 assurance that "independent judges" would be on hand for "determination . . . of . . . Constitutionality" of Congressional laws only sharpened the implication of his Convention statement that he was "at a loss what expedient to substitute" for judicial review.[285] Baldwin's statement in the First Congress, two years removed from the Convention, was made in a House in which sat a group of Framers and Ratifiers, and in which there was virtual unanimity that judicial review was available.[286] Blair had not only advised Washington in 1792 that the court could not act under an unconstitutional statute,

---

[278] Corwin, *Doctrine* 47.

[279] 1 *Ann. Cong.* 457.

[280] Supra, text accompanying note 232.

[281] Supra, text accompanying note 252.

[282] Infra, Chapter 4, text accompanying notes 1 and 2.

[283] Supra, text accompanying notes 244–249.

[284] Supra, text accompanying notes 237–239, 243.

[285] Beard 249. In 1914 Corwin counted Dickinson among those who "definitely asserted" that the Constitution gave courts the "right to pass on the validity of acts of Congress." Supra, text accompanying note 267.

[286] Beard 66; and see infra, Chapter 5, text accompanying notes 11–18; and Corwin, quoted supra, note 254.

but had voted in the First Congress for the Judiciary Act,[287] an Act signed by Washington. Paterson delivered a charge to a jury in 1795, at a remove of eight years from the Convention, and here Beard's reliance is more debateable. Nevertheless, absent political motivation and earlier conflicting statements, it is not unreasonable to infer from a responsible statement in 1795 the reflection of an opinion held in 1787, particularly when it is confirmed by Paterson's vote for the Judiciary Act in 1789.[288] In 1914, Corwin himself included Hamilton, Madison, Randolph, Ellsworth, and Dickinson in the "evidence that is strictly contemporaneous with the framing and ratifying of the Constitution" for judicial review.[289]

Corwin's critique continues:

Again another four are reckoned as favoring the power of judicial review proper on account of judicial utterances antedating the convention from five to seven years, though these utterances, at the time they were made, were in one instance sharply challenged by public opinion or in the other by judicial opinion.

Beard cites the opinions of Blair and Wythe in *Commonwealth v. Caton*, and of Brearley and Livingston in connection with *Holmes v. Walton*.[290] Deletion of Wythe, Brearley, and Livingston was above suggested for other reasons,[291] but one may set to one side Blair's participation in *Caton* in 1782 and still rest on his vote for the Act of 1789 and his judicial expression in 1792 that the Circuit Court could not act under an unconstitutional statute.[292] Here, at least, Corwin scores three, if for debatable reasons.

Corwin goes on to say,

Only eight of the twenty-five acknowledged the power on the floor of the Convention itself, and of those eight three were pretty clearly recent converts to the idea, while some of them seemed to limit the power to its use as a means of self-defense by the court

[287] Supra, text accompanying note 252, 257.
[288] Supra, text accompanying note 258.
[289] Supra, text accompanying note 268.
[290] Beard 48, 68, 69 n. 2.
[291] Supra, text accompanying notes 260–263.
[292] Beard 48.

against legislative encroachment.[293] On the other hand the idea was challenged by four members of the Convention; and though they were outnumbered, so far as the available record shows, two to one by the avowed advocates of judicial review, yet popular discussion previous to the Convention had shown their point of view to have too formidable backing to admit of its being crassly overridden.

Unwittingly Corwin has engaged in statistical juggling, applying one measure to whittle down the majority and quite another to puff up the minority. By limiting the majority to remarks "on the floor of the Convention itself" Corwin shrivels twenty-five to a mere eight, and three of these are damned as "recent converts," although the example of St. Paul should teach that the convictions of a "recent convert" are not to be despised.[294] When Corwin turns to the dissenters, the "on the floor" test goes out the window. Of the four dissenters, Bedford, Mercer, Spaight, and Yates,[295] two spake not on the floor; Spaight wrote a letter to Iredell,[296] and Yates published a critique of the Constitution because, among other things, the Framers had provided for judicial review. So by Corwin's own "floor test," the majority outnumbered the minority not by 8 to 4 but by 8 to 2 or, on my count, by 11, and possibly 13, to 2, a sweeping preponderance. And only one of the two, Mercer, unmistakably "challenged" judicial review while sounding distinct provisional

[293] For discussion of "self-defense" see infra, Chapter 6, text accompanying notes 1–62.

[294] A remark by Sherman illustrates that the men who came to the Convention learned from one another: "He was at first for leaving the matter [criteria of representation in the House] wholly to the discretion of the Legislature; but he had been convinced by the observations of (Mr. Randolph and Mr. Mason) that the *periods* & the *rule* of revising the Representation ought to be fixt by the Constitution." 1 Farrand 582. "Mr. Rutledge animadverted on the shyness of gentlemen on this and other subjects. He said it looked as if they supposed themselves precluded by having frankly disclosed their opinions from afterwards changing them, which he did not take to be the case." Id. at 65. Randolph said, "every member will find [progress] to have taken place in his own [mind], if he will compare his present opinions with those brought with him into the Convention." 2 Farrand 89. Compare Madison, 3 Farrand 517; Corwin, *Doctrine* 41, quoted infra, Chapter 6, text accompanying note 232.

[295] Corwin, *Doctrine* 12; Corwin, *Court Over* 29–30.

[296] Supra, text accompanying notes 165–166. In 1914 Corwin stated that Spaight "later heard the idea [of judicial review] expounded both on the floor of the Philadelphia Convention and the North Carolina Convention without protest." Corwin, *Doctrine* 12.

overtones.[297] Bedford's dissent was directed to the Council of Revision, not to judicial review, and his opposition to "every check on the Legislative"[298] was so far from expressing "formidable backing" as to be disregarded time after time by the Convention as it added cumulative "checks" on the Congress.[299] Their "formidable backing" is further deflated by the fact that each was in effect repudiated by his own State.[300] It therefore required no "crassness" on the part of the Convention to override the expressions of Mercer and Bedford.

Finally, says Corwin,

> Despite, therefore, the sharp issue made in the Convention [by Mercer and Bedford], not a word designed to put the view of the majority beyond the same contingencies of interpretation to which it was at the moment exposed in the state constitutions was inserted in the national constitution, though on the other hand nothing to nullify the manifest hopes of the majority was inserted either.

To argue that "not a word . . . was inserted in the national constitution" runs contrary to the view of Yates, and of others yet to be noted, that the "arising under" clause, not present in State constitutions, embraced the power of judicial review.[301]

In reliance on the remarks of Mercer and Bedford, Corwin had stated in an earlier article that "As the clause 'cases under this Constitution' was inserted in the Constitution less than a fortnight later by unanimous vote of the Convention, it seems plain that it was not intended or understood to confer upon the federal judiciary a branch of power which certain members of the Convention were so loath

---

[297] Supra, text accompanying notes 78–81. In his 1914 book, Corwin stated that "It is by no means impossible that one of the grounds of his [Mercer's] opposition [to adoption] was recognition of the fact that the Constitution established judicial review." Corwin, *Doctrine* 12.

[298] Supra, text accompanying notes 106–108.

[299] In 1938 Corwin said, "Bedford should *perhaps* be placed on the list of opponents on the score of his strong views regarding legislative supremacy." Corwin, *Court Over* 30 (emphasis added).

[300] Mercer was "fiercely opposed to the Constitution," Bowen 262; but his native State, Maryland, ratified it overwhelmingly. Infra, Chapter 4, text accompanying note 50. So too, Bedford's State, Delaware, "unanimously ratified the Constitution," van Doren 193, despite its various "checks" on the Congress.

[301] Supra, text accompanying notes 184–188; and see infra, Chapter 7, text accompanying notes 16–19.

to admit as adhering to the judicial office."[302] Now Bedford's opposition "to *every* check on the Legislative" ran counter to the current, as the various checks thereafter adopted attest. But giving the Bedford and Mercer statements due weight, Corwin's inference is yet far from "plain," as any one who has participated in group deliberations can testify. One who, like Bedford, has expressed a dissenting view and sees the current strongly running the other way may have a variety of reasons for swallowing his differences and joining the majority to make the action unanimous, not the least of which may be that in the interim majority arguments or discussion in the anterooms may have won him over.[303] Corwin's reading would also require us to assume that a majority who have forcibly expressed themselves in favor of judicial review silently surrendered their convictions in order to win the unneeded votes of a couple of dissenters, one of whom unpopularly was opposed to "every" check upon the Legislature. That assumption is also rebutted by the statements some of the majority later made in the Ratification conventions and the First Congress,[304] which show their continued adherence to judicial review as an important part of the constitutional scheme.

Beard's count, subject to the above-mentioned deletions, stands more solidly than the 1913 Corwin critique, which his 1914 *Doctrine* substantially repudiated. Nine, or by my count eleven and possibly thirteen, of the leaders had spoken for judicial review in the Convention;[305] six more, or by my count seven, had indicated a preference for judicial review outside the Convention;[306] six other members voted for the Judiciary Act of 1789.[307] Against this, two members at most disapproved in the Convention;[308] two others dis-

[302] Corwin, 9 *Mich. L. Rev.* 119.

[303] Cf. supra, note 294. Bedford voted for Ratification in Delaware. 1 Elliot 319.

[304] See, e.g., infra, Chapter 4, text accompanying notes 26, 39–41, 88–91; id. Chapter 5, at notes 15, 18.

[305] Beard's list of speakers in the Convention: Dickinson, Gerry, King, Madison, Martin, Mason, G. Morris, Williamson, Wilson. I would add C. Pinckney and Rutledge, plus Strong and Gorham, whose case is weaker, but in Strong's case was confirmed by his vote for the Act of 1789.

[306] Beard's list of speakers outside the Convention: Baldwin, Blair, Ellsworth, Hamilton, Paterson, and Randolph. I would add Davie.

[307] I put to one side Blair, Ellsworth, Paterson, and Strong, whose vote confirms some prior or subsequent approval of judicial review. The other six voters were Bassett, Few, Johnson, R. Morris, Reid, and Washington. Supra, text accompanying note 252.

[308] Bedford and Mercer.

approved outside the Convention;[309] and two more voted against the Act of 1789.[310] Not one of the six was a leader, and the total of 26 to 6 (by my count) interestingly reflects the "on the floor" ratio of either 9 or 11 to 2. If we strip from this list men approved by Corwin in 1914 and later rejected by him on questionable grounds in 1938, namely, Dickinson, Madison, and Pinckney (plus Baldwin),[311] and Gorham (added by me), the score would be 21 to 6, still a sweeping endorsement of judicial review by any test.

Even when tearing down the Beard tally in 1913, Corwin closed by saying that the "manifest hopes of the majority,"

> it must be conceded, had pretty solid ground to rest upon . . . the state legislatures had by 1787 got in bad odor . . . the demand of the day was for methods to check legislative power. In response to this demand the executive veto was created, prohibitions upon State [and upon Congress, Art. I, §9] legislative powers enforceable by the State or national judiciaries were inserted in the national Constitution, and lastly a construction put upon the current doctrine of the separation of powers which left the interpretation of laws exclusively to the courts.
>
> A growing popular sentiment was disgusted with legislators and wanted to check them and to that end was willing to make the courts paramount.

Recognition of that "growing popular sentiment"—which was not really counter-balanced by a coherent opposition—and of "the demand of the day . . . for methods to check legislative power," of insertion of judicial "enforceability" of Constitutional "prohibitions," plus a willingness "to make the courts paramount," should have counseled Corwin to cling throughout to the hospitable reading of the leadership remarks later exhibited in his 1914 "Doctrine." Above all, that "popular sentiment" should make it easier to extrapolate from the 9 to 2 and 26 to 6 ratios the acquiescence of a comparable majority of the remaining silent 29 of the total 55 members, and to infer that that majority likewise shared or approved the views of "fully three-fourths of the leaders." Our own experience in dealing

[309] Spaight and Yates.
[310] Butler and Langdon.
[311] Infra, note 312.

with complex and extensive legislation has taught us to accept statements by the leadership as expressive of the intent of the silent body, and rarely are we furnished with such a confirmatory poll of individual predispositions as is furnished by the records marshaled by Beard. Corwin justifiably stated in 1914 that "On no other feature of the Constitution with reference to which there has been considerable debate is the view of the Convention itself better attested."[312]

True it is that the question whether there should be judicial review was never in terms squarely put to a vote, and in this sense Bickel may be justified in stating that "it will never be entirely clear just where the collective judgment—which alone is decisive—came to rest."[313] But the very casualness with which the leadership assumed that judicial review was available—aside from what the Convention intended by the "arising" and "supremacy" clauses and by the judicial tenure and compensation provisions—suggests that the leaders considered they were dealing with a widely-accepted doctrine.[314] Opponents of ratification thought the Convention had gone with the leadership; they did not conclude that the "collective judgment" had not come to rest on the issue of judicial review. Yates, Martin, and the "Centinel" opposed the Constitution during the campaign for ratification because, among other things, they understood the Constitution to provide for judicial review. Dickin-

---

[312] Corwin, *Doctrine* 12–13. But compare his testimony before Congress on the Court-packing plan, designed to release New Deal legislation from judicial constriction: "I consider [judicial review] far more a matter of doubt [now] than I did then . . . I don't think I gave the weight that should have been given to the objections made by Dickinson and by Madison, and afterwards by Charles Pinckney and by Baldwin." The Pinckney-Baldwin statements, made in 1799 and 1800, are suspect of political coloration. Supra, note 5; text accompanying notes 74–76; compare id. at notes 67–72. Corwin himself insisted in 1914 on "confining ourselves simply to the available evidence that is strictly contemporaneous with the framing and ratifying of the Constitution." Corwin, *Doctrine* 10. Dickinson seems to me to have spoken for judicial review, as did Madison in the federal and Virginia conventions. Supra, text accompanying notes 82, 86, 117–164. If this Corwin "Court-packing" statement is "perhaps the strongest challenge to Beard's proofs," as Professor Westin stated, Westin 26, the opposition to the conventional view is pretty feeble.

[313] Bickel 16. In 1958 Judge Learned Hand said, "I cannot, however, help doubting whether the evidence justifies a certain conclusion that the Convention would have so voted, if the issue had been put to it that the courts should have power to invalidate acts of Congress." Hand 7.

[314] See supra, note 8; infra note 315.

son, Hanson, and Hamilton, who argued for adoption, assured the public there was provision for judicial review. Four of these, Yates, Martin, Dickinson, and Hamilton were Framers; Dickinson and Martin had spoken on the subject in the Convention. And in evaluating the "collective judgment"[315] we may not ignore the repeated assurances in the Ratification conventions that judicial review would protect against congressional excesses.

Another objection to reliance on statements by the leaders is made by John Wofford: "presumably their intents are entitled to special weight," he says; but he argues that, unlike a statute which expressed "the intent of one or two deliberative bodies," the Constitution purports to express "the intent of a widely dispersed and numerically sovereign electorate," hence we must turn to the Ratifying conventions to ascertain the sense it had for those who adopted the Constitution.[316] Those Ratifying conventions, it will appear, confirmed the views of the Convention leadership. But first it may be noticed that the "deliberative bodies" which adopt a federal statute also speak for a "widely dispersed electorate," and seldom, if ever, do they share the great confidence that was reposed in the Framers. From Paris, Jefferson wrote John Adams that the Convention "is really an assembly of demigods";[317] Adams wrote in similar vein to

[315] Boudin 85 makes the point ironically and in different terms: "*notwithstanding the tremendous importance of the subject, it was, nevertheless, never discussed in the Convention,* except as incidental to some other topic, because of an alleged assumption by the leading men in the Convention that the power existed, which led these leading men to assure the Convention, 'over and over again,' that this power would be exercised by the federal judiciary," and asks, "is it conceivable that if the Framers actually wanted the Judiciary to have that power, they would have let it rest on so precarious a foundation? By this time we already know that there were no real precedents for the power." There is no presumption that the Framers knew what "we already [and *now*] know"; to the contrary, there is solid reason to conclude that *they* believed there *were* precedents for judicial review, though such belief may now appear, in part, ill-founded. Supra, Chapter 2, text accompanying notes 135–161. And what seems "precarious" to Boudin may well have seemed self-evident to the leaders, as it subsequently proved to be to their critics such as Yates. Supra, text accompanying notes 180–188; infra, Chapter 7, text accompanying notes 16–19. Boudin himself states, "Of course, if the statements [of the leaders] actually mean what Professor Farrand says they mean, it makes no difference in what connection they were made." Boudin 566, 564.

[316] Wofford, "The Blinding Light: The Uses of History in Constitutional Interpretation," 31 *U. Chi. L. Rev.* 502, 507–508 (1964). Wofford also entertains large doubts as to the value of the Ratification testimony. Infra Chapter 4, note 5.

[317] 3 Farrand 76.

John Jay.[318] The sober, aged Franklin reported that it was *"une assembleé des notables,"*[319] a view that was widely shared,[320] and few today would deny that "They formed such a constellation as never again appeared in the American skies."[321] Who would regard the members of the House who passed the Tuck Bill in 1964 as a more authentic voice of the American people? When we follow Wofford's cue and turn to the Ratification conventions, we will find that those who had spoken behind closed doors in Philadelphia and were now returned by the "sovereign electorate" to the Ratification conventions unhesitatingly spoke up once more for judicial review, generally by way of countering fears of Congressional "excesses." Some of those who had been silent before now took a laboring oar,[322] from which we may at least infer acquiescence in views earlier expressed in Philadelphia and responsiveness to the views of their constituents. The representations made in the Ratification conventions to quiet fears of unlimited Congressional power were impliedly endorsed by those who voted for adoption. Rarely, if ever,

[318] The Convention was composed, Adams wrote to John Jay, "of heroes, sages and demigods to be sure, who want no assistance from me in framing the best possible plan." 8 Adams, *Works* 452 (1853).

[319] Van Doren 13.

[320] Noah Webster wrote in October 1787 that the Convention was composed of "some of the greatest men in America . . . *all* of them distinguished for their acquaintance with ancient and modern governments, as well as with the temper, the passions, the interests and the wishes of the Americans." Ford, *Pamphlets* 29, 64. A. C. Hanson, a delegate to the Maryland convention, said that "almost every state . . . made a determined point of delegating its first characters to this [federal] grand convention." Id. at 221, 246.

Of course, there were animadversions, see Farrand, *Framing* 40, and one may readily agree that not every member was a demigod, a Washington, Madison, Hamilton, or Franklin. But the sprinkling of men like James Wilson, George Mason, Gouverneur Morris, leads one to concur with R. H. Lee, a contemporary critic of the Constitution, that "America probably will never see an assembly of men, of a like number, more respectable." Ford, *Pamphlets* 279, 322. The Farrand statement that "the convention as a whole was composed of men such as would be appointed to a similar gathering at the present time," Farrand, *Framing* 40, gives no weight to the undeniable fact that public life simply has not duplicated the quality of these men "as a whole." One cannot come away from reading the Convention records, those of the Ratification conventions, or of the First Congress, without a sense of wonder at the breadth of reading, the quickness and flexibility of mind, the depth of analytical power and wisdom there exhibited.

[321] Mitchell & Mitchell, *A Biography of the Constitution of the United States* 23 (1964).

[322] E.g., Davie, Ellsworth, Hamilton, Randolph; and Yates, who though opposed the adoption of the Constitution, recognized in clear-cut terms its provision for judicial review.

can statutory legislative history summon such popular approval as was thus expressed of the Framers' views.

IMPLICATIONS OF JUDICIAL INDEPENDENCE

Beard did not examine the implications of remarks by the Founders about judicial "independence," which further light up the issue of judicial review. It was because they presupposed a *function* of judicial review that they were concerned about judicial independence, seeking thereby to ensure judicial fortitude should unconstitutional laws call for annulment, and to shield judges from Congressional retaliation if such laws were declared void. Legislative vengeance did not threaten judges who mistakenly decided that a mule belonged to one farmer rather than another; it had been engendered by judicial refusal to effectuate the legislative will on burning public issues, such as denial of trial by jury to one who refused to accept "paper money."[323] In a number of well-publicized earlier State cases there had been more or less successful attempts at legislative punishment of judges who, so it was thought, had the temerity to declare statutes unconstitutional.[324] Judges were made "independent" in order that they could freely decide such issues without fear of legislative reprisals.

Hamilton emphasized that constitutional limitations would be meaningful only if judges of assured independence were available to enforce them.[325] In this he reflected Convention sentiment. The Virginia Plan, which listed the judiciary among the "checks upon the Legv. and Ex. Powers," advocated protection for judicial tenure and fixed compensation from the beginning.[326] Madison drew the lesson from history in arguing for a Congressional negative on State laws because "confidence can not be put in State Tribunals . . . more or less dependent on the Legislatures." To illustrate his meaning, he referred to Rhode Island where "the judges who refused to execute an unconstitutional law were displaced, and others substituted, by the Legislature who would be willing instruments of the wicked and arbitrary plans."[327] Madison was not condemning legis-

[323] Supra, Chapter 2, text accompanying notes 146–150.
[324] Id. at notes 162–172.
[325] Infra, text accompanying note 334.
[326] 1 Farrand 28, 21.
[327] 2 Farrand 27–28.

lative displacement of such State judges only to propose that federal judges should be left under the thumb of Congress. In fact, he spoke on the same day against Congressional reappointment of judges, "Because they might be tempted to cultivate the Legislature, by an undue complaisance, and thus render the Legislature the virtual expositor, as well as the maker of the laws."[328] His separation of "exposition" from "law-making" also expresses the exclusion of Congress from the task of interpretation.[329] Wilson opposed executive removal of judges on application by Congress because the "judges would be in a bad situation if made to depend on every gust of faction which might prevail in the two branches of our Govt."[330] He made his meaning plainer in the Pennsylvania convention: "The servile dependence of the judges, in some of the states that have neglected to make proper provisions on this subject, endanger the liberty and property of the citizen . . . personal liberty, and private property, depend essentially upon the able and upright determination of independent judges";[331] and to round out his meaning he explained the provisions for judicial review in unmistakable terms.[332] In the Connecticut convention, Ellsworth explained that if Congress "make a law which the Constitution does not authorize, it is void; and the judicial power, the national judges, who to secure

[328] Id. at 34; and see id. at 45.

[329] Supra, text accompanying notes 31–38; and see infra, Chapter 6, text accompanying notes 161–169.

[330] 2 Farrand 429.

[331] 2 Elliot 480–481. So too, he said, "judges independent . . . will behave with intrepidity and refuse to the act [that is "incompatible with the superior power of the Constitution"] the sanction of judicial authority." Id. at 445–446. See also his statement quoted infra, Chapter 4, text accompanying note 4. See also Thacher in New York, 2 Elliot 145. Pendleton said in Virginia, "Whenever . . . the judges are independent, property is secure." 3 Elliot 303. And see infra, Chapter 4, text accompanying note 117.

[332] Infra, Chapter 4, text accompanying note 41. In his 1791 Lectures, Wilson repeated that the legislature "is subject also to another given degree of control by the judiciary department, whenever the laws, though in fact passed, are found to be contradictory to the constitution." 1 Wilson, Works 411. A few pages earlier he had said, "Can dignity or independence be expected from judges, who are liable to be tossed about by every veering gale of politics, and can be secured from destruction, only by dexterously swimming along with every successive tide of party." Id. at 406.

One hundred and forty years later, Charles Evans Hughes said that because of the provisions for judicial independence, "the justices of the Supreme Court dealing so largely with constitutional questions of the gravest sort may address themselves to their work with freedom from anxiety as to their future and unembarrassed by suspicion as to their motives." Hughes 19.

their impartiality, are to be independent, will declare it to be void."[333] Manifestly Ellsworth regarded judicial "independence" as the guarantee that judges would unswervingly declare invalid federal acts void. But it was Hamilton who most clearly spelled out the tie between independence and judicial review in *Federalist* No. 78:

> If, then, the courts are to be considered as the bulwarks of a limited Constitution against legislative encroachments, this consideration will afford a strong argument for the permanent tenure of judicial offices, since nothing will contribute so much as this to that independent spirit in the judges which must be essential to the faithful performance of so arduous a duty.
>
> This independence of the judges is equally requisite to guard the Constitution and the rights of individuals from the effects of those ill humours [of the majority] . . . But it is easy to see, that it would require an uncommon portion of fortitude in judges to do their duty as faithful guardians of the Constitution, where legislative invasions of it have been instigated by the major voice of the community.[334]

The provisions for judicial tenure and fixed compensation therefore premised existence of a function—judicial review—which required protection, and to deny the existence of that function is largely to deprive those provisions of their purpose.

[333] 2 Ellsworth 196.
[334] No. 78 at 507–509.

THE STATE RATIFICATION CONVENTIONS

For Madison, the meaning of the Constitution was to be looked for "in the State Conventions which accepted and ratified the Constitution";[1] and, as President, Jefferson declared that he read the Constitution in accordance with the "meaning contemplated *by the plain understanding of the people at the time of its adoption*—a meaning to be found in the explanation of those who advocated it."[2] True, Madison also said that he would not put "entire confidence in the accuracy" of the published debates,[3] but however imperfect these records, he yet clung "to the sense in which the Constitution was accepted and ratified by the Nation . . . And if that be not the guide in expounding it, there can be no security for a consistent and stable government, more than for a faithful exercise of its powers."[4]

Professor Crosskey finds it "utterly impossible" to accept the Ratification "campaign" statements as "proof of the true opinions of the makers"; indeed he maintains that in their zeal for adoption "advocates of the Constitution" were "misrepresenting the Constitution"

[1] Quoted Warren, *Congress* 67 n. 1.
[2] Quoted 4 Elliot 446. And toward the end of his life, Jefferson stated that he had endeavored to make the government "to conform to the Constitution as understood by the Convention that produced and recommended it, and particularly by the State conventions that *adopted* it." 3 Farrand 534.
R. H. Lee, who fought adoption in Virginia, said of the Ratification conventions, "in them will be collected the solid sense and the real political character of the country . . . If these conventions, after examining the system, adopt it, I shall be properly satisfied." Ford's *Pamphlets*, 279, 322.
[3] Quoted Warren, *Congress* 68 n. 2. In any event, the repeated affirmations in the several Ratification debates that judicial review was contemplated suggests that these at least were not garbled, for inaccuracy is random rather than selected.
[4] 9 Madison *Writings* 191, 372. To the same effect, his letter of December 1831. 3 Farrand 518.

and not expressing "their actual understanding of the document."[5] Centuries ago Chief Justice Brian remarked that "the Devil himself knoweth not the thought of man,"[6] and the search for what men "thought" has not grown less elusive over the years. If what men once "thought" is not to be found in what they said or did, as recorded by contemporary records, it is beyond recovery. "What they actually thought" found no triumphant demonstration at Crosskey's hands, as his mistaken reliance on Hamilton as "proof" should have demonstrated.[7] Against Crosskey's collapsed Hamilton example may be set James Wilson, who spoke unequivocally for judicial review in the Convention, in the Pennsylvania Ratification convention, and again in his 1791 Lectures. There were others.[8] So far as man's "thought" is recoverable from what he does or says, it may be reasonably concluded that the Framers "thought" exactly what they said. Professor Crosskey's too easy attribution of "lack of scruple" to the Founders[9] on the basis of what *he* concludes "they actually thought" is a poor substitute for "naive" acceptance of what they "actually" said, let alone that to inject psychoanalysis into constitutional interpretation is to open Pandora's box.[10]

The overshadowing fact is that the proposed new national govern-

---

[5] Crosskey 1026; Wofford, 31 *U. Chi. L. Rev.* 509, joins Crosskey in giving short shrift to expressions in the Ratifying conventions because the delegates "were advocates, using every possible argument for either the support or the rejection of the Constitution." This would equally discredit the Framers in the Convention, for they were no less "advocates" hoping to prevail, as is only natural when men hold deep convictions on matters of gravest import. Various Framers who sat in the Ratification conventions reiterated views earlier expressed in the Convention. They were surrounded by picked men whose remarks today attest their insight and sagacity. In Virginia opponents of the Constitution such as Patrick Henry yet spoke in praise of judicial review, suggesting that the issue transcended "politics." And the analytical unanimity of those who spoke for judicial review, though separated by the vast distances of the time, lifts their utterances above the level of mere expediency.

[6] Year Book 17 Edw. 4 (1477) PASA, Fo. 2, Pl. 3, cited and approved by Lord Blackburn in Broggen v. Metropolitan Ry. Co. [1877] 2 A.C. 666, 692.

[7] Supra, Chapter 3, text accompanying notes 207–221.

[8] Among others who reaffirmed views expressed in the Convention were Gerry, supra, Chapter 3, text accompanying note 17; Pinckney, id. at notes 71–72; Dickinson, id. at note 85; Madison, id. at notes 146, 151; cf. Mason, id. at note 56.

[9] Hart, Book Review 1481. One who hurls such charges should be immune to countercharges. See comment by Professor Hart, quoted infra, Chapter 8, note 18.

[10] "The process of psycho-analysis," remarked Justice Cardozo, "must not be carried into inquiries as to the motives of legislative bodies." United States v. Constantine, 296 U.S. 287, 298–299 (1935) (dissenting opinion). Courts will not undertake inquiries into legislative motives. Fletcher v. Peck, 6 Cranch 87 (1810).

ment "had been portrayed as an engine of despotism,"[11] and protagonists of the Constitution were hard-pressed to quiet alarm aroused by the sweeping power conferred upon Congress.[12] In Virginia suspicion of centralized tyranny, of unlimited Congressional power, all but overwhelmed the "ex-members of the Federal Convention."[13] They *were* overwhelmed in North Carolina notwithstanding that the Constitution had already been adopted in ten states.[14] Even if the "ex-members" disbelieved their own representations—which remains to be proved—the bitter debates must have convinced them that those who voted in reliance on their representations would never permit repudiation. Any doubts on that score were speedily dispelled by the unrelenting pressure for yet more "limits" on the Congress, which soon found expression in the Bill of Rights. In essence, Crosskey would have us repudiate those representations 175 years after the event on the ground that the makers did not really believe what they were saying![15]

Charles Curtis maintained that only what the Framers "said," that is, the words of the Constitutional text, "was ratified."[16] But the bare text had aroused fears,[17] and only when those fears were quieted by explanations were the ratifiers persuaded to vote for adoption. The "explanation of those who advocated it," to borrow from Jefferson, established the meaning for those who ratified, and their approval, be the political motivations of the spokesmen what they may, is what gives authority to the remarks made in the Ratifying conventions. As White stated in the First Congress during the

[11] Rossiter, *Hamilton* 58. See also supra, Chapter 2, text accompanying notes 14–20, and infra, Chapter 8, text accompanying notes 167–172. Cf. supra, Chapter 2, notes 2 and 3, and text accompanying notes 5 and 8; infra, text accompanying notes 68, 69.

[12] E.g., supra, Chapter 2, text accompanying notes 22–32; cf. id. at notes 8–16. Such assurances are regarded by Crosskey 1026, as a response to the "very great" "temptation to misrepresent the powers of Congress as few and limited, and the Supreme Court as an agency to confine Congress within a few supposedly narrow powers." The "temptation" testifies to the existence of lively fears, entertained by the hearers, of Congressional oppression and powerful pressures to counteract it.

[13] Van Doren 230. The quoted phrase is Crosskey's, 1026.

[14] 4 Elliot 208; Van Doren 235–237.

[15] Supra, Chapter 3, note 123.

[16] Quoted by Wofford, 31 *U. Chi. L. Rev.* at 509.

[17] Davis, *Veto* 72, a critic of judicial review, says "Much alarm was caused by the vague language of the Constitution." Cf. infra, note 44; and see infra, text accompanying notes 68–78, 101–107; Chapter 6, text accompanying note 119.

course of the "removal" debate, after insisting that the federal government must adhere to the limits described in the Constitution:

> This was the ground on which the friends of the Government supported the constitution . . . it could not have been supported on any other. If this principle had not been successfully maintained by its advocates in the convention of the state from which I came, the constitution would never have been ratified.[18]

It would of course be much more satisfying had judicial review been discussed in every convention, or if the issue had been squarely submitted to each[19] (although not every corollary issue was separately voted on), or if we could even approximate the opinions of the membership after the fashion of Beard's research into the opinions of a large segment of the Framers.[20] But the availability of judicial review was stated in unmistakable terms in several of the conventions,[21] often in response to expressions of fear of unbounded Congressional power, that is, as a remedy for an explicitly identified mischief. In Pennsylvania and Connecticut such expressions came from Framers Wilson and Ellsworth, who made the availability of judicial review clear beyond caviling.[22] In Virginia, Patrick Henry, engaged in an all-out struggle to block adoption,[23] joined in praise of judicial review, though he preferred his State judges because of their proven fortitude.[24] No voices were raised in opposition to judicial review, after the manner of Mercer in the federal Convention, in any State convention. The scattering of remarks in favor of judicial review across the country permits us to regard them as a sampling,[25] a sampling in which we may have the more confidence

[18] 1 *Ann. Cong.* 535.

[19] Davis, *Veto* 44–45.

[20] Beard 80.

[21] In stating that "the question was not presented in such a way as to get any clear and unequivocal answer," Davis, *Veto* 45, gives too little weight to the statements hereinafter quoted.

[22] Infra, text accompanying notes 39–41, 26.

[23] Van Doren 219–223, 229–230.

[24] Infra, text accompanying notes 110–111.

[25] Davis, *Veto* 72, conjectures that "if all the debates had been preserved in full, it is probable that we should find considerable argument on the subject." If we proceed from the known to the unknown we find that such debates as are preserved disclose *no* argument on the subject but rather uncontradicted assurances that judicial review would curb feared Congressional excesses. Compare the Virginia opposition joinder in praising judicial review. Infra, text accompanying notes

because the mischief—fear of unlimited Congressional power—was widely perceived. A prudent man in the conduct of his own affairs might reasonably act upon the basis of such a sampling rather than to refrain because it is "insufficient."

In Connecticut, Oliver Ellsworth, one of the Framers who played a leading role, said

> If the general legislature should at any time overleap their limits, the judicial department is a constitutional check. If the United States go beyond their powers, if they make a law which the Constitution does not authorize, it is void; and the judicial power, the national judges . . . will declare it to be void.[26]

Davis, who made the most extended attack upon reliance on the Ratification conventions for proof of judicial review, sought to shake Ellsworth's testimony by resort to the "more popular view" exemplified by three letters published just *before* the convention in the *New Haven Gazette*.[27] In one a citizen wrote that the House "will have a negative upon every legislative act of the other branch. So far, in short as the sphere of federal jurisdiction extends, they will be controulable only by the people."[28] The correspondent's failure to mention the judicial power furnishes a debatable argument against its existence. The second letter states that "the assumption of any powers not necessary to establish justice, ensure domestic tranquillity . . . will be unconstitutional and endanger the existence of Congress." Recognition that action may be "unconstitutional" normally suggests that some one will be empowered to declare it so, and there is no necessary implication in this epistle that the judiciary will be powerless to do so. The third letter, thought to be from Roger Sherman, argues that since members of Congress "can take no im-

---

110–111. Where doubts were raised, it was because the Congressional powers were deemed so broad and vague, without "limits," as to defy judicial policing. Infra, text accompanying notes 43–46, 57–58; note 62; Chapter 8, note 38.

[26] 2 Elliot 196.

[27] Davis, *Veto* 82–84.

[28] Read literally, this would also dispose of the Presidential veto. For analysis of "controulable only by the people" remarks see infra, Chapter 6, text accompanying notes 128–141.

proper steps which will not affect them as much as it does us, we need not apprehend that they will usurp authorities not given to them." This is one of the cumulative assurances to allay fear of Congressional usurpation. If contrary to his prophesy there *is* usurpation, his statement does not necessarily foreclose judicial review. By Davis' own testimony Ellsworth's statement is "clear";[29] it came from a Framer on the floor of the convention, *after* the three letters and may well have been calculated to set such doubts at rest.

MASSACHUSETTS

In Massachusetts, Samuel Adams said of a proposal that "powers not expressly delegated to Congress are reserved to the several states," that it "removes a doubt which many have entertained respecting the matter, and gives assurance that, if any laws made by the Federal Government shall be extended beyond the powers granted by the proposed Constitution . . . it will be . . . adjudged by the Courts of law to be void."[30] Davis states that "Although Adams does not expressly say *state* courts, the strong inference is that he referred to state courts *only* . . . He was discussing . . . limitations to be imposed on the national government in favor of the States; and he mentioned this action of the 'courts of law' as a primary exercise of a reserved power by the States."[31] Were this interpretation sound, it would not vitiate Adams' espousal of judicial review; it would merely make the State courts the sole instrument of such review, a matter hereinafter examined in greater detail. In fact, Adams at no point "mentioned" the "action of the 'courts of law' as a primary exercise of a reserved power by the States." Nor did the proposal to reserve powers not delegated *to Congress* purport either to enlarge or to limit the "judicial power." To derive from a proposal to limit Congress a curtailment of the "judicial power" conferred by Article III plus an exclusive State court jurisdiction,[32] to both of which the proposal had absolutely no reference, is a singular non sequitur.

[29] Davis, *Veto* 82.
[30] 2 Elliot 131.
[31] Davis, *Veto* 88.
[32] This coupling of "reserved" State powers with exclusive State jurisdiction to decide what laws of Congress are unconstitutional smacks of the power vainly asserted in the Virginia-Kentucky Resolutions.

CHAPTER 4

Corwin and Davis quote James Bowdoin's enumeration of checks on Congressional usurpation, which does not include judicial review, and Theophilus Parsons' remark that "an act of usurpation is not law, and any man may be justified in his resistance."[33] Parsons cannot be taken to mean that if a citizen, instead of resort to "resistance," turned to the courts, they alone would be unable to resist usurpation.[34] Indeed, Parsons pointed out that by virtue of the oath state officers (he overlooked that federal officers also must take the oath), including judicial officers, take to support the Constitution, they would be obliged "vigorously to oppose" an "increase of the powers by usurpation."[35] Bowdoin's omission to mention judicial review is outweighed by Adams' and Parsons' explicit reliance on it, without contradiction.[36]

PENNSYLVANIA

In Pennsylvania, Thomas McKean, chief justice of the Pennsylvania Supreme Court, said that "In order to secure liberty and the Constitution, it is absolutely necessary that the legislature should be restrained," among other ways: "1. By the judges deciding agst. the Legislature in Favor of the Constn., 2. By elections . . . 3. By the interposition of the Supreme Power of the People on necessary

[33] Davis, *Veto* 85–86; 2 Elliot 85–87, 93–94; Corwin, *Court Over* 41–43.

[34] That courts would be part of "universal resistance" was plainly stated by Steele in North Carolina. Infra, text accompanying note 79; and see infra, Chapter 6, text accompanying notes 134–141.

[35] See also Parsons' remark, infra, Appendix B, note 52.

[36] The uncertainties of reliance of Bowdoin's omission are pointed up by the William Symmes incident. Originally Symmes said, "This body is not amenable to any tribunal, and therefore this congress can do no wrong." Came proposed amendments patterned on a bill of rights, which would more sharply delimit Congressional powers, followed by Adams' remarks, whereupon, as Davis, *Veto* 89, notes, Symmes stated, "approving the amendments, and firmly believing that they will be adopted, I recall my former opposition," 2 Elliot 71, 174, a graceful confession of ignorance that judicial review was contemplated.

Corwin, *Court Over* 41, would explain Bowdoin's omission by the fact that "the thing feared was the power of the proposed government as a whole, *including its judicial branch.* So even supporters of the Constitution frequently ignored judicial review when mention of it would have been apposite." Fear of the judicial branch derived chiefly from two sources: (1) it would swallow up the State judiciary; and (2) it would favor federal as against State claims. Judicial review of Congressional Acts was something else again, for this, as Corwin notes, was brought forward "as a check on the national legislative power," Corwin, *Court Over* 40. The Judiciary Act of 1789, which left federal questions to State judges, subject to appeal to the Supreme Court, confirms that fear of Congress played the predominant role.

126

occasions."[37] McKean's array of cumulative remedies, his reference to direct action by the people only on "necessary occasions," should go far to undermine reliance upon isolated statements that the "people" alone were to be the "check."[38] James Wilson, a Framer who had recognized the availability of judicial review in the federal Convention, picked up McKean's reference to "restraints" on Congress in the form of "elections," and stressed the "great and last resort . . . the people themselves." And, he continued, "the legislature may be restrained, and kept within its prescribed bounds, by the interposition of the judicial department."

Referring to the possibility that the legislature "may transgress the bounds assigned to it," he said that when the "act comes to be discussed before *the judges,*—when they consider its principles, and find it to be incompatible with the superior power of the Constitution—it is their duty to pronounce it *void*; and judges independent . . . will behave with intrepidity, and refuse to the act the sanction of judicial authority."[39] Later he repelled the suggestion that "Judges are to be impeached because they declare an act null and void, that was made in defiance of the Constitution."[40] And he returned to the subject when discussing the "arising under" clause, and again stated:

If a law should be made inconsistent with those powers vested by this instrument in Congress, the judges, as a consequence of their independence, and the particular powers of government being defined, will declare such law to be null and void.[41]

Davis himself concludes that "there can be no doubt that the principle of judicial control was fully expounded by" McKean and Wilson "and was accepted by the Convention."[42]

[37] McMaster & Stone 766. Smilie had argued for the opposition that "it will be impracticable to stop the progress of tyranny, for there will be no check but the people, and their exertions must be futile and uncertain; since it will be difficult, indeed, to communicate to them the violation that has been committed, and their proceedings will be neither systematical nor unanimous." Id. at 255. Compare M. Smith in the New York convention. 2 Elliot 249. Jefferson desired to make transgressions of the fundamental "law" "nullities, to render unnecessary an appeal to the people." Infra, Chapter 6, text accompanying note 122.

[38] Cf. supra, Chapter 2, note 62; and see infra, Chapter 6, text accompanying notes 131–141.

[39] 2 Elliott 445–446.

[40] Id. at 478.

[41] Id. at 489. Wilson's remarks, made on December 1 and 7, 1787, 2 Elliot 443, 486, anticipate in large part Hamilton's analysis in *Federalist* No. 78, April 1788.

[42] Davis, *Veto* 73.

Opponents of the Constitution, such as John Smilie, argued that the powers *conferred* upon Congress by Article I were "so unlimited in their extent" as to make possible "the most extravagent degree of arbitrary sway."[43] Smilie charged that the Congressional powers were so "loosely" drawn as to render it impossible to prove that they had been exceeded, an attack upon the absence of enforceable standards rather than upon judicial enforcement of Congressional limitations.[44] When the dissenters published their reasons for dissent after the close of the convention, they rejected the assurance "that the words 'pursuant' to the Constitution are a restriction upon the authority of Congress,"[45] echoing Smilie's attack upon lack of enforceable standards rather than objection to judicial review.[46] Essentially the dissenters objected to an "absolute government that will embrace all America in one chain of despotism"[47] rather than to judicial review as an instrument to curb it.

MARYLAND

The brief record of the Maryland convention contains no reference to judicial review, but the attention of the people of Maryland had been drawn to the Constitutional provision for it prior to the convention. First there was the report to the Legislature by Luther Martin, which criticized the provision for judicial review by inferior federal rather than State courts.[48] A. C. Hanson, a proponent of the Constitution, later a delegate to the Maryland convention, and still later State Chancellor, had advised the people of Maryland that objections to the overbroad power of Congress to decide what laws were necessary and proper were met by the fact that every judge "will have a right to reject any act, handed to him as a law, which he may conceive repugnant to the constitution."[49] Opposition to the Con-

[43] McMaster & Stone 284.
[44] Smilie had argued, "So loosely, so inaccurately are the powers which are enumerated in this constitution defined, that it will be impossible, without a test of this kind [a bill of rights] to ascertain when the government has degenerated into oppression," explaining that to a complaint "You have extended the powers of your office, you have oppressed us," the government would reply "you have no test by which you can prove it." McMaster & Stone 255.
[45] Id. at 467.
[46] Davis, *Veto* 73–74, quotes Smilie's remarks without remarking on their significance.
[47] McMaster & Stone 466; see also id. at 255, 258, 269, 283–284.
[48] Supra, Chapter 3, text accompanying notes 45–46.
[49] Ford, *Pamphlets* 221, 234.

stitution, by Mercer among others, was swept aside; ratification carried by 63 to 11; and Davis comments that "In electing the delegates who pursued this course, the people of Maryland had before them" the remarks of Martin and Hanson.[50]

NEW YORK

In New York, the vast bulk of the debate swirled around Article I, for example, "insufficient representation" in the House, eligibility of Senators for reelection, and the taxing power.[51] The real question, to quote Hamilton, was "the *division of powers* between the general and state governments."[52] Opponents rang the changes on the "danger to State governments";[53] "there will not the shadow of liberty be left to the states,"[54] so that Hamilton was driven to insist that *Congress* would never desire "to destroy the state governments"[55] and went on to prove their "entire *safety*."[56] Melancton Smith, leader of the opposition, rejected the "idea that Congress ought to have *unlimited powers*."[57] Williams complained that the powers granted to Congress were "indefinite" and urged that "the greatest care should be taken to define" the powers of the federal government and to "guard against an abuse of authority."[58] The opponents were thus not so much intent on placing Congress beyond review as critical of the Congressional threat to State powers. Smith was concerned because conflicts in this crucial State-federal area "relative to jurisdiction must be decided in a federal court." Whether Congress had invaded State powers, Smith therefore recognized,

[50] Van Doren 207–208; Davis, *Veto* 91. Mercer, who had uttered his disapproval of judicial review in the federal Convention, energetically opposed the Constitution in Maryland, Van Doren 206–207. After the large vote for adoption, the Maryland convention referred some proposed amendments to a committee of which Mercer was a member, 2 Elliot 549; and the committee returned a number of proposals respecting the judiciary, none of which purported to curtail judicial review, id. at 550. A chief object was "to secure the independence of the federal judges, to whom the happiness of the people of this great continent will be so greatly committed by the extensive powers assigned to them," id. at 551, an object which, as has been shown, implicates judicial review.

[51] 2 Elliot 229, 244–249, 252–255, 261, 286 (representation); 289–294, 300, 309 (Senators); 330, 339–340, 342–346, 362–374, 377–378 (taxation).

[52] Id. at 350.

[53] E.g., id. at 374.

[54] Id. at 386.

[55] Id. at 353.

[56] Id. at 356.

[57] Id. at 337.

[58] Id. at 338, 241.

was to be decided by a federal court; and this did not suffice for Smith only because it gave "this advantage" to the general government,[59] that is, because the federal court would presumably lean in favor of federal as against State claims.

Haines cited Smith and Williams as believers that courts "would be obliged to accept and enforce the laws as enacted by Congress,"[60] but in this he erred. Smith declared that the national government *"would have power* to abrogate the laws of the states," and the courts "before whom any disputes on these points should come, whether federal or not, would be bound by oath to give judgment according to the laws of the Union."[61] What Haines overlooked is that Congress "would *have power"* to pass such laws, in which case, of course, courts would be bound to give them effect. Williams stated that there was no "check or impediment" if Congress should judge that "the state governments should be essentially destroyed" "for the common defense and general welfare." The reason was not lack of judicial power but Congress' full constitutional authorization, as Williams own rhetorical question shows: "Are they [Congress] not constitutionally authorized to pass such laws," relying on the fact that "the terms *common defence and general welfare* [are] indefinite, undefinable terms."[62]

In the absence of a pointed attack on judicial review there was no occasion to argue the point, for members of the convention were well acquainted with *The Federalist*.[63] Notwithstanding, the un-

[59] Id. at 322–333.

[60] Haines 141.

[61] 2 Elliot 78 (emphasis added).

[62] Id. at 338. At another point Williams said that "the legislature, under this Constitution, may pass any law which they may think proper . . . what limitation, if any is set to the exercise of this power by the Constitution?" 2 Elliot 330. As his explanation of the "necessary and proper clause," which he also discussed, shows, "A case cannot be conceived which is not included in this power." Id. at 331. Of course, if unlimited power was indeed granted to Congress by the Constitution, there are no limits which call for judicial enforcement. Only when a law is inconsistent with the Constitution may it be declared unconstitutional.

[63] "In these debates, Hamilton gave the Convention so many arguments straight out of 'Publius' that Governor Clinton sarcastically inquired if the young knight-errant of federalism was planning to bring out a second edition." Miller, *Alexander Hamilton: Portrait in Paradox* 212 (1959). Melancton Smith remarked that Hamilton "speaks out very frequently, very long and very vehemently—has, like Publius, very much to say not applicable to the subject." Ibid. In *The Federalist*, Hamilton had "spread abroad" that "an independent judiciary was to guard the personal and property rights of minorities against all legislatures, state and national." Beard 107.

ceasing attack upon unlimited Congressional power induced Hamilton to say, "the laws of Congress are restricted to a certain sphere, and when they depart from this sphere, they are no longer supreme or binding."[64] Davis argues that Hamilton "does not indicate by whom the statute would be pronounced unconstitutional."[65] Given the extreme hostility to unlimited Congressional power, the fear that the States would be "destroyed," the hairs-breadth margin by which ratification was achieved, we may be sure that the convention hardly left to Congress the function of deciding whether it invaded State prerogatives. Where the mischief was so clearly perceived, it is unreasonable to build on silence rejection of the well-advertised remedy. But we need not rely on inference, for Hamilton did not leave us in the dark. He pointed to the division of the legislative branch, to the executive branch, and to the judicial power "still reserved for an independent body," and concluded that "it is next to impossible that an impolitic or wicked measure should pass the scrutiny [of all these] with success."[66] In other words, there would be first an interlegislative Senate-House check, next a Presidential veto, and if a bill survived these hurdles, there was judicial "scrutiny," all of which needed no spelling out to an audience familiar with *The Federalist* and Yates's views that the Constitution provided for judicial review.

Finally, there is the silence of Yates in the convention. He had opposed adoption and limned the features of judicial review in his "Letters of Brutus." Now, though Hamilton and Smith delivered themselves of the quoted remarks, Yates made no attempt at any point to register his objection to judicial review. Perhaps his own preference for curative measures by the "people" may have yielded to the pervasive opposition to unlimited Congressional power and the fact that Melancton Smith had labeled reliance on the "people" for a curb as "absurd."[67]

NORTH CAROLINA

The keynote of the North Carolina convention was sounded at the outset by Goudy: "Let us beware of the iron glove of tyranny;[68]

[64] 2 Elliot 362.
[65] Davis, *Veto* 101.
[66] 2 Elliot 348.
[67] Id. at 249. See also infra, text accompanying notes 81, 82.
[68] 4 Elliott 10; see also id. at 213 (Lancaster).

and on this note he closed: the Constitution will "totally destroy our liberties."[69] Others cried out that the rights of North Carolinians would be "trampled on";[70] Samuel Spencer feared Senate power "so enormous as to enable them to destroy our rights," a contingency "to be strictly guarded against."[71] The "great powers of Congress" gave William Lenoir "great cause for alarm."[72] "Unlimited" power, powers not "sufficiently defined" was the constant challenge;[73] the "great" Congressional powers would "swallow up" the States;[74] there was a tendency in the Constitution "to destroy the state governments."[75] Again and again proponents assured the sceptics that Congress "cannot travel beyond its bounds."[76] "The powers of Congress are all circumscribed, defined and clearly laid down," Governor Johnston emphasized; "So far they may go, but no farther."[77] Despite such assurances, despite the fact of prior adoption by ten States,[78] ratification was overwhelmingly defeated, testimony to the deep-rooted fear of centralized government and of Congress in particular.

Early in the convention John Steele said,

> The judicial power . . . is so well constructed as to be a check . . . If the Congress make laws inconsistent with the Constitution, independent judges will not uphold them, nor will the people obey them. A universal resistance will ensue.[79]

To counter the effect of this unequivocal statement, Davis cites remarks of two fellow-proponents, of Maclaine to show that he "did not accept judicial control," and of Iredell to show that he argued "the

[69] Id. at 93; see also id. at 68 (Spencer).

[70] Id. at 187. "Without the most express restrictions, Congress may trample on your rights." Id. at 167.

[71] Id. at 131–132.

[72] Id. at 203. Meigs, *Relations* 159, states that "before the people [in the various conventions] the burden of discussion related to unauthorized laws of Congress, for one of the dreads of opponents was that the powers of Congress would be indefinitely extended."

[73] 4 Elliot 212, 190, 93.

[74] Id. at 51.

[75] Id. at 93, 180, 70.

[76] Id. at 63 (Maclaine).

[77] Id. at 64; see also id. at 188, 185.

[78] Spaight stated, "It is adopted by ten states already." 4 Elliot 208. When the North Carolina convention voted on August 2 "neither to ratify nor to reject," it probably had not learned that New York had voted to ratify on July 26, making eleven for adoption. Van Doren 234–235.

[79] Id. at 71.

people would restrain Congressional usurpation."[80] If Davis meant that Iredell would substitute popular resistance for judicial review, his citation is singularly unhappy. There is first Iredell's rejection in 1786 of "universal resistance of the people" as the "only remedy" if the Assembly should violate the Constitution, because resistance is "a dreadful expedient indeed"; people suffer a "thousand injuries" first; it requires *"universal oppression."*[81] Nor did he put his faith in elections: "I conceive the remedy by a new election to be of very little consequence, because this would only secure the views of a majority; whereas every citizen in my opinion should have a surer pledge for his constitutional rights than the wisdom and activity of an occasional majority of his fellow citizens, who, if their own rights are in fact unmolested, may care little for his."[82] Then too, Iredell had lucidly espoused judicial review in his 1786 Address; he had in equally clear terms refuted Spaight's critique in 1787;[83] he had been co-counsel in *Bayard v. Singleton* in which the North Carolina court declared a State statute unconstitutional;[84] and he was speaking in a State which was therefore well aware of judicial review as an important instrument of government. His hearers, we may be sure, did not construe his remark that "the people will resist" as a call to the barricades, at least not before judicial review, to which his co-worker Steele had earlier adverted in the convention, proved inadequate to the occasion.

Of the same order is Davis' citation of Maclaine's "If congress should make a law beyond the powers . . . should we not say to

[80] Davis, *Veto* 109.

[81] 2 McRee 147. In Pennsylvania Smilie made a similar objection. See supra note 37. Melancton Smith said in the New York convention that "To say . . . that our security is to depend upon the spirit of the people, who will be watchful of their liberties, and not suffer them to be infringed, is absurd. It would equally prove that we might adopt any form of government." 2 Elliot 249–250.

Perhaps the most thoroughgoing exposition of the "insuperable objections against the proposed recurrence to the people, as a provision in all cases for keeping the departments of power within their constitutional limits" is that of Madison in Nos. 49 and 50 of *The Federalist*. His remedy was in part to give each department the necessary constitutional means and personal motives to resist the encroachments of the others, id. No. 51 at 337, and in part to rely "on the great variety of interests, parties and sects" which were embraced in the United States. Id. at 341.

[82] 2 McRee 175.

[83] Supra, Chapter 3, text accompanying note 168. These statements explain why Iredell is "quoted by all writers as one of the staunchest champions of judicial control." Davis, *Veto* 109.

[84] Supra, Chapter 2, text accompanying notes 142–144.

congress, 'you have no authority to make this law. There are limits beyond which you cannot go. You cannot exceed the power prescribed by the Constitution. This act is unconstitutional. We will disregard it and punish you for the attempt.' "[85] That Maclaine did not hold out cure by election or by revolution is indicated by the next following sentence: "But the gentleman seems to be most tenacious of the judicial power of the states." The implication is that the preceding argument was in part addressed to the question *which* judiciary, State or federal, was to declare an "act is unconstitutional," rather than to a rejection of all judicial control. In truth, the opponents did prefer the State courts,[86] so that Maclaine was constrained to argue that it was "impossible" for State judges "to be impartial in cases where the local laws or interests of" their "state clash with the *laws* of the Union."[87] The corollary of his argument necessarily was that in such a "clash" federal courts could be relied upon "impartially" to hold that Congress had unconstitutionally invaded the province of the State.

Turn to the remarks of Davie, a Framer who had argued *Bayard v. Singleton:* "The judiciary ought to be competent to the decision of *any* question arising out of the Constitution itself."[88] True, in citing illustrations of the necessity for federal jurisdiction "of *all* questions" arising under the Constitution," Davie referred to Constitutional restrictions on the States, saying that

> the Constitution might be violated with impunity if there was no power in the general government to correct and counteract such [violative state] laws. This great object can only be safely and completely obtained by the instrumentality of the federal judiciary . . . This restriction in the Constitution is a fundamental principle, which is not to be violated, but which would have been a dead letter, were there no judiciary constituted to enforce it.[89]

Ex post facto laws, for example, were prohibited both to Congress and the States, and it would be utterly unrealistic to conclude that

[85] Davis, *Veto* 109; 4 Elliot 161–162.
[86] 4 Elliot 136, 164.
[87] Id. at 172 (emphasis added); and see his remarks infra, text accompanying note 92.
[88] Id. at 156 (emphasis added).
[89] Id. at 156–157.

Davie's listeners understood him to mean that judicial correction was limited to State violations and that Congress might "violate" the Constitution "with impunity."[90] Davie spoke to restrictions on the States because they contributed to the fear that the central government "will destroy the state sovereignty";[91] he was compelled to urge that such restrictions simply had to be judicially enforceable. As Maclaine reminded the convention, "The treaty of peace with Great Britain was the supreme law of the land, yet it was disregarded for want of a federal judiciary."[92]

An opposition "alarmed" by the Congressional threat to the States was naturally concerned by federal court policing of restrictions upon the States and as naturally interested in guaranteeing Congressional observance of restrictions upon *its* powers. The opposition goal was at once more freedom for the States and more restrictions upon Congress. Those who had to be persuaded that restrictions upon the States required judicial enforcement were little likely to exempt Congressional "violations" of State prerogatives. The opposition wanted to be protected *against* Congress, not to shield its excesses, and in this they were at one with the proponents. "Restrictions" upon the Congress were no more to be a "dead letter" than those upon the States. Both restrictions were a "fundamental principle" and for both there was a "judiciary constituted to enforce it."[93]

Criticism of the federal courts was not lacking: the additional expense,[94] the distance of the new courts from litigants,[95] the preference for State courts,[96] above all the alleged encroachments on trial by jury through appeals on questions of fact.[97] But never was there a word to rebut Steele's assurance that courts would check federal

[90] Cf. Mason, infra, text accompanying note 119.

[91] 4 Elliot 180, 51, 93, 70.

[92] Id. at 164.

[93] Supra, text accompanying note 89. In Davie's words, "It is therefore absolutely necessary that the judiciary of the Union should have jurisdiction in *all* cases arising in law or equity under the Constitution. Surely there should be somewhere a constitutional authority for carrying into execution *constitutional provisions;* otherwise, as I have already said, they would be a dead letter." Id. at 158 (emphasis added).

[94] Id. at 138.

[95] Id. at 139, 174. Similar objection was made in Virginia, 3 Elliot 526.

[96] 4 Elliot 136, 139; cf. id. at 142. For Virginia, see 3 Elliot 527, 539, 559, 563.

[97] 4 Elliot 151, 170, 202–203, 165–166. For Virginia, see 3 Elliot 528, 540, cf. 519, 572. For Maryland, see 2 Elliot 550–551. See also infra, Chapter 9, text accompanying notes 8–19.

laws which were "inconsistent with the Constitution," a not surprising silence in the State which had fathered *Bayard v. Singleton*,[98] and in which fear of Congressional "tyranny" rode high.

VIRGINIA

Of the State conventions, Virginia's was "the most philosophical and wide-ranging in its debates";[99] it threw into high relief the concerns that echoed and reechoed throughout the land. The tocsin was unceasingly tolled by Patrick Henry. Delicately reminding the convention of his earlier patriotic services—"Twenty three years ago" he had been "supposed a traitor to [his] country"[100]—Henry painted the horrors of incipient despotism in glaring colors. The country was "in extreme danger"; the "great rights of freemen are endangered: in other parts absolutely taken away."[101] "Absolute despotism" must ensue given "unlimited, unbounded authority"; the people would "be oppressed, and the state legislature prostrated."[102] His hortatory torrent spreads over one-fifth of the six hundred pages,[103] and it was only halted by a "violent storm . . . which put the house in such disorder, that Mr. Henry was obliged to conclude."[104] George Mason and James Monroe, among others, richly embroidered his theme.[105]

As in other State conventions, it was argued that the States would be totally annihilated with the aid of the judiciary.[106] Henry looked to the state legislature for the "care and preservation of the people,"[107] an attachment fully appreciated by Madison, who shrewdly turned the tables by urging that this "irresistible bias towards the state governments" would make it "impossible to turn the balance against them."[108]

In the deluge of denunciation, not a word condemning judicial review. To the contrary, it found an adherent in Henry from the

98 Supra, Chapter 2, text accompanying notes 142–144.
99 Van Doren 218.
100 3 Elliot 45.
101 Id. at 21, 47.
102 Id. at 60, 437, 650, 396, 169, 579.
103 Van Doren 222.
104 3 Elliot 625.
105 Id. at 218, 222, 263, 268, 236.
106 Id. at 29, 33, 415, 522.
107 Id. at 156.
108 Id. at 257–258, 259.

outset, but only if the power were wielded by state rather than federal judges: "The honorable gentleman has told us that these powers, given to Congress, are accompanied by a judiciary which will correct all. On examination you will find this very judiciary oppressively constructed, your jury trial destroyed, and the judges dependent on Congress."[109] But he left no doubt that he was a friend to judicial review:

> The honorable gentleman did our judiciary honor in saying that they had firmness to counteract the legislature in some cases. Yes sir, our judges opposed the acts of the legislature . . . They had the fortitude to declare that they were the judiciary, and would oppose unconstitutional acts. Are you sure your federal judiciary will act thus? Is that judiciary as well constructed, as independent of the other branches, as our state judiciary? . . . I take it as the highest encomium on this country, that the acts of the legislature, if unconstitutional, are liable to be opposed by the judiciary.[110]

For one reason or another, he continued to prefer the state to the federal courts:

> I consider the Virginia judiciary as one of the best barriers against strides of power . . . So small are the barriers against the encroachments and usurpations of Congress, that, when I see this last barrier—the independency of [state] judges impaired, I am persuaded I see the prostration of all our rights . . . The [state] judiciary are the sole protection against a tyrannical execution of the laws. But if by this system we lose our judiciary, and they cannot help us, we must sit down quietly, and be oppressed.[111]

Nevertheless, while combating another argument, he said that "If Congress, under the specious pretence of pursuing this clause, altered it, and prohibited appeals as to fact, the federal judges, if they spoke the sentiments of independent men, would declare their prohibition nugatory and void."[112] Henry therefore wanted judicial

---

[109] Id. at 57. Grayson later questioned the independence of federal judges on the ground that their salaries "may be augmented," a method whereby "to corrupt a judge." Id. at 563. For "oppression" and jury trial, see infra, text accompanying notes 129–136.

[110] 3 Elliot 324–325.

[111] Id. at 539.

[112] Id. at 541.

protection against Congressional excesses but very much preferred to rely on State courts.[113]

With judicial review conceded in principle by the leader of the opposition, there was no need constantly to harp on it. The incessant drumbeat of Congressional "oppression," however, prompted the proponents, who acted in concert,[114] to counter from time to time with the corrective role of judicial review. So, Randolph said, "If Congress wish to aggrandize themselves by oppressing the people, the judiciary must first be corrupted."[115] Judge Pendleton said that his judicial brethren had "prevented the operation of some unconstitutional acts";[116] and later said that "oppressive laws will not be warranted by the Constitution," that "independent judges will never admit an oppressive construction," and that he relied on "an honest interpretation from independent judges" whose "peculiar province" it was to give execution to *proper* laws."[117] George Nicholas, a spokesman for the proponents, seeking to calm fears of the "*sweeping* ["necessary and proper"] *clause*," stated,

> But says he [the opposition speaker], who is to determine the extent of such powers? I say, the same power which, in all well-

[113] Davis, *Veto* 97, fairly summarizes Henry's view: "while the federal courts might on occasion declare an act of Congress unconstitutional, the chief reliance of the people ought to be based on the state judiciary." Prior to the Virginia convention, R. H. Lee, who opposed ratification, stated, "It is proper that the federal judiciary should have . . . the power of deciding finally on the laws of the Union." Ford, *Pamphlets* 279, 306.

[114] Van Doren 218.

[115] 3 Elliot 205.

[116] Id. at 299. To show that Pendleton "did not rely" on "judicial annulment," Davis, *Veto* 97, quotes his next sentence, "Notwithstanding those violations [by the legislature], I rely upon the principles of government—that it will produce its own reform, by the responsibility resulting from frequent elections." This merely expresses the hope that a chastened legislature will not "violate" Constitutional bounds; it does not foreclose judicial review if it does. See infra, text accompanying note 117.

At another point, Davis, *Veto* 100, quotes R. H. Lee's remark in the pre-Ratification campaign that the treaty power "is absolute . . . and the judge will be bound to allow full force to whatever . . . the President and senate shall establish by treaty." But Lee, as Davis notices, based his argument on the fact that Article VI does not provide "that these treaties shall be made in pursuance of the Constitution." "Laws" of Congress, on the other hand, were "binding" only if "in pursuance" of the Constitution; and in the same "Letters of a Federal Farmer" Lee said that "It is proper that the federal judiciary should have . . . the power of deciding finally on the laws of the union." Ford, *Pamphlets* 279, 306. For discussion of the treaty power and judicial review, see infra, Appendix B.

[117] 3 Elliot 548 (emphasis added); cf. id. at 303.

regulated communities, determines the extent of the legislative powers. If they exceed those powers, the judges will declare it void, or else the people will have a right to declare it void.[118]

Mason, a leader of the opposition, addressing himself to the prohibition of Congressional ex post facto laws, and noting that "The States are equally precluded," stated,

> Will it not be the duty of the federal court to say that such laws are prohibited? . . . an express power is given to the federal court to take cognizance of such controversies, and to declare null all *ex post facto* laws.[119]

Then there is his subsequent statement that the all-embracing scope of the "arising under" clause would enable the federal courts "to destroy the state governments; for they will be the judges *how far* their [federal] laws operate."[120] If such federal laws went too "far," the implication is that federal courts, assuming they were unbiased, could halt their operation.[121]

Madison, in explaining Article III, said that "Controversies affecting the interest of the United States ought to be determined by their own judiciary, and not left to partial, local tribunals."[122] Whether a federal law should override a State statute would preeminently present such a "controversy"; and since Patrick Henry had already urged that the task of declaring federal laws unconstitutional should be left to State courts, Madison may be taken to mean that in order to prevent "local partiality" that determination should be made by the federal courts. His fellow proponent, Nicholas, had

---

[118] Id. at 443. Note the generally unspoken premise of popular action—a last resort if judicial action proves insufficient.

Nicholas later stated that Congress "cannot legislate in any case but those particularly enumerated." Id. at 451. H. Lee said, "When a question arises with respect to the legality of any power exercised or assumed by congress, it is plain on the side of the governed: *Is it enumerated in the Constitution? If it be, it is legal and just. It is otherwise arbitrary and unconstitutional.*" Id. at 186. Patrick Henry had earlier said that it was the function of the courts so to hold, and proponents later made the inarticulate premise explicit.

[119] Id. at 479–480.

[120] Id. at 521 (emphasis supplied).

[121] Mason had made this quite clear in the Constitutional Convention, supra, Chapter 3, text accompanying note 49.

[122] 3 Elliot 532. This was in reply to attacks on anticipated bias of federal judges. Infra, text accompanying notes 133–134.

earlier made it unmistakably clear that the federal courts would set unconstitutional federal laws aside.

But it is John Marshall's remarks that are of the greatest interest to the student of judicial review. Toward the close of the convention he forthrightly stated that if Congress were to

> go beyond the delegated powers . . . If they were to make a law not warranted by any of the powers enumerated, it would be considered by the judges as an infringement of the Constitution which they are to guard . . . They would declare it void . . . To what quarter will you look for protection from an infringement on the constitution, if you will not give the power to the judiciary? There is no other body that can afford such a protection.[123]

Marshall has often been considered a master sorcerer who, in *Marbury v. Madison,* conjured judicial review from the vasty deep.[124] He is acquitted of sorcery by his remarks in the Virginia convention where, in fact, they echoed a refrain that fell from the lips of proponents and opponents alike, and which still earlier had been uttered by Iredell,[125] Yates,[126] and Hamilton.[127] Indeed, the

---

[123] 3 Elliot 553–554.

[124] For citations see Corwin, *Doctrine* 1 n. 1; cf. Bickel 1–2.

[125] Supra, Chapter 3, text accompanying note 168.

[126] Supra, Chapter 3, text accompanying notes 180–188.

[127] Supra, Chapter 3, text accompanying notes 227–229. By the time of Marbury v. Madison (1803) there had also appeared the Lectures of James Wilson (1791), infra, Chapter 5, text accompanying notes 28–30; the opinions in Kamper v. Hawkins, 1 Va. Cas. 22 (1793), supra, Chapter 2, notes 134 and 179; Judge and Professor St. George Tucker's annotations to Blackstone's *Commentaries* (1802–1803), supra, Chapter 2, note 134; all of which unequivocally state the existence of judicial review, not to speak of several earlier expressions of the Supreme Court Justices on Circuit. See Haines 173–180, 187.

Certainly Marshall had no aura of innovation for his contemporaries if we may judge from the insufficiently-noticed statement of Justice Chase in the year before Marshall was appointed to the Court and three years before Marbury v. Madison was decided: "It is, indeed, a general opinion, it is expressly admitted by all this bar, and some of the judges have, individually, in the circuits, decided that the supreme court can declare an act of congress to be unconstitutional, and, therefore, invalid; but there is no adjudication of the supreme court itself upon the point. I concur, however, in the general sentiment." Cooper v. Telfair, 4 Dallas 14, 18 (1800).

Judge Learned Hand remarked "how closely Marshall's reasoning in Marbury v. Madison followed Hamilton's," Hand 8; and even with respect to the "holding" that Congress is without power to expand the "original" jurisdiction of the Court,

final remark on the subject in the Virginia convention was that of William Grayson, a leader of the opposition. The courts, he said, "are the best check we have; they secure us from encroachments on our privileges"; and he said still later, "If the Congress cannot make a law against the Constitution, I apprehend they cannot make a law to abridge it. The judges are to defend it."[128]

Of course there was criticism of the federal courts: nothing was "left to the state courts";[129] the federal jurisdiction was of "stupendous magnitude"; it would "ultimately destroy the state judiciaries";[130] "the state courts must soon be annihilated."[131] Grayson preferred appeals to the State courts; the appellate jurisdiction of the Supreme Court was "perfectly unnecessary."[132] Federal courts would "be inclined to favor their own officers,"[133] the community could not "place confidence" in federal judges,[134] and there was the travel "distance" to federal courts which would place the "poor man" under burdensome expense.[135] The "greatest objection" against the appellate jurisdiction, acknowledged Judge Pendleton, was to the phrase "both as to law and fact" because of its fancied threat to trial by jury.[136] Not a voice in the chorus of criticism was raised against judicial review.[137] If judicial control of the Congressional

---

he was preceded by his colleague in the Virginia convention, Judge Pendleton, who stated that "the legislature cannot extend its original jurisdiction, which is limited." 3 Elliot 518. It is time to disencumber Marshall of the mantle of creating something out of nothing, and to dwell instead on the fact that he himself had joined with his coworkers in the Virginia convention in asserting that the design of the Framers was to provide judicial review. If no mention of that "intention" is made in Marbury v. Madison and the argument instead is strictly from the text, it may be because the "legislative history" was as yet unpublished. 1 Farrand xii, xv; 1 Elliot iii, iv. Then too, his generation did not customarily resort to such history.

[128] 3 Elliot 563, 567.

[129] Id. at 521, 522, 527, 542.

[130] Id. at 565, 527.

[131] Id. at 542.

[132] Id. at 567.

[133] Id. at 58.

[134] Id. at 524.

[135] Id. at 524, 520, 69.

[136] Id. at 519, 525, 540, 568, 572. Madison also said that this was the "principal criticism" of the appellate jurisdiction. Id. at 534.

[137] My own study of the Ratification convention records confirmed Warren's statement that "so far as reported, there was no challenge, in any Convention, of the existence of the power of the court with reference to Acts of Congress." Warren, Congress 68. And I would agree with Warren, id. at 70, that "any man who has taken part in any Convention will realize that plain statements as to the

ogre by federal judges was not as desirable as review by trusted State judges, it was yet better than nothing.

So clear and convincing are the materials from the Ratification conventions that one reads with astonishment Boudin's remark that "one can not possibly believe that the ratifiers could have possibly known that this great power was contained in the Constitution."[138] Davis, on the other hand, set out to prove that in the Ratification conventions "a vigorous objection to the power [of judicial review] was expressed, especially in the most important states,"[139] but as has been shown his citations do not stand up. If the opponents found in judicial review "an argument against ratification,"[140] as Davis concludes, it was largely because it was to be administered by federal rather than state judges, not because it invaded the sacred precincts of Congress.

Finally, there is the soft impeachment by Corwin in 1938:

> The great argument against the Constitution was, of course, that the proposed government would menace the rights of the states and liberties of the people, and to this argument backers of the proposal occasionally found it convenient to bring forward the idea of judicial review as a check on the national legislative power. Yet the argument was not greatly stressed in the state conventions; nor was it apparently very persuasive—partly because of the absence of a Bill of Rights, and partly because of the broad language of the "necessary and proper" and "Supremacy Clauses," to say nothing of the highly suspect "general welfare" clause of Article I, section 8, and the still vaguer language of the Preamble. Besides the thing feared was the power of the government as a whole, *including its judicial branch.*[141]

---

existence of a power, under any new proposed Constitution or by-law, would, as a matter of common experience, be vigorously attacked and denied, if there were any considerable body of men in the Convention who believed that the power did not, or should not, exist." Cf. Melvin 197–198.

[138] Boudin 97.

[139] Davis, *Veto* 46. See supra, note 137.

[140] Davis, *Veto* 112.

[141] Corwin, *Court Over* 40–41. Davis, Veto 113, also argued that because the "jealousy of federal authority on the part of all the States extended to the judiciary," the people did not contemplate "vesting in the Supreme Court (much less in any inferior court) the power to annul an Act of Congress." The First Congress was shortly to confide exactly that power to State courts, with an appeal to the Supreme Court, Infra, Chapter 8, text accompanying notes 202–244.

Why should the availability of judicial review have been "greatly stressed" in the Ratification conventions when statement of the proposition met with no opposition and, indeed, as in Virginia, found enthusiastic concurrence.[142] Unsparing criticism of *other* aspects of the judicial function[143] indicates that the opposition found no fault with judicial review. To be sure, opponents stressed that the legislative powers were so broad and vague as to defy judicial line-drawing,[144] but the majority vote for adoption connoted acceptance of assurances that judicial review would be effective. To argue that such assurances were not "very persuasive" is to ignore the fact of ratification. The opposition wanted more definite limits because they desired *enforceable*, that is, unquestionable, limits,[145] not because they wanted *no* limits on Congress. Insistence on more tightly defined legislative powers posited judicial review, for without it the tightest limitation would be ineffectual. The opponents were practical men; if their broadly-based opposition to "vague" powers failed they scarcely designed to leave Congress, the transcendent object of their fears and suspicions, utterly unbridled, free to violate even express Constitutional prohibitions. The dreaded menace to States Rights and individual liberties would lead opponents to welcome rather than to discard every additional safeguard.[146] Suspect of partiality as federal courts might be, there was yet the possibility that they might exhibit as much "fortitude" vis-à-vis Congress as the Virginia courts, according to Patrick Henry, had shown against the Assembly. When the States Righters faced the gun in the First Congress, they pushed through *State court* review of Congressional Acts with an appeal to the Supreme Court,[147] thus underlining that their opposition was to the *choice* of courts rather than to the function of overriding unconstitutional federal laws.

---

[142] Wilson addressed himself to judicial review several times in the Pennsylvania convention, for example, supra, text accompanying notes 39–40; the matter was discussed four or five times in Virginia, supra, text at notes 115–118, 123, with opposition figures like Patrick Henry joining in the the chorus of praise for judicial review, id. at notes 110, 111, 128; and it was discussed in North Carolina, id. at notes 79, 87, 89.

[143] See, e.g., infra, Chapter 9, text accompanying notes 7–19; supra, notes 94–97, 129–136.

[144] See supra, note 44; text accompanying note 62.

[145] Cf. supra, note 44.

[146] Cf. Corwin, supra, Chapter 3, text following note 311.

[147] Infra, Chapter 8, text accompanying notes 202–244.

THE FIRST CONGRESS

As an "almost adjourned session" of the Convention, in which sat members of both the Convention and the Ratifying conventions, the First Congress has always been regarded as an authoritative expounder of the Constitution.[1] The debate on the President's "removal" power preceded the debate on the Judiciary Act of 1789, and it is the earlier debate that furnishes the significant utterances about judicial review of Congressional Acts. Crosskey's treatment of these materials will serve as a convenient introduction to the views expressed in the First Congress about judicial review. From his examination of section 25 of the Judiciary Act he concludes that the First Congress "had no interest whatever in the Supreme Court as a reviewing agency . . . in the case of its own acts of legislation," and that "the complete correctness of this conclusion is plainly confirmed by" its decision on the "Presidential power . . . to remove executive officers." The House decided, he asserts, that the President "possessed this power" and this

> deliberate act of Constitutional interpretation was carried through
> in the House . . . in the face of contentions from certain mi-

[1] Warren, *Congress* 99. See Madison's remarks quoted supra, Chapter 3, note 272. What Congressman William Vans Murray said in the House in 1796, "We have all seen the Constitution from its cradle, we know it from its infancy, and have the most perfect knowledge of it and more light than ever a body of men in any country ever had of ascertaining any other Constitution," 5 *Ann. Cong.* 701 (4th Cong. 1st Sess.; Gales & Seaton 1849), was even more true of the First Congress. In 1827, William Johnson, one of the great Justices of the Supreme Court, referred to the "presumption that the contemporaries of the constitution have claims to our deference . . . because they had the best opportunities of informing themselves of the understanding of the framers of the constitution, and of the sense put upon it by the people, when it was adopted by them." Ogden v. Saunders, 12 Wheat. 213, 270, 290 (1827); see also Stuart v. Laird, 1 Cranch 299, 309 (1803); Cohens v. Virginia, 6 Wheat. 264, 418 (1821).

nority speakers there (who were displeased with the decision on the substantive point the majority were about to make), that the right of interpreting the Constitution belonged to the Supreme Court solely . . . The answer to these contentions, which James Madison, the chief majority speaker made, was that "there [was] not one government on the face of the earth, *not one in the United States,* in which provision [was] made for a particular authority to determine the limits of the Constitutional division of power between the branches of the Government." "In all systems, there are points," he said, "which must be adjusted by the departments themselves, to which no one of them is competent." . . . Since, moreover, Madison further insisted that the Court had no "greater" right of constitutional interpretation than any other department, it is plain that, in his estimation, in 1789, the Court's right to interpret *in contravention* of the views of any other department as to the nature of such department's own powers depended upon the involvement in the question at issue, of the Court's powers or duties under the Constitution.

The foregoing views were those, apparently, upon which the majority in the House of Representatives acted. The majority, as a whole, seemed quite convinced, as Madison was, that their interpretation, if the President and Senate should concur . . . would be authoritative; and they appeared to be not at all impressed with the minority's contention that the right to interpret belonged solely to the Supreme Court. These things seem certainly established by the removal-power decision, because upon no other view of the opinions of the House majority, does the elaborate care they took to create an unmistakably clear precedent as to their belief in the existence of Presidential removal power make sense.[2]

It is by no means clear that Madison's remarks may be taken to show that *he* "had no interest whatever in the Supreme Court as a reviewing agency" of Congressional acts that invaded *private* rights, or that he thought the legislative construction would be binding on the Supreme Court.[3] But if Madison did in fact hold such views,

[2] Crosskey 1033–1034; 1 *Ann. Cong.* 520.
[3] Madison had opened by saying that the "decision" of the House "will become the permanent exposition of the Constitution," 1 *Ann. Cong.* 514, and

Crosskey does violence to the facts when he maintains that the "majority in the House" acted on them. To the contrary, as Corwin stated, Madison's "attempt to construe the Constitution" was vigorously protested, "with the result that eventually Madison himself joined in support of a motion striking the exceptionable clause."[4]

The proof is worth close examination. The point at issue was a clause which purported to *grant* to the President the right of removal of the Secretary of Foreign Affairs.[5] It brought forth such a profusion of constitutional theory[6] as to make peculiarly apt Crosskey's statement in an analogous situation: "What theory of power the majority held, was left completely uncertain; for no vote was taken on the various theories, but only on the ultimate question."[7] One thing, however, is clear: the argument that the House lacked power to make the grant carried the day. In the upshot the words "to be removable by the President" were replaced by a declaration of "sentiment" or "sense" of the House "upon the meaning of a *constitutional grant* of power *to the President*," and Madison concurred on the ground that the Legislature is "not in possession of this power."[8] So there was no question of a House construction of the "nature of such department's *own* powers," or as to the boundaries between those powers and those of the other departments, but at most a gratuitous expression as to the scope of the President's

---

from this and remarks that followed Crosskey, 1034, concludes that Madison could "only mean that it would be binding on the one uninterested branch of the Government: the Supreme Court."

[4] Corwin, *Doctrine* 48.

[5] 1 *Ann. Cong.* 385.

[6] John Vining said, "I am confounded with the diversity of arguments used on this occasion." 1 *Ann. Cong.* 593. Many years later Justice Peckham said, "all arguments that could be thought of by men . . . were brought forward." Parsons v. United States, 167 U.S. 324, 329 (1897). To mention a few of the "theories": some believed that the sole power of removal was via impeachment, 1 *Ann. Cong.* 387, 389, 490; others felt that the power of removal like that of appointment resided in both the President and Senate, id. at 388–389, 393, 396; others that it vested in the President alone, id. at 397, 482; others that Congress could confer the power, id. at 392. Madison thought that Congress did not possess this power. Id. at 604.

[7] Crosskey 1037.

[8] 1 *Ann. Cong.* 525, 605, 604. Sherman justly asked, if "the power is vested in the President by the Constitution . . . why are we officiously to intrude our opinion upon the President." 1 *Ann. Cong.* 558. Similar views were expressed by White, Livermore, and Page, id. at 536, 564, 570.

power. The House therefore wisely *refused* to deliver itself of a "deliberate act of Constitutional interpretation." This is not all.

To make his case Crosskey played with the word "majority" in careless fashion. Presumably those who voted for the final measure, that which replaced the words of grant with a mere expression of the sentiment of the House, were the "majority."[9] Madison aside, *no* majority speaker suggested that a Congressional construction stood on a par with that of the Supreme Court. To the contrary, every "majority" speaker who addressed himself to the interpretation issue stressed that the Court would have the last word. They were joined by three members of the "minority"; two other "minority" members who spoke to the matter did so in terms of convenience or of preliminary construction. No "minority" speaker laid claim to Congressional finality. Because the issue is one of scholarly credibility bare assertion cannot suffice; the facts must be allowed to speak for themselves.

Preliminary legislative construction of ambiguous constitutional provisions was and remains a prerequisite to legislating, for as Peter Sylvester (minority member) said, "without such a power we could pass no law whatever."[10] He added that "the Judiciary will be better able to decide the question of constitutionality in this way than in any other. If we are wrong, they can correct our error."[11] John Lawrence (minority) said, "it is proper for the Legislature to speak their sense upon those points on which the constitution is silent. I believe that the judges will never decide that we are guilty of a breach of the constitution, by declaring a legislative opinion in cases where the constitution is silent. If the laws shall be in violation of any part of the constitution, the judges will not hesitate to decide against them."[12] On this issue Lawrence and Sylvester were at one with the "majority." Alexander White (majority) said that "the legislature may construe the constitution with respect to the powers annexed to their department, but subject to the decision of the judges."[13] This was the view of Fisher Ames (majority): "if we

---

[9] Id. at 608.
[10] For a broad discussion of the problem see Morgan, *Congress and the Constitution* (1968).
[11] 1 *Ann. Cong.* 585.
[12] Id. at 505.
[13] Id. at 539.

declare improperly the judiciary will revise our decision";[14] of Abraham Baldwin (majority) a Framer: "It is their [judges'] province to decide upon our laws; if they find this clause to be unconstitutional, they will not hesitate to declare it so."[15] John Page (majority) insisted that the House should "leave the constitution to the proper expositors of it,"[16] that is, the judges. The differentiation between "expounding" and "making" law, it will be recalled, had found frequent expression on the Convention floor. Now William Smith of South Carolina (minority) branded a "legislative construction" as an "infringement of the powers of the Judiciary," and said, "Sir, it is the duty of the Legislature to make laws. Your judges are to expound them."[17] Gerry (majority), a Framer, also said that "The judges are the expositors of the Constitution . . . Our exposition, therefore, would be subject to their revisal." The "judges are the Constitutional umpires on such questions"; and he asked whether they "would not be bound to declare the law a nullity, if this clause is continued in it, and is inconsistent with the Constitution."[18] Two minority speakers were at best equivocal. Elias Boudinot considered that "there may be much inconvenience if the President does not exercise his prerogative until it is decided by the courts of justice." A nonvoting speaker, Michael Stone, said, "I do not think it would do to leave it to the determination of the courts of law hereafter. It should be our duty, in cases like the present [judicially unconstrued ambiguity requiring preliminary legislative construction] to give *our opinion* on the construction of the constitution."[19] The remarks of Boudinot and Stone are far from claiming finality for the Congressional construction, and it is safe to say that, but for Madison, majority and minority were united in recognition of the courts' right to the last word.

Without pausing to dissect Madison's statement, it may be noted that whatever impact it may have had was diluted by his own subsequent statements: "When the question emerges as it does in this

[14] Id. at 496.
[15] Id. at 582.
[16] Id. at 572.
[17] Id. at 488–489; see supra, Chapter 3, text accompanying notes 31–38.
[18] 1 *Ann. Cong.* 596, 492, 524.
[19] For Boudinot's remarks see id. at 488; for Stone, id. at 511 (emphasis added). Cf. Boudinot's praise of judicial review, infra, text accompanying note 32.

bill [requiring a preliminary legislative construction] and much seems to depend on it, I should conceive it highly proper to make a legislative construction."[20] And he concluded in defending the "sentiment" amendment that "the constitution fairly vests the President with the power, and that the amendment declares this to be the sense of the House."[21] Madison could scarcely claim "conclusiveness" for a construction by the House of *Presidential* powers; much less was there need to maintain at this juncture that "the sense of the House" was conclusive on the courts. Madison's statements do not lend themselves to such a reading, and if they are so read, they are overcome by the many unequivocal utterances by both majority and minority spokesmen that construction was the task of the courts. Indeed they would be irreconcilable with his own remark, nine days earlier, that under the proposed Bill of Rights the courts would be an impenetrable bulwark against every assumption of power in the Legislature,"[22] a statement which had been anticipated by Hamilton in *Federalist* No. 78: "the courts of justice are to be considered as the bulwarks of a limited Constitution against legislative encroachments."[23]

[20] Id. at 568; cf. id. at 520. Madison's modified position may not only have resulted from his appreciation that the sentiment of the House ran the other way, but was perhaps also a belated response to the very difficulties he had been the first to point out. In the "removal" debate he remarked that if the departments could not "adjust" points arising from the "division of power between the branches of the Government" "there is no resource left but the will of the community." 1 *Ann. Cong.* 520. Earlier, in *Federalist* No. 49 at 328, he had noted Jefferson's view, expressed in 1782, that no department "can pretend to an exclusive or superior right of settling the boundaries between their respective powers," but concluded that "there appear to be insuperable objections against [Jefferson's] proposed recurrence to the people, as a provision in all cases for keeping the several departments of power within their constitutional limits," objections which he further amplified in No. 50. Those objections have only been sharpened by the passage of time: a national referendum on each question of constitutional limits in our own time is almost unthinkable.

[21] 1 *Ann. Cong.* 605; Corwin, *Doctrine* 48-49.

[22] 1 *Ann. Cong.* 457.

[23] *Federalist* No. 78 at 508. As Hamilton's statement indicates, judicial review was not a resultant of the Bill of Rights but antecedent machinery to enforce rights earlier assumed.

Wilson's statement to the Pennsylvania convention on this score deserves to be remembered:

I cannot say, Mr. President, what were the reasons of every member of that [federal] Convention for not adding a bill of rights. I believe the truth is, that such an idea never entered the mind of many of them. I do not recollect to have heard the subject mentioned till within about three days of the time

With the numerous and clear-cut expressions in the "removal" debate affirming the judicial right to revise or correct Congressional Acts, it is little wonder that the House took the matter for granted in the subsequent debate on the Judiciary Act and found little occasion to stress yet again what had been so generally accepted.[24] Gerry said in passing that "The constitution will be their [the courts'] first law; and so far as your laws conform to that, they will attend to them, but no further." Against this background it sufficed to provide in section 25 for review of Constitutional issues by State courts subject to appeal to the Supreme Court.[25] The First Congress recorded in unmistakable fashion its belief that judicial review of Congressional Acts had been contemplated, and thereby it confirmed the earlier expressions in the Convention and the several Ratifying conventions.

All this was summed up in the testimony of a great contemporary. In 1790–91 James Wilson, who had espoused judicial review in the Federal and Pennsylvania conventions, and was now a Justice of the Supreme Court as well as Professor of Law in Philadelphia, delivered a series of "Lectures on Law." The acrimony of the post-Convention debate had subsided; the submission of the Bill of Rights

---

of rising; and even then, there was no direct motion offered for any thing of the kind . . . But in a government consisting of enumerated powers, such as is proposed for the United States, a bill of rights would not only be unnecessary, but, in my humble judgment, highly imprudent. In all societies, there are many powers and rights which cannot be particularly enumerated. A bill of rights annexed to a constitution is *an enumeration of the powers* reserved. If we attempt an enumeration, every thing that is not enumerated is presumed to be given. The consequence is, that an imperfect enumeration would throw all implied power into the scale of the government. 2 Elliot 435–436.

See also, supra, Chapter 2, note 53, par. 2.

[24] As Melvin 199, said, "a fuller recognition . . . of judicial supervision of Congressional acts could scarcely be desired." In that "removal" debate, said Corwin, *Doctrine* 49 n. 74, there were "at least a half dozen men championing the notions of judicial review who later voted for the Act of 1787." Says Bickel 21, "It is, in fact, extremely likely, that the First Congress thought" that "the Constitution implies judicial review." So far as the First Congress is concerned, my own study confirms Charles Warren's observation that "it is an especially striking fact that Members of Congress, of both parties, should have been united in one sentiment at least, that under the Constitution it was the judiciary which was finally to determine the validity of an Act of Congress." Warren, *Congress* 99.

[25] For quotation by Gerry, see 1 *Ann. Cong.* 861: cf. Stone, quoted infra, Chapter 8, text accompanying note 212. For discussion of section 25 of the Judiciary Act, see infra, Chapter 8, text accompanying notes 234–237, 215–233, and note 216.

had "converted most of those who still opposed the Constitution."[26] Beyond this, Justice Wilson may be absolved of crass political motivation in speaking from the scholar's lectern.[27] After criticizing the doctrine that Parliament is supreme, he exulted that in the United States, "Instead of being uncontrollable, the legislative authority is placed, as it ought to be, under just and strict control. The effect of its extravagencies may be prevented, sometimes by the executive, sometimes by the judicial authority."[28] The independence of the legislative power, he explained, consisted in the power of preparing, debating, and passing or refusing to pass bills. But "after the proceedings of the legislature are finished" then the legislative power is subject "to another given degree of control by the judiciary department, whenever the laws, though in fact passed, are found to be contradictory to the constitution."[29] The "bounds of the legislative power" are "distinctly marked" and "effectual and permanent provision is made, that every transgression of those bounds shall be adjudged and rendered vain and fruitless. What a noble guard against legislative despotism."[30]

Not until the turn of the century was there any significant dissent from this view.[31] Among other things, Wilson had quoted the reply of Elias Boudinot in the third Session of the First Congress to the argument of Antifederalists that the proposed charter to the Bank of the United States might be viewed as unconstitutional by the courts:

It has been objected that, by adopting the bill before us, we expose the measure to be considered and defeated by the judiciary

[26] Morison 319; McCloskey, Introduction 28.

[27] "President Washington, Vice-President Adams, and a galaxy of other republican worthies turned out." McCloskey, Introduction 37. As Professsor McCloskey remarks, Wilson "was widely acknowledged as the preeminent legal scholar of his generation. In such a place and time such a preceptor ["a founding father and a Supreme Court justice"] could expect to be heard and heeded." Ibid.

[28] 1 Wilson, *Works* 182, 210, 211.

[29] Id. at 411. His explanation of the nature of the judicial duty echoes that of Iredell and Hamilton.

[30] Id. at 462.

[31] Writing of the period contemporary with the Constitution, Meigs, *Relation* 160, said, "so far as I know, the existence of the power [of judicial review] was nowhere denied by any writer of repute . . . not one seems to have expressed doubt as to the intention of the Convention to incorporate it in the new Constitution." Warren, *Congress* 122–123, locates the first "instance of a denial by a member of Congress of the Court's power of judicial review" in March 1800.

of the United States, who may adjudge it to be contrary to the constitution, and therefore void, and not lend their aid to carry it into execution. This gives me no uneasiness. I am so far from controverting this right in the judiciary, that it is my boast and confidence. It leads me to greater decision on all subjects of a constitutional nature, when I reflect, that, if from inattention, want of precision, or any other defect, I should do wrong, there is a power in the government, which can constitutionally prevent the operation of a wrong measure from affecting my constituents. I am legislating for a Nation, and for thousands unborn; and it is for the glory of the constitution that there is a remedy for the failure even of the legislature itself.[32]

Thus, on a controversial measure, a proponent welcomed the possibility raised by the opposition that the courts might declare the measure unconstitutional, striking confirmation of the virtually unanimous recognition during the "removal" debate earlier in that Congress that judicial review was part of the constitutional structure. Charles Warren has collected similar early statements by Federalists and Antifederalists.[33] Of special interest is a letter of Madison in April, 1792:

The Judges have also called the attention of the public to Legislative fallibility, by pronouncing a law providing for invalid pensioners unconstitutional and void; perhaps they may be wrong in the execution of their powers, but such an *evidence of its existence* gives inquietude to those who do not wish Congress to be controuled or doubted, whilst its proceedings correspond with their views.[34]

[32] Quoted 1 Wilson, *Works* 463.
[33] Warren, *Congress* 107–124.
[34] Quoted id. at 110 (emphasis supplied). Madison's reference to the case of "invalid pensioners" is presumably to Hayburn's Case, 2 Dallas 409 (1792). "This being the first instance in which a Court of Justice had declared a law of Congress to be unconstitutional, the novelty of the case produced a variety of opinions with respect to measures to be taken on the occasion. At length a Committee of five was appointed to enquire into the facts and to report thereon." Warren comments, "No further action was taken, except that one Congressman suggested, amid no dissent, that a law be passed 'to point out some regular mode in which the Judges shall give official notice of their refusal to act under any law of Congress on the ground of unconstitutionality,'" which Warren considers recognition by Congress that judges possessed the power. Warren, *Congress* 109. Compare Boudin's animadversions. Boudin 181–183.

Madison here says that one may question the wisdom of a particular judicial exercise of the power, but its *existence* is challenged only by those who wish Congress to be free of interference when *their* views are to be overturned. Warren points out that in the "whole excited debate" on the Sedition Act in 1798 "members of both political parties acceded to the view that the judiciary had the power to hold an Act of Congress unconstitutional; and that no one expressed a contrary opinion."[35] Only after enactment of the Alien and Sedition laws, stated Henry Lee of Virginia in 1801, when the federal courts refused to hold them unconstitutional at the insistent call of the Antifederalists, did they turn "in most poignant anathema against the Judiciary of our country."[36]

Before turning to the Constitutional text itself, it will be instructive to consider some of the criticisms that have been leveled at the conventional reliance on the Framers' remarks, and some of the obstacles that are said to strew the path of the "Hamiltonian" analysis.

[35] Warren, *Congress* 121.

[36] Ibid., quoting a speech in the House of Representatives. Cf. Boudin 160. The Virginia-Kentucky Resolutions, which laid claim to the right of a State to decide whether an Act of Congress was unconstitutional, may therefore in considerable part have derived from the fact that resort to the courts had proved unavailing.

CURRENT ARGUMENTS AGAINST

JUDICIAL REVIEW

JUDICIAL "SELF-DEFENSE"

Seizing on several remarks by some of the Framers, some critics would limit judicial review to such Acts as invade the prerogatives of the judiciary itself, that is, to "self-defense." This view had its genesis at the hands of Corwin; in 1913 he said that "some" of the Framers "seemed to limit the power to its use as a means of self-defense by the court against legislative encroachment."[1] Even when reacting to the Supreme Court's assault on New Deal legislation, Corwin still made clear in 1938 that there were yet *other* groups of Framers, including those who claimed a complete right of judicial review, that is, the right to construe Constitutional *"grants* of power to Congress."[2] Boudin, however, with characteristic exaggeration, stated that "The most striking thing about *all* of the references to the Judiciary is the assurance that it was only a weak power in need of defensive weapons to protect itself against encroachments by other departments, particularly the Legislature."[3] With an air of

---

[1] Quoted supra, Chapter 3, text accompanying note 293, and by Westin 28. In 1938 Corwin repeated that "there were those who regarded judicial review as a sort of veto power to be used by the Court chiefly, if not exclusively, in defense of 'judicial power.'" Corwin, *Court Over* 2, 29. He had made the point in 1906. Corwin, 4 *Mich. L. Rev.* 620.

[2] Corwin, *Court Over* 2, 29–31. In 1914, Corwin said without qualification that the Framers "thought the Constitution secured to the courts . . . the right to pass on the validity of acts of Congress." Corwin, *Doctrine* 10, quoted supra, Chapter 3, text accompanying notes 266–268.

[3] Boudin 114 (emphasis added).

fresh discovery,[4] Professor Crosskey bellied out the theory still further. Professor Hart's crushing refutation,[5] should have given "self-defense" its *coup de grâce,* notwithstanding which Professor Westin has since referred to the *problem* whether "the Court could go beyond defense of its own prerogatives."[6]

Common sense may be permitted to sound a timid preliminary note. Can it be that the Framers' resolute attempt to forestall feared Congressional invasions of private and State's rights by fettering Congress with express prohibitions, by confining it strictly within "limits," accompanied by repeated assurances that action outside those "limits" or in derogation of the prohibitions would be judicially declared unconstitutional and void—can it be that all this was designed only to fashion a judiciary that is confined to guarding its *own* prerogatives? Can it be that statutes "merely impairing the rights of the people or of the States"[7] were meant to be unreviewable? This strange discrimination would give rise to two classes of Congressional "usurpation," both of which are "unconstitutional and void" (for the "unconstitutional and void" statements were *never confined* to invasions of judicial prerogatives), but only invasion of judicial prerogatives may be *declared* void by the courts. "Mere" impairments of private rights though no less "void" are left like Mahomet's coffin suspended in mid-air.[8]

No less strange is the Crosskey transmutation of two early State "precedents": they "actually appertained to legislative attempts to invade the judiciary's own prerogatives."[9] In *Trevett v. Weeden* the "fundamental" principle involved was whether the legislature had the power "to destroy trial by jury";[10] *Bayard v. Singleton* held an Act unconstitutional "as depriving the plaintiffs of *their* right to a

---

[4] Crosskey makes no reference to the anticipatory remarks of Corwin and Boudin.

[5] Hart, Book Review 1478–1480.

[6] Westin 30.

[7] Hart, Book Review 1478, paraphrasing Crosskey.

[8] For the Founders' solicitude for private rights, see supra, Chapter 2, text accompanying notes 41–57; and see infra, note 29, and text accompanying note 60.

Hart, Book Review 1461, remarks that all "six principal points" aimed against judicial review by Crosskey "apply with undifferentiable force, in principle to the review of acts of Congress claimed to infringe the prerogatives of the Judiciary." For other internal difficulties presented by the Crosskey differentiation, see id. at 1472–1475.

[9] Crosskey 974; cf. Westin 30.

[10] Crosskey 970, 965–966.

trial by jury."[11] It does not require the admonition of the Seventh Amendment to remind us that "the right of trial by jury" is a *personal* right, a right designed for the protection of the individual, not a "judicial prerogative."[12] Crosskey's conversion of that right into a judicial prerogative underlines the artificiality of the distinction between judicial protection against "mere" impairment of individual rights and against "encroachments" upon the judiciary's own prerogatives.[13]

Randolph's statement in the Virginia convention might suffice to demonstrate that "self-defense" was merely convenient shorthand for judicial review:

> nothing is granted which does not belong to a federal judiciary. Self-defense is its first object. Has not the Constitution said that states shall not use such and such powers, and given exclusive powers to Congress?[14]

Defense of *Congress'* "exclusive powers" clearly is not equivalent to judicial "self-defense." But Corwin's parentage, and Westin's respectful mention, of the doctrine entitle it to closer inspection.

When Corwin suggested that *some* regarded judicial review as a judicial weapon for self-defense against legislative encroachments, he relied on certain remarks of Gerry, Wilson, and Madison. In Crosskey's hands this becomes "the *general* understanding" that "the right could exist *only* as a means for the judges to use for that

[11] Id. at 972 (emphasis added).

[12] "The right of trial by jury shall be preserved and no fact tried by a jury shall be otherwise *re-examined in any court* . . ." (emphasis added). This *denies* rather than confers a judicial "prerogative."

Hart, Book Review 1463, justly states that there is not "the faintest suggestion" in the cases "that the distinction [Crosskey] takes was recognized in the thinking of the time." Fresh currency is lent to the distinction by Westin, who states that "Most of the pre-Convention cases in which state judges had been alleged to have held state laws void had involved laws regulating the courts and judicial proceedings." Westin 30. For additional comment on Crosskey's conversion of the personal "right" to jury trial into "self-defense" of judicial prerogatives, see supra, Chapter 2, note 144.

[13] Crosskey virtually washes out the distinction for practical purposes when he concludes that "The Fourth, Fifth, Sixth, Seventh and Eighth Amendments, taken collectively are . . . primarily applicable to the judicial branch of the Government," Crosskey 1004, and thus fall within the doctrine of "self-defense." The vast bulk of "private" constitutional claims invoke one or the other of these Amendments and are on his theory therefore reviewable.

[14] 3 Elliot 570.

purpose."[15] Of course, this was not "the general understanding," and such interpretation distorts the shorthand expressions of Gerry, Wilson, and Madison. Although Gerry said that a "judicial share in the veto" of the proposed Council of Revision, which was to "guard against Congressional excesses," was unnecessary because "the judiciary would have a sufficient check against encroachments on their own department by their exposition of the laws,"[16] he is a poor witness for "self-defense." In the First Congress debate on whether Congress should construe the President's "removal" power, a subject that did not remotely affect judicial prerogatives, Gerry said that "judges are the constitutional umpires on such questions," and asked whether the judges "would not be bound to declare the law a nullity, if this clause is continued in it and is inconsistent with the Constitution."[17] This and other remarks of Gerry [18] demonstrate that his view of judicial review was not limited to "self-defense" but was all-embracing.

[15] Crosskey 1014.

[16] Crosskey 1013. Gerry is more fully quoted supra, Chapter 3, text accompanying note 13. Crosskey takes off from manifest error. He states that "the men in the Convention who were most interested in using the Supreme Court justices as guards against Congressional excesses, *at first attempted* to provide for the Justices functioning in this way by making them . . . the dominant members of a 'Council of [legislative] Revision.'" Crosskey 1013 (emphasis added). From the outset, the Virginia Plan provided separate "checks" on the legislative powers in the form of "1) a Council of Revision . . . 2) A ntl. Judiciary" 1 Farrand 28. Participation in the Council was designed, in Madison's words, to give the judiciary "an additional [and earlier] opportunity," 2 Farrand 74; or as Wilson put it, the "expository" power of the judges "did not go far enough" because laws might "be unjust . . . unwise" and "yet not be . . . unconstitutional," id. at 73; quoted more fully supra, Chapter 3, text accompanying note 26. Wilson desired that the courts should not only enjoy the power of declaring laws unconstitutional, but should participate in "revision" *prior to effectiveness* of "unwise" laws which might yet be constitutional.

[17] 1 *Ann. Cong.* 492, 524. This also disposes of another inference Crosskey 1016, draws from Gerry's "self-defense" remark: "plainly implying, as it does, that no *general* right of judicial review—no right extending to the defense of [the Executive's rights]—was then in contemplation, [Gerry] manifestly means that cases like Myers v. United States, for example, were beyond what the Convention had in mind." Gerry was among those in the First Congress who considered that the Congressional construction of the President's "removal" power *was* subject to judicial review. See Chapter 5, text accompanying note 18, and at notes 10–17.

[18] 1 *Ann. Cong.* 596, 492, 524. Gerry also stated, "But say Congress, we are the constitutional expounders and your [judges'] decision in this case has been improper. Shall the judges, because Congress have usurped power . . . be impeached . . . for . . . standing in opposition to their usurpation of power? If this is the meaning of the Constitution, it was hardly worth while to have had so much bustle and uneasiness about it." 1 *Ann. Cong.* 558.

It is Wilson who is summoned by Crosskey as chief witness for the "general understanding," in reliance on some remarks Wilson made during discussion of the proposal to join judges with the Executive on a Council of Revision for the veto of Congressional Acts:

> Wilson urged . . . that "the judiciary ought to have an opportunity of remonstrating ag[ain]st projected encroachments on the people as well as themselves." This certainly indicates that Wilson understood the judges would *not* have an "opportunity" to protect "the people" as things then stood; and this in turn, would seem to indicate that he did not consider the judges to be possessed of a *general* right of judicial review. With reference to the judges' defense of their own prerogatives, he reminded the Convention that "it had been said the Judges, *as expositors of the laws,* would have an opportunity of defending *their* constitutional rights." "There was weight in this observation," he conceded, "but this power"—that is, the power to defending "*their* constitutional rights" by setting aside any acts of Congress deemed to invade them—"did not," Wilson thought, "go far enough. [For] laws," he pointed out, "m[ight] be unjust, m[ight] be dangerous, m[ight] be destructive; and yet not be *so* unconstitutional as to justify the Judges in refusing to give them effect." So, merely for the safety of their own prerogatives, the judges, he was apparently arguing, ought to have a share in the veto over national legislation.[19]

On Crosskey's reading, Wilson postulated that judges already possessed the power of "defending *their* constitutional rights" by "refusing to give [unconstitutional laws] effect," and sought to give judges a "share in the veto" over "unwise" laws that fell short of unconstitutionality "merely for the safety of their own prerogatives." This is not the only strange result to which Crosskey's literalism leads. On his reading the Conciliar veto function was either (1) to be divided into two parts, in only one of which—defense of judicial prerogatives—the judiciary would participate, or else (2) the Council veto itself was to be limited to laws that invaded judicial prerogatives. Not a shred of evidence exists for either alternative;

[19] Crosskey 1015. For Wilson's remarks see 2 Farrand 73.

instead, as will be shown, the veto of the Council and that of its judicial participants was to run to *all* laws.

Literalism is subject to yet another infirmity. Both Gerry and Wilson had also spoken of the *Executive* veto in terms of "self-defense." Gerry said that the object of "the Revisionary power was merely to secure the Executive department agst. legislative encroachments. The Executive therefore who will best know and be ready to defend his rights ought also to have the defense of them."[20] "Without such a Self-defense," said Wilson of his earlier proposal of an "absolute veto" that could not be overruled, "the Legislature can at any moment sink it [the Executive] into non-existence."[21] Mason, however, was at pains to say that "The defense of the Executive was not the sole object of the Revisionary power . . . the Legislature . . . would so much resemble that of the individual States, that it must be expected frequently to pass unjust or pernicious laws. This restraining power was therefore essentially necessary."[22] Madison had called attention to the English practice whereunder "the Executive might negative any law whatever."[23] It was generally assumed, as will appear, that both the Executive veto and proposed Conciliar substitute were to run the whole gamut of the laws. Never since has it been intimated that the Executive veto is limited to laws that encroach on Executive "prerogatives"; to the contrary, it is established that the veto extends to all laws whatsoever.[24] So "self-defense" remarks, whether in the context of Executive or Judicial "prerogatives" ought to be read as the shorthand they manifestly are.[25]

---

[20] 2 Farrand 75.

[21] 1 Farrand 98.

[22] 2 Farrand 78. Madison said in the Convention, "whether the object of the revisionary power [of the Council of Revision] was to restrain the Legislature from encroaching on other coordinate departments, or on the rights of the people at large . . . the utility of annexing the wisdom and weight of the Judiciary seems incontestable." 1 Farrand 139. Referring to the Council, he said, "A check is devised for three purposes—to prevent encroachment by the Legislature on the Executive, the Judicial or on private rights." 1 Farrand 144.

[23] 2 Farrand 77.

[24] For the Framers' all-inclusive view of the scope of the veto, see infra, text accompanying notes 37, 38, 43.

[25] "In the course of a debate which was central to the whole problem of balance among the three departments, it was natural that the delegates spoke repeatedly of the danger of 'encroachments' upon one department by another." Hart, Book Review 1478.

Wilson's own words unmistakably repel the narrow views attributed to him by Crosskey. In the Pennsylvania convention Wilson stated that the legislature may be "kept within its prescribed bounds by . . . the judicial department" and should the legislature "transgress" those bounds, the judges would be under "a duty to pronounce it void."[26] He did not leave us in the dark as to the relation between judicial review and private rights. Explaining the judicial tenure provisions, he said that where they are lacking, "the liberty and property of the citizen" are endangered, that "personal liberty, and private property, depend essentially upon the able and upright determinations of independent judges," and that the consequence of judicial independence would be that "private property and personal liberty . . . will be guarded with firmness and watchfulness."[27] This, not jealous guardianship of judicial privileges, was the prime purpose of the judicial power. In his 1791 Lectures Wilson described the judicial power to adjudge "*every* transgression of [constitutional] bounds . . . vain and fruitless" as "a noble guard against legislative despotism."[28] For Wilson, the "purpose" of the "magnificent" constitutional structure was the "accommodation of the sovereign, Man," and to afford a "new security" for *his* rights.[29] Contrast with Wilson's own words Crosskey's statement that Wilson "understood the judges *not* to be possessed of the power of judicial review for any other purpose [than self-defense] whatsoever, and that the majority of the Convention had not been interested in the Supreme Court Justices as agents for the defense of the people as against Congress, at all."[30]

Not the least remarkable aspect of Crosskey's "self-defense" argument is his manner of extracting a "general understanding"[31] from

[26] Quoted supra, Chapter 4, text accompanying notes 39–41. In the federal Convention he said, "It will be better to prevent the passage of an improper law, then to declare it void when passed." 2 Farrand 391.

[27] 2 Elliot 480–481. Madison stressed "the necessity of providing more effectively for the security of private rights, and the steady dispensation of Justice. Interferences with these were evils which had perhaps more than anything else, produced this convention." 1 Farrand 134.

[28] Supra, Chapter 5, text accompanying notes 28–30 (emphasis added).

[29] Supra, Chapter 2, text accompanying note 52.

[30] Crosskey 1015. Compare Madison, supra, note 27; Randolph and Marshall, supra, Chapter 2, text accompanying notes 54–55.

[31] Compare Crosskey 1088: "casually read" parts of the Convention records "give the impression that there were men in the Convention who simply assumed, as a matter of course, that the Supreme Court would have a complete and general right of judicial review against Congress."

Wilson's remarks. First, however, he has to dispose of Martin and Mason. Mason, defending Wilson's motion against Martin's objection that participation in the veto would give judges a "double negative," said that in their judicial capacity they could only "declare an unconstitutional act void. But with regard to *every* law however unjust or oppressive or pernicious, which did not come plainly under this description, they would be under the necessity as judges to give it a free course." Martin too had said that "Constitutionality of laws" would "come before the Judges in their proper official character."[32] "Vaguely general" is how Crosskey labels these remarks, but he concedes that they refer to judicial review in "general," that is, not restricted to "self-defense," "*if* taken in strict literality."[33] King had also stated immediately after Gerry that in "the expounding of those Laws when they come before them . . . they will no doubt stop the operation of such as shall appear repugnant to the Constitution."[34] Crosskey uncomfortably recognizes that King "is recorded, in this note, as having spoken of judicial review, *literally*, at large. Yet the subject was apparently mentioned by King, as it had been by Gerry, in connection with the judiciary's right to protect its own peculiar constitutional prerogatives."[35] This warps the facts, for both Gerry and King spoke "in connection" with judicial participation in the Council veto which knew no limits, and while Gerry described the separate judicial function in "self-defense" shorthand, King did not follow his lead but spoke of the judicial role in ordinary, comprehensive terms.[36] If strict literality has any play at all, it cannot

[32] 2 Farrand 76, 78 (emphasis added).
[33] Crosskey 1017. Crosskey's attempts to show that Martin's and Mason's remarks cannot be taken "literally" were considered supra, Chapter 3, text accompanying notes 47, 48, 50.
[34] 1 Farrand 109.
[35] Crosskey 1014.
[36] Gorham, on the other hand, did follow Wilson's reference to judicial "self-defense," 2 Farrand 73. But Gorham renewed his objection to judicial participation in the veto because "Judges ought to carry into the exposition of the laws no prepossessions with regard to them." 2 Farrand 79. Since the veto was to embrace *all* laws, and since Gorham did not suggest that judicial participation should be excluded only when laws invaded judicial prerogatives, he may be taken to imply that judges should "expound" all laws free of "prepossessions with regard to them."
  Crosskey 1016, also argues that Madison was in "hearty agreement with the sentiments Wilson had urged" respecting "self-defense." The remarks of Madison that are quoted supra, note 22, and infra, text accompanying note 38 plainly run beyond "self-defense." See also supra, Chapter 2, text accompanying notes 126–128.

be used to advance a pet argument—"self-defense"—and blandly ignored to cut down King's unfavorable language. Such a double standard is plainly objectionable. Commonly words are given their ordinary, "literal" meaning unless that conduces to an absurd or unreasonable result. No absurdity results from reading Mason, King, and Martin literally; it does result when the "self-defense" allusions are read with "strict literality." And rejection of that absurdity is confirmed by other remarks of Wilson and Gerry.

In truth, the *Records* overwhelmingly confute Crosskey's evocation of a "general understanding" that judicial review was to be limited to "self-defense." Because it is high time that the "self-defense" theory be decently interred, I shall set out the proof in further detail. The debate on judicial participation in the Conciliar negative, which precipitated the "self-defense" remarks, shows that both the negative and judicial participation ran not merely to protection of judicial prerogatives but to *all* laws. Ellsworth urged that

> The aid of the Judges will give more wisdom & firmness to the Executive. They will possess a systematic and accurate knowledge of the Laws, which the Executive can not be expected always to possess. The law of Nations also will frequently come into question. Of this the Judges alone will have competent information.[37]

Madison considered that the Wilson motion

> would be useful to the Executive, by inspiring additional confidence & firmness in exerting the revisionary power. It would be useful to the Legislature by the valuable assistance it would give in preserving a consistency, conciseness, perspecuity and technical propriety in the laws, qualities peculiarly necessary, and yet shamefully wanting in our Republican Codes. It would moreover be useful to the Community at large as an additional check agst. a pursuit of those unwise and unjust measures which constituted so great a portion of our calamities.[38]

[37] 2 Farrand 73–74.
[38] 2 Farrand 74. Rebutting fears of judicial prepossessions as a result of participation in the Council of Revision, Madison said, "a small portion of the laws coming in question before a judge wd. be such wherein he had been consulted . . . How much good . . . wd. proceed from . . . the systematic character wch. the Code of Law wd. receive from the Judiciary talents." 1 Farrand 138–139.

Mason concurred because the provision

> would give a confidence to the Executive [who could veto *all* laws], which he would not otherwise have, and without which the Revisionary power would be of little avail."[39]

Martin argues that "the confidence of the people" in the "Supreme Judiciary" "will soon be lost, if they are employed in the task of remonstrating agst. popular measures of the Legislature."[40] Summarizing the issues, Gouverneur Morris said,

> Some check being necessary on the Legislature, the question is in what hands should it be lodged. On one side it was contended that the Executive alone ought to exercise it . . . On the other side it was urged that he ought to be reinforced by the Judiciary department . . . It has been said that the Legislature ought to be relied on as the proper Guardian of liberty. The answer was short and conclusive. Either bad laws will be pushed or not. On the latter supposition no check will be wanted. On the former a strong check will be necessary. And this is the proper supposition.[41]

He "could not agree that the Judiciary . . . should be bound to say that a direct violation of the Constitution was law."[42] Mason stated that the Congress

> must be expected frequently to pass unjust and pernicious laws. This restraining [Revisionary] power was therefore essentially necessary . . . It had been said (by Mr. L. Martin) that if the Judges were joined in this check on the laws, they would have a double negative, since in their expository capacity of Judges they would have one negative ["to declare an unconstitutional law void"] . . . He wished the further use to be made of the Judges, of giving aid in preventing *every* improper law. Their aid will be the more valuable as they are in the habit & practice of considering laws in their true principles, and in all their consequences.[43]

---

[39] 2 Farrand 74; see also supra, note 22.
[40] 2 Farrand 77.
[41] Id. at 75–76.
[42] Quoted more fully supra, Chapter 3, text accompanying note 87.
[43] 2 Farrand 78.

These statements so clearly bespeak a *general* Revisionary power over *all* unconstitutional laws, in which Judges were to participate, as to render detailed explication redundant.

A few similar statements may be summarily noted: Dickinson referred "to the power of the Judges to set aside the law."[44] Spaight criticized a judicial negative "on proceedings of the Legislature."[45] Yates affirmed that "the supreme court are authorized in the last resort to determine what is the extent of the powers of Congress."[46] Hamilton stated that every legislative act contrary to authority would be declared void by the courts.[47] The statements of Ellsworth,[48] Baldwin,[49] and Randolph[50] are equally uncluttered by references to "self-defense." Those who wrote about judicial review prior to Ratification—Lee,[51] the "Centinel,"[52] and Hanson[53]—also referred to "any law." It suffices to allude to the similar expressions in the Ratification conventions by Adams,[54] McKean,[55] Steele,[56] Patrick Henry,[57] Pendleton,[58] and Nicholas.[59] Grayson said in Virginia that the courts are "the best check we have. They secure us from encroachments on *our* privileges."[60] Marshall stated that judges would declare void "a law not warranted" by the enumerated powers—"to what [other] quarter will *you* look for protection,"[61] Finally, Madison, in proposing the Bill of Rights in the First Congress, stated that courts will "be an impenetrable bulwark against *every* assumption of power in the Legislature."[62] Needless to say, no one challenged such

[44] Supra, Chapter 3, text accompanying note 82.
[45] Id. at note 166.
[46] Id. at note 187.
[47] Id. at notes 226–229.
[48] Id. at note 232.
[49] Id. at note 234.
[50] Id. at notes 237, 259; and Chapter 4, text accompanying note 117.
[51] Supra, Chapter 3, text accompanying note 179.
[52] Supra, Chapter 3, note 191.
[53] Supra, Chapter 3, note 194.
[54] Supra, Chapter 4, text accompanying note 30.
[55] Id. at note 37.
[56] Id. at note 79.
[57] Id. at notes 110–111.
[58] Id. at notes 116–117.
[59] Id. at note 118.
[60] Id. at note 128 (emphasis added).
[61] Id. at note 123 (emphasis added).
[62] 1 *Ann. Cong.* 457 (emphasis added). Hamilton made "magnificently plain that the institution [of judicial review] exists for the protection of the people and not of the judges." Hart, Book Review 1482. See Tucker, quoted supra, Chapter

statements on the ground that judicial review must be limited to "self-defense," and one may hazard that such a challenge would have been laughed out of court by those who harbored intense suspicions that Congress would invade private rights. In sum, the theory that judicial review was designed to be limited to "self-defense" is a 20th century construct, resting upon an overmagnification of a few shorthand expressions which, in the case of Gerry and Wilson, is repudiated by their own statements, and which does violence to the "general understanding" of those who framed and adopted the Constitution.

PROHIBITIONS ALONE ARE REVIEWABLE

Perhaps the most searching intelligence that has been brought to bear on the subject of judicial review was that of Edward Corwin. In studies stretching over a period of thirty-five years, Corwin substantially contributed to our understanding of how judicial review developed, bringing to the surface complexities that a mere nose-count would overlook. At one time a protagonist of the conventional view, his adherence shrank sharply after New Deal legislation was laid low by the Four Horsemen,[63] illustrating once again that scholarship is not altogether immune from the strains of contemporary events. It is not proposed to tax Corwin with inconsistency but rather to inquire whether some of his influential opinions are solidly rooted, for they seemed to Professor Alan Westin, in his 1962 resurvey of the field, to require consideration thus far withheld.[64] To one who examines Corwin's analysis after immersion in the historical materials, it often seems oversubtle, tending to import into the 1787 debate the refined reflections after the fact of a 20th century

---

2, note 53. "Individual liberty" was the "real reason" for judicial review. Supra, Chapter 2, text accompanying note 57; and see id. at notes 41–56.

[63] In 1934 he stated, "I have no hesitation in avowing a sympathetic interest in the larger features of the New Deal." Corwin, *Twilight of the Supreme Court*, xxvii; and his 1938 volume was admittedly "an effort to treat the role of the Supreme Court in relation to Congress in the fresh perspective afforded by the New Deal." Corwin, *Court Over* vii. Cf. supra, Chapter 3, notes 115, 162. Compare too his astringent 1913 review of Beard, supra, Chapter 3, text accompanying notes 269–301, with his 1914 *Doctrine of Judicial Review*, quoted supra, id. at 266–268; and his 1925 "Progress of Constitutional Theory"; and compare the latter two with his 1938 *Court Over Constitution*, and his 1937 testimony before Congress, quoted supra, Chapter 3, note 312.

[64] Westin 29–30. The points mentioned by Westin are those raised by Corwin.

political scientist. And he seems prone to build too heavily on short-hand expressions, to resort to convenient, particular illustrations of broad general principles in the debates which are not necessarily restrictive and afford an uncertain footing for firm deductions as to the narrowing intent of the Founders. One example of this tendency—his theory that some of the Framers conceived of judicial review as limited to defense of judicial prerogatives—has already been shown to have very slight basis.

When Corwin gave voice to his theory of "self-defense," he also stated that "there were those who apparently confined judicial review to the enforcement of direct *prohibitions* in the Constitution on Congress." And he went so far as to conclude, in reliance on certain remarks of Hamilton, Davie, and Madison, that the "arising under" clause is *confined* to "cases arising in consequence of direct transgressions of specific *prohibitions* of the Constitution."[65] Although this view is deprived of practical effect by his conclusion that, by reserving to the States powers not delegated to the United States, the Tenth Amendment in effect furnished "words of prohibition against those powers being exceeded *lest state powers be invaded*," thereby furnishing a textual basis for the "whole principle of ultra vires,"[66] clarification is required not only in the interest of history but because it serves to illustrate a recurrent flaw in Corwin's judgment.

Although Yates's broad view of the "arising under" clause would have supported Hamilton's argument for judicial review in *Federalist* 78, says Corwin, "Hamilton rejected it for a much narrower conception, which he sets forth in Federalist 80, as follows: 'All the restrictions upon the authority of the *state* legislatures furnish examples of it. They are not, for instance, to emit paper money; but the interdiction results from the Constitution, and will have no connection with any law of the United States.'"[67] Hamilton was

---

[65] Corwin, *Court Over* 2, 37–38.

[66] Id. at 54–55. The Corwin inference seems farfetched. The Tenth Amendment merely nailed down the earlier assurances that the federal government was one of "enumerated" powers and underlined the corollary that powers not delegated remained in the States or the people. See supra, Chapter, 5, note 23. In making the implicit explicit, the Amendment did not convert nonenumeration into "prohibition." On its face the Amendment differentiates between powers "not delegated to the United States" "nor prohibited . . . to the States," indicating that the draftsmen were mindful of the difference.

[67] Corwin, *Court Over* 36 (emphasis added).

addressing himself to the question "what is meant by 'cases arising under the Constitution,' in contradistinction from those 'arising under the laws of the United States?'" And he added, after the Corwin quotation, that controversies respecting *State* emission of paper money "would be cases arising under the Constitution and not the laws of the United States."[68] Because Hamilton mentioned one "for instance" to explain this "contradistinction," Corwin in effect concludes that other instances were excluded. Yet Corwin perceived that Hamilton's remark was "meant to be illustrative rather than exclusive," but this was merely because "it would be strange" if a *Congressional* Act "violative of a direct prohibition of the Constitution" would not likewise give rise to a case "arising under this Constitution."[69] If, however, the remark is thus "illustrative" for one purpose, it becomes essential to advance reasons for transforming it into "exclusive" for all other purposes, a task which Corwin did not undertake. In fact, it would be even more "strange" if after elaborately explaining judicial review in broadest terms in *Federalist* 78, Hamilton should have chosen in *Federalist* 80 to scuttle that analysis merely by resort to an "illustration" for a special purpose. To select only two immediately relevant remarks: Hamilton said in No. 78 that "the courts were designed . . . among other things to keep the [legislature] within the limits assigned to their authority," and in his discussion of agency principles he derided the notion that those who act under delegation "may do not only what their powers do not authorize, but what they forbid."[70] Before we impute to Hamilton a repudiation of his carefully-framed No. 78 analysis, we should have something more solid to rest on than a subsequent "illustration" which Corwin demonstrates is not "exclusive." Corwin himself stated in 1938 that Congress

was presented by the advocates of the Constitution . . . as a legislature of delegated powers . . . It was, therefore, entirely legitimate for Hamilton to argue in the *Federalist* . . . to the

[68] *Federalist* No. 80 at 520.

[69] Corwin, *Court Over* 36. Mason took for granted that the federal courts were given "express power" to deal with prohibited *Congressional* ex post facto laws. Quoted, supra, Chapter 4, text accompanying note 119.

[70] *Federalist* No. 78 at 506. Compare Hamilton's restatement in No. 81 of his rejection in No. 78 of the view that Congress could be left to judge of its own powers. See infra, note 192 and infra, text accompanying note 155.

effect that the grants of power to Congress implied limitations which were judicially construable *no less* than the *prohibitions* on those grants . . . in short, for judicial review of unlimited scope.[71]

So the "advocates" later assured the Ratification conventions.

Davie is merely cited by Corwin, and it is true that Davie also employed an illustration of restrictions on States in discussing the "arising under" clause in North Carolina.[72] But his illustration no more carries an "exclusive" connotation than that of Hamilton. He had opened by saying that the "judiciary ought to be competent to the decision of *any* question arising out of the Constitution itself . . . that the judicial power should be coextensive with the legislative." On this note he closed: "It is therefore absolutely necessary that the judiciary should have jurisdiction in *all* cases arising under the Constitution. Surely there should be somewhere a constitutional authority for carrying into execution constitutional provisions; otherwise . . . they would be a dead letter."[73] He would not have dared in North Carolina to assert a judicial duty to give unquestioning effect to all Congressional Acts that were not expressly prohibited, for his allies repeatedly assured the convention that "Congress cannot travel beyond [the Constitution's] bounds," that every law "repugnant" to the Constitution would be void.[74] Governor Johnston told the doubters that the legislature cannot "assume any other powers than those expressly given them, without a palpable violation of the Constitution."[75] Davie himself had prevailed on the North Carolina court in *Bayard v. Singleton* to hold that a state statute was unconstitutional[76] in a situation that did not arise out of an express "prohibition." There he had argued that "the Assembly had clearly exceeded the limits of the power which the people . . . delegated to their representatives . . . and that an act so illegally

[71] Corwin, *Court Over* 21.

[72] 4 Elliot 156.

[73] Id. at 156, 158 (emphasis added).

[74] 4 Elliot 63–64, 188, 185, 161; and see supra, Chapter 4, text accompanying notes 69–98.

[75] 4 Elliot 142; and see supra, Chapter 2, note 29.

[76] Supra, Chapter 2, text accompanying notes 142–144. In 1938 Corwin classified Davie as a proponent of judicial review on the ground that as Iredell's co-counsel "he had urged the constitutional argument upon the court" in Bayard v. Singleton. Corwin, *Court Over* 31, 24 n. 22.

passed, was not to be looked on as a law."[77] His associate, Iredell, stated in the convention that "The question . . . will always be whether Congress has exceeded its authority."[78] The facts do not sustain Corwin's classification of Davie as one who "confined judicial review to the enforcement of direct prohibitions in the Constitution on the Congress."

Remains Corwin's citation of Madison: "That causes of a federal nature will arise, will be obvious to every gentleman who will recollect that the states are laid under restrictions." But Madison went on to say: "With respect to the laws of the Union, it is so necessary that the judicial power should correspond with the legislative that it has not been objected to. With respect to treaties, there is a peculiar propriety in the judiciary's expounding them."[79] "Exposition" of treaties was not tied to an express prohibition of State violations. From the "peculiar propriety" of "expounding" of treaties we may infer that courts were also to "expound" the "laws"; and "exposition," as was earlier shown, implicated unrestricted judicial review.[80] The "correspondence" of judicial to legislative power, R. H. Lee had explained to Virginia, meant the "power of deciding finally on the laws of the Union."[81] The fact that no one objected in

[77] Meigs, *Relation* 114.
[78] 4 Elliot 179; see also supra, Chapter 3, text accompanying note 168. It needs to be borne in mind that Corwin merely stated that *some* of the Framers "apparently confined judicial review to the enforcement of direct *prohibitions* in the Constitution." He also said, however, that "there were those who claimed for the Court the right to read the Constitution for itself, including the *grants* of power to Congress." Corwin, *Court Over* 2. To mention only a few examples, Wilson stated that if any Congressional Act should be "inconsistent with those powers vested by this instrument in Congress, the judges, as a consequence of their independence, and the particular powers of government being defined, will declare such laws to be null and void." 2 Elliot 489. Maclaine said in the North Carolina convention that "If Congress should make a law beyond the power and spirit of the Constitution, should we not say to Congress, 'you have no authority to make this law. There are limits beyond which you cannot go.'" 4 Elliot 161. Adams said in the Massachusetts convention that the courts would adjudge void "any" federal law "extended beyond the power granted by the proposed Constitution." 2 Elliot 131. And Marshall told the Virginia convention that were Congress to "go beyond the delegated powers," "to make a law not warranted by any of the powers enumerated," the courts would "declare it void." 3 Elliot 553. This was likewise the view of Martin, who opposed the Constitution, but understood the judicial power to extend both to Acts "*contrary to*, or not *warranted* by the Constitution." 3 Farrand 220.
[79] 3 Elliot 532.
[80] Supra, Chapter 3, text accompanying notes 31-38.
[81] Ford, *Pamphlets* 279, 306-307.

the Virginia convention to judicial review of Congressional Acts confirms that Lee's reading of the "correspondence," to borrow Madison's phrase, "ha[d] not been objected too." Then too, Madison spoke after his confrere, Nicholas, had said that the judges were to determine "the extent of legislative powers," and he was shortly followed by Marshall, who declared that the judges would declare void a law that went "beyond the delegated powers."[82] If Madison sought to win the Virginia convention to a more restricted view, he went about it in remarkably obscure and elliptical fashion. It is unnecessary to recapitulate the earlier comprehensive analysis of Madison's several remarks,[83] the sum of which he epitomized in proposing the Bill of Rights to the First Congress: the courts will "be an impregnable bulwark against *every* assumption of power in the Legislative."[84] Like Corwin's companion theory of "self-defense," his theory that *some* proponents of judicial review envisaged it *solely* in terms of policing express constitutional "prohibitions" (illustrated by references to States) rests on very flimsy evidence.

THE CONSTITUTION AS "LAW"

The "weakest link" in the Hamiltonian "syllogism," said Corwin, if I understand him rightly, is the proposition that the "Constitution is law," "fundamental law."[85] If the Constitution "was law," he stated, "it was so in virtue of having been *enacted* by *lawmaking* power; but *whose* lawmaking power? Hamilton's answer was that the Constitution was an act of *popular legislation*. The people themselves, he urged, were the *supreme* legislators, while the ordinary legislators comprised 'mere agents' of the people." True, Corwin said, the people were the "authors," but once they "completed their task they lapsed back . . . save on election days . . . into the every day government, and *especially into the legislative assembly*."[86] Or, as he more vigorously stated upon an earlier occasion, the people

[82] Supra, Chapter 4, text accompanying notes 118, 123.
[83] Supra, Chapter 3, text accompanying notes 126–154.
[84] 1 *Ann. Cong.* 457 (emphasis added).
[85] Corwin, *Court Over* 9–12. Roughly to paraphrase Corwin, that syllogism is: 1. interpretation of the Constitution is the peculiar province of the judges; 2. the Constitution is "law" and "fundamental law"; 3. the judicial version of the law is "the law"; 4. accordingly the function of keeping the legislature within bounds falls to the courts. Id. at 8; cf. Corwin, 9 *Mich. L. Rev.* 107.
[86] Corwin, *Court Over* 10–11.

then "passed out of existence, save as a highly artificial concept," and the "right to *govern* . . . was recoverable by the people only by another act of revolution."[87] In sum, "The power of *enacting* laws . . . was a function of *government*. How then could constitutions . . . the work of the people themselves, be regarded as laws in the strict sense of the term?"[88] So that Hamilton's statement that the legislature comprised "mere agents" of the people who could not " 'substitute their *will* to that of their constituents,' departed radically from what until that time had been practically universal opinion. The *representatives* of the people *were* the people—that is what representation meant."[89]

Corwin offers his interpretation as an attempted version of the 1787 meaning of the Hamiltonian terms in order to avoid the risks of importing the meaning they have for us today,[90] but his version seems highly artificial and debatable at every step. The "constituents" had expressed their "will" in a Constitution, and according to Vattel's widely-accepted apothegm, the "legislators" could not "change it without destroying their authority."[91] As Iredell said in 1786, "The people have chosen to be governed under such and such principles. They have not chosen to be governed or promised to submit upon any other."[92] It is therefore not easy to grasp why the Hamiltonian proposition that the legislative agents "could not substitute their will" for that of their constituents "departed radically" from "universal opinion."[93] Suppose too, contrary to the fact, that

[87] Corwin, 9 *Mich. L. Rev.* 108; Corwin, *Doctrine* 34.

[88] Corwin, *Doctrine* 34. Corwin found "uncertainty" whether early state "constitutions possessed the force of law." Ibid.

[89] Corwin, *Court Over* 12–13. Earlier Corwin said, "The greatest obstacle to the establishment of judicial review" was "the doctrine of legislative sovereignty" resting on the "assumption that the legislature not merely *represents* but *is* the people." Corwin, 9 *Mich. L. Rev.* 306.

[90] Corwin, 9 *Mich. L. Rev.* 107–108.

[91] See supra, Chapter 2, text accompanying note 92; and see id. notes 93, 95. Madison said in the Convention, "it would be a novel and dangerous doctrine—that a Legislative could change the constitution under which it held its existence." 2 Farrand 92–93. Haines 71–72, states that it was "frequently enacted that no part of the constitution should be altered, changed or abolished by the legislature," citing the Maryland constitution, 3 F. N. Thorpe, *Constitutions and Charters, 1690–1691* (1909).

[92] 2 McRee 146.

[93] In his 1785 "Memorial and Remonstrance Against Religious Assessment," Madison stated that "the Legislative Body" "are but the creatures and vice regents" of "the society at large." 2 Madison, *Writings* 185. Compare the view of Locke, quoted infra, text accompanying note 105.

the people "passed out of existence" after constitution-making, it by no means follows that what they had done prior thereto was not "lawmaking." Blackstone, to whom critics of judicial review look for a mirror of 1787 opinion, defined "law" as a "rule of civil conduct prescribed by the supreme power in a state."[94] Although Blackstone did not consider the making of a written constitution, he posited that "in a democracy" the "right of making laws resides in the people at large."[95] At the moment of constitution-making, the people was the "supreme power"; and in laying down *rules* for the exercise of delegated power which the legislature could not change, that is, which it was bound to observe, the people, in Hamilton's sturdy common-sense expression, were the "supreme legislators" and were making "law" in the Blackstonian sense. Corwin himself notices a statement by Madison in the Convention which "quite clearly attributes a law-making capacity to the people at large."[96]

For the theory that the legislature "not merely *represents* but *is* the people," Corwin cited Luther Martin's statement to Maryland after the Convention. Martin had opposed submission of the Constitution directly to the people rather than to the State legislatures, and now he argued that ratification was a function of State governments because "once the people have *exercised their power in establishing and forming themselves* into a State government, it *never devolves* back to them, nor have they a *right* to *resume* or *again to exercise that power*, until such events take place as will amount to a *dissolution* of their State governments."[97] If his theory had represented "the practically universal opinion,"[98] it was repudiated by

[94] 1 Bl. 44.
[95] 1 Bl. 49.
[96] Corwin, *Court Over* 32; 2 Farrand 92–93. There are statements by Justices Wilson and Blair, both Framers, on Circuit, that "in Congress the *whole* legislative power of the United States is not vested. An important part of that power was exercised by the people themselves, when they ordained and established the constitution." Hayburn's Case, 2 Dallas 408, 411 (1792). The matter-of-fact tone of this utterance indicates that Wilson and Blair thought it no "radical departure."
[97] Corwin is quoted supra, note 89. Citations to Martin in Corwin, *Doctrine* 107, 35 n. 49; 3 Farrand 230.
[98] Corwin, *Court Over* 13. In his American edition of Blackstone, vol. 1 at 193 (1803), Professor and Judge St. George Tucker quoted 1 Burgh's *Political Disquisition* 202,

> When we elect persons to represent us in Parliament, we must not be supposed to depart from the smallest right which we have deposited with them. We make a lodgment, not a gift; we *entrust*, but *part with* nothing. And, were

the Convention by a vote of 9 to 1.[99] On Martin's theory, a people "disgusted" with "omnipotent" state legislatures,[100] who, in Jefferson's vivid phrase, had concluded that "An elective despotism was not the government we fought for,"[101] would now rivet upon themselves precisely such a despotism, removable only by a second Revolution. Under the circumstances his appeal to an irrevocable devolution of power bordered on the fatuous, and not surprisingly was stunningly rejected even by his own State of Maryland.[102] True it is that Ellsworth alluded in the Convention to the fact that "a new set of ideas" had "crept in";[103] but his own State of Connecticut voted nonetheless with the nine to override the Martin view.[104] New or not, the people demonstrated that they, not their representatives, were, and meant to remain, monarch.

That determination could rest upon Locke who, as Blackstone owned, held that

there remains still inherent in the people a supreme power to remove or alter the legislative, when they find the legislative act contrary to the trust reposed in them; for, when such trust is abused, it is thereby forfeited, and devolves to those who gave it.[105]

Blackstone, to be sure, argued that this was impractical because "devolution of power" requires nothing less than a "dissolution of

---

it possible that they should attempt to destroy that constitution which we had appointed them to maintain, they can no more be held in the rank of representatives than a factor turned pirate can continue to be called a factor of those merchants whose goods he had plundered.

In this is reflected the view of Locke, infra, text accompanying note 105; and Tucker comments, "However inadmissible this doctrine may be in Great Britain, it seems perfectly adapted to the principles of our government." Ibid. Compare Iredell's remarks in 1786 about the establishment of the North Carolina constitution, supra, Chapter 2, text accompanying note 133.

[99] 2 Farrand 93–94. Mason said in the Convention that "The legislatures have no power to ratify it [the Constitution]. They are the mere creatures of the State Constitutions . . . Whither then must we resort? To the people with whom all the power remains." 2 Farrand 88. See also Maclaine, 4 Elliot 161 ("all power is in the people, not in the state governments").

[100] Corwin, quoted supra, Chapter 3, text accompanying notes 311–312.

[101] Quoted supra, Chapter 2, text accompanying note 8; and see Iredell, quoted supra, id. at note 133.

[102] Van Doren 207–208.

[103] Corwin, *Court Over* 11; 2 Farrand 91.

[104] 2 Farrand 94.

[105] 1 Bl. 162.

the whole form of government established by the people."[106] Not Blackstone but Locke was the lodestar of the Founders, as a number of statements plainly demonstrate. Wilson told the Pennsylvania convention that "absolute and uncontrollable power *remains* with the people," and that they "meant not . . . to part with it to any government whatsoever," and may change the constitution whenever and however they please."[107] Madison stated in the Convention that the "people were in fact, the fountain of all power . . . They could alter constitutions as they pleased."[108] There too, Mason insisted that "all power remains" with the people,[109] as did Maclaine in North Carolina.[110] Iredell stated in North Carolina that "Those in power are [the] servants and agents" of the people, and that "the people, without their consent, may new-model their government whenever they think proper, not merely because it is oppressively exercised, but because they think another form will be more conducive to their welfare."[111] When the "people" met in the several Ratification conventions to adopt the Constitution, which curtailed State legislative powers, they gave proof that this was a basic tenet of the nascent democracy. By the Article V machinery for amendment, the people made explicit their retention of power, freedom to alter the Constitution, and rejection of any notion that they had "passed out of existence."

If adaptation of the common law principle of agency to public law was indeed "radical,"[112] it was not the exclusive Hamiltonian innovation painted by Corwin. It had found expression in Article V of the Massachusetts constitution of 1780: "All power residing originally in the people, and being derived from them, the several magistrates and officers of government, vested with authority, whether legislative, executive or judicial, are their substitutes and agents, and are at all times accountable to them."[113] Lee told the

106 Ibid.
107 2 Elliot 456, 432.
108 2 Farrand 476.
109 2 Farrand 88.
110 4 Elliot 161.
111 Id. at 9; see also Madison, supra note 93.
112 The transition from the Roman law of mandate via Vattel et al. to the theory that legislatures were "agents" of the people merits further study. See supra, Chapter 2, note 34.
113 F. N. Thorp, *Constitutions and Charters, 1890* (1909). This too weighs against Corwin's view that the "people passed out of existence" after forming a constitution. Supra, text accompanying note 87.

Virginia convention, "It would be an insult upon common sense to suppose that the agent could legally transact any business for his principal which was not contained in the commission whereby the powers were delegated."[114] Power, said Wilson in Pennsylvania, *"remains* with the people . . . They can delegate it in such proportions, to such bodies, on such terms, and with such limitations, as they think proper."[115] In North Carolina Iredell stated that "Those in power are . . . servants and agents" of the people, and was joined by Maclaine, who said that "all power is in the people" who can "delegate power to agents," and consequently the people could say to Congress "You cannot exceed the power prescribed by the Constitution,"[116] all of which, parenthetically, is at war with the concept of a people who had "passed out of existence." Charles Pinckney said in South Carolina that power "is delegated" by the people "to their officers" who are "servants of the people."[117] It was not therefore Hamilton alone who "contended" that the legislature "comprise 'mere agents' of the people";[118] proponents of adoption reassured the doubters met in the Ratification conventions that power merely was being delegated and that the delegates, like every agent, could be compelled to stay within bounds.[119]

Let us turn to the concept that a constitution is "fundamental law." That concept was expressed in the Massachusetts Circular Letter of 1768, which stated that a man's right to his property is an "unalterable right . . . ingrafted into the British Constitution, as a fundamental law."[120] Jefferson unhesitatingly identified a constitution with "law" in 1782. Chafing at some "very capital defects" in the Virginia constitution, in his *Notes on Virginia,* among them the fact that the legislature could supersede any provision of the constitution by legislative enactment, Jefferson explained that such

---

[114] 3 Elliot 186.

[115] 2 Elliot 456.

[116] 2 Elliot 9, 161.

[117] 4 Elliot 319.

[118] Corwin, *Court Over* 12. "All in all, Hamilton is to be understood as a man who subscribed, for the most part uncritically, to the 'conventional wisdom' of his generation about constitutions and constitutionalism." Rossiter, *Hamilton* 187.

[119] See also White's statement, supra, Chapter 4, text accompanying note 18.

[120] Quoted Haines 60–61. For claims in 1628 and in 1654 that the rights of Englishmen were protected by "fundamental law," see infra, Appendix A, note 44. Coke spoke of Magna Charta as "ancient, fundamental law." 2 *Inst.* 51. Compare id. at 47, 75. Cf. James Otis' appeal to "fundamental principles of the British Constitution" in 1764, supra, Chapter 2, note 85.

defects resulted from the formation of the constitution when Virginia was "new and unexperienced in the science of government."[121] And he called for a "convention to fix the constitution, to amend its defects, and to bind up the several branches of government by certain [that is, fixed] *laws*, which, when they transgress, their acts shall become nullities; to render unnecessary an appeal to the people."[122] Jefferson was too schooled in political science to be charged with ignorance that contemporary opinion rejected the concept of a constitution as "law," and his easy identification of the two speaks volumes against Corwin's attempted dichotomy. Iredell regarded the identification as undeniable: "It will not be denied, I suppose, that the Constitution *is a law of the State,* as well as an act of Assembly, with this difference only, that it is the *fundamental law,* and unalterable by the legislature."[123] For those who accepted Vattel's maxim that a legislature could not "change" the constitution, it was nothing if not "fundamental."[124] What Jefferson and Iredell made explicit was implicit in the numerous assurances that the federal powers were "limited," for such assurances were meaningful only on the assumption that the "limits" *must* be observed.[125] For it is the essence of "law" that it must be obeyed. Prominent 1787 contemporaries were thus apparently unaware of the doctrinal obstacles which Corwin found strewn in their path, and no mention of such obstacles is to be found in the course of the debate on the Article VI provision that the Constitution shall be the "supreme law of the land."

121 Jefferson, *Writings* 225–227, 222.
122 Id. at 235.
123 2 McRee 148. This was in North Carolina in 1786. Writing in New York in 1788, *before* Hamilton made his "radical" statement, Yates said, "it will not be denied that the constitution is the highest or supreme law." Corwin, *Court Over* 245–246. "It will not be denied" suggests a familiar concept; but if it was an innovation it had caught on with astonishing rapidity.
124 In a letter to John Adams, February 23, 1787, Jefferson wrote, "It has accordingly been the decision of our courts that the [Articles of] Confederation is a part of the law of the land, and superior to the ordinary laws, because it cannot be altered by the legislature of any one state." Corwin, 9 *Mich. L. Rev.* 116. If his understanding of the cases may not reflect the actual holdings, it is significant that he entertained the view with sufficient seriousness to impart it to Adams.
125 In 1910, Corwin, 9 *Mich. L. Rev.* 104, stated that "all the literary evidence goes to establish the idea of legislative power as limited upon a foundation entirely independent of American colonial history, upon the foundation, to wit, of the idea of fundamental law. This idea reaches back far beyond Magna Charta."

WHO WAS TO INTERPRET THE CONSTITUTION?

Suppose that in 1787 the Constitution was thought to be "law," the question then arises, who was to "interpret" it. Today we take for granted that the interpretive function falls to the courts, what Corwin labels the "juristic" doctrine. Apparently, however, he considers that in 1787 there were competing doctrines: the "naive" doctrine, roughly that every man may interpret the Constitution for himself, and the "departmental" doctrine, that each Department was authorized to interpret the Constitution for itself.[126] For present purposes these "doctrines" are of interest only to the extent that they influenced the thinking of the Founders about judicial review, and of such influence there is virtually no trace. Corwin's citations to statements by Parsons and Steele on a closely related matter[127] do not fill the gap.

The "naive" doctrine, states Corwin, is illustrated by the statement that "nobody is bound by an unconstitutional law." Either "this means that everybody—*including judges*—has an equal right to determine what laws he is bound by, or else it means that nobody is bound by a law which has been held to be unconstitutional *by a proper authority,* which of course leaves the essential question of the location of such authority undetermined."[128] Parsons stated in the Massachusetts convention that "an act of usurpation is not obligatory; it is not law; and any man may be justified in his resistance."[129] Everybody has a preliminary right to determine that he will not obey an unconstitutional law,[130] but Parsons scarcely regarded the individual judgment as "final." Nor was he in doubt as to the "proper authority," for he stated that if in consequence of resistance the government brought a criminal prosecution, a jury of the defendant's "own fellow citizens will pronounce him innocent," in a word that the "final" answer would be supplied through resort to judicial machinery.

In an atmosphere charged with fear of centralized "tyranny" the right of "resistance" was often mentioned, but, it is safe to conclude,

[126] Corwin, *Court Over* 4–8; Corwin, *Doctrine* 19–21.
[127] Corwin, *Doctrine* 20 n. 33.
[128] Corwin, *Court Over* 5; Corwin, *Doctrine* 19–20.
[129] 2 Elliot 94.
[130] See Wilson, infra text accompanying note 136.

only as a last resort should judicial review prove unavailing. James Varnum made this quite plain in 1786:

> *But as the legislature is the supreme power in government,* who is to judge whether they have violated the constitutional right of the people?—I answer . . . whenever they attempt to enslave the people, and carry their attempts into execution, *the people themselves will judge, as the only last resort in the last stages of oppression.* But when they [the legislature] proceed no farther than merely to enact what they may call laws, *and refer those laws to the Judiciary* Courts for determination, then (in the discharge of the great trust reposed in them, and to prevent the horrors of civil war, as in the present case) the judges can, and we trust your Honours will, decide upon them.[131]

McKean, also, told the Pennsylvania convention that the Congress should be restrained by the judges, by elections, and by "interposition of the Supreme Power of the People on necessary occasions."[132] What the "necessary occasion" meant was made clear by his co-worker Wilson: "If the error be in the legislature, it may be corrected by the constitution; if in the constitution, it may be corrected by the people"[133]—that is, the people would intervene only if the constitutional machinery proved inadequate for correction of the legislature, and Wilson, it is clear, believed judicial review would be adequate. In the North Carolina convention, Steele said, "If the Congress make laws inconsistent with the Constitution, independent judges will not uphold them, nor will the people obey them. A universal resistance will ensue."[134] When judges "will not uphold" unconstitutional laws, there is no occasion for "universal resistance."[135]

---

131 Quoted Boudin 62–63 n. 4.
132 McMaster & Stone 766.
133 2 Elliot 433.
134 4 Elliot 71.
135 Corwin views the Parsons and Steele statements as "basing judicial review on the right of revolution." Corwin, *Doctrine* 20 n. 33. But Parsons had prefaced his remarks by stating, "The people themselves have it in their power effectually to resist usurpation, without being driven to an appeal to arms." A resister, he said, could rely upon a jury to acquit him. 2 Elliot 94. Steele posited constitutional machinery, "Independent judges" who "will not uphold" laws inconsistent with the Constitution. Quoted supra, Chapter 4, text accompanying note 79. Judicial review, to my mind, was simply part of the machinery for keeping an "agent"

In so far as Corwin's "naive" doctrine derives from remarks such as Parsons' "any man may be justified in his resistance" to an unconstitutional law—for so the doctrine must be tested if we are not to substitute 20th century speculation for 1787 opinion—it needs little more than the similar remarks of Wilson and Iredell to expose its frailty. Wilson had stated in his 1791 Lectures that "Whoever would be obliged to obey a constitutional law, is justified in refusing to obey an unconstitutional act of the legislature—and that, when a question, even of this delicate nature, occurs, every one who is called to act, has a right to judge."[136] Nevertheless, Wilson was no advocate of the "naive" doctrine. Repeatedly he told the Pennsylvania convention that the courts would keep the legislature "within its prescribed bounds," that they would declare a law inconsistent with the Constitution to be "null and void."[137] It was the Judiciary, he said in his 1791 Lectures, that was the "noble guard against legislative despotism,"[138] and the "great and *last resort*," he told the Pennsylvania convention, was "the people themselves."[139] Iredell too had said in the North Carolina convention that "The people will resist if the government usurp powers not delegated to it."[140] But he did not therefore claim for everyman the right finally to determine the issue of constitutionality for himself, nor did he leave in doubt the "proper authority" for that determination. He had categorically opted for judicial review in 1786 and again in 1787, stating the "juristic" doctrine in its full sweep, and he had rejected "universal resistance" as a "dreadful expedient" because "people suffer a thousand injuries first" and because it requires "universal oppression."[141] Assuming therefore that an exposition of the "naive" doctrine was available to the Founders, there is virtually no evidence that it exerted a competing pull in their consideration of judicial review. Reiteration of everyman's right to resist an unconstitutional

---

within bounds. In setting up a Constitution, the Framers were not proceeding from a postulate of a "right of revolution" so much as from a premise of absolute power, only a part of which was being delegated.

[136] 1 J. Wilson, Works 186 (McCloskey ed. 1967).

[137] Quoted supra, Chapter 4, text accompanying notes 39–41.

[138] Quoted supra, Chapter 5, text accompanying note 30.

[139] Quoted supra, Chapter 4, text accompanying note 39 (emphasis added). See Nicholas' remark, supra, id. at note 118.

[140] 4 Elliot 185.

[141] 2 McRee 147; see also supra, Chapter 3, text accompanying note 168, and note 168; Chapter 4, notes 37, 81.

law, which to be effective must mount to "universal resistance," was merely an emphatic reassurance that in the *last resort* the people could call the shots.

The influence of the "departmental" doctrine on the thinking of the Founders is even more tenuous. Corwin states that "There is an early hint of this doctrine in Jefferson's Va. Notes which is criticized by Madison in Fed. No. 49."[142] Jefferson had remarked in 1782 that the coordinate departments could not pretend to an "exclusive or superior right of settling the boundaries between their respective powers" and accordingly recommended an "appeal to the people themselves."[143] In pointing out the impracticability of such "departmental" constructions, he was surely not fathering the "departmental" doctrine; and he at once dismissed the possibility in favor of an appeal to the people, which Madison in turn showed to be unfeasible.[144] In the same Virginia Notes Jefferson had called for "binding" the several branches by "certain," that is, fixed "laws" so that Acts which transgress such "laws" shall "become nullities, to render unnecessary an appeal to the people."[145] Soon Jefferson came to realize that "nullity" without a judiciary to declare it fell short. He wrote to Madison in 1787 that "In the arguments in favor of a declaration of rights, you omit one which has great weight with me, the legal check which it puts into the hands of the judiciary."[146] Since the Bill of Rights was largely addressed to limitations on Congress, this judicial "check" is incompatible with a "departmental" construction by Congress of its own powers. Apart from Jefferson's 1782 statement, Corwin cites only statements subsequent to 1800,[147] at a time when the judiciary was engulfed in bitter political strife,[148] and it cannot be assumed that such statements represent positions taken in 1787. So far as my search could develop,

[142] Corwin, *Doctrine* 66; Corwin, *Court Over* 7.

[143] Quoted *Federalist* No. 49 at 328.

[144] *Ibid.*

[145] Quoted supra, text accompanying note 122.

[146] 5 Jefferson, *Writings* 80–81. After the lines of battle with the Federalists had been drawn, Jefferson became an avowed adherent of "departmental" construction. Corwin, *Court Over* 70 n. 71. But changes of viewpoint under such political stresses should not color appraisal of the events of 1787.

[147] Corwin, *Doctrine* 66; Corwin, *Court Over* 70 n. 71.

[148] Warren, *Congress* 121–122, 125–126 (the struggle over repeal of the appointments of the "midnight judges"); Corwin, *Doctrine* 57. See supra, Chapter 3, note 76.

the only contemporary espousal of "departmental" construction was that of Madison in the course of the debate on the "removal" power in the First Congress.[149] But, as Corwin himself recorded, this "attempt to construe the Constitution" was vigorously protested "with the result that eventually Madison himself joined in support of a motion striking out the exceptionable clause.[150] Of course, every officer, including members of Congress, has the right to "interpret the Constitution preliminary" to taking action thereunder,[151] but in the "removal" debate it was repeatedly emphasized that this right was for *preliminary* purposes only and in no way binding on the courts.[152] In short, there is no evidence that the "departmental" doctrine played a significant role in the thinking of the Founders. Corwin himself stated that the "notion of a departmental right of constitutional construction takes its rise not from the effort to establish judicial review but from an attempt to overthrow it" after 1800.[153] And if what is meant by the "departmental" doctrine, he said in 1914, "is that the three departments have an equal right, when acting in their respective sphere, to determine the validity of their own acts, then it is untrue."[154] This was the view of Hamilton, who, in *Federalist* No. 78, rejected the notion that "the legislative body are themselves the judges of their own powers" and concluded that it was for the courts "to keep" the legislature "within the limits assigned to their authority."[155] Confirmation is furnished by the materials bearing on where the function of "interpreting" the Constitution was lodged.

[149] Supra, Chapter 5, text accompanying notes 2–23.

[150] Corwin, *Doctrine* 48. See supra, Chapter 5, text accompanying notes 2–23.

[151] Corwin, *Doctrine* 20–21; Corwin, *Court Over* 15.

[152] Supra, Chapter 5, text accompanying notes 10–15. Gerry, a Framer, said in the "removal" debate, "The people of America can never be safe, if Congress have a right to exercise the power of giving constructions to the constitution different from the original instrument. Such a power would render the most important clause in the Constitution [the Amendment provision] nugatory, and one without which, I will be bold to say, this system of Government would never have been ratified." 1 *Ann. Cong.* 523.

[153] Corwin, *Doctrine* 58, 21; cf. Corwin, *Court Over* 69–70.

[154] Corwin, *Doctrine* 21. Professor Westin, 20, states that Beard's operative term, "judicial control," "obscured" the problem arising from the "departmental interpretation." Beard was almost entirely concerned with the 1787 roots, in which context the "problem" arising from "departmental interpretation" was virtually nonexistent.

[155] *Federalist* No. 78 at 506, quoted more fully supra, Chapter 3, text accompanying note 226.

Before we conclude by the process of elimination that the task of interpreting the Constitution was lodged in the courts, we should, with Corwin, consider the practice of some early State legislatures, "in the exercise of a species of equity jurisdiction, to reverse decisions of the ordinary courts."[156] Hamilton's objection in *Federalist* No. 81 "that this practice was violative of the principle of the separation of powers," states Corwin, "crowded developments rather brusquely. Not for a generation yet did the interpretation of the principle thus invoked become a generally accepted part of the corpus of American constitutional law and theory."[157] It was not, I suggest, Hamilton who "crowded developments" but Corwin who failed to take account of antecedent events. True, some of the early legislatures reversed ordinary judicial decisions, but such practices were vigorously condemned by Jefferson in 1782, and by the Pennsylvania Council of Censors in 1783,[158] as part of a "constitutional reaction," which, in Corwin's words, "leaped suddenly to its climax in the Philadelphia Convention."[159] To balance early views that the function of interpretation was lodged in the lawmaker,[160] Corwin has shown that the idea that the legislature was excluded "from the business of judging" may be traced to Locke.[161] In 1786 Varnum maintained that "the judiciary have the sole power of judging of laws"; and Iredell stated in 1786 that "the power of judging rests with the courts,"[162] as did John Jay.[163]

[156] Corwin, *Court Over* 13–14.

[157] Ibid.

[158] Corwin, "Progress" 519–520. Both the Notes and the Council Report were summarized by Madison in *Federalist* No. 48 at 324–325.

[159] Corwin, *Doctrine* 37.

[160] Id. at 70.

[161] Corwin, "Progress" 524. "According to Coke's view the common law was the supreme law in the state, and the judges, unfettered and uncontrolled save by the law, were the sole exponents of this supreme law." Holdworth, *Some Makers of English Law* 115 (1938). In 1759 Governor Colden of New York condemned the attempted repeal of a law by one branch of the legislature as the exercise of "a Judicial power of declaring them void, a power which in no wise belonged to them." Quoted Meigs, *Relation* 42. Corwin, *Doctrine* 39 n. 60, cites a 1695 affirmation by the New York Governor that " 'Laws are to be interpreted by Judges' i.e. the judges alone." See also 1 Page Smith, *John Adams* 83.

[162] Quoted Corwin, *Progress* 526; 2 McRee 148–149.

[163] As Secretary of Foreign Affairs for the Confederation, Jay stated in 1786 that state legislatures are not "competent authoritatively to decide on or ascertain the construction of" treaties. The meaning of a treaty, "like all doubts respecting the meaning of a law, are in the first instance mere judicial questions, and are to be heard and decided in courts of justice." Quoted, Corwin, *National Supremacy* 26.

It is not therefore surprising that Strong should say in the Convention "that the power of making ought to be kept distinct from that of expounding, the laws. No maxim was better established."[164] And, added Corwin in 1914, "the utterances of other members bear out his words."[165] So, Madison insisted on judicial independence lest Congress be the "expositors as well as the makers of the laws."[166] Gerry said that "making the Expositors of the Laws, the Legislators . . . ought never to be done."[167] Corwin justly stated in 1914 that "In one form or another, the notion of legislative power as *inherently limited power,* distinct from and exclusive of the power of interpreting the standing law, was reiterated again and again and was never contradicted."[168] Even more clearly, the Framers expected the courts to "expound," to interpret the "law."[169] Instead, therefore, of "brusquely" crowding developments which required yet another "generation" for crystallization, Hamilton, in stating in No. 78 that "The interpretation of the laws is the proper and peculiar province of the courts," was, again to quote Corwin, "here, as at other points, endeavoring to reproduce the matured conclusions of the Convention itself."[170]

Without reference to this history, Marshall put the matter in common-sense terms, felicitously paraphrased by Bickel: "To leave the decision with the legislature, he said, is to allow those whose power is supposed to be limited themselves to set the limits—an absurd invitation to consistent abuse."[171] If this be absurd, retorts

---

[164] 2 Farrand 75.

[165] Corwin, *Doctrine* 42.

[166] Supra, Chapter 3, text accompanying note 37.

[167] Supra, id. at note 31.

[168] Corwin, *Doctrine* 42.

[169] Supra, Chapter 3, text accompanying notes 31–38.

[170] Corwin, *Doctrine* 44. Even in his 1913 critique of Beard, Corwin noted that "the demand of the day was for methods to check legislative power. In response to this demand . . . a construction [was] put [by the Convention] upon the current doctrine of the separation of powers which left the interpretation of laws exclusively with the courts." Quoted more fully, supra, Chapter 3, text following note 311.

[171] Bickel 3. In Marbury v. Madison, 1 Cranch 137, 178 (1803), Marshall, C. J. said, the doctrine "that the courts must close their eyes on the constitution, and see only the law [i. e., statute]" "would declare that an act, which according to the principles and theories of our government, is entirely void, is yet, in practice, completely obligatory. It would declare, that if the legislature shall do what is expressly forbidden, such act, notwithstanding the express prohibition, is in reality effectual. It would be giving to the legislature a practical and real omnipotence, with the same breath which professes to restrict their powers within

Bickel, the Constitution limits "the powers of the courts as well, and it may be equally absurd, therefore, to allow the courts to set the limits."[172] This is well enough as an exercise in logic, but here again "a page of history is worth a volume of logic."[173] Legislative, not judicial, despotism worried the Founders; judges were trusted, legislators were not.[174] Fear of "legislative despotism if in the exercise of their power they are unchecked or unrestrained by another branch"[175] cropped up repeatedly in one guise or another; the specter of judicial "excesses" passed almost unnoticed. Today, with the benefit of hindsight, we can discern the "counter-majoritarian" potential of judicial review.[176] But few—Spaight in his letter to Iredell[177] and Yates in his "Letters of Brutus"[178]—remarked the possibility in the Convention period. Apart from Bedford's general disapproval of all "checks" upon Congress,[179] I found no similar

---

narrow limits." One hundred and thirty-eight years later, though Justice Jackson had no undiluted admiration for the manner in which judicial review had been exercised in the then recent past, he yet said that "Each unit cannot be left to judge the limits of its own power." Jackson, *The Struggle for Judicial Supremacy* 9 (1941). Lord Bryce, bred in the tradition of parliamentary supremacy, nevertheless perceived that Congress could not be left to determine whether its statute exceeded constitutional limitations because "Congress is a party interested. If such a body as Congress were permitted to decide whether the acts it had passed were constitutional, it would of course decide in its own favor and to allow it to decide would be to put the Constitution at its mercy." Bryce 269.

[172] Bickel 3.

[173] New York Trust Co. v. Eisner, 256 U.S. 345, 349 (1921) (per Holmes, J.).

[174] Haines 208, 213. In the First Congress, Madison said that the legislature "is the most powerful and most likely to be abused"; and Smith said that legislative "power is perhaps more liable to abuse than the judicial." 1 *Ann. Cong.* 454, 848.

Corwin said in 1906, "The courts were at once the authors and interpreters of the common law, the most usual source of individual rights; they had often, in both England and Colonies, intervened in defense of individual rights against administrative usurpation; they were the ancient defenders of the Rule of Law against prerogative." Corwin, 4 *Mich. L. Rev.* 626–627.

[175] Wilson in the Convention, 1 Farrand 261. Though uttered in another context, an accompanying remark is worth noting: "The English courts are hitherto pure, just and incorrupt, while their legislature are base and venal." Ibid.

[176] Bickel 16; see also infra, Chapter 7, text accompanying note 47.

[177] Spaight had written to Iredell that to give the courts "an absolute negative on the proceedings of the legislature" would vitiate representative government and "would be more despotic than the Roman decemvirate and equally insufferable." Quoted Haines 119. But in his own State it was dread of Congressional tyranny that dominated the convention. Supra, Chapter 4, text accompanying notes 68–97.

[178] See supra, Chapter 3, text accompanying note 183.

[179] Bedford had opposed "every check on the legislature" because the Congress

utterance in any of the convention records. The Founders, it bears repetition, feared legislative, not judicial, tyranny.[180] Gouverneur Morris, for example, thought the "public liberty in greater danger from legislative usurpation than from any other source."[181] "All agree," said Gorham, "that a check on the Legislature is necessary,"[182] and from the outset the Virginia Plan provided for a "check" on the Legislative by the Judiciary.[183] Not alone is there no mention of a "check" running in the other direction, but the provisions for judicial tenure and compensation were expressly designed to put the Judiciary beyond Congressional reach, to make it "independent" of Congress.[184]

There is also positive evidence of special confidence in the judiciary. Said Madison in the Virginia convention, "Were I to select a power which might be given with confidence, it would be the judicial power."[185] Mason espoused judicial participation in the executive veto because judges "are in the habit and practice of considering law in their true principles, and in all their consequences," a view

---

"were the best judges of what was for" the people's interest. 1 Farrand 100–101. Nevertheless the Convention adopted a Constitution which contained many such "checks," and that Constitution was unanimously ratified by his own State of Delaware. Van Doren 193.

[180] In addition, fear that majorities would oppress minorities weighed heavily with the Founders. Supra, Chapter 2, text accompanying notes 44–45. Professor Rostow states, "The dominance of the popular will through the mechanism of our system of government is achieved in large part by having the courts enforce limitations on the power of elected officials, in the name of constitutional provisions which only the people can alter by amendment." Rostow, "The Supreme Court and the People's Will," 33 Notre Dame Lawyer, 573, 590 (1958).

[181] 2 Farrand 76. Madison said, "The legislative department is everywhere extending the sphere of its activity, and drains all power into its impetuous vortex . . . [I]t is against the enterprising ambition of this department that the people ought to indulge all their jealousy and exhaust all their precautions." Federalist No. 48 at 322–323. For an earlier "vortex" remark by Madison, see 2 Farrand 74: "This was the real source of danger."

[182] Id. at 79.

[183] 1 Farrand 28. For other remarks see supra, Chapter 2, text accompanying notes 6–32.

[184] Supra, Chapter 3, text accompanying notes 325–334. "Dependence" on the legislature, said Madison in Federalist No. 48 at 323, "gives still greater facility to encroachments of the" legislature. And he stated that "the judiciary being described by landmarks still less uncertain, projects of usurpation by . . . [it] would immediately betray and defeat themselves," i.e., no additional "check" was necessary. Federalist No. 49 at 330 remarked on the tendency "to an aggrandizement of the legislative at the expense of the other departments."

[185] 3 Elliot 535.

shared by Ellsworth.[186] In 1787, when Jefferson welcomed the "check" which a Bill of Rights "puts in the hands of the judiciary," he added, "This is a body, which if rendered independent and kept strictly to their own department merits confidence for their learning and integrity."[187] Patrick Henry, who raised a hue and cry against Congress and wished to "see Congressional oppression crushed in embryo," declared it "the highest encomium of this country, that the acts of the legislature, if unconstitutional, are liable to be opposed by the judiciary."[188] When Hamilton, therefore, concluded in *Federalist* No. 78 that it "cannot be the natural presumption" that "the legislative body are themselves the constitutional judges of their own powers" and that "It is far more rational to suppose, that the courts were designed . . . to keep the [legislature] within the limits assigned to their authority,"[189] he spoke not for himself alone but for all those who rejected mere "parchment" barriers and insisted on real protection against legislative "encroachments."[190] Those, for

[186] 2 Farrand 78. Ellsworth advocated judicial participation in the executive veto because it would "give more wisdom and firmness to the Executive," because Judges "will possess a systematic and accurate knowledge of the laws." Id. at 74. Melancton Smith, who led the opposition in the New York convention said, "It was not to be expected that the members of the federal legislature would generally be versed in those subtilties which distinguish the profession of the law. They would not be disposed to make nice distinctions with respect to jurisdiction," in other words, they would be more prone to wander out of bounds. 2 Elliot 377.

Compare with the foregoing remarks, Boudin, 579: *"As far as the debates in the Constitutional Convention disclose, the Framers were not particular admirers of the Judiciary."*

[187] 5 Jefferson, *Writings* 81.

[188] 3 Elliot 546, 325. When the dread of Congressional "tyranny" and "despotism," the insistence on well-defined "limits," enforceable by the courts, which found repeated expression in the Ratification conventions, supra, Chapter 2, text accompanying notes 22–40, are coupled with expressions of confidence in the judiciary, one may question whether the Founders intended to provide for Congressional "alterations of the jurisdiction [of constitutional issues] motivated by hostility to the decisions of the Court." Cf. Wechsler, *Court & Constitution* 1005.

[189] *Federalist* No. 78 at 506.

[190] Madison stated in the Convention that "experience had taught us a distrust" of the "security" of a "Constitutional discrimination of the departments on paper . . . agst. encroachments of the others." 2 Farrand 77. He recurred to this *motif* in *Federalist* No. 48 at 321, when he expressed lack of trust in "parchment barriers against the encroaching spirit of power." The same note was sounded by Hamilton: "commands" without sanctions are "nothing more than advice," *Federalist* No. 15 at 91. Without judicial power to declare void "all acts contrary to the manifest tenor of the Constitution" the "reservations of particular rights or privileges would amount to nothing." *Federalist* No. 78 at 505. Without such power, said G. Morris, "the time employed in framing a bill of rights and form of government was merely thrown away." 3 Sparks, *G. Morris*

example, who heard Iredell's assurance that the question "will always be, whether Congress has exceeded its authority"[191] scarcely conceived that the determination of *that* question was to be left to Congress itself. The Founders were too hardheaded to look to a suspect legislature to adjudge its own actions void.[192] If the courts were not, in Hamilton's words, "the bulwarks of a limited constitution against legislative encroachments,"[193] all the pains to fashion a Congress of limited powers fell short of the mark, all of the assurances—to counteract acute distrust of unlimited legislative power—that any legislative act in excess of those bounds was void were a snare and a delusion.[194]

---

438 (1832). Davie said in the North Carolina convention that constitutional restrictions without a judiciary to enforce them are a "dead letter." 4 Elliot 157. R. H. Lee wrote Patrick Henry, "Your observation is perfectly just that right without power to protect it, is of little avail." Quoted Warren, "New Light" 128. See also Henry's rejections of "paper" checks, 3 Elliot 166. Such misgivings led Corbin to assure the Virginia convention that "public liberty" is "secured by bars and adamantine bolts." 3 Elliot 110.

[191] 4 Elliot 179.

[192] Hamilton spoke to the issue with unrelenting common sense in *Federalist* No. 81 at 524: "From a body which had even a partial agency in passing bad laws, we could rarely expect a disposition to temper and moderate them in the application. The same spirit which had operated in making them, would be too apt in interpreting them; still less could it be expected that men who had infringed the Constitution in the character of legislators would be disposed to repair the breach in the character of judges."

Modern illustration of this all too human trait is furnished in Professor Gellhorn's discussion of the Finnish Chancellor as the government's "legal counsel" concerning the "validity of government action." A former Chancellor acknowledged that "If the act had been done in accord with advice I had given, I was not eager to find anything wrong with it afterward." Gellhorn, "Finland's Official Watchman," 114 *U. Pa. L. Rev.* 327, 331 (1966).

[193] *Federalist* No. 78 at 508.

[194] In the course of his reply to Spaight's criticism of judicial review Iredell stated (1787) that "In any other light . . . the greater part of the provisions of the [North Carolina] Constitution would appear to me ridiculous, since in my opinion nothing could be more so than for the representatives of a people solemnly assembled to form a Constitution, to set down a number of political dogmas, which might or might not be regarded; whereas it must have been intended, as I conceive, that it should be a system of authority, not depending on the casual whim or accidental ideas of a majority." 2 McRee 174. In the First Congress, Gerry rejecting the notion that courts would be bound by a Congressional construction, said, "If this is the meaning of the constitution, it was hardly worth while to have had so much bustle and uneasiness about it." 1 *Ann. Cong.* 557–558. Not without reason did Marshall say in Marbury v. Madison, 1 Cranch 137, 176 (1803), that if the constitution "is alterable when the legislature shall please to alter it" "then written constitutions are absurd attempts, on the part of the people, to limit a power, in its own nature illimitable." See also Meigs, *Relation* 154, 216.

FINALITY OF JUDICIAL INTERPRETATION

Was a judicial decision to be "final," asks Corwin; what deference were Congress and the President *"required by the Constitution to pay relevant judicial versions of the Constitution?"*[195] According to Westin this is a "central issue" in ascertaining the intention of the Framers.[196] In 1787, says Corwin, if I rightly understand him, "there were . . . three views on the question of *effect* or *finality*" of a judicial pronouncement of unconstitutionality: (1) it "merely settles the law of the case . . . and of some such future cases as the Court may choose to apply it to on the strength of the doctrine of *stare decisis*"; (2) such "a pronouncement further operates, unless reversed [by the Court] to strike the condemned statute from the statute books"; and (3) it "also fixes the meaning of the Constitution *against the President and Congress.*"[197] The only evidence cited by Corwin relates to his discussion of "departmental" construction and some pre-1787 legislative practices of reversing "decisions of ordinary courts," points examined above.[198] The triadic distinction drawn by Corwin never surfaced, so far as I could find, in the records of the several conventions, or in such of the contemporary discussions as I have examined. As to the possibility that the Founders considered "what degree of *finality* the endorsers of judicial review were prepared to ascribe to a judicial reading of the Constitution," he concludes that "The probability is that few of them had given the subject a thought."[199] The facts, I submit, prove the contrary: proponents and critics of judicial review both expected the courts to have the "final" word on constitutional limitations.

Let us begin with two early remarks which Corwin cited in 1925 as milestones en route to the claim for exclusive judicial "power in interpreting [the Constitution] with final force and effect." James Varnum argued in 1786 that "the judiciary have the sole power of judging of laws . . . and cannot admit any act of the legislators against the Constitution." Iredell, in his reply to Spaight, stated that "if the power of judging rests with the courts [as he maintained]

---

[195] Corwin, *Court Over* 13–15.
[196] Westin 30.
[197] Corwin, *Court Over* 2–3.
[198] Supra, text accompanying notes 142–184.
[199] *Court Over* 33.

their decision is final."[200] In *Federalist* No. 81, Hamilton commented on the "absurdity in subjecting the decisions of men, selected for their knowledge of the laws, acquired by long and laborious study, to the revision and control of [legislators] who, for want of the same advantage, cannot but be deficient in that knowledge."[201] Prior to the Virginia Ratification convention, R. H. Lee wrote in his *Letters of a Federal Farmer:* "It is proper that the federal judiciary should have . . . the power of deciding finally on the laws of the union."[202]

Then there are the implications of remarks not framed in express terms of "finality." Wilson's assurance to the Pennsylvania convention, iterated by others elsewhere, that "the legislature may be restrained, and kept within its prescribed bounds, by the interposition of the judicial department,"[203] posits "finality." Judicial interposition that the legislature would have been free to disregard would have been ineffective. So too, "finality" may be deduced from the remarks that the judiciary was to control Congress.[204] The frequent state-

---

[200] Quoted Corwin, "Progress" 526; 2 McRee 149. So too, Madison, in *Federalist* No. 39 at 249, stated that the Supreme Court "is ultimately to decide" in "controversies relating to the boundary between" the State and national governments. That he did not distinguish between enforcement against the State and the Nation is illustrated infra, Chapter 8, note 195.

[201] No. 81 at 424–425, quoted supra, Chapter 3, text accompanying note 226.

[202] Ford, *Pamphlets* 279, 306.

[203] 2 Elliot 445; Mason, supra, Chapter 3, text accompanying note 49; Hamilton, id. at note 228; Ellsworth, id. at note 232; McKean, supra, Chapter 4, text accompanying note 37; Wilson, id. at note 39. See also id. at notes 76–77, 79.

[204] Morris, supra, Chapter 3, text accompanying note 87; Wilson, supra, Chapter 5, text accompanying note 28. Relying on Wilson's statement that any one "is justified in refusing to obey an unconstitutional act of the legislature . . . every one who is called on to act has a right to judge," Boudin 100, asserted that Wilson "clearly" was not talking about a final or irrevocable power of interpreting the Constitution, but rather that the Judiciary could adjudicate "without, however, its interpretation being binding upon any other governmental department." Under this "Wilsonian theory," said Boudin, the President, after the Supreme Court had declared a statute unconstitutional, has "the right, nay the duty, to enforce that law." Ibid. Wilson's own utterances repel Boudin's "Wilsonian theory."

In the very same Lectures Wilson said that "the legislative authority is placed . . . under just and strict control," and that its "extravagencies may be prevented . . . by the judicial authority." 1 Wilson, *Works* 211; and see id. at 411. It is the duty of the courts to decide, he said, that a law "repugnant" to the Constitution is "void." Id. at 461. This he regarded as a "permanent provision . . . that every transgression of [legislative] bounds shall be adjudged and rendered vain and fruitless. What a noble guard against legislative despotism!" Id. at 462. He had made similar statements in the Pennsylvania convention, 2 Elliot 446. A law contrary to the Constitution would be judicially declared "null and void" and would "not have the force of law." Id. at 489. How the President

ments that courts would declare void Congressional Acts which overleapt Constitutional bounds[205] also premise that courts were given the last word. That inference may likewise be drawn from the several statements that the legislators were to be the makers, not the expositors of the law,[206] that interpretation was the peculiar province of the courts.[207] These implications were spelled out by Yates, who complained that "the opinions of the supreme court . . . will have the force of law [that is, be binding and therefore "final"] because there is no power that can correct their errors . . . The legislature themselves cannot set aside a judgment of this court . . . the supreme court are authorized in *the last resort* to determine what is the extent of the powers of Congress . . . If, therefore, the legislature pass any laws inconsistent with the sense the judges put upon the constitution, they will declare it void." And he stated, Congress "will not go over the limits by which the courts may adjudge they are confined."[208] Similar views were expressed by Martin and by the "Centinel."[209] Then there are the uncontradicted assertions in

---

could then proceed to "enforce" a void law which no longer had "the force of law" Boudin did not discuss.

It had been feared that if the judges were "to decide against [the constitutionality of] the law," they would be impeached. Wilson repudiated the proposition: "Judges are to be impeached, because they declare an act null and void, that was made in defiance of the Constitution!" Id. at 478. The hypothetical resort to impeachment posits that there was no other alternative; and Wilson's rejection confirms that Congress and the President were not left free to ignore the judicial decision and to reinterpret the Constitution for themselves. See also infra, Chapter 9, note 34. For general discussion see supra, text accompanying notes 128–141.

So too, the remarks in the First Congress, supra, Chapter 5, text accompanying notes 10–18, with respect to judicial review of a preliminary construction by Congress are instinct with the concept that the last word was for the courts.

[205] Ellsworth, supra, Chapter 4, text accompanying note 26; Samuel Adams, id. at note 30; Wilson, id. at note 39; Marshall, id. at note 123; Hamilton, supra, Chapter 3, text accompanying note 228; Yates, id. at note 188; King, id. at note 19.

[206] Gerry, supra, text accompanying note 167; Madison, supra, Chapter 3, text accompanying note 37; Strong, id. at note 39.

[207] Baldwin, supra, Chapter 3, text accompanying note 234; Nicholas, supra, Chapter 4, text accompanying note 118. See also supra, text accompanying notes 164–170. Compare Dickinson's fear that judicial review would make the judiciary the "law-givers"; supra, Chapter 3, text accompanying note 82.

[208] Supra, Chapter 3, text accompanying notes 184–188; Corwin, *Court Over* 237, 245.

[209] Martin said, "Whether therefore, any *laws* or *regulations* of the Congress . . . are *contrary* to, or not *warranted* by the constitution, rests *only* with the judges." 3 Farrand 172, 220.

After stating that it would be the "province" of the Court to determine "the

the First Congress that Congressional interpretations could be corrected and revised by the courts.[210] It is therefore reasonable to infer that in a proper "case" the Founders contemplated that the courts could "strike the condemned statute from the statute books," that is, declare it "void." So too, the implications of the above-quoted statements are that a judicial decision would fix "the meaning of the Constitution against the President and Congress."[211]

An extensive argument to the contrary was made by William Meigs, but he did not notice the quoted remarks of Hamilton, Yates, Martin, and "Centinel" and did not comment on the effect of the other above-examined statements.[212] Only so much of his analysis as is close to the 1787 period will be considered. For the "limited" view judges allegedly took "of their power," Meigs points to a statement by one of the judges in *Kamper v. Hawkins* (Va. 1793) that he did "not consider the judiciary as the champions of the people or of the constitution, bound to sound the alarm and excite an opposition to the Legislature. But when causes of individuals are brought before the judiciary, they are bound to decide," to render "judgment" against one who claims "under an act contrary to the Consti-

---

constitutionality of any law [of Congress] that might be controverted," the "Centinel" stated that "The 1st section of the 3d article gives the supreme court cognizance . . . of all cases arising under the Constitution, which empowers this tribunal to decide upon the Construction of the Constitution itself in the last resort. This is so extraordinary, so unprecedented an authority, that the intention of vesting it must have been to *put it out of the power of Congress,* even by breaking through the Constitution, to compel these defaulters to restore the public treasure." McMaster & Stone 659–660 (emphasis added).

[210] Supra, Chapter 5, text accompanying notes 10–15.

[211] In 1914 Corwin said that "It is not the duty nor yet the power of courts to *decide* cases, but to decide them *in accordance with the law,* of which the consitution is part and parcel; and if the other departments are bound by their decisions it is because they are *presumed* by the constitution itself to be in accordance with the constitution and laws. Otherwise, we should be confronted with the solecism of those sworn to support the constitution obliged to support its violation on occasion. The courts then must ascertain the meaning of the constitution and laws, from which it would seem to follow that those who are bound by the constitution are bound by the judicial view of it in the same general sense as that in which those bound by ordinary law are bound by the judicial view of *it* . . . It is true, of course, that the court does not order the legislature arrested for trying to violate the constitution, but neither does it order a man arrested for trying to make a contract contrary to the statute of frauds . . . The penalty which the legislature and the man suffer in such cases is the same . . . they have their acts disallowed by the court." Corwin, *Doctrine* 24–26.

[212] Meigs, *Relation* 219.

tution, that is, under *no* law."[213] This merely disclaims a roving commission to interfere with legislation, but it expressly affirms that courts may adjudge an act unconstitutional when a proper "cause" is "brought before them."[214] There is no implication in this that the legislature is not bound by a judicial determination in a proper case. In the same *Kamper v. Hawkins,* Judge Tucker said that "it is the duty and office of the judiciary to make" an "exposition" of the Constitution, and he quoted Hamilton's definition of judicial supremacy as "conclusive."[215]

Meigs also cites Hamilton's statement in *Federalist* No. 51 that to maintain the separation of powers each department is given the "necessary constitutional means and personal motives to resist encroachments of the other," and Hamilton's question in No. 49:[216] "The several departments being perfectly coordinated . . . neither of them, it is evident, can pretend to an exclusive or superior right of settling the boundaries between their respective powers; and how are the encroachments of the stronger to be prevented . . . without an appeal to the people themselves?" Hamilton's answer was not, as Meigs mistakenly stated, "that frequent recurrence should be had to the people."[217] The quotation from No. 49 was a paraphrase of Jefferson's view in the *Notes on Virginia,* which Hamilton (No. 49 is attributed to either Madison or Hamilton) then criticized in words immediately following the quoted language: "There appear to be insuperable objections against the proposed recurrence to the people, as a provision in all cases for keeping the several departments within their constitutional limits." We may put to one side whether a difference between departments about "the boundaries between *their* respective departments," for example, whether the President may remove officials without Senate consent, is to be equated with a difference between Congress and a citizen who alleges an unconstitutional invasion of his rights. For Hamilton rejected the view that the legislative body "are themselves the judges of their own powers, and that the construction they put upon them

213 Id. at 217–218.
214 Cf. Iredell, supra, Chapter 3, text accompanying note 168.
215 Kamper v. Hawkins, 1 Va. Cas. 20, 78–79, 81–84 (1793).
216 Meigs, *Relation* 224; *Federalist* No. 51 at 331. Nos. 49 and 51 have been attributed to Madison *or* Hamilton.
217 Meigs, *Relation* 223–224; *Federalist* No. 49 at 328.

is conclusive."[218] He labeled as "absurd" legislative "revision" of judicial decisions.[219] He emphasized that action in excess of delegated power is invalid, that courts are to keep the legislature "within the limits assigned to their authority" and are to serve as the "bulwarks of a limited Constitution against legislative encroachments,"[220] all of which posits that Congress would be bound by an adjudication.

Finally, Meigs relies on remarks of James Wilson.[221] In his 1791 Lectures, Wilson stressed that in *preparing* and passing bills, the Congress should be "uncontrolled." It was in this context that Wilson said that the proceedings of each department "should be formed without restraint, but when they are *once formed,* they should be subject to control." After completion of the enacting process, Congress, said Wilson, was subject to "control by the judiciary department, whenever the laws, *though in fact passed,* are found to be contradictory to the Constitution."[222] In consequence, "the bounds of the legislative power—a power the most apt to overleap its bounds—are not only distinctly marked in the system itself; but effectual and permanent provision is made that every transgression of those bounds shall be adjudged and rendered *vain and fruitless.*"[223] That Congress could then proceed to reinterpret the relevant Constitutional provision after its own heart is at war with the implications of Wilson's statement. Nor was Wilson being an apostle of the "departmental" theory when he said that "In the same manner the President . . . [can] refuse to carry into effect an act that violates the constitution."[224] He proceeded from the contemporary premise that an Act which was incompatible with the Constitution was "void" and therefore not binding on any one, Whether the President's "refusal" or construction would be binding on the courts, whether the President could refuse to effectuate a judicial determination that a statute was void, was not under

---

[218] *Federalist* No. 78 at 506.
[219] Quoted supra, text accompanying note 201.
[220] *Federalist* No. 78 at 508.
[221] Meigs, *Relation* 227.
[222] 1 Wilson, *Works* 410–411 (emphasis added).
[223] Id. at 462 (emphasis added).
[224] Meigs, *Relation* 227; McMaster & Stone 305. A moment earlier he had explained that courts would pronounce a Congressional "transgression" "void." Id. at 304–305.

discussion, and it may be doubted whether Wilson remotely entertained such notions, for he looked to the courts as a "noble guard
against legislative despotism."[225] Meigs citations to the 1787 period
make out a very unconvincing case for the proposition that "the
opinion of the Judiciary was not [meant to be] conclusive."[226]

Marshall did not ask the Virginia convention "To what quarter
will you look for protection from an infringement of the Constitution, if you will not give the power to the judiciary?",[227] Wilson did
not proclaim the judiciary a "noble guard against legislative despotism," only to pave the way for Congressional reinterpretation in
defiance of the judicial construction. If it be true that the Founders
looked to the Court as the "bulwark" against legislative encroachments, if courts were to keep Congress within the limits assigned
to their authority, it seems to follow that a fresh legislative construction is precluded by a judicial determination that the predecessor
Act was "out of bounds" and therefore void. Otherwise the judicial
decision could be set at naught by immediate Congressional re-
enactment of the anulled statute, giving rise to a constitutional tug-
of-war. For me, such a decision fixes "the meaning of the Constitution against the President and Congress."

But I would not suggest that this is a constitutional absolute, if
only for the practical considerations which lie at the root of Hart's
view:

> Because the judicial power is a power to dispose finally of the
> matters immediately in litigation as between the parties to the
> litigation, the incidental power to disregard an act of Congress
> which is found to be unconstitutional is a power to do so with
> the same degree of finality. But of course it is more than this.
> Such a decision, once made, is likely to control future cases duly
> presented for adjudication, since the Court is under an obligation
> to adhere to prior decisions unless satisfied that they are unsound.
> Out of either prudence or respect, accordingly, other branches of
> the government and other persons than the litigants may accept
> the grounds of decision which the Court announces, and usually

[225] 1 Wilson, *Works* 462.
[226] Meigs, *Relation* 223.
[227] Supra, Chapter 4, text accompanying note 123.

do. But the Court has never formally asserted any power to control the judgment of Congress or the President when they are called upon to consider constitutional questions as an incident to the discharge of their own functions. What obligations of respect these branches of the Government owe to the earlier opinions of the judicial branch are for them to decide subject to the review of the electorate and, if occasion arises, the further consideration of the Court. The political branches, in other words, retain at all times the crucial ability to force the Court to reexamine in new contexts the validity of the constitutional positions it has previously taken.[228]

Over the years, the Court has at times changed its constitutional interpretations, and since it can act only in "cases," the way must be kept clear for litigants to reopen the issue, and that in turn may require the impetus of fresh legislation which responds to the needs of a changing world, notwithstanding that it involves an interpretive departure from prevailing judicial decision.[229] The Founders were acutely aware that they were drafting for posterity,[230] and nothing in the records of the several conventions suggests that they meant to bar the way to judicial reevaluation of a mistaken or inadequate constitutional construction and to freeze it. True, *stare decisis* was a less flexible doctrine in 1787 than it is today, but it flourished in an atmosphere where mistaken judicial common law tort or contract rules could be replaced with little fuss by a Parliamentary statute. There had been no occasion to consider the doctrine in the context of the interpretation of a written Constitution where *stare decisis* would require resort to the cumbersome and generally insurmountable amending process if the Court was to be released from its mistakes.

Yet given the historical basis for the view that Congress is "bound" by a judicial construction of the Constitution, I should prefer a less latitudinarian formulation than the freedom of the other branches

---

[228] Hart, Book Review 1457–1458.

[229] Compare the adventures of "soft-coal" legislation after the Supreme Court, in 1935, declared the National Recovery Administration Act unconstitutional. Morgan, *Congress and the Constitution* 163–183 (1966).

[230] 1 Farrand 424, 431, 490, 515; and see Corwin, *Court Over* 222–223.

to decide "what obligations of respect" they owe to judicial interpretations of the Constitution. Something more than a departure from "prudence and respect"—which carry connotations of "comity"—is involved when Congressional reinterpretation runs the risk of judicial disallowance.[231] Reinterpretation by the other branches may be justified, I suggest, not because those branches are free to depart from "respect," but as a response to exigencies that no longer may be denied, for example, the pressure for minimum wage and hour legislation in a fast shifting society. The "bonds" of a judicial construction can then be relaxed by a preliminary legislative reinterpretation because circumstances demand that the Court be enabled "to re-examine in new contexts the validity of constitutional positions [it] has previously taken." Judicious reinterpretation by the other branches does not, in this light, mark a deviation from "respect" but rather constitutes a necessary part of the constitutional machinery whereby the Court is better enabled to fulfill its own continuing function.

The weary reader who has patiently toiled over Corwin's obstacle course will, it is hoped, agree that in large part the Founders were apparently oblivious to the presence of the obstacles he portrayed, and that the influence of those "obstacles" on the framing and adoption of the Constitution was virtually nil. That trek should have served, however, to show that the Framers were aware of the underlying implications of judicial review, for example, the rejection of "legislative omnipotence," the concept of the Constitution as "fundamental law," the ideas that the function of "interpretation" was for the courts, not the legislature, that judicial interpretation would necessarily be "final," and the like. It cannot be assumed that the interrelation of these ideas, which today seems so plain, was lost upon the perceptive Founders, and it was in fact explicitly formulated by Iredell and Hamilton. As Corwin said in 1914, after drawing up a more comprehensive list:

---

231 Yates said that when the principles upon which the Court acted "become fixed, by a course of decisions, [they] will be adopted by the Legislature, and will be the rule by which they will explain their own powers. This appears evident from this consideration, that if the legislature pass laws, which, in the judgment of the court, they are not authorized to do by the constitution, the court will not take notice of them, for it will not be denied that the constitution is the highest or supreme law . . . . [T]hey will not readily pass laws which they know the courts will not execute." Quoted, Corwin, *Court Over* 245–246.

Probably no one public man of the time shared all these ideas when the Philadelphia Convention met. But the able membership of that famous body was in a position to compare views drawn from every section of the country. Slowly, by process of discussion and conversation, these men, most of them trained in the legal way of thinking, discovered the intrinsic harmony of the ideas just passed in review; discovered, in other words, that the acceptance of one of them more or less constrained the acceptance of the others also, that each implied a system embracing all.[232]

He considered that judicial review was "the natural outgrowth of ideas that were common property in the period when the Constitution was established," and agreed that "a considerable portion of the body that framed the Constitution are on record as having personally favored judicial review at one time or another, either before, during, or after the Convention."[233]

[232] Corwin, *Doctrine* 41. See supra, Chapter 3, note 294; and cf. supra, Chapter 4, note 36.

[233] Corwin, *Doctrine* 2. In 1938 Corwin stated that while Hamilton's *"Juristic* theory of judicial review frequently invoked conceptions which were the common currency of political discussions in 1787, it affixed to those conceptions a sharpness of definition and application which had not been theirs before. It was thus no mere ratification of history, it was creative as well." Corwin, *Court Over* 16–17. Contrast this with Corwin's 1925 statement, quoted supra, Chapter 3, text accompanying note 230, that Varnum and Iredell had earlier set forth "all the premises of the doctrine of judicial review . . . Federalist No. 78 improves on the statement of these premises but adds nothing essential to them." When we add Iredell's earlier "sharpness of definition," supra, Chapter 3, note 168, and that of Yates and of Wilson, supra, Chapter 3, text accompanying notes 182–186, Chapter 4, text accompanying note 39, we may at least conclude that the "conceptions which were the common currency of political discussion" in the years immediately preceding the Convention were not fuzzy, be their provenance what it may.

THE CONSTITUTIONAL TEXT

AND JUDICIAL REVIEW: "ALL CASES . . .

ARISING UNDER THIS CONSTITUTION"

If one agrees that the records of the several conventions disclose an assumption by the leadership that judicial review would be available to keep Congress within Constitutional "limits," the question presents itself why did not the Framers so expressly provide—a question which Professor Crosskey regards as conclusive.[1] One thing is clear: the leaders were not concealing their intentions,[2] for again and again they openly avowed their belief that judicial review would be available.[3] Crosskey's rhetorical question would override a basic rule cf documentary interpretation that comes into play precisely when a text is ambiguous, the rule that the task of construction is to search out the intention of the draftsmen and to give it effect.[4]

[1] Professor Crosskey 968, 971, 973, rings the changes on items which "must surely have enforced the necessity of clearly stipulating the right of judicial review if the Supreme Court was to have that right."

[2] Lewis, *Interpreting the Constitution* 12 (1937), quoted Jackson, *The Struggle for Judicial Supremacy* 4 n. 4 (1941).

[3] Commenting on the omission to "choose language apt" for the purpose of judicial review, Corwin, *Doctrine* 17, discards the possibility that the Framers "desired to conceal their intentions at this point" because "the fact is, that they proclaimed them and that judicial review was universally regarded as a feature of the new system while its adoption was pending." Corwin's rejection of "concealment" is fortified by the fact that Madison did not shrink from saying in the Convention that he "thought it best on the whole to be silent on the subject" of ceded lands where that seemed appropriate. 2 Farrand 465; cf. Boudin 84–85.

[4] Crosskey 364 himself tells us that the "rules" of interpretation of the period "were calculated to give a just and well-rounded interpretation to every document, in light of its declared purpose, or if its purpose was not declared, then in the light of its apparent purpose, so far as it could be discovered." The principle has

And Crosskey's "triumphant question"[5] would leave a clearly recognized mischief largely uncured, contrary to the principle familiar to the Founders and still valid today.[6] In place of the Crosskey query, I suggest, the question should be, rather, how did the *Founders* understand the Constitutional text; did *they* consider that it gave adequate expression to their belief in the availability of judicial review. For it is *their* understanding rather than our 20th century doubts that should be controlling.

Preliminarily let us consider the question asked by Corwin in 1914: what did the Framers "*do* with reference" to judicial review —that is, were the "ideas" above discussed "by contemporary understanding, incorporated in the Constitution for" the purpose of judicial review, and were they "logically sufficient for it"?[7] His answer was that "no clause was inserted in the Constitution for the specific purpose of bestowing this power on the courts, but that the power rests upon certain general principles thought by its framers to have been embodied in the Constitution," "principles which in their estimation made specific provision for it unnecessary."[8] Corwin felt

---

found frequent application in statutory construction. In an oft-cited case, Justice Holmes, on circuit, said that if the legislature "has intimated its will, however indirectly, that will should be recognized and obeyed." Johnson v. United States, 163 Fed. 20, 32 (1st Cir. 1908). See also Federal Deposit Ins. Corp. v. Tremaine, 133 F.2d 827, 830 (2d Cir. 1943) (per Learned Hand, J.); Hawaii v. Mankichi, 190 U.S. 197, 212 (1903).

[5] Hart, Book Review 462, remarked, "Professor Crosskey is a devotee of that technique of interpretation which reaches its apogee of persuasiveness in the triumphant question, 'If that's what they meant, why didn't they say so.'"

[6] See infra, note 95. Crosskey 366, quotes Blackstone, "the cause which moved the legislature to enact it" is "the most universal and effectual way of discovering the meaning of a law, when the words are dubious." He himself points out that Yates (who found unmistakable provision for judicial review in the Constitution) properly employed Blackstone's criterion in construing the "judiciary powers," Crosskey 712 (cf. Chapter 2, text accompanying notes 184–193), though in justice to Professor Crosskey it must be noticed that it was a segment of the powers that he favors, not deplores.

[7] Corwin, *Doctrine* 2–3.

[8] Id. at 10, 17. Crosskey 1018 states that "casually read," parts of the Convention records "give the impression that there were men in the Convention who simply assumed, as a matter of course, that the Supreme Court would have a complete and general right of review against Congress, without any particular provision for it in the Constitution." Since most of the remarks about judicial review were made during discussion of the legislative and veto powers, it is not surprising that the Framers did not interrupt the debates to spell out the mechanics of judicial review. Discussion of Article III came much later, and the interpolations then made are discussed hereafter. See also infra, note 28, and supra, Chapter 3, note 315.

"driven to [this] conclusion" because he found that neither the "arising under" nor the "supremacy" clause was designed to comprehend review of Congressional Acts.[9] The "supremacy clause," as I shall hereafter seek to show, does not purport to confer "jurisdiction" on either State or federal courts. Federal jurisdiction is a creature of grant, that is, the federal courts have only such jurisdiction as was expressly conferred upon them. The sole grant of such jurisdiction is that conferred by Article III. If federal jurisdiction cannot be found in Article III it cannot, I consider, be drawn from "general principles."[10] Article III, moreover, does not purport to confer "judicial power" in bulk but only as circumscribed by the enumerated "cases and controversies," among them "cases arising under this Constitution." Consequently a violation of the Constitution by State or federal law was either comprehended in the "arising under" clause or it seems ineluctably to follow that "judicial power" to deal with it was withheld. If it does not "arise under" that clause, it "arises" nowhere, and the First to Ninth Amendments become empty promises so far as judicial sanctions are concerned. To discard the "arising under" clause, therefore, is to throw judicial review out the window.

True, Hamilton said in *Federalist* No. 81 at 524 that "the Constitution ought to be the standard for construction for the laws, and that wherever there is evident opposition, the laws ought to give place to the Constitution. But this doctrine is not deducible from any circumstance peculiar to the plan of the Convention but from the general theory of a limited Constitution." Yet he was cognizant of the effect of both the "supremacy" and "arising under" clauses. In *Federalist* No. 33 at 201–202, he stated that federal laws "not pursuant" to constitutional power, which are an "invasion" of "residuary" State powers, would be "merely acts of usurpation," and that the Supremacy Clause *"expressly confines this supremacy* to laws made *pursuant to the Constitution."* So the supremacy of the Constitution, by his own analysis, found explicit expression in the Supremacy Clause. And although Hamilton, in analyzing the "arising under this Constitution" phrase (*Federalist* No. 80 at 520) employs as an illustration a restriction upon the States, see infra, text accompanying notes 23–28, he nonetheless exhibits an awareness that the Constitution had thereby provided machinery to carry out the plan. He described his survey of the several categories of "cases of controversies" as a "review of the particular *powers* of the federal judiciary, *as marked out* in the Constitution." No. 80 at 522 (emphasis added).

[9] Corwin, *Doctrine* 17, 13–16.

[10] Wright 14; Dred Scott v. Sandford, 19 How. 393, 401–402 (1857). Note Madison's statement respecting Article III, "The right of expounding the Constitution in cases not of this ["judiciary"] nature ought not to be *given* to that Department." 2 Farrand 430 (emphasis added). Madison was well aware that Article III was designed to "give" jurisdiction, i.e., that jurisdiction would not arise from "general principles."

That was not Corwin's intention; his resort to "general principles" sought to give effect to the utterances of the Framers who "thought that the Constitution secured to the courts in the United States the right to pass on the validity of acts of Congress."[11] To such utterances may be added the frequent rejection of an "omnipotent legislature," the constant invocation of "checks" and "limits" on legislative power, which disclose a keen appreciation of the "mischief to be cured."[12] Were the language of the "arising under" clause less apt, we would therefore be justified in straining to accomplish rather than defeat the purpose of the Founders. But more important, the Founders considered, as I shall now attempt to show, that by the "arising under" clause they were, Corwin to the contrary notwithstanding,[13] conferring the power of judicial review.

Article III, section 2, provides in part that "The judicial power shall extend to all cases . . . arising under this Constitution." The clause has appeared ambiguous or inadequate to more than one student, for example, Corwin, Crosskey, and Bickel.[14] To ascertain the meaning of the Constitution. Crosskey would employ the "obvious and natural" interpretive standard, "the probable opinion of an intelligent and well-informed man of the time, based on a reasoned analysis of the Constitution, in the light of antecedent [nonsuspect] materials."[15] History enables us to employ an even more exacting standard, to substitute for "probable" opinions the actual and unequivocal opinions of contemporaries who were exceptionally well situated to form them. Those opinions reveal that the "arising under" clause spoke plainly enough to the men of 1787 and was understood by them to provide for judicial review.

Let us begin with a vigorous critic of the Constitution, Justice Yates of New York, who opposed it precisely for the reason, among others, that it provided for judicial review. Yates had been a delegate to the Convention, and notwithstanding sporadic attendance, should qualify as well informed. He scrutinized the Constitutional text

[11] Corwin, *Doctrine* 10.

[12] Supra, note 6; infra, note 95.

[13] Corwin, *Court Over* 37–38, published in 1938, reflects a less restrictive view; there he relies on Hamilton to show that the "arising under" clause is confined to policing express "prohibitions," i.e., it *grants* limited jurisdiction.

[14] Corwin, *Doctrine* 14–16; Corwin, *Court Over* 35–38; Crosskey 983; Bickel 5–6.

[15] Crosskey 1028. The citations that follow are not open to the charge of tampering by Madison or others, made by Crosskey 1009–1010; 952–960.

attentively and concluded that "The cases arising under the Constitution must include such, as bring into question its meaning, and will require an explanation of the nature and extent of the powers of the different departments under it." And, he said, Congress "will not go over the limits by which the courts may adjudge they are confined."[16] Martin, a delegate from Maryland and also an opponent of adoption, addressed himself to the "arising under" clause and concluded that "Whether therefore, any *laws* or *regulations* of the *Congress*, or any *acts* of its *President* or *other officers*, are *contrary to*, or *not warranted by* the Constitution, rests only with the judges."[17] Wilson, explaining the "arising under" clause to the Pennsylvania convention, stated that "If a law should be inconsistent with those powers vested by this instrument in Congress, the judges . . . will declare such law to be null and void."[18] So too did the Pennsylvania dissenters, for whom the "Centinel" spoke, understand the matter: "The 1st section of the 3d article gives the supreme court cognizance of not only the laws, but of all cases arising under the constitution, which empowers this tribunal to decide upon the construction of the constitution itself in the last resort." And under such "arising under" jurisdiction, it was the "supreme court of the Union, whose province it would be to determine the constitutionality of any law [of Congress] that may be controverted.[19] In Virginia, Pendleton spoke to the "arising under" clause and stated that courts must "confine [federal officers] to the line of their duty," that "oppressive laws will not be warranted by the Constitution," and that "independent judges will never admit an oppressive construction."[20] Marshall, who discussed the "arising under" clause after Pendleton, also said that a federal law "not warranted by any of the powers enumerated" would be judicially declared void.[21] Not once was it suggested that

[16] Corwin, *Court Over* 235, 245.

[17] 3 Farrand 220.

[18] 2 Elliot 489.

[19] McMaster & Stone 659–660; for additional citations see supra, Chapter 6, note 207.

[20] 3 Elliot 548.

[21] Id. at 553. In the Virginia convention, Mason, referring to the prohibition of Congressional ex post facto laws (Art. I §9 (3)), asked rhetorically, would it not be the "duty of the federal court to say that such laws are prohibited," as "an *express power* is given to the federal court to take cognizance of such controversies." 3 Elliot 479–480. His reference postulates that the "arising under" clause embraced Congressional violation of an express prohibition.

the "arising under" clause did not accomplish these purposes. On the contrary, Mason objected that the jurisdiction conferred "in all cases arising under the system . . . may be said to be unlimited"; and Grayson also considered the jurisdiction "of stupendous magnitude . . . it is impossible . . . to trace its extent."[22] In view of the striking unanimity as to the scope of the "arising under" clause among those who opposed and those who advocated adoption of the Constitution, only a powerful showing should lead us to substitute 20th century speculation for the meaning ascribed to the "arising under" clause by the Founders who explained its meaning in 1788.

That showing is not made by Corwin. Yates's broad reading, says Corwin, was "logical," but Hamilton allegedly "rejected" it "for a much narrower conception," one limited to enforcement of constitutional *prohibitions*.[23] So read, I showed, *Federalist* No. 80[24] collides with Hamilton's express rejection in No. 78 of the notion "that men acting by virtue of powers [under a "delegated authority"] may do not only what their powers *do not authorize,* but what they forbid," and his emphasis that courts are "the bulwarks of a *limited* Constitution," that is, *both* prohibitions and limitations were to be judicially enforceable.[25] Corwin's reading of No. 80 rests upon Hamilton's illustrative reference to express restrictions upon the States.[26] Ordinarily the use of an illustration to explain broad language does not narrow its breadth unless it appears that the purpose of the illustration was restrictive, an element here absent. Corwin would attribute to Hamilton the design—after bas-

---

[22] Id. at 523, 565. And Tyler complained that there was no "limitation of, or restriction on, the federal judicial power." Id. at 638–639. Mason, a Framer and opponent of adoption, said in the Virginia convention that the "arising under" cases "take in *all* the officers of the government . . . what is done by them to others." Id. at 524 (emphasis added). Though an advocate of adoption, Randolph likewise considered the jurisdiction too broad. Speaking of the phrase "all cases in law and equity arising under the Constitution," he said "What are these cases of law and equity? Do they not involve *all* rights, from an inchoate right to a complete right, arising *from* this Constitution?" 3 Elliot 572 (emphasis added).

[23] Corwin, *Court Over* 39–40, 36.

[24] Supra, Chapter 6, text accompanying notes 67–71.

[25] *Federalist* No. 78 at 505–506 (emphasis added); see supra, Chapter 3, text accompanying notes 227–229.

[26] Compare his conclusion that Hamilton's illustrative reference to enforcement of prohibitions on States inferentially must embrace similar enforcement against Congress under the "arising under" clause. Infra, Chapter 8, note 152.

ing his analysis in No. 78 upon the principle that the act of an agent beyond his "delegated authority" is void, after explaining that the courts were designed to "keep the [legislature] within the limits assigned to their authority"[27]—to disable the courts from performing this function by restricting the jurisdiction which would render performance possible. It is not reasonable to attribute to Hamilton's resort to a readily-comprehended illustration in *Federalist* No. 80 an intention thus to abort his carefully designed scheme of judicial review in No. 78. Were we to give Hamilton's illustration this strange effect, it would yet not dispose of the fact that the views expressed in No. 78 were the views of his opponent Yates, shared by Martin, another opponent, and by Hamilton's allies, Marshall, Pendleton, and Wilson, not to stress that other Founders conceived of judicial review in broad terms that went beyond enforcement of express "prohibitions" to "limits" and "enumerated" powers.[28] If it

---

[27] *Federalist* No. 78 at 506, 505.

[28] Supra, Chapter 6, note 78. Corwin, *Doctrine* 16, asks how "is the fact to be explained that most of the advocates of judicial review in the Convention of 1787 had declared their belief that this power would reside in the national courts long before they had heard or thought of the 'arising under' clause." The explanation may lie in the familiar lag between discussion or assumption of basic, controlling concepts in a legislative body and their subsequent reduction to formulae by the draftsmen. Remarks about judicial review were made in various relevant contexts as the Convention proceeded from the legislative to the executive to the judicial power. Large preliminary problems agitated the Convention, e.g., the Small States resolutely opposed Large State domination; and only when the dust of such controversies settled could the functions of a national judiciary be more clearly envisaged. For example, Large State espousal of a Congressional negative on State laws was only laid to rest on July 17, when the Convention turned to the Paterson-Martin "supremacy" formula whereby federal laws and treaties would bind State judges. 2 Farrand 28–29; and see infra, Chapter 8, text accompanying notes 5–12. So too, judicial participation in a Council of Revision which could veto Congressional Acts was voted down on July 21. 2 Farrand 80.

The first "arising under" phrase occurred on July 18, one day after adoption of the Paterson-Martin "supremacy" clause; it provided that jurisdiction "shall extend to cases arising under laws passed by the general Legislature and to such other questions as involve the National peace and harmony," 2 Farrand 39, 46. Such questions, one may surmise, would comprehend State violations of mooted Constitutional prohibitions such as the emission of paper money, 1 Farrand 317–318, and the "harmony" phrase may therefore be regarded as a forerunner of "arising under this Constitution." And the "arising under" phrase itself may be viewed as an attempt to coordinate Article III jurisdiction with the newly-fashioned Supremacy Clause; see Chapter 8, text accompanying note 100. That clause, sponsored by the jealous Small States, contemplated that State courts would enforce only such laws as they determined were "in pursuance" of the Articles of Union. Infra, Chapter 8, text accompanying notes 199–212.

It is true that the insertion of the words "this Constitution" in the "arising

may safely be concluded that such Founders expressed the sense of the Convention and the Ratifying conventions, then we should be slow to read the "arising under" clause, which some of them expressly stated embraced judicial review, in such a way as to defeat their design.

Another Corwin argument is that so far as the "arising under" clause would extend the judicial power of review to Congressional Acts it would have been "mere surplusage, for the simple reason that [such cases] were already there." This he deduces from the absence of the "pursuance" clause from Article III so that the "judicial power . . . extends to *every* Act of Congress whether made in pursuance of the Constitution or not," that is, the courts can consider whether an Act of Congress "be made within the limits of its delegated power or be an assumption of power beyond the grants in the Constitution."[29] The "judicial power" is not enlarged by omission; it is the product of express grant, so that the omission of the "pursuance" clause from Article III supplied nothing that could take the place of the express grant of "arising under" jurisdiction.[30] Article III did not purport to grant unbounded "judicial power" but power limited to enumerated "cases or controversies"; in consequence the threshold inquiry is always whether a given case falls into one of the enumerated categories.[31] The courts are authorized to consider whether an Act of Congress is "within the limits of its delegated power or an [unconstitutional] assumption of power"[32] only because a statutory invasion of a constitutional right presents a case "arising under" the Constitution.[33] At this point Corwin might have asked: How do courts obtain jurisdiction where

---

under" clause came quite late in the day. 2 Farrand 423, 430. But from the beginning the Virginia Plan had contemplated that the Judiciary would act as a "check" on the national legislature. Supra, Chapter 3, text accompanying notes 11–12. Although there was likewise general agreement on needed judicial review of treaties, the word "treaties" was also a late insertion in the "arising under" clause. 2 Farrand 424, 431. In short, the several insertions were made when what is now Article III, §2, was "taken up" by the Convention in order, presumably, to give effect to the earlier consensus.

[29] Corwin, *Doctrine* 14–15.

[30] The absence of "in pursuance" from Article III is discussed infra, Chapter 8, text accompanying notes 104–108.

[31] Wright 14.

[32] Corwin, *Doctrine* 15.

[33] Corwin, *Doctrine* 15, said, "No doubt it must be allowed that cases involving the question of constitutionality with reference to acts of Congress are describable

a statute does not in fact invade constitutional rights? The explanation lies in administrative exigency. A court cannot know until it examines a given charge whether the statute is unconstitutional or not, so of necessity it must, in legal parlance, have "jurisdiction to determine jurisdiction"[34] if it is to act at all. Upon such examination it may determine that the charge is unfounded, dismiss the case, and leave the statute untouched. But that examination and that determination are only possible because the judicial power was expressly extended to cases "arising under" the Constitution.

Professor Bickel apparently is among those who find the "arising under" clause inadequate to carry the burden of judicial review. Taking off from Marshall's it is "too extravagent to be maintained" that those who granted the "arising under" jurisdiction meant that such cases would be decided without judicial examination of the Constitution in the course of decision, he concludes that this reading, "although out of line with the general scheme of Article III, may be possible; but it is optional."[35] When he turns from bare text to history, he concludes that

> it is as clear as such matters can be that the Framers of the Constitution specifically, if tacitly, expected that the federal courts would assume a power—of whatever exact dimensions—to pass on the constitutionality of actions of the Congress and the President . . . Moreover, not even a colorable showing of decisive historical evidence to the contrary can be made.[36]

as 'cases arising under this Constitution.'" But he asked, "why, if the Framers wanted judicial review and still thought it necessary to provide for it specifically, did they not choose language . . . as explicit and unmistakable as that describing, for example, the veto power of the President?" Id. at 16–17. Article I, §7 (2)—which requires that before a bill "become a law" it be submitted for approval by the President; if approval is withheld, reconsideration by both Houses and re-passage by a two-thirds vote is required to make a bill "law"—could state simply the narrow purpose of the veto. But the functions of the judicial power are multiple and complex, not as susceptible of succinct statement. Besides, the meaning of the language chosen was plain enough to the Founders. Supra, text accompanying notes 16–21.

[34] United States v. United Mine Workers of America, 330 U.S. 258, 292 n. 57 (1947); Wright 44.

[35] Bickel 5–6.

[36] Id. at 15–16. He dilutes the force of this remark by stating that "it will never be entirely clear just exactly where the collective judgment—which alone is decisive—came to rest." But cf. supra, Chapter 3, text accompanying notes 312–322.

That history constrains one to give the "arising under" clause a construction that would effectuate this "expectation," in response to the basic doctrine of documentary interpretation: give effect to the intention of the draftsmen.[37]

Professor Bickel, if I do not misunderstand him, does not make this correlation, apparently because—in reliance on Holmes's "Continuity with the past is not a duty; it is merely a necessity," and Holmes's statement that it is "revolting" to adhere to a rule of law the grounds of which "have vanished long since"—he concludes that judicial review "represents a choice that men have made and ultimately we must justify it in our own time."[38] Holmes was discussing the judicial role in fashioning the common law, for example, rules of tort and contract, a domain in which courts traditionally have played a creative role, and where legislatures are free to alter judge-made rules. But interpretation of the Constitution is something else again; here judges enjoy nothing like the latitude they exercise in formulating or revising the common law. Changes in the Constitution were meant to be accomplished by Amendment,[39] and although Chief Justice Hughes remarked that the Constitution is what the Court says it is, the stark implications of that dictum have yet to win conscious acceptance by the American people.[40] A Constitution refashioned to the heart's desire of the Court might be a better document than one which the people could redesign by

[37] See supra, note 4. We "cannot rightly prefer" a meaning "which will defeat rather than effectuate the Constitutional purpose." United States v. Classic, 313 U.S. 299, 316 (1941). In the First Congress, Gerry stated, "why should we construe any part of the Constitution in such a manner as to destroy its essential principles, when a more consonant construction can be obtained?" 1 *Ann. Cong.* 491.

[38] Bickel 16.

[39] Compare Gerry's statement in the First Congress, quoted infra, Chapter 8, text accompanying note 244. In Bell v. Maryland, 378 U.S. 226, 318, 342 (1964), Justice Black stated, "changes in the Constitution, when thought necessary, are to be proposed by Congress or conventions and ratified by the States. The Founders gave no such amending power to this Court" (dissenting opinion, Harlan and White, JJ. concurring). Justice Black himself has not hesitated to "amend" the Constitution in reliance on very dubious history. Berger, "Constructive Contempt: A Post-Mortem," 9 *U. Chi. L. Rev.* 602, 614–627 (1942).

[40] Professor Frankfurter wrote President Roosevelt about the "Court-packing" plan, "People have been taught to believe that when the Supreme Court speaks it is not they who speak but the Constitution, whereas, of course, in so many vital cases, it is *they* who speak and *not* the Constitution. And I verily believe that that is what the country most needs to understand." Freedman, *Roosevelt and Frankfurter, Their Correspondence*, 383 (1967).

Amendment,[41] but the Constitution is revered by the people precisely because it is deemed a permanent safeguard of rights that were secured from alteration except by Amendment.[42]

If judicial review "represents a choice that men have made," that choice was made either by the Founders or presumably by the acquiescence of the American people in the Court's construction of the Constitution over a period of 166 years, which one might regard as a form of ratification.[43] But such "ratification" would sidestep the Constitutional requirement that change be made by Amendment, and usurpation would become sanctified by inertia. Judicial "lawlessness" cannot be legitimated by the passage of time, as *Erie Ry. Co. v. Tompkins* startlingly demonstrated.[44] Let it be assumed, however, that one way or another a "choice" was made, "ultimately," says Bickel, "we must justify it as a choice in our own time,"[45] which means, I suppose, that it is open to us to repudiate it. Professor Bickel's interesting "justification" of judicial review removes that choice to the closet of contemporary political philosophers, but the substitution of their views for those of Hamilton, Iredell, James Wilson, and others does not add up to a "choice" by the people. Because judicial review is "counter-majoritarian," as Bickel justly reminds us,[46] because experience has taught us the

[41] For the view that the Court must be a leader and educator of opinion, see Bickel 239, 250, 267, cf. id. at 27; and see Rostow, "The Supreme Court and the People's Will," 33 *Notre Dame Lawyer* 573, 594, 596 (1958).

[42] See Gerry's remark in the First Congress, quoted supra, Chapter 6, note 152; and see supra, note 40. Cf. Corwin, *Court Over* 210–216.

[43] "The weight of one hundred and sixty-nine years of history is evidence that people do expect the courts to interpret, declare, adapt and apply these constitutional provisions, as one of their main protections against the possibility of abuse by Presidents and legislatures." Rostow, supra, note 41 at 590. Cf. Bickel, quoted infra, Chapter 8, note 32. The rejection of the "Court-packing" Plan in 1937, at the height of popular frustration with judicial invalidation of much-desired New Deal legislation, furnishes significant confirmation for the Rostow view. As A. L. Todd recently said in a Book Review, Baker, *Back to Back, The Duel Between FDR and the Supreme Court*, "the overriding lesson taught by the 1937 Supreme Court fight" is "the deep-seated devotion of the American people to the independence of their judiciary." *New York Times Book Review,* September 24, 1967, p. 39.

[44] After almost 100 years, Justice Brandeis said of the course upon which the Court had embarked in Swift v. Tyson, 16 Pet. 1 (1842), that the "unconstitutionality of the course pursued has now been made clear, and compels us" to "abandon" the "doctrine so widely applied throughout nearly a century." Erie Ry. Co. v. Tompkins, 304 U.S. 64, 77–78 (1938).

[45] Bickel 16.

[46] Ibid.

cost of obstruction to necessary social change by a wilful majority of the Court which identified its prejudices with Constitutional dogma,[47] the people have a right to be consulted today if they were not consulted in the past. If the power of judicial review is not to be found in the Constitutional text, if it was not ratified by the "collective judgment" of the Convention, which Bickel considers "alone is decisive,"[48] it is high time that judicial review should be legitimized and that the people should be permitted to "choose" in the form of an Amendment.

Let us consider Bickel's conclusion that Marshall's reading is "out of line with the general scheme of Article III," apparently because Article III furnishes no guide to the "nature and extent of the function of the Court—the judicial power," no answer to the question whether the Court is empowered "when it decides a case, to declare that a duly enacted statute violates the Constitution," because "it does not purport to tell the court how to decide cases; it only specifies what kinds of cases the Court shall have jurisdiction to deal with at all."[49] "Note well," he states, "that what the Constitution extends to cases arising under it is 'the judicial power,'" and asks, "What are the nature and extent of the function of the Court—the judicial power?" Professor Bickel wraps the words in mystery they did not have for the Framers; for them the words had no recondite significance but were merely another name for courts or judges.[50] "Judicial power" was substituted without debate by the Convention for the words "The jurisdiction of the Supreme Court,"[50a] perhaps as a succinct way of comprehending the jurisdic-

---

[47] In 1937, Frankfurter wrote President Roosevelt that "the Supreme Court for about a quarter of a century has distorted the power of judicial review into a revision of legislative policy, thereby usurping powers belonging to the Congress and to the legislatures of the several states." Freedman, *Roosevelt and Frankfurter, Their Correspondence* 384 (1967). Compare dissenting opinion of Justice Holmes in Lochner v. New York, 198 U.S. 45, 75 (1905); Charles Clark, Introduction to Corwin, *Twilight of the Supreme Court* xviii-xix (1934); Berger, "Constructive Contempt: A Post-Mortem," 9 *U. Chi. L. Rev.* 602, 605, 641–642 (1942).

[48] Bickel 16.

[49] Bickel 5.

[50] Iredell referred to the courts as the "judicial power, in exercise of their authority." 2 McRee 173. Ellsworth said of "a law which the Constitution does not authorize" that "the judicial power, the national . . . judges will declare it void." 2 Elliot 196. The Declaration of Independence complains of the King's refusal of "assent to laws for establishing Judiciary Powers," i.e., courts.

[50a] 2 Farrand 431. Instead of viewing "judicial power" as a crystal-ball, we do

tion of the inferior courts. It is simpler, I suggest, to read "judicial power" as the synonym for jurisdiction, for which the words had been substituted, and to deduce that judges were merely expected to act as such within the circumscribed jurisdiction conferred by Article III, just as today when a court is given jurisdiction of cases arising under the Sherman Antitrust law, it is expected to act after the fashion of a court, that is, to apply the law to the particular case.

For the moment let us shift to "what kind of cases the Court shall have jurisdiction to deal with at all." One kind is "cases arising under this Constitution," which Randolph equated with "cases arising *from* this Constitution."[51] The citizen who not unjustifiably looks to the Constitution for protection and gives those words their ordinary meaning, as well he may,[52] properly may conclude that a statute which violates his constitutionally guaranteed right presents a case "arising under" or "from" the Constitution, and, in consequence, that he may ask a court to "deal" with his case. Despite his misgivings, Corwin said, "No doubt it must be allowed that cases involving the question of constitutionality with reference to acts of Congress are describable as 'cases arising under this Constitution.'"[53] One would be hard put to reject this inference from the ordinary meaning of the words. "Jurisdiction" of such a claim is

---

well to ponder on Maitland's remark about the antecedent word "jurisdiction": "We puzzle foreigners by our lax use of the word 'jurisdiction' and it is remarkable enough. Whatever the justice has had to do has become the exercise of a jurisdiction, whether he was refusing a license or sentencing a thief, this was an exercise of jurisdiction, *an application of the law to a particular case.*" Maitland, *Collected Papers* 478 (1911).

[51] Quoted supra, note 22.

[52] The reason that "every word employed in the Constitution is to be expounded in its plain, obvious, and common sense, unless the context furnishes some ground to control, qualify or enlarge it," as Justice Story early stated, is that "The people make [constitutions], the people adopt them, the people must be supposed to read them, with the help of common sense, and cannot be presumed to admit in them any recondite reading or extraordinary gloss." Story *On the Constitution* §451 (4th ed. 1873). Yates took for granted in 1788 that judges would be bound to "give such meaning to the constitution, as comports best with the common, generally received acceptation of the words in which it is expressed, regarding their ordinary and popular use." Quoted Corwin, *Court Over* 235. In the North Carolina convention, Lenoir said, "A constitution ought to be understood by every one. The most humble and trifling characters . . . have a right to know what foundation they stand upon." 4 Elliot 201.

[53] Corwin, *Doctrine* 14. But see Corwin, 4 *Mich. L. Rev.* 618–619. A case arises under the Constitution "whenever its correct decision depends upon the construction of" the Constitution. Tennessee v. Davis, 100 U.S. 257, 264 (1880). This was Yates's 1788 view; supra, text accompanying note 16.

therefore a reasonable inference from the text, and if that be conceded, it would be a singular conclusion that a court is powerless to
"declare" that the "statute violates the Constitution" when the
jurisdiction is invoked. So to conclude is to give and abort jurisdiction at one stroke. It cannot be pure coincidence that Ellsworth
should say of an unconstitutional law that "the *judicial power,* the
national . . . judges will declare it void," particularly since Mason
expressly identified the grant of jurisdiction with the power to
"declare" a statute void. Speaking in the Virginia convention with
reference to the prohibition of ex post facto laws, Mason stated,
"Will it not be the duty of the federal court to say that such laws
are prohibited? . . . an express power is given to the federal court
to *take cognizance* of such controversies, and *to declare* null all *ex
post facto* laws."[54]

Professor Bickel's demand that the grant of jurisdiction should
"tell the court how to decide cases" is, to say the least, novel. Seldom
did an innovatory grant of jurisdiction tell that to the courts. When
the path-breaking Statute of Westminster II (1285),[55] for example,
gave rise to the vast jurisdiction of Action on the Case, it merely
authorized the issuance of writs in cases "of like nature" lest it
happen that the court should fail "to minister justice unto the com-
plainants." How justice was to be "ministered," what the ingredients
of judgment were to be, traditionally was left to the judges. The
early judges "were almost compelled to be original,"[56] for they were
"dealing with an unprecedented state of affairs, meeting new facts
by new expedients,"[57] precisely the situation that would confront

[54] The Ellsworth quotation is in 2 Elliot 196. Mason is quoted 3 Elliot 479–480
(emphasis added). See also "Centinel," supra, text accompanying note 19.
[55] 13 Edw. I, Ch. 24.
[56] Pollock, *Expansion of the Common Law* 49 (1904).
[57] Pollock & Maitland, *History of English Law* 108 (2d ed. 1899). "The
judicial system . . . as it existed at the beginning of the 19th century . . .
was compounded in all its parts of a 'heterogeneous growth of complex past expedients.'" 1 Holdsworth, *History of English Law* 402 (1903). While this was
said in a discussion of the profusion of English types of courts, it is no less true of
the development of procedure and the common law by the courts. Cf. id. at
406–407; Pollock, *Expansion of the Common Law* 50 (1904). One of the greatest bursts of English judicial creativity, the development of "negligence" doctrine, took place after 1787. See Green, *Traffic Victims: Tort Law and Insurance*
10–19 (1958).
"The powers inherent in the judicial office when Holt was Lord Chief Justice
exist in undiminished force today. One does not extinguish them by saying that

the new judges under the unprecedented Constitution. Judicial creativity has been the sustaining source of the common law, and one of the most creative of the judicial innovators, Lord Mansfield, was a contemporary of the Founders. Every novel grant of jurisdiction, I submit, therefore posited that judges, in deciding disputes, would exercise powers that were suitable to the jurisdiction conferred. But, it may be asked, if we are to look to English law for the scope of "judicial power," as indeed we must, does not that law show that English judges had no authority in the process of decision to set aside an Act of Parliament? "Legislative omnipotence," however, had unmistakably been brushed aside by the Founders.[58] Then too, English judges had never been called upon to deal with a written Constitution, and one which expressly prohibited certain legislative acts, which carefully enumerated the powers conferred upon the legislature,[59] which then extended the "judicial power" to cases "arising under this Constitution," and which declared in the cognate Supremacy Clause that the Constitution was to be the "supreme law of the land," and that "laws made in pursuance thereof" were equally to be the "supreme law," the plain implication being that laws *not* "in pursuance thereof," that is, inconsistent with the Constitution, were *not* to be the "supreme law."[60] These considerations preclude an assumption that earlier "limitations" of judicial authority as against the Parliament were being imported into a revolutionary document that for the first time *explicitly confined* legislative power. Faced with such unprecedented legislative limitations and the novel jurisdiction, the judges could be expected to do what English judges ever had been wont to do, to "supplement and enlarge the law . . . as the novelty of questions coming before

---

the earlier centuries were formative." Cardozo, *Paradoxes of Legal Science* 21 (1928).

[58] Supra, Chapter 2, text accompanying notes 128–134; cf. Chapter 3, text following note 311.

[59] The significance of those facts was writ large in the minds of the Founders. For example, Governor Johnston said in North Carolina, "a parallel has been drawn between the British Parliament and Congress. The powers of Congress are all circumscribed, defined and clearly laid down. So far they may go, but no farther. But, sir, what are the powers of the British Parliament? They have no written constitution in Britain." 4 Elliott 64. See also supra, Chapter 2, text accompanying notes 128–132.

[60] The implications of "in pursuance" and of the Supremacy Clause are discussed infra, Chapter 8, text accompanying notes 1–244.

them may require,"[61] in a word, to "declare" what the jurisdiction conferred required in the premises. And, as will appear, the Article VI definition of the "supreme law" in fact furnished a guide to the courts for the exercise of the "arising under" jurisdiction.

Professor Bickel's analysis is not readily reconciled with his view that the Court *can* "declare" that a *State* statute violates the Constitution. The Court, he states, can apply the Constitution "against inconsistent state law throughout the country," and it is possible to read the "arising under" clause restrictively, for example, to confine it to "acts of states."[62] Nothing in the "arising under" clause tells the Court that it may "declare that a duly enacted [State] statute violates the Constitution," yet Bickel experiences no difficulty on *that* score. Nor does the Clause tell the Court that *only* a State "duly enacted statute" may be so declared, that federal statutes are excluded. Every textual omission marshaled by Bickel against review of a Congressional Act may as plausibly be invoked when a State statute collides with the Constitution. Article III no more tells the Court "how to decide" a conflict between Constitution and State law than between federal law and Constitution. It no more answers the question whether the Court is empowered to "declare that a duly enacted [State] statute violates the Constitution" than it does when a violation by federal Act is charged. So far as the *text* of Article III is concerned, if an infringement of Constitutional rights by State "statute" presents an "arising under" case, as Bickel must necessarily postulate, inescapably a violation by federal "statute" does the same. His restrictive reading is an importation, not at all compelled by the language or "scheme" of Article III. To contract the ordinary meaning of broad constitutional terms, something more is required than a "possibility" that they may be read

---

[61] Pollock, *Expansion of the Common Law* 49 (1904). In citing such language I do not of course suggest that the Court was given a free hand to refashion the substantive terms of the Constitution, see supra, text accompanying notes 39–42, and see notes 39, 40, but rather that if it was alleged that a statute violated the Constitution and therefore constituted a case "arising under" the Constitution, the judges were expected under the novel jurisdiction to "declare" the violation, if so they found. As Lord Mansfield said in Rex v. Barker, 3 Burr. 1265, 1267, 97 Eng. Rep. 823, 825 (1762), "The right itself being recent, there can be no direct ancient precedent." See also Rex v. Electricity Commissioners [1924] 1 K.B. Div. 171, 192.

[62] Bickel 13, 6; Crosskey 1107 also considers that judicial review "was meant to be provided generally as to the Acts of the States."

restrictively, something amounting to a clear indication that so the Founders plainly intended that the broad language should be read.[63] Nor should the "arising under" clause be read in total isolation from Article VI,[64] which defines the "supreme law" to include laws "in pursuance" of the Constitution, impliedly directing that laws not "in pursuance thereof" shall not be given effect, of which more anon.[65]

Professor Crosskey argues that the "arising under" clause was required in order to authorize enforcement of the Constitution "upon the States," and consequently the clause "does not necessarily include" review of Congressional Acts, so it must be proven by "other provisions of the Constitution that such review was intended."[66] His demand for proof reflects his presumption of "legislative omnipotence," which the Founders rejected.[67] Use of extrinsic evidence to justify coverage of one type—State violations—of "arising under" issue does not "necessarily" restrict the ordinary meaning of "arising under"; rather it invites the use of other extrinsic evidence that the broad language includes other instances as well. Crosskey, moreover, reverses the normal order of things: Article III provides that "The judicial power shall extend to *all* cases . . . arising under this Constitution"; it adds to the ordinary meaning of "arising under" the comprehensive word "all." One who would make "all" mean less than all has the burden of proving why the ordinary meaning should not prevail, of advancing "a strong and independent reason for rejection of the excluded applications, such as the rescue of the general provisions from absurdity."[68] Indeed, Crosskey himself opens up the "arising under" clause for review of some *federal* Acts "within certain circumscribed areas," for example, acts trenching on judicial "self-defense," when he

[63] Cf. supra, note 52, and infra, text accompanying note 68.

[64] "Of course, the document must be read as a whole, and any particular phrase is informed by the purpose of the whole." Bickel 12.

[65] Infra, Chapter 8, text accompanying notes 27–61.

[66] Crosskey 983.

[67] Supra, Chapter 2, text accompanying notes 128–134; Chapter 3, text following note 311.

[68] Hart, Book Review 1465; and see supra, note 52. "If the text be clear and distinct," said Justice Story, "no restriction upon its plain and obvious import ought to be admitted, unless the inference is irresistible." Martin v. Hunter's Lessee, 1 Wheat. 304, 338 (1816); see also Sturges v. Crowninshield, 4 Wheat. 122, 202 (1819).

concludes that "the Supreme Court appears to have justly, against Congress, a right of judicial review."[69] Like an accordion, the clause is thus made to expand or contract according to Crosskey's taste in extrinsic evidence. But so far as the *textual* analysis goes, one may logically claim that if the "arising under" clause embraces one type of violation by federal statutes, and all violations by State statutes, then *any* statutory violation of Constitutional rights, including violations by all federal statutes, presents a "case arising under this Constitution."

Professor Bickel would dispose of "all" by pointing to the fact that in some cases "under . . . the laws" courts "often leave determinations of issues of fact and even issues that may be thought 'of law' to administrative agencies. And under both 'the Laws . . . and Treaties,' much of the decision concerning meaning and applicability may be received ready-made from the Congress and the President. In some cases of all three descriptions, judicial decision may be withheld altogether—and it is for this reason that it will not do to place reliance on the word 'all.' "[70] Over the years, it is true, the Court has in a number of instances "arising under *the laws*" self-denyingly restricted review. For example, in working out a division of labor with administrative agencies, the Court, with a bow to alleged administrative expertise, has insulated findings of fact from review—provided that they are supported by "adequate" evidence.[71] Never, it may be added, has it expressly abdicated the function of inquiring into administrative *jurisdiction*,[72] and it has in fact stated, per Justice Frankfurter, that "An agency may not finally determine the limits of its statutory power."[73] Professor Bickel cited no case in which the Court declined review of cases involving denials of Constitutional rights, that is, "arising under the Constitution" as distinguished from "under the laws." And since he looks for light as to the meaning of "all" to the Court's own process of inclusion and exclusion, how can he reject Marshall's very early

[69] Crosskey 1002–1003, 1007. See Hart's critique of this shift. Hart, Book Review 1471–1475.
[70] Bickel 6.
[71] Morgan v. United States, 298 U.S. 468, 480 (1936).
[72] Elsewhere I have questioned whether, under the Constitution, it can do so. Berger, "Administrative Arbitrariness and Judicial Review," 65 *Colum. L. Rev.* 55, 89 (1965).
[73] Social Security Bd. v. Nierotko, 327 U.S. 358, 369 (1940).

inclusion in "all" of conflicts between federal laws and the Constitution, an inclusion from which the Court has never wavered?[74]

The Convention itself indicated that "all" was to be read comprehensively. Toward the close of the Convention, when it was proposed to interpolate the words "this Constitution" in the "arising under" clause, Madison

> doubted whether it was not going too far to extend the jurisdiction of the Court *generally* to cases arising under the Constitution, and whether it ought not to be *limited* to cases of a Judiciary Nature. The right of *expounding* the Constitution in cases not of this nature ought not to be given that Department.

The Convention concluded that the "jurisdiction given was constructively limited to cases of a Judiciary Nature," presumably by the words "cases or controversies," and the interpolation was adopted.[75] Although the magnitude of the jurisdiction was thus brought before the Convention,[76] although Madison's reference to

[74] Marshall's inclusion of conflicts between federal laws and the Constitution was implicit in Marbury v. Madison, 1 Cranch 137 (1803), wherein he asserted the power of the Court to declare a Congressional Act unconstitutional. Consider too his statement in Cohens v. Virginia, 6 Wheat. 264, 392 (1821): "Why" should a State prosecution in violation of Constitutional rights "be excepted from that provision which expressly extends the judicial power of the Union to *all* cases arising under the constitution and laws."

It may be thought that the doctrine of "political questions" marks an area in which the Court declined to review denials of Constitutional rights. That doctrine largely proceeds from the premise that jurisdiction to decide has been lodged by the Constitution in some other department than the judiciary. Berger, "Executive Privilege v. Congressional Inquiry," 12 *U.C.L.A. L. Rev.* 288, 1352–1355 (1965). But from the outset, Luther v. Borden, 7 How. 1, 47 (1849), differentiated the "high power" of determining whether Congressional and Presidential acts "are beyond the limits of power marked out for them . . . by the Constitution." And in Baker v. Carr, 369 U.S. 186, 211 (1962), the Court declared that it is "error to suppose that every case or controversy which touches foreign relations [an important "political question" category] lies beyond judicial cognizance." Reid v. Covert, 354 U.S. 1 (1957), illustrates that constitutional guarantees will be enforced in this area.

[75] 2 Farrand 430 (emphasis added). By cases of a "judiciary nature" was meant cases submitted by adversary parties for judicial determination as distinguished from a roving commission to veto Congressional legislation. Compare Iredell's remark, supra, Chapter 3, text accompanying note 168; see also infra, Chapter 9, note 5.

[76] Compare subsequent criticism in the Ratification conventions of the "unlimited" jurisdiction conferred by the "arising under" clause. Supra, text accompanying note 22, and note 22.

"giving" the "right of expounding the Constitution" recalled, if it was not geared into, the earlier remarks that identified "expounding" with judicial review,[77] no one suggested that review of Congressional Acts be excluded. The only "limitation" upon the interpolated "this Constitution" to which reference was made was to "cases of a Judiciary Nature," which itself suggests that the engrafting of further limitations would be amendatory rather than interpretive.

A restrictive reading of the "arising under" clause can not be extracted from textual compulsions, but in each instance will be found to rest on certain presuppositions *dehors* the text, assumptions about "legislative omnipotence," about a "tradition" that English laws were not overturnable by judges, and the like. And the "question to be decided" is what role did these presuppositions play in the thinking of the Founders, a question which exclusive focus on the *text* removes to the realm of speculation. *History,* on the other hand, shows that Parliamentary and legislative supremacy were roundly rejected, that "interpretation" was regarded as a judicial function, that the Constitution was regarded as "fundamental law." The interrelation of these concepts was perceived by leading Founders. To recall only one, Iredell regarded a constitution as "fundamental law," so that "the judicial power, in exercise of their authority must take notice of it," and "as no article of the Constitution can be repealed by a Legislature . . . the *fundamental unrepealable law* must be obeyed by rejection of an act unwarranted by or inconsistent with it." When an Act is necessarily brought before the courts, he said, they must "unavoidably, determine one way or another" "whether the Assembly have or have not violated the Constitution."[78] This was likewise underscored by Yates,[79] it was reiterated by Hamilton,[80] and it is in substance the argument made by Marshall in *Marbury v. Madison.*[81] Nor should it be doubted, I suggest, that the Founders deemed the phrase "cases arising under this Constitution" an adequate vehicle for the effectuation of these concepts. In the preratification debate, and in the Ratifying con-

[77] Supra, Chapter 3, text accompanying notes 31–38.
[78] 2 McRee 173.
[79] Supra, Chapter 3, text accompanying notes 180–188.
[80] *Federalist* No. 78 at 506.
[81] 1 Cranch 137, 176–177 (1803).

ventions, leading figures, as we have seen, were agreed that the "arising under" clause embraced Congressional Acts. The matter was put with unmistakable clarity by Yates, who opposed adoption:

> The cases arising under the constitution must include such as bring into question its meaning, and will require an explanation of the nature and extent of the power of the different departments under it.
>
> This article, therefore, vests the judicial with a power to resolve all questions that may arise on any case on the construction of the constitution.

And he concluded that "the supreme court are authorized in the last resort to determine what is the extent of the powers of Congress."[82]

To such of the Founders and their critics as recorded their understanding—we cannot conjure evidence to the contrary out of thin air—[83] the "arising under" clause spoke plainly enough. "The eighteenth century draftsman," Crosskey himself stated, "felt no obligation to spell out every last detail in the documents he drew."[84] For a Convention, the leadership of which from the outset had expressly recognized the availability of judicial review,[85] the common-sense meaning of "arising under" needed no spelling out. Having conferred jurisdiction of cases "arising under" the Constitution, the draftsmen could reasonably assume, for example, that a Congressional violation of a Constitutional prohibition would "arise under"

[82] Quoted Corwin, *Court Over* 235, 352; and see supra, text accompanying notes 16–21.

[83] In the conduct of litigation, courts are accustomed to act on this rule; even when tempted to disbelieve a witness: "mere disbelief of testimony [not inherently incredible] is not the equivalent of proof to the contrary." Phillips v. Gookin, 231 Mass. 250, 251, 120 N.E. 691 (1918); Messon v. Liberty Fast Freight Co., 124 F.2d 448, 450 (2d Cir. 1942); Eckenrode v. Pennsylvania R. Co., 164 F.2d 996, 999 n.8 (3d Cir. 1947); cf. Miller v. Herzfeld, 4 F.2d 355, 356 (3d Cir. 1925); Magg v. Miller, 296 Fed. 973, 979 (D.C. Cir. 1924).

[84] Crosskey 364.

[85] Bowen 248, cites R. H. Lee, "fiercely anti-constitutionalist, who, commenting on the Convention's omission of a bill of rights, stated, "that when men have long and early understood certain matters as the common concerns of the country, they are apt to suppose those things are understood by others and need not be expressed." Lee himself understood that the Constitution provided for judicial review. Supra, Chapter 3, text accompanying note 153.

the Constitution. That assumption was confirmed by the fact that so the Ratifiers plainly understood. To my mind, these considerations furnish a sufficient answer to the question: "Then why didn't they say so?" To require more is to permit doubts harbored by present day students to displace the understanding of the Founders.[86] If we fail to discern what they perceived, the fault may lie with us.

Let us now examine Judge Learned Hand's "interpolation" theory against this background. In his 1958 Lectures, Judge Hand, though "unwilling to rest on the historical evidence,"[87] was prepared to "interpolate"[88] a power of judicial review in order to "keep the States, Congress, and the President within their prescribed powers."[89] Otherwise Congress would have been "substantially omnipotent" and the government "would almost certainly have foundered."[90] This, he stated, is "not a logical deduction from the structure of the Constitution but only a practical condition upon its successful operation."[91] Now the Founders unequivocally rejected "legislative omnipotence";[92] they saw quite clearly the "mischief to be cured." It was because of this that "limits" were provided and endlessly stressed. Aside from remarks by the leadership in the several conventions that the judiciary was the final instrument that would make these limits effective, how can we attribute to the most enlightened students of government ever produced by our country a failure to perceive that judicial review was the "practical condition" to meet the need? Indeed, they recorded that perception.[93] And if that insight cannot be denied, are we not constrained to conclude that the "arising under" language they employed in Article III was designed to confer power to deal with the evil. The problem therefore, I suggest, is not one of "interpolation" but of "interpretation,"[94] of construing constitutional language which is adapted to the purpose to cure a plainly perceived evil—a rule of interpretation with

[86] Cf. supra, text accompanying note 15.
[87] Bickel 46.
[88] Hand 14.
[89] Hand 15.
[90] Hand 11, 15.
[91] Hand 15.
[92] Supra, Chapter 2, text accompanying notes 128–133.
[93] Supra, Chapters 3 and 4.
[94] Professor Bickel regards it as "remarkable" that Professor Wechsler "believes that the existing power of the Supreme Court is grounded in the language of the Constitution and is not a mere interpolation." Bickel 49.

which the Founders were familiar.[95] That approach can draw support from the view of informed contemporaries that the "arising under" clause would embrace judicial review, and from expressions by the leadership in the several conventions that judicial review would be available to accomplish the cure.

In summary of the textual analysis, a claim that a statute invades a constitutionally protected right requires an inquiry whether the Constitution does in fact protect that right, and to the ordinary understanding it "arises under" the Constitution. Those who consider that the Court has jurisdiction to determine whether a State statute is repugnant to the Constitution confirm that understanding. Nothing contained in Article III indicates that jurisdiction is to turn on the provenance of the offending statute and that federal statutes which violate constitutional rights cannot present an "arising under" case. The understanding of the Founders was to the contrary, as is evidenced by the remarks of Marshall in Virginia, and of Yates, Martin, Pendleton, Wilson, and others. With due deference to Professor Bickel, Marshall's construction of the "arising under" clause in *Marbury v. Madison* is not merely a "possible" reading; it is not "out of line with the general scheme of Article III"; but, in the words of Yates, it represents the ordinary understanding of the "general scheme" of Article III and the function of the "arising under" clause.

No discussion of "arising under" is complete without a glance at Gouverneur Morris' letter of 1814, 27 years after the Convention, to which Beard and Horace Davis attach great importance from

---

[95] "Under principles coming down from Heydon's Case [3 Co. Rep. 7a, 76 Eng. Rept. 637 (1584), a court faced with the task of construction must endeavor to appreciate the mischief the framers were seeking to alleviate." Friendly, "The Bill of Rights as a Code of Criminal Procedure," 53 *Calif. L. Rev.* 929, 943 (1965). Randolph observed at the outset of the Convention that: "the general object was to provide a cure for the evils under which the U.S. labored." 1 Farrand 51. In the Virginia convention, Judge Pendleton, who presided, said that "The Federal Convention devised the paper on your table as a remedy to remove our political diseases." 3 Elliot 36. In 1830 Madison wrote that a "just guide" for interpretation of the Constitution was "The evils & defects for the curing which the Constitution was called for & introduced." 9 Madison, *Writings* 372. See the 18th century interpretive "rules" collected by Crosskey, one which is quoted supra, note 4; and see supra, note 6. Also counseling against a reading that would balk the remedy is the "sense of mission" which, as Corwin stated, animated the Framers because of the feeling that "if adequate remedies could not be devised for the shortcomings of the existing system . . . republican government itself must disappear from the earth." Corwin, *Court Over* 222; see also 1 Farrand 424, 431, 490, 515; 2 Elliot 240.

their very different vantage points. Morris stated that his fingers had written the Constitution, and that on the subject of the judiciary "conflicting opinions had been maintained with so much professional astuteness, that it became necessary to select phrases which, expressing my own notions, would not alarm others nor shock their self-love."[96] From this Davis infers that "the power of judicial control . . . was intentionally omitted."[97] In fact, the "arising under" clause came to the Committee on Style, of which Morris was a member, virtually in its final form.[98] The key words "judicial power" and "this Constitution" had been added on the floor of the Convention.[99] Nothing that affects judicial review was either added or omitted by that Committee. As to the "conflicting opinions," a "conflict" respecting judicial review is at best rested on Mercer's solitary "disapproval."[100] There *were* conflicts, for example, the States Righters opposed the creation of inferior federal courts;[101] there was opposition, if we may judge from the storm that blew up in the subsequent Ratification conventions, to appellate jurisdiction of questions of fact, which was thought to imperil trial by jury,[102] but here too the controlling phraseology had also been framed prior to the Committee's labors.[103] So far as the provision by Article III for judicial review is concerned, Morris' letter therefore affords scant support for Beard's inference that "the Constitution was not designed to be perfectly explicit on all points and to embody definitely the opinions of the majority of the Convention."[104]

[96] Beard 78–79; Davis, *Veto* 68.
[97] Davis, *Veto* 69.
[98] 2 Farrand 172, 186, 423–424, 430–431, 576, 600–601.
[99] Id. at 423, 424, 430–431.
[100] Supra, Chapter 3, text accompanying notes 78–80.
[101] Beard 79 n. 1. See e.g., 2 Farrand 45–46; 3 Elliot 527, 539.
[102] E.g., 4 Elliot 166, 144, 151, 165, 170; and see infra, Chapter 9 text accompanying notes 7–19. Iredell, who apparently had discussed the matter with Spaight, a Framer, said that "Everything could be agreed upon except the regulation of trial by jury in civil cases." 4 Elliot 166. Madison stated in the Virginia convention that the "principal criticism which has been made was against the appellate cognizance as well of fact as of law." 3 Elliot 572.
[103] 2 Farrand 424.
[104] Beard 79. Nor is Beard helped by Baldwin's statement in 1796 that among the questions "left a little ambiguous or uncertain" were "some question respecting the judiciary." This may serve to explain the fact that Congress was given the power to make "exceptions" to the Supreme Court's appellate jurisdiction in order to handle the many problems presented by appeals on *questions of fact*, which no single formula could settle. Infra, Chapter 9, text accompanying notes 7–19.

Let us pause to take stock. Beard's demonstration that the leadership of the Convention considered that judicial review would be available and that many silent members favored it seems to me unshaken; the few disapproving voices were greatly outnumbered. In the Ratifying conventions the promise of judicial review as a check on unbridled Congressional power emerges more clearly and without dissent. And, but for some equivocal remarks by Madison in the First Congress, balanced by his statement that the courts would be a "bulwark" for the Bill of Rights, that Congress, without regard to party lines, considered that judicial power to set aside unconstitutional Acts of Congress was part of the Constitutional scheme. The jurisdiction of "all cases . . . arising under this Constitution" conferred by Article III is broad enough to comprehend power to set aside Congressional Acts which are inconsistent with the Constitution. No basis for a restrictive reading of that clause is furnished by the several convention records; to the contrary, they confirm the contemporary understanding that "arising under" was intended to confer that power. The problem, in my view, is not therefore one of "implying" a power in the absence of appropriate language but of interpreting broad terms well-suited to the task, which confer power, to effectuate the intention of the Founders.[105]

Thus far discussion has proceeded in the frame of federal court review. The perspective broadens when the problem is viewed from the standpoint of State court determination of Constitutional issues, subject to Supreme Court review.

[105] See supra, note 4, and infra, Chapter 10, text accompanying note 161. The President's "removal" power is derived from his power to "appoint," and seems much more a creature of "implication," unilluminated by Convention or Ratification remarks, than does the construction of "arising under" to comprehend Congressional violations of the Constitution. Cf. Corwin, *Doctrine* 17.

THE CONSTITUTIONAL TEXT AND

JUDICIAL REVIEW: THE SUPREMACY

CLAUSE—STATE COURT REVIEW

The second of the Constitutional texts which bears on judicial review is the so-called "Supremacy Clause" contained in Article VI, section 2:

> This Constitution and the Laws of the United States which shall be made in Pursuance thereof; and all Treaties made, or which shall be made, under the authority of the United States, shall be the supreme law of the land; and the judges in every State shall be bound thereby, anything in the Constitution or Laws of any State to the contrary notwithstanding.

The origin of the Clause as a substitute for a proposed Congressional negative on State laws that contravene the Constitution lights up its purposes. What Madison called the "centrifugal tendency of the States" to "destroy the order and harmony of the political system" had led, to employ his own bill of particulars, to State violations of national treaties, to encroachments on federal authority, and to collisions of State interests.[1] So well known were these facts that the Virginia Plan proposal to empower the national legislature to "negative all laws passed by the several States, contravening in the opinion of the National Legislature the articles of Union," was, with the addition of the words "any Treaties," accepted at the outset without

[1] 1 Farrand 165, 164; see also Randolph, id. at 25–26; Wilson, id. at 166.

debate.[2] Charles Pinckney's subsequent proposal to expand the veto to all laws which the national legislature "should judge to be improper"[3] touched off a reaction inspired largely by fears of diminished State sovereignty. As Gerry stated, "The Natl. Legislature with such a power may enslave the States," and Bedford of Delaware feared that the "large states [would] crush the small ones." Pinckney's expansion was voted down.[4] Then, on June 15th, Paterson introduced the New Jersey, small-State Plan, the sixth resolution of which contained the germ of the Supremacy Clause, whereby State judges would be "bound" by national laws and treaties.[5] The earlier "negative" proposal came up again on July 25th, at which juncture Sherman argued that it was "unnecessary, as the Courts of the States would not consider as valid any law contravening the Authority of the Union."[6] In reply, Madison did not dispute the *power* of State judges, but said that "Confidence can [not] be put in State tribunals as guardians of the Ntl. authority and interests" because of the dependence of State judges on State legislatures, citing as an example, "In R. Island the judges who refused to execute an unconstitutional law were displaced, and others substituted by the Legislature."[7] Gouverneur Morris rejoined that "A law that ought to be negatived will be set aside in the judiciary department" and that the proposed Congressional power "was likely to be terrible to the States."[8] Sounding his earlier note, Sherman added that the legislative "negative" "involves a wrong principle, to wit, that a law of a State, contrary to the articles of the Union, would if not negatived, be valid and operative."[9] At this point, Luther Martin pro-

[2] Id. at 21, 54.

[3] Id. at 164.

[4] Id. at 165, 167, 168. Dickinson had said, "We must either subject the States to the danger of being injured by the power of the Natl. Govt. or the latter to the danger of being injured by that of the States. He thought the danger greater from the States." Id. at 167. See Butler's "vehement" opposition on State grounds, id. at 168; and Morris' "likely to be terrible to the States," 2 Farrand 27; see also id. at 28, 391.

[5] 1 Farrand 245.

[6] 2 Farrand 27.

[7] Id. at 27–28. Such considerations had led Madison to advocate judicial independence of Congress. Supra, Chapter 3, text accompanying notes 327–328. Madison's concern "was not with the powers but with the predispositions of the state courts." Hart, Book Review 1468.

[8] 2 Farrand 27–28.

[9] Id. at 28.

posed the original Supremacy Clause, which would make federal laws and treaties "the supreme law of the respective States" and binding on State courts; and this was adopted without dissent.[10] Pinckney reopened the matter on August 23d; but Sherman thought a Congressional negative "unnecessary, the laws of the General Government being Supreme and paramount to the State laws according to the Plan as it now stands."[11] After the motion to refer the matter to a committee was voted down, Pinckney withdrew his motion.[12]

Professor Crosskey agrees that the Supremacy Clause came into the Constitution "as a substitute for the general negative over all state legislative acts," but concludes that the object of the negative was to empower Congress to deal with the "difficulty growing from the normal and usual duty of judges to yield obedience to the acts of their own particular legislatures," a duty which he speedily converts to "absolute obedience."[13] For this he relies on Yates's record of Madison's early statement that "The judges of the State must give state laws their operation, although the law abridges the right of the ntl. govt."[14] Crosskey's attribution to Madison of a judicial "obedience" doctrine was earlier shown to be untenable.[15] Here it suffices to repeat that State judges understandably might be expected to give State laws and constitutions preeminence over *federal* laws, for they were servants of the State. Their higher duty to the nation was a developing concept and was yet to be forged by the provision that State judges were to be "bound" by the "supreme law of the land," "anything in the Constitution or laws of any State to the contrary notwithstanding." It required specific absolution, so some thought, before a State judge could give *federal* law overriding effect.[16] Nothing in Madison's statement suggests that State judges

---

[10] Id. at 28–29.

[11] Id. at 390.

[12] Id. at 391–392.

[13] Crosskey 985–986.

[14] 1 Farrand 169.

[15] Supra, Chapter 3, text accompanying notes 137–144.

[16] Supra, Chapter 3, text accompanying notes 137–144. Compare Luther Martin's explanation of his proposed original Supremacy Clause, 3 Farrand 286–287, discussed infra, text accompanying notes 77–80; and see supra, Chapter 3, text accompanying notes 139–140. Sherman considered that State courts would hold invalid State laws that contravened the Constitution. Supra, text accompanying note 6.

were required to yield "absolute obedience" to *State* laws that were repugnant to *State* constitutions, and such an inference is foreclosed by his implicit praise of Rhode Island judges who had declared a State statute unconstitutional.[17] Crosskey's theory that the proposed Congressional negative of State laws was a means of dealing with a supposed State court duty of "absolute obedience" to State legislatures finds scant support in the facts.[18]

Even after adoption of the Supremacy Clause Wilson continued to press for the Congressional negative because "The firmness of the judges is not of itself sufficient. Something further is requisite . . . It will be better to prevent the passage of an improper law, than to declare it void when passed."[19] Still enamored of the "negative," Madison wrote Jefferson shortly after the Convention in terms reminiscent of Wilson, "it may be said that the judicial authority, under our new system will keep the States within their proper limits, and supply the place of a negative on their laws. The answer is, that it is more convenient to prevent the passage of a law than to declare it void after it is passed."[20] He preferred the "preventive" to the "corrective" approach,[21] and like Wilson desired a preventive power *before* "enactments became effective."[22] But the Convention stood firm; and its preference for courts rather than a Congressional "negative" on State laws topples another Crosskey fetish—the predominant role of English "legislative supremacy" in the thinking

[17] Quoted supra, text accompanying note 7; and see Hart, Book Review 1469–1470.

[18] Professor Hart branded Crosskey's use of the Yates recorded Madison statement to prove the "usual duty of judges to yield obedience to the acts of their own particular legislature" as constituting "as baldly unprincipled a use of a single fragment of evidence to the complete distortion of the record as a whole as [the reader] is likely to discover anywhere in American historiography." Hart, Book Review 1468.

[19] 2 Farrand 391.

[20] October 24, 1787; 3 Farrand 131, 134.

[21] Writing to John Tyler in 1833, Madison said of the "mode of controul on the Individual Legislatures, this might be either preventive or corrective. The former by a negative on the State laws; the latter by a Legislative repeal by a Judicial supersedeas . . . The preventive mode as the best if equally practicable with the corrective, was brought by Mr. R[andolph] to the consideration of the Convention." 3 Farrand 524, 527.

[22] Madison stated that the States "can pass laws which will accomplish their injurious objects before they can be repealed by the General Legislature or be set aside by the National Tribunals," 2 Farrand 27, consequences that could be averted by a veto before effectiveness.

of the Framers.[23] Twice Madison called attention to the familiar vetoes, "legislative" in nature, of Colonial legislation by the Privy Council,[24] and although he was joined by another important leader, James Wilson, in strenuous advocacy, the Convention flatly rejected Congress as the arbiter whether a State law contravened the Constitution. Alive to the undeniable need to keep States within bounds and to compel compliance with express prohibitions, confronted by a choice weighted in favor of Congress by the English practice, the Convention nevertheless refused to confide the task to Blackstone's "omnipotent legislature" and by the Supremacy Clause turned to the courts instead. In the upshot, State courts were preferred to Congress as the interpreters of Constitutional limitations on the States.[25] The fact that State courts may thus set aside State laws has implications for federal court review of federal laws that have not been sufficiently appreciated.

First, however, let us recur to the terms of the Supremacy Clause and consider the problems it presents under a number of headings: (1) What is the meaning of the words "in pursuance thereof"? (2) Is the clause "binding" on federal as well as State judges? (3) Does it purport to confer jurisdiction on either State or federal courts? (4) What are the implications of State court review of State laws for federal court review of federal laws? (5) Does the Clause contemplate that State judges may determine the constitutionality of Congressional Acts? and (6) Are such State court decisions reviewable by the Supreme Court?[26]

[23] For example, speaking of "judicial review of a *general* character," Crosskey stated that "the men of the Convention probably regarded the English law as the standing American *national* law upon this subject anyway." Cf. supra, Chapter 2, text accompanying notes 65, 101.

[24] Madison, 1 Farrand 168; 2 Farrand 28. Pinckney stated that the "negative of the Crown had been found beneficial." 1 Farrand 164; and see Corwin, *Court Over* 18, 28.

[25] Jefferson had written Madison on June 20, 1787, i.e., early in the Convention, "The negative proposed them [Congress] on all acts of the several legislatures is now for the first time suggested to my mind. *Prima facie*, I do not like it. Would not an appeal from the State judicatures to a federal court be as effectual a remedy?" Quoted Warren, *Congress* 30. His view was adopted in the Judiciary Act of 1789.

[26] Brinton Coxe stated that the words "law of the land" contained in the Supremacy Clause had a "distinct meaning, constituting a body of laws and privileges . . . which it was particularly the duty of the judiciary to enforce." Coxe vi (as reconstructed by Meigs). This aspect of "the law of the land" merits further investigation. Williamson's comment in the Convention respecting the

"IN PURSUANCE THEREOF"

It had commonly been assumed that "in pursuance thereof" means "consistent with," "not repugnant to," the Constitution,[27] until Corwin pointed in 1938 to several statements contemporary with the Constitution that " 'in pursuance of the Constitution' meant only in consequence of it."[28] This has been elaborated by Crosskey, who found in Dr. Johnson's 1755 *Dictionary* that the "only" meaning assigned to "pursuant" was "done in consequence or prosecution of anything"—in Crosskey's example, goods shipped "pursuant to" a contract but not "in accord with" its requirements. Prudently he added that "while it might possibly be wrong to conclude that 'in pursuance of' could not be used, in the eighteenth century, to mean 'in consistency with' when such meaning was in some way indicated in a particular context, it does seem proper to conclude that Johnson's definition truly indicates what seemed to him the general and usual meaning."[29] Dr. Johnson's opinion is inconclusive if it was not shared by the Founders.

Although the Crosskey interpretation was cogently criticized by Hart,[30] it has since been reformulated by Bickel. Confining himself to the text, Bickel states that "it fully meets all else that is compelling

---

"14th Resolve" of the Virginia Plan ("the Legislature, Executive & Judiciary powers within the several States ought to be bound by oath to support the articles of Union," 1 Farrand 22) that "This resolve will be unnecessary, as the union will become the law of the land," id. at 207, implies that the Judiciary would therefore be bound to enforce it. A similar suggestion is contained in Jefferson's letter to Adams in 1787, stating that "It has . . . been the decision of our courts that the Confederation is a part of the law of the land and superior to the ordinary laws." Quoted Corwin, *National Supremacy* 30. Note also Wilson's "justice must be administered according to the law of the land." Quoted infra, text accompanying note 40. Cf. Maclaine, infra note 75.

Then there is Hamilton's statement in his "Letters from Phocion," 4 Hamilton, *Works* 232, 237: "If we enquire what is meant by the law of the land, the best commentators will tell us that it means due process of law, that is by indictment or presentment of good and lawful men, and trial and conviction in consequence." And, he repeated, "the constitutional mode of ascertaining whether this forfeiture [deprivation of a right] has been incurred, is by legal process, trial and conviction." Id. at 10. For Hamilton, we may infer, "the law of the land" spelled judicial enforcement of individual rights.

[27] Marbury v. Madison, 5 U.S. (1 Cranch) 137, 180 (1803). E.g., Ableman v. Booth, 21 How. (62 U.S.) 506, 520 (1858); Ware v. Hylton, 3 Dallas 199, 235 (1796), quoted infra, note 43.

[28] Corwin, *Court Over* 35.

[29] Crosskey 991–992.

[30] Hart, Book Review 1470.

in the language of the clause simply to conclude that the proviso that only those federal statutes are to be supreme which are made in pursuance of the Constitution means that the statutes must carry the outer indicia of validity lent them by enactment in accordance with the constitutional forms. If so enacted, a federal statute is constitutional," which is "to be taken as a given fact by state courts."[31] It is far from "simple" to conclude that words which have carried an accepted meaning for 175 years now mean something altogether different;[32] yet I would not rest on acquiescence over the years but rather would seek out the meaning that the "language of the clause" had for the Founders.

Professor Crosskey tells us that he "found no talks of 'pursuing, not violating, a constitution,' or 'a law' in the years before the Federal Convention assembled."[33] Let that be assumed and the lack is yet of no moment if the records of the several conventions supply such "talk." Crosskey proffers a remark by David Caldwell in the North Carolina convention: "The word *pursuance* is equivocal and ambiguous; a plainer word would be better."[34] But Crosskey overlooked Governor Johnston's immediate response:

> I do not know a word in the English language so good as the word *pursuance,* to express the idea meant and intended by the Constitution. Can any one understand the word other than this? . . . Every law *consistent* with the Constitution will have been made *in pursuance* of the powers granted by it. Every *usurpation* or law repugnant to it *cannot* have been made *in pursuance* of its powers. The latter will be nugatory and void.[35]

[31] Bickel 9. By the "forms," Professor Bickel means "the mechanical provisions that describe how a federal law is to be enacted—by the concurrence of both Houses and with the signature of the President." Ibid.
Compare Locke's teaching: "laws which transgressed . . . certain fundamental principles were not laws 'properly so called.'" Haines 40.

[32] Compare supra, Chapter 7, note 43. Speaking generally of judicial review, Professor Bickel stated that the "doctrines have held sway for roughly over a century and a half . . . Settled expectations have formed around them . . . It is late for radical changes." Bickel 14.

[33] Crosskey 960.

[34] Id. at 992; 4 Elliot 187.

[35] 4 Elliot 188 (emphasis supplied). Examining another portion of Crosskey's work, Professor Goebel comments, "This lack of candor in presenting evidence . . . is by no means a solitary example." Goebel, "Ex Parte Clio," 54 *Colum. L. Rev.* 450, 457 (1954). Compare Crosskey's partial citations of Tucker and Otis, supra, Chapter 2, note 134.

Johnston was not alone in this, and there were no dissenting voices. At the risk of tedium, I shall pile up the proof in the hope of stilling further useless debate on this score.

In the North Carolina convention, where Governor Johnston had spoken, Davie, who had been a member of the federal Convention, said

> it is not the supreme law in the exercise of a power not granted. It can be supreme *only in cases consistent* with the powers specially granted, and not in usurpations. If you grant any power to the federal government, the laws made *in pursuance of that power* must be supreme.[36]

His colleague Iredell said that "Everything is the law of the land . . . provided it be consistent with the Constitution." In discussing Article VI, he said that

> when the Congress passes a law consistent with the Constitution, it is to be binding on the people. If Congress, under pretense of executing one power, should, in fact, usurp another, they will violate the Constitution,

an "explanation," he said, "which appears to me, the plainest in the world." And, he stated, "The question, then, under this clause, will always be, whether Congress has exceeded its authority."[37] "Repugnancy," "usurpation," "consistent with," "excess of authority,"

Crosskey 972, states that "there are in James Madison's notes of the debates in the Federal Convention, for July 23d, certain uses of the word 'pursue' in the sense of 'observe,' and of the word 'pursuance' in the sense of 'observance,' which, if they can be relied upon as not fabricated . . . tend to indicate that such, perhaps, may have been the sense in which 'in Pursuance' was used in the Supremacy Clause." But he regards this as inconclusive because Wilson allegedly appeared to be unaware that the "primitive Supremacy Clause . . . had provided for judicial review, as to all the legislation of Congress," citing 2 Farrand 73. At the cited point, Wilson had renewed his attempt to unite the judges with the Executive in the veto, because he desired to give to judges a power reaching *beyond* unconstitutional laws to those that were merely "unjust," "unwise." See supra, Chapter 3, text accompanying note 26; and compare infra, text accompanying note 39.

[36] 4 Elliot 182 (emphasis added).
[37] Id. at 28, 178, 179.

were to be the tests under the Supremacy Clause whether a law was "in pursuance," "binding," or the "law of the land," not mere compliance with the "forms" of enactment.

The same view was taken in Pennsylvania. An opponent of the Constitution, Whitehill, had argued that "Laws may be made in *Pursuance* of the Constitution, though not agreeably to it."[38] Wilson, a Framer, and leader of the adoption forces, whose Notes record this remark, stated,

> it is possible that the legislature . . . may transgress the bounds assigned to it, and an act may pass, in the *usual* [that is, proper] *mode,* notwithstanding that transgression; but when it comes to be discussed before *the judges*—when they consider its principles, and find it to be incompatible with the superior power of the Constitution,—it is their duty to pronounce it *void.*[39]

Passage in the "usual mode" in Bickel's phrase, "in accordance with the constitutional forms" was therefore to provide no insulation from review. In his 1791 Lectures, Wilson repeated that if the "legislature should pass an act, manifestly repugnant to some part of the constitution," it is "the duty of the court to decide . . . for justice must

---

[38] McMaster & Stone 780. Corwin, *Court Over* 35 n. 35, cites McMaster & Stone 562. Nothing germane to "in pursuance" is to be found at that page. But at page 467, the minority dissent, published after the convention, said, "It has been alleged that the words 'pursuant to the constitution,' are a restriction upon the authority of Congress; but when it is considered that by other sections they are vested with every efficient power of government, and which may be exercised to the absolute destruction of the State governments, without any violation of even the forms of the constitution, this seeming restriction . . . appears to be nugatory and delusive." And see the "Centinel," id. at 611. Observe that the dissenters acknowledge the majority view that "in pursuance" would serve as a "restriction" upon Congress; they do not protest against the claimed power. As Corwin, *Doctrine* 66, remarked, "The absence of a Bill of Rights and the presence of the 'general welfare' and 'necessary and proper' clauses caused opponents of the Constitution to charge that the judges would never be able to stamp any act of Congress as invalid, that Congress' power was practically unlimited to begin with." It was not maintained that the judges lacked the power of judicial review, or that "in pursuance" would not lend itself to that purpose, but rather that the power would be ineffectual because Congress was given virtually unlimited power, i.e., judicial review is useful only to police "limits."

[39] 2 Elliot 446. See also Wilson, supra, Chapter 6, text accompanying notes 222–223. Yates too remarked that the legislature might "pass laws" which "they are not authorized to do by the Constitution." Quoted supra, Chapter 6, note 231.

be administered according to the law of the land."[40] Since only laws "in pursuance" of the Constitution were to be the "law of the land," Wilson pretty clearly equated "in pursuance" of with "not repugnant" to the Constitution.

In the Virginia convention, Pendleton, discussing "laws made in pursuance thereof," said that "The fair inference is, that oppressive laws will not be warranted by the Constitution . . . and that independent judges will never admit an oppressive construction."[41] And there is Hamilton's statement in *Federalist* No. 33 respecting "the supreme law of the land," that "it will not follow from this doctrine that acts of the larger society which are *not pursuant* to its constitutional powers, but which are invasions of the residuary authorities of the smaller societies, will become the supreme law of the land. These will be merely acts of usurpation, and will deserve to be treated as such." He emphasized that the clause "*expressly* confines this supremacy to laws made *pursuant to the* Constitution."[42] The repeated identification of "pursuance" with consistent or nonrepugnant need not be labored. Opposed, therefore, to Crosskey's alleged

[40] 1 Wilson, *Works* 461. And he stated that the legislative power "is subject also to another given degree of control by the judiciary department, whenever the laws, though in fact passed, are found to be contradictory to the Constitution." Id. at 411.

[41] 3 Elliot 548.

[42] No. 33 at 201–202. In *Federalist* No. 80 at 515, Hamilton said, "It seems scarcely to admit of controversy, that the judicial authority of the union ought to extend to these several descriptions of cases: 1st, to all those which arise out of the laws of the United States, passed in pursuance of their *just and constitutional* powers of legislation" (emphasis supplied). He repeated in the New York convention that "the laws of Congress are restricted to a certain sphere, and when they depart from this sphere, they are no longer supreme and binding." 2 Elliot 362. Crosskey makes no mention of these remarks, nor of those made in the North Carolina, Pennsylvania, and Virginia conventions, but leans instead on "a writer in a New York newspaper" who said that "pursuance" "is a vague term" which "generally implies little more that [sic] 'in consequence.'" Crosskey 992. Such selectivity condemns itself.

In his report of Commonwealth v. Caton, 4 Call (Va.) 5, the reporter, Daniel Call, said that Judge Pendleton stated that the Virginia "legislature had pursued, not violated, the constitution." Because Crosskey "found no talk of 'pursuing, and not violating, a constitution' . . . in the years before the Federal Convention assembled," he concluded that Call (writing 45 years after the case was decided, Crosskey 952) "was simply manufacturing, in ex post facto manner, a little much needed pre-Constitutional usage of 'pursuance' in this important sense." Crosskey 960. When one balances against Crosskey's failure to find evidence of pre-constitutional usage the remarks of Hamilton and others, including Pendleton in the Ratification conventions, which offer the strongest substantiation of Call's version of Judge Pendleton's judicial statement, supra, text accompanying notes 35–42, cf. id. at notes 44–54, Crosskey's charge of falsification is deplorable.

18th century usage, and to Bickel's 20th century speculative interpretations, we have here the Founders' own explanation that they understood "pursuant to" to mean "consistent with," and this to ensure that only laws that were not "repugnant" to the Constitution would be the "supreme law of the land." That it is capable of carrying that meaning is admitted by both Bickel and Crosskey.[43] So much for the direct evidence.

The indirect evidence confirms that the Founders understood that only laws consistent with the Constitution would be the supreme law. The constant stress upon the federal system as a government of "limited" powers, upon the voidness of laws in excess of those powers, and the duty of the courts so to declare, was earlier noticed;[44] and a few reminiscent highlights will here suffice. In the Convention, it was said that the courts would set aside laws which were "repugnant" to the Constitution,[45] or were "unconstitutional,"[46] or "violations" of the Constitution and "encroachments,"[47] or "usurpations"[48] by Congress. After the submission of the Constitution to the people, Yates wrote in New York that the Court would "determine what is the extent of the powers of Congress";[49] Hanson wrote in Maryland that judges would reject Acts "repugnant" to the Constitution;[50] Martin, who introduced the Supremacy Clause, advised Maryland that whether laws of Congress "are *contrary* to, or *not warranted* by the constitution rests only with the courts."[51] In the Ratification conventions, Ellsworth said that a court would declare void a law which is not "authorized" by the Constitution.[52] If a law extended "beyond the powers granted," said Adams, or if Congress "exceeded" its powers, said Nicholas, the courts would declare the

---

[43] Crosskey, supra, text accompanying note 29; Bickel 9. That meaning was taken for granted in an early opinion by Justice Chase: "it is the duty of its courts of justice not to question the validity of any laws made *in pursuance* of the constitution. There is no question that the act of the Virginia legislature . . . was *within the authority* granted to them by the people." Ware v. Hylton, 3 Dallas 199, 235 (1796).

[44] Supra, Chapter 2, text accompanying notes 22–40. See also 2 Elliot 131, 196, 445–446; 3 Elliot 186, 553; 4 Elliot 71, 141.

[45] Supra, Chapter 3, text accompanying note 19.

[46] Id. at 49.

[47] Id. at 87.

[48] Id. at 146.

[49] Id. at 187.

[50] Supra, Chapter 4, text accompanying note 49.

[51] 3 Farrand 220.

[52] Supra, Chapter 4, text accompanying note 26.

law void.[53] A law would be declared void, said Marshall, if it was "not warranted" by the powers enumerated.[54] Is it reasonable to conclude that if a law undeniably was enacted in the teeth of an express constitutional "prohibition" the Founders intended it to become the supreme "law of the land" merely because Congress had complied with the formalities of enactment? Such prohibitions would be writ in water.

The prolonged and at last successful struggle to make State courts the initial arbiters of State-federal conflicts was not waged for the empty privilege of checking whether Congress had complied with the formalities of enactment but because State courts were trusted to protect against Congressional "usurpations." Obviously the Founders had something more in mind than mere compliance with the punctilio of enactment; they demanded that laws should be warranted by and not in excess of the powers grudgingly granted.[55] Since the words "in pursuance thereof" do not, to say the least, exclude the meaning of "consistent with," they should be read to effectuate rather than defeat the intentions of the Founders. The implications of the indirect evidence, I submit, confirm the other unmistakable expressions of the Founders that only federal laws which were not repugnant to the Constitution were to be deemed "in pursuance thereof," and that those laws alone were to be the "supreme law of the land."

A distinction is made by the Supremacy Clause between "laws" and "treaties": *laws* made "in *pursuance*" of the Constitution are to be the "supreme law," in contrast to *treaties* "made, or which shall be made, *under the authority* of the United States." As the differentiation in the treaty phrase between "made" and "which shall be made" immediately suggests, the phrase was to comprehend subsisting treaties which had been made under the Articles of Confederation, as well as post-Convention treaties.[56] State noncompli-

---

[53] Id. at notes 30, 118.

[54] Id. at note 123.

[55] Supra, text accompanying note 39. Judge Pendleton stated in the Virginia convention, "I rely on an honest interpretation from independent judges . . . To give execution to *proper* laws, in a proper manner, is their peculiar province." 3 Elliot 548 (emphasis added).

[56] Madison's Notes explain that the insertion of the words "or which shall be made" was "meant to obviate all doubt concerning the force of treaties pre-existing, by making the words 'all treaties made' to refer to them, as the words

ance with the British treaty, for example, had been a festering source of irritation,[57] and existing treaties had to be preserved if only to avoid the risk of renegotiation in changed circumstances. So I would agree with Professor Crosskey that it was desired to ensure the "desired retrospective application in the case of treaties."[58] No such exigency existed with respect to unilateral enactment of "laws"; Congress could be relied upon to adopt such existing laws as seemed useful and to replace others by new laws of their own design. Crosskey maintains that "in pursuance" was employed solely to accomplish this demarcation,[59] that is, "pursuance" was to have a temporal, "prospective" connotation only. Neither the explicit understanding of the Ratifiers nor the purposes of the Framers would have been served by such a reading, and the reading is in fact at odds with history.

The differentiated treatment of "laws" and "treaties" antedates the Supremacy Clause, and it originated as a distinction between subsisting treaties and *laws* that *"contravened"* the Constitution. The Clause, it will be recalled, replaced the proposed Congressional "negative" which had its inception in the Virginia Plan provision for a negative on "acts *contravening* . . . the Articles of Union." Franklin, who had been a participant in the British Treaty negotiations, added "or any Treaties subsisting under the authority of the union."[60] There is no evidence whatsoever that subsequent resort to "in pursuance thereof" was designed to scrap the "contravened" approach and to function solely as a reference to prospective laws. "In pursuance" may be regarded as another version of "contravened"; certainly the Founders, as has appeared, left no doubt that *laws* which "contravened" the Constitution would *not* be "in pursuance thereof." The fortuitous circumstance that "in pursuance" was not employed for treaties because it had an undesirable "side-effect" in that setting—it would cut off existing treaties—does not

---

inserted would refer to future treaties." 2 Farrand 417. See also Rawle, *A View of the Constitution* 60 (1st ed. 1825); Reid v. Covert, 354 U.S. 1, 16–17 (1957) (opinion by Black, J., Warren, C. J., Douglas and Brennan, J. J. concurring); Henkin, *Arms Control and Inspection in American Law* 169, 170 (1958).

[57] Corwin, "Progress" 529; see infra, note 75.
[58] Crosskey 998.
[59] Ibid.
[60] 1 Farrand 21, 47.

rob the words of the anticontravention meaning they had for the Founders as applied to *laws*.

Then too, the primitive Supremacy Clause, embodied in the New Jersey small-State plan, covered both acts made "in pursuance of the powers hereby & by the articles of confederation vested in them, and all Treaties made & ratified under the authority of the U. States."[61] In its inception, therefore, "in pursuance" was *not* employed to distinguish prospective from existing laws; it comprehended both. Nor may we reasonably impute to the small States which would not trust Congress with a negative over *their* laws an intention by "in pursuance" to confer on Congress a power to *bind them* with federal laws that "contravened" the Constitution.

"THE JUDGES IN EVERY STATE SHALL BE BOUND" AND THE "OATH" PROVISION

It is not my purpose to wrest from the Supremacy Clause "power" to set Congressional Acts aside. My point, assuming that "judicial power" is elsewhere conferred, is that Article VI, section 2 furnishes a guide to its employment,[62] a guide no less applicable to federal than to state courts. Section 2 first *defines* the "supreme law of the land" and then goes on in another clause to make the "supreme law" "binding" on State judges. Although the "binding" clause is not "addressed to federal courts" but to "state judges alone," as Bickel states,[63] it is hardly maintainable that in consequence federal judges are not bound by the preceding *definition* of the "supreme law."[64]

[61] Id. at 245.

[62] Infra, text accompanying notes 83–88.

[63] Bickel 8, 12. The point was made by Hand 5, and by Crosskey 985. Crosskey concluded that "this pointed difference of provision with respect to state 'Laws' and national 'Laws' would surely have given rise to a very strong inference that judicial review had *not* been intended, under the Constitution, as to laws of Congress." In matters touching "self-defense" of judicial prerogatives, however, Crosskey affirms that federal acts were to be reviewable. Crosskey 990, 1107. But as Professor Hart remarked, Crosskey does not explain why the Supremacy Clause, which he has "presented as 'so plainly drawn to exclude . . . by implication' any 'judicial review of Congressional enactments,' without qualification, should now suddenly open up and admit a qualification." Hart, Book Review 1472.

[64] Chief Justice Marshall declared that "The 2d clause of the 6th article declares, that 'this constitution, and the laws of the United States, which shall be made in pursuance thereof, shall be the supreme law of the land.' The clause which gives exclusive jurisdiction is, unquestionably, a part of the constitution, and as such, binds all the United States." Cohens v. Virginia, 6 Wheat. 264, 424 (1821).

Were we to regard that definition as wedded exclusively to the "binding" clause, we would have the anomaly that "state judges alone" would be "bound" by the "Constitution and the laws . . . made in pursuance thereof," and that all other officers, federal and State, would not. That anomaly is sharpened by the fact that the correlated "oath" provision in section 3 of Article VI requires all officers only to "support this Constitution," so that on a literal reading no official could be sworn to "support" "laws made in pursuance" of the Constitution, particularly because in contrast State judges *explicitly* are to be "bound" by such laws. Literalism therefore has its pitfalls. No evidence has been adduced to show that "state judges alone" were to be "bound" by the "Constitution and laws made in pursuance thereof"; and there is in fact evidence to the contrary.[65]

Moreover, section 2 of Article VI must be read in conjunction with section 3, the related "oath" provision which declares that all legislators, executive and judicial officers, State and federal, "shall be bound by oath . . . to support this Constitution." The section 2 definition of the "supreme law," which only made explicit what seemed implicit to Hamilton and Davie,[66] is general in terms and,

---

[65] Iredell spoke of the Supremacy Clause in broadest terms before the North Carolina convention: "when the Congress passes a law consistent with the Constitution, it is to be binding on the people." 4 Elliot 179. The "people" are no more named in the "binding" clause than federal and State officials other than State judges, and if they were deemed "bound," so too were their representatives. Compare the frequent comments that laws inconsistent with the Constitution would *not* be binding on the people. Supra, Chapter 6, text accompanying notes 129, 134, 136. In the New York convention, Hamilton stated that "The States, as well as individuals, are bound by law." 2 Elliot 362. And Washington said in his Farewell Address that "The Constitution . . . is sacredly binding on all." Quoted Rossiter, *Hamilton* 177. At an early date Justice Story said that "the legislatures of the states . . . in every case, are under the Constitution, bound by the permanent authority of the United States." Martin v. Hunter's Lessee, 1 Wheat. 304, 343-344 (1816). See also Hamilton's remark, quoted infra, text accompanying note 68; cf. Hanson, supra, Chapter 3, note 194.

[66] In *Federalist* No. 33 at 201-202, Hamilton said,

A LAW, by the very meaning of the term, includes supremacy . . . the clause which declares the supremacy of the laws of the Union . . . only declares a truth, which flows immediately and necessarily from the institution of a federal government. It will not, I presume, have escaped observation, that it *expressly* confines this supremacy to laws made *pursuant to the Constitution;* which I mention merely as an instance of caution in the convention; since the limitation would have been understood, though it had not been expressed.

See also id. at 199. Davie told the North Carolina convention, "To say that you have vested the federal government with power to legislate for the Union, and then deny the supremacy of the laws, is a solecism in terms." 4 Elliot 182.

unlike the second "binding" portion of section 2, is not addressed to "state judges alone." The definition is a part of the Constitution which officers are to be sworn to "support," and one so sworn to "support" the Constitution as the "supreme law" is as good as "bound" by it.[67] To differentiate in this context between "support" and "bound by" would be a task worthy of a scholastic. Not alone does the structure of Article VI suggest that the "supreme law" definition and "oath" provision were integrated, but so a number of Framers conceived.

The "laws," stated Hamilton in *Federalist* No. 20, "will become the SUPREME LAW of the land; to the observance of which all officers, legislative, executive and judicial in each State, will be bound by the sanctity of an *oath*."[68] His opponent in the New York convention, Melancton Smith, said that "all courts . . . whether federal or not, would be bound by *oath* to give judgment according to the laws of the Union," that is, the "law of the land."[69] And in a pre-*Marbury v. Madison* opinion, Justice Chase, who had opposed the Constitution in the Maryland convention, stated in 1796 that "it is the declared duty of the state judge to determine any constitution or laws of any state, contrary to that treaty . . . null and void. National and federal judges are bound by duty and oath to the same

[67] Initially the Virginia Plan contemplated that only State legislators and executive and judicial officers were to be "bound by oath to support the articles of Union." 1 Farrand 26. Randolph, who introduced the Plan, explained that unless State judges were so sworn they would "determine in favor of their State laws," resembling not a little the factor that lay behind the Supremacy Clause. 1 Farrand 203, 207. The extension of the "oath" to federal officers was inspired by Gerry's fear that national legislators might "annihilate" the State constitutions. 1 Farrand 207; 2 Farrand 84, 87. The terminological difference between the §2 "bound" and the §3 "support" may derive from the fact that the two provisions were of different provenance—the Supremacy Clause came via Martin from the New Jersey Plan as a substitute for a Congressional "negative," while the "oath" originated in the Virginia Plan.

[68] *Federalist* No. 20 at 169 (emphasis added). His example was framed in terms of State officials because it was State compliance that was under discussion. Williamson considered the "oath" was "unnecessary" because officials were duty-bound to support the "law of the land." 1 Farrand 203, 207.

[69] 2 Elliot 378 (emphasis added). And he said that "The states, as well as individuals, are bound by the laws" of the United States. Id. at 362. It is worth noting that both Hamilton and Smith include "laws" within the sweep of the "oath" provision, although it speaks only of support of the "Constitution," an indication that they did not approach the provision in a spirit of literalism. Cf. Parsons, infra, note 211. In 1819, Chief Justice Marshall, who had participated in the Virginia convention, said that State officials, legislative, executive, and judicial, take the "oath of fidelity" to the Constitution as the "supreme law of the land." McCulloch v. Maryland, 4 Wheat. 316, 406 (1819).

conduct."[70] Contemporary opinion, it is reasonable to deduce, regarded all officers as bound to the observance of the "supreme law" by the "oath" provision;[71] and there is good reason to believe that the additional admonition to State judges contained in section 2 constitutes an overlap for a special purpose, as will now appear.

There was some diversity of opinion whether State judges would automatically be "bound" to give overriding effect to federal over State law. Charles Pinckney thought that adoption of the Constitution would "operate as a complete repeal of all the constitutions and state laws, so far as they were inconsistent with the new government," a view apparently shared by Sherman and Williamson.[72] On the other hand, Madison, in discussing the Congressional "negative" over State laws, said that "The judges of the state must give the state laws their operation although the laws abridge the rights of the national government."[73] Randolph had said at the outset that "No judge will say that the *confederation* is paramount to a State constition" [sic],[74] and experience with treaty enforcement under the Confederation would appear to substantiate his view. As secretary of Foreign Affairs under the Confederation, John Jay had argued that treaties were binding on every State; nevertheless he recommended that the States "should pass acts" that courts shall decide "according to the treaty."[75] Martin's original Supremacy Clause responded to the Madison-Randolph view.

The Supremacy Clause had its origin in the New Jersey Plan, which provided for a "supreme tribunal" only, and declared in an

[70] Ware v. Hylton, 3 Dallas 199, 237.

[71] In 1833, Madison referred to the "Declaration" in the Constitution that it "should be the supreme law of the Land, and as such should be obligatory on the Authorities of the States as well as those of the United States." 3 Farrand 524, 527.

[72] 1 Farrand 170. Sherman thought the Congressional negative "unnecessary, as the courts of the States would not Consider as valid any law contravening the Authority of the Union." 2 Farrand 27. Williamson, speaking of the proposed "oath" for the State officers to observe the "National Constitution and laws," said, "it will be unnecessary, as the union will become the law of the land." 1 Farrand 203, 207.

[73] 1 Farrand 169.

[74] Id. at 26.

[75] Corwin, *National Supremacy* 26–27. In the North Carolina convention Maclaine stated, "The treaty of peace with Great Britain was the supreme law of the land; yet it was disregarded, for want of a federal judiciary. The state courts did not enforce an observance of it." 4 Elliot 164. Precisely this issue was presented in Rutgers v. Waddington, Haines 100; supra, Chapter 2, text accompanying notes 158–159. In the Convention Madison commented that the files of Congress contained complaints from almost every nation with whom treaties had been made of State violations. 1 Farrand 316.

adjoining section that "the Judiciary of the several States shall be bound [by federal treaties and statutes] in their decisions, anything in the respective laws [not constitutions] of the Individual States to the contrary notwithstanding."[76] When the original Supremacy Clause of Luther Martin, patterned on that section, was unanimously adopted,[77] there was as yet no provision, he later explained, for inferior federal courts. He had hoped that every question involving federal treaties and statutes "would have been determined in the first instance in the courts of the respective states." The "necessity" that these "should be binding on the state judiciaries," he added, "must be evident."[78] Martin's proposal was bottomed on the premise that otherwise State courts would *not* be "bound" by federal laws, as is underscored by his further explanation that by virtue of the omission of State "constitutions" from his proposal, State judges would "be bound to reject" federal laws and treaties that were "inconsistent with our [State] constitutions."[79] In other words, they would not be bound to give overriding effect to federal laws over State constitutions because no provision to absolve them of their primary duty to the State constitution had yet been made. The "supreme Tribunal," on the other hand, was not subject to the conflicting loyalties by which State judges would be torn, and which required a special dispensation from State laws "to the contrary." Since the paramount duty of the "supreme Tribunal" plainly ran to the federal system, it may well have seemed gratuitous to *bind*

[76] 1 Farrand 244–245.

[77] 2 Farrand 28–29.

[78] 3 Farrand 287. The problem had been foreseen by Madison, in a letter to Randolph of April 8, 1787, i.e., prior to the Convention: "If the judges in the last resort depend on the States, and are bound by their oaths to them and not to the Union, the intention of the law and interests of the Union may be defeated by the obsequiousness of the tribunals to the policy or prejudices of the States." 2 Madison, *Writings* 339.

[79] 3 Farrand 287. Because the original Martin clause omitted the federal Constitution from the definition of the "supreme law," Boudin 123, concludes that the State judiciaries would have been "compelled . . . to enforce every act of the federal legislature, whether constitutional or unconstitutional." And, he asserts, the "destructive effects" of his analysis "upon the argument" for the judicial power "from the text of the Constitution is simply overwhelming." Boudin overlooked that Martin also omitted *State constitutions,* and because of that omission State judges would "be bound to reject" federal laws that were "inconsistent with our [State] constitution." States Righters relied much more heavily on their own state constitutions with their bill of rights than upon the proposed Constitution which had none.

it, for like the State courts it was evidently under a duty to give effect to the Constitution and valid laws of its *own* government, supplemented by the "oath" that its judges swore to "support" the Constitution.

In sum, the reason that the "binding" provision of the Supremacy Clause is addressed to "state judges alone" is, as Corwin remarked, that they are "judges of an independent jurisdiction. Their duty to take cognizance of national laws *at all* had therefore to be declared in unmistakable terms."[80] The "binding" clause dealt "with a special problem peculiar to the state judges, of a conflict between the commands of their own government and those of a different government,"[81] a problem by which judges of a "supreme Tribunal" were untouched, and to whom, it will appear, appeals from State courts were contemplated. To give to the Supremacy Clause naming of "state judges alone" an exclusory effect is to disregard both its origin and the fact that contemporaries read it broadly, as well as to invite anomalous consequences that attend a literal reading, for example, to absolve federal judges from enforcement of the "supreme law of the land" as defined by section 2.[82] It is not therefore necessary to warp the "binding" clause which is addressed to "state judges alone" to arrive at the conclusion that federal judges are "bound by oath" to enforce the "supreme law of the land."

Given the contemporary understanding of "in pursuance thereof" as "consistent with" the Constitution, and the Founders' understanding that the task of final interpretation was committed to the courts,[83] the first or "definition" portion of the Supremacy Clause has important sequelae. In providing that "laws . . . made in pur-

---

[80] Corwin, *Doctrine* 13–14.

[81] Hart, Book Review 1470. Wechsler, *Principles* 6, states that the "binding" clause is "a special and emphatic admonition that it binds the judges of the previously independent states."

Brinton Coxe, whom the carping Boudin 25 credits with "genuine scholarship," made the point that in declaring what the "supreme law" shall be, the Clause bound all and sundry, instancing statutes which "bind the King" and which are not construed to mean "that they bind only the king but they bind even him, as well as every one else." Coxe vii.

[82] Some of these anomalies were earlier mentioned. Additionally, it would be unreasonable to suppose that on appeal from a State court that was "bound," the "supreme Tribunal" was not "bound" by a valid federal law. See Wechsler, infra, note 216.

[83] See supra, text accompanying notes 27–55; Chapter 6, text accompanying notes 126–227.

suance" of the Constitution "shall be the supreme law of the land," the definition by necessary implication directed that laws *not* made "in pursuance thereof" shall *not* be the "law of the land." Such was the import of Hamilton's statement to the New York convention:

> the laws of Congress are restricted to a certain sphere, and when they depart from that sphere they are no longer supreme and binding.[84]

Similar statements were made by Davie and Iredell in North Carolina; and in Virginia Steele said, "If the Congress make laws inconsistent with the Constitution, independent judges will not uphold them."[85] No judge, it follows, would be required to give effect to such laws. Gerry asked, would not judges "be bound to declare the law a nullity if this clause [of the bill] . . . is inconsistent with the Constitution?" And he further stated in the First Congress, "so far as your laws conform" to the Constitution the courts "will attend to them, but no further."[86] The Founders believed, I submit, that the terms of the section 2 definition constrained a judge to determine whether a given law was "consistent" with the Constitution, and if it was not, so to declare.[87] That implication was again drawn by Justice Chase with respect to the duty of *all* judges to set aside State laws contrary to *treaty;* and whatever distinction may be drawn between setting aside State laws and federal laws, the fact remains that Chase casually included federal judges among those "bound" to enforce the "supreme law."[88]

[84] 2 Elliot 362. See also supra, text accompanying notes 41–54. Compare the frequent statements that laws inconsistent with the Constitution would not be binding on the people. Supra, Chapter 6, text accompanying notes 129, 134, 136. See also Hamilton, quoted supra, note 66.

[85] For Davie and Iredell see supra, text accompanying notes 36, 37; for Steele, 4 Elliot 71.

[86] 1 *Ann. Cong.* 524; 1 *Ann. Cong.* 861. See also infra, text accompanying notes 202–212. Although Professor Bickel recognizes that "State judges need enforce, however, only such federal law as is made in pursuance of the Constitution," Bickel 9, he would read "in pursuance" as a reference to "just the mechanical provisions that describe how a federal law is to be enacted," a reading refuted by history; supra, text accompanying notes 34–55. And he declares that an authorization to State judges "to measure federal law against the federal Constitution and uphold it or strike it down in accordance with their understanding of the relevant constitutional provision . . . standing alone would have been . . . self-destructive," Bickel 9, a point hereinafter considered.

[87] See Wilson, quoted supra, text accompanying note 39.

[88] Supra, text accompanying note 70.

Chief Justice Marshall relied on the "oath" provision as an additional argument for judicial review; but says Professor Bickel,

> Far from supporting Marshall, the oath is perhaps the strongest textual argument against him. For it would seem to obligate each of these officers, in the performance of his functions, to support the Constitution. On one reading, the consequence might be utter chaos—everyone at every juncture interprets and applies the Constitution for himself. Or as we have seen, it may be deduced that everyone is to construe the Constitution with finality in so far as it addresses itself to the performance of his own peculiar functions. Surely the language lends itself more readily to this interpretation than to Marshall's apparent conclusion.[89]

In isolating discussion of one textual provision from another, thereby shutting off the light they shed reciprocally,[90] and in compartmentalizing analysis of the text from its historical background, Bickel departs from his acknowledgment that "the document must be read as a whole, and any particular phraseology is informed by the purpose of the whole."[91] That purpose is better derived from history than from textual speculation. Of course everyone—legislators, executives, no less than judges—is sworn to "support" the Constitution, but each within the frame of his own "peculiar functions." History shows that the legislature was to be *excluded* from the task of *interpreting or expounding* the Constitution,[92] and nothing contained in the "oath" provision transforms the "peculiar function" of the legislature as "maker" of the laws into the "interpreter." Against Bickel's optional "everyone is to construe the Constitution with finality in so far as it addresses itself to the performance of his own peculiar functions" may be counterbalanced Judge Hand's view that such a reading would conduce to an "omnipotent" Congress and the government "would almost certainly have

[89] Bickel 8.
[90] See supra, Chapter 1, note 16. As Hart, Book Review 1465, said of Crosskey in similar circumstances,

> Professor Crosskey wrestles separately with several of these provisions, and satisfies himself that each, standing alone, is insufficient. The conclusions in the case of each provision are unpersuasive. But they leave untouched in any event the fact that the provisions do not stand alone but together.

[91] Bickel 12.
[92] Supra, Chapter 6, text accompanying notes 161–170, 189–194.

foundered,"[93] the Founders' categorical rejection of an "omnipotent" Congress, and their statements that the task of "final" interpretation was for the courts. Because the "consequences" of an "oath" to support the Constitution according to how each State and federal officer interprets it, in Bickel's words, "might be utter chaos,"[94] such a reading cannot be seriously entertained.

Marshall's "apparent conclusion" that every official is sworn "to support the Constitution as the judges, in pursuance of the same oath, have construed it, rather than as his own conscience may dictate"[95] may be debatable when viewed solely in the frame of the "oath" provision, but it faithfully reflects the Founders' intention that the courts should have the final power of interpretation.[96] And it is buttressed by the fact that under the definition of the "supreme law" State courts (subject to an appeal to the Supreme Court) plainly were to enforce only such "laws" as were "in pursuance" of or "consistent with" the Constitution, notwithstanding a Congressional interpretation to the contrary, a matter to which I shall recur in more closely examining the power of State judges to declare federal laws not "consistent with" the Constitution.

THE SUPREMACY CLAUSE DOES NOT CONFER JURISDICTION

The Supremacy Clause, it has been said, was viewed by Judge Learned Hand "as a grant of jurisdiction to state courts."[97] If this means that State courts were thereby given or vested with judicial

[93] Supra, Chapter 7, text accompanying notes 87–91.
[94] Bickel 8.
[95] Ibid.
[96] Said Bickel 15, "it is as clear as such matters can be that the Framers of the Constitution specifically, if tacitly, expected that the federal courts would assume a power—of whatever exact dimensions—to pass on the constitutionality of actions of the Congress and the President." I would substitute "exercise" for "assume," for there is no tinge of arrogation in satifying an "expectation"; and I would strike "tacitly" because a large proportion of the Framers explicitly affirmed the availability of judicial review, and, in the words of Professor Bickel, "not even a colorable showing of decisive historical evidence to the contrary can be made." Ibid.
[97] Wechsler, *Principles* 5–6. Judge Hand noted that under the Supremacy Clause "state courts would at times have to decide whether state laws and constitutions, or even a federal statute, were in conflict with the federal constitution"; and he added that "the fact that this jurisdiction was confined to such occasions, and that it was thought necessary specifically to provide such a limited jurisdiction, looks rather against than in favor of a general jurisdiction." Hand 28.

power to decide certain controversies, it runs afoul of the fact that the Clause does not purport to grant authority to hear and decide cases, in contrast to Article III, which *vests* "judicial power" in federal courts and defines the areas in which that power may be exercised.[98] Then too, jurisdiction is normally vested in *courts,* in the manner of Article III, not in *judges,* and it is State "judges" who, by the terms of Article VI, are "bound." For me, as for Brinton Coxe, the Supremacy Clause "enacts what the law shall be,"[99] it defines the governing "supreme law," and *if* a State court *has* jurisdiction, it commands that that law shall govern. *A fortiori,* if the Supremacy Clause confers no jurisdiction on State courts, it confers none on the there unmentioned federal courts.

Some confirmation for this inference is furnished by the fact that on the day after adoption of Martin's Supremacy Clause, which provided that "the Legislative acts of the U.S. . . . shall be the supreme law," Madison proposed that the Resolution dealing with "The jurisdiction of Ntl. Judiciary" be amended to read "the jurisdiction shall extend to all cases arising under the Natl. laws."[100] Adopted by unanimous agreement, this amendment minimally indicates the Convention view that the Supremacy Clause had not conferred federal *jurisdiction* of such cases. And it may be regarded as an attempt to integrate federal jurisdiction with the newly-born definition of the "supreme law," that is, a question presented by virtue of Article VI was deemed a question "arising under" within the meaning of Article III.[101] A similar integration of Article III with Article VI was later made by Rutledge. After the words "or which shall be made" had been added to the "treaty" phrase of Article VI, the same words were added on his motion of August

[98] When the Founders conferred "power" they said so in specific terms. Article I, §8 (1); Article II, §1 (1); Article III, §1. And see statements that no jurisdiction can be conferred by one sovereign on another. Ames, infra, text accompanying note 135; Frankfurter, J., id. at note 109.

[99] Coxe v.

[100] 2 Farrand 46, 39; cf. Meigs, *Relation* 138.

[101] Compare Wechlser's statement that in so far as federal courts "enforce the Constitution" they do so because "they must decide a litigated issue that is otherwise within their jurisdiction and in doing so must give effect to the supreme law of the land." Wechsler, "Courts & Constitution" 1006. What is the "supreme law of the land" presents a "judicial question," and the "judicial power necessarily extends to a judicial question and hence extends to questions arising under 2, VI," Coxe vii–viii, assuming, of course, a proper "case" within the Wechsler formulation.

CHAPTER 8

27th to the "arising under" clause of Article III.[102] Considerable force is therefore lent to Brinton Coxe's view that the two Articles must be read side by side, as if integrated.[103]

One can only speculate why the words "in pursuance" were not similarly added to Article III, for no answer is furnished by the records. Conceivably the inclusion of "in pursuance" might have given rise to jurisdictional doubts; it might, by negative implication, have been interpreted to exclude cognizance of statutes that were *not* "in pursuance"; and access to the federal courts for claims that federal statutes were *not* "in pursuance" of the Constitution might thus have been befogged. By omitting "in pursuance" from Article III, the Framers left the unqualified "arising under" phrase broad enough to embrace cognizance both of statutes that were "in pursuance" of the Constitution and of those that were not, to enforce the former and to deny enforcement or to set aside the latter. Possibly this is what Chief Justice Taney meant when he stated in *Ableman v. Booth* that the "judicial power covers every legislative act of Congress, whether it be made within the limits of its delegated powers, or be an assumption of power beyond the grants in the Constitution."[104] To build on the absence of "in pursuance" from Article III would present yet another anomaly: State courts are "bound" by Article VI to set aside federal laws "inconsistent" with the Constitution,[105] but the Supreme Court, on this theory, can not. Since appeals from State courts to the Supreme Court were contemplated, such a double standard would defeat the very "uniformity" of interpretation that such appeals were to ensure.[106] Finally, although there were a few criticisms of the allegedly equivocal nature of the "in pursuance" language itself,[107] no one, so far as I could ascertain, complained that the federal courts could not reach invalid "National laws" because "in pursuance" was absent from Article III. Despite the fact that the Ratifying conventions required frequent assurances that courts would declare "void" federal laws which were not consistent with the Constitution, despite representations that the "aris-

[102] 2 Farrand 409, 417, 431.
[103] Quoted Westin 21.
[104] 21 How. 506, 520 (1858).
[105] Supra, text accompanying notes 83–88; infra, id. at notes 202–212.
[106] Infra, text accompanying notes 216–229.
[107] Supra, text accompanying note 34; cf. id. at note 38; and see id. at note 42.

ing under" clause would reach such situations,[108] not one voice was raised to recommend that "in pursuance" be added to Article III to place the matter beyond doubt. It is not easy therefore to deduce from the omission of "in pursuance" from Article III a design to withhold jurisdiction of federal statutes that contravened the Constitution. To recur to the general framework of the Supremacy Clause: given jurisdiction, which federal courts have by virtue of Article III, and which State courts have by force of factors to be considered, both sets of courts are to be governed in the exercise of their jurisdiction by the "supreme law of the land."

STATE COURT JURISDICTION AND ARTICLE III

Whence do State courts derive jurisdiction of federal questions if not from the Supremacy Clause? Not, I suggest, from Article III, nor from Congressional grants that would draw upon it. Article III provides that "The judicial power of the United States shall be vested in one Supreme Court and in such inferior courts as the Congress may from time to time ordain and establish." To the ordinary understanding, "inferior" courts "established" by Congress means federal courts; the grant of federal judicial power to a State court is not the *establishment* of an "inferior" court; and it is in federal courts that the "judicial power" is "vested." Then too, the jealous insistence upon State sovereignty in the 1787 period underscores the point made by Justice Frankfurter: "Neither Congress nor the British Parliament nor the Vermont Legislature has power to confer jurisdiction upon the New York courts."[109]

There was no discussion in the Convention whether Article III power could or should be vested in State courts, perhaps because protagonists of State courts assumed that those courts *had* jurisdiction. That assumption looms large in the New Jersey Plan, which provided solely for a "supreme tribunal," and declared in an adjoining section that "the Judiciary of the several States shall be bound [by federal laws and treaties] in their decisions";[110] the implication

---

[108] Supra, Chapter 7, text accompanying notes 16–22.

[109] Brown v. Gerdes, 321 U.S. 178, 188 (1944) (concurring opinion); Claflin v. Houseman, 93 U.S. 130, 141 (1876) ("Not that Congress could confer jurisdiction upon the State courts.") The point was vigorously made in the First Congress, infra, text accompanying notes 131–135.

[110] 1 Farrand 244–245.

being that State courts already had jurisdiction to hear federal questions and that no more was required than to make federal law "binding" in their decision. Rutledge said that the establishment of inferior courts "was making an unnecessary *encroachment* on the jurisdiction of the States," and urged that State courts "ought to be *left* in all cases to decide in the first instance."[111] Sherman thought a Congressional veto of State laws was "unnecessary, as the Courts of the States would not consider as valid any law contravening the Authority of the Union."[112] Martin's explanation of his original Supremacy Clause posited that State judiciaries would be bound to reject national laws that were inconsistent with State constitutions.[113] Both Sherman and Martin obviously assumed that State courts had jurisdiction to entertain such issues. Distrust of local bias rather than disbelief in the existence of State judicial jurisdiction led Madison to express lack of confidence of State courts.[114]

Post-Convention events exhibit some divergence of opinion, although the substantial preponderance remained with the believers in existing State court power. Hamilton's discussions of the matter in two issues of *The Federalist* appear to look in different directions and may turn on a puzzling distinction between cases arising under the "Constitution" and those arising under the "laws" of the United States. In *Federalist* No. 81, he stated that "a necessary part of the plan" was "to empower the national legislature to commit to [State courts] the cognizance of causes arising out of the national Constitution. To confer the power of determining such causes upon the

---

[111] 1 Farrand 124–128 (emphasis added).

[112] 2 Farrand 27. But after the Convention he said, "'tis probable that the courts of the particular States will be authorized by the laws of the Union, as had been heretofore done in cases of piracy." Quoted, Warren, "New Light," 37 *Harv. L. Rev.* at 66.

[113] 3 Farrand 287. This was contained in Martin's reply of March 19, 1788, to Oliver Ellsworth, 3 Farrand 271, and postulated that at the introduction of the Supremacy Clause "it was not established that inferior continental courts should be appointed for trial of all questions arising on treaties and on the laws of the general government." Id. at 287. But in reporting on the completed Constitution to the Maryland legislature on November 29, 1787, id. at 172, he stated that the Article III "courts, and *these only*, will have a right to decide upon the laws of the United States . . . to which the courts . . . of the respective States . . . are rendered incompetent." He also said, "To the courts of the general government are also confined all cases in law or equity, arising under the proposed constitution." Id. at 220. As will appear, the decided preponderance of opinion ran the other way.

[114] 2 Farrand 27–28; Hart, Book Review 1468.

existing courts of the several States, would perhaps be as much 'to constitute tribunals,' as to create new courts with the like power." . In *Federalist* No. 82, on the other hand, he stated that Congress might "commit the decision of causes arising upon a particular regulation to the federal courts solely . . . ; but I hold that the State courts will be divested of no part of their primitive jurisdiction," and "I am even of opinion that in every case in which they are not expressly excluded by future acts of the national legislature, they will of course take cognizance of the causes to which those acts may give birth." In other words, "the State courts would have a concurrent jurisdiction in all cases arising under the laws of the Union, where it was not expressly prohibited." He laid it "down as a rule, that the State courts will *retain* the jurisdiction they now have, unless it was taken away in one of the enumerated modes."[115] And he rejected the possibility that the Article III vesting of the judicial power in the federal courts might be deemed exclusive of States courts because this would entail an "alienation of state power by implication." But if judicial power was thus "retained"—States Righters finally succeeded in leaving to State courts in the first instance questions whether State laws contravened the Constitution[116] —there was no occasion to "commit" the "cognizance of causes arising out of the national Constitution" to State courts. Nor was Hamilton content to rest State court jurisdiction on bare assertion, but based it on a familiar "conflict of laws" principle that still finds everyday application:

> The judiciary power of every government looks beyond its own local or municipal laws, and in civil cases lays hold of all subjects of litigation between parties within its jurisdiction, though the causes of the dispute are relative to the laws of the most distant

---

[115] *Federalist* No. 81 at 527–528. *Federalist* No. 82 at 536, 535. In *Federalist* No. 32 at 194, he had formulated the general principle that "the State governments would clearly retain all the rights of sovereignty which they before had, and which were not by that act [the Constitution], *exclusively* delegated to the United States." For the application of that principle to State court jurisdiction and the formulation of exclusivity tests, see *Federalist* No. 82 at 534–535.

In *Federalist* No. 27 at 169–170, Hamilton had said that the fact that State officials were "bound by oath" (Article VI, §3) to support this Constitution rendered all State courts "auxiliary to the enforcement of its laws." I would read this to require the exercise of existing State jurisdiction to enforce federal laws.

[116] Infra, note 143; cf. text accompanying notes 182–185, 217–222.

part of the globe. Those of Japan, not less than of New York, may furnish the objects of legal discussion in our courts. When in addition to this we consider the State governments, and the national government, as they truly are, in the light of kindred systems, and as parts of ONE WHOLE, the inference seems to be conclusive, that the State courts would have a concurrent jurisdiction in all cases arising under the laws of the union, where it was not expressly prohibited.[117]

The different points of view were expressed in the Virginia convention. Madison, referring to captures at sea, stated that, "It will also be in the power of Congress to vest this power in the State courts," though he was to adopt a contrary view when the subject was debated in the First Congress.[118] Pendleton, like Madison, a proponent of the Constitution, said in Virginia that "I think it highly probable that [Congress'] first experiment will be, to appoint the state courts to have inferior federal jurisdiction."[119] Mason, who opposed adoption, said Congress "may also pass a law vesting the federal power in the state judiciaries."[120] On the other hand, R. H. Lee, prior to the Virginia convention, said of Article III, section 2, that "Actions in all these cases, except against a state government, are now brought and finally determined in the law courts of the states respectively and as there are no words to exclude these courts of their jurisdiction in these cases, they will have concurrent jurisdiction with the inferior federal courts in them."[121] In the

117 *Federalist* No. 82 at 535–536. In modern restatement, "the jurisdiction conferred upon [State courts] by the only authority that has power to create them and confer jurisdiction upon them—namely the law-making power of the State . . . enables them to enforce rights no matter what the legislative source of the rights may be." Brown v. Gerdes, 321 U.S. 178, 188 (1944) (Frankfurter, J., concurring). Hart, "The Relation Between State and Federal Law," 54 *Colum. L. Rev.* 489, 507 (1954). ("Absent a special prohibition, express or implied, the state courts enforce federal law as they do their own.") Cf. Claflin v. Houseman, 93 U.S. 130, 136–137 (1876).

118 3 Elliot 536. Madison expressed a similar view in *Federalist* No. 45 at 302: "it is extremely probable that . . . in the organization of the judicial power, the officers of the State will be clothed with correspondent authority of the Union." But see his later remark, infra, text accompanying note 133.

119 3 Elliot 517.

120 Id. at 584.

121 Ford, *Pamphlets* 279, 307. In the First Congress, Lee opposed federal jurisdiction and proposed that "federal interference shall be limited to appeals only from the State courts to the Supreme Federal Court." Quoted Warren, "New Light," 37 *Harv. L. Rev.* 67. Warren casts some doubt on the authenticity of this statement.

Virginia convention, Randolph, referring to oppression by the federal government, said that if the federal judiciary "will not do justice to the persons injured, may they not go into our own state judiciaries, and obtain it?"[122] Opponents of adoption expressed confidence in State courts that did not extend to federal courts. It was forcibly expressed by Patrick Henry:

> The honorable gentleman did our judiciary honor in saying that they had firmness to counteract the legislature in some cases. Yes, sir, our judges opposed the acts of the legislature. We have this landmark to guide us. They had fortitude to declare that they were the judiciary, and would oppose unconstitutional acts. Are you sure that your federal judiciary will act thus?[123]

It was to meet arguments that the federal jurisdiction would "annihilate the state courts" that Marshall said in the Virginia convention that,

> The state courts will not lose jurisdiction of the cases they now decide. They have a concurrence of jurisdiction with the federal courts in those cases in which the latter have cognizance . . . There is no clause in the Constitution which bars the individual member injured from applying ["for protection from an infringement on the Constitution"] to the state courts to give him redress.[124]

Such was the force of the State court tide that, after ratification by the Virginia convention, the committee, which had been requested to prepare suggested amendments under the chairmanship of George Wythe, proposed that the judicial power be vested in the Supreme Court (omitting inferior federal jurisdiction altogether), that the Court "shall have original jurisdiction" in ambassadorial and state-

---

[122] 3 Elliot 468.

[123] Id. at 324–325. Probably such sentiments led Pendleton, a leader in the struggle for adoption, to say, "I think it highly probable that [Congress'] first experiment will be to appoint the state courts to have the inferior federal jurisdiction, because it would be best calculated to give general satisfaction." Id. at 517. In the event, the First Congress did in fact leave initial jurisdiction of the bulk of federal questions to State courts. Infra, text accompanying notes 234–244, and note 143.

[124] 3 Elliot 554. Grayson, in opposition, concurred that the State courts "are the best check we have" but objected that they were "to be subordinated to the federal judiciary." Id. at 563.

party cases, and that "in all other cases before mentioned," which had been drastically curtailed, "the Supreme Court shall have appellate jurisdiction."[125] Appellate jurisdiction premised initial jurisdiction in State courts which, unlike the Supreme Court, were *not given* such jurisdiction by the amendment but were presumed to have it, therein resembling the subsequent section 25 of the Judiciary Act of 1789. The amendment was adopted and may be considered to represent the mature view of the Virginia convention that State courts enjoyed power as State instrumentalities to entertain "federal questions." Such an amendment was likewise adopted by the North Carolina convention,[126] and it was vigorously pressed in the First Congress.[127]

In the North Carolina convention, Governor Johnston, responding to a remark that the "federal courts have exclusive jurisdiction of all cases . . . arising under the Constitution and laws of the United States," said that

> they will, in these cases, as well as in several others, have concurrent jurisdiction with the state courts, and not exclusive jurisdiction . . . this I am sure of, that the state judiciaries are not divested of their present judicial cognizance.[128]

He too was addressing himself to the fear that the Constitution tended to "destroy their state judiciaries"; but for opponents such as Bloodworth this was not enough, and Iredell undertook to dispel the anticipated "danger [to State courts] of concurrent jurisdiction."[129] In the Pennsylvania convention, Wilson enumerated the various "cases or controversies" and said that these "powers given to the federal courts . . . are not exclusively given. In all instances,

[125] 3 Elliot 657, 660.
[126] 4 Elliot 246. In New York, opponents of the Constitution submitted an amendment against the establishment of inferior federal courts which provided that Article III cases should be tried in State courts with an appeal to the Supreme Court. 2 Elliot 408. Compare remarks of Melancton Smith, supra, Chapter 4, text accompanying note 61.
[127] Tucker of Virginia led the struggle in the Senate to eliminate the power to create inferior federal courts and to abolish the power of vesting judicial power in such courts, maintaining that "State courts fully adequate to deal with all federal matters." See Warren, "New Light," 37 *Harv. L. Rev.* 119, 123.
[128] 4 Elliot 141–142.
[129] Id. at 142–144, 146; see also id. at 153, 164.

the parties may commence suits in the courts of the several states."[130] The preponderance of such assurances in the Ratification conventions, it may fairly be concluded, indicates a widespread view that State courts had independent, that is, State-created, jurisdiction of federal questions.

In the First Congress debate on the Judiciary Act, there were sharp differences of opinion between proponents of a federal court system and of the existing State courts; but on one thing there was virtually no disagreement: Congress could not vest federal jurisdiction in State courts. A leading Federalist, William Smith of South Carolina, said,

> It is declared by [Article III] that the judicial power of the United States shall be vested in one supreme, and in such inferior courts as Congress shall from time to time establish. Here is no discretion, then, in Congress to vest the judicial power of the United States in any other tribunal.[131]

Subsequently he asked, after analyzing Article III, "Does not, then, the constitution, in the plainest and most unequivocal language, preclude us from alloting [vesting] any part of the judicial authority of the Union to the State judicatures."[132] Madison "did not see how it could be made compatible with the Constitution . . . to make a transfer of the Federal jurisdiction to the State courts"[133] Gerry, a Framer, said, "You cannot make Federal courts of the State courts,

---

[130] 2 Elliot 491. Ellsworth wrote in Connecticut on December 10, 1787, "Nothing hinders . . . that all the cases except the few in which it (the Supreme Court) has original and not appellate jurisdiction, may in the first instance be had in the State courts." Quoted, Warren, *The Making of the Constitution* 541 (1928).

[131] 1 *Ann. Cong.* 831–832. Ellsworth stated in 1789 that "To annex to State courts jurisdiction which they had not before, as of admiralty cases, and perhaps offenses against the United States, would be constituting the Judges of them, *pro tanto* Federal Judges." Quoted, Warren, "New Light" 66. Justice Story said in 1816 that "Congress can not vest any portion of the judicial power of the United States, except in courts ordained and established by itself." Martin v. Hunter's Lessee, 1 Wheat. 304, 330 (1816).

[132] 1 *Ann. Cong.* 850. For Smith "vesting" merely meant leaving State courts in possession: "It has been observed that the constitution is no bar to vesting the State courts with federal power" on the ground that the Congressional power to establish inferior courts "impl[ies] that Congress may not institute them; and if they are not instituted, these powers must of course remain with the State courts." Id. at 849.

[133] Id. at 844.

because the Constitution is an insuperable bar."[134] Ames stated that federal law "could not enlarge [State court] powers."[135]

Adherents of State courts did not maintain that the Constitution authorized the "vesting" of "judicial power" in State courts, but rather that they already possessed the jurisdiction. Samuel Livermore stated that "The State courts have hitherto decided all cases of a national or local import," that "the State courts have hitherto had cognizance of" maritime captures. And he stated that if Article III "had taken from State courts all cognizance of Federal causes, something might be said, but this is not the case. The State courts are allowed jurisdiction in these cases."[136] Jackson said that by section 11 of the Judiciary bill submitted by the Senate, the State courts "are acknowledged to have concurrent jurisdiction to a large extent, where the United States and an alien are a party . . . And if the jurisdiction is acknowledged in some points, it must be so in the fullest extent."[137] The Federalist Ames agreed that "The State courts were not supposed to be deprived by the Constitution of the jurisdiction that they had exercised before, over many causes that may now be tried in the national courts."[138]

But, Ames asked, how could State courts have jurisdiction of "a new created action? Here jurisdiction is made *de novo*."[139] Or, as Smith put it, "The State courts have no jurisdiction of causes arising from a national impost law, because no such law heretofore existed."[140] To this Jackson and Stone made vigorous replies. Pointing to the Supremacy Clause whereby State judges are bound to notice the Constitution, laws, and treaties as the "supreme law," and supposing a State trial of a state criminal offense wherein the defendant justified under a federal law, Jackson said, "If there was

---

[134] Id. at 860.

[135] Id. at 839.

[136] Id. at 814, 852.

[137] Id. at 845–846. Replying to the argument that if inferior courts "are not instituted, these powers must of course remain with the State courts," Smith did not deny State court jurisdiction but insisted that Congress could not omit to establish federal courts. Id. at 849–850.

[138] Id. at 838.

[139] The point had been anticipated in Hanson's remarks to the people of Maryland, yet he assumed at the same time that "every judge in the union, whether of federal or state appointment . . . will have a right to reject any act, handed to him as a law, which he may conceive repugnant to the constitution." Ford, *Pamphlets* 231, 234, 238.

[140] 1 *Ann. Cong.* 830.

no jurisdiction, neither could [State judges] notice the law."[141] Stone added that "A judge binds himself not only to act upon the laws which have already passed, but to obey all that may hereafter pass. If it is admitted that the judges cannot take cognizance of the laws *de novo*, you annihilate the Judicial capacity at a blow; they cannot notice the adoption of the Federal constitution or any law passed after appointment."[142] Hamilton, it will be recalled, based State court jurisdiction of "federal" causes on the traditional power of enforcing claims that originate under "foreign" law; and such laws may have been enacted after the institution of the enforcing court. It was this idea of a preexisting, extra-Constitutional State court jurisdiction, of which they were not "divested," that animated Governor Johnston, Marshall, Wilson, and others in the Ratification conventions, and the pro-State adherents in the First Congress. The fact that Congress left "federal questions" to the State courts[143] indicates that that view was embodied in the Judiciary Act.

The contrary view was expressed by the Supreme Court in *Testa v. Katt*: "The first Congress . . . conferred jurisdiction upon the state courts to enforce important federal civil laws," citing section 9 of the Judiciary Act.[144] That section provided that "the district

[141] Id. at 845. Jackson's argument was elaborated by Justice Story in Martin v. Hunter's Lessee, 1 Wheat. 304, 341–342 (1816), to show the "unquestionable" jurisdiction of the State courts. And, he said, the Framers contemplated that "cases within the judicial cognizance of the United States not only might but would arise in the state courts, in the exercise of their ordinary jurisdiction." Id. at 340. He found this view expressed in the Supremacy Clause: "It was foreseen that in the exercise of their ordinary jurisdiction, state courts would incidentally take cognizance of cases arising under the constitution, the laws and treaties of the United States." Id. at 342. History amply bears him out.

[142] 1 *Ann. Cong.* 856.

[143] The First Judiciary Act established the principle that "private litigants must look to the state tribunals in the first instance for vindication of federal claims." Hart & Wechsler 727. See infra, text accompanying notes 234–244, 184–191. It "was not until 1875 that Congress gave the federal courts jurisdiction over such cases." Wright 48.

[144] 330 U.S. 386, 389–390 (1947). Though I would differ with the implications of grant in this statement, I am yet in agreement with the holding that "State courts are not free to refuse enforcement of" claims arising under a federal act, assuming that they have jurisdiction. One may agree with Professors Hart & Wechsler 397 that some of the authorities upon which *Testa* relied "were concerned with whether state courts may take jurisdiction, not whether they must do so." But given inherent State court jurisdiction, the Court's determination that State courts are "bound" by the Supremacy Clause is persuasive. Although the clause may be read to bind judges in deciding a case of which they *take* jurisdiction, rather than to *require* them to take jurisdiction, States Righters' insistence

courts *shall have* exclusively of the courts of the several States" jurisdiction of certain criminal offenses against the United States, and that they *"shall have* also *cognizance,* concurrent with the courts of the several States . . . of all causes" pertaining to certain torts by an alien and of suits by the United States.[145] First there is the distinction between the express grant of cognizance to district courts and the *exclusion* of State courts. Were State court jurisdiction solely a creature of Congressional grant, it would have sufficed merely to make the grant to the district courts, for there would have been no need to exclude a nonexistent State jurisdiction. Resort to exclusory terms pre-supposes existing State court jurisdiction which had to be curtailed.[146] Then too, the provision that the district courts "shall have cognizance, concurrent [that is, side by side] with" the State courts purports only to grant jurisdiction to district courts, while arguably recognizing existing State court jurisdiction "with" which district court "cognizance" shall be "concurrent." In both cases the federal courts alone were *given cognizance;* in one case State courts were *excluded,* in the other their jurisdiction was left untouched, except that it was to be shared by district courts. The legislative history seems to me to confirm this analysis of the statutory terms. The undisputed Federalist view that Article III jurisdiction could not be vested in State courts explains why sections 9 and 11 did not unambiguously provide that both federal courts and State courts *shall have* cognizance of the described causes. Resort instead to "concurrent with" State courts, I suggest, indicates that the terms of the statute responded both to Federalist denials that federal jurisdiction could be conferred on State courts and to States Righters' claims of existing State court jurisdiction.

---

that federal questions be left to State courts, which produced the compromise leaving establishment of inferior federal courts to Congressional discretion, and which prevailed in the Judiciary Act of 1789, may be taken to imply the corollary obligation to enforce federal claims. Their drive for State courts embodied a demand for *more* protection of rights secured by the Constitution, not for *no* protection. The colorful history of this issue is detailed in Warren, "New Light" 71; and in part analyzed by Hart & Wechsler 359–399; Wright 147–150. See also, infra, text accompanying notes 182–191, 246–249.

145 1 Stat. 73, 77 (emphasis supplied).

146 Cf. infra, text accompanying note 149.

Governor Johnston had emphasized that federal courts would "have concurrent jurisdiction with the state courts," which were "not divested of their present judicial cognizance." See supra, text accompanying note 128.

Similar implications may be drawn from section 25 of the Judiciary Act, which expressly authorizes the Supreme court to review certain State court decisions of constitutional issues, but breathes not a word that would authorize State courts to "have cognizance" of such causes initially, thereby recognizing that State courts had "retained" and not been "divested" of such jurisdiction. Jackson said that by the section 11 provisions for circuit courts, which like section 9 alternated between "exclusive" and "concurrent" jurisdiction, the State courts "are acknowledged to have concurrent jurisdiction to a large extent . . . And if jurisdiction is acknowledged in some points, it must be so to the fullest extent,"[147] that is, in the areas that were unmentioned. Vastly more was left to the State courts altogether without mention, for example, the "federal question" jurisdiction,[148] then the fragments of federal jurisdiction that were parceled out to district and circuit courts "concurrent with" State courts. Both the history and terms of the Judiciary Act therefore disclose that reliance was had on existing State court jurisdiction, not drawn from the Article III "judicial power."

This is made more plain in the memorandum submitted by Attorney General Randolph in December 1790 in response to a request by the House for a report on the Judiciary Act of 1789. He noted that State courts are not expressly excluded from jurisdiction of the Article III cases and controversies, that the extension of federal jurisdiction to these categories "which would of course be embraced" by State courts "had no such extension been made, cannot of itself, deprive [a State court] of its pre-existing rights," and that the State courts did not rely for their concurrent jurisdiction "upon any cession in the Constitution." But he concluded that the "nature" of some of the categories "shuts out the jurisdiction of the State courts," and proposed a provision "That no State court shall take cognizance of, or exercise jurisdiction" in the important categories he enumerated.[149] In short, Randolph proposed that the Act be amended to *exclude* State court jurisdiction of his categories. Thus the independent nature of State court jurisdiction and a plea for

---

[147] Supra, text accompanying note 137.

[148] Wright 4; supra, note 143.

[149] *American State Papers, Misc.* 1 (1789–1809) 22, 23, 26. In his note 4 to p. 26, Randolph states that "Some exclusions of the State courts are delineated in the original law [the Judiciary Act]."

its exclusion was once more drawn to the attention of Congress; and the fact that it left the Act untouched justifies the inference that once again it was satisfied to rely upon *existing* State court jurisdiction.[150]

The Supremacy Clause declares that State judges are "bound" by the federal Constitution and "laws in pursuance thereof," anything in State laws and constitution "to the contrary notwithstanding." Even severe critics of the conventional approach to the Clause are agreed, in the words of Bickel, that State judges are therefore under "a duty to enforce the supreme federal law above any contrary state law."[151] To the extent that "legislative omnipotence" constituted a barrier to judicial review, the Supremacy Clause represents an undeniable breakthrough: State judges were directed to set aside enactments of their "own" legislature when they conflicted with requirements of federal laws and Constitution. Once the dike was thus breached, why should Congressional violations of Constitutional limits have been regarded more tenderly?[152] Corwin drew

---

[150] The contrary view was taken in Tennessee v. Davis, 100 U.S. 257, 267 (1880), where the Court said that before adoption of the Constitution, the State judicial power "extended to every legal question that could arise. But when the Constitution was adopted, a portion of that judicial power became vested in the new government created, and so far as thus vested it was withdrawn from the sovereignty of the State." That view seems to me at odds with history. It was not shared by Chief Justice Marshall. In Slocum v. Mayberry, 2 Wheat. 1, 12 (1817), he said, echoing his earlier view in the Virginia convention, supra, text accompanying note 124, as well as that of Hamilton, id. at note 116, that "the Act of Congress neither expressly, nor by implication, forbids the state courts to take cognizance of such suits instituted for property in possession of an officer of the United States, nor detained under some law of the United States; consequently their jurisdiction remains.

[151] Bickel 9; and see Crosskey 989.

[152] Discussing the text of Article III in 1938 in the context of a narrow illustration employed by *The Federalist,* Corwin said, "Certainly it would be strange if a state act violative of a direct prohibition would give rise to a case 'under this Constitution' and yet a similar act of Congress could not. That the phrase may well have been intended to comprise both categories of cases is also borne out when we turn to the proceedings in the Convention itself." Corwin, *Court Over 36;* and see infra, note 191.

Crosskey, however, finds it "utterly impossible to believe" that the Founders did not intend by this omission "by plain implication" to exclude "the laws of Congress" from judicial review. Crosskey 989. The "rational impossibility of any other conclusion upon this subject seems very clear, indeed." Id. at 990. The

a distinction that has become fashionable: review of action by a "subordinate" State is "vastly different" from review of the acts of a "coordinate" branch, the Congress.[153] Yet State courts were directed to set aside acts of *their* coordinate branch, the State legislature. Professor Westin, restating Beard's critics, explains that "quite different questions of policy and politics are involved in judicial review of national legislation and in judicial review of State laws . . . many members of the Convention may have felt that, while review of state laws by the Court was essential to preserve the federal system and insure uniformity of rules, nothing was as compelling in the case of Congress or the President possessing the power to judge the constitutionality of their own measures and to stand accountable to the electorate for their judgments."[154]

That supposition, to my mind, is far removed from the presuppositions of the Founders. The State was the tried and true;[155] many

---

fact that State judges had to be released from their duty to effectuate State constitutions and valid state laws, the implications of the Framers' rejection of a *Congressional* negative for judicial enforcement, are not noticed by Crosskey. See supra, text accompanying notes 14–25. And if the "in pursuance" phrase be given the meaning it had for the Founders, supra, text accompanying notes 35–42, why was this not a "direction" to disregard Congressional laws that were repugnant to the Constitution. See supra, text accompanying notes 83–88; and infra, text accompanying notes 182–205.

[153] "How vastly different this veto of the central government upon the legislation of the local law-making bodies is—even though it is exercised by the judicial organ of the central government—from a veto upon the acts of any legislature, whether central or local, by a merely coordinate judiciary—it is hardly necessary to dwell upon at length. Only imagine the judicial committee of the British Privy Council, which vetoes a number of acts of colonial legislation every year, interposing its veto upon an Act of Parliament." Corwin, 4 *Mich. L. Rev.* 619. Compare his remarks with note 152, supra. But the Founders rejected the notion of Parliamentary supremacy, supra, Chapter 2, text accompanying notes 128–133, and see the remarks assuring the Ratification conventions that Congressional transgressions of "limits" would be reviewable.

Corwin repeated his opinion in *Court Over* 28; it was expressed by Boudin 98; Westin 29; cf. Crosskey 990. Yet "such nice distinctions," Melvin 201, stated in 1914, "as to the principle involved were scarcely voiced at the adoption nor during the early interpretations of the Constitution." No contemporary remark drawing the distinction cropped up in my own research. For contrary views by Ellsworth and Madison, see infra, text accompanying notes 193–197. In echoing the distinction, Boudin 98 himself illustrates the hazard, noted by him, of regarding "historic events from our own point of view in judging the attitude of their contemporaries towards them." Id. at 234.

[154] Westin 29–30. For a well-reasoned, contemporary dismissal of reliance on the "electorate" to correct constitutional transgressions, see Iredell's comment, supra, Chapter 4, text accompanying note 82; and see note 81.

[155] In Virginia, Pendleton assured the convention that "Our dearest rights

feared the new federal system as a potential oppressor. Wilson grasped the "dread, that the boasted *state sovereignties* will, under this system, be disrobed of part of their power";[156] and the last thing contemplated by those who dreaded Congressional invasions was to leave to Congress the final judgment on how far the disrobing should proceed. Although "uniformity of rule" for the several States was a desideratum, it was not deemed nearly "as compelling" as protection against feared Congressional "usurpations," as the great disproportion between discussion of the two issues in the records itself would persuade. Nor did the Founders proceed from the premise of "subordinate" States. It took the fires of a Civil War to forge the claims of an overriding Union.[157] In the beginning was a pervasive, powerful attachment to the States, a deep-rooted bias for local autonomy.[158] Hamilton adverted in the New York convention to a "strong and uniform attachment" exhibited by members of the Continental Congress "to the interests of their own States" which "have too often been preferred to the welfare of the Union."[159] "State attachments, and State importance," said Gouverneur Morris in the Convention, "have been the bane of this country."[160] Midway in the Convention Washington wrote, "independent sovereignty is so ardently contended for . . . the local views of each State . . . will not yield to a more enlarged scale of politicks."[161] "This passion for separate sovereignty," as Benjamin Rush

---

. . . as Virginians, are still in the hands of our state legislature." 3 Elliot 301. In the federal Convention, Martin agreed with Mason "as to the importance of the State Govts. he would support them at the expense of the Genl. Govt." 1 Farrand 340, 347. See also infra, text accompanying note 171; and 2 Elliot 393, 373, 250.

[156] 2 Elliot 443. The advocates of the Constitution sought to allay such fears. In the Convention, Dr. Johnson said that if "patrons" of the New Jersey Plan could be shown "that the individuality of the States would not be endangered, many of their objections would no doubt be removed." 1 Farrand 355. And see the comments of Wilson and Madison, id. at 355–356; see also 2 Elliot 217, 228, 242, 266, 304, 353, 354–355, 356, 438, 440, 443; McMaster & Stone 263, 265; 3 Elliot 301; 4 Elliot 58, 70, 180. Marshall was moved to say that "the friends of the Constitution are as tenacious of liberty as are its enemies." 3 Elliot 226.

[157] The "fundamental issues over the extent of federal supremacy," said Testa v. Katt, 330 U.S. 386, 390 (1940), "had been resolved by war." See also McCloskey, Introduction 33.

[158] See supra, note 156; cf. Chapter 2, text accompanying notes 113–127.

[159] 2 Elliot 266.

[160] 1 Farrand 530.

[161] 3 Farrand 51. Read said, "Too much attachment is betrayed to the State Governments." 1 Farrand 136.

observed in the Pennsylvania convention, persisted.[162] Men feared to trust their local interests to a remote centralized government that might be dominated by hostile sectional opposition.[163] Bedford made no bones about it in the Convention: *"I do not, gentlemen, trust you."*[164] Those who had "all their lives been inhabitants of Pennsylvania, could not quickly think of themselves as citizens of the United States."[165] When Hamilton took up the cudgels in *The Federalist,* he well knew that he was fighting for "a plan of government that had been portrayed as an engine of despotism."[166] And so it continued to be pictured, to mention only Patrick Henry's declamatory "I trust I shall see congressional oppression crushed in embryo."[167]

Opponents of adoption cried alarm at the threatened "destruction" of the States;[168] the argument, as Pennsylvania illustrated, was that "Unprotected by their States, the citizens would be at the mercy of the general government."[169] In New York, Melancton Smith said that in framing the Articles of Confederation, "we placed the state legislatures . . . between Congress and the people."[170] It was to "state governments," Ellsworth had said in the

---

[162] McMaster & Stone 299–300.

[163] See supra, Chapter 2, text accompanying notes 116–127, and note 127. "The people as a whole were by no means prepared for the creation of a vigorous central government. Apart from local pride and mutual jealousy, questions of unequal practical advantage made the favorable reception of the new plan a matter of the greatest uncertainty." Davis, *Veto* 70. And "The identification of remote and centralized government with political frustration and economic restraint was easy to make in the 1780's." Brown, 67 *Harv. L. Rev.* 1440; compare Chapter 2, note 127.

[164] 1 Farrand 500.

[165] Van Doren 187.

[166] Rossiter, *Hamilton* 58.

[167] 3 Elliot 546. Gerry charged that advocates of the Constitution sought "to lock the strong chains of domestic despotism on the country." Ford, *Pamphlets* 1, 6; see supra, Chapter 2, text accompanying notes 1–20.

[168] 1 Farrand 257, 345, 445; 2 Elliot 134, 241–242, 338, 374, 386; 3 Elliot 29, 415; cf. id. at 156, 171, 325, 579; 4 Elliot 51, 53, 93; McMaster & Stone 262–263, 284, 300. Hartley, a proponent of adoption in the Pennsylvania convention, noted that this objection "seems to spread the greatest alarm." Id. at 292. In the North Carolina convention Iredell, a leader in the struggle for adoption, said, "I heartily agree . . . that, if any thing in this Constitution tended to the annihilation of the state government, instead of exciting the admiration of any man, it ought to excite the resentment and execration. No such wicked intention ought to be suffered." 4 Elliot 53.

[169] Van Doren 180; see supra, note 155.

[170] 2 Elliot 250.

Convention, that "he turned his eyes . . . for the preservation of his rights."[171] There too Gerry asked, "Will any man say that liberty will be as safe in the hands of eighty or a hundred men taken from the whole continent, as in the hands of two or three hundred taken from a single State?"[172] Such fears were fed by the absence of a Bill of Rights and the feared consequent threat to rights secured by States constitutions.[173] True, Gouverneur Morris would have met the problem head on and "perhaps taken the teeth out of the serpents,"[174] but the leadership was better attuned to the temper of the times. Madison acknowledged in the Convention this "habitual attachment of the people," and seeking to convert weakness into strength, urged that the "whole force of this tie is on the side of the State government."[175] He pressed the point in *The Federalist,* and again in the Virginia convention: "The People will be attached to their state legislatures from a thousand causes . . . that scale will preponderate."[176] Such was also the position taken by Hamilton in the New York convention and in *The Federalist.*[177]

Attachment to the States had to yield in part to the necessity for national action in selected areas;[178] but power was grudgingly conferred and then only on repeated assurances that unauthorized acts of the new "agent" would be "void."[179] There is no inkling that the Founders considered that thereby they were reducing the States to "subordinate" status. "It was generally admitted," said Wilson in the Convention, "that a jealousy and rivalship would be felt between the Genl. & particular Govts."[180] The "inherent advantages"

171 1 Farrand 492.

172 2 Farrand 386.

173 E.g., Mason, 3 Elliot 266.

174 1 Farrand 530. Yet Morris said that the proposed *Congressional* negative was "likely to be terrible to the States." 2 Farrand 27.

175 1 Farrand 284.

176 *Federalist* No. 46 at 306; 3 Elliot 258.

177 2 Elliot 304; *Federalist* No. 17 at 103.

178 E.g., Hartley, a proponent of adoption in the Pennsylvania convention, said "That the rights now possessed by the States will in some degree be abridged by adoption of the proposed system, has never been denied; but it is only in that degree which is necessary and proper to promote the great purposes of the Union." McMaster & Stone 292–293; cf. 2 Elliot 443.

179 Supra, Chapter 2, text accompanying notes 33–40.

180 1 Farrand 355. "The same opposition of interests will probably ever remain, and the members of Congress will retain the same disposition to regard as their principal object the genuine good of their respective states." Lansing, 2 Elliot 294.

possessed by the States, said Hamilton in the New York convention, "will ever give them an influence and ascendancy over the national government."[181] The States remained the cherished first bastion,[182] as was soon hammered home when initial review of challenged State laws was left by the Act of 1789 to *State* courts. Those who did not trust Congress to determine whether State laws were repugnant to Congressional laws—for from such distrust sprang the Supremacy Clause—were in no mood to leave to Congress the final determination whether Congressional laws invaded the rights of a State or its citizens. Instead, the State courts were relied upon to prevent Congress itself from encroaching on rights of States and their citizens.[183] State courts, as Corwin said, were "thus assumed to be the *final* guardians of both State laws and State *constitutions*."[184] It was because many, like Grayson in Virginia, felt that "State courts were the principal defense of the states," their "only defensive armor,"[185] that the stubborn insistence on State court arbitrament of federal-State conflicts persisted and was ultimately expressed in the Judiciary Act of 1789. When deep-seated loyalty to the State could give way to the need for compulsion of State compliance with Constitutional prohibitions,[186] it was little likely that a suspect, untried Congress would be left free to violate

---

[181] 2 Elliot 239.

[182] E.g., supra, note 155.

[183] Cf. infra, note 191.

[184] Corwin, *Doctrine* 14; and see supra, note 143.

[185] 3 Elliot 563. See also supra, Chapter 4, text accompanying note 111. Of course, proponents of a federal system, such as Madison, expressed lack of confidence in State courts, supra, text accompanying note 7. His views were shared by Randolph, 2 Farrand 103; 2 Farrand 46; by Maclaine in North Carolina, 4 Elliot 164, where the sentiment ran powerfully the other way, cf. Bloodworth, id. at 142–143; Iredell, id. at 146. And see the remarks of Sedgwick and Vining in the First Congress, 1 *Ann. Cong.* 836, 853. Yet in the upshot it was the State courts that won out.

When Rutledge's motion in the federal Convention to reconsider and expunge the clause authorizing the establishment of inferior federal courts carried by a narrowly divided vote, Madison and Wilson sagaciously moved to amend the clause so that Congress would be "empowered to institute inferior tribunals," leaving it in the "discretion" of Congress to establish them. 1 Farrand 124–125. This was sweepingly adopted, later accompanied by Sherman's admonition "to make use of the State tribunals wherever it could be done," 2 Farrand 46, foreshadowing the subsequent compromise of 1789, whereby inferior federal courts were "established" but the bulk of "federal question" jurisdiction was left, as Rutledge had desired, to State courts. 1 Farrand 124.

[186] E.g., Davie, 4 Elliot 156.

Constitutional prohibitions at will.[187] To the contrary, although some urged that suits *against a State* be precluded, not one voice was heard to urge that suits against the United States be foreclosed.[188] Professor Crosskey's assumption that Congress must be the "constitutional judge of its own powers," that it was not left to "every petty 'judge in every State'" to judge of the powers of the "'Supreme Legislative of the nation,'"[189] would attribute to the Founders predilections held by few.[190] Prospective Congressional laws were not regarded with awe but with apprehension. To conclude against this background that the Founders could coolly permit State judges to overturn prized State constitutions but recoiled from judicial overthrow of a federal law that was thought to invade rights protected by State as well as federal Constitutions is to strain at the gnat and swallow the camel.[191]

[187] Mason understood that federal courts would indifferently enforce prohibitions both against Congress and the States. Supra, Chapter 4, text accompanying note 119.

[188] Compare the proposed New York amendment that would expressly bar suits *against a State*. Infra, Chapter 10, text accompanying notes 72–73. Mason declared that suits against the United States were required by reciprocity but rejected suits against a State. Id. at note 144. Some maintained that a *State* could not be sued, id. at notes 76–78, but Nicholas alone stated that Congress cannot be sued for debts, id. at note 143.

[189] Crosskey 990–991.

[190] Bedford, supra, Chapter 3, text accompanying notes 106–108; Mercer, id. at notes 78–80; Spaight, id. at notes 165–166. And see id. at notes 296–300.

Corwin early stated that "the men of 1787 expended no small fraction of their united ingenuity in devising an elaborate system of checks and balances, with the view of holding the government of their creation—particularly the popular organ thereof, the legislature—in permanent leash." After enumerating the various checks devised by them, he stated, "It was then but a step farther, and a very rational one, to set the judiciary against the legislature . . . The courts . . . had often, in both England and the Colonies, intervened in the defense of individual rights against administrative usurpation; they were the ancient defenders of the Rule of Law against prerogative." Corwin, 4 *Mich. L. Rev.* 626–627.

Meigs, *Relation* 151, could not suppose that the "careful" Framers "actually meant to leave each Congress free in its uncontrolled discretion to interpret the instrument to mean what that body might at the moment think expedient. If any one believes this possible, he can have little knowledge of the jealousy of power which was then almost universally prevalent. Had the Constitution been supposed to carry this meaning, there can be no shadow of doubt but that the smaller States would all have instantly rejected the instrument, rather than submit themselves to the absolute power of the larger States. The possibility of this interpretation was seen to some extent, and the fear of it was one cause of alarm, but the many answers made in the *Federalist* and other publications, as well as in the Ratifying Conventions, were in general found satisfactory." The materials earlier set forth abundantly confirm Meigs's judgment.

[191] Corwin, who first formulated the distinction between the "subordinate" State and the "coordinate" Congress, cf. supra, note 153, added in 1938, "Never-

Lastly, members of the Federal Convention made clear that Congressional laws which contravened the Constitution were no less subject to judicial review than violative State laws. Mason took for granted that federal courts would enforce prohibitions against both Congress and the States.[192] Ellsworth told the Connecticut convention that

> This Constitution defines the extent of the powers of the general government. If the general legislature should at any time overleap their limits, the judicial department is a constitutional check. If the United States go beyond their powers, if they make a law which the Constitution does not authorize, it is void; and the judicial power, the national . . . judges will declare it void. On the other hand, if the states go beyond their limits, if they make a law which is a usurpation upon the general government, the law is void; and upright, independent judges will declare it to be so.[193]

A similar view was expressed by Stone in the First Congress,[194] and analogous comparisons between judicial review of State laws and federal laws were made by Madison,[195] and by Hamilton.[196] One

---

theless, once it was decided to rely upon *courts* rather than a political agency [Congressional negative] to maintain the supremacy of national law in all its branches, a long step had been taken towards stamping the Constitution, even when considered by itself, as a judicially cognizable source of law for other purposes." *Court Over* 28; see also supra, note 152.

[192] Supra, Chapter 4, text accompanying note 119.

[193] 2 Elliott 196.

[194] Quoted infra, text accompanying note 212. See also Parsons' remarks, infra, note 211.

[195] In *Federalist* No. 44 at 295, Madison said that if Congress "shall exercise powers not warranted by" the Constitution, the answer would be "the same . . . as if the State legislatures should violate their respective authorities. In the first instance the success of the usurpation will depend on the the the executive and judiciary departments." Compare his remark late in the Convention, on August 28th, with respect to State infractions of the "obligation of contracts" clause, that the "prohibition of *ex post facto* laws . . . will oblige the judges to declare such interferences void." 2 Farrand 440. Manifestly he relied on existing judicial machinery. In the First Congress he said, "If there was reason for restraining the State governments from exercising this power [general warrants] there is like reason for restraining the Federal Government." 1 *Ann. Cong.* 456.

[196] In *Federalist* No. 81 at 524, Hamilton said, "the Constitution ought to be the standard of construction for the laws . . . There can be no objection, therefore, on this account, to the federal judiciary which will not lie against the local [State] judiciaries in general, and which will not serve to condemn any constitution that attempts to set bounds to legislative discretion."

vainly searches for contemporary opposition to the parallel thus drawn between judicial protection against State and Congressional excesses, for a remark that only State, not Congressional Acts, were to be declared void if in contravention of the Constitution.[197] On the other hand, Adams, Hamilton, Ellsworth, Wilson, Nicholas, and Marshall unequivocally stated that the courts were to set aside Congressional Acts that went beyond the powers conferred.[198] Plainly the men of 1787 did not share the view, much later fashioned by Corwin and Crosskey, that the "coordinate" Congress stood on a loftier pinnacle than the "subordinate" State, a pinnacle that judicial review could not reach. For in either case, the Founders contemplated that Constitutional limits were to be enforced even-handedly by the judiciary.

STATE COURT POWER TO DECLARE

FEDERAL LAWS UNCONSTITUTIONAL

Power to declare federal statutes unconstitutional is "conceded to state courts," asserts Bickel, only "in order to enable one to lodge it in the federal courts also, and for no other reason."[199] One who, like Hart, considers that the State courts "are the primary guarantors of constitutional rights, and in many cases they may be the ultimate ones,"[200] might consider that a good enough reason. Even though that guarantee has become somewhat tarnished,[201] the power of the State courts ought to be considered on its own merits and can stand on its own bottom.

That the Founders expected State courts to declare void Congressional Acts which were inconsistent with the Constitution should in large part have emerged from the preceding pages. To pull a few threads together, there is the fact that only laws "in pursuance" of the Constitution were made "binding" on State judges, that the Founders equated "in pursuance" to "consistent with." By necessary implication State judges were *not* bound by laws "inconsistent with" with Constitution, and before overriding a State Constitu-

---

[197] The expressions of Mercer, supra, Chapter 3, text accompanying note 78, and of Spaight, id. at note 166, may be viewed as the exceptions.

[198] See supra, Chapter 2, text accompanying note 36; id. Chapter 3 at note 227; id. Chapter 4 at notes 26, 39–41, 118, 123.

[199] Bickel 11.

[200] Hart, "Dialectic," quoted Hart & Wechsler 339.

[201] Cf. Norris v. Alabama, 294 U.S. 587 (1935); NAACP v. Alabama, 357 U.S. 449 (1958).

tion or law, they had perforce to determine whether the Congressional "law" was or was not "consistent with" the federal Constitution. This view is confirmed by the many assurances that Congress would be kept within "limits" and that laws not authorized by the Constitution would be declared void. In addition, there is the sustained and at last successful struggle to leave federal questions to State rather than to inferior federal courts because State courts were counted on to defend rights of the individual and the State.[202] Adherents of State courts did not wage battle in order to guarantee supine enforcement of Congressional "usurpations"; they did not command State courts to become blind enforcers of impermissible invasions of rights sheltered by State or federal constitutions. To the contrary, Hamilton assured the New York convention, "the laws of Congress are restricted to a certain sphere, and when they depart from that sphere, they are no longer supreme and binding."[203] Davie and Iredell made similar assurances to the North Carolina convention.[204] "The question then, under this [Supremacy] clause," added Iredell, "will always be whether Congress has exceeded its authority."[205] Neither Hamilton nor Iredell, much less those who feared and opposed a federal system, meant to leave the decision of that question to Congress itself.[206]

Hamilton amplified his view of the Supremacy Clause in *Federalist* No. 33. The Clause, he stated, "*expressly* confines this supremacy to laws made *pursuant to the Constitution*"; federal acts "which are *not pursuant*" thereto but "are invasions of the residuary powers of the smaller societies . . . will be merely acts of usurpation and will deserve to be treated as such."[207] Thus State judges were not "bound" by "acts of usurpation" and could treat them as such only if they were free preliminarily to decide whether the

[202] See Grayson, supra, text accompanying note 185; Henry, id. at note 123; Martin, infra, id. at note 209; Rutledge, infra, id. at note 218.

[203] 2 Elliot 362. Compare Gerry: "so far as your laws conform" to the Constitution, the courts "will attend to them, but no further." 1 *Ann. Cong.* 361. Compare too his rhetorical question, "would not [the courts] be bound to declare the law a nullity, if this clause is continued in it and is inconsistent with the Constitution?" 1 *Ann. Cong.* 524.

[204] Supra, Chapter 4, text accompanying note 85; supra, text accompanying notes 36–37.

[205] 4 Elliot 179. For a similar remark by Lee in Virginia, see supra, Chapter 4, note 118.

[206] For Hamilton, see supra, Chapter 3, text accompanying notes 226–229; Iredell, id. at note 168.

[207] *Federalist* No. 33 at 201–202.

federal statute *was* a usurpation. This also appears to be the implication of Hamilton's remark in *Federalist* No. 27, when he concluded from the "oath" taken by State officers to observe the "Supreme Law of the land" that all State courts "will be incorporated into the operations of the national government *as far as its just and constitutional authority extends.*" The phrase, italicized by Hamilton himself, was gratuitous if State courts could not determine whether the federal Act was within the "constitutional authority," if, in other words, they were bound by *every* duly enacted federal law.[208] So too, Luther Martin explained that by virtue of the initial omission of State *constitutions* from the "to the contrary notwithstanding" phrase of the original Supremacy Clause, State judges "would be bound to *reject*" federal laws that were "inconsistent with our own [State] constitution."[209] When State constitutions were interpolated in the clause, it is highly improbable that the Framers intended to place them at the mercy of Congress in the exercise of powers that were *not* "in purusuance" of the Constitution. Rather, it is more reasonable to infer that State judges remained "bound to reject" federal laws that were "inconsistent with" the federal Constitution and consequently encroached wrongfully on State constitutions.[210]

The point was made again by Gerry in the debate on the Judiciary Act of 1789: "the State judges would not be bound by any law altering the State constitution, unless such law was necessary to carry into operation the constitution of the Union."[211] In the same debate,

[208] *Federalist* No. 27 at 169–170.

[209] 3 Farrand 287.

[210] Cf. supra, text accompanying notes 123, 185.

[211] 1 *Ann. Cong.* 864. See also Gerry's remarks, quoted supra, note 203. Hanson told Maryland that "every judge in the Union, whether of federal or State appointment . . . will have a right to reject any act, handed to him as a law, which he may conceive repugnant to the constitution." Ford, *Pamphlets* 233–234.

Parsons, speaking in the Massachusetts convention about the "checks the people have against usurpation, and the abuse of power," said, "The oath of the several legislative, executive and judicial officers of the several states take to support the federal Constitution, is as effectual a *security* against the *usurpation* of the general government as it is against the encroachments of the state governments . . . an increase of powers by usurpation is as clearly a violation of the federal Constitution" which the oath obliges the State officers "vigorously to oppose." 2 Elliot 93–94.

Judge Learned Hand stated that under the Supremacy Clause "state courts would at times have to decide whether state laws and constitutions, or even a federal statute, were in conflict with the federal constitution." Hand 28.

a middle-of-the-roader, Stone, who urged that State courts be given a trial before the establishment of federal courts, reminded the First Congress about the stakes that were involved:

> I believe that the scheme of the present Government was considered by those who framed it as dangerous to the liberties of the United States; if they had not considered it from this point of view, they would not have guarded it in the manner they have done. They supposed that it had a natural tendency to destroy the State Governments; or, on the other hand, they supposed that State Governments had a tendency to abridge the powers of the General Government; therefore it was necessary to guard against either taking place, and this was to be done properly by establishing a Judiciary of the United States. This Judiciary was likewise absolutely necessary because a great many purposes of the Union could not be accomplished by the States from the principle of their Government, and could not be executed from a defect of their power [for example, "could not determine between State and State"]. But all these, I presume, are involved in the jurisdiction of the Supreme Federal Court. I apprehend in everything else the State courts might have had complete and adequate jurisdiction.[212]

State courts, in a word, might "guard" against the federal "tendency" to destroy the State governments, and the Supreme Court could "guard" against the State tendency "to abridge" national power.

Apparently Professor Bickel is of a contrary opinion; he states that an authority to State judges "to measure federal law against the federal Constitution and to uphold it or to strike it down in accordance with their understanding of the relevant constitutional provision . . . *standing alone,* would have been extraordinary, and it would have been self-destructive." If, he continues, "state judges were to have *final power* to strike down federal statutes" the "purpose of the clause . . . to make federal authority supreme over the state" would have been balked.[213] His hypothesis runs counter

[212] 1 *Ann. Cong.* 840–841. Haines 147, said of the debate on the 1789 Act that there was "general agreement that state courts might declare federal laws contrary to the Constitution invalid."
[213] Bickel 9 (emphasis supplied).

to the facts. "Federal authority" was not a blank check; it was "limited" authority, "binding" only if "consistent with" the Constitution. Nor were State court judgments either to "stand alone" or to be "final." What has gone before should have demonstrated that State courts were only relied on to determine the validity of federal laws "in the first instance." And section 25 of the Judiciary Act expressly anticipated the situation in which the validity of federal statutes would be questioned and the State court decision would be "against their validity."[214] It was not left "standing alone." As Corwin stated in 1910, "the constitutional fathers intended that appeals should lie from State courts to the United States Supreme Court."[215] The point has been so generally accepted[216] that it would be laboring the obvious to collate supporting materials but for Bickel's thesis that the argument for State court power is merely a device whereby to clothe federal courts with the power of judicial review.

The Convention records show that Supreme Court review of State court action was contemplated. Reflecting the New Jersey Plan,[217] Rutledge, a vigorous proponent of States Rights, urged that "State tribunals might and ought to be left in all cases to decide in the first instance the right of appeal being sufficient to secure national right and uniformity of Judgmts."[218] It was on his motion that

[214] 1 *Stat.* 73 85; the relevant portions are quoted in Hart & Wechsler 41.

[215] Corwin, 9 *Mich. L. Rev.* 299. Says Charles Warren, *The Making of the Constitution* 539 (1928): "The fact is that the Framers of the Constitution, as well as its advocates in the State conventions, expected practically all cases to go from the State courts to the Supreme Court . . . All expected and desired that the State courts should take cognizance of all other [than admiralty and maritime] cases in the first instance with a right of appeal to the Supreme Court."

[216] Wechsler, *Principles* 7, says of the "arising under" and "appellate jurisdiction" clauses of Article III, "Surely this means, as section 25 of the Judiciary Act of 1789 took it to mean, that if a state court passes on a constitutional issue, as the supremacy clause provides that it should, its judgment is reviewable, subject to congressional exceptions, by the Supreme Court, in which event that Court must have no less authority and duty to accord priority to constitutional provisions than the court that it reviews." And see Hart, Book Review 1469; Tucker's *Blackstone* 183; Corwin, *Doctrine* 55; Warren, *Congress* 104; Haines 147; Frankfurter and Landis, *Business of the Supreme Court* 4 (1928); Wright 420.

[217] Supra, text accompanying note 110.

[218] 1 Farrand 134. Pierce records Rutledge as "of opinion that it would be right to make the adjudications of the State judges appealable to the national judicial." Id. at 128. Jefferson suggested to Madison in June 1787 that the proposed Congressional "negative" be replaced by "an appeal from the State judicatures to a federal court." Supra, note 25. An amendment proposed in the New York convention provided for the trial of federal questions in "the State courts with the right of appeal to the Supreme Court." 2 Elliot 408.

the provision for "inferior courts" was expunged, leading to the adoption of the Madison-Wilson compromise motion that institution of such courts be left in the discretion of Congress,[219] the formula embodied in Article III. When the matter moved from the Committee of the Whole to the Convention, the struggle was renewed by opponents of inferior federal courts, but the Madison-Wilson compromise was adopted, accompanied by Sherman's admonition that Congress should "make use of the State tribunals whenever it could be done with safety to the general interest,"[220] as the First Congress in fact later did. This history led Corwin to remark that State court "jurisdiction in the first instance . . . with subsequent appeal to the United State Supreme Court, was the maximum concession that was demanded in the Convention by the Pro-State party."[221] To this may be added the explanation of the original Supremacy Clause by Luther Martin, an ardent States Righter, that it was his wish to have the question involved "determined in the first instance in the courts of the respective states," and that he "voted an appeal should lay to the supreme judiciary of the United States."[222] So Hamilton also understood. In *Federalist* No. 82, he stated that an "appeal would certainly lie from" State courts "to the Supreme Court . . . The Constitution in direct terms gives an appellate jurisdiction to the Supreme Court . . . without a single expression to confine its operation to the inferior federal courts"; the appellate jurisdiction "ought to be construed to extend to the State tribunals." He furnished a "weighty reason":

> Either this must be the case, or the local courts must be excluded from a concurrent jurisdiction in matters of national concern, else the judiciary authority of the Union may be eluded at the pleasure of every plaintiff or prosecutor. Neither of these consequences ought, without evident necessity to be involved; the latter would be entirely inadmissible, as it would defeat some of the most important and avowed purposes of the proposed government . . .

[219] 1 Farrand 125.

[220] 2 Farrand 45–46.

[221] Corwin, 9 *Mich. L. Rev.* 123. See amendment proposed in New York convention, 2 Elliot 408; Spencer in North Carolina, 4 Elliot 155.

[222] 3 Farrand 287. Hanson advised Maryland that an appeal would lie to the Supreme Court from both state and federal courts. Ford, *Pamphlets* 238. See also Randolph, 3 Elliot 570.

The evident aim of the plan of the convention is, that all causes of the specified classes shall, for weighty reasons, receive their original or final determination in the courts of the Union.[223]

His analysis was reiterated by Smith in the First Congress and by Justice Story in 1816.[224]

Considerations of "uniformity" alone would call for such an interpretation. Professor Bickel himself referred to the "obvious interest, if for no other interest than uniformity of application, in having federal law construed as well as declared by an institution of the general government."[225] That "interest" was also "obvious" to the Founders. The need for a Supreme tribunal to ensure "uniformity" had been mentioned in the Convention by Rutledge, and in *The Federalist* by Hamilton.[226] The point was made in the Ratification conventions, by Madison and Pendleton in Virginia, by Davie and Iredell in North Carolina, and by Charles Pinckney in North Carolina.[227] As Iredell stated, "There can be no other way of securing the administration of justice uniformly in the several States. There might be, otherwise, as many different adjudications on the

---

[223] *Federalist* No. 82 at 536–537. Appeals from State courts to the Supreme Courts were contemplated prior to the Virginia convention; supra, note 121. Undeniably, said Charles Pinckney in the North Carolina convention, the "supreme federal jurisdiction was indispensable" so that, among other things, "the state judiciary would confine themselves within their proper spheres." 4 Elliot 257–258.

[224] 1 *Ann. Cong.* 829; Martin v. Hunter's Lessee, 1 Wheat. 304, 339 (1816). But Smith, a proponent of federal courts, argued that "the constant control of the Supreme Court over adjudications of the State courts, would dissatisfy the people, and weaken the authority and importance of the State judges." 1 *Ann. Cong.* 829. Later he argued that the appeal to the Supreme Court could not come from a State court, but "it must come from a federal tribunal." Id. at 850. Anticipating such arguments, Hamilton had said that "The objects of the appeal, not the tribunals from which it is to be made, are alone contemplated." *Federalist* No. 82 at 536.

If Article III be ambiguous on this score, the ambiguity was resolved by the States Righters acceptance in the conventions and in the First Congress of an appeal from State courts to the Supreme Court. Compare amendments proposed in several Ratification conventions, which eliminated inferior federal courts but retained Supreme Court appellate jurisdiction. Supra, text accompanying note 125; and infra, id. at note 229. The Hamilton-Story analysis has the concurrence of Crosskey, 811–813. The controversy about State court appeals is summarized by Wright 420.

[225] Bickel 10.

[226] Infra, text accompanying note 228; *Federalist* No. 22 at 138. And see 2 Wilson, *Works* 290.

[227] 3 Elliot 518, 532; 4 Elliot 158, 147, 258. And see Spencer, an opponent of adoption, 4 Elliot 155.

same subject as there are States," a point earlier made by Hamilton.[228]

Amendments proposed in the North Carolina, New York, and Virginia conventions sought to supplant inferior federal courts with State courts but with an appeal to the Supreme Court.[229] Such views found expression in the debate on the Judiciary Act in the First Congress. In the House, the debate revolved around the Senate bill which ultimately became the Act. Opinions ranged from that of Livermore, who was altogether opposed to federal jurisdiction, even to a Supreme Court,[230] through Federalists like Smith, who maintained that establishment of inferior federal courts with comprehensive federal jurisdiction was required by the Constitution,[231] to pro-State men like Jackson, who defended the Senate bill with its recognition of existing State court jurisdiction from which appeal on certain federal questions would lie on the Supreme Court.[232] It was the latter who carried the day, for by the Judiciary Act of 1789 the First Congress left the great bulk of federal jurisdiction to the State courts with provision for an appeal to the Supreme Court.

With good reason, therefore, did Justice Story state in 1816 that "It is an historical fact, that this exposition of the constitution, extending its appellate power to state courts, was, previous to its adoption, uniformly and publicly avowed by its friends, and admitted by its enemies, as the basis of their respective reasonings, both in and out of the state conventions." And when the Judiciary Act was deliberated in the First Congress, he continued, "the same exposition was explicitly declared and admitted by the friends and opponents of that system."[233]

---

[228] 4 Elliot 147. "Thirteen independent courts of final jurisdiction over the same causes, arising under the same laws," said Hamilton, "is a hydra in government, from which nothing but contradiction and confusion can proceed." *Federalist* No. 80 at 516. And see id. No. 22 at 139; Ratner 165 n. 41.

[229] New York, 2 Elliot 408; Virginia, 3 Elliot 657, 660; North Carolina, 4 Elliot 246.

[230] 1 *Ann. Cong.* 813–814.

[231] Id. at 850.

[232] Jackson, id. at 833–834; Stone, id. at 840; Livermore, id. at 827; Smith, id. at 828–829. And see Corwin, *Doctrine* 55.

[233] Martin v. Hunter's Lessee, 1 Wheat. (4 U.S.) 304, 351 (1816). Marshall, C. J. regarded the Judiciary Act as an authoritative "contemporary exposition" of the Constitution, and said that "not a single individual, so far as is known, supposed that part of the act which gives the Supreme Court appellate jurisdiction over the judgments of the state courts . . . to be unauthorized by the con-

Roughly speaking, section 25 of the Act of 1789 provided for Supreme Court review of final State court judgments in three categories: Clause 1: where the validity of a federal statute or treaty is challenged and the decision is *against* their validity; Clause 2: where a State statute or exercise of authority is challenged as repugnant to federal Constitution, law, or treaty and decision is in *favor* of their validity; and Clause 3: where the construction of the federal Constitution, law, or treaty is drawn in question and decision is *against* the right specially claimed by either party thereunder.[234] In each of these situations the decision may be "reversed or affirmed" by the Supreme Court. Patently Clause 1 contemplates that a State court may hold that a federal law is *not valid,* and that the Supreme Court, by affirming, may hold the same.[235] Nevertheless, Crosskey maintains that the draftsmen "were interested in the [Supreme] Court as an *enforcing* agency only. Their sole concern was that the acts of Congress and the nation's treaties should be *obeyed.*" Anything else "seems utterly impossible to believe," he states, because section 25 permitted Supreme Court review only when State courts "denied" the validity of a federal law.[236] The factual premises of the

---

stitution." Cohens v. Virginia, 6 Wheat. (9 U.S.) 264, 420 (1821). So far as I could find, only Smith maintained that the appeal must come from a federal court. 1 *Ann. Cong.* 850.

[234] 1 Stat. 73, 85.

[235] Warren, *Congress* 104, states, "Power to affirm necessarily implied power to hold the Act of Congress unconstitutional, since the State court decision, so affirmed, would have made that holding." See also Wechsler, supra, n. 216.

[236] Crosskey 1032. In part, Crosskey rests his argument on the claim that there is no power to decide against the "validity of a treaty," first, because the constitutional power "is in terms absolutely general," Crosskey 1030, meaning presumably that whereas "laws" under the Supremacy Clause must be "in pursuance" of the Constitution, it suffices that "treaties" are "under the authority of the United States." But as Crosskey himself has pointed out, the "under the authority" phrase was designed to ensure the "desired retrospective application in the case of treaties" in order to preserve those that had been made prior to the Constitution. Supra, text accompanying notes 58–60. The Convention records indicate that the Founders did not intend to create an unlimited treaty-making power. See Appendix B.

Second, Crosskey asserts, the treaty-power "from the very nature of the exigencies it must meet" has to be "unlimited in its character"; moreover the Court itself has expressed "doubt of its power to review in the premises," citing Missouri v. Holland, 252 U.S. 416, 433 (1920). In consequence, "it manifestly is a pretty far-fetched view that our first President and first Senate, having just been vested with the unlimited treaty-making power, agreed to a statute 'explicitly' recognizing a right in the Supreme Court to review the constitutionality of the treaties they might make thereunder . . . And this being true, a strong presumption surely arises that the argument requiring this improbable assumption is not, in fact, a sound one, either with respect to treaties or with respect

Crosskey argument are at least debatable,[237] but if they be assumed, his conclusion does not follow.

---

to acts of Congress." Crosskey 1030. What this boils down to is that when the First Congress and President Washington expressly provided by §25 that State courts might decide "against the validity" of "treaties" they did not know what they were about. Against express statutory terms Crosskey pits his conviction that the treaty-power must be unlimited and therefore the First Congress could not have meant what it said. It is simpler to conclude that when the First Congress expressly made "treaties" reviewable, it confirmed that the "under the authority" differentiation of the Supremacy Clause was not designed to confer unreviewable, unlimited treaty-making power. Congressional "usurpations," it has been shown, *were* to be reviewable, so that the inclusion of "statutes" in §25 confirms the assurances made in the various conventions. Lee, who alluded to the "absolute" treaty power, Appendix B, text accompanying note 1, yet conceded to the courts the "power of deciding finally on the laws of the union." The coupling of "treaties" with "statutes" in §25 works against rather than for Professor Crosskey.

Missouri v. Holland is a strange citation. The Court said, "We do not mean to imply that there are no qualifications to the treaty-making power." "The only question to whether [the treaty] is forbidden by some invisible radiation from the general terms of the Tenth Amendment"; and it held that State interest had to yield to "a national interest of very nearly the first magnitude." 252 U.S. at 433–435. See Reid v. Covert, 354, U.S. 1, 18 (1957). Why, too, must we attach so much importance to what a solitary case allegedly intimated about "unlimited" treaty power 130 years after the event when Crosskey unhesitatingly consigns to deepest limbo Marbury v. Madison (1803) and all its progeny because they cross *his* view of what the Constitution meant in 1789? Assume *arguendo* that the treaty provision of §25 is fatally vulnerable, does it necessarily follow that review of "statutes" must also fall? Where are the "exigencies" which require "unlimited" Congressional power to enact "laws," and what of all the outcries against "unlimited" Congressional power?

[237] Professor Hart points out that "State court decisions upholding a federal statute or treaty against a challenge under the federal Constitution were reviewable under a different category [Clause 3], giving jurisdiction in cases in which the construction of the Constitution had been drawn in question and the decision was against a right specially set up under the Constitution." Hart, Book Review 1484. The point had been made in Treblicock v. Wilson, 12 Wall. 687, 692–694 (1872), where the State court had held in favor of a plaintiff who relied upon a federal statute, so that there was no jurisdiction under Clause 1, but defendant had invoked the Constitution to invalidate the statute and the State court had held *against* him within the meaning of Clause 3. Chief Justice Marshall had recognized this Clause 3 jurisdiction in Gordon v. Coldcleugh, 3 Cranch 268 (1806).

As to State statutes under Clause 2, Professor Wright points out that until the Act of 1914, the "Supreme Court could not review state court decisions which upheld the federal claim and found a state act invalid." Wright 420. A decision that a State statute is, as claimed, repugnant to federal law or the Constitution and is therefore not reviewable under Clause 2 should find no review under Clause 3 because the "construction" of the law or Constitution would be in favor of the "claim" thereunder, not "against" it. To this extent, Professor Crosskey's argument has some factual footing.

Professor Hart also notes that Crosskey's restriction of review to "state court *denials* of federal rights" conflicts with his theory "that it was a matter of common agreement in the Convention that the Court should have the function of establishing nationwide uniformity of judicial decision generally." Hart, Book Review 1484 n. 80.

The logic of the Crosskey argument limits the Supreme Court to *reversal* of a State adjudication that a federal law is invalid, and reversal must be automatic because to "affirm" is not to act as "an *enforcing* agency only" of federal laws. The argument is oblivious to the special purpose of initial State court jurisdiction, which was to serve as a first line of defense against Congressional "usurpations." The draftsmen might reasonably conclude that no further inquiry into "validity" of a federal law was necessary when it passed muster with a jealous-eyed State court, as Clause 2 plainly discloses in shutting off review where a State court holds that a *State* statute *is* repugnant to federal law or Constitution.[238] The same draftsmen, moreover, who "omitted" review of State judgments of "validity" went on to provide that the Supreme Court could *either* "reverse" or "affirm" judgments that federal laws were *invalid*. The narrow purpose attributed to the draftsmen by Crosskey could have been satisfied by a provision for reversal. Why did they add "affirm"? One who would deprive a statutory term of effect—on Crosskey's reading, "affirm" minimally becomes inapplicable to Clause 1—carries the burden of showing that such rewriting or elision is essential to effectuate the intention of the draftsmen or to avoid an unreasonable result. No such showing is made by Crosskey, and in fact his version thwarts the expressed intention of the draftsmen and *produces* an unreasonable result. If the draftsmen's "sole concern" was that Congressional statutes "should be obeyed," section 25 represents a useless meander around Robin Hood's barn. Instead of issuing what amounts to a futile invitation to State courts to hold a federal law invalid, which the Supreme Court was then required automatically to reverse, it would have been simpler to provide that federal laws duly enacted—to pick up the Crosskey-Bickel version of "in pursuance" of the Constitution—were to be accepted without more as valid and binding.[239] In fact, however, the struggle for initial State

---

[238] Professor Wright states that "The reason for such a distinction [in §25] was clear enough. When the state court had yielded to the authority of the federal government, and had held its own statute invalid, appeal to the Supreme Court was thought unnecessary to protect the federal government in the exercise of its rightful powers." Wright 420.

[239] Consequently I cannot concur in Professor Bickel's view, respecting the §25 provision for review of holdings of "invalidity," that "Reading no presuppositions into it, one may as easily conclude that the Supreme Court was meant only to enforce against state courts a rule that duly enacted statutes are constitutional by virtue of their due enactment." Bickel 13. Cf. supra, text accompanying notes

court review was not waged to protect Congressional "usurpation" from overturn but to provide greater security for State and individual prerogatives. The States Righters accepted review by a supreme tribunal in the interests of "uniformity" and because of the seriousness of state-federal conflicts; but minimally they contemplated a fair and sober determination on appeal, not a cut-and-dried reversal. Their struggle would have been meaningless if State court judgments that Congressional "usurpations" were invalid were to be automatically reversible.

The records of the First Congress also read against Crosskey. That Congress expressed *no* concern about the Court's duty to make State courts "obey" federal statutes which contravened the Constitution; but it did unmistakably record its conviction that the Court could "revise" or "correct" Congressional action which exceeded Constitutional limits. Some weeks earlier the debate on the President's "removal" power had elicited numerous affirmations of the judicial corrective power[240] by men who, as Corwin remarked, went on to vote for the Judiciary Act.[241] So preponderant were such views, so slight the dissent, that it is safe to infer that the House found no occasion to reargue a point so widely accepted. Even so, without challenge, Gerry remarked in the course of the Judiciary Act debate itself that "so far as your laws conform" to the Constitution, the courts "will attend to them, but no further";[242] and Stone emphasized that a judiciary was provided in part to prevent the federal government from "destroying" State governments.[243]

The members of the First Congress knew well enough what was at stake, as may be gathered from the remarks of Gerry in the course of the "removal" debate:

> The people of America can never be safe, if Congress have a right to exercise the power of giving constructions to the constitution different from the original instrument . . . If the people

---

28–55, and id. at note 39. Nor can the text of §25 be read *in vacuo;* the express recognition by the First Congress of judicial power to set aside Congressional Acts must be taken into account. Supra, Chapter 5, text accompanying notes 11–18, 24–25; infra, id. at notes 240–244; cf. supra, text accompanying notes 44–54.

[240] Supra, Chapter 5, text accompanying notes 11–18.

[241] Corwin, *Doctrine* 49 n. 74.

[242] 1 *Ann. Cong.* 861. See also supra, text accompanying note 211.

[243] Id. at 840.

were to find that Congress meant to alter it in this way; . . . it would be repugnant to the principles of the revolution . . .

But if the . . . judges are bound by our decisions, we may alter that part of the constitution which is secured from being amended by the fifth article . . .

Shall the judges, because Congress have usurped power . . . be impeached . . . for doing a meritorious act, and standing in opposition to their usurpation of power? If this is the meaning of the constitution, it was hardly worth so much bustle and uneasiness about it.[244]

In his dry, common-sense way, Gerry reminds us that it was not the purpose of the Founders to leave Congress to judge for itself whether its own laws contravened the Constitution.

The power of State courts, and of the Supreme Court on appeal, to declare a federal law unconstitutional seems therefore quite clear. This is not because the Supremacy Clause conferred jurisdiction on either, but rather because the Founders relied on the inherent State court jurisdiction and the Article III appellate jurisdiction of the Supreme Court. What the Supremacy Clause added was first, to define the content of the "supreme law of the land," and second, to make clear that State judges were "bound" by federal laws and Constitution when these were opposed to those of the State, but only when federal "laws" were "in pursuance of," that is, "consistent with" the Constitution. Necessarily this provision contemplated that State courts would determine whether or not federal laws were consistent with the Constitution. It was because State courts were trusted to perform this protective function, to serve as a first line of defense against Congressional invasion, that States Righters obstinately fought to leave federal jurisdiction to State courts. And they prevailed, first in the Convention, which left the establishment of inferior federal courts in the discretion of Congress, and then in the First Congress, which by the Judiciary Act of 1789 left the vast bulk

---

[244] Id. at 523, 557–558. So too, Iredell, after exposition of the argument for judicial review, stated that "In any other light than as I have stated it, the greater part of the provisions of the [North Carolina] Constitution would appear to me to be ridiculous, since in my opinion nothing could be more so than for representatives of a people solemnly assembled to form a Constitution, to set down a number of political dogmas, which might or might not be regarded." 2 McRee 174.

of "federal question" jurisdiction to the State courts, subject to appeal to the Supreme Court. That Act constitutes an authoritative construction by those who were quite familiar with what the Convention and the several Ratifying conventions had contemplated. Nevertheless, it would be a mistake to rely over-much on State courts for reasons now to be noticed.

<h2 style="text-align:center">MUST STATE COURTS EXERCISE JURISDICTION?</h2>

If State courts have jurisdiction, must they exercise it? The States Righters, who had opposed the establishment of inferior federal courts and stubbornly insisted that matters of federal import be left in the first instance to State courts, could not very well maintain that State courts were at liberty to shut their doors to assertion of federal rights.[245] They had urged that State courts were the best reliance of the individual; for example, Patrick Henry declared that the Virginia judiciary was "was one of the best barriers against strides of power" and was therefore to be preferred to an untried federal judiciary.[246] It was because many looked for protection to State courts that Marshall assured the Virginia convention that "There is no clause in the Constitution which bars the individual member from applying ["for protection from an infringement of the Constitution"] to the state courts to give him redress."[247] Anxiety about access to such redress underlies the frequent assurances that State courts would have "concurrent" jurisdiction.[248] States Righters, I suggest, did not wage battle for State court availability, "concurrent" or "exclusive," only to have their efforts to secure better protection—as they then thought—aborted by the State courts themselves. *More* protection of constitutional rights was the mainspring of the drive for State court administration of "federal questions," not *no* protection.

More concrete evidence for the mandatory exercise of State court jurisdiction is furnished by remarks of Hamilton and Parsons. In

---

[245] Compare Chief Justice Taney, dissenting in Prigg v. Pennsylvania, 16 Pet. 539, 631 (1842).

[246] Supra, Chapter 4, text accompanying note 111. See also Grayson, supra, text accompanying note 185.

[247] Supra, text accompanying note 124; cf. supra, Chapter 4, text accompanying notes 96, 132.

[248] Supra, text accompanying notes 124–129; cf. id. at notes 182–187.

Federalist No. 82 Hamilton emphasized that "The evident aim of the plan of the convention" was that Article III "causes" shall "receive their original *or* final determination in the courts of the Union." Appeal must lie from State courts to the Supreme Court "or the local courts must be excluded from a concurrent jurisdiction in matters of national concern, else the judiciary authority of the Union may be eluded."[249] If State courts were confided with "exclusive" federal jurisdiction, as the Judiciary Act of 1789 in large part provided, Hamilton posited that it must be exercised; otherwise there could be no appeal to the Supreme Court, and therefore "no original or final determination in the courts of the Union," thus "eluding" its judicial authority.

Hamilton went beyond this in his analysis of the "oath" provision (Article III, section 3) in *Federalist* No. 27, to affirm that the fact that State officers were "bound by oath" to support the Constitution rendered State courts "auxiliary to the enforcement of [national] laws," that all State courts "will [by that oath] be incorporated into the operations of the national government *as far as its just and constitutional authority extends.*"[250] In short, State judges were by "oath" "incorporated" into the federal government, and "bound by oath" to "enforcement of its laws." Similar views were expressed in Massachusetts by Parsons: "The oath the . . . judicial officers of the several states take to support the federal Constitution, is . . . a *security* against the *usurpations* of the general government" which the oath obliges the State judges, as well as other State officers "vigorously to oppose."[251] To my mind the views of Hamilton and Parsons are faithful to the ordinary meaning of the "oath" provision. A judge who takes an "oath" to support the Constitution, and is then by its terms "bound by oath" to do so surely may not refuse to hear a claim that federal or state action is in violation of the Constitution. Nor may a State frustrate the Constitutional "oath" requirement simply by depriving the State court of jurisdiction to hear a claim of unconstitutional infringement.[252] Nevertheless, State courts, under the stress of "fugitive slave" actions, began to assert early in the 1800's that they were not required to entertain federal

[249] No. 82 at 537.
[250] *Federalist* No. 27 at 169–170.
[251] 2 Elliot 93–94.
[252] See infra, text accompanying notes 265–266.

claims,[253] and that view was expressed by the Supreme Court in *Prigg v. Pennsylvania.*[254] But the 1947 *Testa v. Katt*[255] seems to come closer to the original intention in holding that "State courts are not free to refuse enforcement" of a claim that arises under a federal law, and even less, of a constitutional right.[256]

Reliance on State courts, however, for vindication of constitutional rights is a weak reed. First, there is the depressing treatment accorded to Negro rights by some Southern courts, which time and again has led to Supreme Court reversals.[257] And there is the possibility that access to State courts may be barred by Congress under the power to "vest exclusive jurisdiction in the federal courts,"[258] a power which, as we have seen, was asserted by Congress in some areas from the very beginning.

MAY CONGRESS CONSTITUTIONALLY CREATE
A JURISDICTIONAL VACUUM?

The grant of exclusive jurisdiction to a federal court leaves access open to a judicial tribunal for assertion of a federal right. Suppose however that conjointly with a bar of State court jurisdiction Congress also bars or withdraws jurisdiction from inferior federal courts under its power to "ordain or establish" inferior federal courts,[259] as it did in the Fair Labor Standards Act ("Portal to Portal"),[260] what then becomes of the State court as the "ultimate guarantor" of con-

---

[253] For citations see Warren, 37 *Harv. L. Rev.* 71 n. 50.

[254] Prigg v. Pennsylvania, 16 Pet. 539, 615 (1842).

[255] 330 U.S. 386, 394 (1947).

[256] In 1816, Justice Story asked respecting a State court suit involving an "impairment of contracts," "If Congress shall not have passed a law providing for the removal of such a suit to the courts of the United States, must not the state court proceed to hear and determine it?" Can the State "prohibit an inquiry . . . when no other tribunal exists to whom judicial cognizance of such cases is confided?" parenthetically postulating original State court jurisdiction. "Unless the state courts," continued Story, "would sustain jurisdiction in such cases, this [Supremacy] clause of the sixth article would be without meaning or effect." Martin v. Hunter's Lessee, 1 Wheat. 304, 341, 342.

[257] Supra, note 201.

[258] The Moses Taylor, 4 Wall. 411, 429–430 (1867). There are, of course, still other problems, e.g., the rule that no State court may issue a writ of habeas corpus for a person held by a federal officer. Tarble's Cases, 13 Wall. 397 (1872). See also Hart & Wechsler 373–399.

[259] "[H]aving a right to prescribe, Congress may withhold from any court of its creation jurisdiction of any of the enumerated controversies." Sheldon v. Sill, 8 How. 441, 449 (1850).

[260] 52 *Stat.* 1060, 29 U.S.C. §201 (1938), quoted Hart & Wechsler 301.

stitutional rights? Indeed, what becomes of the rights themselves? Apart from its power to make "exceptions" to the Supreme Court's appellate jurisdiction, may Congress contract it by depriving *both* State and inferior federal courts of jurisdiction over constitutional claims? An "appellate" jurisdiction without *either* State or inferior federal court jurisdiction from which appeals may be taken is an empty shell; and, it may be ventured, such a state of affairs was never contemplated. Men differed over State versus inferior federal court jurisdiction; there were those, like Patrick Henry, who put their trust in State courts for defense against Congressional oppression;[261] but there was little dissent from the view that judicial review of some sort was indispensable if a suspect Congress was to be kept in bounds. And a Supreme federal tribunal was accepted by virtually all.[262] Hamilton justly concluded in *Federalist* No. 82 that the "evident aim" of the Convention was that the cases enumerated in Article III shall either "receive their original or final determination in the courts of the Union."[263]

When Congress, as in the "Portal to Portal" Act, seeks to bar *all* access to the courts for assertion of Constitutional rights by an admixture of its power to "exclude" State courts, to "disestablish" inferior federal courts, and to make "exceptions" to Supreme Court appellate jurisdiction, it raises questions of utmost gravity. Whatever the scope of Congressional power to exclude State courts and to withhold jurisdiction from federal courts may be when *viewed separately*, these powers cannot be so employed as to defeat one "of the most important and avowed purposes of the proposed government"—judicial protection of constitutional rights.[264] One or the other court must remain open, and the last word must be left to the Supreme Court. In a State context, the Supreme Court declared in *General Oil Co. v. Crain,*

> If a suit against state officers is precluded in the national courts by the Eleventh Amendment, and may be forbidden by a State to its courts, . . . without power of review in this court, it must

261 Supra, text accompanying notes 123, 185.

262 Hamilton stated in *Federalist* No. 81 at 523, "That there ought to be one supreme and final jurisdiction, is a proposition which is not likely to be contested." See also Ratner 161; and supra, text accompanying notes 215–233.

263 *Federalist* No. 82 at 537; see also supra, text accompanying notes 221–222.

264 Hamilton, quoted supra, text accompanying note 223.

be evident that an easy way is open to prevent the enforcement of many provisions of the Constitution, and the Fourteenth Amendment, which is directed at State action, could be nullified as to much of its operation.[265]

Subsequently Justice Holmes stated, "it is plain that a State cannot escape its constitutional obligations by the simple device of denying jurisdiction in such cases to courts otherwise competent."[266] It is no less "evident" that the Fifth Amendment, "which is directed at" Congressional action would equally "be nullified" were Congress to bar all access to the courts,[267] and that "an easy way is open to prevent the enforcement of many provisions of the Constitution" which were squarely aimed *at Congress.* And if State courts are to have exclusive initial jurisdiction, then, said Hamilton, an appeal to the Supreme Court is required lest the "judiciary authority of the Union . . . be eluded."[268]

Access to the courts was designed for the protection of the citizen. In the Convention, the Ratification conventions, and the First Congress, the Founders postulated that the judiciary would be available to curb Congressional "usurpations." To close every court to claims

[265] 209 U.S. 211, 226 (1908) (State court was deprived of jurisdiction to entertain suit against State officer to enjoin collection of State tax as burden on interstate commerce). An important aspect of the decision is that the Supreme Court has jurisdiction of an appeal from a State court's *refusal to act.* Compare Bayard v. Singleton, 1 Martin 42, 45 (N.C. 1787):

if the Legislature could take away this right [to trial by jury], and require him to stand condemned in his property without a trial, it might with as much authority require his life to be taken away without a trial by jury.

In the course of the 1964 debate on the Tuck Bill, Chairman Celler, of the House Judiciary Committee, stated that "If Congress can provide that no court of the United State . . . may hear a case arising under the Constitution, then the rights guaranteed by that same constitution become nullities." 110 *Cong. Rec.* 20238.

[266] Kenney v. Supreme Lodge, 252 U.S. 411, 415 (1920).

[267] Compare General Motors v. Battaglia, quoted infra, Chapter 9, text accompanying note 53. In the 1964 debate on the Tuck Bill, Congressman McCulloch, a proponent, stated, "although the Congress has the power under the Constitution to limit the jurisdiction of Federal courts, if the exercise of that power operates in such a fashion as to deprive an individual of a constitutional right, it is possible that the Court will declare the statute unconstitutional [he had noticed General Motors v. Battaglia, supra]. A statutory withdrawal of the jurisdiction of Federal courts over questions of apportionment does not suffer from this defect because of the availability of the State courts for redress; courts which are bound by the Constitution to enforce the Federal rights thereunder." 110 *Cong. Rec.* 20250.

[268] Supra, text accompanying note 223.

of unconstitutional Congressional invasions is to frustrate the protection which they contemplated. History and effectuation of that design undergird Hart's "necessary postulate of constitutional government" that "a court must always be available to pass on claims of constitutional right to judicial process."[269]

It remains to inquire what role the "exceptions" clause was designed to play in the original Constitutional scheme, and to examine the effect on the clause of the subsequent Bill of Rights.

[269] Hart, "Dialectic" 1372.

In St. Joseph Stockyards Co. v. United States, 298 U.S. 38, 84 (1936), Justice Brandeis in a concurring opinion, joined by Stone and Cardozo, JJ., stated that "The supremacy of law demands that there shall be an opportunity to have some court decide whether an erroneous rule of law was applied," and *a fortiori*, whether there has been a deprivation of constitutional right. In Estep v. United States, 327 U.S. 114, 120 (1946), it was said that "except when the Constitution requires it, judicial review of administrative action may be granted or withheld as Congress chooses." There is also the statement in Yakus v. United States, 321 U.S. 414, 444 (1944), "There is no constitutional requirement" that the "test of the validity of a regulation be made in one tribunal rather than another, so long as there is an opportunity for judicial review which satisfied the demands of due process." But these are merely straws in the wind, for the Supreme Court has had no occasion to decide whether the "exceptions" power may be applied conjointly with other Congressional powers to preclude *all* judicial review of a constitutional claim.

THE CONGRESSIONAL POWER TO MAKE

"EXCEPTIONS" TO THE

APPELLATE JURISDICTION

Article III, section 2, provides that

> . . . the Supreme Court shall have appellate jurisdiction, both as to law and fact, with such exceptions and under such regulations, as Congress shall make.

"It follows from this," we are told by Professor Wechsler, "that Congress has the power by enactment of a statute to strike at what it deems judicial excess by delimitations . . . of the Supreme Court's appellate jurisdiction."[1] The inference is warranted if we look no further than the terms of the clause itself; and Supreme Court dicta frequently allude to the plenary Congressional power

---

[1] Wechsler, "Courts & Constitution" 1005.

With the aid of legal usage and dictionaries of the 1787 period, Professor Ratner demonstrates that an "exception cannot nullify the rule," that it must "necessarily have a narrower application," and that a regulation does not "ordinarily include the power to prohibit the entire sphere of activity that is subject to regulation." Ratner 169, 171. One may agree and yet find the problem unsolved. An exception which would preserve to the courts the power of adjudicating whether the *application* of federal statutes was unconstitutional while withdrawing the issue of their *validity* would not swallow the whole but would go only to a part. Or Congress might withdraw the validity of federal statutes and leave the constitutionality of State statutes, or withdraw all constitutional issues and leave the diversity jurisdiction and still remain within the definitional scope of "exception" and "regulation." Nothing in the definition of these terms seems to me to serve as a guide, whether one part or another may be "excepted" or "regulated."

over the appellate jurisdiction, notably in *Ex Parte McCardle*.[2] But
apart from references to the impeachment power, there is scarcely
a hint in the records, much less in the intensive debate churned up
by the clause, that the Founders intended to entrust Congress with
a power to curb judicial "excess."[3] The records, as we have seen,
disclose that the Founders were deeply concerned with, and in no
little part designed judicial review as a restraint on, *Congressional*
excesses.[4] If the Court was intended to curb Congressional excesses
in appropriately presented "cases or controversies,"[5] and if an attempt to exercise that power might in turn be blocked by Congress
as a judicial "excess," then the Convention was aimlessly going in
circles. Professor Hart justly suggests that a literal reading of the
"exceptions" clause would serve to "destroy the essential role of the
Supreme Court in the constitutional plan."[6] So far as can be
gathered from the records, that was not the purpose of the "exceptions" clause.

The "exceptions" clause was the subject of prolonged debate
which turned not at all on a curb on judicial "excess," but was solely

[2] Supra, Chapter 1, text accompanying notes 4–5. "Literalism," stated Judge
Friendly, is "peculiarly inappropriate in constitutional adjudication." Supra,
Chapter 1, note 13.

[3] In fact, the provisions for tenure and fixed compensation were designed to
protect the judiciary from Congress. Supra, Chapter 3, text accompanying notes
325–334; cf. Chapter 6, text accompanying notes 174–184.

[4] Supra, Chapter 2, text accompanying notes 1–40.

[5] It needs to be borne in mind that "Federal courts . . . pass on constitutional
questions because . . . they must decide a litigated issue that is otherwise
within their jurisdiction and in doing so must give effect to the supreme law of
the land." Wechsler, "Courts & Constitution" 1006; and see Hart, Book Review
1457–1458, 1461. See also Iredell, quoted supra, Chapter 3, text accompanying
note 168; and Chapter 7, text accompanying note 75.

[6] Hart, "Dialectic," 66 *Harv. L. Rev.* 1365. Believing as I do that appeals from
State courts to the Supreme Court were contemplated by the Founders, supra,
Chapter 8, text accompanying notes 215–237, I am constrained to dissent from
Professor Wechsler's rejection of a "narrow meaning" for the "exceptions" clause,
i.e., "not including cases that have constitutional dimension." He considers that
meaning to be "antithetical to the plan of the Constitution for the courts—
which was quite simply that Congress would decide from time to time how
far the federal judicial institution should be used within the limits of the federal
judicial power; or stated differently, how far the judicial jurisdiction should be
left to the state courts." Wechsler, "Courts & Constitution" 1005. For it seems
quite clear that it was only "initial," original, *not final*, jurisdiction that was to
be "left to the state courts," subject to an appeal to the Supreme Court. Supra,
Chapter 8, text accompanying notes 215–241. See also Ratner 158, 160–165.

concerned with review of matters of "fact." Such review was "bitterly denounced" by opponents of the Constitution on the ground that it infringed the right of trial by jury.[7] The issue is clearly expressed in Luther Martin's report to Maryland:

> the proposed constitution . . . by its appellate jurisdiction, *absolutely takes away that inestimable privilege* [trial by jury]; since it expressly declares that the Supreme Court shall have appellate jurisdiction both as to law and *fact* . . . The Supreme Court is to take up *all questions of fact . . . to decide upon them* as if they *had never been tried by a jury*.[8]

Embarrassed by the issue, Judge Pendleton, the venerable presiding officer in the Virginia convention, wished that the words "both as to law and fact" "had been buried in oblivion. If they had, it would have silenced the greatest objections against the section."[9] Randolph, another advocate of the Constitution, concurred that these words were "unfortunate, and my lamentations over it would be incessant, were there no remedy . . . were I not satisfied that it contains its own cure, in the following words 'with such exceptions and under such regulations as Congress shall make.' "[10]

The difficulty, in a nutshell, was the greatly varied practice in the States respecting review of facts, not alone in jury trials but in admiralty and equity as well.[11] As Spaight, a member of the federal Convention, told the North Carolina convention, "the subject took up a considerable time to investigate it. It was impossible to make any one uniform regulation for all the states, or that would include all cases where it would be necessary."[12] This was the explanation also made by two other Framers, Pinckney in South Carolina,[13] and

---

[7] Warren, *Making Constitution* 543.

[8] 3 Farrand 221.

[9] 3 Elliot 519. Madison also said that this was the "principal criticism which had been made" of the appellate jurisdiction. Id. at 534.

[10] Id. at 572.

[11] Some of the difficulties were sketched by Iredell in North Carolina, 4 Elliot 165–166, 144–145, by Wilson in Pennsylvania, 2 Elliot 488, and by Hamilton in *Federalist* No. 81 at 530–532. See also 3 Elliot 550; 4 Elliot 144, 170.

[12] 4 Elliot 144. He later added, "It was three or four days before them. There were a variety of objections to any one mode." Id. at 208.

[13] Id. at 260.

Wilson in Pennsylvania: "no particular mode of trial by jury could be discovered that would suit them all."[14] Because of such difficulties, said Iredell, paraphrasing Spaight, the Framers "thought it better to leave all such regulations to the legislature itself."[15] Randolph, also a Framer, said, "The appellate jurisdiction might be corrected as to matters of fact by the exceptions and regulations of Congress."[16] This was also Madison's explanation in Virginia— cheek by jowl with his statement, "Were I to select a power which might be given with confidence, it would be the judicial power"[17]— of Wilson in Pennsylvania, of Maclaine in North Carolina,[18] and of Pendleton and Marshall in Virginia. The "exceptions" power, said Marshall, would "go to the cure of the mischief apprehended."[19] Such assurances notwithstanding, the imperious demand to be doubly sure was shortly to find expression in the Seventh Amendment provision that "no fact tried by a jury shall be otherwise examined in any court of the United States."

The purpose of the "exceptions" clause, in Madison's words, was "to provide against inconveniences,"[20] to serve the "convenience and secure the liberty," said Maclaine and Marshall, of the people.[21] It "can hardly be supposed," said Pinckney, "that [Congress] will exercise it in a manner injurious to their constituents."[22] It was not to "be presumed," said Hanson in Maryland, "that, in making regulations and exceptions, this appellate power shall be calculated

---

[14] 2 Elliot 488. Iredell said, "Everything could be agreed upon except the regulation of trial by jury in civil cases. They were all anxious to establish it upon the best footing, but found they could fix no permanent rule that was not liable to great objections and difficulties." 4 Elliot 166; see also McKean, 2 Elliot 539–540; and Thomas Dawes, 2 Elliot 114.

[15] 4 Elliot 166, 144.

[16] 3 Elliot 576.

[17] 3 Elliot 534–535. Cf. supra, Chapter 6, text accompanying notes 186–194.

[18] 2 Elliot 488; 4 Elliot 151–152.

[19] 3 Elliot 520, 560.

[20] 3 Elliot 535. Said Hamilton, "To avoid all inconveniences, it will be safest to declare generally, that the Supreme Court shall possess appellate jurisdiction both as to law and *fact*, and that this jurisdiction shall be subject to such *exceptions* and regulations as the national legislature may prescribe." *Federalist* No. 81 at 532. Hamilton regarded judicial review as indispensable, by no means an "inconvenience" which Congress could remove.

[21] 4 Elliot 152; 3 Elliot 560. Explaining the "exceptions" clause, Noah Webster said that "in small actions, Congress will doubtless direct that a sentence in a subordinate court shall, to a certain amount, be definite and final." Ford's *Pamphlets* 29, 54.

[22] 4 Elliot 307.

as an instrument of oppression."[23] As an advocate of judicial review, Hanson, it may safely be inferred, would have regarded deprivation of judicial protection for constitutional rights as "oppressive." No more would his fellow advocate of judicial review, Marshall, regard removal of that safeguard as in the "interest" of the people.

In sum, discussion of the "exceptions" power in the Ratification conventions revolved almost exclusively about the retrial of facts found by a jury. So complicated were the varying practices that it was concluded to leave the problem for handling by the Congress through the medium of the "exceptions" clause, fashioned to meet the "principal criticism" of the appellate jurisdiction, its inclusion of matters of "fact." Questions of constitutionality are "matters of law," and as Hamilton said, "The propriety of this appellate jurisdiction has scarcely been called in question in regard to matters of law; but the clamors have been loud against it as applied to matters of fact."[24] Constitutional issues therefore fell outside the remedial purposes of the "exceptions" clause. Indeed, even States Righters agreed that there must be appeals on such issues from the State courts.[25]

There is not the faintest intimation in the several convention records, nor in the contemporary prints, that the "exceptions" clause was designed to enable Congress to withdraw jurisdiction to declare an Act of Congress void. No aspect of Article III was as intensively debated in the Ratification conventions as the "exceptions" clause.[26] Yet, although opponents of the Constitution required frequent assurances that the courts would keep the Congress within Consti-

[23] Ford,, *Pamphlets* 221, 238–239. Iredell said, "It is not to be presumed that the Congress would dare to deprive the people of this valuable privilege [trial by jury]," 4 Elliot 145. Would he have felt less strongly about Congressional deprivation of access to judicial protection against Congressional invasions of other Constitutional rights?

[24] *Federalist* No. 81 at 530. Madison stated in the Virginia convention that the "principal criticism which has been made, was against the appellate cognizance as well of fact as of law." 3 Elliot 534. Randolph said, "I can see no reason for giving it jurisdiction with respect to fact as well as law." 3 Elliot 572. Mason said, "I would confine the appellate jurisdiction to matters of law only." 3 Elliot 525. Cf. Iredell, supra note 14. Randolph stated that "The appellate jurisdiction might be corrected, as to matters of fact, by the exceptions and regulations of Congress." 3 Elliot 576. In Maryland an amendment was proposed that would "prevent the appeal from fact." 2 Elliot 550.

[25] Supra, Chapter 8, text accompanying notes 215–232.

[26] Cf. supra, note 12.

tutional "limits," though some argued that overwide delegations to Congress made judicial review meaningless, though even States Righters recognized the need for a Supreme tribunal in the national interest and in the interest of "uniformity," no one thought to torpedo such assurances by citing Congress' power to withdraw Supreme Court jurisdiction. The acute Yates minutely examined Article III and concluded that "the supreme court has the power, in the last resort, to determine all questions on the meaning . . . of the constitution," and that the "legislature can not deprive the former of this right."[27] The same meaning attaches to Hamilton's acknowledgment of judicial "finality" and explanation that Congress would not be left to adjudge the validity of its own laws.[28] Literal reading of the "exceptions" clause requires us to conclude that Yates and Hamilton, and those who like Marshall and Iredell relied on judicial review for "protection from [Congressional] infringement of the Constitution,"[29] completely overlooked the fact that Congress had but to enact an "exception" to the "appellate" jurisdiction to deprive the Supreme Court of the power to decide that a Congressional Act was contrary to the Constitution—an egregious oversight indeed. If the "exceptions" clause was truly designed to make that withdrawal of jurisdiction possible, the short answer to fears of unlimited judicial power expressed by Mason and Grayson in the Virginia convention[30] would have been: not while the "exceptions" power exists. Indeed, Tyler said toward the close of that convention, "Is there any limitation or restriction on the federal judicial power? I think not."[31]

The sole reference to a curb on the "independence" and "responsibility" of the judiciary which I could find was to the impeachment power. This, said Hamilton, "is the *only* provision on the point which is consistent with the necessary independence of the judicial character."[32] He expanded on the matter in *Federalist* No. 81, wherein he envisaged occasional judicial "contraventions of the will

[27] Corwin, *Court Over* 244.
[28] *Federalist* No. 78 at 506, No. 81 at 524–525.
[29] 3 Elliot 554; and supra, Chapter 3, text accompanying notes 168, 228–229; and Chapter 4, text accompanying note 123.
[30] 3 Elliot 521, 523, 565.
[31] Id. at 638–639.
[32] *Federalist* No. 80 at 514 (emphasis supplied).

of the legislature," but did not consider that "the supposed danger of judiciary encroachments on the legislative authority" was serious because of the peculiar nature of judicial jurisdiction; and concluded that judges would be deterred from "deliberate usurpations on the authority of the legislature" by the overhanging threat of impeachment.[33] If the "exceptions" power was available to Congress in order to curb judicial "excesses," Hamilton's reference to impeachment substituted a steamhammer where a nutcracker would suffice. And even as regards impeachment, Wilson, and later Gerry, indignantly rejected the notion that judges might be impeached if they were to "decide against the law,"

> The judges are to be impeached, because they decide an act null and void, that was made in defiance of the Constitution! What House of Representatives would dare to impeach, or Senate to commit, judges for the performance of their duty?[34]

It is hardly to be supposed that Wilson would stomach the withdrawal of jurisdiction because judges decided an act was void—"for the performance of their duty."

Least of all should that inference be drawn by a generation that saw the most popular President in decades, Franklin D. Roosevelt, thrown back by Congress when he sought its help to "pack" a Court that had repeatedly invalidated legislation designed to rescue the nation from the depths of the Depression.[35] The "Court-packing" plan, wrote President Roosevelt to then Professor Frankfurter, was "arrived at by a process of elimination" after searching through "all the other proposals for legislative action."[36] It enlisted the aid, behind-the-scenes, of Frankfurter,[37] himself the leading authority on

[33] Id. at No. 81 at 526–527.

[34] 2 Elliot 478. Gerry expressed the same view in the First Congress. Supra, Chapter 8, text accompanying note 244. Prior to the federal Convention, the New Hampshire Legislature, by a vote of 56 to 21 refused to impeach judges who had declared a statute unconstitutional. Crosskey 970. An attempt to rebuke North Carolina judges was similarly defeated, id. at 971–972. Compare New York and Rhode Island, id. at 964, 968.

[35] Baker, *Back to Back: The Duel Between FDR and the Supreme Court* (1967); Barrett, *Constitutional Law* 219; Elliot, "Court-Curbing Proposals in Congress," 33 *Notre Dame Lawyer* 596, 605–606 (1958); cf. Westin 25–26.

[36] Freedman, *Roosevelt and Frankfurter, Their Correspondence* 381–382 (1967).

[37] Id. at 383–417.

federal jurisdiction, the lore of the Constitution, and the Court. How could Roosevelt and Frankfurter, with a corps of brilliant New Deal lawyers at their command, have overlooked the "simple" alternative: a Congressional exercise of Article III power to "strike at . . . judicial excess" by delimiting jurisdiction of constitutional controversies?[38] All the hullabaloo about "Court-packing" was so easily avoidable if this alternative is so legitimate and available. The explanation, I suggest, lies not merely in the devotion of the people to the Court,[39] but in the Congressional rejection of the view that "when the Court stands in the way of a legislative enactment, the Congress may reverse it by enlarging the Court. When such a principle is adopted, our constitutional system is overthrown."[40] As the veteran Chairman of the House Judiciary Committee, Emanuel Celler, reminded the House in the course of the 1964 debate on the Tuck Bill, "The rationale of this reasoning clearly applies with equal force to [a Congressional] attempt to impose its will on the Court by seeking to limit its jurisdiction rather than by enlarging [the Court]."[41]

[38] Wechsler "Courts & Constitution" 1005.

[39] The "over-riding lesson taught by the 1937 Supreme Court fight" was "the deep-seated devotion of the American people to the independence of their judiciary." Dodd, Book Review, *New York Times Book Review*, September 24, 1967, p. 40.

Frankfurter put his finger on the heart of the problem, the need to educate the people about the realities of judicial review: "A majority of the Court have, as it were, been exploiting the public's devotion because they have been exploiting the mystery which so largely envelops the Court. People have been taught to believe that when the Supreme Court speaks it is not they who speak but the Constitution, whereas, of course, in so many vital cases, it is *they* who speak and *not* the Constitution. And I verily believe that that is what the country needs most to understand." Freedman, *Roosevelt & Frankfurter* 383; see also id. at 390.

The belief that the Court was guilty of judicial "excess" was summed up by Frankfurter: "the Supreme Court for about a quarter of a century has distorted the power of judicial review into a revision of legislative policy, thereby usurping powers belonging to the Congress and the legislatures of the several states, always by a divided court and always over the protest of its most distinguished members. With increasing frequency a majority of the Court have not hesitated to exercise a negative power over any legislation, state or federal, which does not confirm to their own economic notions." Id. at 384. Few today would quarrel with Frankfurter's judgment that the majority were reading their own social and economic predilections into the Constitution, blocking desperately needed social reconstruction. If ever there was a case for correcting "judicial excess" it was at this moment, to change what Frankfurter termed "the long course of judicial abuse in preventing not only national but state action." Id. at 390.

[40] S. Rept. 771, 75th Cong. 1st Sess. p. 14, quoted 100 *Cong. Rec.* 20240 (August 19, 1964).

[41] 100 *Cong. Rec.* 20240. "Court-packing" is hardly a more serious threat to

CONGRESSIONAL POWER TO MAKE "EXCEPTIONS"

Judicial enforcement of "limits" on Congressional power and of "prohibitions" of certain Congressional action was a cardinal element in the Constitutional scheme. The debate in the Ratification conventions on the "exceptions" clause furnishes a persuasive historical basis for Congressman Celler's conclusion in August 1964 that the "power vested in Congress to make 'exceptions' and 'regulations'" with respect to the appellate jurisdiction was not designed "to upset the entire constitutional plan and to defeat the precise purposes for which the Federal Judiciary was established."[42] The power which the Constitution "confers on the one hand," said Chief Justice White, "it does not immediately take away on the other."[43]

Were the argument based on the purpose and structure of the Constitution more doubtful than appears, the immediate enactment of the Bill of Rights put the matter in fresh perspective. Insistent demands during the Ratification debates, which persisted after adoption of the Constitution, for more explicit guarantees against encroachment by a much-feared central government[44]—fears that clustered in the main around "legislative despotism"[45]—led to the adoption of the Bill of Rights. Notwithstanding repeated assurances

---

judicial independence than an attempt to deprive the courts of jurisdiction. In the 1788 Virginia Remonstrance, the Virginia court said, "vain would be the precautions of the founders of our government to secure liberty, if the legislature, though restrained from changing the tenure of judicial officers, are at liberty . . . by lessening the duties to render offices almost sinecures; the independence of the judiciary is in either case annihilated." Quoted in Kamper v. Hawkins, 1 Va. Case. 22, 106–107 (1793). See also Boehle v. Electro Metallurgical Co., 72 F. Supp. 21 (Ore. 1947).

Not the least of the Crosskean *curiosa* is that he, who so caustically impeaches the bases for judicial review, should yet find it a "natural conclusion" that "the Federal Convention expected the Supreme Court to exercise" certain rights "without regard to any acts of Congress interfering unconstitutionally with them" through the "excepting power." Crosskey 1003; and see id. at 616; Hart, Book Review 1473 n. 54. Similarly, Boudin, 64, an inveterate foe of judicial review, declared that "the legislature may not prohibit the judiciary from taking cognizance of any judicial matter."

[42] 110 *Cong. Rec.* 20240.

[43] Billings v. United States, 232 U.S. 261, 282 (1914).

[44] Supra, Chapter 2, text accompanying note 51. Gerry, for example, said in the First Congress, "we see a great body of our constituents opposed to the constitution as it now stands, who are apprehensive of the enormous powers of Government." 1 *Ann. Cong.* 463.

[45] Supra, Chapter 2, text accompanying notes 2–21. In profferring the Amendments to the First Congress, Madison said that the "guard against abuse" "must be levelled against the legislative, for it is the most powerful, most likely to be abused." 1 *Ann. Cong.* 454.

during the Ratification debates on the "exceptions" clause that trial by jury would be adequately protected by Congress through the instrumentality of that clause,[46] the Fathers preferred to nail down that protection firmly by means of the Seventh Amendment. Is it reasonable to conclude that in riveting the accompanying guarantees against Congressional invasions of liberty and property without due process or just compensation, they intended through the medium of the "exceptions" clause to leave those rights at the mercy of Congress? A Congress not trusted to preserve trial by jury was little likely to be trusted as Protector of other precious rights; and it is even less likely that the Founders intended to leave with Congress the power to bar judicial protection of those rights.

So much emerges from Madison's explanation of the proposed Amendments to the First Congress: laws may "be considered necessary and proper by Congress . . . which laws in themselves are neither necessary nor proper; as well as improper laws could be enacted by State legislatures . . . If there was reason for restraining the State governments from exercising this power ["general warrants"], there is like reason for restraining the Federal Government." And, he went on to say, if these Amendments

> are incorporated into the Constitution, independent tribunals of justice will consider themselves in a peculiar manner the guardians of those rights; they will be an impenetrable bulwark against every assumption of power in the legislative or executive.[47]

No challenge was made to this statement;[48] and indeed, shortly thereafter, in the course of the debate on the President's "removal" power, a decided preponderance of the spokesmen in the House expressly recognized that the courts were the ultimate arbiters whether Congressional Acts were consistent with the Constitution.[49] An "impenetrable bulwark" against Congressional oppression

---

[46] Supra, Chapter 1, text accompanying notes 16–19.

[47] 1 *Ann. Cong.* 456–457. Madison's phraseology had been anticipated by Hamilton in *Federalist* No. 78 at 508: "If, then, the courts of justice are to be considered as the bulwarks of a limited Constitution against legislative encroachments, this consideration will afford a strong argument for the permanent tenure of judicial offices." In his 1791 Lectures, Justice Wilson referred to judicial review as "a noble guard against legislative despotism." 1 Wilson, *Works* 462.

[48] Warren, *Congress* 93.

[49] Supra, Chapter 5, text accompanying notes 11–18.

that could easily be flanked by Congressional withdrawal of jurisdiction from the courts would be no bulwark at all. Common sense shrinks from a reading which would reduce the "bulwark" to a stage-setting that Congress can remove to the flies by a flick of the "exceptions" switch.[50] One who has toiled over the records cannot attribute to the Founders an intention to make that possible.

In the sheaf of Congressional powers, the power to make "exceptions" to the appellate jurisdiction scarcely ranks higher, when measured by indispensability to the largest national purposes, than the commerce, tax, and war powers; yet each of these is subject to the Fifth Amendment.[51] Like these, "The power to regulate jurisdic-

---

[50] "How can there be a duty to decide 'all Cases' conformably to the Constitution, acts of Congress to the contrary notwithstanding, if Congress can defeat this duty by a jurisdictional act? Would not this be 'to overthrow in fact what was established in theory?' Would it not seem 'an absurdity too gross to be insisted on?' Congress, to be sure, is authorized to regulate the Court's appellate jurisdiction and to make exceptions in it, but that cannot be the whole answer." Bickel 124–125.

Senator Sam J. Ervin, Chairman of the Senate Subcommittee on Constitutional Rights, noted that "to give a people a constitutional right and then deny them opportunity to vindicate that right, in case of its denial, is certainly making a hollow mockery of the Constitution." Hearings before said Subcommittee on S.2097, 89th Cong., 2d Sess. (March 1966) at 283–284; cf. id. at 34, 66, 91, 278. "No right," he said, "is worthwhile unless it can be protected . . . no substantive right can exist . . . unless there is a procedural right to enforce it," id. at 312. He found it "inconceivable" that the Founders adopted Constitutional prohibitions of certain Congressional actions and at the same time barred the courts from inquiry whether such prohibitions had been violated, id. at 100, 65, 150, 233.

Yet, although he repeatedly stressed in 1966 that "the final power to make definitive interpretations of the meaning of the Constitution rests with the Supreme Court of the United States rather than in Congress," id. at 89, 15, 29, 36, 37, 152, that it "is fortunate that we have a court that can adjudge invalid provisions of law in cases where Congress exceeds its legislative powers under the Constitution," id. at 89, cf. id. at 264, that "a citizen ought to have a right to find out whether the Constitution of his country is being violated," id. at 26, cf. id. at 35, 278, he could maintain one year later that the power over appellate jurisdiction authorized the Congress to "discipline and correct" the Supreme Court when "in their judgment the Court is behaving improperly." Supra, Chapter 1, note 12.

[51] "[L]ike the other powers granted to Congress by the Constitution, the power to regulate commerce is subject to all the limitations imposed by such instrument, and among them is the Fifth Amendment." Monongahela Navigation Co. v. United States, 148 U.S. 312, 336 (1893). "The war power of the United States, like its other powers . . . is subject to applicable constitutional limitations," including the Fifth Amendment. Hamilton v. Kentucky Distilleries, 251 U.S. 146, 156 (1919). Cf. Heiner v. Donnan, 285 U.S. 312, 326 (1932). And see Louisville Bank v. Radford, 295 U.S. 555, 589 (1935); North American Co. v. SEC, 327 U.S. 686, 704, 705 (1946).

tion," in the words of Hart, "is subject . . . to the other provisions of the Constitution."[52] History affords a sure footing, in my opinion, for the statement by the Second Circuit in *General Motors v. Battaglia* that Congress must not so exercise its "undoubted power to give, withhold, or restrict the jurisdiction" of the federal courts "as to deprive any person of life, liberty or property without due process of law or to take private property without just compensation."[53]

[52] Hart, "Dialectic" 1372.
[53] 169 F.2d 254, 257 (2d Cir. 1948); cf. United States v. Kissinger, 250 F.2d 940, 941–942 (3d Cir. 1958).

SOVEREIGN IMMUNITY: WITHHOLDING

CONSENT TO SUIT ON

CONSTITUTIONAL CLAIMS

The Congressional arsenal boasts another bar to relief for unconstitutional invasions of private rights: Congress can withhold or withdraw consent to a suit against the United States under the doctrine of sovereign immunity. Unlike the express Congressional authorization to make "exceptions" to the appellate jurisdiction, sovereign immunity can draw upon no textual provision. It is a judicial importation pure and simple, which would limit express Constitutional jurisdiction of the courts and which departs from a well-reasoned early decision by the Court on which sat Justice Wilson, a leading Framer.[1] If the express "exceptions" power cannot bar access to judicial protection of Constitutional rights, as the preceding pages sought to demonstrate, how can judicial protection of such rights be balked by withholding a "consent" that has no textual warrant? The rhetorical question that James Wilson put in the Federal Convention, in another context, places the matter in proper perspective:

[1] Chisholm v. Georgia, 2 Dallas 419 (1793). In analyzing the case, Corwin, 9 *Mich. L. Rev.* 294, states, "the question at issue was whether the United States Supreme Court could take jurisdiction of a suit instituted by a citizen of South Carolina against the State of Georgia. The language of the Constitution was perfectly explicit in favor of the jurisdiction but the attorneys of the defendant State contended that this language must be construed in the light of the principle that a sovereign can be sued only in its own courts and at its own consent . . . In other words State sovereignty was set up as a sort of interpretative principle limiting the operation of the Constitution." Four of the five Justices rejected the claim.

For whom do we form a constitution, for men, or for *imaginary beings* called states, a mere metaphysical distinction? Will a regard to *state* rights justify the sacrifice of the rights of men?[2]

A dictum of Justice Brandeis in *Lynch v. United States*[3] that withdrawal by the federal government of consent to suit infringes no constitutional "right" brings the problem into focus. An insurance policy had been issued by the government pursuant to statute; the beneficiary had paid premiums; and the Court held that a contract had arisen which "bound" the United States and enjoyed the protection of the Fifth Amendment.[4] Justice Brandeis, however, distinguished between the contract "right" and the remedy: withdrawal of the remedy after such a right arose was sheltered by the doctrine of sovereign immunity;[5] consent to suit is a "privilege accorded, not the grant of a property right protected by the Fifth Amendment."[6] But, he concluded, Congress had gone too far; it had destroyed the legal obligation.[7] Even one nourished on legal refinements may well experience some difficulty with the proposition that the government may not destroy a "right" arising out of its contractual obligation but is nevertheless free to render it unenforceable. For an unenforceable "right" is an empty shell; from Roman times onward a "right" has been deemed inseparable from a remedy.[8] The Court's remarks about sovereign immunity represent

---

[2] 1 Farrand 494. In Chisholm v. Georgia, 2 Dallas at 468, Justice Cushing said, "The rights of individuals and the justice due to them are as dear and precious as those of states."

[3] 292 U.S. 571 (1934).

[4] Id. at 580, 579.

[5] Id. at 580–582. Perry v. United States, 294 U.S. 330, 354 (1935), explained that "The fact that the United States may not be sued without its consent is a matter of *procedure* which does not affect the legal and binding character of its contracts." Nonenforcement is an "infirmity of procedure." See also Pflueger v. United States, 121 F.2d 732, 735 (D.Col. Cir. 1941): "the immunity of the sovereign from suit is paramount even over rights founded on the Constitution."

[6] 292 U.S. at 581. Sovereign immunity, said the Court in Lynch, applies to causes of action "arising from some violation of rights conferred upon the citizen by the constitution," 292 U.S. at 582.

[7] 292 U.S. 583.

[8] At Roman law a right which was not protected from invasion was not a legal right. Morey, *Outlines of Roman Law* 224, 387 (1913); Declareuil, *Rome the Law-Giver* 191 (1927). The maxim "Ubi jus, ibi remedium"—where there is a right, there is a remedy—was taken up in English law. See Co. Litt. 197b; cf. Bracton, quoted by Wilson, infra text accompanying note 150. Blackstone stated that "it is a general and indisputable rule, that where there is a legal

the sheerest dictum—repeatedly the Court emphasized that "Congress did not aim at the remedy"; it did not seek to withdraw the "privilege to sue the United States"; it was "not concerned with the consent to sue the United States"—and not being necessary to decision may the more freely be re-examined.[9]

The view that a constitutional right can be emptied by withholding consent to suit calls for reevaluation in light of the current disrepute of sovereign immunity. Sovereign immunity is "discredited,"[10] said Justice Frankfurter, and runs "counter to democratic notions of the moral responsibility of the States,"[11] let alone that it bars access to judicial protection of constitutional rights. In substantial part the doctrine has been circumvented by resort to the fiction that

---

right, there is also a legal remedy by suit, or action at law, whenever that right is invaded." Quoted, Marbury v. Madison, 1 Cranch 137, 163 (1803). Madison stated in *Federalist* No. 43 at 282, that "a right implies a remedy." The Founders placed no faith in "parchment barriers." Supra, Chapter 6, notes 190, 194.

"Nothing can be more material to the obligation than the means of enforcement. Without the remedy the contract may indeed . . . be said not to exist, and both are parts of the obligation which is guaranteed by the Constitution against invasion." Von Hoffman v. City of Quincy, 4 Wall. 535, 552 (1867). "The State and the corporation . . . are equally bound." Id. at 555. "Legal obligations that exist but can not be enforced are ghosts." De la Rama S.S. Co. v. United States, 344 U.S. 386, 390 (1953). Said Judge Jerome Frank, "It is idle chatter to speak of a legal wrong for which there is no legal redress; a so-called legal right without a legal remedy is . . . but a shabby mythical entity like the 'grin without a cat' which Lewis Carroll's Alice justifiably could not understand." Hammond-Knowlton v. United States, 121 F.2d 192, 205 n. 37 (2d Cir. 1941); cf. Parden v. Terminal Ry. Co. of Alabama, 377 U.S. 184, 192, 197 (1964).

[9] 292 U.S. at 583, 585. When some of Chief Justice Marshall's own remarks in Marbury v. Madison were pressed upon him in a later case, he stated, "It is a maxim, not to be disregarded, that general expressions, in every opinion, are to be taken in connection with the case in which these expressions are used. If they go beyond the case, they may be respected, but ought not to control the judgment in a subsequent suit, when the very point is presented for decision. The reason for the maxim is obvious. The question actually before the court is investigated with great care, and considered in its full extent. Other principles which may serve to illustrate it, are considered in their relation to the case decided, but their possible bearing on all other cases is seldom completely investigated." Cohens v. Virginia, 6 Wheat. 264, 399 (1821).

[10] Kennecott Copper Co. v. Tax Comm., 327 U.S. 573, 581 (1946) (dissenting opinion). He had earlier said on behalf of the Court that the doctrine was in "disfavor." Keifer & Keifer v. RFC, 306 U.S. 381, 391 (1939); and in National Bank v. Republic of China, 348 U.S. 356, 359 (1955), he repeated that the doctrine had "not been favored by the test of time."

[11] Kennecott Copper, supra, note 10 at 80. To the same effect, National Bank, supra, note 10 at 359.

when an officer acts in excess of constitutional or statutory authority,[12] a suit brought against him in his "individual" capacity is not a suit against the state but against a "wrongdoer" stripped of his authority because he acted illegally.[13] Such suits are allowed because, as the Court said in *United States v. Lee,* "it cannot be denied" that "the rights of the citizen" were "intended to be enforced by the judiciary."[14] Large doubts remain, however, as to the scope or availability of "individual wrongdoer suits," including the question whether the United States is bound in terms of *res judicata* by a judgment against an officer in his individual capacity.[15] Even under an ameliatory proposal that no violation of private rights should be shielded in the "absence of clear statutory authority," Congress would still be left free "to authorize government infringement of the legal rights of private parties without judicial redress."[16] It merits inquiry whether Congress is indeed free to do so; then, too, "legal history still has its claims."[17]

But for the early survey of English law by Justice Iredell in his dissenting opinion in *Chisholm v. Georgia,*[18] the Supreme Court itself acknowledged that the "principle" of sovereign immunity has

[12] Hammond-Knowlton v. United States, 121 F.2d 192, 194 (2d Cir. 1941) (per Frank, J.): the absence of consent was "surmounted by a doctrine plainly devised to avoid injustice to the citizen." See Larson v. Domestic & Foreign Commerce Corp., 337 U.S. 682, 709 (1949) (Frankfurter, J., dissenting).

After a survey of early English law, Professor Jaffe stated, "It is sometimes said that actions and proceedings against officers for their official conduct rests on a fiction designed to avoid the effects of sovereign immunity. But in the light of history which we have traversed this would seem to be a latter day explanation of the phenomenon." Jaffe, *Judicial Control* 212. For Iredell, suits against officers were an accepted fact of English law; quoted infra, text accompanying note 38. See also note 38. Chief Justice Marshall said in Marbury v. Madison, 1 Cranch 137, 170 (1803), "If one of the heads of departments commits any illegal act, under color of his office, by which an individual sustains an injury, it cannot be pretended that his office alone exempts him from being sued."

[13] The leading federal officer case is United States v. Lee, 106 U.S. 196 (1882); the State officer case, Ex Parte Young, 209 U.S. 123 (1908). See Jaffe, *Judicial Control* 215 et seq.

[14] 106 U.S. at 220. There "is no safety for the citizen except in the protection of the judicial tribunals, for rights which have been invaded by the officers of the Government." Id. at 219.

[15] See Sawyer v. Dollar, 190 F.2d 623, 645 (D.Col. Cir. 1951); 3 Davis §27.10 and §27.06.

[16] Davis §27.10 at 614–615.

[17] Federal Power Comm. v. Natural Gas Pipeline Co., 315 U.S. 575, 609 (1942).

[18] 2 Dallas 419, 429 (1793).

"never been discussed or the reasons for it given, but it has always been treated as an established doctrine."[19] And Iredell's carefully hedged dictum, which he himself stated was unnecessary to decision,[20] is not today thought to reflect pre-1789 English law. In a valuable survey, Professor Louis Jaffe concluded that the King or State "has been suable throughout the whole range of the law, sometimes with its consent, sometimes without, and whether that consent was necessary was determined by expediency rather than by abstract theory as to whether the action was really against the state." When "it was necessary to sue the Crown *eo nomine* consent apparently was given as of course." The catch-phrase "The King can do no wrong," there is good reason to believe, originally meant that the King was "not entitled to do wrong." And his grant of consent was "based precisely on the proposition that the King has acted contrary to law." In a word, the "so-called doctrine of sovereign immunity was largely an abstract idea without determinative impact on the subject's right to relief against government illegality."[21]

[19] United States v. Lee, 106 U.S. 196, 207 (1882).

[20] "[L]ooking at the Act of Congress, which I consider is on this occasion the limit of our authority (whatever further might be constitutionally enacted)," "My opinion being, that even if the constitution would admit of the exercise of such a power . . . no part of the existing law [i.e., the statute] applies . . . So much, however, has been said on the constitution, that it may not be improper to intimate, that my present opinion is strongly against any construction of it which will admit, under any circumstances, a compulsive suit against a state for the recovery of money . . . This opinion, I hold however, with all the reserve proper for one, which . . . may be deemed in some measure extra-judicial." 2 Dallas 436, 449–450.

[21] Jaffe, *Judicial Control* 198, 197, 199, 212. The "common [law] lawyers, in common with many other mediaeval thinkers, laid it down that, the law was a rule of conduct binding all members of the state including the king; and political writers argued in the fourteenth and fifteenth centuries, as they had argued in the thirteenth, that this was no diminution of the royal power. It merely limited the king's power to do evil, and this was no limitation—an idea which is perhaps one of the roots of the later doctrine that the king can do no wrong." 2 Holdsworth, *History* 435 (4th ed. 1936). Says Professor Wade, "The maxim that 'the king can do no wrong' does not in fact have much to do with this procedural immunity. Its true meaning is that the king has no legal power to do wrong." Wade, *Administrative Law* 253 (1967). See also Rex v. Speyer (1915) 1 K.B. 595, 619.

Respecting an invasion of private rights by the Crown, 3 Blackstone 255 states, "yet the law hath furnished the subject with a decent and respectful mode of removing that invasion, by informing the king of the true state of the matter in dispute; and, as it presumes that to *know* of any injury and to *redress* it are inseparable in the royal breast, it then issues as of course, in the king's own name, his orders to his judges to do justice to the party aggrieved." United States

CHAPTER 10

It remained for the American courts to convert this not really inconvenient abstraction into inflexible doctrine.[22] On the latter view, the Founders, in repudiating Crown prerogative and embracing democratic principles of accountability,[23] interposed a barrier to accountability in the shape of an alleged offshoot of the prerogative—sovereign immunity. But this view was a product of a later time. When the issue was first presented to the Court in *Chisholm v. Georgia* (1793),[24] four Justices concluded that Constitutional purposes and simple honesty and justice found expression in the Article III grant of jurisdiction, and they held that that jurisdiction was not left subject to the whim of the States.[25] Chief Justice Jay, among other things, pointed to the preamble of the Constitution which recites that the Union was founded "in order . . . to establish justice," found in Article III machinery for its establishment, and considered that to make this jurisdiction subject to State consent would do violence to the basic principle of the Nation: "to ensure justice for all."[26] With a wealth of reasoning, Justice Wilson[27] declared that the notion of sovereign immunity was unsuited to a government formed by consent for the benefit of all.[28] Of what good,

---

v. O'Keefe, 11 Wall. (78 U.S.) 178, 183–184 (1870), comments, "It is of no consequence that theoretically speaking, the permission of the Crown is necessary to the filing of the petition, because it is the duty of the King to grant it, and the right of the subject to demand it." See also Muskopf v. Corning Hospital District, 55 C.2d 211, 215 n. 1, 357 P.2d 457 (1961) (per Justice Traynor). Among the variety of "devices for getting relief against government" there were "suits against the king brought as petitions of right requiring his consent [which issued as of course]; this type of remedy has been over-generalized into the broad abstraction of sovereign immunity." Jaffe, *Judicial Control* at 198. For other procedures, see id. at 201–203.

[22] Hans v. Louisiana, 134 U.S. 1, 16, 15 (1890), Mr. Justice Bradley stated that "The suability of a State without its consent was a thing unknown to the law," and that "the cognizance of suits unknown to the law, forbidden by the law, was not contemplated by the Constitution."

[23] See infra, text accompanying notes 37–41.

[24] 2 Dallas 419 (1793).

[25] Id. at 450–451, 455, 464, 467, 476.

[26] Id. at 477, 476.

[27] Hale v. Henkel, 201 U.S. 43, 61 (1906), says of one of his lectures in 1791 that he "may be assumed to have known the current practice." He "was commonly accepted . . . as the most learned and profound legal scholar of his generation." McCloskey, Introduction 2.

[28] "To the constitution . . . the term *sovereign* is totally unknown." 2 Dallas at 454. Wilson defined a "state" as a "body of free persons united for their common benefit . . . [and] to do justice to others," and rejected the notion that a

he asked, are such provisions as the ban on "impairment of contracts" if a State may withhold consent to its enforcement.[29] Justice Iredell alone dissented, resting on an interpretation of the statute which conferred jurisdiction "where a state is a party."[30] This he read, substituting "can be" for "is," as referring to controversies "in which a state *can* be a party";[31] and looking to English law, he concluded that a sovereign could not be made a party without its consent, though in England that consent issued as of course and was purely formal. His constitutional dictum was carefully limited to a "suit against a state for the recovery of money," and was tendered "with all the reserve proper" to an "extra-judicial" utterance.[32] It is at least questionable whether Iredell, one of the foremost proponents of the judicial power to set aside unconstitutional laws for the protection of citizens,[33] meant to hamstring that power by a doctrine that would permit Congress to bar access to the courts.

Almost 100 years later, Justice Bradley, overlooking how cautiously Iredell had framed his dictum, exalted it above the opinions of "the other justices [who] were more swayed by a close observance of the letter of the Constitution, without regard to former experi-

---

state "ought not to do justice and fulfill engagements." Id. at 455–456. He would not permit a state to "insult" a creditor "and justice, by declaring I am a sovereign state" when sued. Id. at 456. He repudiated Blackstone's "all jurisdiction implies superiority of power" as the foundation of despotism. Id. at 458, 461, 462. Attorney General Randolph, counsel for plaintiff, relied upon both the letter and "spirit" of the Constitution, id. at 421, and concluded that "Government itself would be useless" without a sanction for its laws. Id. at 422.

[29] 2 Dallas at 465. Justice Cushing expressed some doubt whether the reasons for making a State suable equally extended to the United States, but did "not think it necessary to enter fully into the question." 2 Dallas at 469. Wilson had lumped the two together in his 1791 Lectures, infra, text accompanying note 54. Chief Justice Jay expressed a doubt derived from an assumed lack of power to enforce a decree against the federal government, but expressed the wish that "the whole nation could . . . be compelled to do justice, and be sued by individual citizens. Whether that is, or is not, now the case . . . I leave it a question." 2 Dallas at 478.

[30] Id. at 430. The *Constitutional* phrase does not employ the statutory "party" but refers to controversies "between a state and citizens of another state."

[31] Id. at 436. For the dubiety of this conclusion, see infra note 104.

[32] Supra, note 20.

[33] Supra, Chapter 3, text accompanying note 168, and note 168. At no point in his dissenting opinion did Iredell consider the point made by Wilson and Randolph, that sovereign immunity would render constitutional guarantees ineffectual. Infra, text accompanying notes 150–151.

ence and usage."[34] Before "usage" is permitted to override the "letter of the Constitution," it should at least be entirely clear that the usage was both plainly established and within the contemplation of the Founders, both of which factors are open to challenge. The usage presumably was expressed in Blackstone's statement that "no suit can be brought against the King"; but he himself stated that consent to a petition of right issued "as of course,"[35] and this practice, as Jaffe has shown, persisted into the "time the American Constitution was drafted."[36] The actual state of English law in 1787 need not be regarded as conclusive; more important, if there was a usage requiring consent to suit, is whether it was adopted by the Founders, and since the evidence on that score is, to say the least, mixed, whether it was compatible with the overriding purpose of the Founders to provide a government of limited powers which a judiciary was to keep in bounds.

Suppose that I have misconceived Blackstone's "as of course" qualification, his views were by no means accepted as Gospel when they collided with democratic principles; his statements on "legislative omnipotence" had been unmistakably repudiated, and by none more forcibly than by Iredell.[37] So too, Iredell had declaimed against the Crown prerogative in the North Carolina convention. Adverting to the maxim that the King "can do no wrong," he stated, "We have experienced that he can do wrong, yet no man can say so in his own country. There are no courts to try him for any high crimes." Iredell did not infer from this that acts of misgovernment were therefore unassailable, for he went on to say,

It is, therefore, of the utmost moment in that country that whoever is the instrument of *any act* of government should be personally responsible for it, since the king is not, that *no act* of

[34] Hans v. Louisiana, 134 U.S. 1, 12 (1890). He did the majority an injustice, for Bradley himself did not bring to the issue the broad analysis in terms of constitutional purposes, text, underlying democratic principles that it received at the hands of the majority. Marshall showed in Cohens v. Virginia, 6 Wheat. 264 (1821) that the argument for overriding the letter of Article III was inadequate and would defeat the purpose of the Founders. See infra, text accompanying notes 110–117, 126.

[35] 1 Bl. 242, 3 Bl. 255, quoted supra, note 21. See also Justice Wilson's discussion of the suit by petition, 2 Dallas at 460: "the difference is only in the form, not the thing."

[36] Jaffe, *Judicial Control* 197.

[37] Supra, Chapter 2, text accompanying notes 128–133.

government should be exercised but by the instrumentality of some person who can be accountable for it.[38]

Though Iredell mistakenly assumed that English law barred suit against the Crown, he understood that relief against any wrongful act of the government was available through the medium of suits against officers, foreshadowing our own suits against an officer as a wrongdoer in his individual capacity. And he underlined the "happier" American provision whereby even the President can be tried for criminal acts.[39] Wilson stated in the federal Convention that he "did not consider the prerogatives of the British Monarch a proper guide in defining the Executive powers";[40] and we know from his 1791 Lectures that he considered one debatable aspect of that "prerogative," sovereign immunity, incompatible with democratic principles.[41]

On what ground can we attribute to the Founders an intention, by the substitution of democratic principles for Crown prerogative, to fasten on the American people a dubious branch of the prerogative that would balk enforcement of carefully fashioned constitutional guarantees. One ground assigned by Justice Bradley in 1890 was that the jurisdiction of suits against States had "been expressly disclaimed and even resented by the great defenders of the constitution," that is, by Madison and Marshall in the Virginia convention, and by Hamilton in *The Federalist*.[42] Bradley made no mention of opposing views; he did not appraise the implications of the fact that these remarks were made in the narrow compass of pre-Constitution creditors' claims during a discussion of a "controversies"

[38] 4 Elliot 109 (italics added). "The Crown's immunity in tort never extended to its servants personally. It was, and is, a principle of first importance that officials of all kinds, high or low, are personally liable for any injury for which they cannot produce legal authority. The orders of the Crown are not legal authority, unless it is one of the rare acts which the prerogative justifies, such as the detention of an enemy alien in time of war." Wade, *Administrative Law* 256 (1967).

[39] 4 Elliot 109.

[40] 1 Farrand 65. For repudiation of the royal prerogative, see Goebel, "Ex Parte Clio," 54 *Colum. L. Rev.* 450, 474, 469 (1954).

[41] Supra, text accompanying note 28, and note 28; and see Wilson's opinion in Chisholm v. Georgia, 2 Dallas at 458, 462. Chief Justice Jay stated that in England sovereignty "exist[s] on feudal principles . . . No such ideas obtain here; at the revolution, the sovereignty devolved on the people; and they are the sovereigns of the country." Chisholm v. Georgia, 2 Dallas at 471.

[42] Hans v. Louisiana, 134 U.S. 1, 12–14 (1890).

phrase, not the "arising under" clause. Nor did he inquire whether Hamilton, for example, after vigorous espousal of judicial review, intended, by speaking for sovereign immunity in the context of creditors' suits against States, to bar enforcement of constitutional guarantees except with the permission of Congress. The history calls for sifting; and I may be indulged for setting it out in some detail because my findings run counter to conventional learning.

Preliminarily it is to be noted that the Hamilton-Madison-Marshall remarks fall within that Article III category which governs controversies "between a State and citizens of another State." Jurisdiction of other categories, for example, controversies "to which the United States shall be a party,"[43] "between two or more States,"[44] was accepted without demur. Chief Justice Jay justifiably deduced that "suability and state sovereignty are not incompatible";[45] so we start not from a blanket sovereign immunity doctrine but an immunity that was highly selective, and that responded not so much to emanations from "established doctrine" as to a tax-payers' revolt against enrichment of speculators who had purchased government paper at ruinous discounts.[46] Other expressions not invoked by Justice Bradley, which on their face might be thought to favor his view, arose in the course of tenacious opposition to direct taxation by the Congress. Requisitions made upon the States by the Continental Congress had collapsed ignominiously, and apologists for the direct tax repeatedly asked was the Congress to collect from the States by force of arms and precipitate civil war. Better to lay a tax directly on the "individual" which the judiciary could peaceably enforce.[47] This responds to an assumed incapacity to enforce a

---

[43] See Wilson, infra, text accompanying notes 67–71; proposed Virginia and North Carolina amendments, id. at notes 81, 105.

[44] See Wilson, 2 Elliot 462; Madison, 3 Elliot 532; Randolph, id. at 571; proposed Virginia and North Carolina amendments, 3 Elliot 660; 4 Elliot 246. Justice Cushing, looking at "controversies between two or more States," said, "If it was not the intent . . . that a State might be made defendant, why was it so expressed as naturally to lead to and comprehend that idea? Why was not an exception made, if one was intended?" 2 Dallas 460. Chief Justice Jay also asked if Article III "meant to exclude a certain class of these controversies, why were they not expressly excepted." Id. at 476.

[45] Chisholm v. Georgia, 2 Dallas at 472.

[46] See infra, note 130.

[47] E.g., Marshall in Virginia: "requisitions cannot be rendered efficient without a civil war." "By direct taxation, the necessities of the government will be supplied in a peaceable manner." 3 Elliot 228. See Corbin, id. at 105; Nicholas, id. at 243; Iredell, 4 Elliot 146.

proper demand against a State—which in the case of suits by State against State, or by the United States against a State,[48] time has proven can be undertaken without bloodshed—rather than to doctrinal considerations. Such remarks were unaccompanied by reference to Article III or consideration of how Constitutional prohibitions, federal laws, and treaties were to be enforced upon the States.

Opponents of the Constitution fought fiercely for State sovereignty, but this was to preserve political power against feared federal "annihilation" rather than because of allegiance to a jural concept.[49] The concept did not enjoy high esteem with eminent proponents of the Constitution. Wilson's insistence that "sovereignty resides in the people, not in States,"[50] was a corollary of a widely held postulate: power remains in the people; they delegated some of it to their agents and servants and can at any time withdraw it;[51] they can, in Wilson's words, "distribute one portion of power [to] state governments; they can also furnish another proportion to the government of the United States."[52] Charles Pinckney also spelled out the implications of this postulate: "Where absolute, uncontrollable power resides" there is "the sovereign or supreme power of the state. With us the sovereignty of the Union is in the people."[53] As Wilson emphasized in his 1791 Lectures, the purpose of the new system was for the accommodation "of the sovereign, Man," and the "primary and principal object" was "to acquire a new security" for *his* rights.[54] It ill accords with that purpose to bar him from the courts, which were erected to secure those rights, in the name of "imaginary beings called states."[55] Let us now canvass the history.

Addressing the Connecticut convention, Oliver Ellsworth, later Chief Justice of the Supreme Court, began by stating that without "coercive power" "government is ineffective, or rather is no government at all . . . Do not states do wrong?" For want of coercive power, "treaties are not performed by the States," and "if

---

[48] Rhode Island v. Massachusetts, 12 Pet. 657 (1838); South Dakota v. North Carolina, 192 U.S. 286 (1904). United States v. North Carolina, 136 U.S. 211 (1890).
[49] Supra, Chapter 8, text accompanying notes 156–177.
[50] McCloskey, Introduction 33; 2 Elliot 443; cf. supra, note 28.
[51] Supra, Chapter 6, text accompanying notes 107–111.
[52] 2 Elliot 244.
[53] 4 Elliot 317–318.
[54] Supra, Chapter 2, text accompanying note 52.
[55] Supra, text accompanying note 2.

the states go beyond their limits, if they make a law which is a usurpation upon the general government, the law is void; and upright, independent judges will declare it so."[56] One might infer that a State which did "wrong" would be coerced to do right, to "perform" a treaty; but any implication that in consequence States could be brought into court is at odds with a remark Ellsworth later made in rounding out his discussion of direct taxation: "Hence we see how necessary for the Union is a coercive principle. No man pretends to the contrary: we all see and feel this necessity. The only question is, Shall it be a coercion of law, or a coercion of arms? There is no other alternative . . . I am for coercion by law—that coercion which acts only upon delinquent individuals. This Constitution does not attempt to coerce sovereign bodies, states in their political capacity. No coercion is applicable to such bodies but that of an armed force."[57] There are a number of similar remarks in other States by speakers who were defending the substitution of direct taxation for fruitless requisitions.[58]

Direct taxes could be collected from "individuals" but how were States to be compelled to perform treaties, observe Constitutional prohibitions, and respect constitutional guarantees? In searching for an answer we must not ascribe to the Founders foreknowledge of the development that stretched over a century whereby the individual wrongdoer's suit became a means of testing constitutionality of statutes and official action, in some, not all, circumstances. For some Founders, at least, enforcement against the individual embraced what courts today are pleased to denominate a suit against the State. Although Marshall declared it unthinkable, in speaking of a creditor's suit, that a "state will be called at the bar of a federal court," he added in the next breath "are there not many cases in which the legislature of Virginia is a party, and yet the state is not sued."[59] It is true, as Randolph stated, that "the body of a state" cannot be "put in prison,"[60] but that of a Governor can. Certainly this was how Iredell understood the practice when he stated that in England "no act of government [could] be exercised but by

[56] 2 Elliot 189, 196.
[57] Id. at 197.
[58] Supra, note 46; and see Hamilton, 2 Elliot 233; Davie, 4 Elliot 22.
[59] 3 Elliot 555.
[60] Id. at 373.

the instrumentality of some person who can be accountable for it."[61] This might have afforded an adequate mechanism of enforcement against the State or federal governments but for the frequent practice of American courts to peer behind the "individual" action against the official to discern a suit against the State or nation,[62] often denying all redress; although the Court itself has said that undeniably "the rights of the citizen" were "intended to be enforced by the judiciary."[63] But enough for the moment that Ellsworth's logic need not be pressed to the attenuation of constitutional guarantees because he shrank from enforcing requisitions by resort to arms against a defiant State.

As Ellsworth noted, there was virtual unanimity on the need for "coercive power." "Was it not a political farce," asked Randolph in Virginia, "to pretend to vest powers without accompanying them with the means of execution?" And, he observed, the pre-1787 "Congress could not even enforce the observance of treaties."[64] In Massachusetts, Thomas Thacher, after enumerating State refusals to comply "with the requisitions of Congress," laws "made directly against the treaty of peace," statutes "which clashed directly against any federal union," said that a "coervice power" is necessary.[65] In North Carolina, Iredell stated that Congress had been powerless to "compel the observance of treaties"; and Davie pointed to the Constitutional prohibition against the laying of "imposts or duties on imports and exports," and said,

the importing states might make laws laying duties notwithstanding, and the Constitution might be violated with impunity, if there was no power in the general government to correct or counteract such laws. This great object can only be safely and completely obtained by the instrumentality of the federal judi-

[61] Supra, text accompanying note 38.

[62] Cf. Morrison v. Work, 266 U.S. 481 (1925) (allegedly unconstitutional official action); Mine Safety Appliances Co. v. Forrestal, 326 U.S. 371 (1945) (allegedly unconstitutional statute).

[63] Supra, text accompanying note 14.

[64] 3 Elliot 26, 27; see also Maclaine in North Carolina, supra, Chapter 4, text accompanying note 92; supra, Chapter 2, text accompanying notes 158–161; infra, note 119.

[65] 2 Elliot 144; see also Connecticut, Governor Huntington, id. at 198; Virginia, Corbin, 3 Elliot 106; Grayson, id. at 279; Madison, id. at 414; North Carolina, Iredell, 4 Elliot 145–146.

ciary . . . This restriction would have been a dead letter, were no judiciary constituted to enforce obedience to it.[66]

Wilson it was who boldly faced up in the Pennsylvania convention to the implications of coercive power in the confines of Article III. With respect to State boundary and jurisdictional disputes, he said that the earlier Congress "had no power to carry the decree into execution"; and when he came to the "controversies between two or more States," he stated that the power of enforcing decrees in such cases is "necessary, and I presume no exception will be taken to it."[67] As to controversies "Between a state and citizens of another state," he said, "When a citizen has a controversy with another state, there ought to be a tribunal where both parties may stand on a just and equal footing."[68] Objection was made to the jurisdiction of "controversies to which the United States shall be a party" on the ground that "the sovereignty of the states is destroyed, if they should be engaged in a controversy with the United States, because a suitor in a court must acknowledge the jurisdiction of that court, and it is not the custom of sovereigns to suffer their names to be made use of in this manner." Wilson stated, "The answer is plain and easy; the government of each state ought to be subordinate to the government of the United States."[69] He did not shrink from compulsion. "Let us suppose," he said, "that a wicked law is made in one of the states, enabling a debtor to pay his creditor with the . . . sixth part of the real value of the debt," that a foreign subject then complained to his sovereign who then applied for redress to the United States which "must be accountable." "If the United States," he continued, "are answerable for the injury, ought they not possess

---

[66] 4 Elliot 157. Even in rejecting the Constitution, the North Carolina convention proposed an amendment that would retain controversies "to which the United States shall be a party." 4 Elliot 246. Davie was also mindful of laws that struck at individuals, and said it was necessary that "the hands of the states should be bound from making paper money, instalment laws, or *pine barren acts*. By such iniquitous laws the merchant or farmer may be defrauded of a considerable part of his just claim." 4 Elliot 159. In Massachusetts, Thacher said, "In South Carolina creditors, by law, were obliged to receive barren and useless land for contracts made in gold and silver." 2 Elliot 144.

[67] 2 Elliot 462, 490–491.

[68] Id. at 491.

[69] Id. at 490.

the means of compelling the faulty state to repair it? They ought; and this is what is done here."[70]

These views were amplified by Wilson in his 1791 Lectures, delivered two years before *Chisholm v. Georgia:* In controversies to which the state or nation is a party,

> the state or nation ought itself to be amenable before the judicial powers. This principle, dignified because it is just is expressly ratified by the constitution of Pennsylvania. It declares that suits may be brought against the commonwealth.

As to the "sovereignty of the states," he said,

> Is a man degraded by the manly declaration, that he renders himself amenable to justice? Can a similar declaration degrade a state?
>
> To be privileged from the awards of equal justice, is a disgrace instead of being an honor; but a state claims a privilege from the awards of equal justice, when she refuses to become a party . . .
>
> In the Mirrour of Justices, we have an account of the first constitutions ordained by the ancient kings of England . . . Among these constitutions, we find the following very remarkable one. "It was ordained that the king's court should be open to all plaintiffs; from which they should have, without delay, remedial writs, *as well against the king or queen* as against any *other* people."[71]

At the close of the New York convention an amendment was proposed that "nothing in the Constitution . . . is to be construed to authorize any suit to be brought against any state, in any manner whatever."[72] This proposal was cut down in the New York Instrument of Ratification to a declaration that the Judicial Power "does not authorize a suit by any Person against a State";[73] from which it

---

[70] Id. at 493.

[71] 2 Wilson, *Works* 292, 295. Attorney General Randolph later argued in Chisholm v. Georgia that it was "no degradation of sovereignty, in the States, to submit to the supreme judiciary of the United States." 2 Dallas at 425. Chief Justice Jay echoed the phrase. Id. at 473.

[72] 2 Elliot 409.

[73] De Pauw, *The Eleventh Pillar* 296 (1966).

may be gathered both that express language was deemed essential to lift sovereign immunity above the Article III jurisdiction, and that except as modified the Article III jurisdiction was unobjectionable. Similarly, the Massachusetts convention proposed an amendment that the "Supreme Federal Judicial Court shall have no jurisdiction of causes between citizens of different states, unless the matter in dispute . . . be one of the value of three thousand dollars at least."[74] Such a minute revision makes it difficult to conclude that Massachusetts overlooked the Article III encroachment on sovereign immunity, and it is not unreasonable to deduce that Massachusetts also found this acceptable. Maryland had been told that the Constitution provided for judicial review, but amendments designed to strengthen judicial independence were proposed to its convention,[75] again suggesting that the jurisdiction conferred was acceptable.

Let us now consider the Hamilton-Madison-Marshall remarks upon which Justice Bradley relied, bearing in mind that whatever the force of the Madison-Marshall remarks in the Virginia convention, they represent at best the views of one state only and do not tip the scales against views expressed explicitly in Pennsylvania, and by implication in New York and Massachusetts. Madison referred to the "much objected to" jurisdiction of controversies between a State and citizens of another State, and said that it "is not in the power of individuals to call any state into court."[76] At the same time he said of the jurisdiction "where two or more states are the parties," this "is not objected to,"[77] parenthetically, a gratuitous remark if all suits against a State were subject to "consent" to suit. Marshall, also speaking "with respect to disputes between a state and citizens of another state" said, "its jurisdiction had been decried with unusual vehemence. I hope that no gentleman will think that a state will be called at the bar of the federal court."[78] Nevertheless, Pendleton, a member of the Virginia Supreme Court,

---

[74] 2 Elliot 177.

[75] Id. at 550–554. A chief object of such proposals as were made was "to secure the independence of the federal judges, to whom the happiness of the people of this great continent will be so greatly committed by the extensive powers assigned to them," 2 Elliot 551, an object ill-served by an assumption of overriding federal immunity.

[76] 3 Elliot 533.

[77] Id. at 532.

[78] Id. at 555.

President of the Convention, and a proponent of adoption, stated thereafter that "The impossibility of calling a sovereign state before the jurisdiction of another sovereign state, shows the propriety and necessity of vesting this tribunal with the decisions to which a state shall be a party."[79] Marshall himself, as Chief Justice, later withdrew questions "arising under" the Constitution both from any doctrine of sovereign immunity and from the scope of the Eleventh Amendment.[80] In Virginia, finally, the convention proposed an Amendment which was forwarded with its Ratification, and which retained in Article III "Controversies to which the United States shall be a party, [and] controversies between two or more States."[81] As in the case of New York, Virginia relied *on deletion,* not on a supra-constitutional doctrine of sovereign immunity, to restrict the terms of Article III.

Hamilton had contented himself in *Federalist* No. 80 with a perfunctory outline of the several categories of Article III "controversies" and the "arising under" jurisdiction, and concluded that these "particular powers of the federal judiciary . . . are all conformable to the principles which ought to have governed the structure of that department," "calculated to avoid general mischiefs and to obtain general advantages,"[82] which had been delineated in considerable detail in No. 78. His casual treatment suggests that he anticipated no objections. But apparently some criticism reached him thereafter, for in the next issue, *Federalist* No. 81, he "digressed" to counter "a supposition which has excited some alarm" with respect to *one* of these categories, "controversies between a state and citizens of a different state," alarm lest "an assignment of the public securities of one State to the citizens of another, would enable them to prosecute that State in the federal courts for the amount

---

[79] Id. at 549. Grayson argued the Constitution made States parties without requiring their consent. Id. at 567. P. Henry and R. H. Lee said States were answerable to an individual. Id. at 543, and Ford's *Pamphlets,* 279, 309. For Mason, see Chapter 8, n. 188. "A citizen," said "Letters of Agrippa," reprinted, Ford, *Essays on the Constitution* (1892), 93, 97, possessed "of the notes of another state may bring his action." Chief Justice Jay deduced from the provision for suits between the States that "suability and state sovereignty are not incompatible." Chisholm v. Georgia, 2 Dallas at 472.

[80] See infra, text accompanying notes 110–117.

[81] 3 Elliot 660.

[82] *Federalist* at 521–522.

of those securities." To quiet this alarm, he stated that "It is inherent in the nature of sovereignty not to be amenable to the suit of an individual without its consent."[83] Limited to an individual, this remark is further limited by the words that followed: "Unless, therefore there is a surrender of this immunity in the plan of the convention, it will remain with the States . . . The circumstances which are necessary to produce an alienation of State sovereignty were discussed in considering the article of taxation, and need not be repeated here."[84] In that piece, *Federalist* No. 32, Hamilton had stated, "the State governments would clearly retain all the rights of sovereignty which they before had, and which were not by that act [Constitution] *exclusively* delegated to the United States."[85] These "surrender" remarks have been translated by the Supreme Court into a doctrine that the States must have "consented" to suit or "waived" immunity "within the plan of the convention,"[86] in effect grafting an extrinsic qualification on an explicit constitutional grant.[87]

It is a singular interpretive approach that would accord clear terms effectiveness only if they are confirmed by extrinsic evidence. The rule is to the contrary: express terms are given literal effect unless the result is absurd or unreasonable, or unless the "intention" of the draftsmen manifestly requires a different result.[88] "It would

---

[83] Id. at 529.

[84] Id. at 529–530. Justice Blair, discussing controversies "between a State and citizens of another State" in Chisholm v. Georgia, stated, "if sovereignty be an exemption from suit . . . it follows that when a state by adopting the constitution, has agreed to be amenable to the judicial power of the United States, she has, in that respect, given up her right of sovereignty." 2 Dallas at 452. No internal logic compels a differentiation of "consents" so as to exclude any Article III category.

[85] Id. at 194. "This exclusive delegation, or rather this alienation of state sovereignty, would only exist in three cases: where the Amendment in express terms granted an exclusive authority to the Union; where it granted in one instance an authority to the Union, and in another prohibited the States from exercising the like authority; and where it granted an authority to the Union, to which a similar authority would be absolutely and totally *contradictory* and *repugnant*."

[86] Monaco v. Mississippi, 292 U.S. 313, 324, 328–329 (1934).

[87] As Corwin, 9 *Mich. L. Rev.* 294, said of the argument on behalf of Georgia in Chisholm v. Georgia, "State sovereignty was set up as a sort of interpretive principle limiting the operation of the Constitution."

[88] Said Chief Justice Marshall, if "the plain meaning of a provision . . . is to be disregarded, because we believe that the framers of the instrument could not intend what they say, it must be one in which the absurdity and injustice of

be dangerous in the extreme," said Chief Justice Marshall, "to infer from extrinsic circumstances, that a case for which the words of an instrument expressly provide, shall be exempted from its operation." Judges have continued to attach great weight to the words set down by the Founders.[89] Moreover, Hamilton's "exclusive delegation" criterion, which served well enough to reassure that State local taxation was not endangered, is patently insufficient to explain at least one instance that comes to mind—the "waiver" spelled out by the Supreme Court in controversies between sister States.[90] Outside the terms of Article III the Constitution nowhere makes an "exclusive delegation" to the federal government of all subjects that may become embroiled in controversy between sister States; and as we have seen, the Court looks outside Article III for "consent." To find consent to suits between States the Court returned to Hamilton's statement in No. 80 that such jurisdiction "was essential to the peace of the Union."[91] Such flexibility licenses us to wander beyond the "surrender" confines for still other purposes that fall within the "plan of the Constitution." For example, Article I, section 10(1) declares that "No State shall . . . pass any . . . law impairing the obligation of contracts." That provision was made for the benefit of the individual citizen and was a response to State excesses

---

applying the provision to the case, would be so monstrous, that all mankind would without hesitation, unite in rejecting the application." Sturges v. Crowninshield, 4 Wheat. 122, 202 (1819); see also United States v. Kirby, 7 Wall. 482, 486–487 (1868). Literal terms will be disregarded when it is found the intention of the legislators was to the contrary. Hawaii v. Mankichi, 190 U.S. 197, 212 (1903); Hand 24–25 (to effect the "obvious design"). Compare Crooks v. Harrelson, 282 U.S. 55, 60 (1930). The only discoverable "intention" pertains to creditors' suits and is based on remarks in the Virginia convention which, in my judgment, are outweighed by the evidence in other States.

[89] Marshall quoted from Sturges v. Crowninshield, 4 Wheat. 122, 202 (1819); see also infra, text accompanying note 107. Chief Justice Taney stated that "in expounding the constitution . . . every word must have its due force, and appropriate meaning; for it is evident from the whole instrument, that no word was unnecessarily used, or needlessly added . . . Every word appears to have been weighed with the utmost deliberation, and in its force and effect to have been fully understood. No word in the instrument, therefore, can be rejected as superfluous or unmeaning." Holmes v. Jenison, 14 Pet. 540, 570–571 (1840). See also Blake v. McClung, 172 U.S. 239, 260–261 (1898). Nor by the same token can any word be qualified by an unexpressed meaning except on the strongest evidence.

[90] Monaco v. Mississippi, 292 U.S. 313, 328–329 (1934).

[91] Id. at 328.

which had impaired individual rights.[92] Suppose an impairment
case where relief is available solely by direct suit against the State,
and consider Hamilton's own rhetorical question in *Federalist* No.
80, "What, for instance, would avail restrictions on the authority
of State legislatures, without some constitutional mode of enforcing the observance of them?" His answer was that there must be
"an authority in the federal courts to overrule such [State laws]
as might be in manifest contravention of the Articles of Union,"[93]
a remark that was in consonance with his earlier statement in No.
78 that the courts would be "the bulwarks of a limited Constitution
against legislative encroachment," "equally requisite to guard the
Constitution and the rights of individuals from the effects of those
ill humors" of majorities which had occasioned "serious oppression
of the minor party in the community."[94] I cannot bring myself to
believe that in hurriedly fielding a hot potato—creditors' suits—
Hamilton meant to abandon his painstakingly articulated structure
of judicial review as a "bulwark" for the individual, a formulation
that expressed the Founders' design that judicial review would protect the individual against legislative excesses, both State and federal.
Certainly his own state, New York, did not accept the view that
sovereign immunity qualified Article III, for by its proposed amendment it demonstrated that an amendment was thought necessary
to remove a suit against a State from Article III. Such an amendment was superfluous if a State could block jurisdiction by withholding consent to suit. In Pennsylvania Wilson, rated by Max
Farrand as "second only to Madison and almost on a par with
him,"[95] flatfootedly defended Article III against sovereign immunity. And the implication of the Massachusetts amendment also
speaks against an overbroad gloss on the Hamilton "creditors' suits"
remarks.[96]

---

[92] Even an opponent of the Constitution, R. H. Lee, testified that such "abuse
of power" fed sentiment for a change of government. Quoted supra, Chapter 2
n. 12. See also id., text accompanying notes 9–15, 41–47; and supra, note 66.

[93] *Federalist* No. 80 at 516.

[94] Id. at 508. See supra, notes 92 and 66.

[95] Farrand, *Framing* 197; McCloskey, Introduction 6.

[96] One should notice the somewhat garbled utterance of Randolph, concluding, "Would it not be [disgraceful] that Virginia, after eight states had adopted
the government, none of which opposed the jurisdiction in this case, rejected it
on this account?" 3 Elliot 573, 576.

Other incongruities emerge when we compare the Court's contrasting treatment of suits by a State versus the United States, where the United States is sheltered by an "established doctrine" of sovereign immunity, with suits by the United States versus a State, where the doctrine is breached on the theory that the State "consented" to such suit. Let us begin with suits by the United States, and the paradox that Chief Justice Marshall, who had labored so convincingly to cut down the literal exemption from suit conferred upon States by the Eleventh Amendment,[97] should in the very same opinion effortlessly rise above the implications of his own reasoning and drop the dictum that "The universally received opinion is, that no suit can be commenced or prosecuted against the United States."[98] At a later time, Chief Justice Hughes explained that "there is no express provision that the United States may not be sued in the absence of consent. Clause one . . . extends the judicial power 'to Controversies to which the United States shall be a Party.' Literally, this includes such controversies, whether the United States be party plaintiff or defendant. . . . But by reason of the *established doctrine* of the immunity of the sovereign from suit except upon consent, the provision of clause one . . . does not authorize the maintenance of suits against the United States."[99] It would be tedious again to rehearse the materials which impeach the assumption of an "established doctrine." Consider rather the reverse of the medal, suit by the United States *against* a State. Said Chief Justice Hughes, "While that jurisdiction is not conferred by the Constitution in express words, it is inherent in the constitutional plan . . . Without such a provision . . . 'the permanence of the Union might be endangered.' "[100] Thus sovereign immunity yields to a purpose "inherent in the constitutional plan." Agreed that enforcement of constitutional restrictions upon the States and protection of constitutional guarantees requires that the Article III jurisdiction of "controversies to which the United States is a party" be given such effect. It is no less "inherent in the constitutional plan," however, that States should have access to the courts for protection of the rights reserved by the Constitution to them.

[97] Infra, text accompanying notes 110–117.
[98] Cohens v. Virginia, 6 Wheat. 264, 411–412 (1821).
[99] Monaco v. Mississippi, 292 U.S. 313, 321 (1934) (emphasis added).
[100] Id. at 329.

CHAPTER 10

In 1787, the State, not the federal government, was the darling of the people. Fear that the "permanence of the Union might be endangered" was not nearly as intense as dread that the States would be "annihilated," swallowed up by the federal ogre. Opponents were repeatedly assured that Congressional powers were limited, that they could always be called in question, and that Acts in excess of those powers would be held void.[101] History renders untenable the assumption that the Founders intended to bar suits by the States versus the United States to protest against unconstitutional encroachments. With the exception of one remark by Nicholas,[102] the debate in the Ratification conventions revolved entirely about the impact Article III might have on a State; and Wilson said in 1791 that both State and nation must be amenable to judicial process.[103] Given the meaning that Chief Justice Hughes justifiably put on "party" as embracing both plaintiff and defendant,[104] it is especially noteworthy that in no State was objection made to Article III jurisdiction of the United States as a "party." Instead, in Virginia, where determined opposition nearly overwhelmed the proponents, and in North Carolina, where adoption of the Constitution was de-

[101] Supra, Chapter 2, text accompanying notes 25–40; Chapter 4, id. at notes 52–55, 73–77, 106–108; Chapter 8, id. at notes 45–54, 156–187.

[102] 3 Elliot 476–477 (no clause gives "speculators" power to sue for public debt).

[103] Supra, text accompanying note 71.

[104] Justice Iredell, in dissenting, regarded the word "party" as meaning where a State "can be" a party; supra, text accompanying notes 30–31. His thinking departed from that of the Founders. In Virginia, Judge Pendleton said that "The impossibility of calling a sovereign state before the jurisdiction of another sovereign state, shows the propriety and necessity of vesting this tribunal with the decision to which a state shall be a party." 3 Elliot 549. Thus a State could be a party-defendant when "called" into federal court. Although Article III speaks of "controversies between two or more States," Madison, like Pendleton, rendered it as "where two or more states are the parties," 3 Elliot 532, in a situation where either State might be plaintiff or defendant. Finally, said Wilson in his 1791 Lectures, "In controversies to which the state or nation is a party, the state or nation itself ought to be amenable before the judicial powers." Supra, text accompanying note 71. Patently, Pendleton, Madison, and Wilson regarded "party" as inclusive of plaintiff and defendant, so that Chief Justice Hughes's statement that "party" literally includes the United States as plaintiff or defendant can summon the support of history.

Governor Caswell wrote to Spaight, a delegate from North Carolina to the federal Convention, that he wished for "an independent Judicial department to decide any contest that may happen between the United States and individual States & between one State and another." 3 Farrand 64.

feated, chiefly because of deep-seated suspicion of unbounded Congressional powers, amendments were proposed which curtailed Article III but *preserved* the "controversies where the United States is a party."[105] Will it be maintained that these States sought to preserve suits *by* the United States but disclaimed those a State might bring *against* the United States? Is it reasonable to infer that Davie, fighting a losing battle for the Constitution in North Carolina, pleading for enforcement of Constitutional restrictions on the States lest the Constitution be "violated with impunity," saying of one such restriction that it "would have been a dead letter, were there no judiciary to enforce it," intended that *Congress* could violate Constitutional restrictions "with impunity," that such restrictions were a "dead letter" as to *it*, and this in a State where Congressional "tyranny" was the shibboleth? The people required assurances that the Congressional hobgoblin could be effectively curbed; but they had to be persuaded that an effective federal government required enforcement of restrictions on the States. The Framers, in the words of Stone in the First Congress, "supposed" that the federal government "had a natural tendency to destroy the State Governments: . . . they supposed that State Governments had a tendency to abridge the powers of the General Government; therefore it was necessary to guard against either taking place, and this was to be done properly by establishing a judiciary of the United States."[106] To exhibit solicitude for federal suits against a State while barring States themselves from suing the United States is to stand history on its head.

The entire doctrine of sovereign immunity, it can not be sufficiently stressed, rests upon an *assumption* that it was "established doctrine" at the adoption of the Constitution and upon debatable proof that the Founders acted upon that proposition. Instead of an easy assumption, for which there is little historical warrant, whereby a limitation is grafted upon a clear text, the long-held rule requires, as Justice Story declared in 1816, that "If the text be clear and distinct, no restriction upon its plain and obvious import ought to be admitted, unless the inference is irresistible."[107] Given the

[105] 3 Elliot 660; 4 Elliot 246, 251.
[106] Supra, Chapter 8, text accompanying note 212.
[107] Martin v. Hunters' Lessee, 1 Wheat. 304, 338 (1816).

express terms of Article III, our approach should be that of Chief Justice Marshall:

> The jurisdiction of the court, then, being extended by the letter of the constitution to all cases arising under it, or under the laws of the United States, it follows, that those who would withdraw any case of this description from that jurisdiction must sustain the exemption they claim, on the spirit and true meaning of the constitution, which spirit and meaning *must be so apparent* as to over-rule the words which its framers have employed.[108]

He found no such "spirit" in the case before him; and if my analysis of the historical materials is valid, the "spirit" of the Constitution speaks against, not for, sovereign immunity. That spirit need not be sought in an impalpable distillation from its terms and structure, for the Founders made amply plain that they aimed to protect the individual from both State and federal excesses, and to put teeth into Constitutional guarantees.

In sum: (1) Some of the Founders stated that direct taxation was preferable to war with States which refused to honor Congressional requisitions, without mention of Article III or consideration of how States were to be compelled to honor Constitutional prohibitions, federal treaties, and laws. No one claimed that *these* must be unenforceable. (2) Hamilton, Madison, and Marshall sought to quiet alarm over creditors' suits which could threaten the financial security of some States, whereas Pennsylvania and New York recognized there was no such immunity; and in Virginia itself, Judge Pendleton stated that the federal courts must be enabled to "call" a State before their bar. (3) The need for suits by sister States and by the United States was virtually undisputed, thus undercutting Justice Bradley's inference of a blanket sovereign immunity doctrine. The argument that such an immunity was assumed and that the States consented to waive it in particular circumstances seems to me opposed to the facts and to run counter to accepted canons of construction. (4) There is no suggestion that those, like

---

[108] Cohens v. Virginia, 6 Wheat. 264, 379–380 (1821) (emphasis added).

Hamilton and Marshall, who affirmed that Courts were to be the bulwarks of constitutional rights, conceived that sovereign immunity would bar judicial protection of such rights. (5) *Chisholm v. Georgia,* a contemporary decision by a Court which included Justice Wilson, a Framer who had categoricaliy rejected sovereign immunity, represents a 4 to 1 adoption of the Wilson view, even in the case of creditors' suits.[109]

In 1821 Chief Justice Marshall, far from affirming that *Chisholm* had misconceived both common law and constitutional requirements, was at pains to state that "the court maintained its jurisdiction,"[110] and then to demonstrate the limited effect of the Eleventh Amendment in restoring sovereign immunity. *Chisholm* was in fact powerfully fortified by Marshall's incisive analysis in *Cohens v. Virginia.*[111] He pointed out that Article III empowers the courts to act in two quite separate categories: (1) "all cases . . . arising under this Constitution," and (2) "controversies . . . between two or more States; between a State and citizens of another State . . . between citizens of different States." In category 2, he stated, "the jurisdiction of the court is founded entirely on the character of the parties; the nature of the controversy is not contemplated by the constitution." In category 1, "the jurisdiction is founded entirely on the character of the case, and the parties are not contemplated by the constitution."[112] That discrimination has become a familiar staple of federal jurisdiction. For example, a suit "between citizens of different states" need not rise to constitutional dimensions and may be brought in the absence of a constitutional question under the "diversity jurisdiction."[113] Though "diversity jurisdiction" is lacking, a citizen may come into federal court to assert a constitutional right under the "federal question" jurisdiction. As Marshall underscored, "If jurisdiction depended entirely on the character of the parties," the provision "which extends the judicial

---

[109] Some contemporary opinion regarded Chisholm as a sweeping rejection of all sovereign immunity. Warren, *Supreme Court in History* 96.

[110] Cohens v. Virginia, 6 Wheat. at 406.

[111] 6 Wheat. 264 (1821).

[112] Id. at 398. Marshall had been anticipated in part by Justice Wilson, who said of Article III, "Causes, and not parties to causes, are weighed by justice, in her equal scales; on the former solely, her attention is fixed: to the latter, she is, as painted, blind." Chisholm v. Georgia, 2 Dallas at 466.

[113] See Forrester & Currier, *Federal Jurisdiction & Procedure* 69 (1962).

CHAPTER 10

power to all cases arising under the Constitution . . . would be mere surplusage. It is to give jurisdiction, where the character of the parties would not give it, that this very important part of the clause was inserted."[114] The Marshall "surplusage" argument is reinforced by a cognate canon of constitutional construction: no provision of the Constitution should be so construed as to deprive another provision of effect unless that is unavoidable. The several remarks about creditors' suits were clustered around the Article III "controversies between a State and citizens of another State"; no mention was made of the separate clause, "cases . . . arising under this Constitution." That clause was in no wise involved in the discussion, and under the circumstances it is gratuitous to charge Hamilton and Marshall with abandonment of judicial enforcement of *constitutional* rights. All intendments are to the contrary and they are reinforced by the canon that if at all possible effect should be given to each separate provision.[115]

Marshall found nothing in the "spirit of the Constitution" to control the express terms, and concluded that "a case arising under the Constitution or laws of the United States is cognizable in the courts of the Union, whoever may be the parties to that case."[116] Thus Marshall's reasoning renders the "nature of the party" irrelevant when constitutional rights are at stake. And he asked, "why should such a case be excepted from the provision which expressly extends the judicial provision of the Union to *all* cases arising under the Constitution?"[117] The answer that to him seemed self-evident is fortified by the emphasis during the several conventions upon the necessity of enforcing Constitutional prohibitions against the

[114] 6 Wheat. at 391.
[115] "It cannot be presumed," said Marshall, C. J., "that any clause in the Constitution is designed to be without effect; and therefore such a construction is inadmissible, unless the words require it." Marbury v. Madison, 1 Cranch 137, 178 (1803). Constitutional provisions "are of equal dignity, and neither must be so enforced as to nullify or substantially impair the other." Dick v. United States, 208 U.S. 340, 353 (1908). As Chief Justice White said in Billings v. United States, 232 U.S. 261, 282 (1914), "the powers which [the Constitution] confers on the one hand it does not immediately take away on the other."
[116] 6 Wheat. at 382. Marshall purportedly confined himself to a prosecution *brought* by a State, 6 Wheat. 390–391, 392, 403, wisely deciding the case at bar. But the logic of his reasoning will not be so confined, and inescapably embraces the cases in which a citizen seeks judicial aid against a State violation of constitutional rights.
[117] 6 Wheat. at 392.

States,[118] of enforcing treaties which States had ignored to the detriment of the Confederation,[119] and upon the need for protection against State excesses which had threatened liberty and property.[120] In imposing such restrictions, the Founders may be acquitted of framing mere "parchment barriers," of contenting themselves with toothless exhortations for which they recorded their contempt.[121]

Marshall's views were dismissed by Justice Bradley as "unnecessary to the decision,"[122] although Marshall's careful and extended analysis may well be regarded as another ground of decision and therefore not subject to dismissal as dictum.[123] His Court was closer to the crucial events than was Bradley, and his cogent reasoning, in my view, is keyed to history and is far more convincing than Bradley's "presumption that no anomalous and unheard of proceedings or suits were intended to be raised by the Constitution."[124] If suits

[118] E.g., Davie, quoted supra, Chapter 4, text accompanying note 89. Hamilton asked, "What, for instance would avail restrictions on the authority of the State legislatures, without some constitutional mode of enforcing the observance of them?" *Federalist* No. 80 at 516.

[119] Corbin said in the Virginia convention, "Fatal experience has proved that treaties would never be complied with if their observance depended on the will of states, and the consequences would be constant war." 3 Elliot 510. To the same effect, Nicholas and Madison, id. at 507, 515. In the North Carolina convention, Maclaine stated, "The treaty of peace with Great Britain was the supreme law of the land, yet it was disregarded for want of a federal judiciary. The state courts did not enforce an observance of it." 4 Elliot 164. This was exactly the issue presented in Rutgers v. Waddington, supra, chapter 2, text accompanying notes 158–159. Wilson cited Article III in Pennsylvania to show that "the judges . . . will be enabled to carry [a treaty] into effect, let the legislatures of the different states do what they may." 2 Elliot 490. See also Appendix B, note 72.

[120] Supra, Chapter 2, text accompanying notes 7–15, 43–45; and see Corwin, quoted supra, Chapter 3, text following note 311.

[121] See supra, Chapter 6, note 190. And see 3 Elliot 26; *Federalist* No. 80 at 516, No. 78 at 505, No. 15 at 91; Gerry, quoted supra, Chapter 8, text accompanying note 244; Iredell, quoted supra, Chapter 8, note 244; Davie quoted supra, text accompanying note 66; Hamilton, quoted id. at note 93; Randolph, quoted supra, note 28.

[122] Hans v. Louisiana, 134 U.S. 1, 20 (1890).

[123] "[W]here a decision rests on two or more grounds, none can be relegated to the category of *obiter* dictum." Woods v. Interstate Realty Co., 337 U.S. 535, 537 (1949).

[124] Hans v. Louisiana, 134 U.S. at 18. For the weight attached to contemporary opinion, see supra, Chapter 5, note 1. Bradley conceded that at the establishment of the judicial power, "Some things, undoubtedly were made justiciable which were not known as such at the common law; such, for example, as controversies between States as to boundary lines," though he mentioned some early

against the state were indeed "unknown to the common law," as Justice Bradley asserted, the Constitution, first and last, was itself a prodigious novelty; and novelty cannot defeat the intention of the Founders to bind the States to observance of the Constitution. Novelty cannot serve as a basis for reading out of the Constitution the express grant of jurisdiction designed to make observance enforceable. Once the Framers acknowledged that restrictions on the States were inescapable, and that observance of such Constitutional restrictions must therefore be enforceable, they would be little likely to stumble over the "novelty" of a suit against the state. "Had no important step been taken by the leaders of the Revolution for which a precedent could not be discovered," said Madison in *Federalist* No. 14, "the people of the United States might . . . have been numbered among the melancholy victims of misguided councils."[125] Still less is a reading supportable that thwarts access to the courts for the protection of the individual whose Constitutional rights are invaded. In the words of Chief Justice Marshall,

> The constitution gave to every person having a claim upon a state, a right to submit his case to the court of the nation . . . Can it be imagined, that the same persons [Framers] considered a case involving the constitution of our country as withdrawn from this tribunal, because a state is a party.[126]

THE ELEVENTH AMENDMENT

When Justice Frankfurter stated that "The vehement speed with which the Eleventh Amendment displaced the decision in Chisholm v. Georgia . . . proves how deeply rooted the doctrine was in

---

cases to suggest that such controversies were "not unknown to the courts." Id. at 15. No mention of such cases is to be found in the several conventions. Jurisdiction of such suits was thought requisite to fulfill a constitutional purpose—preservation of peace between the States. Hamilton, *Federalist* No. 80 at 517; Randolph, 3 Elliot 571; Monaco v. Mississippi, 292 U.S. 313, 328 (1934).

[125] Quoted fully supra, Chapter 2, note 177. In Massachusetts Brooks replied to the objection that "biennial elections were a novelty," "we are not to consider whether a measure was new, but whether it was proper." 2 Elliot 14.

[126] 6 Wheat. at 383. The Supreme Court, however, has followed Bradley, not Marshall: "although a case may arise under the Constitution and laws of the United States, the judicial power does not extend to it if the suit is sought to be prosecuted against a State, without her consent, by one of her own citizens." Monaco v. Mississippi, 292 U.S. 313, 322 (1934).

the early days of the Republic,"[127] he overlooked the very narrow scope of the Amendment and the throbbing grievances behind the sovereignty façade. Passions were not aroused by abstract juridical doctrine but by fear of taxation to make amends to Tories or refugees who sued the States to recover properties sequestered during the Revolution. As the *Independent Chronicle* wrote after *Chisholm v. Georgia,* which was a suit on behalf of an expatriate colonial to recover against sequestered property of refugee debtors,[128]

> Nothing remains but to give the key of our treasury to the agents of the Refugees, Tories and men who were inimical to our Revolution, to distribute the hard money now deposited in that office to persons of that description.[129]

The citizenry was up in arms against taxation that would only serve to enrich Tories and speculators who had bought State obligations for a few cents on the dollar. This it was, not a "deeply-rooted" doctrine of sovereign immunity, that led to the Eleventh Amendment.[130]

---

[127] Larson v. Domestic & Foreign Commerce Corp., 337 U.S. 682, 705, 708 (1949) (dissenting opinion).

[128] Warren, *Supreme Court in History* 99.

[129] Quoted id. at 99 n. 1.

[130] Said Warren, id. at 99, "While this opposition to the Court's decision was to some extent based on divergencies of political theories as to State sovereignty, the real source of the attack on the *Chisholm Case* was the very concrete fear of 'numerous prosecutions that will immediately issue from the various claims of refugees, Tories, etc. as will throw every State in the Union into the greatest confusion.' In the crucial condition of the finances of most of the States at that time only disaster was to be expected if suits could be successfully maintained by holders of State issues of paper and other credits, or by Loyalist refugees to recover property confiscated or sequestered by the States." As the *Independent Chronicle,* July 25, 1793, wrote, "The subject is now but of infinite importance to the rights and property of every individual citizen." Ibid.

In Cohens v. Virginia, 6 Wheat. 264, 406 (1821), Marshall explained that the "motive" of the Eleventh Amendment "was not to maintain the sovereignty of a State from the degradation supposed to attend a compulsory appearance before the Supreme Court," but to prevent suits by its "creditors." At the time "of the adoption of the Constitution," he said, "all the states were greatly indebted."

"Farmers, discharged soldiers, petty shopkeepers, and the like who held government securities representing service rendered, goods supplied, or money advanced during the war, had been forced to part with them at a ruinous discount during the hard times that followed. By 1789 the bulk of the public debt was in the hands of the 'right people' at Philadelphia, New York, Boston; and the nation was taxed [under the federal funding of Hamilton] to pay them at par for what they had purchased at a tremendous discount." 1 Morison & Commager,

CHAPTER 10

Judicial repudiation of sovereign immunity in *Chisholm v. Georgia* set the stage for enthronement of sovereign immunity in full panoply; the bitter resentment against suits by speculators and Loyalists made the moment propitious for adoption of full-scale immunity. Earlier a resolution had been introduced in the New York convention which would disallow "any suit to be brought against any state, in any manner whatever."[131] Notwithstanding that the House likewise had before it a Resolution which would preclude both individual suits against a State and suits "by any body politic or corporate within or without the United States,"[132] despite the passions aroused by the *Chisholm* decision,[133] no such sweeping exclusion was incorporated in the Amendment approved and submitted by Congress[134] and ratified by the States. The rejection of the broader Resolution underlines the limited objectives of the Eleventh Amendment: it withdrew jurisdiction only of suits against a State by citizens (1) of another State, and (2) of a foreign state, leaving intact suits by (1) a sister State, (2) the United States, and (3) a citizen against his own State. That limited withdrawal refutes a "postulate" of overriding sovereign immunity. With the problem squarely presented, the draftsmen did not delete from Article III all suits against a State and substitute therefor "consent" by a State to suits by sister States or the United States. Instead they prohibited only two types of Article III suits and left the remaining categories intact, whereby they confirmed that sovereign immunity constitutes no bar to suits which were not forbidden.[135]

The Growth of the American Republic 336 (4th ed. 1952). Such considerations led Mason heatedly to say in the Virginia convention of the proposed funding of State debts, "are we to part with every shilling of our property and be reduced to the lowest insignificancy, to aggrandize a few speculators?" 3 Elliot 479.

[131] 2 Elliot 409.

[132] Warren, *Supreme Court in History* 101.

[133] Id. at 94–100.

[134] 3 *Ann. Cong.* 35, 30, 476–477 (1794).

[135] "The decision in Chisholm v. Georgia . . . was shortly followed by the adoption of the Eleventh Amendment, but this fact, far from impairing the logic of that decision, seems rather to confirm it." Corwin, 9 *Mich. L. Rev.* 295.

Compare also the interpretive rule of express mention-implied exclusion: "Affirmative words are often, in their operation, negative of other objects than those affirmed." Marbury v. Madison, 1 Cranch 137, 174 (1803). See also Botany Worsted Mills v. United States, 278 U.S. 282, 289 (1929). In terms of the Eleventh Amendment, only the expressly proscribed suits were banned and therefore required consent; all others could be brought without consent.

Manifestly the Amendment was not a response to demands of entrenched doctrine, even less of a symmetrical jurisprudence, but was carefully tailored to meet the immediate practical problem that confronted the States—suits by creditors and the like who were citizens of other States. Marshall later stated—as a participant in the Virginia convention and member of the Virginia Assembly from 1782 to 1791 he presumably knew where the bones were buried—that foreign states and sister States were excluded because there "was not much reason to fear" that they "would be creditors to any considerable amount."[136] One might hazard the guess that the depreciated securities were likewise not held in "any considerable amount" by citizens of the debtor States, for the "public debt was in the hands of the 'right people' at Philadelphia, New York and Boston,"[137] so that the exclusion of a citizen of his own State from the Amendment was not quite as irrational as Justice Bradley much later assumed out of hand.[138] Chief Justice Marshall was therefore on solid ground in concluding that the "motive" of the Amendment was "not to maintain the sovereignty of a State from the degradation supposed to attend a compulsory appearance before the tribunal of the nation," but to "inhibit" the described creditors' suits.[139] Preservation of suits between States, between States and the United States, and between a State and its own citizens, constituted recognition that constitutional purposes had to override sovereign immunity.[140] When the States later invoked the absence of consent to suit in order to bar suits by sister States, the Article III jurisdiction was sustained on the theory that the States had "agreed" to subject themselves to such suits.[141] No less had they "agreed" to suits by their own citizens, including suits under a separate category for the protection of rights "arising under this Constitution."

---

[136] Cohens v. Virginia, 6 Wheat. 264, 406 (1821).

[137] Supra, note 130.

[138] Hans v. Louisiana, 134 U.S. 1, 15 (1890).

[139] Cohens v. Virginia, 6 Wheat. 264, 406 (1821). See also, supra, note 130.

[140] After noting the improbability that State debts were held in considerable amounts by sister States and foreign states, Marshall said, "there was reason to retain the jurisdiction of the court in those cases, because it might be essential to the preservation of peace." 6 Wheat. at 407.

[141] United States v. Texas, 143 U.S. 621, 646 (1892); South Dakota v. North Carolina, 192 U.S. 286, 316 (1904). Cf. supra, note 84. Marshall had stated in Cohens v. Virginia that by adoption of the Constitution "the State has submitted to be sued." 6 Wheat. at 380.

In summary, the Eleventh Amendment, to borrow from Chief Justice Marshall,

> was intended for those cases, and for those only, in which some *demand* against a state is made by an individual, in the courts of the Union . . . A general interest might well be felt in leaving to a state the full power of consulting its convenience in the adjustment of its debts, or of any other claims upon it [for example, wartime confiscations], but no interest could be felt in ["stripping"] the government of the means of protecting, by the instrumentality of its courts, the constitution and laws from active violation.[142]

It is a perversion of the Eleventh Amendment, designed by the people to forestall taxation for restitution to Loyalists who had been inimical to the cause for which they bled or for the enrichment of speculators who had fattened on their misery, to read it so as to deprive the people of access to the courts which were to be the guardians of their constitutional rights.

FEDERAL IMMUNITY

Whatever the merits of a construction of the Eleventh Amendment that would expand State immunity, the Amendment is not at all addressed to federal immunity. Federal immunity is altogether without textual warrant; and but for Nicholas' remark that Congress cannot be sued for debts by the "speculators,"[143] it can invoke no recognition by the Framers or Ratifiers. To the contrary, Wilson declared that both State and nation were amenable to suit; and although Mason rejected suits against a State, he said that reciprocity required suits against the United States.[144] For the people were strongly attached to the States, not to the jealously-eyed newcomer, Congress, as the Tenth Amendment should confirm and as is reflected by the omission of all mention of the federal government from the Eleventh Amendment itself. It is food for thought that the people, who knew well enough how to saddle the federal govern-

[142] 6 Wheat. at 407 (emphasis supplied).
[143] 3 Elliot 476–477.
[144] Id. at 480, 527.

ment with additional limitations in the first Ten Amendments, were completely indifferent to a declaration in its favor in the Eleventh.

If judicial review is indeed built into the Constitution, in Hamilton's words, as a "bulwark of a limited Constitution against legislative encroachment" "equally requisite to guard the Constitution and the rights of individuals," it follows that Congress cannot bar the courts to complaints of Congressional injuries, whether by the "exceptions" power or by resort to sovereign immunity, which lacks even the textual basis of the "exceptions" power. The Hamilton-Madison-Marshall remarks, confined to creditors' suits against the States and outweighed by sentiment in other States, furnish flimsy historical warrant for a design to provide an escape hatch from judicial protection against Congressional "despotism." True it is that Marshall, a fervent advocate of judicial protection against Congressional oppression, yet found it possible later to say in *Cohens v. Virginia* that the United States is immune to suit; but his own reasoning undercuts his passing remark. To adapt what he said in the context of State immunity then before the Court,

> the great purpose for which jurisdiction over all cases arising under the constitution and laws of the United States is confided to the judicial department [does not leave the Court] at liberty to insert in this general grant an exception of those cases in which [the federal government] may be a party.[145]

In his own words, an "arising under" case "is cognizable in the courts of the Union, whoever may be the parties to that case."[146] Viewed against the terms of Article III and its history, the claim of federal immunity would deprive expressly granted jurisdiction of effect; it would thwart enforcement of constitutional guarantees on the basis of a doctrine of dubious historical merit, which a Court that had hardly emerged from the shadow of the Convention declared in *Chisholm v. Georgia* to be incompatible with the purposes of the Constitution and spirit of American democracy. That Court had no occasion to inquire into the effect of the Fifth Amendment, for no claim against the United States was presented; but it is open to us

[145] Cohens v. Virginia, 6 Wheat. at 382.
[146] Quoted supra, text accompanying note 116.

to examine the impact of the Amendment on the claim of federal immunity.

To dismiss that issue with the statement that "consent" to suit is a "privilege," its absence a mere "procedural infirmity," unprotected by the Fifth Amendment,[147] is to assume the very point in issue, to substitute labels for analysis.[148] The Founders again and again decried mere "parchment barriers"; they well knew that constitutional restrictions without judicial enforcement would be a "dead letter."[149] It was against this background that Justice Wilson adverted in *Chisholm v. Georgia* to the enduring value of Bracton's maxim, "It would be superfluous to make laws, unless those laws, when made, were to be enforced," and then inquired, what was the good of the "impairment of contracts" clause if a state would "be amenable, for such a violation of right, to no controlling power."[150] Attorney General Randolph, a former member of both the federal and Virginia conventions, asked in *Chisholm*, "What is to be done, if . . . the estate of a citizen shall be confiscated, and deposited in the treasury of a state . . . These evils cannot be corrected without a suit against a state."[151]

Precisely such conduct by Congress was barred by the Fifth Amendment declaration that private property shall not "be taken for public use without just compensation." One who seeks recovery for property taken without compensation only to be denied redress because Congress has not consented to suit has in practical effect been deprived of his protection against such takings.[152] Not for this

---

[147] Supra, text accompanying notes 3–6; and notes 5, 6.

[148] "Both liberty and property are specifically protected by the Fourteenth Amendment against any state deprivation which does not meet the standards of due process, and this protection is not to be avoided by the simple label a state chooses to fasten upon its conduct or its statute." Giaccio v. Pennsylvania, 382 U.S. 520, 540 (1965). What was said of State employed "labels" is no less applicable to the Court itself. " 'Constitutional rights would be of little value if they could be . . . indirectly denied' . . . or 'manipulated out of existence.' " Harmon v. Forsennius, 380 U.S. 520, 540 (1965).

[149] Supra, text accompanying note 66; Chapter 6, notes 190, 194.

[150] 2 Dallas at 464, 465.

[151] Id. at 422.

[152] The fact that there is a "standing consent" to such suits, 28 U.S.C. §1346 (7), §1491 (1), Hart & Wechsler 317, would not bar withdrawal of the consent. It "will not do to say that the argument is drawn from extremes. Constitutional provisions are based on the possibility of extremes." General Oil Co. v. Crain, 209 U.S. 211, 226–227 (1908). And the argument was made in a State context by Attorney General Randolph in 1793; supra, text accompanying note

did the Nation demand immediate adoption of the Bill of Rights. The first Ten Amendments responded to a demand to "guard against the abuse of power," a demand for "security against the apprehended encroachments of the general government."[153]

The farsighted men who sharply delimited federal powers by the Bill of Rights, and were told by Madison that the courts would be a "bulwark" of the rights thereby guaranteed, scarcely envisioned that Congress was left free to abort those rights by withholding consent to suit. Were sovereign immunity less shaky historically than Jaffe has shown it to be, were it more widely accepted than the contemporary records indicate, it would yet have to yield to the Fifth Amendment if the rights guaranteed thereby were to be protected. In this light "consent to suit" may not be regarded as a "privilege" to be accorded or withheld without regard to the Amendment, but rather as an ineluctable corollary of the right to just compensation and other Constitutional rights, an indefeasible *right to sue* the government for the invasion of those rights.[154]

Additional support for this analysis is furnished by the holdings

---

151. Then too, there remain inadequate remedies in the area for "persons adversely affected by unconstitutional actions of government." Barrett 75–76.

[153] See supra, Chapter 2, text accompanying note 51. A few examples will suffice. In the Virginia convention Mason explained insistence on a bill of rights, "We wish to withhold such powers as are not absolutely necessary in themselves, but are extremely dangerous." 3 Elliot 271. In the First Congress, Madison stated that a "considerable part" of the community are "anxious to secure those rights which they are apprehensive are endangered by the present constitution." 1 *Ann. Cong.* 733. Gerry referred to "a great body of our constituents [who] are opposed to the constitution as it now stands, who are apprehensive of the enormous powers of Government"; id. at 463; and he later added, "This declaration of rights . . . is intended to secure the people against mal-administration of the Government." Id. at 778.

[154] So held the Supreme Court in Von Hoffman v. City of Quincy, 4 Wall. 535, 552 (1867), quoted, supra, note 8. As Judge Madden stated in his Review of Davis, *Administrative Law Treatise: 1963 Pocket Parts*, 17 *Stanford L. Rev.* 165 (1964), "the fifth amendment provision that private property should not be taken for public use without just compensation to the owner, coupled with the Article III provision for federal court jurisdiction of suits to which the United States is a party, might well have been regarded as creating a *constitutional right* in an owner whose property had been taken by the government under an unfounded claim of right *to sue* the government for the value of the property taken" (emphasis added). Speaking of the Article III jurisdiction, Chief Justice Marshall said, "The Constitution gave to every person having a claim upon a State a *right* to submit his case to the court of the nation." Cohens v. Virginia, 6 Wheat. 264, 383 (1821) (emphasis added).

that contracts between persons are "impaired" "whenever the right to enforce them by legal process is taken away or materially lessened."[155] For purposes of the "impairment" clause a remedy is inseparable from a contract "right," and an early case held that this was no less true of a State's own contract. A test of contract impairment, it was there stated, is that "its value has by legislation been diminished."[156] The logic which impels the conclusion that deprival of a State remedy "impairs" Article I rights equally should compel the conclusion that deprival of a federal remedy diminishes Fifth Amendment rights.[157] The "impairment" cases were distinguished in *Lynch v. United States* on the ground that they involved contracts between individuals, although that is not altogether the fact, whereas "contracts between a Nation and an individual" "are only binding on the conscience of the sovereign and have no pretensions to compulsive force."[158] This is sovereign immunity dressed in different rhetoric; it does not explain, it merely rationalizes. Morality dictates that the government be the first to honor its obligations, by compulsion if need be.[159] The *Lynch* explanation that there is no

[155] E.g., Von Hoffman v. City of Quincy, supra, note 8; cf. Brinkerhof-Faris Trust Co. v. Hill, 281 U.S. 673, 682 (1930).

[156] Planters' Bank v. Sharp, 6 How. 301, 326, 327, 328 (1848). The time has come to substitute reality for fiction and to "hold that the Eleventh Amendment does not contemplate a suit based on State action contrary to the United States Constitution." Louisiana State Board of Education v. Baker, 339 F. 2d 911, 914 (5th Cir. 1964). In Sawyer v. Dollar, 190 F.2d 623, 645 (D.Col. Cir. 1951), where government officers, after defeat in an "individual wrongdoer's action" to recover property which they held, filed suit in a second court on behalf of the United States, alleging that the decision was not res judicata as to it, the first court then held them in contempt, and said that the rule of sovereign immunity "should not be permitted to thwart fundamental principles of greater importance." The case was then settled, and vacated as moot. 344 U.S. 806 (1952).

[157] Cf. General Oil Co. v. Crain, 209 U.S. 211, 226 (1908): "If a suit against these officers is precluded in the national courts by the Eleventh Amendment, and may be forbidden by a State to its courts . . . without power of review in this court, it must be evident that an easy way is open to prevent the enforcement of many provisions of the Constitution, and the Fourteenth Amendment, which is directed to State action, could be nullified as to much of its operation." The Fifth Amendment could equally be "nullified" were Congress permitted to invoke sovereign immunity when sued for unconstitutional infractions.

[158] Lynch v. United States, 292 U.S. 571, 580-581 (1934). For impairment by a State of its *own* contract, see supra, text accompanying note 101.

[159] Government action should exhibit even "more scrupulous regard to justice and a higher morality" than is required of individuals. Woodruff v. Trapnall, 10 How. 190, 207 (1850). "It would derogate from the King's honor," said Baron Atkyns, "to imagine, that what is equity against a common person, should not be equity against him." Pawlett v. Attorney General, Hardres 465, 469 (1667). In

right of enforcement against the government allows sovereign immunity to override express Fifth Amendment guarantees. That view is the more anomalous in that one *express* constitutional power after another—the power to tax, to regulate commerce, the war power—has been held subject to the Fifth Amendment,[160] whereas under the *Lynch* dictum, an immunity derived by implication, nowhere mentioned in the Constitution, is permitted to rise above the Amendment. It is not at all self-evident that immunity from suit is more vital to national functioning than the tax, commerce, and war powers; indeed the mass of "individual wrongdoer" suits against federal officers testifies to the contrary. We "cannot rightly prefer" a meaning, the Court has stated, "which will defeat rather than effectuate the constitutional purpose";[161] "no constitutional guarantee" "should suffer subordination or deletion."[162]

In sum, sovereign immunity was not solidly entrenched English doctrine in 1787; "consent to suit" issued "as of course." So far as it may be credited, its roots in Crown prerogative were alien to the democratic principles that animated the Founders, as was emphasized by Wilson; and its adoption requires reading an exception into the Article III text. The Hamilton-Madison-Marshall remarks invoked in its behalf were made in the context of creditors' claims, as to which there was substantial contrary opinion. Let those remarks be given hospitable scope and they yet fall short of blanket immunity because suits by sister States were recognized in the Ratification conventions, and suits by the United States were all but unchallenged. There was no suggestion that judicial enforcement of constitutional guarantees was to be subject to Congressional consent. *Chisholm v. Georgia*, decided by the Court not long after these conventions, rejected sovereign immunity even in creditors' suits; and in cutting down that decision, the Eleventh Amendment studiously avoided a comprehensive State immunity and made no men-

---

Chisholm v. Georgia, Justice Wilson rejected the notion that a state "ought not to do justice and fulfill engagements." 2 Dallas at 455–456. See also supra, text accompanying note 54. Fulfillment is required by "democratic notions of the moral responsibility of the State." Kennecott Copper Corp. v. Tax Comm., 327 U.S. 573, 581 (1946) (Frankfurter, J. dissenting).

[160] See Chapter 9, note 51.
[161] United States v. Classic, 313 U.S. 299, 316 (1941).
[162] Ullmann v. United States, 350 U.S. 422, 428 (1956).

tion whatever of federal immunity. Had federal immunity been framed in express terms in the Constitution, it must still be subject to the later Fifth Amendment, as are other express federal powers, lest the rights protected by the Amendment be defeated by a bar to judicial enforcement. The mass of "individual wrongdoer" suits for action in excess of constitutional authority testify that such action cannot be tolerated. Replacement of the fictional suit by a suit against the United States would not only recognize realities, it would give full effect to the Founders' intention to afford judicial protection against governmental invasions of constitutional guarantees.

CONCLUSION

Far from leaving "the record vague and conflicting as to judicial review,"[1] the Framers, I consider, made reasonably plain that such review was part of the Constitutional scheme. Throughout the Convention the availability of judicial review was repeatedly asserted by the leadership, while the voices of dissenters were few and feeble.[2] Balance, for example, Spaight's statement that judicial review was undesirable, which was not communicated to Convention or public, against the published analyses of Yates and Martin, opponents of adoption, affirming that the Constitution provided for judicial review. The conclusion they drew from the Constitutional text is entirely intelligible today. When the Article VI Supremacy Clause provision that laws made "pursuant to" this Constitution shall be "the Supreme Law of the Land" is read in conjunction with the Article III grant of jurisdiction to entertain "cases . . . arising under this Constitution," it seems plain that courts were authorized to decide that laws which were *not* pursuant to the Constitution were *not* the "Supreme Law of the Land." To the ordinary understanding, a claim that a federal "law" is not "pursuant" to the Constitution presents a question "arising" thereunder. The attempts to deprive those texts of their ordinary meaning seem to me altogether unconvincing, and they are repelled by the expressions of the

---

[1] Westin 34.

[2] On one point, at least, there can be little doubt. The Convention proceedings, as Professor Hart remarked, put "intractable difficulties" "in the way of any unqualified denial of the process of judicial review." Hart, Book Review 1471. Professor Charles Black suggested that the doctrine of judicial review "had decidedly better claims than its contradictory." Black, *The People and the Court* 26 (1960). My own study led me to concur in both statements.

Founders who pointed out that those provisions made judicial review available.

Certainly the unmistakable assurances made in the several Ratification conventions, in order to quiet the fear of Congressional excesses, that courts would declare Congressional transgressions of Constitutional limits to be void, go far to dispel lingering doubts. In those conventions, *no* dissentient voices were raised, either in condemnation of judicial review or in pleas for legislative supremacy. To the contrary, in the crucial and searching Virginia debate, Patrick Henry, leader of the opposition, added his praise of judicial review as an instrument to curb unconstitutional legislation. The First Congress, in which sat a goodly number of Framers and participants in the Ratification conventions, made abundantly clear in the debate on the President's "removal" power that the courts were empowered to set aside unconstitutional Congressional Acts; and it went on to provide by the Judiciary Act that State courts might set such Acts aside, subject to an appeal to the Supreme Court. It is not necessary to label those who entertain views to the contrary as "incompetents or outraged partisans deprived of reason."[3] Let the reader determine whether their criticisms of conventional reliance on the Founder's statements and Constitutional text are strained and insubstantial.

One who singles out for special emphasis any one factor in a complex situation may appear to some to be ridden by an *idée fixe*. Nevertheless, my own sifting of the historical materials left me with the conviction that fear of Congressional despotism bulked large in the thinking of the Founders. And if that be so, their assurances that judicial review would serve as an effective "check" gain added weight and counsel a hospitable construction of the Constitutional text.

Once the legitimacy of judicial review and its central role in the Constitutional scheme are granted, the power of Congress to make "exceptions" to the Supreme Court's appellate jurisdiction cannot properly be given unlimited scope. There is no indication whatever that the Founders conceived the "exceptions" clause as a check on the Court's Constitutional decisions. It seems hardly reasonable to conclude that they designed an effective curb on Congressional

[3] Westin 2.

CONCLUSION

excesses and simultaneously furnished Congress with an easy means of circumventing it. To attribute that dual intention to the Founders is to charge them with chasing their tails around a stump. So far as can be gathered from the intensive discussions of the "exceptions" clause in the Ratification conventions, its purpose was narrow and altogether unrelated to a power to deprive the Court of jurisdiction of Constitutional claims. And as is the case with other powers, the "exceptions" power cannot override the guarantees of the Fifth Amendment, which without judicial enforcement are mere "parchment" barriers.

Today the battleground has moved from the existence of the power to the criteria for its exercise.[4] Many would concede, said McCloskey, that a law which clearly violated the Constitution, such as a duty on state exports in violation of Article I, section 9, would surely be something which the judges should not enforce. The real question for them "would arise when the statute was not a *clear* violation of the Constitution,"[5] reflecting James Bradley Thayer's rule that courts may strike down a statute as unconstitutional only when the legislators "have made a very clear [mistake],—so clear that it is not open to rational question."[6] Thayer merely purported to restate the law as he found it after a survey of the cases. As late as 1873 the Court could say that

> It is an axiom in American jurisprudence that a statute is not to be pronounced void . . . unless the repugnancy to the constitution be clear, and the conclusion that it exists inevitable. Every doubt is to be resolved in support of the enactment.[7]

The tide is now running the other way, and thoughtful men look to the Court as "educator of public opinion,"[8] national conscience

[4] Wechsler, "Toward Neutral Principles of Constitutional Law," 73 *Harv. L. Rev.* 1 (1959); Miller & Howell, "The Myth of Neutrality in Constitutional Adjudication," 27 *U. Chi. L. Rev.* 661, 684 (1960); Pollak, "Constitutional Adjudication: Relative or Absolute Neutrality," 11 *Jour. Pub. Law* 48 (1962); Henkin, "Some Reflections on Current Constitutional Controversies," 109 *U. Pa. L. Rev.* 637 (1961); Bickel 49–65. For additional citations see Morgan, *Congress and the Constitution* 390–391, nn. 34 and 35 (1966).
[5] McCloskey, *The American Supreme Court* (1960).
[6] Thayer, "The Origin and Scope of the American Doctrine of Constitutional Law," 7 *Harv. L. Rev.* 129, 144 (1893).
[7] Pine Grove Township v. Talcott, 19 Wall. 666, 673 (1873).
[8] Bickel 26, 69.

for the American people,[9] "leader" in the resolution of tormenting social problems.[10] The "clear mistake" rule has its limitations in our dizzily changing world.[11] On the other hand, asked Judge Learned Hand, should the Court act as a "third legislative Chamber," going beyond the function of keeping "the States, Congress, and the President within their prescribed powers" to passing on the propriety of making choices within those boundaries?[12] That question poses too large an issue for casual comment at the tail of a historical study. It is, however, relevant to inquire into the historical footing of the "clear mistake" rule, for which Thayer marshaled some judicial worthies. Justice Iredell said in 1798 that because the authority to declare a legislative Act, federal or State, "void, is of a delicate and awful nature, the Court will never resort to that authority but in a clear and unjust case," "a very clear case," said Justice Chase.[13] In *McCulloch v. Maryland*, Marshall indicated that something like a "bold and plain usurpation, to which the constitution gave no countenance," was required to invoke the exercise of judicial annulment.[14] Unlike Jefferson and Madison, who were "strict construc-

[9] "Acting at least in part as a 'national conscience,' the Court should help articulate in broad principle the goals of American society." Miller & Howell, supra, note 4 at 689, 686, 962.

[10] Bickel considers the Court is "a leader of opinion, not a mere register of it," and that its "principles are required to gain assent, not necessarily to have it." Bickel 239, 251; and see id. at 26, 27. Professor Cox poses the issue in a balanced evaluation of the problem: "Should the Court play an active, creative role in shaping our destiny, equally with the executive and legislative branches?" Cox, *The Warren Court: Constitutional Decision as an Instrument of Reform* (1968).

It is chastening to recall one disastrous attempt at judicial "leadership," Dred Scott v. Sandford, 19 How. 393 (1857). "Chief Justice Taney and the four Southerners among the associate justices saw in this case an opportunity to settle the question of slavery in the territories by extending it legally to all United States territory." Morrison 593. See also Hockett, *Constitutional History of the United States (1826–1876)* 239 (1939); 1 Morison & Commager, *Growth of the American Republic* 651 (5th ed. 1962). Dred Scott, says Professor Bickel, "was more than a crime; it was a blunder." The *"casus belli"* of the Civil War, he states, "was the act repealing the Missouri Compromise (and all the more so, the Dred Scott decision)." Bickel 45, 68.

[11] Bickel 36–45.

[12] Quoted Bickel 46–48.

[13] Calder v. Bull, 3 Dallas 386, 399, 395 (1798). Earlier Iredell, rebutting Spaight's criticism of judicial review in August 1787 had stressed, "In all doubtful cases, to be sure, the Act ought to be supported: it should be unconstitutional beyond dispute before it is pronounced such." 2 McRee 175.

[14] 4 Wheat. 316, 402 (1819); Bickel 37. In Fletcher v. Peck, 6 Cranch 83, 123 (1810), Marshall said, "The question, whether a law be void for its repugnancy

tionists,"[15] Marshall was a "loose constructionist,"[16] well aware, as he said in *McCulloch* itself, that the Constitution was "to be adapted to various crises of human affairs,"[17] yet taking a narrowing view of the "scope of the Court's power to negative legislative and executive choices."[18] Were such views responsive to those of the Founders?

Although confidence in the legislature had been badly eroded by legislative excesses in the 1776–1787 period, not even the most ardent advocate of judicial review suggested that legislative policy-making be supplanted by judicial review. No one, so far as I could find, looked to the courts for "leadership" in resolving problems that the Congress had failed to solve. As the Fathers conceived it, the judicial role was to "negative" or set aside unauthorized action rather than to initiate policy. They looked to the courts to "check" legislative excesses, to "restrain" Congress within its Constitutional "limits," to prevent the "abuse" of power, to guard against the "usurpation" of power withheld. A few illustrations must suffice. The need, in Madison's words, was to give "every *defensive* authority to the other departments" in order to cope with the "danger" that the Legislature would "absorb all power into its vortex."[19] It was necessary, said

---

to the constitution, is, at all times, a question of much delicacy, which ought seldom, if ever, to be decided in the affirmative, in a doubtful case . . . The opposition between the constitution and the law should be such that the judge feels a clear and strong conviction of their incompatibility with each other." This attitude carried over, as is evidenced by the remark of Justice Bushrod Washington in 1827, "It is but a decent respect due to the wisdom, the integrity, and the patriotism of the legislative body by which any law is passed, to presume in favor of its validity until its violation of the Constitution is proved beyond all reasonable doubt." Ogden v. Saunders, 12 Wheat. 213, 270 (1827).

[15] Supra, Chapter 4, text accompanying notes 1–4. Madison said of the "sense in which the Constitution was accepted and ratified by the Natiton," "In that sense alone it is the legitimate Constitution. And if that be not the guide in expounding it, there can be no security for a consistent and stable government, more than for a faithful exercise of its powers." 9 Madison, *Writings* 191, 372. Writing in 1819 to Judge Roane, he said, "it was anticipated, I believe, by few, if any friends of the Constitution, that a rule of construction would be introduced as broad and pliant as what has occurred. And those who recollect, and still more, those who shared in what passed in the State conventions, through which the people ratified the Constitution, with respect to the extent of the powers vested in the Congress, cannot easily be persuaded that the avowal of such a rule would not have prevented its ratification." 3 Farrand 435.

[16] Bickel 36.

[17] 4 Wheat. at 407.

[18] Bickel 36.

[19] 2 Farrand 74 (emphasis added).

McKean, that "the legislature should be restrained,"[20] and Wilson added, "kept within its prescribed bounds."[21] The courts, said Ellsworth, were a "check" if Congress should "overleap their limits," "make a law which the Constitution does not authorize."[22] Judges, said Marshall in the Virginia convention, would declare void "a law not warranted by any of the powers enumerated."[23] Patrick Henry's reliance on State courts to act as "barriers against the encroachments and usurpations of Congress,"[24] echoing Hamilton's "barriers to the encroachments and oppressions of the representative body,"[25] reflected Wilson's reliance on the judiciary to "remonstrate" against "encroachments on the people."[26] "Controul over the legislature might have its inconveniences," said Gouverneur Morris, but "Encroachments of the popular branch of the Government ought to be guarded against."[27] In an atmosphere crackling with distrust of Congress, it is significant that advocates of judicial review cast the courts in the role of a nay-sayer, with never a hint that they were to serve as a "leader" of public opinion.

There is in fact plainer indication that the Founders did not contemplate judges in the "legislative," policy-making role. Gorham, arguing against judicial participation in the Council of Revision, stated, "As judges they are not presumed to possess any peculiar knowledge of mere policy of public measures."[28] Instead they were expected to add legal expertise to the Council, as may be gathered from Ellsworth's remark: "They will possess a systematic and accurate knowledge of the Laws, which the Executive can not be expected always to possess. The law of nations also will frequently come into question. Of this the judges alone will have competent information."[29] In 1787, when Jefferson welcomed the "check"

---

[20] McMaster & Stone 766.

[21] 2 Elliot 445.

[22] Id. at 196.

[23] 3 Elliot 553. Similar remarks were made by Adams, supra, Chapter 4, text accompanying note 30; by Nicholas, id. at note 118. See also summary, supra, Chapter 8, text accompanying notes 45–54.

[24] 3 Elliot 539. Madison said courts were to guard against Congressional "usurpations." *Federalist* No. 44 at 295.

[25] *Federalist* No. 78 at 503.

[26] 2 Farrand 73.

[27] Id. at 299.

[28] 2 Farrand 73.

[29] Id. at 74.

which a Bill of Rights "puts in the hands of the judiciary," he added, "This is a body which if rendered independent and kept strictly to their own department merits confidence for their learning and integrity."[30] The connotation of "kept strictly to their own department" stands forth in Dickinson's reluctant acceptance of judicial review because he saw no alternative, while cautioning that "The Justiciary of Aragon . . . became by degrees the lawgivers."[31] Were the judiciary "employed in remonstrating agst. popular measures of the Legislature," said Martin, "the confidence of the people . . . will soon be lost."[32] The Framers made tolerably clear that they were not casting judges as "law givers."

For this there is yet other evidence. When Mason argued for participation of judges in a Council of Revision that could "negative," that is, veto, a Congressional Act before it became effective, he recognized that judges already

> could declare an unconstitutional act void. But with regard to every law however unjust oppressive or pernicious which did *not plainly* come under this description, they would be under the necessity as Judges to give it a free course. He wished further use to be made of the Judges, of giving aid in *preventing every improper law.*[33]

In rejecting the Council, the Convention inferably dispensed with judicial aid "in preventing every improper law," and thereby indicated that far less did they look to judges to *initiate* proper laws, that is, to act as a policy-making "leader." That is likewise the implication of Wilson's statement:

> Laws may be unjust, may be unwise, may be dangerous, may be destructive; and yet not be so unconstitutional as to justify the judges in refusing to give them effect. Let them have a share in the Revisionary power [in order to "counteract"] the improper views of the Legislature.[34]

[30] 5 Jefferson, *Writings* 81.
[31] 2 Farrand 299.
[32] Id. at 77.
[33] Id. at 78 (emphasis added).
[34] Id. at 73.

Wilson did not equate unconstitutionality with laws that were merely "improper," or even "unjust, dangerous, destructive"; for him the *judicial* function was not to decide whether laws were "improper" but whether they fell outside Constitutional "limits."

It fell to a vigorous advocate of judicial review, Gerry, to explain that he opposed judicial participation in the Council because,

> It was quite foreign from the nature of ye. office to make them judges of the policy of public measures . . . It was making Statesmen of the Judges; and setting them up as guardians of the people. He relied, for his part on the Representatives of the people [Congress] as the guardians of their Rights and interests.[35]

Charles Pinckney also "opposed the interference of the Judges in the legislative business; it will involve them in parties."[36] In reply to Gerry's objections, Morris did not propose that judicial guardians must displace the legislative guardians but insisted rather on a judicial "check" on the legislative guardians,

> It has been said that Legislatures ought to be relied on as the proper Guardians of liberty. The answer was short and conclusive. Either bad laws will be pushed or not. On the latter supposition no check will be wanted. On the former a strong check will be necessary. And this is the proper supposition.[37]

Absent a "bad" law there was nothing to "check," and in this there was tacit acceptance of Gerry's view that it was the legislature that was the policy-maker. Gerry's view was a survival of the prevalent "partiality" for the legislative, noted by Wilson, because of the fact

[35] 1 Farrand 97–98; 2 Farrand 75. King's notes contain a comment, apparently by himself, "the judges must interpret the Laws they ought not to be legislators." 1 Farrand 108. See also Rutledge, supra, Chapter 3, text accompanying note 63.

Professor Benjamin F. Wright states, "Gerry is not alone in this, for the same point of view is expressed by almost every man who says anything at all on this subject in the Convention and in that ratification controversy." Wright, *The Growth of American Constitutional Law* 18 (1942). "The judiciary," he concludes, "would not be concerned with the policy, the reasonableness or arbitrariness, the wisdom of the legislation." Id. at 244; see also id. at 19–20.

Many months after my manuscript went to the publisher I found with mingled pleasure and regret that Professor Wright had anticipated my analysis and had remarked that the point "seems to me to be of great, and contemporary importance." Id. at 18. So far as my reading goes, his analysis has received no judicial notice, nor has it been noticed by contemporary proponents of judicial "leadership."

[36] 2 Farrand 298.
[37] Id. at 76.

that judges had been thrust upon the Colonists by the Crown whereas the Assemblies were chosen by themselves. Though resort was had to the courts to correct legislative excesses, the "fond predilection" for a wayward child was not shaken off overnight.[38] As Gouverneur Morris later said, it was the judicial function to reject a "direct violation of the Constitution,"[39] in which vibrate few overtones of "leadership." But to pass from words to deeds: rejection by the Framers of judicial participation in the Council after they had been warned that laws might be oppressive and destructive and still fall short of unconstitutionality, indicates to my mind that the Framers refused to allocate a larger role to the judges than annulment of laws that plainly went out of bounds. Even less than in the 1790's was the country, to borrow the words of McCloskey, "prepared to accept the judicial leadership of later years."[40]

[38] See supra, Chapter 2, note 109.

[39] 2 Farrand 299.

[40] McCloskey, Introduction 30. Yates, a vigorous *opponent* of the Constitution, alone declared that the courts "will not confine themselves to any fixed or established rules, but will determine, according to what appears to them, the reason and spirit of the construction." Corwin, *Court Over* 236–237. Wright remarks that "no one before him, either in the Convention, or in the ratification controversy, had entertained the idea that the courts would have so broad and inclusive a power of interpretation." Wright, supra, note 35 at 22.

Wright considers that in No. 78 of *The Federalist,* Hamilton took "the fears of Yates and made them an extraordinary effective substitute . . . against the excesses of popular majorities," not being "content with a brief statement that the courts would declare acts contrary to the Constitution void," and assigning to the judiciary "final authority, to interpret the meaning of the Constitution." Id. at 24–25. Hamilton was not alone in claiming the exclusive role of interpretation for the courts and in giving it "finality," see supra, Chapter 6, text accompanying notes 126–127, but nowhere were such claims linked to substituted judicial "leadership." If Professor Wright means that Hamilton adopted and went beyond Yates attribution to the courts of a free-wheeling power to determine the scope of judicial review "according to what appears to them the reason and spirit of the constitution," I am constrained to dissent. In No. 81 at 524, Hamilton expressly disclaimed the broad implications of Yates's words: "there is not a syllable" in the Constitution "which *directly* empowers the national courts to construe the laws according to the spirit of the Constitution . . . I admit, however . . . that wherever there is *evident* [emphasis added] opposition, the laws ought to give place to the Constitution." He dismissed the "supposed danger of judiciary encroachments on the legislative authority" as "in reality a phantom." Id. at 526.

Subsequently, Professor Wright emphasized that in No. 78 "the courts of justice are obligated not merely to hold void acts in clear conflict with the Constitution. They are also 'to declare all acts contrary to the manifest tenor of the Constitution void.'" Introduction, *The Federalist* 75 (Wright ed. 1961). As a lawyer reading a legal document, Hamilton may well have employed "tenor" in its technical legal sense, i.e., "implying the actual wording of a document," *Oxford English Dictionary,* Bouvier's *Law Dictionary.* Suppose that he employed its general connotation, the "general sense or meaning of a document," *Oxford*

Of course, the pricking out of limits itself may involve close questions which turn on value judgments; but there are indications that judicial intervention was envisaged only when encroachments were plain. Legislative authority, said Wilson, is placed under strict control so that the "effect of its *extravagencies* may be prevented."[41] The duty of the courts, Hamilton stated, was to "declare all acts contrary to the *manifest* tenor of the Constitution void."[42] Mason considered that laws would be declared unconstitutional only if they "plainly come under this description";[43] and as we have seen, Justice Iredell, who had been a powerful advocate of judicial review, before long echoed, "in a clear case."

Was adoption of the Bill of Rights designed to alter the judicial role? Despite earlier assurances that there was no need for a Bill of Rights because the powers of Congress were enumerated and therefore limited,[44] ratification left in its wake many who remained "apprehensive of the enormous powers of Government."[45] Dwelling on the necessity of conciliating such critics, Madison said that they "disliked [the Constitution] because it did not contain effectual provisions against *encroachments* on particular rights, and those safeguards which they have been *long accustomed* to have interposed

---

English Dictionary, it is qualified by "manifest," a term defined as "obvious to the understanding," "clearly evident," a synonym of "self-evident." Webster's *Collegiate Dictionary*. Read in the entire context of No. 78, "manifest tenor" reflects the "usual attitude of the proponents of the Constitution . . . that the courts would [merely] protect against usurpations of undelegated power by the Congress," Wright, supra, note 35 at 20, as I now propose to show. Hamilton repeatedly stressed in No. 78 that judicial tenure is "an excellent barrier to the encroachments and oppressions of the representative body," No. 78 at 503; that the courts were designed to keep the legislature "within the limits assigned to their authority," id. at 506; that it was the duty of the courts to "adhere" to the Constitution whenever "a particular statute contravenes" it, id. at 507. After his "manifest tenor" statement, id. at 505, there follow the statements that the courts are "the bulwarks of a limited Constitution against legislative encroachments," id. at 508, and the rebuttal of Yates's claim that courts "will not confine themselves to any fixed or established rules," supra—"To avoid an arbitrary discretion in the courts, it is indispensable that they should be bound down by strict rules and precedents," No. 78 at 510. It is not easy to read into No. 78 a broad charter for "judicial leadership" as opposed to judicial protection against legislative usurpations.

41 1 Wilson, *Works* 211.
42 *Federalist* No. 78 at 505.
43 Quoted more fully supra, text accompanying note 33.
44 Supra, Chapter 5, note 23; Chapter 2, note 53, par. 2.
45 Supra, Chapter 10, notes 153.

between them and the magistrate who exercises the sovereign power."[46] He thought it wise to reconcile them by "*expressly* declar-[ing] the great rights of mankind secured under this constitution."[47] Like the original purpose of the judiciary, that of the Amendments was to guard against "encroachments," in particular by the "legislative," which power Madison considered the "most likely to be abused"; and to this end safeguards were "expressed" to which men had "been long accustomed."[48] To Madison fell the task of explaining the proposed Amendments, and he faced up to the accommodation between a broad Congressional power and a protected right:

> It is true the powers of the General Government are circumscribed . . . but even if Government keeps within those limits, it has certain discretionary powers with respect to the means, which may admit of abuse to a certain extent . . . because in the constitution of the United States, there is a clause granting to Congress the power to make all laws which shall be necessary and proper for carrying into execution all the powers vested in the Government of the United States . . . Now, may not laws be considered necessary and proper by Congress, for it is for them to judge of the necessity and propriety to accomplish those special purposes which they may have in contemplation, which laws in themselves are neither necessary nor proper . . . I will state an instance, which I think in point, and proves that this might be the case. The General Government has a right to pass all laws which shall be necessary to collect its revenue; the means for enforcing the collection are within the direction of the Legislature: may not general warrants be considered necessary for this purpose . . . If there was reason for restraining the State Government from exercising this power, there is like reason for restraining the Federal Government.[49]

Given already "circumscribed powers," Madison felt constrained to explain the need for a Bill of Rights as a means for countering "abuse" of the "means" whereby those powers were exercised. It may be doubted whether he contemplated that the Court, under the

[46] 1 *Ann. Cong.* 450 (emphasis added).
[47] Id. at 449 (emphasis added).
[48] Id. at 454.
[49] Id. at 455–456.

guise of protecting the individual "rights" thus secured, may *expand* the "circumscribed powers" of the General Government. And it is not a little remarkable that he should have paused to affirm that Congress was itself the judge of its broad "necessary and proper" power and then to mark its limits by resort to the flagrant "general warrants" example that had set the Colonies aflame.[50] I would not suggest that Madison's illustration must be given restrictive effect, but rather that he was fencing off the powers of Congress from rights to which men had "been long accustomed" and which therefore presumably had familiar and more or less definite content, and that those rights were not regarded as amorphous charters under which courts rather than Congress would serve as formulator of policy.[51] The function of the courts, rather, remained the policing of boundaries, the earlier negative "check." In Madison's closing words, the courts were to

> be an impenetrable *bulwark* against every *assumption* of power in the legislative or executive . . . to *resist* every *encroachment* upon rights expressly stipulated for in the constitution by the declaration of rights.[52]

What I have said with respect to the scope of judicial review is uttered in no dogmatic spirit but rather to prompt further study of the judicial role in light of its historical origins. To those who would turn away from history and maintain that the choices are for us to make,[53] I would suggest that the most generous interpretation of the Constitutional text must still rely on history to buttress the legitimacy of judicial review, and that it would be arbitrary to invoke history for the establishment of the power and to repudiate it when the scope of the power comes in question.

[50] Morison 183.

[51] In Massachusetts, Stillman acknowledged that the Congressional powers were "great and extensive," but maintained that they are "defined and limited, and . . . sufficiently checked." 2 Elliot 166. Wilson said, the "bounds of the legislative power" are "distinctly marked," 1 Wilson, *Works* 462. In consequence of "the particular powers of government being defined," judges "will declare" laws "inconsistent with those powers" void. 2 Elliot 489.

[52] 1 *Ann. Cong.* 457 (emphasis added).

[53] See e.g., remarks of Charles Curtis in Cahn, "Supreme Court and Supreme Law" 68, 70 (symposium 1954); reviewed by Swisher, Book Review, 67 *Harv. L. Rev.* 1487 (1954). See also Bickel 16; Wofford, passim; Berger, "Executive Privilege v. Congressional Inquiry," 12 *U.C.L.A. L. Rev.* 1044, 1046–1048 (1965).

APPENDICES   BIBLIOGRAPHY

INDEX OF CASES   GENERAL INDEX

DR. BONHAM'S CASE

Whether or not Coke was "right," I attempted to show,[1] was of no moment if the Colonists *believed* that he was. Although adequate grounds for that belief are not essential to sustain the structure which the Colonists went on to build, I suggest—recognizing that current opinion is to the contrary—that there were such grounds. The case contra is well-stated by Professor Bailyn: "Coke had not meant, as Professor Thorne has made clear, 'that there were superior principles of right and justice which Acts of Parliament might not contravene.'" By "saying that courts might 'void' a legislative provision that violated the constitution he meant only that the Courts were to construe statutes so as to bring them into conformity with recognized legal principles."[2] In short, Coke stated "a familiar common law canon of statutory construction rather than a constitutional theory."[3]

It would be tedious yet again to restate the facts of *Bonham's Case,* so I shall assume that they are familiar to the interested reader,[4] and shall plunge into the issue whether Royal College of Physicians was empowered by statute to fine unlicensed as distinguished from incompetent physicians, and more particularly the *Fourth* reason adduced by Coke to deny the power. Since the College was to receive one-half of the fine, said Coke, they were judges in their own cause, a practice contrary to the common law:

> It appears in our books, that in many cases, the common law will controul Acts of Parliament, and sometimes adjudge them to be utterly void; for when an Act of Parliament is against common right and reason, or repugnant, or impossible to be performed, the common law will controul it, and adjudge such Act to be void.[5]

[1] Supra, Chapter 2, text accompanying note 91.
[2] Bailyn 177.
[3] Editorial note, 2 John Adams, *Legal Papers* 118.
[4] For citations to the literature, see Thorne, 54 *L.Q.R.* 543; Gough 32.
[5] 8 Co. Rep. 113b, 118a, 77 Eng. Rep. 646, 652 (1610).

APPENDIX A

Let it be assumed that Coke construed the statute as not conferring power to fine in the premises because that construction would render it void, in modern terms, a construction to avoid a "constitutional" doubt. To describe Coke's statement as a "canon of statutory construction" by no means, however, exhausts its implications; there remains his affirmation that a statute which makes a party judge in his own cause is contrary to "common right and reason" and therefore void. That statement is not deprived of "constitutional" significance because it was uttered in the process of "construction." We would, of course, be attributing to Coke an as yet undreamed of conceptualization were we to conclude that he deemed himself engaged in fashioning "constitutional theory." Nevertheless, attachment of the label "construction" to the germinal concept—an Act of Parliament which makes a party judge in his own case is against "reason" and void—does not make what we term the "constitutional" problem disappear. Strictly speaking, I venture to add, there was no problem of construction so far as the *Fourth* reason goes. The words, Professor Thorne justly states, "were straight forward";[6] they plainly made the College judge in its own case. Nor would I concur that in measuring these particular words Coke "was concerned only with the application of a statute."[7] This was not the case of excepting the single unjust application of words which *generally* were applicable justly;[8] instead this part of the Act was void in the only application it might have.

Professor Thorne has put the issue into sharper focus: did Coke mean that the statute was void *ab initio* or merely "ineffective"?

Coke seems to be asserting that there were acts of Parliament void *ab initio* since they conflicted with common right and reason, but if this interpretation of his words is adopted one has difficulty in explaining both the absence of the familiar passages in the *Doctor and Stu-*

[6] Thorne, Introduction 85.

[7] "Coke was concerned only with the application of a statute that led to results 'encounter common droit & reason,' not with the theory that 'an Act of Parliament may be void from its first creation' because of a conflict between its provisions and fundamental, natural, or 'higher' law." Thorne, Introduction 89.

[8] "St. Germain recognized [certain cases 'in which statutes had not been applied in particular cases because of the injustice that would ensue'] as . . . 'an exception of the law of god, or the law of reason, from the general rules of the law of man, when they by reason of their generalty would in any particular case iudge against the law of god, or the law of reason.'" Thorne, Introduction 77–78.

The law of nature and of reason, states Holdsworth, required "abstract justice to be done in each individual case, even at the cost of dispensing (if necessary) with the law of the State." Holdsworth, *Some Makers of English Law* 93 (1938). Even as an "exception" to avoid an unjust "application" the rationale differed little from the general rule which governed laws in conflict with the law of reason. See infra, text accompanying notes 15, 16, 20.

dent, and elsewhere, that might have been usefully cited, and his references in the same sentence to repugnant statutes and acts impossible to be performed. Such acts he likewise considered "void," but clearly that section of an act which is inconsistent with another portion of it need only be considered ineffective, nor need the authority and validity of a statute that is impossible to apply be impugned.

Coke, continues Professor Thorne,

> must be understood to say that "in many cases the common law will control acts of parliament"—that is, will restrict their words in order to reach sound results; and "sometimes it will adjudge them to be completely void"—that is, will reject them completely if modification cannot serve.[9]

One who would differ with Professor Thorne must tread warily for it is he who has made us aware of the shifting currents in the early centuries, of the need for assaying judicial treatment of statutes in the light of the developing and changing authority of Parliament.[10] Even so, his analysis stirs doubts in my mind which I set forth with deference, realizing that my own suggestions may excite still other doubts. In my view, there is little or no evidence that the distinction drawn between void *ab initio* and "ineffectiveness" played an appreciable role in Coke's time. Our own theorizing to one side, a 17th century lawyer and a later Colonial might well have understood, as in fact they did, Coke to mean *simpliciter* that no Act of Parliament could contravene "fundamental" law. But first a closer look at the suggested distinction.

To begin with Coke's noncitation of the "familiar passages" which "Coke had used . . . in Calvin's Case,"[11] that case, decided only one year before *Bonham,* in 1609, was argued by almost all the notables of the day and decided by the Lord Chancellor and twelve judges; Coke observed that it was "the longest and weightiest that ever was argued in any Court."[12] There Coke said that "the law of nature is part of the law of England"; he cited *Doctor and Student,* a work published in 1518, for the proposition that it is "immutable," and went on to say, "Parliament could not take away that protection which the law of nature

[9] Thorne, Introduction at 86–87, 88.
[10] See Thorne, Introduction; Thorne, "The Equity of a Statute and Heydon's Case," 31 *Ill. L. Rev.* 202 (1936). His analysis of Bonham in terms of statutory construction rather than constitutional theory has been widely accepted. See Bailyn 177; 2 John Adams, *Legal Papers* 118. For earlier views to the same effect see Gough 35.
[11] Thorne, Introduction 86 n. 184.
[12] 7 Co. Rep. 1a, 2a, 3b, 77 Eng. Rep. 377, 379, 380, 381 (1608).

giveth unto him, and therefore notwithstanding that statute, the King may protect and pardon him."[13] Here was judicial recognition that "notwithstanding statute" a subject could not be deprived of rights protected by the law of nature.

Why did not Coke cite *Doctor and Student* in *Bonham?* The argument from silence is inconclusive, and against it may be urged that having recently examined the point in a "great case" wherein Coke said that law on the point "appeareth plainly and plentifully in our books,"[14] he might well feel no need to repeat citations for a proposition so generally accepted. From Coke's citation of *Doctor and Student,* it may also be inferred that he employed "reason" as equivalent to the law of nature, for that Dialogue stated that "The law of nature . . . is also called the law of reason," and that English lawyers were accustomed to say that if anything "be prohibited by the law of nature" "it is against reason," precisely the words employed by Coke.[15] In the circumstances a 17th century lawyer might reasonably assume that Coke's "against common right and reason" was a familiar version of against the "law of nature."[16] From this follow important consequences.

Medieval law, said Gierke, "declared that every act of the Sovereign which broke the bounds drawn by Natural Law was formally null and void."[17] It is safe to conclude that so early English lawyers regarded

[13] 7 Co. Rep. 12b, 13b, 14a, 77 Eng. Rep. 391, 392–393. Gough 45 states that "we need not read more into Coke's opinion than a willingness . . . to adopt a strict interpretation of the law. We can find support for this in Bacon's speech in Calvin's behalf in the course of the same case." Because, said Bacon, "civil and national laws" "tend to abridge the law of nature, the law favoreth not them, but takes them strictly." With Bacon's argument in his ears, Coke significantly spoke, not in terms of strict construction, but of "protection" "notwithstanding that statute."

[14] 7 Co. Rep. 13b, 77 Eng. Rep. 392–393, quoted infra, note 31.

[15] Chapter 2 p. 4; Chapter 5, p. 9 (1607 ed.). The same identification of the law of nature with reason was made 41 years after *Bonham* by John Milton in his Defense of the People of England (1751). The "foundation of all laws," he said, is the "principle, which likewise all our lawyers recognize, that if any law or custom be contrary to the law of God or of nature, or in fine, to reason, it shall not be held a valid law." 7 J. Milton, *Works* 427 (1932).

[16] It has been said that "Coke does not use the concept of 'reason' the way the mediaevalist did . . . he does not equate 'fundamental' law with the orthodox sense of 'higher' or 'natural' law." "For Coke . . . law is a work of reason in this sense, that it is the nature of law to be reasonable; and the test of its reasonableness, he thinks, is its ability to withstand the test of time." Lewis, "Coke's Theory of 'Artificial Reason' as a Context for Modern Basic Legal Theory," 84 L.Q.R. 330, 338, 339 (1968). A Colonial who read his Calvin Case remarks might justly conclude that Coke considered that a statute had to yield to the law of nature or "reason" in its "orthodox sense."

[17] Quoted McIlwain 272.

it;[18] and J. W. Gough says we must extend: "belief in natural law from mediaeval lawyers to lawyers of the sixteenth and seventeenth centuries,"[19] as in fact Coke recorded in *Calvin's Case*. Gierke's version of medieval law was that of *Doctor and Student:*

> if any law made of men bind any person to any thing that is against the said laws [of reason] it is no law, but a corruption.[20]

On the assumption that Coke, who had cited *Doctor and Student* in 1608, meant by his 1610 reference to "against reason" to state the law of nature summarily, it is inferable that he meant the Act was void *ab initio,* if the refined distinction we now draw occurred to him at all.

Does his use of "void" to comprehend "repugnant or impossible to perform" compel the inference that he merely meant "ineffective"? Coke had lumped together Acts which were "against common right and reason, or repugnant, or impossible to be performed," and all three were indifferently cited as examples of Acts that courts would adjudge to be "utterly void." The word "impossible" was discussed in 1673 by Chief Justice Vaughan as if it were analogous to breaches of natural law, and so too of "contradictions,"[21] which being "impossible to obey" are "no

---

[18] "[N]o human law which was contrary to these universal laws [of "nature or reason"] was valid." 4 Holdsworth 280 (2d ed. 1937). "The distinction between law natural and law positive . . . was part of the mediaeval equipment. In fifteenth century England it was a commonplace of jurisprudence." Pickthorn 164. "The prevalent mediaeval conceptions about law and politics would certainly have led lawyers and statesmen to deny the proposition that there were no limits to the things which could be effected by a statute." 2 Holdsworth 444 (4th ed. 1936). Says Plucknett, *Concise History* 319, "Of course, there is no doubt that the mediaeval mind would never think of postulating the absolute sovereignty of Parliament or State."

[19] Gough 45. In 1604 the Speaker of the House of Commons included the law of nature and of reason in the laws "whereby the ark of this government hath ever been steered." Quoted McIlwain 63 n. 1. In his Defense of the People of England, Milton adverts to "that fundamental maxim in our law . . . by which nothing that is contrary to the laws of God and to reason can be accounted a law." Supra, note 15 at 445.

[20] Chapter 19, p. 34 (1607 ed.). See Holdsworth's comment, supra, note 18. Pickthorn 134, states that "Every judge of the later fifteenth century . . . however reluctant to 'annul any act made in parliament,' would have agreed with a legal writer [St. Germain, author of *Doctor & Student*] a generation later that 'against that law (of reason), prescription, statute nor custom may not prevail, and if any be brought against it, they be not prescriptions, statutes, nor customs, but things void and against justice.' " *Doctor and Student,* Chapter 2, p. 4 (1607 ed.).

[21] Thorne has called attention to early learning explaining "repugnancy" in terms of "contradiction":

> But what yf the wordes of an estatute be contraryent or repugnant, what is there then to be saide? And suerlie therein we ought to make our construccion

353

law."[22] Vaughan was far closer in time to Coke, and therefore perhaps in sympathetic understanding, than are we; consequently Coke's enumeration of "impossible" and "repugnant" makes it no more difficult to conclude that by "void" he meant null *ab initio* than to arrive at "ineffective." The fact that language suggesting "ineffective" was employed on one occasion[23] whereas reference to void was made on another does not without more prove that the judges had a firm distinction in mind. There is danger of reading back into Coke's mind a differentiation which is clear enough today but to which a 17th century lawyer may have been oblivious.[24] To give a meaning to words in the process of "construction" that was "quite contrary to the text" in order to make them agree with "reason" might well have appeared to that lawyer "nullification" in fact.

---

as nyghe as we can in such sorte that nothinge be repugnant; yet yf yt cannot be avoided but that a repugnancie nedes must be, then is the former sayenge good & the thynge repugnant void . . . and therefore are the former wordes good and the later, because they make a jarre by reason of the repugnancye, shalbe omytted.

Thorne ed. *Discourse Upon the Exposicion & Understandinge of Statutes* 132–133 (1942). Probably the *Discourse* was written ca. 1567. Thorne, Introduction 11. See also Thorne, 54 *L.Q.R.* 549.

[22] After explaining that murder signifies unlawful killing, stealing is unlawful taking, and that a royal "dispensation" (i.e., an authorization to kill as distinguished from a pardon after the fact) would make them "lawful" Chief Justice Vaughan said, "So the same thing, at the same time, would be both lawful and unlawful, which is impossible. For the same reason, a law making murther, stealing . . . lawful, would be a void law in itself. For a law which a man cannot obey, nor act according to it, is void, and no law; and it is impossible to obey contradictions, or act according to them." Thomas v. Sorrell, Vaughn 330, 336–337, 124 Eng. Rep. 1098, 1101–1102 (1673). Is it far-fetched to infer that for Vaughan "impossible," "contradiction" (repugnancy) were synonymous with "against . . . reason" or the law of nature?

[23] Thorne, Introduction 87 n. 186.

[24] What McIlwain 146–147 said is relevant: "Institutions that are now narrow and definite become as we trace them back indistinguishable from others that we have always considered equally definite. To ignore this fact is fatal. To read the same definiteness into the earlier institutions is not necessarily to put words into men's mouths which they never uttered, but it is to put ideas into their heads that they never dreamed of." Cf. Thorne, Introduction 28: "No judge or serjeant had regarded the non-extension of the act to ancient demesne as an 'exception out' of the statute, accomplished through an exercise of judicial discretion, for to say that ancient demesne was bound by an enactment but saved from its operation is a refinement (superfluous in a private law scheme) for which no contemporary support can be found."

We are cited to no use of the words void *ab initio* either by Coke or his predecessors (in the present context); what they said was that when positive law contravenes natural law it is "no law" and void. Vaughan, C. J. said as much about "impossible" and "contradictions." In 1712 counsel, seeking apparently to restrain application of the Bonham doctrine to a "very clear case," posited that it meant "void *ab initio*." Quoted infra, text accompanying note 89.

Would it ultimately matter to that lawyer that a crucial portion of a statute was held void from its creation rather than because the "repugnant" section must be "omitted"?[25] The difference matters to us because we attach importance to concepts, such as the separation of powers, which were yet unborn.[26] To the mind of a 17th century lawyer, we may conjecture, rejection of a statute as "ineffective," that is, rejection, to borrow Thorne's phrase, "completely if modification cannot serve," would as effectively negate it for practical purposes as would a flat declaration that it was "no law" and null, as indeed Chief Justice Vaughan was later to say about "impossible" and "contradiction." And so much may be deduced from the excoriation of Coke by his eminent contemporary Lord Ellsmere, for "reversing" the Parliament, for "trampling" on and "blowing away" an Act of Parliament "as vain and of no value."[27] If the distinction we draw today between "ineffective" and *void ab initio* lurks in Coke's phrase, Ellsmere's diatribes suggest that it was then of no practical consequence.

What Coke failed to state—"the theory that any act of the sovereign that broke the bounds of natural law was formally void"—was in Thorne's view "soon advanced" by Chief Justice Hobart.[28] Patently restating *Bonham*, though without mention of it,[29] Hobart said, "even an Act of Parliament, made against natural equity, as to make a man Judge in his own case, is void in itself, for jura naturae sunt immutabilia, and they are leges legum."[30] So far as I can discern, Hobart differs from *Bonham* only in substituting "natural equity" for "common right and reason" and inclusion of the Latin phrase, which Coke had earlier quoted in *Calvin's Case*, citing *Doctor and Student*[31] but which he omitted in *Bonham*. Coke's "against reason," *Doctor and Student* explains, was the familiar reference to the law of nature, including its immutability.

Let us now consider the matter in the perspective of "constitutional theory." Commenting on judicial disregard of statutes in the 14th century, Plucknett states that "constitutional questions" "were not asked." If it was desirable

[25] See infra, note 35, and supra, note 21.
[26] Gough 46, 48.
[27] See infra, text accompanying notes 71–74.
[28] Thorne, Introduction 91.
[29] Possibly Hobart did not cite Bonham's Case, says Plucknett, because his "natural caution warned him against too open a tribute to one whose fortunes had already begun to decline." Plucknett 50.
[30] Day v. Savadge, Hobart 85, 87, 80 Eng. Rep. 235, 237 (1614).
[31] 7 Co. Rep. 13b, 77 Eng. Rep. 392–393: "it is certainly true that *jura naturalis sunt immutabilia* . . . And herewith agreeth Bracton . . . Doctor and Student . . . And this appeareth plainly and plentifully in our books."

to neglect some words of a statute, then they were quietly set aside, but in doing so neither counsel nor judges enquired into the nature of statutes and legislation, the sovereignty of Parliament, the supremacy of the common law, the functions of the judicature, and all the other questions which the modern mind finds so absorbingly interesting.[32]

Thorne arrives at the same conclusion.[33] This "free and easy attitude" begins to disappear in the middle of the 14th century, we are told by Plucknett,[34] yet as we pass through the 15th century into the age of Coke, "the power of the courts to construe or misconstrue legislation was unimpaired, and indeed increased . . . Plowden gloried in the liberty which courts enjoyed in playing fast and loose with statutes."[35]

All this to be sure was in the domain of "private law," "public law" being still in the womb of the future. But as Thorne observes, "That rights would have been infringed or unjust results would have ensued upon the application of a statute had previously [before the 16th century] been sufficient to hold it ineffective."[36] It is therefore of no moment in weighing *Bonham* and its 17th century successors that they "had nothing to do with the great constitutional questions of the age," that "they were entirely private disputes."[37] For the important thing, the

[32] Plucknett, *Concise History* 314.
[33] Thorne, "The Equity of a Statute and Heydon's Case," 31 *Ill. L. Rev.* 202, 206–207 (1936). He refers in Thorne, Introduction 71, to "a group of decisions that permitted acts of Parliament phrased in unambiguous terms to be completely disregarded since they led to results that were considered improper. No principle of jurisprudence, or political theory that might serve as an explanation was offered."
[34] Plucknett, *Concise History* 315.
[35] Id. at 316–317. In Fulmerston v. Steward, 1 Plowden 101, 109, 75 Eng. Rep. 160, 171 (1554), Justice Bromley stated, "it is most reasonable to expound the words, which seem contrary to reason, according to good reason and equity. And so the Judges, who were our predecessors, have sometimes expounded the words quite contrary to the text, and sometimes have taken things by equity contrary to the text, in order to make them agree with reason and equity," thereby exhibiting a sense of continuity with the past. And in Partridge v. Strange & Croker, 1 Plowden 77, 88, 75 Eng. Rep. 123, 140 (1553), Chief Justice Montague said, "And that, which law and reason allows, shall be taken to be in force against the words of statutes." Holdsworth explains that "the rules of equity were really special applications of the overriding law of God or of reason or nature to the treatment by merely human law of particular cases." 4 Holdsworth 280 (2d ed. 1937).
In the 16th century, states Professor Thorne, "statutes were not yet thought to be exact formulas emanating from supreme parliamentary authority." Thorne, Introduction 56. The whereabouts of sovereignty at this point, i.e., the need to have a sovereign power somewhere, was but dimly understood by Parliament itself. Infra, text accompanying note 41.
[36] Thorne, Introduction 41.
[37] Gough 49. Speaking of the later distinction "between the laws of property

seed from which "constitutional theory" was to germinate, is that when a statute was deemed unjustly to prejudice one of the parties to a "private dispute," Coke, like his predecessors, was ready to shelter private rights from statutory infringement.

By importing our own preoccupations into analysis of *Bonham* we becloud the issue that faced Coke. Coke was not confronted by a dispute with Parliament but by an existing statute which invaded private rights, and the pivot of his thinking, I hazard, was protection of private rights rather than a challenge to Parliament. To Coke "the question of whether the legislature was sovereign or non-sovereign did not occur, and indeed did not arise."[38] Parliament itself was "slow to understand" the "whereabouts of the sovereign power of the state," and Holdsworth remarks that Coke "hardly saw" the necessity "to have a sovereign power somewhere."[39] There was no occasion to fashion a new theory to deal with a statute which infringed private rights; he could meet the case before him by resort to the old. For him "the political theory ["supremacy of the law"] which he found in his mediaeval law books," says Holdsworth, "was good enough for the seventeenth century."[40] Little or no reason exists to saddle him with our refined analysis, with a belief in the "separation of powers," "judicial review," concepts that were to be formulated in much later times.[41]

But if our "judicial review" conceptualization was unknown to him, "fundamental law" was not. Pickthorn refers to the "mediaeval idea of

---

and those of Government," Plucknett, 40 *Harv. L. Rev.* 52, observes that "To the middle ages they were all one." As a conscious bearer of the medieval tradition, albeit he was on the threshold of modern political thought, Coke, one may hazard, found no occasion to draw the distinction. Even in the early 17th century, it would appear, "every litigated issue of constitutional right was primarily a question of private law, was raised by private law procedure, and was settled not as an affair of state but as a matter of general law." Goebel, "Constitutional History and Constitutional Law," 38 *Colum. L. Rev.* 555, 559 (1938).

[38] Gough 48.

[39] 6 Holdsworth, *History* 83–84 (2d ed. 1937). "Definition of law in terms of sovereign will and the theories of its binding force entailed by them made a relatively late appearance in the history of jurisprudence—certainly long after Coke's time." Lewis, "Coke's Theory of 'Artificial Reason' as a Context for Modern Basic Legal Theory," 84 *L.Q.R.* 330 (1968).

[40] 6 Holdsworth, *History* 84 (2d ed. 1937). Plucknett, 40 *Harv. L. Rev.* 30–31, considers that Coke had "a presentiment of the coming conflict of Crown and Parliament" and "felt the necessity of curbing the arising arrogance of both" that his "solution" was "a fundamental law that limited Crown and Parliament indifferently" and that he found the means in the old books. This seems a retroactive speculative reading into Coke of a theory which succeeding generations distilled from his action, action that squared well enough with accepted doctrine and with what his predecessors had done.

[41] Gough 46, 48.

the supremacy of the law, an idea of which it is hardly too much to say that before the sixteenth century it was all there was in England in the way of a constitution, [and] that during the seventeenth century it was most of what there was."[42] Coke, we have seen, believed in the overriding force of the law of nature; and, with Bacon, he believed that Magna Charta was unalterable.[43] English subjects considered that their rights and liberties were protected against the King's prerogative; and in 1628 Coke himself joined in assertion of the claim.[44] But, argues Gough, "Fundamental laws (and Magna Charta itself) were valued for the protection they afforded against the arbitrary power of kings. There was no suggestion yet that the people's representatives themselves . . . might be tyrannical."[45] Because fundamental law was invoked against existing tyranny it does not follow that unanticipated Parliamentary tyranny would be deemed to rise above fundamental law. To the contrary, both the law of nature and Magna Charta were considered to override *all* conflicting law,[46] so that an appeal to fundamental law against a statute

[42] Pickthorn 55; cf. Coke, supra, text accompanying note 40.

[43] McIlwain 64. Coke spoke of Magna Charta as an "ancient, fundamental law." 2 Inst. 51. He also stated that if any statute be made contrary to "Magna Charta it shall be holden for none. And therefore if [a statute] . . . be contrary thereunto, it is repealed." 3 Inst. 111; see also 2 Inst. 37. If Magna Charta was alterable by subsequent Parliaments, the fact that it was confirmed by later Parliaments upwards of forty times must have impressed "on later generations the conviction that Magna Charta was no ordinary statute but of special permanence and importance." Gough 16.

[44] Gough 61, 62. After marshaling a group of instances in which Parliament had spoken for fundamental liberties and rights of Englishmen, William Prynne said that "The people of England have both ancient Fundamental Rights, Liberties, Franchises, Laws" which may not be altered, violated, or innovated upon any pretense. Prynne, *Historical and Legal Vindication of Fundamental Liberties, Rights and Laws of England* 24, 54 (1654). "In a conference between the houses in 1628, the Archbishop of Canterbury, on the part of the House of Lords, promised 'to maintain and support the fundamental Liberties of the Subject.' Sir Dudley Digges in reply expressed the gratification of the Commons at the willingness of the Lords 'to maintain and support the fundamental laws and liberties of England.'" McIlwain 82.
Protection of private rights was also the theme of a Massachusetts judge in 1657, infra, note 79. In 1765 Lieutenant Governor Thomas Hutchinson of Massachusetts relayed the claim to protection of "the peculiar rights of Englishmen," quoted by Plucknett, 40 *Harv. L. Rev.* 63. Jefferson identified the British constitution with "what is called British Rights." Quoted by Corwin, *Doctrine* 31; and in 1785 Madison praised English courts for maintaining "private rights against all corruptions of the two other departments." 2 Madison, *Writings* 166, 170. Blackstone himself enumerated the "absolute rights" of Englishmen, and stated that the law "will not authorize the least violation of" private property. 1 Bl. 127–129, 139.

[45] Gough 65.

[46] "No human law which was contrary to these universal laws was valid." 4 Holdsworth, *History* 280 (2d ed. 1937); see also supra, note 43.

was entirely logical.[47] "All through his life," said Holdsworth, Coke "had held firmly to the idea that the law must be supreme."[48] When *Bonham* came down, Parliament was struggling for power and as yet could lay no claim to a greater than royal prerogative. Indeed, the arguments used by the Parliamentary opposition to overweening royal claims "encouraged the belief that in the common law there might be found a store of principles which could be used to demonstrate the illegality of particular exercises of arbitrary power."[49] One like Coke, who could offer the Petition of Right (1628), which grew out of his bill for "the better securing of every freeman touching the propriety of his goods and liberty of his person,"[50] in the teeth of arrogant claims to absolute royal power would scarcely shrink from condemning an infringing arbitrary statute. There is no need to assume that Englishmen who were preparing to shed their blood in defense of their rights against royal arbitrariness were ready to suffer arbitrariness from their own elected Parliament. They turned to Parliament because they trusted it to protect their rights against royal despotism, not to substitute Parliamentary

[47] Gough 49, says of Bonham's Case and Day v. Savadge, "fundamental law was not mentioned in them. Coke and his colleagues certainly talked of fundamental law (though not in court), and there was indeed a connexion between this idea and their judicial decisions, but it was only a connexion, not an identity. Indeed there could not be an identity, for fundamental law in the seventeenth century was an ill-defined term which covered a wide field, and could not be identified with any one thing." Nonetheless, Gough states, "Fundamental law (and Magna Charta) were valued for the protection they afforded against the arbitrary power of kings." Gough 65. He also called attention to "other passages in Coke's writings which lend colour to the theory that he believed in the existence of a body of fundamental law." Gough 40. Compare Coke's a statute contrary to Magna Charta "shall be holden for none." Supra, note 43. And in his Postscript, Gough 222 adds that "In the seventeenth century it was constitutional limitations to absolute power—generally to the power of the monarchy, but sometime also to the power of Parliament—which above all were claimed as fundamental." Whether or not Coke and his fellows attached the label "fundamental" to the law of "nature" or "reason" or "natural equity," it was certainly so regarded in fact in the particular case. Coke left no doubt that Magna Charta was "fundamental," and presumably he felt no need to separate and ticket the various strands of "fundamental law."

[48] 5 Holdsworth, *History* 454 (2d ed. 1937). Said Holdsworth, "According to Coke's view the common law was the supreme law in the state, and the judges, unfettered and uncontrolled save by the law, were the sole exponents of this supreme law." Holdsworth, *Some Makers of English Law* 115 (1938). Coke "preserved the mediaeval idea of the supremacy of the law, at a time when political speculation was tending to assert the necessity of the supremacy of a sovereign person or body, which was above the law." Id. at 126. The "establishment of the rule of law" was "due mainly to Coke's insistence on the supremacy of the common law." Id. at 131–132.

[49] 5 Holdsworth, *History* 435 (2d ed. 1937).

[50] Id. at 451–452.

tyranny. As Jefferson was much later to say, after the battle against Parliament had been won and the issue was arbitrariness of State legislatures, "An elective despotism was not the government we fought for."[51]

Having no reason to suspect that Parliament would be arbitrary, Coke could assume there was no deliberate arbitrariness in the statute before him, the more so because Parliament "had always contended for the mediaeval idea of the supremacy of law."[52] Untroubled by "Parliamentary sovereignty," he could like his predecessors decide the "private dispute" without reference to "constitutional questions." If no predecessor had actually declared than an Act which contravened natural law is void,[53] many acts had been "quietly set aside" for the protection of private rights. Cokes "advance" was to make the tacit explicit, to identify a statute as an Act of Parliament, to articulate judicially what was generally accepted doctrine—a law contrary to "reason" is void—and to proceed from "quietly" setting a statute aside "upon dictates of legal reasonableness"[54] to explicit recognition that a statute contrary to "reason" is to be *declared* void, a process to which *we* assign the label "nullification."[55] That Coke believed himself supported by early precedents does not, in my view, militate against an appeal to "any fundamental, higher or normal law."[56] Plucknett considers that Coke "added" his "against common right and reason" phrase to one of his early citations wherein

51 Supra, Chapter 1, text accompanying note 8. So too, Iredell said, "We had not only been sickened and disgusted for years with the high and almost impious language from Great Britain, of the omnipotent power of the British Parliament, but had severely smarted under its effects. We . . . should have been guilty of . . . the grossest folly, if in the same moment when we spurned at the *insolent despotism* of Great Britain, we had established a *despotic power* among ourselves." 2 McRee 145–146.

52 6 Holdsworth, *History* 243 (2d ed. 1937); cf. supra, note 44. Holdsworth remarks on the "old alliance between Parliament and the common law, to which in the past both the common law and the Parliament had owed so much." 5 Holdsworth, *History* 444 (2d ed. 1937).

53 Plucknett, *Concise History* 319: "we do not find in mediaeval English cases any decisions which clearly hold that a statute is void because it contravenes some fundamental principle." Gough 145 says, "We shall look in vain for a case where statutes were actually nullified by a judicial decision." Compare Gough's reference to "judicial nullification or judicial review." Gough 48.

54 Thorne, "The Equity of a Statute and Heydon's Case," 31 *Ill. L. Rev.* 202, 206–207 (1936).

55 See Gough, supra, note 53. If I do not misunderstand him, Professor Thorne considers that Coke could have reached his result on the "theory that any act of the sovereign that broke the bounds of natural law was formally null and void," Thorne, Introduction 91, but that words which might have accomplished this, and which he employed in Calvin's Case, are missing from Bonham. Supra, text accompanying notes 9, 11–14.

56 Gough 40.

the court had merely "ignored" the statute,[57] thereby equating a "quiet" setting aside with application of the law of reason.[58] When this is viewed in light of his assertion in *Calvin's Case* that "parliament could not take away that protection which the law of nature giveth unto" a subject,[59] his later statement in the Institutes that a statute made contrary to Magna Charta "shall be holden for none," plus the fact that his "against common right and reason" may be fairly regarded as shorthand for Magna Charta and the law of nature, it is easier, for me at least, to regard these several expressions as part of a coherent political-legal theory rather than as unrelated and compartmentalized utterances.[60]

Let us now turn to other arguments advanced for the view that Coke was engaged in "construction," beginning with the juxtaposed *Fifth* reason that unless the two clauses of the statute were distinct, an unlicensed physician would be liable to a fine under the first clause and also to fine under the second, an absurdity, for no one should be punished twice for the same offense.[61] Thorne would read Coke's argument thus: "just as it would be absurd to interpret the statute" to permit two punishments for one offense, "so it would be absurd to interpret it to permit the college . . . to assess fines in which it shares." Brownlow's report of *Bonham* does indeed state that if the college shall be "judges and parties also" this "is absurd."[62] But in his own report Coke was at pains to confine his argument of absurdity to the *Fifth* reason, and we should not be too quick to join what he kept asunder. Moreover, points out Plucknett, Coke had "added" to the report of the ancient "Cessavit 42" the words "Because it would be against common right and

[57] In citing an ancient case wherein the court had merely "ignored" the statute, Coke, in Bonham's case, "added" the phrase "because it would be against common right and reason, the common law adjudges the said act of parliament as to that point void." Plucknett 36.

In 1320, Hugh le Despenser and his son complained to King Edward II of an award of banishment made by the assembled barons as being made "wrongfully against the laws and usages of the realm and against common right and reason." 1 *Howell State Trials* 23, 33.

[58] Under Coke's reasoning, "The newer decisions had not changed the law—they had merely developed or explained the truth to be found concealed in the oldest authorities." 5 Holdsworth, *History* 473 (2d ed. 1937).

[59] Supra, text accompanying note 13.

[60] For Magna Charta and the Institutes, see supra, note 43. Coke, Holdsworth stated, "preserved the mediaeval idea of the supremacy of the law"; for him "the common law was the supreme law in the state" of which the judges "were the sole exponents"; and he "had demonstrated from the bench that the common law was the greatest safeguard against arbitrary power." Holdsworth, *Some Makers of English Law* 126, 115, 116 (1938).

[61] 8 Co. Rep. 118b, 77 Eng. Rep. 654. The argument is more fully spelled out in Thorne, 54 *L.Q.R.* 547.

[62] Thorne, 54 *L.Q.R.* 548; 2 Brownlow 255, 265, 123 Eng. Rep. 928, 933.

reason, the common law adjudges the said act of parliament as to that point void," when according to Plucknett the judges had merely "ignored the statute."[63] Such pains are incompatible with an effort merely to restate "absurdity" in novel and involved fashion, but breathe rather of an intention to furnish an additional reason. With Plucknett I would say that "Coke has really added an explanation and a theory all his own,"[64] adding only that it was an explanation rooted in the past.

There remains the other portion of the *Fourth* reason phrase, "repugnant or impossible to be performed." Repugnancy, Thorne concluded from an early 17th century treatise on statutory construction, is "a contradiction; it occurs when a statute provides one thing, and then through oversight, perhaps, its opposite," in which case according to the treatise "are the former words good, and the latter, because they make a jarre by reason of the repugnancy, shall be omytted."[65] Faced by contradictory provisions a court would save something from the collision rather than let the statute fail; and Thorne justly infers that there "is no conscious constitutional problem raised here, but only one of statutory construction." He then suggests that "Though not technically a repugnancy, certainly a statute making a man judge in his own case and a self-contradictory statute might well be regarded as cognate," a conclusion to which the precedents might have led Coke.[66] But why dress that result in an additional formula when "impossibility and repugnancy" might have sufficed, particularly since he imposed his "reason" gloss upon "Cessavit 42," and because his resort to "against reason" suggests a reference to the law of nature which no Act could contravene.

Still another comment by Coke needs to be taken into account: in the Second Institute, Coke, explaining an old case wherein the statute provided that the assize should not be held except in the counties of the parties concerned, said that a writ was allowed out of the county so that a party in a particular case would not be both judge and party lest "he should have right and no remedy by law given for the wrong done unto him, which the law will not suffer, and therefore this case of ne-

---

[63] Plucknett, 40 *Harv. L. Rev.* 36; 8 Co. Rep. 118a, 77 Eng. Rep. 653.

[64] Plucknett, 40 *Harv. L. Rev.* 36. He said it was a "revival" of earlier "law." Id. at 45.

[65] Supra, note 21.

[66] Thorne, 54 *L.Q.R.* 549. Coke, it seems to me, was too fastidious to regard mere "contradiction" as "cognate" with the judge-party situation that was morally "wrong" and *mala in se*. One need only recall that he did not follow Bacon's suggestion of "strict interpretation" in Calvin's Case, supra, note 40, that he eschewed the argument of "absurdity" in the Fourth reason which he then made in the Fifth reason, supra, text accompanying notes 58–59, and that he preferred not to rest on an "exception by construction," an argument which his fellow Judge Daniel was ready to adopt, infra, text accompanying notes 65–66.

cessity is by construction excepted out of the statute."[67] "More pointed comment on Bonham's case," says Gough, is hardly needed."[68] Coke, however, plainly avoided putting decision in *Bonham* on "exception by construction." Justice Daniel was prepared to rule that a doctor was excepted from the Act,[69] but Coke recorded that he did not speak to this point because "he and Warburton and Daniel agreed, that this action was clearly maintainable for two other points."[70] *Bonham* cannot therefore be explained in terms of a statutory construction doctrine which Coke, by his own statement of the case, felt it unnecessary to consider.

Such doubts as to Coke's meaning as might have been entertained by a Colonial lawyer might well have been dispelled by the strictures of Lord Ellsmere. In his address at the installation of Sir Henry Montague as successor to Coke in the Chief Justiceship, Ellsmere called attention to the demotion of Montague's predecessor and admonished him to follow the practice of his own Grandfather "when he sate Chief Justice in the Common Pleas." *He* did not claim for the judges

> power to judge Statutes and Acts of Parliament to be void, if they conceived them to be against common right and reason [a shaft at Coke]; but left the King and the Parliament to judge what was common right and reason. I speak not of impossibilities or direct repugnancies.[71]

Thorne suggests that the qualifying adjective "direct" seems to indicate that to Ellsmere "Coke's theory was directed toward interpretation broadened to indirect repugnances, that is contradiction not on the statute's face."[72] But Ellsmere "left the King and Parliament to judge what was common right and reason" and carefully preserved legitimate "repugnancy" for the Judges; his separation of the two indicates concern with a differentiation of *functions* rather than a sharpening of definition to guide the judges. His qualifying "direct" repugnancy is of a piece with his counsel not to "strain the statute" or to make "an absurd or inept new construction"; exercise of a power "left to King and Parliament" was something else again; this was to overthrow rather than to misconstrue a statute.

[67] 2 Inst. 25.
[68] Gough 36.
[69] 8 Co. Rep. 116b, 77 Eng. Rep. 650.
[70] Ibid.; Thorne, 54 *L.Q.R.* 546. Thorne considers that exception from the statute by construction was not possible for several reasons, and therefore Coke turned from that path.
[71] Moore K. B. 826, 828, 72 Eng. Rep. 931, 932.
[72] Thorne, 54 *L.Q.R.* 552.

That it was overthrow or "reversal" of a Parliamentary Act which Ellsmere had in mind is suggested by another Ellsmere critique of Coke in the *Earl of Oxford's Case*:

It seemeth, by the Lord Coke's report, in *Dr. Bonham's Case*, that the statutes are not so sacred as that the equity of them may not be examined. For he saith, that in many cases the common law hath such a prerogative, as that it can control Acts of Parliament, and adjudge them void; as if they are against common right or reason, or repugnant or impossible to be performed . . . And yet our books are that the Acts and Statutes of Parliament ought to be reversed by Parliament (only), and not otherwise.

After thus reproaching Coke for "reversing" Parliament, Ellsmere turned to the "Judges" usurpation of the Chancellor's role, of "making construction of [statutes] according to equity . . . and enlarging them *pro bono publico* against the letter and intent of the makers."[73] Again a Colonial lawyer might conclude that Ellsmere had distinguished the "reversal" of Parliament by resort to "common right and reason" from the act of "construction." On still another occasion Ellsmere chided Coke for *Dr. Bonham's Case* because he "tramples upon the Act of Parliament . . . whereby that patent [to the College] was confirmed, blowing them both away as vain and of no value,"[74] once more indicating that he was taking aim at Coke's declaration that a statute was void because "against reason."

Let us move from Coke to Hobart, Chief Justice of Common Pleas, who, in *Day v. Savadge* (1614), stated that "even an Act of Parliament, made against natural equity, as to make a man Judge in his own case, in void in it self, for jura naturae sunt immutabilia, and they are leges legum."[75] Here the *Bonham* "against reason" stands alone, unaccompanied by "repugnancy"; and Hobart's reference to the immutable law of nature again suggests that Coke employed "reason" in the sense earlier explained by *Doctor and Student*. Plucknett observes, "Clearly, then

---

[73] 1 Ch. Rep. 1, 11–13, 21 Eng. Rep. 485, 487–488 (1615).

[74] Ellsmere, *Observations on the [Coke] Reports* 21, quoted in footnote to Bonham's Case, 8 Co. Rep. 118a, 77 Eng. Rep. 652. In the same footnote there is quoted, from Serjeant Hill's copy of the *Observations*, Hill's comment "on the strictures of Lord Ellsmere," the meat of which for present purposes is that Ellsmere condemned Coke's statement "that a statute against reason is void" notwithstanding Coke "is supported by many authorities." Like the Colonists, Hill singled out "against reason," leaving "construction" by the wayside.

[75] Hobart 85, 87, 80 Eng. Rep. 235, 237. See also Thorne, quoted supra, text accompanying note 28.

in Hobart's opinion, the truth of [the *Bonham*] doctrine was beyond dispute";[76] at least a Colonial lawyer might so conclude.

Additional confirmation for such a reading is furnished by a treatise published in 1627 by Sir Henry Finch, serjeant-at-law, wherein he states, "It is truly said, and all men must agree, that laws indeed repugnant to the law of reason are as well void as those that cross the law of nature."[77] This, says Gough, "indicates the atmosphere in which lawyers were educated in the seventeenth century,"[78] and to a Colonial lawyer who did not bring finely-honed modern scholarship to exegesis of Finch, the latter might well seem to justify acceptance of Coke's "against common right and reason" at face value.[79] Consider too Bishop Burnett's summary of the 1676 debate on the exclusion of the Duke of York from the Succession: "All lawyers had great regard to fundamental laws. And it was a great maxim among our lawyers, that even an act of parliament against Magna Charta was null of itself."[80]

Praise of Coke's statement came in 1702 from no less a figure than Chief Justice Holt:

what my Lord Coke says in Dr. Bonham's Case . . . is far from any extravagency, for it is a very reasonable and true saying, that if an Act of Parliament should ordain that the same person should be party

[76] Plucknett, 40 *Harv. L. Rev.* 49.
[77] Quoted by Gough 34.
[78] Ibid.
[79] A 1657 Massachusetts case, Giddings v. Browne, 2 Hutchinson, *Papers* 1 (Prince Soc. 1865), exhibits that understanding. A town-meeting had voted 100 pounds for the gift of a house to the minister; some of the minority refused to pay, were distrained, and brought suit. Justice Symonds held for them, saying that "fundamentall law" included "That every subject shall and may enjoy what he hath a civill right or title unto, soe as it cannot be taken from him." Id. at 2, 4. Arguing "from the greater to the lesse," Symonds said that "if noe kinge or parliament can justly enact and cause that one man's estate . . . may be taken from him and given to another without his owne consent, then surely the major part of a towne or other inferior powers cannot doe it." Id. at 5. He cited the 1627 Finch treatise: "laws positive doe lose their force and are noe lawes at all, which are directly contrary to . . . fundamentall [law]." Id. at 5. Justice Symonds was reversed by the General Court, which did not, however, reject his principles, but found instead that such a gift to the minister was customary and lawful, that the minority were heard at the town-meeting, that the vote was carried by a majority and was binding on the minority. Id. at 22–23.
Justice Symonds' view was partially embodied in the Massachusetts constitution of 1780: "no part of the property of any individual, can, with justice be taken from him, or applied to public uses without his own consent, or that of the representative body of the people . . . And whenever the public exigencies require, that the property of any individual should be appropriated to public uses, he shall receive a reasonable compensation therefor." First Part, Art. X.
[80] Quoted by Gough 148. But see 6 Holdsworth, *History* 186 n. 2 (2d ed. 1937).

and judge . . . it would be a void Act of Parliament; for it is impossible that one should be judge and party . . . and an Act of Parliament can do no wrong, though it may do several things that look pretty odd . . . but it cannot make one who lives under a government Judge and party. An Act of Parliament may not make adultery lawful, that is, it cannot make it lawful for A. to lie with the wife of B.[81]

Although Holt is torn between conflicting concepts, between respect for an Act of Parliament and the conviction that it cannot make wrong lawful,[82] he begins and ends with restatement of the *Bonham* doctrine, paying lip-service to the dawning theory of legislative supremacy.[83] Pre-Revolutionary America seized on that portion of Holt which seemed consonant with what had gone before and which responded to its own needs.

Residual doubts could to a considerable extent have been allayed by the fact that the *Bonham* principle had been repeated in the Viner, Bacon, and Comyns *Abridgments.*[84] "A lot of American law," said Professor Goebel, "came out of Bacon's and Viner's Abridgments."[85] Comyns

---

[81] City of London v. Wood, 12 Mod. 669, 687–688, 88 Eng. Rep. 1592, 1602.

[82] Plucknett, 40 *Harv. L. Rev.* 55.

[83] Compare Holt's earlier statement in The King v. Earl of Banbury, Skinner 517, 526, 90 Eng. Rep. 231, 236 (1693): "the Earl of Banbury can not be ousted of his dignity but by attainder, or Act of Parliament . . . but if there was any such law and custom of Parliament . . . yet when this comes incidently in question before them [the judges], they ought to adjudge and intermeddle with it, and they adjudge things of as high a nature every day; for they construe and expound Acts of Parliament, and adjudge them to be void."

Gough 11, asks whether the "true explanation of Holt's remarks [in the Wood case] may not be that the older view of the relations between the courts and acts of parliament, which Coke had expounded, had not yet been entirely superseded."

Sir Frederick Pollock stated that "The omnipotence of Parliament was not the orthodox theory of English law, if orthodox at all, even in Holt's time. It was first formally adopted, and then not without lip-service to natural law, in Blackstone's Commentaries . . . Down to the Revolution the common legal opinion was that statutes might be void as 'contrary to common right.'" Pollock, "A Plea for Historical Interpretation," 39 *L.Q.R.* 163, 165 (1923).

[84] 19 Viner's *Abridgment* 512–513, "Statutes" (E.6) (1744); 4 Bacon's *Abridgment* 649, "Statutes" (E) (1759); 4 Comyns' *Digest* 340, "Parliament" (R. 10) (1766).

[85] Ex Parte Clio, 54 *Colum. L. Rev.* 450, 455 (1954). James Otis cited Bonham's Case "from the extract of it in 19 Viner, Abridgment." 2 John Adams, *Legal Papers* 128 n. 73; id. at 144. A quick search of the Adams volume discloses frequent citations of Viner and Bacon by Otis, Adams, and Blower, id. at 163, 228, 269, 284, 341, 348, 350, 424, 427, 428, 430. The *Abridgments* remain respected authority in the English courts, cf. Martin v. Mackonochie [1878] L. R. 3 Q.B.D. 730, 749–750; Mayor of London v. Cox [1867] L. R. 2 E.&I. App. 239, 290.

was Chief Baron of the Court of Exchequer, and as late as 1851 his *Digest* was referred to by Lord Campbell as a book "of the highest authority."[86]

But for *Streater's Case* (1653), wherein John Streater sought habeas corpus from a commitment by order of the Long Parliament for publishing seditious pamphlets, I found no departure from the Coke doctrine prior to the American Revolution. In *Streater* Chief Justice Rolle said, "an inferior court cannot control what the Parliament does."[87] Whether this was because of Cromwell's mighty shadow or because the commitment was deemed to resemble Parliament's established power to protect itself from "insult"[88] deserves exploration. Plucknett, on the other hand, considers Blackstone's conclusion that no power can control Parliament "typical of the best judicial opinion,[89] expressed in such cases as *The Duchess of Hamilton's case*,[90] *Great Charte v. Kennington*,[91] *Mersey Docks Trustee v. Gibbs*."[92] *Mersey*, an 1866 decision, may be regarded as irrelevant to judicial opinion in 1765. In the *Hamilton* case, says Plucknett, counsel for plaintiff *argued* that Hobart stated, "an Act of Parliament may be void from its first creation, as an act against natural equity. But this must be a very clear case, and Judges will strain hard rather than interpret an Act void *ab initio*." Plucknett concludes that the "application of Coke's principle is now to be decently veiled under the cloak of 'interpretation.'"[93] Plaintiff's counsel was indeed primarily concerned with a genuine question of "interpretation," that is, the meaning of the statute,[94] rather than an acknowledged meaning, for example, judge and party in the same cause, that made the statute "void," and a reading that led to a judgment that the statute is void was not lightly to be made. If *Hamilton* has any relevance to *Bonham* it is robbed of impact by the fact that judgment went *against* plaintiff who made the argument. Remains *Kennington*; this, said Plucknett, was "a decisive step in the destruction" of the Cokean theory, when it held that "although it was a good principle that a man should not be judge and party, yet if

---

[86] Wadsworth v. The Queen of Spain, 17 Q.B. 171, 214, 117 Eng. Rep. 1246, 1262.

[87] 5 Howell *State Trials* 365, 386; and see Gough 130–132. Pickthorn 134, observes that "it would be easy to hang too much on the expressions of [judicial] timidity" at a moment of revolutionary crisis.

[88] Cf. Berger, "Constructive Contempt: A Post-Mortem," 9 *U. Chi. L. Rev.* 602, 611 (1942).

[89] Plucknett 40 *Harv. L. Rev.* 60.

[90] Thornby v. Fleetwood, 10 Mod. 114, 88 Eng. Rep. 651 (C.P. 1712).

[91] 2 Strange 1173, 93 Eng. Rep. 1107 (K.B. 1742).

[92] L.R.1 E.&I. App. 93 (1866).

[93] Plucknett 40 *Harv. L. Rev.* 58.

[94] 10 Mod. 115, 88 Eng. Rep. 653.

APPENDIX A

a situation arose in which the only competent judge assigned by statute was interested in the dispute, he could, and ought to proceed notwithstanding."[95] As *Grand Junction Canal Co. v. Dimes* explained, "a failure of justice was . . . considered to be a greater evil than a departure from that fundamental rule, that a party interested cannot be a Judge."[96] Neither court touched upon the setting aside of Parliamentary Acts; and the fact that an exception was grafted upon a particular rule which had furnished the occasion for articulation of the *Bonham* "against reason" in nowise diminished the doctrine.

It is idle to think that one can assign to words uttered by Coke 360 years ago a definitive meaning. The glosses put by present-day scholars upon his words seem to me, however, oversubtle and debatable, and therefore I elected at the risk of being "simplistic"—the eighth deadly sin—to construe "against reason" as did his immediate predecessor, *Doctor and Student,* that is, as prohibited by the law of nature. It did not require acceptance of such later concepts as the separation of powers to declare judicially what was generally accepted: a "positive" law which violated the law of nature was "no law." Although the words were uttered in deciding a "private dispute" and presumably were devoid of any implication of challenge to Parliament they readily lent themselves to direct defiance of Parliamentary arbitrariness. When the Colonists concluded that Parliament was intolerably abusing its power, they not unjustifiably took Coke's words, which meanwhile had been repeated respectfully for 150 years by Judges and in the *Abridgments,* at face value. That they went on to fashion from Coke's phrase "constitutional theory" which did not enter into his thinking does not rob it of the meaning the words bear on their face: an Act of Parliament "against common right and reason" is void. And if it is indeed "void," what more logical than that a court may say so.

95 Plucknett, 40 *Harv. L. Rev.* 58.
96 12 Beav. 63, 77, 50 Eng. Rep. 984, 989 (1849).

368

TREATIES "UNDER THE AUTHORITY

OF THE UNITED STATES"

The conjunction in the "Supremacy Clause" of *treaties* "under the authority of the United States" with *laws* made "in pursuance" of the Constitution, it has been noted, did not deprive the latter phrase of its "not-in-contravention" of the Constitution meaning as applied to laws. What, however, did the Founders intend by "under the authority of the United States" with respect to treaties? Did they mean by the contrasting terms to confer an *unlimited* treaty power, as R. H. Lee, an opponent of the Constitution, considered?[1]

Franklin's addition, it will be recalled, to the provision for a Congressional negative on State "acts contravening . . . the Articles of Union," of the phrase "or any treaties subsisting under the authority of the Union," was designed to preserve existing treaties.[2] The words "subsisting under the authority" do not necessarily imply that *future* treaties might be inconsistent with the new Articles of Union. When the Paterson or New Jersey Plan offered a "Supremacy Clause" in place of the Congressional negative of State laws, it echoed the Franklin composite: all acts of Congress "made by virtue and in pursuance of the powers hereby . . . vested in them, and all Treaties made and ratified under the authority of the United States shall be the supreme law."[3] Paterson was a small-state man who sought to diminish rather than enlarge federal powers;[4] and it may be doubted that he intended to confer an unlimited treaty power, whereby President and Senate could evade Constitutional restraints imposed by the "in pursuance" phrase and the Constitution on the entire Congress and the President in the enactment of "laws." It is more reasonable to regard "under the authority,"

[1] See infra, text accompanying note 27.
[2] Supra, Chapter 8, text accompanying notes 56–60; 1 Farrand 47.
[3] 1 Farrand 245.
[4] Bowen 104–107; van Doren 85–86.

APPENDIX B

which originated in Franklin's desire to preserve existing treaties, as a
fortuitous survival, attributable to an oversight that is likely to occur
in the drafting process when the original purpose of a phrase is overlooked, rather than a means whereby constitutional limitations on the
executive and legislative branches may be circumvented, the more so
because to the Founders the notion of unlimited power was anathema.[5]

A rejection of unlimited treaty power is confirmed by the several
convention records. And although remarks addressed to judicial review of treaty power are wanting, once unlimited power is rejected the
logic of judicial review extends to judicial enforcement of constitutional
limits on the treaty power. To prick out those limits, however, is a
formidable task which lies outside the scope of this study.[6]

A few preliminary remarks about the nature of the treaty power and
how it is exercised may facilitate consideration of several problems
mooted in the course of the convention debates. As Hamilton noticed,
the power, strictly speaking, is neither executive nor legislative, though
it partakes "more of the legislative than of the executive character," because, though an agreement between sovereigns, it is to have "the force
of law."[7] The power, John Jay stated, was committed "to a distinct body
from the legislature [and] the executive."[8] The fact that Article II,
section 2 (1) provides that the President "shall have power, by and with
the consent of the Senate, to make treaties," should not blind us to
the fact that the Senate has a real voice in the *making* of treaties. For
secrecy, dispatch, and the like, *negotiation* was entrusted to the President alone;[9] but Hamilton remarked on Senate participation "in the
office of making" treaties;[10] and in the Pennsylvania convention, Wilson
stated that "Senate and President possess the power of making treaties"
and that "Neither the President nor the Senate solely can complete a

[5] Supra, Chapter 2, text accompanying notes 22–40; cf. id. at notes 1–21. As
Melancton Smith said in the New York Ratification convention, "The idea that
Congress ought to have unlimited powers is entirely novel." 2 Elliot 333. "Unlimited power," said Bodman in the Massachusetts convention, was "dangerous."
2 Elliot 60. See Pierce, id. at 77; Stillman, id. at 166; cf. infra, text accompanying notes 90 and 107.
[6] Madison said in Virginia, "Would it be right to define all cases in which
Congress could exercise this authority? The definition might, and probably
would, be defective." 3 Elliot 514–515. While Vice-President, Jefferson, *A Manual
of Parliamentary Practice* (1801) §52, "Treaties," said, "To what subjects this
power extends, has not been defined in detail by the Constitution; nor are we
entirely agreed among ourselves" (hereafter cited, Jefferson, *Manual*). See infra,
text accompanying notes 49–53.
[7] *Federalist* No. 75 at 486.
[8] Id. No. 64 at 421; and see id. at 486.
[9] Id. at 419–420.
[10] Id. No. 75 at 486.

treaty,"[11] as Woodrow Wilson bitterly found when the Senate rejected his Versailles treaty.[12] It was because of the "operation of treaties as laws"[13] that participation was sought for the House.[14]

THE FEDERAL CONVENTION

The sparse remarks about the treaty power in the federal Convention shed little light on the scope of the power. At an early stage the power to make treaties was lodged in the Senate.[15] Mercer contended that the Executive rather than the Senate should have the treaty power, but that "Treaties would not be final so as to alter the law of the land, till ratified by legislative authority."[16] Mason, whose prior remark had prompted Mercer, commented that "he did not say that a Treaty would repeal a law,"[17] perhaps suggesting that the Mercer proviso was redundant. Subsequently Gouveneur Morris proposed an amendment to the Senate power provision: "No Treaty shall be binding on the United States which is not ratified by a law."[18] Madison "suggested the inconvenience of requiring a legal *ratification* of treaties of alliance for purposes of war etc."[19] Gorham pointed to other "disadvantages" if treaties of peace and all negotiations "are to be previously ratified—and if not previously, the Ministers would be at a loss how to proceed" without instructions.[20] The Morris motion was defeated,[21] and the entire matter was referred to a committee,[22] which reported back, "The President by and with the

---

[11] 2 Elliot 506–507. He also said, "The Senate can make no treaties; they can approve of none, unless the President of the United States lays it before them." Id. at 466.

[12] Morison 881–883.

[13] *Federalist* No. 75 at 486.

[14] See infra, text accompanying note 24.

[15] 2 Farrand 155, 169.

[16] Id. at 297.

[17] Ibid.

[18] 2 Farrand 383, 392.

[19] Id. at 382.

[20] Ibid.

[21] Id. at 383, 394. When President Washington pointed to this rejection of the Morris motion to support his view that "the assent of the House of Representatives is not necessary to the validity of a Treaty [Jay Treaty]," 3 Farrand 371, Madison commented in the House that the term "ratify . . . had a technical meaning different from the agency claimed by the House on the subject of Treaties." Id. at 374.

[22] 2 Farrand 383, 394. Madison "hinted for consideration, whether a distinction might not be made between different sorts of Treaties—Allowing the President and Senate to make Treaties eventual and of Alliance for limited terms —and requiring the concurrence of the whole legislature in other Treaties." Id. at 394.

consent of the Senate shall have power to make treaties."[23] Wilson later moved to add the House of Representatives: "As treaties he said are to have the operation of laws, they ought to have the sanction of laws also"; but his motion was voted down.[24]

In the main, this history shows an effort to obtain a share of the treaty power for the House, which failed largely on grounds of convenience,[25] and because the small States insisted on an equal voice in treaty-making through equal representation in the Senate.[26] Whether that failure indicates that treaties were meant to override federal "laws" is at least doubtful—*vide* Mason. The meager evidence from the Convention affords no affirmative evidence that the treaty power was to be unlimited, that President and Senate were empowered to accomplish by treaty what President and the entire Congress could not achieve by "laws." Perhaps an implication to the contrary may be found in Wilson's comparison to the "operation" and "sanction of laws," which *were* to be limited.

THE VIRGINIA RATIFICATION CONVENTION

No Unlimited Treaty Power

R. H. Lee, who opposed adoption of the Constitution in the pre-Ratification campaign, noted that Article VI does not provide that "treaties shall be made in pursuance of the Constitution," and concluded that the treaty power "is absolute . . . the Judges will be bound to allow full force to whatever . . . the President and Senate shall establish by treaty."[27] But that view was disclaimed in the Virginia Ratification convention by proponents of the Constitution.

Spearheading the opposition, Patrick Henry led an attack on an "unlimited" power that would invade both State and individual rights; he inveighed against a treaty that would be "paramount to the Constitution and laws of the States."[28] Proponent Francis Corbin remarked that "Fatal

[23] Id. at 495.
[24] Id. at 538.
[25] Secrecy was thought incompatible with participation of a large popular assembly. See the remarks of Butler and General Pinckney in the South Carolina convention, quoted infra note 84, of Wilson in the Pennsylvania convention, 2 Elliot 506, of Corbin in the Virginia convention, 3 Elliot 509. Jay added that the staggered 6-year term would permit Senators to familiarize themselves with national concerns, *Federalist* No. 64 at 418, a familiarity not then expected from the "fluctuating" House. Id. No. 75 at 488.
[26] Infra, text accompanying note 88. General Pinckney also explained in South Carolina that one reason for choosing the Senate was "the equality of power which each State has in it." 4 Elliot 281.
[27] Ford, *Pamphlets* 279, 306.
[28] 3 Elliot 500, 504, 512.

experience has proved that treaties would never be complied with, if their observance depended on the will of states; and the consequences would be constant war."[29] When the treaty power was analogized to that of the King, Henry cited an instance where the Queen stated that compliance with a Russian demand "exceeded her power . . . because it was contrary to the Constitution and laws."[30] Mason concurred that the King could make no "treaty contrary to the constitution of his country," that is, the body of "inviolable maxims."[31] Henry expanded this: "if the King of England attempted to take away the rights of individuals, the law would stand against him." That safeguard, he maintained, was lacking because no bill of rights was contained in the Constitution.[32]

No proponent of the Constitution laid claim to an unlimited treaty power. To the contrary, Madison made explicit at the outset of the discussion that "He did not say that his [the King's] power was unlimited,"[33] and toward the end he disclaimed that the treaty power "is absolute and unlimited."[34] Speaking for adoption, Nicholas stated that the treaty power of King and Congress "were on the same foundation, and that every possible security which existed in the one instance was to be found in the other."[35] Madison denied that "power is given to the President and Senate . . . to alienate any great, essential right."[36]

The idea that treaties can no more be inconsistent with the Constitution than "laws" was put forth by Nicholas. Under Article VI, he said, no treaty can be made

which shall be repugnant to the spirit of the Constitution, or inconsistent with the delegated powers[37] . . . It is sufficiently secured be-

[29] Id. at 510; to the same effect Nicholas and Madison, id. at 507, 515.
[30] Id. at 503.
[31] Id. at 508.
[32] Id. at 513, 504.
[33] Id. at 501.
[34] Id. at 514.
[35] Id. at 506.
[36] Id. at 514. And he closed by saying, "as far as the bills of rights in the states do not express anything foreign to the nature of such things and express fundamental principles essential to liberty, and those privileges which are declared necessary to free people, these rights are not encroached on by this grant." Id. at 516. Compare Iredell's statement in the North Carolina convention, "The power to make treaties can never be supposed to include a right to establish a foreign religion among ourselves." 4 Elliot 194.
In Ware v. Hylton, 3 Dallas 199, 278 (1796), Justice Iredell said, "Though Congress possibly might, as the price of peace," surrender rights of private persons by treaty, the "individual might have been entitled to compensation."
[37] Corwin says that in identifying "the authority of the United States" with the delegated power of the United States, Nicholas intended "to reduce the treaty-power from its rank as a substantive power to that of a mere ancillary

373

cause it only declares that, in pursuance of the powers given they shall be the supreme law of the land.[38]

To attempt by treaty that which would be inconsistent with the Constitution if done by "law" would be "repugnant to the spirit of the Constitution" and "inconsistent with the delegated powers." And in stating that treaties shall be the "supreme law" only "in pursuance of the powers given," Nicholas apparently assumed the applicability of the "in pursuance" concept to treaties, thereby confirming the inference that "under the authority" owed its employment to Franklin's early attempt to preserve "subsisting" treaties, and underlining the existence of limits on the treaty power.

Madison stated that

> The exercise of the power must be consistent with the object of the delegation . . . The object of treaties is the regulation of intercourse with foreign nations, and is external . . . Would it not be considered as a *dangerous principle* in the British government were the king to have the *same power in internal* regulations as he has in the external business of treaties.[39]

What Madison "had in mind," comments Corwin, "was merely the fact that through the treaty-making power the nation deals with other nations and secures American interests and rights abroad. He *certainly* did

---

power, a mode of exercising the *other* delegated powers of the United States. This is the extreme State-rights position with respect to the treaty power." Corwin, *National Supremacy* 73, 74, 121. Nicholas was defending the power against the incessant onslaught of Patrick Henry, and his statement, extreme or not, may be regarded as an informed evaluation of the most that the Virginia convention was prepared to accept.

Corwin divided the States-right view of the treaty power into three aspects, id. at 121–124, the most "objectionable" of which is the "notion that the States possess certain *inalienable rights, rights which therefore they have never alienated to any extent.*" Id. at 124. Among his criticisms of this view is that "it infers logically the doctrine of secession as a constitutional right of a State." Ibid. But that logic first surfaced in a later political struggle, the recoil from the Alien and Sedition Laws that found expression in the Virginia-Kentucky Resolutions, supra, Chapter 3, text accompanying notes 75–76, and note 76. Before long, Madison, author of the Virginia resolves, Morison 354, abandoned his "entire case for interposition." Corwin, *Doctrine* 55–56, 104. See also supra, Chapter 5, text accompanying notes 35–36. So far as the bearing of Nicholas' "extreme State-rights position" on judicial review is concerned, it must be borne in mind that he was a vigorous advocate of judicial review, supra, Chapter 5, text accompanying note 118, and that in this very portion of the treaty debate, his associates Corbin and Madison had emphasized that compliance with treaties could not be left dependent upon the "will of the states." Supra, text accompanying note 29, and note 29.

[38] 3 Elliot 507.
[39] Id. at 514–515 (emphasis added).

not have it in mind to deny that it must and could grant reciprocity at home."[40] Undeniably, "reciprocity" might require that "internal" effect be given to a treaty notwithstanding a *State* law to the contrary, for that lay at the heart of the whole treaty problem. But it does not follow that this "dangerous principle" could override limitations imposed on the *federal* departments by the Constitution itself. Madison's "internal" differentiation seems of a piece with his repeated assurances that treaties could not encroach on "fundamental principles essential to liberty," that the power was not "absolute and unlimited."[41]

Earlier, Corbin, also a proponent of adoption, had said that

A commercial treaty [as distinguished, for example, from a treaty of peace] must be submitted to the consideration of the parliament, because such treaties will render it necessary to alter some laws, add new clauses to some, and repeal others, If this be not done, the treaty is void, *quoad hoc.*[42]

Tieing this in to the touchy issue of a feared surrender by treaty of the right to navigate the Mississippi, Corbin stated that it could not be accomplished by a "common treaty," but, if at all, by a "commercial treaty" to which "the consent of the House of Representatives would be re-

[40] Corwin, *National Supremacy* 72.

[41] 3 Elliot 516. Corwin notes that Randolph and Madison rested their case "for the most part, upon general principle: to wit, that a grant of power comprises in its very terms a limitation upon that power, that all power is a trust to be exercised for the ends for which it is bestowed, that no power can be deemed to have been surrendered to be exercised to the derogation of fundamental rights." Corwin, *National Supremacy* 69–70. But Randolph, as Corwin's own quotation discloses, was somewhat less "general," pointing out that the "President and Senate [will] be restrained" by the "Constitution." Quoted in full infra, text accompanying note 59.

[42] 3 Elliot 511. A similar view was expressed in South Carolina by John Rutledge, a delegate to the federal Convention, "There was an obvious difference between treaties of peace and those of commerce, because commercial treaties frequently clashed with the laws upon that subject; so that it was necessary to be ratified in Parliament." 4 Elliot 267. Extenuating the nonparticipation of the House, Wilson told the Pennsylvania convention, "In England, if the king and his ministers find themselves, during their negotiations, to be embarrassed because an existing law is not repealed, or a new law not enacted, they give notice to the legislature of their situation, and inform them that it will be necessary, before the treaty can operate, that some law be repealed, or some be made. And will not the same thing take place here." 2 Elliot 506–507. A somewhat similar suggestion by Madison in the federal convention, supra, note 22, had not found acceptance.

In his *Manual,* Vice-President Jefferson stated (§52) that in England if treaties "touch the laws of the land they must be approved by the Parliament. Ware v. Hylton, 3 Dall. rep. 273 . . . An Act of Parliament was necessary to validate the American treaty of 1783." Both Madison and Jefferson put their faith in the meaning put upon the Constitution by the Ratification conventions. Supra, Chapter 4, text accompanying notes 1–4.

quisite,"[43] thereby assimilating such treaties to laws which must be "in pursuance" of the Constitution.

Although Corwin was critical of a narrow construction of the treaty power, he nonetheless concluded that the Virginia convention espoused the "idea that the treaty-power was substantially restricted by constitutional limitations in the strict sense of the term."[44]

The Virginia expressions are supplemented by the interpretation of the treaty power Jefferson set forth in his *Manual of Parliamentary Practice* when he was Vice-President.[45] The weight that his interpretation carries because of his prior diplomatic experience, his service as Secretary of State and his Executive post, however, possibly needs to be discounted because party strife was then mounting.[46] Nevertheless, his interpretation is in some respects plainly reminiscent of the earlier Virginia remarks, for example, his "the Constitution must have been intended to comprehend only those subjects which are usually regulated by treaty and cannot otherwise be regulated,"[47] is supported by the earlier quoted remarks of Nicholas, Madison, and Corbin.[48] When Jefferson said that the Constitution "must have meant to except out of this [treaty power] rights reserved to the States: for surely the President cannot do by treaty what the whole government is interdicted from doing any way,"[49] he could rest on Nicholas' disclaimer that a treaty could be "inconsistent with the delegated powers."[50] Nicholas' remark reflected frequent assurances in the Ratification conventions that Congress would have only enumerated powers,[51] assurances that speedily were trans-

[43] 3 Elliot 511.
[44] Corwin, *National Supremacy* 68.
[45] *Manual* §52, "Treaties," is quoted by Corwin, *National Supremacy* 122–123.
[46] Cf. Morison 353–354.
[47] *Manual* §52.
[48] For Nicholas, see supra, text accompanying note 35; for Madison, id. at notes 33, 36, 39; for Corbin, id. at 42, 43.
[49] *Manual* §52.
[50] Supra, text accompanying note 38.
[51] Supra, Chapter 2, text accompanying notes 25–32. In the Massachusetts convention, Stillman said that the powers granted to Congress "are defined and limited." 2 Elliot 166. The functions of the President were largely conceived in terms of faithful execution of the laws. See Berger, Executive Privilege and Congressional Inquiry, 12 *U.C.L.A. L. Rev.* 1044, 1071–1076 (1965). As Bowdoin explained to the Massachusetts convention, "The legislative powers of the President are precisely those of the governor of this state and those of New York—rather negative than positive powers, given with a view to secure the independence of the executive, and to preserve a uniformity in the laws which are committed to them to execute." 2 Elliot 128. See also, Berger, id. at 1073 n. 153. In the first American constitutions, "Executive power was . . . left entirely

lated into the express Tenth Amendment reservation of undelegated powers to the States. Jefferson's reference to the "whole government," I suggest, may largely be taken to mean the Congress, upon whom the vast bulk of federal powers was conferred. Express "interdictions" on the power of Congress were set out in Article I, section 9, and the subsequent interdictions incorporated in the Bill of Rights were, so the Ratifying conventions had been assured, implicit in the Constitution as originally submitted.[52]

Lastly, said Jefferson, there was an intention "to except those subjects of legislation in which [the Constitution] gave a participation to the House of Representatives. This last is denied by some on the ground that it would leave very little matter for the treaty power to work on. The less the better, say others."[53] So far, at least, as treaties are to have an *internal* effect, there is some confirmation, first, in Madison's statement that it would be "a dangerous principle . . . were the king to have the same power in internal regulations as he has in the external business of treaties."[54] Second, Mason said in the federal Convention that a treaty "would not repeal a law" of the land;[55] and third, Wilson, Rutledge, and Corbin, as above noted, stated that where a treaty re-

---

to legislative definition and was cut off from all resources of the common law and the annals of English royalty." Corwin, *Twilight of the Supreme Court* 123–124 (1934). And see Berger, supra at 1074 n. 157.

[52] In South Carolina General Pinckney explained that "we had no bill of rights inserted in our constitution; for, as we might perhaps have omitted the enumeration of some of our rights, it might thereafter be said we had delegated to the general government a power to take away such of our rights as we had not enumerated; but by delegating express powers, we certainly reserve to ourselves every right not mentioned in the Constitution." 4 Elliot 316. In the Massachusetts convention, Parsons "demonstrated the impracticability of forming a bill, in the national constitution, for securing individual rights, and showed the inutility of the measure, from the ideas that no power was given to Congress to infringe on any one of the natural rights of the people by this Constitution; and should they attempt it without constitutional authority, the act would be a nullity, and could not be enforced." 2 Elliot 161–162. Wilson said in Pennsylvania that "in a government of enumerated powers . . . a bill of rights would not only be unnecessary, but in my humble judgment highly imprudent" for the reason that "If we attempt an enumeration, everything that is not enumerated is presumed to be given." Id. at 436 and 453. So too, Chief Justice McKean there said that a bill of rights "is unnecessary; for the powers of Congress, being derived from the people in the mode pointed out by this Constitution, and being there enumerated and *positively* granted, can be no other than what this positive grant conveys." Id. at 540. Cf. Randolph in Virginia, 3 Elliot 464; compare Madison, supra, text accompanying note 36, and note 36.

[53] *Manual* §52.

[54] 3 Elliot 514–515.

[55] 2 Farrand 297.

quires repeal of an existing law or enactment of a new one, Congress, like the Parliament, would be called on.[56]

Commenting on Jefferson's construction, Corwin states,

> admit all this, and what field is left within which the treaty-power may operate independently? "The less the better," remarks Jefferson. But this flippancy hardly meets the situation. For if there is no field in which the treaty-power can operate independently, what becomes of the constitutional designation of treaties as part of "the law of the land?" It would seem to be wholly gratuitous.[57]

"Wholly gratuitous" is overstated. Jefferson scarcely meant to deprive treaty makers of power to enter into an alliance or a compact terminating hostilities, notwithstanding Congress has no power to do so. Nor should his remark too quickly be read to foreclose a compact governing "external" affairs with which Congress has no power to deal, for his disciple, Madison, had told the Virginia convention that the King's power over "external" affairs was broader than over "internal" matters. Such power, where it was withheld from Congress, was thus impliedly claimed for treaty makers. Indeed, Jefferson himself recognized that the treaty power extended to "those subjects which are usually regulated by treaty and cannot otherwise be regulated."

To the extent that there is implicit in Corwin's criticism a plea for a treaty power "independent" of Constitutional restrictions upon the "whole government," his alternative is even less inviting than the consequences he draws from Jefferson's interpretation. The Founders did not fashion a government of limited powers, they did not circumscribe Congress by an enumeration of powers supplemented by express prohibitions, they did not make the Executive little more than an instrument for execution of the laws[58] all of which was designed to protect the individual and the powers reserved to the States—only to turn over to the President and Senate an unbounded power to set all these limitations at naught. In the words of Governor Randolph in the Virginia convention,

> Will not the President and the Senate be restrained? Being creatures of the Constitution, can they destroy it? . . . When the Constitution marks out the powers to be exercised by particular departments, I say no innovation can take place.[59]

[56] Supra, text accompanying note 42, and note 42; cf. infra, text accompanying notes 66–67.

[57] Corwin, *National Supremacy* 123–124.

[58] See supra, notes 51 and 52.

[59] 3 Elliot 504.

It can hardly be doubted that Jefferson expressed Virginia's "idea that the treaty power was substantially restricted by constitutional limitations."[60]

Corwin levels several other objections at the Jeffersonian interpretation. First, the "historical" difficulty, that is, the "power has repeatedly passed beyond the domain otherwise assigned to the National Government and has often invaded the field of power otherwise left with the States."[61] If Jefferson correctly divined the intention of the Founders— the assurances of Madison, Nicholas, and Corbin sustain him—then it is *that history* which must serve as a guide to interpretation.[62] Power withheld and thereafter usurped is not legitimated by repeated exercise. Though one may assume the impracticality of turning back the clock, "legal history still has its claims";[63] and we have the example of *Erie Ry. Co. v. Tompkins,* where the Court declared that the course it had pursued over a period of 100 years was "unconstitutional."[64] Second, Corwin poses the "logical" difficulty: "For if the legislative power of the States [presumably in areas reserved to the States by the Constitution] opposes a barrier to the treaty power, then, certainly, the legislative powers of Congress must also oppose a barrier, since even by State-

---

[60] The quoted words are from Corwin, *National Supremacy* 68. History seems to me aptly summarized in Reid v. Covert, 354 U.S. 1, 16–17, (1957):

> There is nothing in this language [the "Supremacy Clause"] which intimates that treaties and laws enacted pursuant to them do not have to comply with the provisions of the Constitution. Nor is there anything in the debates which accompanied the drafting and ratification of the Constitution which even suggested such a result. These debates as well as the history that surround the adoption of the treaty provision in Article VI make it clear that the reason treaties was not limited to those in "pursuance" of the Constitution was so that agreements made by the United States under the Articles of Confederation, including the important peace treaties which concluded the Revolutionary War, would remain in effect. It would be manifestly contrary to the objectives of those who created the Constitution, as well as those who were responsible for the Bill of Rights—let alone alien to our entire constitutional history and tradition—to construe Article VI as permitting the United States to exercise power under an international agreement without observing constitutional prohibitions . . . The prohibitions of the Constitution were designed to apply to all branches of the National Government and they cannot be nullified by the Executive or by the Executive and Senate combined.

The Ratification debates, it may be added, include express disclaimers of unlimited treaty power or power that could invade fundamental rights.

[61] Corwin, *National Supremacy* 123.

[62] See Berger, "Executive Privilege vs. Congressional Inquiry," 12 *U.C.L.A. L. Rev.* 1044, 1046–1048 (1965).

[63] Federal Power Comm. v. Natural Gas Pipe Line Co., 315 U.S. 575, 609 (1942).

[64] 304 U.S. 64, 79–80 (1938).

right principles, Congress, within the range of its power, is constitutionally the equal of the State legislatures," as "was seen by Jefferson."[65] The analogy is imperfect because the Constitution reserves to the States powers not granted to the United States, whereas it does not purport to exempt the granted area of Congressional "law" making from the national treaty power. In fact, however, the legislative power of Congress with respect to treaties, was set above that of the States in several convention utterances. To the argument that the treaty would be "paramount to the Constitution itself, and the laws of Congress," Corbin replied that "It is as clear as that two and two make four, that the treaties made are to be binding on the states only."[66] His view had the concurrence of Madison, who stated, "I think the argument of the gentleman who restrained the supremacy of these to the laws of the particular states, and not to Congress, is rational."[67] It was the States who had repeatedly violated the treaty of peace to the mortification of the pre-Constitution Congress,[68] and it was the States, therefore, who had to be bound by treaties. Displacement of federal laws, it was stated in one way or another, would require the assent of Congress.[69]

Enforcement of "Limits"

Thus far the discussion has been concerned with the *definition* of the "supreme law." *Enforcement* is the subject of the second branch of the "supremacy clause," which makes the "supreme law" binding on the "judges in every State." In *Rutgers v. Waddington*, it will be recalled, Hamilton besought a New York court to invalidate a State law which was in conflict with the treaty of peace.[70] John Jay, when Secretary for Foreign Affairs, proposed in 1786 that the States should authorize State courts to enforce treaties, any State law to the contrary notwithstanding. His proposal was adopted by the Congress and transmitted to the several States.[71] The necessity of requiring State compliance was emphasized in the Virginia debate by Corbin and by Madison,[72] and it is scarcely debateable that the "binding" clause contemplated that State courts were

[65] Corwin, *National Supremacy* 123.
[66] Elliot 510. See also supra, text accompanying notes 17, 42.
[67] 3 Elliot 514. The accommodation of treaties to federal "laws" was stressed in several conventions. Supra, note 42.
[68] See supra, text accompanying note 29.
[69] Supra, text accompanying notes 42–43.
[70] Supra, Chapter 2, text accompanying notes 158–161.
[71] Corwin, *National Supremacy* 27; Haines 100.
[72] Supra, text accompanying note 29; see also supra, Chapter 8, note 75; Chapter 10, note 119.

to enforce treaties notwithstanding State laws to the contrary.[73] Once it is concluded that the treaty power exercised "under the authority of the United States" is not "absolute and unlimited" but is "restrained" by the Constitution, the reasoning which earlier impelled the conclusion that State courts were expected to ascertain whether "laws" were consistent with the Constitution warrants similar scrutiny of "treaties."[74] Judicial review, we have seen, was in large part designed to keep the Congress in check, and it needs to be demonstrated that there was an intention by confiding the treaty power to a part of Congress and the President to exempt treaties from such checks.

Such an exemption, it may be thought, can be drawn from several remarks in the Virginia convention during the debate on the treaty power. For example, Madison stated that the President would be impeached if he summoned only a few States;[75] Nicholas said that the President would be "checked" by the electors;[76] Corbin adverted to resistance by the people of Kentucky should the Mississippi be dismembered.[77] Checks on the Congress other than the judicial had been mooted and some were adopted, but these, it was earlier noted, were cumulative rather than designed to be exclusive of judicial review.[78] Bearing in mind that "treaties" as well as "laws" were to bind State judges, that the treaty power was not "absolute and unlimited" but was "restrained" by the Constitution, one may conclude that all the considerations which were adduced for judicial review of "laws" are little less persuasive with respect to review of treaties. Given Nicholas' and Marshall's ringing affirmations of judicial review as a curb on Congressional excesses, one

[73] In Pennsylvania Wilson cited Article III to show that "the judges of the United States will be enabled to carry it [a treaty] into effect, let the legislatures of the different states do what they may." 2 Elliot 490. Having stressed that judges would declare that laws "inconsistent with those powers vested by this instrument in Congress" would be "null and void," id. at 489, Wilson (if it be assumed that, in Madison's words, the treaty power was not "absolute and unlimited") would have looked to courts to deal with out-of-bounds treaties in the same fashion. See also Parson's statement, quoted supra, note 52; and infra, text accompanying notes 71, 99; and see supra, Chapter 3, note 37, and text accompanying notes 208–210; Chapter 4, id. at note 92; Chapter 6, note 163.

Chase, J. remarked in Ware v. Hylton, 3 Dall. 199, 235 (1796), "A treaty cannot be the supreme law of the land . . . if any act of a state legislature can stand in the way."

[74] Supra, Chapter 8, text accompanying notes 83–88, 151–244.

[75] 3 Elliot 500; cf. id. at 516.

[76] Id. at 502. But Nicholas, it needs to be remembered, was an unequivocal advocate of judicial review. Supra, Chapter 4, text accompanying note 118; cf. Chapter 6, text accompanying notes 128–135.

[77] 3 Elliot 511.

[78] Supra, Chapter 2, text accompanying notes 58–64.

can only speculate why no reference was made in the hurly-burly of the Virginia debate to judicial review of treaties. But something more than allusions to "impeachment" and "elections,"[79] I suggest, should be required before judicial enforcement of constitutional limitations is excluded from the treaty area.

May the remarks in the Virginia debate be taken to indicate a general sentiment in the several States? In its entirety, that debate reflects the widespread fear of uncurbed Congressional power and the belief in the availability of judicial review as a check.[80] Then too, the interpretation placed by Vice-President Jefferson on the treaty power closely parallels the Virginia view. It is therefore not unreasonable to regard the Virginia treaty debate as no less symptomatic of the general sentiment respecting treaties than on the issue of judicial review in general, at least in the absence of evidence to the contrary. Such "evidence" was collected by Corwin, and he considers that to "some, the term 'authority of the United States' seemed to signify merely 'commission of the United States.' "[81]

THE NORTH CAROLINA RATIFICATION CONVENTION

Let us begin with Corwin's examples from the North Carolina convention. William Porter, an opponent of the Constitution, asked respecting the "power vested in the Senate and President to make treaties . . . Which among us can call them to account."[82] His remark, as well as others to be considered, must be viewed in the setting, which reflected two concerns: (1) a slender group of Senators, two-thirds of a quorum, possibly seven or eight, could bind the Nation; in M'Dowall's words, it "was extremely dangerous" to give "such extensive powers to so few men in the Senate";[83] and (2) absence of popular participation through the medium of the House of Representatives.[84] Both concerns go not to the

[79] Cf. supra, Chapter 4, text accompanying notes 118, 123.

[80] In the debate on the Constitution and proposed amendments in Massachusetts, Adams said, "I have observed the sentiments of gentlemen on the subject as far as Virginia, and I have found that the objections were similar in the newspapers, and in some of the conventions." 2 Elliot 124. See also, supra, Chapter 4, text accompanying notes 21–25.

[81] Corwin, *National Supremacy* 66.

[82] Ibid; 4 Elliot 115; M'Dowall, id. at 119.

[83] Id. at 124, 115, 119. To the same effect Lowndes in South Carolina, 4 Elliot 265. Governor Johnston replied that no Senator would be absent when the interests of his State "are most immediately affected." 4 Elliot 116. See also Spaight, id. at 124.

[84] Id. at 119; cf. supra, notes 25 and 26. Davie stated that the small States had insisted on Senatorial participation to ensure "an equal voice in formation of treaties." 4 Elliot 120. In South Carolina, Butler, who "was one of a committee that drew up" the clause vesting the treaty power in the President with advice and

existence of unlimited power to act but rather to an objectionable allocation of power.[85]

True, Spaight had countered the "call them to account" query with the question "what mode there was of calling the *present* Congress to account."[86] But the Articles of Confederation made no provision for a national judiciary with the powers conferred by Article III. So far as Spaight's remark may have overtones of unaccountability for action inconsistent with the Constitution, it is outweighed by the flat statement of his fellow proponent Steele that "If the Congress makes laws inconsistent with the Constitution, independent judges will not uphold them."[87]

Corwin also quotes Davie, who advocated adoption in the convention:

As the Senate represents the sovereignty of the States, whatever might affect the States in their political capacity, ought to be left to them [the Senate]. This is the certain means of preventing a consolidation of the States. How extremely absurd it is to call that disposition of power a consolidation of the State, which must to all eternity prevent it! I have only to add the principle upon which the General Convention went—that the power of making treaties could nowhere be so safely lodged as in the President and Senate; and the extreme jealousy subsisting between some of the States would not admit of it elsewhere.[88]

"Here, then," comments Corwin, "there is no hint of any sort of constitutional limits."[89] If, as Corwin himself states, "the notion of unlimited

---

consent of the Senate, said that the House was excluded because "negotiation always required the greatest secrecy, which could not be expected in a large body." 4 Elliot 263. General Pinckney, who was also a member of the federal convention, listed secrecy as one of several impelling factors in the choice of the Senate, among them "the equality of power which each State has in it." Id. at 281.

[85] 4 Elliot 124. Impeachment, replied Spencer, was an unsatisfactory remedy because, having advised the President to make the treaty, the Senate could hardly be expected to punish him for making it. Id. at 125. The point was recognized by Wilson in Pennsylvania, 2 Elliot 477; see also Pendleton in South Carolina, 4 Elliot 263. Iredell, like Spaight, an advocate of the Constitution, emphasized that impeachment for mistakes of judgment would render government service hazardous, and must be confined to acceptance of a bribe or action based on corrupt motives, id. at 126–127. It would not lie against legislators, id. at 127; and see Spaight, id. at 124. Thus a leading proponent did not regard impeachment as an adequate means of dealing with treaty excesses, which could nonetheless be honestly motivated.

[86] Id. at 115 (emphasis added).

[87] Id. at 71; quoted supra, Chapter 4, text accompanying note 70.

[88] Corwin, *National Supremacy* 67; 4 Elliot 123–124.

[89] Corwin, *National Supremacy* 67.

power, wherever lodged, has always been to the American mind an uncongenial one,"[90] we should look rather for a hint of "unlimited" power. Further, there was no occasion for a hint of limited power because Davie was not addressing himself to the scope of the power or correction of transgressions, but was explaining that the House was excluded because it was the Senate that was looked to for protection of State interests. As he pointed out, the small States had insisted on Senate participation in treaty-making to ensure "an equal voice in formation of treaties."[91] The House, said Iredell, would have been "able to prevent the Senate from protecting the sovereignty of the states."[92]

Iredell, Davie's colleague in *Bayard v. Singleton,* a notable early precedent for judicial review, and a leader in the struggle for adoption was, as has been noted, a forceful advocate of judicial review.[93] It is against this background that his remarks during the treaty debate should be read:

> The only real security of liberty, in any country, is the jealousy and circumspection of the people themselves. Let them be watchful over their rulers. Should they find a combination against their liberties, and *all other methods appear insufficient* to preserve them, they have, thank God, an *ultimate remedy* . . . amendments can be made in a regular method, in a mode prescribed by the Constitution itself.[94]

For Iredell, recourse to an "ultimate remedy," he had made unmistakably clear, was a last resort if judicial review proved inadequate.[95] In the upshot, the North Carolina convention rejected the Constitution, notwithstanding its adoption by ten States, chiefly because of fear of centralized tyranny.[96] Men like Steele, who strove to reassure the convention that the judiciary would reject an Act that was inconsistent with

90 Id. at 5; see also supra, note 5.

91 See supra, note 84.

92 4 Elliot 133.

93 Supra, Chapter 3, text accompanying note 168; Chapter 2, id. at notes 142–144.

94 4 Elliot 130 (emphasis added). Bodman said in Massachusetts that people ought to be "jealous of their rulers," "one of the greatest securities of the people." 2 Elliot 60.

95 Supra, Chapter 4, text accompanying notes 80–84. Sitting as Justice in the landmark treaty-power case, Ware v. Hylton, 3 Dall. 199, 265 (1796), Iredell said,

> The power of the legislatures [contrary to Parliament] is limited; . . . of the legislature of the Union, [limited] by the Constitution. Beyond these limitations, I have no doubt, their acts are void, because they are not warranted by the authority given.

96 Supra, Chapter 4, text accompanying notes 68–78.

the Constitution, though passed by both branches of Congress with the President's approval, hardly contemplated that one branch and the President by resort to the treaty power could accomplish unchecked what was denied to both branches and the President.

THE SOUTH CAROLINA RATIFICATION CONVENTION

Just as he found "no hint of any sort of constitutional limit" in the several remarks in the North Carolina convention, so Corwin concludes that "the same deduction is to be made from the utterances of General Pinckney and Rutledge in the South Carolina legislature which called the ratifying convention in that State, asserting the supremacy of all treaties entered into over all State laws whatsoever."[97] Rawlin Lowndes had argued for opponents of the Constitution that it was not "consistent with prudence to vest so much power in the hands of so small a body of men [two-thirds of a quorum or ten], who might supersede every existing law in the Union."[98] This may be regarded as a plea for broader popular participation through the medium of the House rather than an assertion that the power, wherever lodged, was without constitutional limits. Lowndes in fact considered that treaties, as will appear, were limited by the law of the land. In replying to Lowndes, General Pinckney, a proponent of adoption, stated that the treaty of peace "had been adjudged, in a variety of cases, to be part of the law of the land . . . If this had not been the case, and any individual state possessed a right to disregard a treaty made by Congress, no nation would have entered into a treaty with us."[99] That a treaty must override a State law had been the lesson of recent experience; and the Supremacy Clause in no small part owed its origin to this inexorable fact.[100] But Pinckney's remark does not tell us whether all treaties must have this effect or only those which were not inconsistent with the Constitution. Lowndes's challenge to the wisdom of vesting "so much power" in the hands of so few men did not call upon Pinckney to dwell on the limits of a not easily definable power.[101] Under the circumstances it is not to be wondered that Pinckney gave "no hint of any sort of constitutional limit."

[97] Corwin, *National Supremacy* 67.
[98] 4 Elliot 65.
[99] Id. at 266. This was also the view of Jefferson, quoted Corwin, *National Supremacy* 30. In fact some States did disregard the treaty, cf. Rutgers v. Waddington (N.Y.), supra, Chapter 2, text accompanying notes 158–161; and John Jay called on the States to authorize their courts to enforce the treaty notwithstanding State laws to the contrary. Supra, Chapter 6, note 163; Maclaine, supra, Chapter 4, text accompanying note 92.
[100] See, e.g., supra, text accompanying note 29; and note 99.
[101] See supra, note 6.

That hint was supplied by others. Lowndes stated that "no treaty concluded contrary to the laws of the land could be valid," later amplifying that the King was without power to ratify a treaty "which trenched on the fundamental laws of the country."[102] Not a voice was raised on behalf of an unlimited treaty power; to the contrary, the Speaker, John J. Pringle, stated that although the treaties the President and Senate made

> may have the force of laws when made, they have not therefore, legislative power. It would be *dangerous,* indeed, to *trust them* with the power of making laws to affect the rights of individuals.[103]

Pringle spoke for a limited treaty power; and he added that treaties "exceeding the powers with which the makers were intrusted ought to be annulled."[104]

Corwin cites John Rutledge to indicate reliance upon a "political check.[105] Rutledge, here more fully quoted, said that a treaty would

> be a sufficient bar to any local or municipal laws. What sort of power is that which leaves individuals full power to reject or approve? Suppose a treaty was unexpectedly concluded between two nations at war; could individual subjects ravage and plunder under letters of marque and reprisal? Certainly not . . . Pray what solid reasons could be urged to support gentlemen's fears that our new governors would unite to promote measures injurious to their native land.[106]

In this there is neither hint of unlimited treaty power nor reliance upon a political check for enforcement of constitutional limits. Instead, Rutledge responded to a recurrent fear of granting power because it might be abused, a fear which threads its way through the several Ratification debates.[107] But as Edward Rutledge remarked, "The very idea of power included a possibility of doing harm," and arguments resting on abuse of

[102] 4 Elliot 271, 308.
[103] Id. at 269.
[104] Id. at 270. But cf. General Pinckney, id. at 277: treaty of peace made by king binding, though censured by House of Commons. But see note 42, supra.
[105] Corwin, *National Supremacy* 68.
[106] 4 Elliot 268. It has been shown that the Founders did not regard the "in pursuance" phrase as satisfied by mere compliance with the formalities of enactment, supra, Chapter 8, text accompanying notes 39, 53–55; and it is highly unlikely that State judges who were to be "bound" by treaties "under the authority of the United States" were merely to inquire whether two-thirds of a Senate quorum had concurred with the President. Jealousy for State and individual rights was not so easily sunk.
[107] E.g., 2 Elliot 68, 74, 113, 157, 85, 91, 97, 241, 345; cf. supra, Chapter 2, text accompanying notes 22–52; cf. Chapter 8, id. at notes 158–182.

power "tend to destruction of all confidence—the withholding of all power—the annihilation of all government."[108] Representatives of the people in the federal government, it was often remarked, would no more become monsters than their State counterparts.[109] But although the grant of power was an inescapable condition of government, few were defendants of unchecked power. Rutledge's remarks appear to be addressed to prevalent fears of granting power rather than to methods whereby abuses might be checked. Indeed, in these same remarks, he adverted to an objection that a treaty might do away with a State "instalment law," and asked, "supposing a person gave security conformable to that law, whether judging from precedent, the judges would permit any further proceeding contrary to it," suggesting, minimally, that judges would weigh whether the treaty constitutionally overrode State law. Rutledge had alluded in the federal Convention to the fact that the "supreme court is to judge between the U.S. and particular States," and there is reason to believe that he envisaged umpiring that embraced issues of constitutionality.[110]

There were, however, remarks which refer to a "political check." Speaker Pringle said,

> If the President and Senate make such [treaties] as violate the fundamental laws, or subvert the Constitution . . . the evils, equally oppressing all, will be removed as soon as felt, as those who are oppressed have the power and means of redress.[111]

And Edward Rutledge said that "If the President or the Senators abused their trust, they were liable to impeachment and punishment,"[112] a view

---

[108] 4 Elliot 276. In the Massachusetts convention, Bowdoin said, "Possibility of abuse . . . is by itself no sufficient reason for withholding the delegation. If it were a sufficient one, no power could be delegated." 2 Elliot 85; to same effect, Stillman, id. at 166. In North Carolina Iredell said, "No power, of any kind or degree, can be given but what may be abused; we have, therefore, only to consider whether any particular power is absolutely necessary. If it be, the power must be given, and we must run the risk of the abuse." 4 Elliot 95.

[109] In New York, Hamilton ridiculed the notion that "the moment you put men into a national council, they become corrupt and tyrannical, and lose all affection for their fellow citizens." 2 Elliot 304. In Pennsylvania, Wilson said that the Framers "did not suppose that the legislature, under this Constitution, would be an *association of demons*." Id. at 486. Yet no one more strongly affirmed the need and availability of judicial review than did Wilson and Hamilton.

[110] Supra, Chapter 3, text accompanying note 64. In this light, Rutledge's doubt that a President "would be such a fool and a knave as to join with ten others [Senators] to tear up liberty by the roots, when a full Senate was competent to impeach him," 4 Elliot 268, may refer to a cumulative rather than exclusive remedy.

[111] 4 Elliot 270.

[112] Id. at 276.

shared by General Pinckney.[113] Though Pringle and Edward Rutledge referred to other than judicial checks, their statements do not compel the inference that those other checks were to be exclusive.

It seems safe to conclude that unlimited treaty power found no favor in South Carolina, and that the equivocal remarks of General Pinckney and John Rutledge are outweighed by the unanimity of opposition leader Lowndes and Speaker Pringle, who flatly declared, without contradiction, that the treaty power is limited. Treaties "exceeding the power with which the makers were entrusted ought to be annulled," said Pringle, and one who felt so strongly would not readily reject the possibility of judicial review. In truth, judicial review had received no such exposition in South Carolina as it had been given in Virginia and Pennsylvania. Nevertheless, Charles Pinckney, like John Rutledge, had stated in the federal Convention that the "judges will be umpire between the U. States and individual States,"[114] and in South Carolina he said that judges would "decide all national questions which arise within the Union"—can it be doubted that whether a treaty overrode a State law would present such a "national question"—and that "licentiousness" of Congress would be "checked and corrected by" the other departments.[115] For such men it was enough that the States must yield to the legitimate exercise of federal power; if a treaty went out of bounds, the "umpire" would be expected to make the call.

THE NEW YORK RATIFICATION CONVENTION

Finally, Corwin cites an amendment proposed in the New York convention:

> . . . no treaty ought to operate to alter the constitution of any State; nor ought any commercial treaty to operate so as to abrogate any law of the United States.[116]

As Luther Martin noted, the struggle to preserve State constitutions from overriding federal laws had been lost,[117] and that would hold equally true of treaties. But States Righters minimally would insist that a federal law or treaty should not be repugnant to the Constitution. As to the impact of a treaty upon a "law of the United States," several ratifying conventions had been told of the English practice to turn to Parliament

[113] Id. at 281.
[114] 2 Farrand 248.
[115] Supra, Chapter 3, text accompanying notes 71–72.
[116] Corwin, *National Supremacy* 68; 2 Elliot 409.
[117] Cf. supra, Chapter 8, text accompanying notes 78–79.

to repeal or enact laws in aid of "commercial treaties,"[118] and that a similar practice was contemplated under the Constitution. Whether an amendment was needed for that purpose may have been debatable, but the proposed amendment only confirms the general sentiment.

SUMMARY

The Virginia convention, and later Jefferson, as Vice-President, quite plainly conceived the treaty power to be restricted by constitutional limitations. No unequivocal hint of an unlimited treaty power is to be found in the North and South Carolina conventions; instead there were clear-cut rejections of an unlimited power in South Carolina. Judicial review is something else again. There are no statements comparable to those which stressed the availability of judicial review to curb transgressions of constitutional limits on the "law" making power, though there were references to other "checks." But given the rejection of an "unlimited" treaty power, one cannot out of hand conclude that treatymaking was to be immune from the judicial check to which Congress and President were subject when engaged in "law" making. Although it is odd that no reference was made to judicial review of treaty-making, it is no less odd that in Virginia, for example, no one commented that the much-feared transgressions by treaty-makers, unlike those of "law" makers, must go unchecked by the courts. The fact that "law" making was to be subject to judicial check, that Article III conferred jurisdiction of "all cases . . . arising . . . under the laws of the United States, and treaties made . . . under their authority" without reference to "pursuant thereto" in either case, that the difference between laws "in pursuance thereof" and treaties "under their authority" is readily explicable by Franklin's desire to save "subsisting" treaties, call for a demonstration, I suggest, that treaties were intended to be exempted from judicial review. In the absence of such demonstration, I would conclude that action in excess of constitutional limits upon the treaty-power—whatever they may be—would, like unconstitutional "laws," be subject to judicial "annulment."

[118] Supra, text accompanying note 42; cf. id. at notes 17, 68–69.

BIBLIOGRAPHY

BOOKS

Adams, Henry. *John Randolph.* Boston: Houghton, Mifflin, 1882.

Adams, John. *Legal Papers of John Adams,* ed. L. Kinvin Wroth and Heller B. Zobel. 3 vols. Cambridge, Mass.: Harvard University Press, 1965.

—————— *Works,* ed. Charles Francis Adams. 10 vols. Boston: Little, Brown, 1850–1856.

American State Papers: Documents, Legislative and Executive. 38 vols. Washington: Gales and Seaton, 1832–1861. *Misc.* I (1789–1809).

1 *Annals of Congress* (1789). Washington: Gales & Seaton, 1834. There are two prints of this volume, bearing identical title pages but having quite different pagination. Citations herein are to the print having the running page-title "Gales & Seaton's History of Debates in Congress."

Bacon, Matthew. *Abridgment,* 3d ed. London, 1768.

Bailyn, Bernard. *The Ideological Origins of the American Revolution.* Cambridge, Mass.: Harvard University Press, 1967.

Baker, Leonard. *Back to Back: The Duel Between FDR and the Supreme Court.* New York: Macmillan, 1967.

Bancroft, George. *History of the Formation of the Constitution of the United States of America.* 2 vols. New York: D. Appleton, 1882.

Barrett, Edward L., Paul W. Bruton, and John Honnold. *Constitutional Law: Cases and Materials,* 2d ed. Brooklyn: Foundation Press, 1963.

Beard, Charles A. *The Supreme Court and the Constitution.* Englewood Cliffs, N.J.: Prentice-Hall, 1962 (paperback ed.).

Bickel, Alexander. *The Least Dangerous Branch: The Supreme Court at the Bar of Politics.* Indianapolis: Bobbs-Merrill, 1962 (paperback ed.).

Black, Charles L. *The People and the Court: Judicial Review in a Democracy.* New York: Macmillan, 1960.

Blackstone, Sir William. *Commentaries on the Laws of England.* Oxford: Clarendon Press, 1765–1769.

Boudin, Louis B. *Government by Judiciary.* New York: W. Godwin, 1932.

Bowen, Catherine D. *Miracle at Philadelphia: The Story of the Constitutional Convention, May to September, 1787.* Boston: Little, Brown, 1966.

Bryce, James. *American Commonwealth,* 2d ed. rev. 2 vols. New York: Commonwealth Publishing Co., 1908.

Cahn, Edmond, ed. *Supreme Court and Supreme Law*. Bloomington, Ind.: Indiana University Press, 1954.

Cardozo, Benjamin N. *Paradoxes of Legal Science*. New York: Columbia University Press, 1928.

Comyns, Sir John. *A Digest of the Laws of England*. 5 vols. London, 1762–1767.

Corwin, Edward S. *Court Over Constitution: A Study of Judicial Review as an Instrument of Popular Government*. Princeton: Princeton University Press, 1938.

——— *The Doctrine of Judicial Review: Its Legal and Historical Basis, and Other Essays*. Gloucester, Mass.: Peter Smith, 1963.

——— *National Supremacy: Treaty Power vs. State Power*. New York: H. Holt, 1913.

——— *Twilight of the Supreme Court: A History of Our Constitutional Theory*. New Haven: Yale University Press, 1934.

Cox, Archibald. *The Warren Court: Constitutional Decision as an Instrument of Reform*. Cambridge, Mass.: Harvard University Press, 1968.

Coxe, Brinton. *An Essay on Judicial Power and Unconstitutional Legislation, Being a Commentary on Parts of the Constitution of the United States*. Philadelphia: Kay and Brother, 1893.

Crosskey, William W. *Politics and the Constitution in the History of the United States*. Chicago: University of Chicago Press, 1953.

Davis, Horace A. *The Judicial Veto*. Boston: Houghton, Mifflin, 1914.

Davis, Kenneth C. *Administrative Law Treatise*. 4 vols. St. Paul, Minn.: West Publishing Co., 1958.

Declareuil, Joseph. *Rome the Law-Giver*, trans. E. A. Parker. New York: A. A. Knopf, 1927.

De Pauw, Linda G. *The Eleventh Pillar: New York State and the Federal Constitution*. Ithaca: Cornell University Press, 1966.

A Discourse Upon the Exposicion and Understanding of Statutes, ed. Samuel E. Thorne. San Marino, Calif.: Huntington Library, 1942.

Elliot, Jonathan. *Debates in the Several State Conventions on the Adoption of the Federal Constitution*, 2d ed. 5 vols. Philadelphia: J. B. Lippincott, 1881.

Farrand, Max. *The Framing of the Constitution of the United States*. New Haven: Yale University Press, 1913.

——— *The Records of the Federal Convention of 1787*. 4 vols. New Haven: Yale University Press, 1911.

The Federalist. New York: Random House (Modern Library), 1937.

Ford, Paul L., ed. *Pamphlets on the Constitution of the United States, Published During Its Discussion by the People, 1787–1788*. Brooklyn, 1888.

Forrester, Ray, and Thomas J. Currier. *Federal Jurisdiction*. St. Paul, Minn.: West Publishing Co., 1962.

Frankfurter, Felix, and James M. Landis. *The Business of the Supreme Court: A Study in the Federal Judicial System*. New York: Macmillan, 1928.

Freedman, Max, ed. *Roosevelt and Frankfurter, Their Correspondence, 1928–1945*. Boston: Little, Brown (Atlantic Monthly Press), 1967.

BIBLIOGRAPHY

Gough, John W. *Fundamental Law in English Constitutional History*, 2d ed. Oxford: Clarendon Press, 1961.

Green, Leon. *Traffic Victims: Tort Law and Insurance*. Evanston, Ill.: Northwestern University Press, 1958.

Haines, Charles G. *The American Doctrine of Judicial Supremacy*, 2d ed. Berkeley, Calif.: University of California Press, 1932.

Hamilton, Alexander. *Works*, ed. H. C. Lodge. 12 vols. New York: Knickerbocker Press, 1904.

Hamlin, Paul M. *Legal Education in Colonial New York*. New York: New York University, Law Quarterly Review, 1939.

Hand, Learned. *The Bill of Rights*. Cambridge, Mass.: Harvard University Press, 1958.

Hart, Henry M., and Herbert Wechsler. *The Federal Courts and the Federal System*. Brooklyn: Foundation Press, 1953.

Henkin, Louis. *Arms Control and Inspection in American Law*. New York: Columbia University Press, 1958.

Hockett, Homer C. *Constitutional History of the United States, 1826–1876*. New York: Macmillan, 1939.

———— *Political and Social History of the United States, 1492–1828*. New York: Macmillan, 1929.

Holdsworth, Sir William. *A History of English Law*. 12 vols. London: Methuen, 1903–1938.

———— *Some Makers of English Law*. Cambridge, Eng.: Cambridge University Press, 1938.

Holmes, Oliver W. *Collected Legal Papers*. New York: Harcourt, Brace, 1920.

Howell, Thomas B. *Cobbett's Complete Collection of State Trials*. 33 vols. London: R. Bagshaw, 1809–1826.

Hughes, Charles E. *The Supreme Court of the United States: Its Foundation, Methods and Achievements, an Interpretation*. New York: Columbia University Press, 1928.

Hutchinson, Thomas. *Hutchinson Papers*. 2 vols. Albany: Prince Society, 1865.

Hyneman, Charles. *The Supreme Court on Trial*. New York: Atherton Press, 1963.

Jackson, Robert H. *The Struggle for Judicial Supremacy: A Study of a Crisis in American Power Politics*. New York: A. A. Knopf, 1941.

Jaffe, Louis L. *Judicial Control of Administrative Action*. Boston: Little, Brown, 1965.

Jameson, John F. *Essays in the Constitutional History of the U.S. in the Formative Period, 1775–1789*. Boston: Houghton, Mifflin, 1889.

Jefferson, Thomas. *A Manual of Parliamentary Practice for the Use of the Senate of the United States*. Washington: S. H. Smith, 1801.

———— *The Writings of Thomas Jefferson*, ed. Paul Leicester Ford. 10 vols. New York: G. P. Putnam's Sons, 1892–1899.

Lewis, William D. *Interpreting the Constitution*. Charlottesville, Va.: Michie, 1937.

McCloskey, Robert G. *The American Supreme Court*. Chicago: University of Chicago Press, 1960.

————, ed. Introduction to *The Works of James Wilson*. 2 vols. Cambridge, Mass.: Harvard University Press, 1967.

McDonald, Forrest. *We the People*. Chicago: University of Chicago Press, 1958.

McIlwain, Charles H. *The High Court of Parliament and Its Supremacy: An Historical Essay on the Boundaries between Legislation and Adjudication in England*. Hamden, Conn.: Archon Books, 1962.

McMaster, John B. *History of the People of the United States, from the Revolution to the Civil War*. 8 vols. New York: Appleton, 1913.

———— and F. D. Stone, eds. *Pennsylvania and the Federal Constitution, 1787–1788*. Lancaster: Inquirer Printing and Publishing, 1888.

McRee, Griffith J. *Life and Correspondence of James Iredell*. 2 vols. New York: D. Appleton, 1857–1858.

Madison, James. *The Writings of James Madison*, ed. Gaillard Hunt. 9 vols. New York: G. P. Putnam's Sons, 1900–1910.

Maitland, F. W. *The Collected Papers of Frederic William Maitland*, ed. H. A. L. Fisher. Cambridge, Eng.: Cambridge University Press, 1911.

Marke, Julius. *Vignettes of Legal History*. South Hackensack, N.J.: F. B. Rothman, 1965.

Meigs, William M. *The Relation of the Judiciary to the Constitution*. New York: The Neale Publishing Co., 1919.

Miller, John C. *Alexander Hamilton: A Portrait in Paradox*. New York: Harper & Row, 1959.

Milton, John. *Works*. 18 vols. New York: Columbia University Press, 1932.

Mitchell, Broadus, and Louise P. Mitchell. *A Biography of the Constitution of the United States: Its Origin, Formation, Adoption, and Interpretation*. New York: Oxford University Press, 1964.

Montesquieu, C. L. de S. *Spirit of the Laws* (American translation). 2 vols. Worcester: Isaiah Thomas, 1802.

Morey, William C. *Outlines of Roman Law*, 2d ed. New York: G. P. Putnam's Sons, 1913.

Morgan, Donald G. *Congress and the Constitution: A Study of Responsibility*. Cambridge, Mass.: Harvard University Press, 1966.

Morison, Samuel E. *Oxford History of the American People*. New York: Oxford University Press, 1965.

———— and Henry S. Commager. *Growth of the American Republic*, 5th ed. 2 vols. New York: Oxford University Press, 1962.

Morse, John T. *John Adams*. Boston: Houghton, Mifflin, 1898.

Muller, Herbert. *Uses of the Past: Profiles of Former Societies*. New York: Mentor (New American Library), 1954.

Patterson, Caleb P. *The Constitutional Principles of Thomas Jefferson*. Austin: University of Texas Press, 1953.

Pickthorn, Sir Kenneth W. M. *Early Tudor Government: Henry VII*. Cambridge, Eng.: Cambridge University Press, 1934.

Plucknett, Theodore F. T. *A Concise History of the Common Law*, 4th ed. London: Butterworth, 1948.

Pollock, Frederick. *Expansion of the Common Law*. London: Stevens and Sons, 1904.

————— and F. W. Maitland. *History of English Law before the Time of Edward I*, 2d ed. Boston: Little, Brown, 1899.

Prynne, William. *A Seasonable, Legal, and Historicall Vindication and Chronologicall Collection of the Good, Old, Fundamentall, Liberties, Franchises, Rights, Laws of All English Freemen*. London, 1654–1657.

Rawle, William. *A View of the Constitution of the United States of America*. Philadelphia: H. C. Carey & I. Lea, 1825.

Richardson, James D. *Compilation of the Messages and Papers of the Presidents, 1789–1897*. 10 vols. Washington, 1907.

Rossiter, Clinton. *Alexander Hamilton and the Constitution*. New York: Harcourt, Brace, 1964.

Saint Germain, Christopher. *The Dialogue in English, Betweene a Doctor of Divinitie, and a Student of the Lawes of England*. London, 1607.

Smith, Page. *John Adams*. 2 vols. Garden City, N.Y.: Doubleday, 1962.

Sparks, Jared. *Life of Gouverneur Morris*. Boston: Gray & Bowen, 1832.

Story, Joseph. *Commentaries on the Constitution of the U.S.*, 4th ed. 2 vols. Boston: Little, Brown, 1873.

Thayer, James B. *Cases on Constitutional Law*. 2 vols. Cambridge, Mass.: G. H. Kent, 1894–1895.

Thorne, Samuel E., ed. Introduction to *A Discourse Upon the Exposicion and Understanding of Statutes*. San Marino, Calif.: Huntington Library, 1942.

Thorpe, Francis N. *The Federal and State Constitutions, Colonial Charters, and Other Organic Laws*. 7 vols. Washington: Government Printing Office, 1909.

Tuchman, Barbara. *Proud Tower: A Portrait of the World Before the War, 1890–1914*. New York: Macmillan, 1965.

Tucker, St. George, ed. *Blackstone's Commentaries*. 5 vols. Philadelphia: Birch & Small, 1803.

Van Doren, Carl. *The Great Rehearsal: The Story of the Making and Ratifying of the Constitution of the United States*. New York: Viking, 1948.

Vattel, Emmerich de. *The Law of Nations* (English translation). London, 1760.

Viner, Charles. *General Abridgment of Law and Equity*. 23 vols. London, 1742–1753.

Wade, H. W. R. *Administrative Law*, 2d ed. Oxford: Clarendon Press, 1967.

Warren, Charles. *Congress, the Constitution and the Supreme Court*. Boston: Little, Brown, 1925.

————— *The Making of the Constitution*. Boston: Little, Brown, 1928.

————— *The Supreme Court in United States History*. Boston: Little, Brown, 1922.

Wechsler, Herbert. *Principles, Politics, and Fundamental Law: Selected Essays*. Cambridge, Mass.: Harvard University Press, 1961.

Westin, Alan F. Introduction to Beard, *The Supreme Court and the Constitution* (paperback ed. 1962).

Wilson, James. *The Works of James Wilson*. 2 vols. Philadelphia: Bronson & Chauncey, 1804.

Wright, Benjamin F. *The Growth of American Constitutional Law.* Boston: Houghton, Mifflin, 1942.

Wright, Charles A. *Handbook on the Law of Federal Courts.* St. Paul, Minn.: West Publishing Co., 1963.

ARTICLES

Berger, Raoul. "Administrative Arbitrariness and Judicial Review," 65 *Columbia Law Review* 55 (1965).

———— "Constructive Contempt: A Post-Mortem," 9 *University of Chicago Law Review* 602 (1942).

———— "Executive Privilege v. Congressional Inquiry," 12 *U.C.L.A. Law Review* 1044, 1288 (1965).

Boorstin, Daniel. "Paperbacks and History, Benson, Turner and Beard: American Historical Writing Reconsidered," *New York Times Book Review,* Nov. 28, 1965.

Brant, Irving. "Mr. Crosskey and Mr. Madison," 54 *Columbia Law Review* 443 (1954).

Brown, Ernest J. Book Review of Crosskey, *Politics and the Constitution,* in 67 *Harvard Law Review* 1439 (1954).

Burton, Harold. "Two Significant Decisions: Ex Parte Milligan and Ex Parte McArdle," 41 *American Bar Association Journal* 124 (1955).

Corwin, Edward S. Book Review of Beard, *The Supreme Court and the Constitution,* in 7 *American Political Science Review* 330 (1913).

———— "The Establishment of Judicial Review," 9 *Michigan Law Review* 102 (1910).

———— "The Progress of Constitutional Theory Between the Declaration of Independence and the Meeting of the Philadelphia Convention," 30 *American Historical Review* 511 (1925).

———— "The Supreme Court and Unconstitutional Laws of Congress," 4 *Michigan Law Review* 616 (1906).

Davis, Horace. "Annulment of Legislation by the Supreme Court," 7 *American Political Science Review* 541 (1913).

Dodd, A. L. Book Review of Baker, *Back to Back,* in *New York Times Book Review,* Sept. 24, 1967, p. 40.

Elliot, Shelden D. "Court-Curbing Proposals in Congress," 33 *Notre Dame Lawyer* 597 (1958).

Fenwick, Charles G. "The Authority of Vattel," 7 *American Political Science Review* 395 (1913).

Frankfurter, Felix. "A Note on Advisory Opinions," 37 *Harvard Law Review* 1002 (1924).

Friendly, Henry J. "The Bill of Rights as a Code of Criminal Procedure," 53 *California Law Review* 929 (1965).

———— "In Praise of Erie—and of the New Federal Common Law," 39 *New York University Law Review* 383 (1964).

Gellhorn, Walter. "Finland's Official Watchman," 14 *University of Pennsylvania Law Review* 327 (1966).

Goebel, Julius. "Constitutional History and Constitutional Law," 38 *Columbia Law Review* 555 (1938).

———— "Ex Parte Clio," 54 *Columbia Law Review* 450 (1954).

BIBLIOGRAPHY

Hart, Henry M., Jr. Book Review, "Professor Crosskey and Judicial Review," in 67 *Harvard Law Review* 1456 (1954).
—— "The Power of Congress to Limit the Jurisdiction of Federal Courts: An Exercise in Dialectic," 66 *Harvard Law Review* 1362 (1953).
—— "The Relation Between State and Federal Law," 54 *Columbia Law Review* 489 (1954).
Henkin, Louis. "Some Reflections on Current Constitutional Controversies," 109 *University of Pennsylvania Law Review* 637 (1961).
Jaffe, Louis L. "The Right to Judicial Review," 71 *Harvard Law Review* 401 (1958).
Keeffe, Arthur J. "Practicing Lawyers' Guide to the Current Law Magazines," 53 *American Bar Association Journal* 91 (1967).
Lewis, John U. "Coke's Theory of 'Artificial Reason' as a Context for Modern Basic Legal Theory," 84 *Law Quarterly Review* 330 (1968).
McGowan, Carl. "The Problems of Historical Perspective," 33 *Notre Dame Lawyer* 527 (1958).
Madden, J. Warren. Book Review of Davis, *Administrative Law Treatise: 1963 Pocket Parts,* in 17 *Stanford Law Review* 165 (1964).
Melvin, Frank E. "The Judicial Bulwark of the Constitution," 8 *American Political Science Review* 167 (1914).
Miller, Arthur, and R. F. Howell. "The Myth of Neutrality in Constitutional Adjudication," 27 *University of Chicago Law Review* 661 (1960).
Plucknett, Theodore F. T. "Bonham's Case and Judicial Review," 40 *Harvard Law Review* 30 (1926).
Pollak, Louis H. "Constitutional Adjudication: Relative or Absolute Neutrality," 11 *Journal of Public Law* 48 (1962).
—— "Racial Discrimination and Judicial Integrity: A Reply to Professor Wechsler," 108 *University of Pennsylvania Law Review* 1 (1959).
Pollock, Sir Frederick. "A Plea for Historical Interpretation," 39 *Law Quarterly Review* 163 (1923).
Ratner, Leonard G. "Congressional Power Over the Appellate Jurisdiction of the Supreme Court," 109 *University of Pennsylvania Law Review* 157 (1960).
Roberts, Owen J. "Fortifying the Supreme Court's Independence," 35 *American Bar Association Journal* 1 (1949).
Rostow, Eugene V. "The Supreme Court and the People's Will," 33 *Notre Dame Lawyer* 573 (1958).
Salvemini, Gaetano. "The Concepts of Democracy and Liberty in the Eighteenth Century," in Conyers Read, ed., *The Constitution Reconsidered.* New York: Columbia University Press, 1938.
Swisher, Carl B. Book review of Cahn, ed., *Supreme Court and Supreme Law,* in 67 *Harvard Law Review* 1487 (1954).
Thayer, James B. "The Origins and Scope of the American Doctrine of Constitutional Law," 7 *Harvard Law Review* 129 (1893).
Thorne, Samuel E. "Dr. Bonham's Case," 54 *Law Quarterly Review* 543 (1938).
—— "The Equity of a Statute and Heydon's Case," 31 *Illinois Law Review* 202 (1936).

BIBLIOGRAPHY

Trevor-Roper, Hugh. Book Review of Elton, *The Practice of History,* in London *Times,* Oct. 15, 1967, p. 33.

Warren, Charles. "New Light on the History of the Federal Judiciary Act of 1789," 37 *Harvard Law Review* 49 (1923).

Wechsler, Herbert. "The Courts and the Constitution," 65 *Columbia Law Review* 1001 (1965).

———— "Toward Neutral Principles of Constitutional Law," 73 *Harvard Law Review* 1 (1959).

Wofford, John G. "The Blinding Light: The Uses of History in Constitutional Interpretation," 31 *University of Chicago Law Review* 502 (1964).

PAMPHLETS

Reprinted in Ford, Paul L. *Pamphlets on the Constitution of the United States.* Brooklyn, 1888.

Hanson, Alexander. *Remarks to the People of Maryland.* 1788.

Iredell, James. *Answer to George Mason's Objections.* 1788.

Lee, R. H. *Letters of a Federal Farmer.* 1787.

Webster, Peletiah. *The Weakness of Brutus Exposed.* 1788.

Otis, James. *Rights of the British Colonies Asserted and Proved,* 3d ed. Boston, 1766.

INDEX OF CASES

Ableman v. Booth, 21 How. 506 (1858), 228n, 246

Baker v. Carr, 369 U.S. 186 (1962), 216n

Barron v. Mayor and City of Baltimore, 7 Peters 243 (1833), 18n

Battaglia v. General Motors Corp., 169 F.2d 254 (2d Cir. 1948), 2n, 296

Bayard v. Singleton, 1 Martin (N.C. 1787), 27n, 35n, 38, 39n, 84, 133, 134, 155, 168, 283n

Bell v. Maryland, 378 U.S. 226 (1964), 207n

Billings v. United States, 232 U.S. 261 (1914), 293n, 322n

Blake v. McClung, 172 U.S. 239 (1898), 315n

Boehle v. Electro Metallurgical Co., 72 F. Supp. 21 (D. Ore. 1947), 293n

Bonham's Case, 8 Co. Rep. 113b (1610), 23, 349, 361

Botany Worsted Mills v. United States, 278 U.S. 282 (1929), 326n

Brinkerhof-Faris Trust Co. v. Hill, 281 U.S. 673 (1930), 332n

Broggen v. Metropolitan Ry. Co. [1877] 2 A.C. 666, 121n

Brown v. Gerdes, 321 U.S. 178 (1944), 247n, 250n

Calder v. Bull, 3 Dallas 386 (1798), 338n

Calvin's Case, 7 Co. Rep. 1a (1608), 351, 355

Chisholm v. Georgia, 2 Dallas 419 (1793), 297n, 298n, 300, 302, 305n, 311n, 321n, 325, 326

City of London v. Wood, 12 Mod. 669 (1702), 23n, 366n

Claflin v. Houseman, 93 U.S. 130 (1876), 247n

Cohens v. Virginia, 6 Wheat. 264 (1821), 90n, 144n, 216n, 236n, 274n, 299n, 304n, 317n, 320n, 321, 327n, 329n, 331n

Commonwealth v. Caton, 4 Call 5 (Va. 1782), 103n, 109, 232n

Crooks v. Harrelson, 282 U.S. 55 (1930), 315n

Day v. Savadge, Hobart 85 (1614), 24n, 355n, 364

De la Rama SS. Co. v. United States, 344 U.S. 386 (1953), 299n

Despensers's Case, 1 Howell *State Trials* 23 (1320), 361n

Dick v. United States, 208 U.S. 340 (1908), 322n

Dred Scott v. Sandford, 19 How. 393 (1857), 200n, 338n

Earl of Oxford's Case, 21 Eng. Rep. 487 (1616), 364n

Eckenrode v. Penn. R. Co., 164 F.2d 458 (2d Cir. 1942), 218n

Erie Ry. Co. v. Tompkins, 304 U.S. 64 (1938), 208, 379

Estep v. United States, 327 U.S. 114 (1946), 284n

Ex Parte McCardle, 7 Wall. 506 (1869), 2–3, 286

Ex Parte Yerger, 8 Wall. 85 (1869), 2n

Ex Parte Young, 209 U.S. 123 (1908), 300n

Federal Deposit Ins. Co. v. Tremaine, 133 F.2d 827 (2d Cir. 1943), 199n

399

GENERAL INDEX

Abridgments: quote Coke, 24n, 366; quoted by Otis, Varnum, 24n

Act of 1789, *see* Judiciary Act

Adams, Henry: Founders feared despotism, 9

Adams, John: approves Cushing's "void," 26n; borrows Otis' argument, 25; Otis' impact, 25n; on Framers, 116n

    Discussed by Boudin, Morison, 31n

Adams, John, *Legal Papers*, 349n, 351n, 366n

Adams, Samuel: courts should determine unconstitutional laws, 15, 125, 169n, 233; noted similarity of sentiment in Ratification conventions, 382n

Agency: Colonial charters limited agency, 15n; Congress is agent, 14, 15, 171n, 173n, 174, 175; in Massachusetts constitution of 1780, 174

Alien and Sedition laws: Justices attacked for refusal to hold unconstitutional, 62

Ames, Fisher: refutation begets proof, 6n; "removal" debate, 147; State court jurisdiction, 254

"Arising under" clause, 198–222

    Bickel: "all" cases, 215; can declare State statute unconstitutional, 213–214; grants jurisdiction, no guidance to exercise, 206–207, 209

    Construction of: as entirety, 214n; contemporary understanding, 201–203; ordinary meaning, 210; Yates, must include constitutionality, 218

    Corwin: ambiguous, 201; came late in day, 204n; confined to prohibitions, 166; thus limited by Hamilton, 203; surplusage, 205; why no ex-

plicit judicial review, 206n; mentioned, 213n, 214

    Crosskey: requires proof of federal inclusion, 214; some federal acts excepted, 214–215; State statute can be held unconstitutional, 213n; mentioned, 351n

    Integration with Supremacy Clause, Madison and Rutledge, 245–246

    Origin, 204n

    Too broad: Mason and Grayson, 203; Tyler and Randolph, 203n

Bacon, Matthew, 24n, 366

Bailyn, Bernard: Coke, 349; Colonial fear of power, 9n; Colonial view of judicial function, 25n; parliamentary absolutism, 29

Baker, Leonard, 291n

Baldwin, Abraham: judiciary provision ambiguous, 221n; courts should determine unconstitutional laws, 98, 108, 148; later contra, 98n; notes party strife, 49n

Bancroft, George, 8n, 9n, 35n, 88n

Barrett, Edward L., 19n, 291n

Bassett, Richard: voted for Judiciary Act, 101

Bayard v. Singleton: Davie and Iredell co-counsel, 133; deprivation of jury trial, 35n; held State statute unconstitutional, 38, 133, 134, 168; judicial "self-defense," 39n, 155; Vattel influence, 27n

Beard, Charles A.: Framers' remarks, 47–104, 112; deletions from his tally, 103

    Convention aims, 17n; effect of "usurpation" argument, 4n, thought he settled it, 47; Madison's fear of

GENERAL INDEX

Coke, 23n, 25; summation of Convention, 104–105, 114

Founders: believed interpretation for courts, 28n; borrowed from Coke, 23n, 25; borrowed ideas, not institutions, 46; influenced by 17th-century England, 30n; influenced by fellow Founders, 197; competing doctrines on interpretation, 177–182; finality judicial interpretation, 188; legislature excluded from interpretation, 55n, 183, 264n; exclusion breach with tradition, 27n

Judicial review: acts as check on Congress, 126n; Congressional power too broad for effective review, 231n; Convention sought to cure evils, 220n; courts as cumulative check, 264n; differentiates review of State Acts, 258–259; for protection of individual rights, 19–20, 184n, 264n; Framers did not conceal intentions, 198n; Hamilton anticipated by Varnum, Iredell, 82, 97, 197n; First Congress, 150n; natural outgrowth, 197; no explicit provision for, 199–200, 206n; related to expounding, 56; secured by Constitution Framers thought, 201; Virginia Plan overlooked it, 50n

Judicial review and Framers: Baldwin, 114n; Bedford, 69n, 111n; Bowdoin, 21n, 126n; Davie, 84, 168; Dickinson, 64, 114n, 312n; Gerry, 50n; Hamilton, 82n, 92n, 97, 105n, 107, 170–171, 182; Madison, 70, 76, 79n, 80n, 107, 108, 169, 181; Mason, 55, 58, 59, 60n; Mercer, 111n; Morris, 66n; Pinckney, 61, 114n; Rutledge, 60; Spaight, 110n; Williamson, 68; Yates, 86–87. Additions to Beard's list, 105n

Judicial review: as "self-defense," 154, 156; Constitution as "law," 170–176; enforcement of prohibitions only, 165–170, 258; "fundamental law," 170–176

Legislative power: agency familiarized by Charters, 15n; Assemblies stood for Colonial interest, 31; excesses led to Convention, 12n; reaction to excesses, 10n; stress on delegation-agency, 14n

On: bias for local autonomy, 10n; Davis, 101n; Eleventh Amendment,

326n; executive power, 376–377n; Privy Council disallowance of Colonial Acts, 28n; Ratification conventions, 142; "removal" debate, 146; shifting views, 97n, 105n, 106n, 109, 114, 165n, 197n

State courts: as guardians, 263; review federal acts, 271; plus appeals to Supreme Court, 270, 271

Treaty power: Jefferson's construction, 376, 378–379; Madison, 374–375; New York amendment, 388; Nicholas, 373–374n; Gen. Pinckney and Rutledge, 385, 386–387; unlimited, 383, 385; unlimited power uncongenial, 383

Mentioned, 5n, 10n, 11n, 20n, 24n, 25n, 26n, 39n, 42n, 60n, 62n, 82n, 85n, 87n, 90n, 111n, 149n, 175n, 176n, 178n, 182, 189n, 195n, 200, 201n, 202n, 204n, 205, 210n, 220n, 222n, 228n, 235n, 239n, 273n, 277, 290n, 358n, 376n, 380n, 382n

Council of Censors: (Pa.), 10n, 182

Council of Revision: not substitute for judicial review, 157n; opposition to judicial participation, 50–53, 55–57, 60; proposed by Virginia Plan, 50, 53; proponents' arguments for judicial participation, 53–54, 58, 61, 63, 157n, 158, 161, 162, 163, 226; veto ran to all laws, 162–164

Court-packing plan, 291–292; Celler, 292

Courts: coextensive jurisdiction, 78, 85; jurisdiction given only by Article III, 200; to protect private rights, see Private rights; to protect States, Stone, 277; to upset both federal and State laws, 265, 269

Check on Congress: Bowdoin, 21; Hamilton, 149; Grayson, 141; Madison, 76–77, 119; Mason, 58, 139; Morris, 65; Nicholas, 138–139; Pinckney, 61; Randolph, 138

Confidence in: Madison, 185, 186; Ellsworth, 186; Jefferson, 186; Henry, 186; Haines, 184; M. Smith, 186n; Wilson, 184n; contra, Boudin, 186n

Declare laws unconstitutional, some sources, 15n; Coke, 23; S. Adams, 15; Baldwin, 98; "Centinel," 87n; Davie, 134; Dickinson,

407

GENERAL INDEX

tional jealousy, 33–34; suspicion of
distant government, 32–33n; Virginia
convention, 136n, 138n; mentioned,
47n, 116n, 122n, 123n, 129n, 132n,
136n, 138n, 173n, 185n, 261n, 369n
Vanhorne v. Dorrance, 102; Boudin and
Davis on, 102n
Varnum, James: courts exclusive in-
terpreter, 28n, 182; Corwin says
Varnum anticipated Hamilton, 97;
General Revolutionary War, 39;
people as last resort, 178; quotes
Bacon's *Abridgment,* 24n; quotes
Coke, 26; quotes Vattel, 27
Vattel, Emerich de: legislature cannot
change Constitution, 171; various
citations of, 27, 34n, 171n
Vaughan, Chief Justice John: "impos-
sibility"-contradictions, 353–354
Viner, Charles, 24n, 71n, 366
Vining, John: "removal" debate, 146n
Virginia-Kentucky Resolutions: fathered
by Madison, 70, who later abandoned
argument, 70n, 374n; result of politi-
cal strife, 62, 153
    Comments by: Davis, 62n; Mori-
son, 62
Virginia Plan, 50, 53, 185, 223

Wade, H. W. R.: removal of judges in
England, 24n; crown immunity, 305n
Warren, Charles: Alien and Sedition
Act, 62n; approval of judicial review
after the Convention, 152; Baldwin,
98n; Congress and Hayburn's case,
152n; Congressman's first denial of
judicial review, 151n; judicial review unchallenged in Ratification
conventions, 141n; "midnight
judges," 180n; review of "fact," 287;
Sedition Act debate and judicial review, 153; sovereign immunity, 321n
    First Congress, 106n; as adjourned
session Convention, 144n; judicial review in, 150n
    Mentioned, 13n, 120n, 152, 153,
227n, 248n, 250n, 252n, 253n, 256n,
281n, 294n, 325n, 326n
Washington, Justice Bushrod: presumption Act valid, 339n
Washington, George: came to Convention for private rights, 16; constitution or anarchy, 8n; Constitution not
factional product, 48n; jealousy for

State sovereignty, 9n, 260; Judiciary
Act, 101; to Hamilton on *Federalist,*
89, 105n; treaty power, 371n
Webster, Noah: Convention members,
116n; "exceptions" clause, 288n
Webster, Pelatiah: Yates, 88n
Wechsler, Herbert: Congress may limit
appellate jurisdiction, 3, though
motivated by hostility, 186n; "exceptions" power, 3, 285, 286n, 292;
nature of judicial power, 245n; on
appeal Supreme Court same power
as State court, 270n, 286n; mentioned, 4n, 244n, 245n, 274n, 337n
Westin, Alan F.: Beard's use of State
Act review, 104; Boudin, 47n; Corwin's strong challenge of Beard,
114n; Crosskey, 47n; departmental
interpretation, 181n; distinguishes review State action, 259; "finality,"
188; judicial review debate, 6n; "self-
defense," 155, 156n; "usurpation"
by Court, 6
White, Alexander: Constitution secured
personal liberty, 17n; ratified on
representation government limited,
122–123; "removal" debate, 146n,
147
Whitehill, Robert: criticizes unlimited
power, 13; feared despotism, 8n
Williams, John: Congress' powers too
indefinite, 129, 130; trusts Congress
no more than Parliament, 34n
Williamson, Hugh: "oath" unnecessary, 239n; on law of land, 227n;
recognized judicial review, 68
    Comment by: Beard, Corwin,
Crosskey, and Davis, 68
Wilson, James: active in Convention,
54; Bill of Rights, 149n; Congressional negative, 226; executive veto,
159; federal officers, 387n; inferior
federal courts, 263n; judicial participation in Council of Revision, 53–54;
notes bias for State, 260, 262; people
last resort, 127, 178; people retain
power, 174, 175; quotes Boudinot,
20n, 151; rejects impeachment
judges, 127, 290; review of "fact,"
287n, 288; State court jurisdiction,
252–253; Supreme Court evaluation
of, 16n, 302n
    Construction of Constitution, 4n;
"arising under," 202; designed to
protect private rights, 18

423

Date Due

~~DEC 8 '86~~			
~~FEB 9 '87~~			
~~APR 6 '87~~			
APR 2 7 '87			
APR 17 '95			
JAN 0 2 '96			